LEE INVADES THE NORTH

A COMPARISON OF THE ANTIETAM AND GETTYSBURG CAMPAIGNS

Bradley M. Gottfried

Turning Point Publications
Fayetteville, Pennsylvania

Copyright: 2022 Bradley M. Gottfried

Second Printing: 2023

Library of Congress Control Number: 2022904826

All rights reserved. No part of this publication may be reproduced, stored in a retrieval system, or transmitted, in any form or by any means, electronic, mechanical, photocopying, recording, or otherwise, without written permission of the publisher. Printed in the United States of America.

Designed by Linda I. Gottfried
Set in Garamond

ISBN: 978-0-578-39410-7

Published by Turning Point Publications

Cover: Left illustration: Antietam by Thure de Thulstrup (the Louis Prang Co.); right illustration by Paul Phillippoteaux (from the Gettysburg Cyclorama); Lee illustration by H. A. Ogden

TABLE OF CONTENTS

PART 1: WHY THE INVASIONS AND PREPARATION

Chapter 1: War Comes to the North: The Military Situation on September 1, 1862 and June 1, 1863....10
Chapter 2: Why Lee Invaded the North in 1862 & 1863....13
Chapter 3: The Armies and Their Leaders....25
- The Army Commanders....25
- The Organization of the Armies....35
- The Size and Experience of the Armies....41
- The Artillery....47
- The Cavalry....57
- The Officer Corps....62

Chapter 4: Supplies, Morale, and Caring for the Men....72
- Supplies....72
- Morale & Straggling....74
- The Men's Condition....80

PART 2: GETTING TO THE BATTLEFIELD

Chapter 5: Intelligence Gathering....85
- Military Intelligence....85
- The Signal Corps....88
- The Cavalry....90
- Happy/Unhappy Accidents....93

Chapter 6: The Two Campaigns Begin (September 4-8, 1862 and June 3-12, 1863)....95

Chapter 7: The Campaigns in Mid-Stream (September 9-12, 1862 and June 13-21, 1863)....120

Chapter 8: The Two Armies Approach the Battlefield (September 13- 17, 1862 and June 22-July 2, 1863)....153

Chapter 9: A Comparison of How the Armies Reached the Battlefield....188
- Distances Traveled and Duration....188
- The Nature of the Marches....189
- Concentrating the Armies....190
- Location of the Armies at the Beginning of Battle....191
- Preliminary Fights....192

- Condition of the Armies....192
- Collecting Supplies....193
- Command Changes....193
- General Orders....193

Chapter 10: The Preliminary Fights....196
- Harpers Ferry....196
- South Mountain....203
- Fox's Gap....204
- Frosttown Gap/Plateau....206
- Turner's Gap....208
- Crampton's Gap....208
- Winchester....212
- Stephenson's Depot....213
- Cavalry Battles....216

Chapter 11: The Final March to the Battlefield....221
Chapter 12: Battlefield Terrain....228
- Antietam Battlefield....228
- Gettysburg Battlefield....229

Chapter 13: Initial Encounters on the Battlefield Prior to the Battle....235

PART 3: THE MAJOR BATTLES OF THE CAMPAIGNS

Chapter 14: Battle Plans....240
Chapter 15: The First Phase of the Battles....250
- Miller Cornfield/East Woods....250
- The West Woods....264
- Initial Fight for the Ridges West of Town....267
- Initial Fighting North of Town....272
- The Confederates Crush the Union Lines....274
- Lost Opportunities....278

Chapter 16: The Second Phase of the Battles....292
- The Sunken Road....292
- Piper Farm....298
- The Strong Union Defensive Line....299
- Lee Takes Position....300
- An Unhappy Dan Sickles....302
- Longstreet Launches His Attack....304
- Houck's Ridge, Devil's Den, and the Slaughter Pen....305

- Little Round Top....306
- Wheatfield/Stony Hill/Rose Woods....307
- Peach Orchard/Along Emmitsburg Road....310
- Plum Run....313
- Cemetery Ridge....316
- Valley of Death....317
- Cemetery and Culp's Hills....317

Chapter 17: The Third or Final Phase of the Battles....330
- The Lower Bridge....330
- The Final Attack....334
- Middle Bridge Sector....338
- Culp's Hill....341
- The Bliss Farm....343
- The Pickett-Pettigrew-Trimble Charge....343
- Cavalry actions....349

Chapter 18: Lee Re-crosses the Potomac River....360

PART 4: AFTER THE BATTLES—END OF THE CAMPAIGNS

Chapter 19: The Army Commanders and Their Commanders-in-Chief....371
Chapter 20: Post-Campaign Events....378
Chapter 21: Final Thoughts....381
- The Armies....381
- The Leaders....381
- Role of Leaders, Civilian and Military, Outside of the Armies....382
- Travel to the Battlefields....384
- Nature of the marches to the battlefield....386
- Travel Logistics....386
- Preliminary Fights....387
- Gambles, Risks, and Blunders....388
- Battlefield Preliminaries....389
- Tactical Plans....391
- The Three Phases of the Battles....392
- Coordination....393
- Luck Smiles on the Defenders but not the Aggressors....394
- Some Noteworthy Actions....395
- Duration....395

- Losses....396
- Returning to Virginia....396
- Lee and His Strategic Goals....397
- Aftermath of Each Campaign....397

Orders of Battle....398

Appendicies:
- Appendix 1: Comparison of Casulties in the Two Campaigns....425
- Appendix 2: Comparison of the Loss of Corps/Wing, Division, and Brigade Commanders in the Two Campaigns....327

Endnotes....432

Index...482

LIST OF MAPS

Map 1: The Road to Antietam (September 4, 1862)…99
Map 2: The Road to Antietam (September 7-9, 1862)….107
Map 3: The Road to Gettysburg (June 3-4, 1863)…109
Map 4: The Road to Gettysburg (June 9-11, 1863)…113
Map 5: The Road to Antietam (September 10, 1862)…127
Map 6: The Road to Antietam (September 12, 1862)…133
Map 7: The Road to Gettysburg (June 15, 1863)…138
Map 8: The Road to Gettysburg (June 19-20, 1863)…147
Map 9: The Road to Antietam (September 14, 1862)…158
Map 10: The Road to Antietam (September 15-16, 1862)…161
Map 11: The Road to Gettysburg (June 23-24, 1863)….165
Map 12: The Road to Gettysburg (June 26, 1863)…170
Map 13: The Road to Gettysburg (June 29, 1863)…178
Map 14: The Preliminary Antietam Battles (Harpers Ferry/Fox's Gap)….201
Map 15: The Preliminary Antietam Campaign Battles (Turner's/Crampton's Gap…209
Map 16: The Preliminary Gettysburg Campaign Battles….215
Map 17: Antietam Environs…230
Map 18: Gettysburg Environs…232
Map 19: The Antietam Battlefield on the Eve of the Battle…237
Map 20: The Cornfield…258
Map 21: The West Woods…266
Map 22: The Morning Fight at Gettysburg (Chambersburg Road fights)…271
Map 23: The Fighting North of Gettysburg…275
Map 24: Final Attack on Seminary Ridge…279
Map 25: The Sunken Road…296
Map 26: The Armies on the Eve of the Fighting on July 2…303
Map 27: Gettysburg—July 2 (Little Round Top/Houck's Ridge)…308
Map 28: Gettysburg—July 2 (Wheatfield/The Peach Orchard)…311
Map 29: Gettysburg—July 2 (Plum Run/Cemetery Ridge)…315
Map 30: Gettysburg—July 2 (Culp's Hill/Cemetery Hill)…318
Map 31: The Bridges During the Third Phase at Antietam…335
Map 32: The Final Actions of the Maryland Campaign…339
Map 33: Culp's Hill (July 3)…342
Map 34: The Pickett-Pettigrew-Trimble Charge…348
Map 35: Lee's Retreat from Gettysburg…366

TABLES

Table 1: Comparison of Military Situation Prior to Each Campaign…12
Table 2: Comparison of Why Lee Invaded the North…24
Table 3: Comparison of the Army Leaders…34
Table 4: Comparison of the Structure of the Armies…40
Table 5: Comparison of the Size and Experience of the Armies…47
Table 6: Comparison of the Size and Organization of the Artillery…55
Table 7: Comparison of the Size and Use of the Cavalry…62
Table 8: Comparison of the Size and Experience of the Infantry…71
Table 9: Comparison of Supplies and Morale…83
Table 10: Comparison of Intelligence Gathering…94
Table 11: Comparison of the First Phase of Traveling to the Battlefield…118
Table 12: Comparison of the Second Phase of Traveling to the Battlefield…152
Table 13: Comparison of the Final Phase of Traveling to the Battlefield…186
Table 14: Comparison of Getting to the Major Battlefield…194
Table 15: Comparison of the Preliminary Fights…220
Table 16: Comparison of the Final Marches to the Battlefield…227
Table 17: Comparison of the Battlefield Terrain…234
Table 18: Comparison of the Initial Interactions on the Battlefield…239
Table 19: Comparison of the Tactics Used in the Battles…249
Table 20: Comparison of the First Phase of the Battles…290
Table 21: Comparison of the Second Phase of the Battles…328
Table 22: Comparison of the Third Phase of the Battles…358
Table 23: Comparison of the Aftermath of the Battles…370
Table 24: Comparison of Casulties in the Two Campaigns…426
Table 25: Comparison of the Loss of Senior Officers…428

FORWARD

I have spent significant time studying both the Maryland and Gettysburg Campaigns, resulting in a number of books on both invasions. As a Gettysburg Licensed Town Guide and an Antietam Certified Battlefield Guide, I spend considerable time interacting with guests whose knowledge ranges from rudimentary to all-embracing. I've learned that few are conversant in both battles, and this perception also extends to most historians. While checking the literature, I found no books comparing the two campaigns; hence the birth of this book.

Robert E. Lee and his Army of Northern Virginia invaded the North twice. In both instances, his ultimate goal was to draw the Union Army of the Potomac away from the friendly confines of Washington and deal a deadly blow. Lee failed in both undertakings, but the similarities of the two campaigns are fascinating, as are the differences. This book attempts to explain how the two campaigns compared and why Lee was ultimately turned back in both.

I struggled coming to terms with the intended audience of this book. Should it be for the novice, who can learn more about each campaign, or the experienced reader, who knows about each campaign, but wants an analysis of the differences? In the end, I decided to address both audiences. For those who are not familiar with both campaigns, this book strives to provide a good grounding. Those familiar with the basics can simply skip over to the "Comparisons" sections which provide a deep dive into the similarities and differences of multiple variables (sorry, that's my science background).

The book contains a large number of maps and will be familiar to those who have read my *Maps of Antietam* and *Maps of Gettysburg* books. There can never be enough maps in a book and this volume contains many.

I was aided in this endeavor by a number of individuals who provided yeoman service. They include Matt Borders, Jared Peatman, and Tim Smith, who read the manuscript and provided valuable suggestions.

I can't thank Ed Marfut enough for spending countless hours reading multiple versions of the manuscript, pointing out factual errors, inconsistencies, and grammar issues.

My loving wife, Linda, provided ongoing support, helped format the book, and created its wonderful cover.

I hope you enjoy reading this book as much as I liked writing it. There are always additional points to be made, but I think I covered the major ones.

Bradley M. Gottfried

PART 1: WHY THE INVASIONS AND PREPARATION

Chapter 1: War Comes to the North: The Military/Political Situation on September 1, 1862 and June 1, 1863

The Maryland Campaign of 1862

The Confederacy enjoyed a productive 1861, but experienced several setbacks the following year. April saw Maj. Gen. Ulysses S. Grant best a large Confederate army at the bloody battle of Shiloh and Maj. Gen. John Pope and his command capture *Island No. 10* on the Mississippi River in Tennessee. In addition, two forts, *Pulaski* in Georgia and *Macon* in North Carolina also fell, as did the vital city of New Orleans. Further north, the mighty Army of the Potomac under Maj. Gen. George McClellan, the "Young Napoleon," prepared to move against Richmond by way of the Virginia Peninsula. Everything was falling into place for the Union. However, events changed rapidly as spring gave way to summer in 1862. Gen. Robert E. Lee, now in command of the Army of Northern Virginia, blunted McClellan's drive toward Richmond as July found the Yanks ensconced along the James River at Harrison's Landing. Only Union gunboats prevented Lee from unleashing an attack to destroy the defeated army.

No amount of President Abraham Lincoln's coaxing could get McClellan from his camps along the James River. In desperation, Lincoln issued Special Order Number 103 in late June establishing the Army of Virginia and selecting Maj. Gen. John Pope as its leader. The army was formed by combining three existing departments: Maj. Gen. John Fremont's Mountain Department, Maj. Gen. Irvin McDowell's Department of the Rappahannock, and Maj. Gen. Nathaniel Banks' Department of the Shenandoah. All had been beaten by Maj. Gen. Thomas "Stonewall" Jackson in the Shenandoah Valley Campaign. Brig. Gen. Samuel Sturgis' brigade from the Military District of Washington was also added to the mix. Pope organized this ragtag force into three corps totaling 50,000 men. Three of McClellan's corps from the Army of the Potomac also arrived to fight with Pope during the Second Bull Run Campaign, waged at the end of August. Pope managed to antagonize many officers and men with his first address to them which included: "I have come to you from the West where we have always seen the backs of our enemies . . . I desire you to dismiss from your minds certain phrases, which I am sorry to find so much in vogue among you. I hear constantly of 'taking strong positions and holding them,' of 'lines of retreat,' and of 'bases of supply.' Let us discard such ideas."

The optimism accompanying Pope's ascension faded by September 1, 1862, as Lee decisively beat the Army of Virginia during the Second Bull Run Campaign. The major battle is considered a masterpiece of cooperation between the two wings of Lee's army, as one held Pope in place while the other hit his flank and rear, causing his decisive defeat. The Union army fell back, literally huddling in the defenses of Washington as seven Confederate columns, from western Virginia to northern Mississippi, drove north to relieve some of the Union armies' pressure on the South. What began as a promising year for the North was rapidly becoming a nightmare.

Other major issues waited in the wings, including foreign recognition of the South and the North's looming mid-term elections.[1]

The Pennsylvania Campaign of 1863

The situation was very different nine months later, on June 1, 1863. Every Confederate thrust the previous autumn had been turned back and large chunks of Southern real estate were now in Northern hands. Union forces realized victories at the battles of Iuka, Sabine Pass, Corinth, Jackson, Stones River, Franklin, Cape Girardeau, to name just a few. Perhaps most significant was Grant's stranglehold on Vicksburg, Mississippi, a vital town on the Mississippi River. There were a number of Confederate victories, to be sure, that discouraged Lincoln, such as at Fredericksburg, Galveston, and Chancellorsville, but the continual Confederate setbacks in the West certainly made it appear that the tide was beginning to move against the South.

Many consider Lee's victory at Chancellorsville in early May 1863 to be his greatest victory. Although dramatically outnumbered, Lee drove the Union army from its position by a devastating flank attack led by Stonewall Jackson's corps. The latter's mortal wound soured the fruits of victory.[2]

Comparisons of the Two Campaigns

Both campaigns began on a high note for Lee's Confederate army and a low one for its Union counterpart. The defeat of portions of the Army of the Potomac and the Army of Virginia at Second Bull Run in 1862 not only demoralized the troops and the North, it also forced a reorganization of the two armies into one, as Lee began his invasion. In 1863, Lee's victory at Chancellorsville was considered to be one of his finest efforts. Therefore, both Confederate invasions were preceded victories that buoyed their army's confidence and dampened their counterpart's spirits.

The broader military situation was very different during the two campaigns. In 1862, several Confederate armies were moving toward the North. While not coordinated movements, they put considerable pressure on Lincoln and his Cabinet. Almost a year after Lee's first invasion, the Confederates were pushed back on their heels, having lost large swatches of territory to Union armies; most distressing was the possible loss of Vicksburg, Mississippi.

Table 1: Comparison of Military Situation Prior to Each Campaign

Issue	Maryland Campaign	Gettysburg Campaign
Military situation:	- Several Southern columns heading north - Lee's army victorious - South begins losing important regions	- Continued defeats of Southern armies in the West - Lee's army victorious - Loss of Southern territory continues
Prior battle:	Second Bull Run	Chancellorsville

Chapter 2: Why Lee Invaded the North in 1862 & 1863

Lee never fully explained his rationale for either of his invasions. However, many historians speculate a considerable overlap in the causes, but also some distinct differences.

The Maryland Campaign of 1862

There were a variety of reasons for Lee to invade the North in 1862. As many as seven Confederate columns were making their way through Kentucky and Tennessee, heading for Ohio. The movement of so many columns may have influenced Lee, but he never articulated it and some historians doubt whether he knew the exact nature of these movements. Lee primarily concentrated on his own situation. Most immediate was what to do now that he had bested two Union armies. Should he stay put or attempt to capture Washington? Joe Johnston had adopted the former strategy after the First Battle of Bull Run, allowing the Union army to reorganize, grow in size, and launch a powerful offensive against Richmond the following year. This was certainly not a viable option.

Lee also discounted the idea of attacking Washington. He wrote after the campaign, "I had no intention of attacking him [the enemy] in his fortifications, and am not prepared to invest them." Lee keenly watched for additional troops appearing in Washington after Lincoln called up 300,000 men on July 2, 1862, to bring the war "to a speedy and satisfactory conclusion," and when they began pouring into Washington, he attempted to ascertain their potential effectiveness. These were not the only troops making their way to Washington. McClellan's setbacks on the Virginia Peninsula caused Lincoln to strip garrisons within 100 miles of Washington to reinforce the capital.[1]

The South was unable to precisely ascertain the number of men in the ranks of its own armies, let alone the enemy who faced them, causing Lee to have only a sense of the growing disparity in the number of men in his army and McClellan's. According to historian Joseph Harsh, the South probably fielded 477,000 men in all its armies in July/August 1862 to the North's 624,000. Although Lee did not know the actual imbalance, he probably realized that with time it would grow even more disproportionately. The time to strike was now, he concluded. There was another part of Lee's philosophy involved: never cede the offensive to the enemy. Lee had held it since assuming command on June 1 and he was not about to relinquish it.[2]

In his communication to President Jefferson Davis on September 3, 1862, Lee noted:

> The present seems to be the most propitious time since the commencement of the war for the Confederate Army to enter Maryland. The two grand armies of the United States that have been operating in Virginia, though now united, are much weakened and demoralized. Their new levies, of which I understand 60,000 men have already been posted in Washington, are not yet organized, and will take some time to prepare for the field. If it is ever desired to give material aid to Maryland and afford her an opportunity of throwing off the oppression to which she is now subject, this would seem the most favorable.[3]

Pennsylvania was Lee's destination. He wrote Jefferson Davis on September 4: "Should the results of the expedition [through Maryland] justify it, I propose to enter Pennsylvania, unless you should deem it unadvisable upon political or other grounds. He first needed to move his army through Maryland and establish a secure line of communications through the Shenandoah Valley.[4]

Although not explicitly stated by Lee, his favored tactics may have also played a role in considering of an invasion of the North. Lee had been commander of the Army of Northern Virginia since June 1—a mere three months. Every time he came against a strong enemy position, he used a turning motion to neutralize it. He did this as many as four times since assuming command of the army. If he couldn't launch a frontal attack on Washington, he would employ a turning movement. Given the location of Washington, Virginia offered no room for such a maneuver, causing him to consider moving into Maryland. Such a movement would threaten Washington's supply lines (e.g., the C & O Canal and the B & O Railroad), forcing McClellan to come out and fight in the open with his demoralized and increasingly inexperienced army. Indeed, historian John Ropes noted, that Lee "probably never would find the Federal army in poorer condition for a great struggle." Lee running wild in Maryland also posed other threats to Washington, such as the safety of Harrisburg and Philadelphia. Equally important, Lee would retain the offensive and potentially inflict a major defeat, bigger than Second Bull Run, on the Union army. The impact could be devastating to the North.[5]

Lee was cognizant of his men's limitations. They had fought several battles in the past three months and marched hundreds of miles, taking their toll on the men's stamina and condition of their clothes and equipment. Lee wrote to Jefferson Davis, "The army is not properly equipped for an invasion of an enemy's territory. It lacks much of the material of war, is feeble in transportation, the animals being much reduced, and the men are poorly provided with clothes, and in thousands of instances are destitute of shoes." Concern about adequate supplies and forage was a primary reason for Lee to move his army north to the Leesburg area after besting Pope at Second Bull Run. Davis may not have been happy with Lee's move into northern Virginia, but the army commander sought to placate him by writing that he could still threaten "the approaches to Washington . . . [and] menace their [the Union army's] possession of the Shenandoah Valley." Despite his men's shortcomings, Lee noted, "We cannot afford to be idle, and though weaker than our opponents in men and military equipment, must endeavor to harass if we cannot destroy them."

The following day, September 4, when his army's vanguard was crossing the Potomac River to begin the invasion, Lee again conveyed his concern about "ammunition and subsistence" to Davis. He needed assistance from Richmond for ammunition, but as for food, he informed Davis, "I am taking measures to obtain all that this region will afford." He explicitly noted the bountiful region across the Potomac River, "but to be able to obtain supplies to advantage in Maryland, I think it important to have the services of some one known to, and acquainted with the resources of the country." This was the first indication that resupply of his army was another goal of the invasion.[6]

Lee also understood the deleterious impact of the armies on Virginia and this became another rationale for the invasion. By moving into Maryland, he told Davis, he could "detain the enemy upon the northern frontier until the approach of winter should render his advance into Virginia difficult, if not impracticable." This would serve to not only protect Richmond from another attack, but also allow the Virginia farmers to harvest their crops without interference from warring armies. Brig. Gen. Bradley Johnson recalled a conference in Leesburg on September 4 when Lee said, "When I left Richmond, I told the President that I would, if possible, relieve Virginia of the pressure of these two armies."[7]

Although Lee did not articulate other desirable outcomes of a successful invasion of the North, one of the most important was foreign recognition. The stakes were probably much higher in 1862 as foreign recognition was more probable than in 1863. The Confederacy sent a three-man delegation to London in 1861 to protest the Union blockade of Southern ports and seek recognition for the fledgling government. The United States had countered with a new and more effective minister. Emotions boiled over when a United States war ship stopped the *HMS Trent* and removed Confederate representatives bound for Europe. The issue was resolved with the release of the emissaries, but uneasiness simmered between the two nations.

Britain was ambivalent about recognizing the Confederacy. On one hand, they needed cotton to fuel their massive textile operations, but slavery was anathema, so they waivered in recognizing the Confederacy. Britain also harbored the hope that the United States' breakup would counter the possibility of a strong competitor on the world stage. Indeed, *The Times* of London had written in August 1862, a breakup would cause a "riddance of a nightmare." With the succession of Confederate battlefield victories, Britain began softening its stance. It, along with France, however, would not recognize the South until it could prove its military staying power. The North also worried about this scenario. The *New York Times* wrote in February 1862: "If our armies now advancing shall generally be stopped or beaten back, France, England, and Spain will make haste to recognize Jeff's Confederacy as an independent power." England's Prime Minister, Henry John Temple, 3rd Viscount Palmerston, indicated the possibility of recognizing the Confederacy at a cabinet meeting during the late summer, indicating he could potentially support a mediation proposal between the North and South. That was a tacit way of suggesting he would support the separation of the United States. Palmerston explicitly stated how a victory on Northern soil could propel recognition of the Confederacy. All eyes were now on Lee and the outcome of his invasion of the North.[8]

Lee had no interest in a long-term occupation of Northern soil. His aide, Charles Marshall, noted "General Lee's policy was not to capture any portion of Federal territory but to prosecute the war by breaking up the enemy's campaigns and so bringing about the pecuniary exhaustion of the North." The latter was especially important, as the United States' midterm elections were a mere two months away. A successful invasion of the North in September 1862 could have a dramatic impact on their outcome and subsequently, the way Lincoln was able to wage war. The Democratic Party, while not necessarily pro-South, was certainly less ardent about keeping the Union together if it meant excessive bloodshed. The same was true about the slavery issue. "Let the Southerners go off with their slaves," was a common refrain of many Democrats. The 1860 Congressional elections were a setback for the Democrats; they lost 53 seats in the House and 8 more in the Senate. The Democrats were now in the minority, although they retained a vocal voice in both chambers of Congress. Continued Union army losses could dramatically change the calculus and launch the Democrats into leadership positions in one or both chambers. The success of the several Confederate columns moving north could be the impetus for such a change.[9]

Lee spoke to the impact of the invasion on the upcoming election in a September 8, 1862 dispatch to Davis, when the army was already in Frederick, Maryland. He suggested that the Confederate government should,

> propose with propriety to that of the United States the recognition of our independence . . . Such a proposition coming from us at this time, could in no way be regarded as suing for peace, but being made when it is in our power to inflict injury upon our adversary, would show conclusively to the world that our sole object is the establishment of our independence, and the attainment of an honorable peace. His rejection of this offer would prove to the country that the responsibility of the continuance of the war does not rest upon us, but that the party in power in the United States elect to prosecute it for the purposes of their own. The proposal of peace would enable the people of the United States to determine at their coming elections whether they will support those who favor a prolongation of the war, or those who wish to bring it to a

termination, which can but be productive of good to both parties without affect the honor of either.[10]

In addition to taking on a weakened Union army, the prospect of securing needed supplies, getting the armies out of Virginia, the enhanced possibility of foreign recognition, and impacting the outcome of the midterm elections, the South still harbored the unlikely possibility that Maryland, a slave and border state remaining with the Union, could cast its lot with the Confederacy. The South had watched with dismay as Confederacy-leaning citizens were arrested in defiance of *habeas corpus* laws and many felt Maryland would change alliances "if the boot of the Federal Government were released from its throat." In a summary of the campaign penned in August 1863, Lee explicitly stated how he "hoped the invasion might afford us an opportunity to aid the citizens of Maryland in any efforts they might be disposed to make to recover their liberties." Lee also expected to attract thousands of young Marylanders to his ranks. Hundreds of Marylanders had already made their way to Virginia to enlist and several Maryland units had, or were already, part of Lee's army. This included several batteries as well as the 1st Maryland Infantry Battalion (not with Lee at this time).[11]

Lee was fully aware of the risks posed by an invasion, including the possible loss of Richmond, as his army would be too distant to provide assistance if attacked. "I am aware that the movement is attended with much risk," he wrote, "yet I do not consider success impossible, and shall endeavor to guard it [Richmond] from loss. As long as the army of the enemy are employed on this frontier I have no fears for the safety of Richmond. . . A respectable force can be collected to defend its approaches by land, and the steamer *Richmond*, I hope, is now ready to clear the river of hostile vessels."[12]

Interestingly, Lee never asked the President for permission to launch the invasion, instead explaining the desirability of such a movement. Lee did write to Davis, "Since my last communication to you with reference to the movements I propose to make with this army, I am more fully persuaded of the benefits that will result from an expedition into Maryland, and I shall proceed to make the movement at once, unless you should signify your disapprobation." Since it took about six days for communications to flow between the army and Richmond, the decision to invade was probably made before Davis could weigh in. Lee may have, however, discussed this strategy with Davis before his army left the environs of Richmond.[13]

While the risks were high, so too were the potential rewards. The invasion of 1862 was Lee's best chance of impacting the outcome of the war.

The Pennsylvania Campaign of 1863

When Lee decided to invade the North after the Maryland Campaign is unknown. He never spoke or wrote about it, but according to historian Wilbur Nye, "he must have had it in his mind for a long time, probably ever since September 17, 1862." The landscape, both politically and militarily was quite different a mere nine months later. Lee had by this time discarded the possibility of Maryland "throwing out the tyrants" and joining the Confederacy. The midterm elections had come and gone and the presidential election was more than a year away. There were state elections that could have impacted policy at a more local level, however. Supplies, or actually a lack of them, continued plaguing Lee while the verdant fields of Pennsylvania beckoned. Perhaps most importantly, Lincoln's Emancipation Proclamation, first publicized five days after the battle of Antietam, and put into effect on January 1, 1863, changed the dynamics of the war. The conflict now took on the moral imperative of ending slavery, extinguishing the last glimmer of hope for foreign recognition. A fuller explanation of the Emancipation Proclamation can be found in Chapter 20.[14]

The two earliest indications of Lee's desire to again invade the North occurred in April 1863. In a letter to Secretary of War James Seddon on April 9, Lee suggested the best way of relieving the enemy's pressure in Tennessee and Mississippi would be an invasion of Maryland by his army (see below). A mere two days later, Lee ordered his Chief of his Engineers, Col. J. F. Gilmer, to send a 550-foot pontoon bridge to Orange County, Virginia, warning him to "keep this matter as quiet as possible." While a distance from the Potomac River, a span that long could only be used for such a wide waterway. Earlier in the year, February 23, Stonewall Jackson called upon his chief cartographer, Jedediah Hotchkiss to prepare a map of the Shenandoah Valley that extended all the way to Harrisburg and Philadelphia. This also was to be kept secret.[15]

Worrying about adequate supplies for his men and the possible future activities of the Army of the Potomac took a back seat when Confederate President Davis asked Lee to "detach a corps for service in the West" to alleviate pressure on Vicksburg. Sec. of War Seddon wrote to Lee on April 6 how it was "very important to re-enforce General Bragg's army; but the Department, after anxiously surveying all the resources at [its] command, is unable to find troops at its disposal for that end . . . If two or three brigades, say of Pickett's division, to be united with another that may be possibly made up from General Samuel Jones' command, could be spared, they would be an encouraging re-enforcement to the Army of the West." Lee received another direct request for troops on April 14, this time from Samuel Cooper, the Adjutant and Inspector, for him to "spare Hood's or Pickett's division from your command for this purpose." Lee parried these requests by informing Richmond of the enemy's mounting activities, portending another drive toward Richmond. He also suggested a victory by his army on Northern soil could result in shifting enemy forces from other theaters, thus relieving pressure on various parts of the South. Lee was summoned to Richmond in mid-May for a series of conversations about the war in the West. Lee's plan to invade the North was embraced by Davis' entire cabinet, except for Postmaster General John Reagan.[16]

Lee's report of the campaign, dated July 31, 1863 gives a clear idea of his thinking about the campaign:

> The position occupied by the enemy opposite Fredericksburg being one in which he could not be attacked to advantage, it was determined to draw him from it. The execution of this purpose embraced the relief of the Shenandoah Valley from the troops that had occupied the lower part of it during the winter and spring, and, if practicable, the transfer of the scene of hostilities north of the Potomac. It was thought that the corresponding movements on the part of the enemy to which those contemplated by us would probably give rise, might offer a fair opportunity to strike a blow at the army then commanded by General Hooker, and that in any event that army would be compelled to leave Virginia, and, possibly, to draw to its support troops designed to operate against other parts of the country. In this way it was supposed that the enemy's plan of

campaign for the summer would be broken up, and part of the season of active operations be consumed in the formation of new combinations, and the preparations that they would require. In addition to these advantages, it was hoped that other valuable results might be attained by military success. Actuated by these and other important considerations that may hereafter be presented, the movement began on June 3.[17]

Lee's report explicitly cites several reasons for the invasion:
- Impracticality of attacking Hooker's strong position along the Rappahannock River, so maneuver to draw him out in the open
- Relieve the Shenandoah Valley of the Union troops occupying it
- Draw enemy troops from other parts of the country
- Break up the enemy's plans for the summer and take the offensive

After the war ended and Lee's died, Gen. Henry Heth recounted a conversation with the venerable leader in 1864 relating to his rationale for launching the invasion that confirms his report.

> If I could do so—unfortunately I cannot—I would again cross the Potomac and invade Pennsylvania. I believe it to be our true policy, notwithstanding the failure of last year. An invasion of the enemy's country breaks up all of his preconceived plans, relieves our country of his presence, and we subsist while there on his resources. The question of food for this army gives me more trouble and uneasiness than every thing else combined; the absence of the army from Virginia gives our people an opportunity to collect supplies ahead. The legitimate fruits of a victory, if gained in Pennsylvania, could be more readily reaped than on our own soil. We would have been in a few days' march of Philadelphia, and the occupation of that city would have given us peace.[18]

If accurate, Lee's major reasons for invading the North in 1863 were similar to those in 1862: gain much needed supplies for his army, get the armies out of Virginia, allowing it to heal from the constant onslaught of thousands of hungry soldiers, and allow him to maintain the offensive by breaking up "all of his [the enemy's] preconceived plans." During a conversation in 1868, William Allen (a Confederate officer whose veracity has been questioned by some historians) recorded Lee saying "he did not intend to give general battle in Pa. if he could avoid it—The South was too weak to carry on a war of invasion. And his offensive movements against the North were never intended except as parts of a defensive system." Lee did expect it would be necessary "to give battle before his return in the fall, as it would have been difficult to retreat without it." His major goal was to "move about, to maneuver & alarm the enemy, threaten their cities, hit any blows he might be able to do without risking a general battle, & then towards Fall return nearer his base." These plans were dashed as "he did not know the Federal army was at Gettysburg, could not believe it, as [Maj. Gen. Jeb] Stuart had been specifically ordered to cover his movements & keep him informed of the position of the enemy & he (Stuart) had sent no word." According to Allen, Lee did not expect to fight the Union army, but was forced into the conflict.[19]

Lee noted on June 25, 1863, "[E]verything that will tend to repress the war feeling in the Federal States will inure to our benefit. I do not know that we can do anything to promote the pacific feeling, but our course ought to be so shaped as not to discourage it." This was a long shot for Lee and probably not a cause for an invasion, but a possible off-shoot.[20]

Comparisons of the Two Campaigns

The two invasions of the North have several common underlying features, including securing needed supplies, getting the armies out of Virginia to relieve pressures on the farmers, maintaining the offensive, and striking before the Union army could recuperate and strike south toward Richmond. The political and emotional impact of a smashing Confederate victory on Northern territory cannot be underestimated.

The two campaigns also differed in several important ways. Political implications of the invasion were much more important in 1862. British and French recognition were very much in play prior to the Maryland Campaign. Lee's loss at Antietam and Lincoln's subsequent issuance of the Emancipation Proclamation all but ended the South's hope of gaining its independence through foreign diplomacy.

Both campaigns preceded fall elections that had the potential of providing succor to the South. During the Maryland Campaign, the Confederate authorities were cognizant of the Northern population's growing discontent over the war as casualty lists grew with little progress to show for it. A major victory on Northern soil by Lee's men had the potential to sway the election and possibly return the Democrats to power in one or both houses of Congress. The urgency of an upcoming election was not nearly as profound during the Pennsylvania Campaign as it was still more than a year away, but could influence policy at a state-wide level.

Prior to the Maryland Campaign, Lee explicitly believed moving his army into Maryland might encourage its state leaders to again consider leaving the United States and join the Confederacy. Absent that, Lee at least hoped for thousands of young Marylanders joining his army. Both scenarios failed to materialize. By 1863, Lee realized that Maryland was no longer in play, but the prospects of capturing Harrisburg and Philadelphia were much more desirable.

Lee had several reasons for invading the North in 1863 that were not important during the prior year. With portions of the South under attack, Lee believed the most effective way of ending this slow erosion of territory under its control was by siphoning off troops to the East so the Western Confederate armies could have greater potential for success. While it is unclear whether Lee intended to capture large cities, such as Harrisburg and Philadelphia during the Maryland Campaign, it appears it was a more viable goal in 1863.

Table 2: Comparison of Why Lee Invaded the North

Issue	Maryland Campaign	Pennsylvania Campaign
Gather needed supplies	Yes	Yes
Maintain the offensive	Yes	Yes
Strike while enemy was weakened	Yes	Yes
Remove armies from Virginia	Yes	Yes
Encourage civilians to sue for peace	Yes	Yes
Encourage foreign recognition	Yes	No
Influence a nation-wide Union election	Yes	No
Capture/ransom Union towns	No	Yes
Siphon troops from other theaters	No	Yes

Chapter 3: The Armies and Their Leaders

The Army Commanders

The Maryland Campaign of 1862

Army commanders, Gen. George B. McClellan (36 years old) and Gen. Robert E. Lee (55 years old), shared a number of similarities. Both hailed from distinguished families, the former in Connecticut and Pennsylvania; the latter from Virginia. Both graduated second in their classes from West Point and served as engineers before the war. Both saw action in Gen. Winfield Scott's army during the War with Mexico where they were recognized for their abilities. This is where their paths diverged. Lee remained in the army, becoming Superintendent of the West Point Military Academy, and serving as lieutenant colonel of the 2nd U. S. Cavalry in the West. McClellan left the army in 1855 to become chief engineer for the Illinois Central Railroad, and by the outbreak of the Civil War, was president of the Ohio & Mississippi Railroad.

They also took different paths to command of their respective armies. After rejecting an offer to assume command of the army being formed in Washington, Lee cast his lot with the Confederacy and tangled with McClellan in the Allegheny Mountains during the winter of 1861-62. He then left army command to inspect the South's forts along the South Atlantic seaboard before becoming Jefferson Davis' military advisor. The unexpected wounding of Gen. Joseph Johnston at the Battle of Seven Pines thrust Lee into command of the Army of Northern Virginia at its darkest hour—when the powerful Union army was at Richmond's gates. There was little time to become familiar with the army or make changes, as the campaign continued in full force.

McClellan began the war in charge of a department that included Kentucky and what is now West Virginia. He successfully kept Kentucky in the Union and held off Confederate forces in West Virginia. After Gen. Irvin McDowell's Bull Run defeat, McClellan was brought East to assume command of the new Army of the Potomac, and later succeeded Winfield Scott as General-in-Chief. He did a masterful job of whipping the demoralized core of the army, and its new additions, into a large and effective fighting force.[1]

The two commanders' relations with their respective presidents had a profound influence on each man's ultimate success. Although a West Point graduate and former Secretary of War in the Franklin Pierce administration, Jefferson Davis usually took a hands-off approach in working with Lee. As military advisor, Lee was a keen observer of Davis' personality and how he related to others. He learned a few "simple" rules to keep him in good stead with his commander-in-chief: Don't question him, don't challenge him, keep him fully informed at all times, do not attack his friends and allies, stay away from the press, and most importantly, show your loyalty to him. Lee, the Virginia gentleman had no problems following these rules and they helped keep him in good stead. It also helped that Lee was both aggressive and successful in his field operations.[2]

McClellan enjoyed a less cordial relationship with Abraham Lincoln, probably stemming from Lincoln's active role in directing strategy. His problems with Abraham Lincoln began almost immediately when the president selected corps and divisional commanders, without input from McClellan. The two also tangled over how best to drive the Confederate army from the gates of Washington. McClellan prevailed and he sailed his army down the Potomac River to the Chesapeake Bay and landed it on the Virginia Peninsula, where he and Lee crossed swords at the critically important "The Seven Days Battles." Lincoln became increasingly frustrated and the number of prodding communications increased when he felt McClellan was dragging his feet. An animus developed between the two men, fueled by the former's insistence on having the final say on strategic decisions; the latter refusing to share his plans with Lincoln and at times, spoke negatively about him behind his back.[3]

Both army commanders' reputations have undergone an evolution since the war. Lee assumed an almost God-like persona during the latter stages of the war, which continued for decades. His untarnished reputation was curried by a corps of Virginia officers who served in his army. In recent years, Lee's propensity to launch attacks that lost thousands of irreplaceable men, has called his judgment into question. McClellan's reputation as a plodding general with an aversion to battle only solidified as time went on. These assertions began in earnest after McClellan ran against Lincoln in the 1864 presidential election. Recent scholarship has been less negative toward McClellan and has shown him to be neither slow nor ineffective. A recent author claimed, "George McClellan wasn't overly cautious; he understood that doing great things entailed risk and that that risk was best managed and mitigated by deliberate, thorough planning."[4]

The fortunes of each commander were on different trajectories at the start of the Maryland Campaign of 1862. The initial reactions to Lee's appointment to army command were a mixed bag. He had earned a reputation as the "Great Entrencher" for his penchant for ordering his men to dig entrenchments during his campaign against McClellan earlier in the war. When an artilleryman in the Army of Northern Virginia expressed his doubts about Lee's ability to lead such a complex force, an officer who had served with Lee on Jefferson Davis' staff replied: "Lee is audacity personified. His name is audacity and you need not be afraid of not seeing all of it that you will want to see."

George McClellan also underestimated Lee's abilities, writing, "I prefer Lee to Johnston. The former is too cautious and weak under grave responsibility – personally brave and energetic to a fault, he yet is wanting in moral firmness when pressed by heavy responsibility and is likely to be timid and irresolute in action." The next few weeks proved the folly of McClellan's predictions, as Lee launched a series of vicious attacks on the Army of the Potomac that drove it back to the James River. Lee's decisive victories at Cedar Mountain and Second Bull Run only heightened his image and the army's sense of invincibleness. At the start of the Maryland Campaign, Lee had been in command of the army a mere three months and his men and officers were still learning about him.[5]

Lee felt anything but invincible as the Maryland Campaign began. The Second Bull Run campaign was still going strong on a rainy August 31, when Lee threw on rubber overalls and a rubber poncho to keep dry while directing his army's movements against Pope. When the cry of "Yankee cavalry!" unnerved his horse, "Traveler," Lee moved quickly to calm him by grabbing the reins, but he tripped on his rubberized clothing and fell forward, throwing out his hands to catch his fall. The result was a small broken bone on one hand and a bad sprain on the other. Both hands were heavily wrapped and his arms in a sling. Lee was forced to spend the next two weeks and more, riding in an ambulance, under a tremendous amount of discomfort during the time he needed to make critical decisions at the beginning of the Maryland Campaign.[6]

McClellan's star was in the nadir. His ambitious drive against Richmond foiled, McClellan and his army holed up beside the James River. Only his gunboats prevented Lee from launching a full scale attack to finish off the Union army. Lincoln was so disillusioned with McClellan's leadership that he pulled together a new army, "The Army of Virginia," commanded by Maj. Gen. John Pope. After Pope's army's inglorious defeat at Second Bull Run, Lincoln was forced change leadership again and finally settled on McClellan to lead the combined army because it was the best of the few options available during this desperate time. Lincoln told Gideon Welles, "I must have McClellan to organize the army and bring it out of chaos." The decision did not sit well with the Cabinet, as Welles related: "There was a more disturbed and desponding feeling than I have ever witnessed in council." Attorney General Edward Bates related that Lincoln "said he felt almost ready to hang himself...that he was so distressed, precisely because he knew we were earnestly sincere." With or without his Cabinet's support, Lincoln knew full well how McClellan had built the army and how its men loved him. Lincoln told his secretary, John Hay, "We must use what tools we have. There is no man in the Army who can man these fortifications and lick these troops of ours into shape half as well as he [McClellan]. If he can't fight himself, he excels in making others ready to fight." It is to Lincoln's credit that he was able to put his personal relations with McClellan aside and appoint him to army command when the country needed his steady hand most.[7]

Although McClellan often interacted directly with Lincoln, he was actually under the supervision of General-in-Chief, Henry Halleck. The two officers had an adversarial relationship from the start, as McClellan had previously served as General-in-Chief until replaced by Lincoln. McClellan now reported directly to Halleck, his replacement-- never a good situation.

The Pennsylvania Campaign of 1863

In the nine months following the Maryland Campaign of 1862, Lee's army decisively bested the Union army two times more: first at Fredericksburg in December 1862 and then at Chancellorsville in May 1863. The latter is considered Lee's greatest victory. At the start of the Pennsylvania Campaign, the Confederate army's morale was high—perhaps higher than it had ever been. Although the army had lost many senior officers, including Stonewall Jackson, Lee had risen to almost God-like status among his men who would follow him to the gates of Hell, if ordered.

As with the first invasion of the North, Lee was not functioning at his highest levels. During the Battle of Gettysburg, Lee was fighting diarrhea, possibly caused by eating too much fruit. An aide to Jeb Stuart observed Lee, "come out of his tent hurriedly and go to the rear several times . . . he walked…as if he was weak and in pain." Some historians believe he may have suffered a heart attack and possibly a recurrence of his old bout with malaria. Whatever the cause, Lee was again hampered when he needed all of his mental and physical faculties.[8]

The Union army had two commanders after McClellan was removed from command. Maj. Gen. Ambrose Burnside, who formerly commanded the IX Corps, took over from his friend in November 1862 and was decisively beaten at the Battle of Fredericksburg in mid-December, when most armies were in winter quarters. V Corps commander (he commanded the I Corps at Antietam), Maj. Gen. Joseph Hooker, assumed command of the army in January 1863 only to lose decisively at the battle of Chancellorsville. The Gettysburg Campaign began with a demoralized Hooker still in command of the army. Provost Marshal Marsena Patrick was frustrated by Hooker's inactivity and wrote in his diary, "He knows that Lee is his master & is afraid to meet him in fair battle." Hooker had powerful political connections that prevented Lincoln from removing him. Only his resignation could rid Lincoln of his less-than effective army commander. That occurred on June 27 when Lincoln forced his hand. Hooker traveled to Harpers Ferry on the morning of June 27 and telegraphed Halleck shortly after noon: "I find 10,000 men here, in condition to take the field. Here they are of no earthly account…they are but a bait for the rebels, should they return." He therefore requested the addition of the garrison to his army. Hooker did not wait for

Halleck's response. Increasingly frustrated by his inability to pull the Harpers Ferry garrison under his banner, he reminded Halleck of his orders to "cover Harpers Ferry and Washington…I beg to be understood, respectfully, but firmly, that I am unable to comply with this condition with the means at my disposal, and earnestly request that I may at once be relieved from the position I occupy."[9]

With Lee's army already in Pennsylvania, Lincoln did not have the luxury of time to consider who would succeed Hooker. Lincoln met with Halleck and Stanton during the night of June 27 to discuss their options. After agreeing to accept Hooker's resignation, they moved on to selecting his replacement. Their first choice, Maj. Gen. John Reynolds, had begged off when Lincoln would not step back from his active role in directing the Army of the Potomac. George Meade, commander of the V Corps had a resume that accorded him the opportunity to command the army. The 48-year old Pennsylvanian had fought in several major campaigns, effectively leading a brigade, division, and corps in battle. He did not, however, have the seniority to command the army. However, those who did had rejected the notion of taking command as it was a career-killer. Most openly supported Meade even though he was their junior in seniority. Meade had frequently bemoaned to his wife how his lack of political connections would preclude him from ever becoming an army commander. When Lincoln proved him wrong, it was only three days before the seminal battle. Because the two armies would collide soon, Lincoln and his aides did not have the luxury of asking Meade if he would accept the post—they ordered his acceptance. Changing horses in midstream put Meade at a distinct disadvantage, compounded by an ignorance of the location of Lee's army, as well as the whereabouts of his own. He immediately went to work preparing for his encounter with Lee. Unlike most of the previous commanders of the Army of the Potomac, Meade was anything but flamboyant, but a hard worker who believed (perhaps naively) that good service would bring rewards. A historian considered him a "curious blend of diffidence and authoritarianism." His officers and men "looked upon him with trust but little affection." His temper was legendary--his aide-de-camp called him a "slasher" because he "cuts up people without much mercy." His heavy eyelids and eyeglasses caused one of his men to call him a "damned old goggle-eyed snapping turtle!" This "reptile" was just what the army needed as July 1863 approached.[10]

An inexperienced army commander, thrust into his position a mere days before meeting the enemy, needed guidance from Washington. As will be seen in later chapters, the Union high command was content to issue overarching requirements and expect the army commander to carry them to the best of his abilities. This led to a stream of exchanges between first Hooker and then Meade with General-in-Chief Halleck and Lincoln. Hooker, whose army was so badly defeated by Lee at Chancellorsville in May, threw out many ideas about the possibility of striking south to capture Richmond while Lee headed north. All were squashed by Lincoln and Halleck. When inexperienced Meade assumed command of the army on June 28, he was told by Halleck, "You will not be hampered by any minute instructions from these headquarters. Your army is free to act as you may deem proper under the circumstances as they arise." The only guidance Meade received was to protect Washington and Baltimore.[11]

Comparisons of the Two Campaigns

The Confederate army had the advantage of retaining the same army commander at Antietam and Gettysburg, providing needed continuity. During the intervening period, Lee's star continued to rise as the men learned to trust his leadership. This was not the case for the Army of the Potomac. The cavalcade of Union commanders destabilized the army and sapped its effectiveness. Just as the troops became familiar with a leader, he was removed and replaced by another. The men knew and loved McClellan, so his re-appointment to command the combined Armies of the Potomac and Virginia was an easy transition for the men. The case was not the same for George Meade. Most outside of the V Corps did not know him, and those who did were often unimpressed because of his testy temperament.

All four leaders (Lee, McClellan, Hooker, and Meade) had the requisite ability to lead their respective armies. They were seasoned professionals who had fought on many a battlefield. Of the four, Meade had the steepest learning curve as he had never led such a large organization. Fortunately, he had experienced corps and divisional commanders who counseled him and provided important insights.

Being physically able to command an army was a different matter. While Hooker, McClellan and Meade had no physical limitations, the same was not true of Lee, who suffered from hand/wrist injuries at Antietam and chronic diarrhea and possibly a heart attack at Gettysburg. These aliments unquestionably affected his ability to function at the highest level required for success.

The relationships of the army leaders with their commander-in-chief also differed and had a profound impact on their ability to direct the armies as they desired. Lee maintained a cordial relationship with Jefferson Davis. He generally kept Davis in the loop and was deferential in his communications with him. As a result, Davis took more of a hands-off approach than his Union counterpart. Lincoln was perhaps the most hands-on commander-in-chief who ever occupied the White House before or since. He was on a mission to maintain the Union and would do anything necessary to achieve that goal. This in evidently brought him into conflict with army leaders, particularly those he thought too slow, too lenient, or too unmotivated. It did not help that McClellan was a Democrat and not a staunch supporter of the war effort. He would work to keep the Union together, but did not have the flame burning in his belly that other leaders did, such as U. S. Grant. Lincoln could become belligerent when he became frustrated and was want to give detailed advice to his army commanders. This rubbed an experienced general like George McClellan to the core and he often rebelled. Only hard feelings could result from these interactions. The same was not yet true of George Meade's relationship with Lincoln. He had only three days of dealings with Lincoln before the battle of Gettysburg and his commander-in-chief was largely deferential during this period. When Lincoln perceived that Meade did not have the needed intensity to finish off Lee after the battle of Gettysburg, he reassumed the mantle of a hands-on commander-in-chief. Meade handled it very differently than McClellan. Rather than lashing out or being sarcastic, Meade often sulked and offered his resignation.

Their relationships with Lincoln probably had a negative impact on McClellan and Meade—more so than Lee with Jefferson Davis. McClellan has been praised for his aggressive advance north to engage Lee. How much of this could be ascribed to Lincoln breathing over his shoulder can only be hypothesized. Still, all of us have had poor relations with our bosses and it usually leads to stress and a greater possibility of making mistakes.

All three Union army commanders operated directly under General-in-Chief, Henry Halleck. McClellan was experienced enough to know what to do, so required little supervision, but his replacements during the Gettysburg Campaign (with Ambrose Burnside in between) Hooker and Meade, required more guidance, but Halleck was unwilling to provide it. He operated under the tenant: "a general in the field is the best judge of conditions." Halleck suffered from a variety of maladies, both physical and mental, that may have affected his behavior. According to Halleck's and Meade's biographers, Halleck was in constant pain from chronic diarrhea and hemorrhoids, and may have taken opium to relieve the discomfort and alcohol to counter the effects of the opium. He may have also "struggled with indecision, like due to a lack of confidence." Lincoln's Secretary of the Navy, Gideon Welles, recorded in his diary, Halleck "originates nothing, anticipates nothing…takes no responsibility, plans nothing, suggests nothing, is good for nothing." Lincoln had various opinions about Halleck, but he liked the ability to have his unsavory decisions being carried out by his subordinate.[12]

Table 3: Comparison of the Army Leaders

Issue	Maryland Campaign	Pennsylvania Campaign
Army commander	**Confederate:** Lee **Union:** McClellan	**Confederate:** Lee **Union:** Hooker/Meade
Experience of leader as army commander	**Confederate:** Extensive **Union:** Extensive	**Confederate:** Extensive **Union:** Extensive (Hooker); Novice (Meade)
Health of army commander	**Confederate:** Issues **Union:** Good	**Confederate:** Issues **Union:** Good
Relations with President	**Confederate:** Good **Union:** Poor	**Confederate:** Good **Union:** Poor (Hooker); Good (Meade)
Relations with General-in-Chief Henry Halleck	McClellan: Poor	Hooker: Poor Meade: Initially good, then soured
How men viewed their army commander	**Confederate:** Positive **Union:** Positive	**Confederate:** Positive **Union:** Concerned (Hooker); Uncertain (Meade)
Cloud over army commander	**Confederate:** No **Union:** Yes	**Confederate:** No **Union:** Yes (Hooker); No (Meade)

The Organization of the Armies

The Maryland Campaign of 1862

The lightning attacks of Lee's Army of Northern Virginia on the Army of the Potomac terrified Washington, causing Lincoln and Halleck to take immediate steps to bolster its security. The garrisons along the Virginia and North Carolina coasts were stripped and their men sent north to be incorporated into the Union army. The IX Corps was the most notable addition. It had gained significant success in securing the North Carolina seacoast, but now it was needed to ward off Lee. The same was true of the Kanawha Division from what is now West Virginia. By the end of the August, two Union armies in the East had sustained major losses during the Seven Days (15,849) and Second Bull Run campaigns (14,462), causing many units to be under-strength and lacking effective commissioned and noncommissioned officers. By combining the two armies, the IX Corps and other units scrounged from other theaters, and thousands of new recruits, McClellan hoped to assemble an effective fighting force that could protect Washington and keep Lee out of Pennsylvania. How to integrate these units and who would lead them occupied much of McClellan's time from September 3 through September 6.

McClellan moved quickly to integrate the two armies into one, along with the additional units being added to the mix. During his drive toward Richmond earlier that summer, McClellan divided his army into corps, each with two divisions of three brigades. With the increased number of troops and questionable ability to find men to effectively lead the new corps, McClellan settled on nine corps (I, II, III, IV [with one division], V, VI, IX, XI, XII), each with three divisions. He undertook some gymnastics to achieve this plan. For example, he created a new Third Division and added it to the veteran II Corps, placing Brig. Gen. William French at its head. The Pennsylvania Reserve Division which had previously fought with the V Corps was transferred to the new I Corps and it was replaced with a new division of eight rookie regiments under Brig. Gen. Andrew Humphreys. Maj. Gen. Darius Couch's division of the IV Corps was attached to the VI Corps, essentially increasing it to three divisions as well. To the IX Corps, McClellan added the Kanawha Division and a second from the North

Carolina coast, increasing the number of its divisions to four, but each contained only two brigades. McClellan also renumbered the corps in the former Army of Virginia to avoid overlap with the Army of the Potomac's. Pope's III Corps became the I Corps with Maj. Gen. Joseph Hooker at its head. Pope's I Corps under Maj. Gen. Franz Sigel was renumbered the XI Corps, and Maj. Gen. Nathaniel Banks' II Corps was designated the XII Corps.[13]

Several of these units remained behind as McClellan ventured north to face Lee's invaders in early September. His army at Antietam was composed of the I Corps (3 divisions), II Corps (3 divisions), V Corps (2 divisions), VI Corps (2 divisions), IX Corps (4 divisions) and XII Corps (2 divisions). These corps provided McClellan with 16 infantry divisions, 44 infantry brigades, and 180 regiments.

Lincoln's call for 300,000 men issued on July 2 added additional cannon fodder to the mix. It was more politically expedient to form them into new regiments than restock existing ones. The Army of the Potomac received 30,000 green recruits—36 regiments—and McClellan moved quickly to integrate them, beginning on September 6, when Lee was already across the Potomac River and approaching Frederick. Special Orders No. 3 distributed 4-6 of these regiments to each corps.[14]

McClellan also grappled with a leadership vacuum, as three of the corps commanders were either no longer with the army or had a cloud over them. These included Maj. Gen. Irvin McDowell (relieved of duty) Maj. Gen. Fitz John Porter and Maj. Gen. William Franklin (both suspended pending a court martial proceeding). Two division commanders were dead (Maj. Gen. Philip Kearny and Brig. Gen. Isaac Stevens), two were wounded or ill (Brig. Gen. Robert Schenck and Brig. Gen. Rufus King), and a number of brigade commanders were out of action (three dead, four wounded, and one suspended). McClellan negotiated the return of three of his generals (Porter, Franklin, and Brig. Gen. Charles Griffin) who had been placed under arrest by Pope. Their trials could wait; their experience was needed.

The Confederate army's organization was much more fluid than its counterpart. A corps level had not yet been authorized by the Confederate Congress, so divisions were the largest sanctioned units. They could contain anywhere from two to six brigades, but most of Lee's army contained four.

Two of Lee's divisions contained six brigades because of consolidations. For example, Brig. Gen. Cadmus Wilcox's three-brigade division was combined with Maj. Gen. Richard Anderson's three in the middle of the campaign to form a larger unit under the latter's command. Similarly, Brig. Gen. James Kemper's three brigades were consolidated with Maj. Gen. D. R. Jones' three, under the latter commander. Why Lee consolidated these units is unknown, but may have been to homogenize the size of his divisions by reducing the number of small ones. He may have also been disappointed in the performances of Wilcox and Kemper. Wilcox would again command a division, but not for nearly two years. A serious wound at Gettysburg deprived Kemper of a larger field command. As a result of these consolidations, Lee would march into Maryland with nine infantry divisions, one cavalry division, and an independent infantry brigade (Brig. Gen. Nathan "Shanks" Evans').[15]

Like the Union army, the brigade was the basic tactical unit in the Confederate army. Lee fielded nine divisions, 40 brigades and 187 regiments. Because of hard fighting, most brigades numbered between 1,000 and 2,000 men, but some, such as the Stonewall Brigade, counted fewer than 500 muskets.

Lee realized he could not effectively keep track of nine divisions so he established unofficial corps, calling them "wings" or "commands." He tapped his ablest leaders to head them: Maj. Gen. Thomas "Stonewall" Jackson and Maj. Gen. James Longstreet. Some divisions were not assigned to either wing, further confusing the issue. This included, Brig. Gen. John Walker's, Maj. Gen. D. H. Hill's, Maj. Gen. Lafayette McLaws' divisions. Despite the ambiguity, the army functioned effectively, as Lee developed a leadership team with Jackson and Longstreet. Historian Scott Hartwig summed up the differences of the Union and Confederate high command: "The harmony, trust, and unity in purpose of Lee's high command contrasted starkly with the disharmony and distrust existing in the command structure of the Army of the Potomac. It gave the Army of Northern Virginia an important operational advantage over their Union adversaries."[16]

The Pennsylvania Campaign of 1863

The organization of the Army of the Potomac marching toward Gettysburg was similar to its former self at Antietam with some minor differences. The I, II, V, VI, and XII Corps were present during both campaigns. Two others, the III and XI, were in existence during the Maryland Campaign, but remained behind in Washington. The XI Corps missed the Battle of Fredericksburg, but would see action at Chancellorsville in May 1863, where all seven corps marched and fought with the Army of the Potomac. This structure continued into the Gettysburg Campaign and through the end of 1863. The IX Corps, which fought with the Army of the Potomac through the fall and winter of 1862-63, did not see action at Gettysburg because one of its divisions was transferred to Newport News, Virginia on February 5, 1863; the remainder headed to the Department of Ohio.

Gettysburg was the last major campaign where the Army of the Potomac would be composed of seven corps. During the fall of 1863, the XI and XII Corps were sent to Maj. Gen. William Rosecrans' besieged army in Chattanooga. The I and III Corps, so badly bruised at Gettysburg, were consolidated with other units in March 1864, and passed out of existence.[17]

Most infantry corps in the Army of the Potomac were composed of three divisions. These included the I, II, V, and XI Corps. The VI Corps also officially contained three divisions with the permanent addition of Couch's division, which was removed from the IV Corps. Only two corps retained two divisions-- the III Corps and the XII Corps. The Army of the Potomac's 19 infantry divisions included 51 brigades and 241 regiments during the Gettysburg Campaign.

Robert E. Lee faced a very difficult command decision after Stonewall Jackson's mortal wounding at Chancellorsville. The two-corps structure, made official after the battle of Antietam, placed a very large number of men under each commander. It only worked well because of its two highly competent leaders. With Jackson out of the picture, Lee sought to identify a replacement, but no one rose to the fore. Complicating matters were the high expectations that would be heaped on Jackson's successor. The *Richmond Whig* noted, "The leader who succeeds him...will be impelled, as by supernatural impulse, to emulate his matchless deeds. Jackson's men will demand to be led in 'Stonewall Jackson's way'." Lee eventually realized no one could replace Jackson, and with his concerns about so many men being in each of the two corps, divided the army into three corps at the end of May 1863.[18]

The creation of a third army corps, allowed Lee to shift brigades to form nine divisions, the same number as at Sharpsburg, but three more than at Chancellorsville. Each corps contained the same number of divisions, three, requiring Lee to shift brigades. Longstreet's First Corps retained McLaws' and Hood's divisions, and Pickett's division was sent up from Richmond. Richard Ewell's Second Corps retained D. H. Hill's division, now under Maj. Gen. Robert Rodes, Jubal Early's division, and the old Stonewall Division, now under Maj. Gen. Edward Johnson. A. P. Hill's new Third Corps contained his own Light Division, but it was reduced from six brigades to four and Maj. Gen. Dorsey Pender was placed in command. The other two brigades, Brig. Gen. Henry Heth's and Brig. Gen. James Archer's, formed the nucleus of a new division under Heth. Two additional brigades were added: Brig. Gen. James Pettigrew's, newly arrived from North Carolina and Brig. Gen. Joseph Davis', formed by combining new and old regiments. To create parity, Maj. Gen. Richard Anderson's division from the First Corps was added to the Third Corps. Lee undertook the second invasion of the North with a new command structure with two untested leaders at the corps level overseeing two-thirds of his army.[19]

Lee's nine infantry divisions each contained four brigades, except for Rodes' and Anderson's, which contained five, and Pickett's division, only three—its other two brigades remained around Richmond. This meant that Lee marched North with 37 brigades and 171 regiments.

Comparisons of the Two Campaigns

The Union army fielded the same number of corps in each campaign—seven-- but they were not the same ones. The I, II, V, VI, and XII Corps participated in both campaigns, but the IV Corps (one division) and IX Corps were present during the Maryland Campaign, but not at Gettysburg. The III and XI Corps were at Gettysburg, but not at Antietam. Both of the latter corps existed, but were left behind in Washington as McClellan moved north.

The changes in the Army of Northern Virginia's organization in the two campaigns were more dramatic. A corps structure did not exist during the Maryland Campaign, forcing Lee to use an improvised "wing" structure, under Stonewall Jackson and James Longstreet. The Confederate Congress authorized corps after the Maryland Campaign and Lee's two leaders slipped into these positions. With the death of Stonewall Jackson, Lee expanded his corps structure to three.[20]

The Confederate army was significantly larger at Gettysburg than at Antietam. Yet, Lee's smaller army at Antietam actually had more brigades (three more) and more regiments (16 more) than at Gettysburg. This reflects a "bulking up" of the regiments rather than increasing the number of units.

The Army of the Potomac took a different tack to increase its size at Gettysburg. It contained three additional divisions, seven additional brigades (14% more than at Antietam) and 44 additional regiments (18% more than at Antietam).

The number of brigades and regiments of the two armies was closer at Antietam than at Gettysburg.

Table 4: Comparison of the Structure of the Armies

Issue	Maryland Campaign	Pennsylvania Campaign
Number of corps present	**Confederate:** None **Union:** 6	**Confederate:** 3 **Union:** 7
Corps present	**Confederate:** None **Union:** I, II, V, VI, IX, XII	**Confederate:** First, Second, Third **Union:** I, II, III, V, VI, XI, XII
Number of divisions	**Confederate:** 9 **Union:** 16	**Confederate:** 9 **Union:** 19
Infantry brigade #'s	**Confederate:** 40 **Union:** 44	**Confederate:** 37 **Union:** 51
Infantry regiment #'s	**Confederate:** 187 **Union:** 197	**Confederate:** 171 **Union:** 241

of the main body..." However, he explained, "there are [some] individuals who...do it no credit."[30]

The Pennsylvania Campaign of 1863

Both armies were in rough shape after the Battle of Chancellorsville. Hooker's Army of the Potomac lost over 17,000 men and Lee's Army of Northern Virginia more than 13,000. Hooker informed Lincoln on May 13 about the condition of his army. His "marching force of infantry is cut down to about 80,000, while I have artillery for an army of more than double that number." On top of these losses, Hooker worried about the potential loss of 31,000 men whose enlistments were up in July.[31]

The armies enjoyed the remainder of May resting, so were in relatively good shape at the onset of the Pennsylvania Campaign. Supplies remained a problem for both armies. Although the Army of the Potomac received few additional units during this time, returning men, either through recovery from wounds, prisoner exchange, or the Enrollment Act passed in March, helped replace some of the battle losses prior to the campaigns. The Union army that marched toward Gettysburg was a battle-hardened and experienced group of units. Only three brigades were new additions to the army: Brig. Gen. Henry Lockwood's, Brig. Gen. George Stannard's, and Brig. Gen. George Willard's, totaling about 5,300 men, but had limited battlefield experience.

Unlike Hooker, Lee received an infusion of troops during the month of May. He welcomed back two of James Longstreet's divisions, from their unsuccessful attempt to recapture the city of Suffolk, Virginia. The army also received three additional brigades—two of them very large. Brig. Gen. Daniel's large, but raw North Carolina brigade was exchanged for Alfred Colquitt's worn out veterans. Two other brigades did not require an exchange: Brig. Gen. Johnston Pettigrew's inexperienced but large North Carolina brigade and Brig. Gen. Joseph Davis' Mississippi and North Carolina brigade was a mix of veterans and green troops. When he accepted these units, Lee agreed he would not receive Micah Jenkins' or Robert Ransom's brigades protecting around Richmond. The new units added almost 7,400 muskets to Lee's army.[32]

By the time the armies reached Gettysburg, the Army of the Potomac had 112,735 men on the rolls, of which 93,921 were combat troops. The Army of Northern Virginia was smaller, totaling 80,202 of which 71,699 were combat ready.[33]

Comparisons of the Two Campaigns

The two campaigns differed dramatically in the condition and size of the armies. During the Maryland Campaign, the two armies were tired from their almost nonstop campaigning from early spring through the Maryland Campaign. Even the well-stocked Union authorities lacked adequate time to resupply the Army of the Potomac before it hastily marched to meet the invading Confederate army. For Lee, supplies were always an issue and remained so during the Maryland Campaign. Many of the men's uniforms were in tatters and shoes continued to be a problem. Lee probably made a wise decision to leave his shoeless men behind. Although this reduced his army by at least 5,000, they would not fall by the wayside during the harsh marches and possibly fall into enemy hands. The armies prior to the Pennsylvania Campaign were relatively rested after spending most of May in camps along the Rappahannock River.

Both armies added manpower prior to both campaigns. McClellan was the beneficiary of a bevy of troops that significantly swelled the size of the army, but as many as 20% were green recruits and certainly not ready for action. This included a division from what is now West Virginia and an additional 15,000 troops who answered Abraham Lincoln's call for 300,000 new troops earlier in the summer. Lee also welcomed additional troops not present during the Second Bull Run campaign. However, most of these were his veterans who had not travelled north fast enough to rejoin the army in time for that battle. Lee gained some conscripts, but that number was more than offset by the relatively large number troops left behind when the army crossed the Potomac River.

Whereas 20% of McClellan's army at Antietam was green, only 6% of Meade's army was inexperienced at Gettysburg. The Confederates saw an opposite trend. As many as 10% of Lee's troops were rookies at both battles.

In sum, the Union and Confederate armies were significantly larger and more experienced during the Pennsylvania Campaign.

Table 5: Comparison of the Size and Experience of the Armies

Issue	Maryland Campaign	Pennsylvania Campaign
Physical condition of both armies at start of the campaign	Exhausted	Rested
Addition of new units	**Confederate:** Significant numbers **Union:** Significant numbers	**Confederate:** Additional brigades **Union:** Relatively few
Number of effectives at the battle	**Confederate:** about 36,000 **Union:** about 58,000	**Confederate:** about 72,000 **Union:** about 94,000

The Artillery

The Maryland Campaign of 1862

McClellan's plan of placing four batteries with each division, one regular and three volunteer, was not completely realized as the army began moving north. McClellan grasped the necessity of shaking up his long arm and found the right officer in Col. Henry Hunt, whom he promoted from the head of the Artillery Reserve to command his artillery. It was a monumental task, and with only a staff of seven, Hunt worked tirelessly to determine the status of each battery and then address its issues. Many of those batteries engaged during the Second Bull Run Campaign were woefully deficient in ammunition, so Hunt ordered up 300 wagonloads. Missing or broken down horses were replaced and infantrymen recruited to replace lost cannoneers. Divisions deficient in batteries were reinforced from the artillery reserve and those batteries in the worst shape were sent back to Washington to be refitted to action readiness or retired. Henry Hunt literally rebuilt the artillery arm while on the fly as the army marched north through Maryland. He did little to change the artillery's organizational structure, however, leaving most of the batteries associated with infantry divisions.

Brig. Gen. William Pendleton was Hunt's Confederate counterpart, but he was not up to the task of effectively overseeing Lee's artillery. Prior to the Maryland Campaign, Pendleton created an Artillery Reserve composed of five battalions, but the remaining batteries were scattered among the infantry brigades. The dispersal of these batteries guaranteed they could not be sent to those parts of the battlefield in greatest need, but would be glued to their infantry brigades. The folly of such an organization graphically showed itself at the battle of Malvern Hill where Lee's individual batteries were outgunned by massed enemy artillery fire. Lee corrected this problem prior to the Maryland Campaign by grouping each division's artillery under one battalion chief. He also removed batteries from the Reserve and distributed them to various divisions to increase their firepower. Jackson and Longstreet's wings each received a reserve battalion as well. Infantry brigades would no longer control batteries. Like Hunt, Lee also ordered all of his batteries inspected prior to the move into Maryland, leaving behind deficient ones, dispersing the men and able horses to other batteries. Neither Lee nor Pendleton apparently reviewed the distribution of batteries prior to the campaign, for D. R. Jones' division had only one battery assigned to it during the Maryland Campaign when all the others had two to five.

An analysis by Curt Johnson and Richard Anderson found the Army of the Potomac headed north into Maryland with 64 batteries: 22 regular and 42 volunteer, sporting a total of 323 guns. However, several were not present or engaged at Antietam, reducing the number to 57 batteries and 293 cannon. Most of the batteries contained five or six guns, most of the same type. To supply the divisions, Hunt raided the Artillery Reserve, leaving it with a mere seven batteries (totaling 34 guns). Four batteries were equipped with big 20 lb. Parrotts that could pack a punch, but their mobility was limited. By distributing batteries from the Reserve to stock the divisions, Hunt knew he was surrendering the ability to bring artillery into play where and when needed, as so many of his guns were decentralized. Worse, the batteries continued to be commanded by infantry division commanders who usually had little formal experience in the effective use of artillery. Each division did have a "chief of artillery," but this was mainly an administrative function, and when the shells began flying, he returned to command his own battery. Only the corps commander could truly concentrate his divisions' artillery into an effective force, but he often was too preoccupied with his own infantry.

The Army of Northern Virginia artillery's array is less clear, as not all units were counted or their armament is unknown. Johnson and Anderson surmised that Lee had 57 batteries with 246 cannon. Unlike the uniform Union batteries, each Confederate battery generally sported several different types and calibers of cannon. For example, Capt. John Brockenbrough's battery in action near the West Woods was composed of a Blakely Rifle, a 10 lb. Parrott, a three-inch Ordnance Rifle, and a 12 lb. Napoleon. There were pros and cons to this approach. A battery could effectively engage the enemy a mile away or within 200 yards but was limited in its firepower, and there was a far greater possibility of mixing the wrong types of ammunition in the limbers.

What the Union artillery arm lacked in organization, it more than made up for in the quality of the guns and their ammunition. The armament of the Army of the Potomac was as follows: 20 lb. Parrotts (rifled) = 30; 10 lb. Parrotts (rifled) = 58; 12 lb. Howitzers (smooth) = 16; 12 lb. Napoleons = 112; 3 in. Ordnance (rifled) = 102; 12 lb. Dahlgren boat howitzers (smooth) = 5. The regular batteries were among the best in the world and they set an example for the volunteer units in each division. Hunt was peeved by the volunteers' penchant for firing rapidly and often indiscriminately, quickly using up their ammunition, and heading to the safety of the rear. At the battle of Antietam, Hunt rode tirelessly among his batteries, giving orders to "fire slowly and deliberately; stating that rapid firing did little execution and was a waste of ammunition."

Equipping the Confederate long arm was more of a challenge as the army was raised from scratch. Most of the guns came through capture, purchase abroad, or manufacture by the Tredegar Iron Works in Richmond. Second Bull Run had provided Lee with a large number of captured Union artillery that was quickly redistributed to his army. As a result, Lee's array of armament was a hodgepodge of guns, creating a nightmare for ordnance officers attempting to supply each battery. The Army of Northern Virginia had the following cannon: 20 lb. Parrotts (rifled) = 4; 10 lb. Parrotts (rifled) = 36; 12 lb. Howitzers (smooth) = 34; 24 lb. Howitzers (smooth)= 4; 12 lb.

Napoleons (smooth) = 27; 3 in. Ordnance (rifled) = 40; Whitworth Rifle = 2; Blakely Rifle = 2; 6 lb. guns (smooth) = 45; guns of unknown caliber = 52.[34]

Not only did McClellan's army possess more cannon (323 vs. 246), they were also of a higher quality. Whereas only 21 of McClellan's 323 were considered to be obsolete (7%); 83 of Lee's 194 known cannon (43%) needed to be replaced with modern cannon.

Sufficient quantities of quality ammunition were of supreme concern to Lee at the onset of the campaign. He wrote to Jefferson Davis on September 3, 1862: "I beg you will instruct the Ordnance Department to spare no pains in manufacturing a sufficient amount of the best kind, & to be particular in preparing that for the artillery, to provide three times as much of the long range ammunition as of that for smooth bore or short range guns." Lee again told the president, on September 5, of his uneasiness in stocking adequate levels of ammunition and the location where these supplies should be delivered.[35]

The Confederate artillery's effectiveness was also reduced by defective fuses, which were notorious for causing premature ignition of the shells--sometimes within the cannon barrel. The Ordnance Department had authorized production of large numbers of modified Bormann fuses early in the war that proved wanting. However, they could not be replaced until the stocks on hand were exhausted.[36]

The Pennsylvania Campaign of 1863

Lee's artillery underwent a face lift between the Maryland and Pennsylvania Campaigns. The frustration with dispersing batteries among brigades and divisions was explained by Gen. William Pendleton, the nominal head of Lee's artillery on February, 11 1863:

> Burdened as are brigade and division commanders, they can scarcely extend to batteries thus assigned that minute supervision which they require, and the supply officers, whose chief care lies with considerable bodies of infantry, cannot devote to one or more batteries the time and attention they imperatively need. This is most injuriously experienced in times of pressure. The existing arrangement moreover affords insufficient scope for field officers of artillery. Batteries, besides, permanently attached in this way, can

scarcely be assigned elsewhere, whatever the emergency, without producing some difficulty, almost as if a vested right was violated.

Pendleton recommended greater consistency in how artillery was distributed to each division. Each would receive a battalion composed of four batteries. While still under an infantry commander's control, the prospects of massing the artillery was much greater because Pendleton recommended the creation of an artillery reserve. Two such battalions would be assigned to each of the corps. It did not take long for Lee to embrace these recommendations, and he put them into effect on February 15, 1863. Each corps received three regular battalions and two reserve battalions. But, Lee did not trust Pendleton in battle so he did not maintain an artillery reserve for the army, unlike the Army of the Potomac. Instead, he downgraded Pendleton's position to primarily an administrative role. By the time Lee's army reached Gettysburg, its artillery arm was composed of 15 battalions with 62 batteries and 246 cannon. The vast majority of the batteries continued sporting four guns, often of different types and calibers, but attempts were being made to reduce the number of batteries, increase the number of guns in each, and strive for uniformity.[37]

Hunt remained in charge of the Union artillery during the Pennsylvania Campaign. He had high hopes when Joseph Hooker assumed command of the army, but they were never realized. According to one historian, "Hooker had reduced Hunt to the status of an adviser on artillery matters with no personal authority whatsoever." Hooker restored Hunt's status after the Chancellorsville fiasco and he would perform exceptionally well at Gettysburg. Thirty-seven batteries were distributed among the seven artillery brigades-- one to each corps-- headed by an effective artillery officer. Each artillery brigade had between four and eight batteries. Hunt also created an artillery reserve, composed of four brigades with 21 batteries that operated independently of the infantry and could be sent anywhere needing additional firepower. The Union army fielded a total of eleven artillery brigades, 58 batteries, and 331 guns operating with the infantry corps.[38]

The armament of the Army of the Potomac (excluding the cavalry's artillery) was as follows: 20 lb. Parrotts (rifled) = 6; 10 lb. Parrotts (rifled) = 60; 12 lb. Howitzers (smooth) = 2; 12 lb. Napoleons = 142; 3 in. Ordnance (rifled) = 109; 14-pounder James Rifles = 4; 4.5-inch Rifle = 8.

The Confederate army's armament at Gettysburg is not definitively known, but is suspected to number about 250, including: 20 lb. Parrotts (rifled) = 12; 10 lb. Parrotts (rifled) = 38; 12 lb. Howitzers (smooth) = 24; 24 lb. Howitzers (smooth)= 4; 12 lb. Napoleons (smooth) = 100; 3 in. Ordnance (rifled) = 65; Whitworth Rifle = 2; 6 lb. guns (smooth) = 1.

The number of the Army of Northern Virginia's deadly Napoleons dramatically increased after Antietam because Lee sent all of his obsolete bronze howitzers to the Tredegar Iron Works to be melted down and to create Napoleons at a ratio of three to two. Therefore, only 29 of his 246 cannon were obsolete (1.3%). Most of the Army of the Potomac's howitzers were removed by Gettysburg, leaving Meade with only two (less than 1%) in his army.

Adequate ammunition was an issue for both armies. Meade expressed grave concern about his batteries running out of ammunition because their supply wagons were far in the rear. Hunt was not as concerned, for he had created a special wagon train to bring up additional ammunition, ensuring the Union guns would have an adequate supply to tear up enemy infantry formations and their artillery. Lee was less concerned about having sufficient stocks of ammunition, possibly because there was time for restocking after Chancellorsville. Fuses remained an issue. While the situation had improved somewhat at Chancellorsville, it continued to plague the artillery at Gettysburg. Compounding the problem was a terrible explosion at a plant in Richmond on March 13, 1863, killing 43 women and maiming 25 others. The destroyed plant would be rebuilt, but in the meantime, the army needed fuses shipped in from Charleston that proved different from their Richmond counterparts, and this resulted in woe for the Confederate artillerymen trying to accurately throw their projectiles at the enemy.[39]

Comparisons of the Two Campaigns

Artillery was highly respected by both armies. The long arm was in transition during the Maryland Campaign and was vastly improved nine months later during the Pennsylvania Campaign, probably because their commanders remained fairly constant during the two campaigns. Hunt performed outstanding work at Antietam, and by Gettysburg the Union artillery was a highly effective and feared part of the Army of the Potomac.

The same cannot be said about William Pendleton and his artillery. Rather than placing a more competent officer in charge, Lee worked around his deficient head of artillery and it cost him dearly in both campaigns.

At Antietam, the Confederate artillery, organized into battalions, was better organized than its Union counterpart. Hunt was so preoccupied with getting his batteries into a serviceable condition that he lacked time to reorganize them. He corrected this shortcoming by the Gettysburg Campaign, when the batteries were organized into brigades associated with corps, not divisions. While still tied to infantry commands, each artillery brigade was headed by an effective artillery chief who could operate at least somewhat autonomously. The Confederate organization also changed with a more consistent placement of artillery within each division. The long arm was still at the mercy of the division commander, who in battle, often forgot about the artillery as he concentrated his attention on his own infantry.

Both armies realized the importance of a strong artillery reserve, but Hunt did a better job of enlarging his army's after Antietam. By Gettysburg, he had a reserve of over 100 cannon that he could direct to any part of the battlefield needing additional firepower. Lee would not dare put artillery directly under Pendleton, so two artillery battalions were assigned to each corps, which operated as a reserve. While an improvement over Antietam, it did not permit artillery to travel outside of a corps commander's realm, unless he expressly permitted it.

The number of batteries were reduced in both armies (Union: 64 at Antietam versus 58 at Gettysburg; Confederate: 73 at Antietam versus 62 at Gettysburg) and a slight increase in the number of cannon from Antietam to Gettysburg (Union: 323 at Antietam versus 331 at Gettysburg; Confederate: 246 at Antietam versus 250 at Gettysburg). These changes were driven by the complement of guns in each battery. The Union army fielded six cannon in 51% of its batteries at Antietam. By Gettysburg, this number had swelled to 73%. The Confederates relied extensively on four-cannon batteries, which were most prevalent at Antietam (56%) and Gettysburg (78%); only 26% of Lee's batteries counted six cannon at Antietam and the number shrank to 7% at Gettysburg. There were a larger number of Confederate batteries consisting of one, two, three, and five cannon at Gettysburg.

Armament quality also differed in both armies and in both campaigns. The Union army lugged 21 obsolete howitzers to Antietam, but only two were present at Gettysburg. Similarly, the Confederates brought 83 ancient smoothbore cannon with them to Antietam, but only 29 to Gettysburg. The Confederates exchanged their obsolete cannon with additional three-inch ordnance rifles (25 more) and Napoleons (73 more). The Union army fielded many fewer large and difficult to maneuver 20-lb. Parrotts at Gettysburg (6 versus 30) and more Napoleons (142 vs. 112). Although Lee was able to improve the quality of his artillery, his long arm was still deficient in modern cannon, compared with its Union counterpart. The greatest disparity was the Union's number of Napoleons (142 versus 100) and 3-inch Ordnance Rifles (150 versus 65).[40]

Ammunition, both quality and quantity, plagued Lee during both campaigns. Not only did he worry about sufficient quantities, his cannoneers questioned whether a charge would explode when expected or if at all.

Table 6: Comparison of the Size and Organization of the Artillery

Issue	Maryland Campaign	Pennsylvania Campaign
Organization	Confederate: Battalions assigned to divisions Union: Most batteries assigned to divisions	Confederate: Battalions assigned to divisions Union: Brigades assigned to Corps
Artillery Reserve	Confederate: Reserve assigned to Corps Union: 7 batteries/34 guns	Confederate: Reserve assigned to corps Union: 4 brigades/21 batteries/ over 100 guns
Number of batteries	Confederate: 73 Union: 64	Confederate: 62 Union: 58
Number of cannon	Confederate: 246 Union: 323	Confederate: 250 Union: 331
Percentage of batteries with six cannon	Confederate: 26% Union: 51%	Confederate: 7% Union: 73%
Percentage of batteries with four cannon	Confederate: 56% Union: 48%	Confederate: 78% Union: 27%
Types of guns in Union batteries: - Three-inch Ordnance Rifles - 10-pounder Parrotts	 102 58	 109 60

Issue	Maryland Campaign	Pennsylvania Campaign
- 20-pounder Parrotts	30	6
- Napoleons	112	142
- 12 lbs. Howitzers	16	2
- 12 lbs. Dahlgren boat howitzers	5	-
- James Rifles	-	4
- 4.5 inch Rifles	-	8
Types of guns in Confederate batteries:		
- Three-inch Ordnance Rifles	40	65
- 10-pounder Parrotts	36	38
- 20-pounder Parrotts	4	12
- Napoleons	27	100
- 12 lbs. Howitzers	34	24
- 24 lbs. Howitzers	4	4
- Blakely Rifles	2	2
- 1861 6-pounder	45	-
- 3" Navy Rifles	-	1
- Whitworth Rifles	-	2
- Unknown	52	-

The Cavalry

The Maryland Campaign of 1862

On paper, McClellan could boast a cavalry division composed of 14 regiments and four batteries of horse artillery totaling 4,300 men and 22 cannon under the tactical control of Brig. Gen. Alfred Pleasonton. Eleven of the regiments were formed into four brigades; the remainder were either assigned to headquarters or unattached. McClellan did not formally create the cavalry division until September 12, and the regiments operated fairly independently during the campaign. The exception was Brig. Gen. John Farnsworth's brigade, which operated as a more cohesive unit. A number of regiments were still down on the Peninsula and the others, when active, were tasked with patrolling and scouting responsibilities. Over 50 companies were detached as headquarter guards, escorts, and couriers to provide provost marshal responsibilities during the Maryland Campaign. This amounted to four regiments, reducing Pleasonton's overall effectiveness. Disease also contributed to Pleasonton's woes, such as "greased heel," a disease afflicting as many as 4,000 horses.[41]

Lee organized his cavalry into one division of three brigades totaling about 5,300 men. Each brigade possessed one horse artillery battery. Maj. Gen. Jeb Stuart commanded this highly mobile force that generally provided accurate information on the enemy's movements, screened the infantry, and packed a punch when confronted by Union cavalry. Stuart was able to keep his regiments intact, and unlike his Union counterpart, brigades operated cohesively. However, as we will see, the demands of the army caused Stuart to disperse his three brigades, and they never fought as a cohesive division during the Maryland Campaign. Their horses were generally of superior quality because each cavalryman was responsible for his own mount; the Union cavalrymen relied on horses provided by the Government. The Confederate system did have its shortcoming, however, for a lost horse forced its owner to return home for another mount or follow the column on foot and fight as an infantryman.[42]

McClellan tasked Pleasonton with scouting the enemy to determine the size and whereabouts of Lee's army. He reported Lee's crossing of the Potomac River on September 5 and his subsequent movement to Frederick.

Pleasonton also accurately reported Lee's strength on September 5 at about 45,000, but he increased the number as the campaign progressed, until September 9, when he reported an enemy army of 115,000 men with massive artillery.[43]

Brig. Gen. William Averell, an experienced cavalryman explained that while on the march, "Cavalry should extend well away from the main body…like antennae to mask its movements and to discover any movement of the enemy." Jeb Stuart's cavalry was adept at these activities and the Maryland Campaign was a good example. Lee ordered him across the river at Edward's Ferry and then toward Poolesville, where he was to screen and protect the army's right flank as it crossed the river and headed for Frederick, Maryland. A couple of regiments from Fitz Lee's brigade encountered three companies of the 1st Massachusetts Cavalry and sent them packing with heavy losses. When Lee enacted Special Orders No. 191, breaking up the army into several pieces, the majority of his infantry headed toward Harpers Ferry to capture or disperse the Federal garrison there. Stuart and his three brigades were tasked with riding in the rear of the army to provide timely notice of the advance of the Army of the Potomac. At times, Stuart failed to accurately communicate enemy activities, and when he did, it was somewhat inaccurate. For example, prior to the South Mountain fight on September 14, Stuart told the Confederate division commander defending the gaps that he was only up against a small Union force, when in reality, it was the entire IX Corps.[44]

The Pennsylvania Campaign of 1863

The Union cavalry was a cohesive and effective fighting force on the eve of the Gettysburg Campaign, and the action at Kelly's Ford in March 1863 showed the Northern horsemen could hold their own against Jeb Stuart's troopers. During the Gettysburg Campaign, the Army of the Potomac's cavalry arm was generally organized into a corps with three divisions. This was true at the start of the campaign, when Pleasonton had three divisions at the battle of Brandy Station. After that fight, as cavalry chief, Pleasonton consolidated them to form two larger divisions under Brig. Gens. John Buford and David Gregg, before creating a third division later in the campaign (see below).

The number of brigades and regiments remained the same through most of the campaign: six brigades and 27 regiments—far more than Pleasonton's divisional strength at Antietam. Political maneuvering allowed Pleasonton to get his hands on Maj. Gen. Julius Stahel's division, assigned to the defenses of Washington. With the transfer, Pleasonton quickly assigned Brig. Gen. Judson Kilpatrick to command the division and its two brigades were assigned to Captains George Custer and Elon Farnsworth who were jumped several ranks to brigadier general. Although green, these new leaders quickly proved themselves worthy of their promotions. With the new division, Pleasonton's cavalry arm grew to three divisions, eight brigades and 37 regiments.

The number of Pleasonton's troopers actually engaged at Gettysburg has been pegged at 11,846. This does not include Gregg's 2nd Brigade, under Col. Pennock Huey, which pulled guard duty and was still in Maryland during the battle of Gettysburg. Two brigades of horse artillery (under Captains James Robertson and John Tidball) sporting nine batteries containing 44 cannon, also fell under Pleasonton's command.[45]

The Union cavalry operated differently than it had during the Maryland Campaign. While it continued scouting and screening infantry movements, the units were permitted, even encouraged, to fight. They engaged in tough engagements at Brandy Station, Aldie, Middleburg, Upperville, Hanover, and Hunterstown before the Gettysburg fight. The elevation of George Meade to command of the Army of the Potomac created some friction with Pleasonton, as the new army commander believed cavalry's role was the more traditional one of scouting and screening, much to the chagrin of the cavalry chief. To emphasize the old role and to assist the new army commander, Meade forced Pleasonton to pitch his tent close to his, thus depriving the cavalry their chief's presence.[46]

As in the Maryland Campaign, Jeb Stuart's Confederate cavalry remained a division. The creation of a corps would not come until after the Gettysburg Campaign (September 9, 1863). Stuart initially had five brigades at his disposal: Brig. Gen. Wade Hampton's, Brig. Gen. Fitz Lee's, Brig. Gen. Rooney Lee's brigade (under John Chambliss after Lee's wounding at Brandy Station), Brig. Gen. Beverly Robertson's and Brig. Gen. William Jones'. Two other mounted brigades also operated in conjunction with Lee's army during the campaign: Brig. Gen. Albert Jenkins' brigade of mounted infantry would screen the Second Corps and fight with Stuart at Gettysburg. Brig. Gen. John Imboden's brigade joined in time to assist in the retreat from the battlefield. Stuart's 25 regiments carried 8,105 men into the campaign.[47]

Stuart's horsemen were augmented by Maj. Robert Beckham's Horse Artillery. The battalion was composed of five batteries and 21 guns or half the number of Pleasonton's long arm.[48]

Stuart continued thriving under the support of his army commander. Always seeking opportunities beyond scouting and screening, Stuart played an outsized role in the Confederate army's fortunes during Lee's second invasion.

Comparisons of the Two Campaigns

Lee's infantry and artillery were dwarfed in size, armament, and supplies available to it, but its cavalry was a different story, at least during the Maryland Campaign, where Jeb Stuart's cavalry arm was better organized than its Union counterpart. Both forces scouted and screened infantry, and occasionally fought, but Lee's cavalry provided much more effective service. This disparity changed by the Pennsylvania Campaign in a number of ways.

While both mounted forces were larger during the Gettysburg Campaign, the Union cavalry arm was more effectively organized into a corps with several divisions. With this structure, Pleasonton, was able to add another layer of leadership and he had two outstanding division commanders in John Buford and David Gregg. Newly elevated Judson Kilpatrick would take time to make the transition from brigade to division commander. Stuart gained additional brigades, but remained a division commander. He was hampered by having to keep track of five brigades, and later in the campaign, seven.

The mounted arms retained the same commanders, Stuart and Pleasonton during both campaigns. This continuity certainly improved the growth and effectiveness of each army's cavalry. While Stuart provided good service during the early stages of the Pennsylvania Campaign, Pleasonton continued struggling to collect accurate information on the enemy's strength and location.

Two of the three Confederate cavalry brigade leaders at Antietam (Fitz Lee and Wade Hampton) also led their units at Gettysburg and a third was on the field in charge of his regiment. Such was not the case with Pleasonton's command, where none of the five brigade commanders at Antietam commanded brigades at Gettysburg. Stuart's top leadership was therefore potentially more experienced at Gettysburg, but the results were not as clear-cut as Pleasonton's division and his less experienced brigade commanders performed quite well during the Pennsylvania Campaign.

The Union cavalry arm was also more confident of its abilities during the Pennsylvania Campaign compared with the Maryland Campaign. It had fought effectively and shown its mettle against Stuart's forces on several battlefields between the two campaigns. The Confederate cavalry retained its autonomy during the Pennsylvania Campaign because of the confidence Lee placed in Jeb Stuart. This was certainly not the case with Pleasonton's cavalry. Starting with Gen. McClellan, and continuing with Hooker and Meade, the Union army commanders did not trust Pleasonton's judgment or abilities and kept him on a short leash.

As we will see, the cavalry played a more pivotal role in the Pennsylvania Campaign compared with Lee's earlier invasion.

Table 7: Comparison of the Size and Use of the Cavalry

Issue	Maryland Campaign	Pennsylvania Campaign
Organization	**Confederate:** Division **Union:** Division being formed	**Confederate:** Division **Union:** Corps
Cavalry Commander	**Confederate:** Stuart **Union:** Pleasonton	**Confederate:** Stuart **Union:** Pleasonton
Number of cavalry divisions	**Confederate:** 1 **Union:** 1	**Confederate:** 1 **Union:** 2-3
Number of cavalry brigades	**Confederate:** 3 **Union:** 4	**Confederate:** 5 (plus Jenkins and Imboden later in campaign) **Union:** 8
Strength of cavalry	**Confederate:** 5,300 **Union:** 4,300	**Confederate:** 8,105 **Union:** 11,846
Confidence by army chief	**Confederate:** High **Union:** Low	**Confederate:** High **Union:** Low

The Officer Corps

The Maryland Campaign of 1862

Five of the six Union infantry corps commanders at Antietam were led by West Point graduates and all but one had already seen significant action during the war. Maj. Gen. Joseph Hooker may have been the most effective of the bunch. Known for his aggressive nature and clear thinking on the battlefield, he ascended to command the Army of the Potomac's new I Corps a mere three weeks before the battle. His troops were among the first (after the IX Corps at Fox's Gap) to engage Lee's men at Turner's Gap and the Frosttown Plateau on September 14, and they opened the battle of Antietam on the morning of September 17. Hooker's star rose in the winter of 1862-63 when he was placed in command of the Army of the Potomac.[49]

At 62, Maj. Gen. Edwin Sumner was the most experienced, but he never attended West Point. He entered the army as a second lieutenant in 1819 and he saw extensive action during war and peace prior to the Civil War. Sumner rose quickly in command during the early portion of the Civil War, and was the initial commander of the large II Corps. Nicknamed "Bull" because a bullet bounced off his head during the Mexican War, his was a fitting sobriquet as he could be stubborn and rash, but he was able to get the most out of his troops. He lost command in the Army of the Potomac after the Fredericksburg fiasco in the winter of 1862-63 and died soon after.[50]

A black veil hung over the commanders of the V and VI Corps. Maj. Gens. Fitz John Porter and William Franklin were fast friends with McClellan and fought under him during the Peninsula Campaign. But when Maj. Gen. John Pope assumed command of the Army of Virginia and was decisively beaten at the Battle of Second Bull Run, he scapegoated both officers and preferred charges against them. McClellan moved quickly to get them back with their commands when he assumed command of the expanded Army of the Potomac. Both participated in the Maryland Campaign, but the cloud remained over their heads and potentially influenced their actions. Antietam would be the last campaign for Porter, who was cashiered from the army; Franklin lasted through the Fredericksburg Campaign before being sent elsewhere.[51]

Maj. Gen. Ambrose Burnside was a close personal friend of McClellan's from their West Point days. Although generally vilified for his actions during the Maryland and Fredericksburg Campaigns, and later for the Crater disaster, he was generally considered an effective general, particularly early in the war when he deployed a land/sea approach to capture much of the North Carolina seacoast, and later in capturing Knoxville, Tennessee. He assumed command of the Army of the Potomac after McClellan's removal in November 1862, and because of continual prodding from Lincoln, felt compelled to fight into the winter, where his army suffered perhaps its worst defeat at the Battle of Fredericksburg.[52]

The most questionable character of the group of Union corps commanders was 59-year old Maj. Gen. Joseph Mansfield. Although he had remained in the army since graduating from West Point, Mansfield had seen limited action. During the Civil War, he commanded the Washington defenses and then became a brigade and division commander in North Carolina, but saw no action there. He was not a fan of a volunteer army and combined with his age and inexperience, the Union high command was reluctant to assign him a combat role. Still, he had friends in high places, and was elevated to command of the XII Corps a mere two days before the battle.[53]

A total of 16 Union infantry divisions and the cavalry division participated in the Maryland Campaign, although not all were engaged. Their commanders were highly trained and for the most part, skilled military men. All but two were West Pointers. Eleven had experience leading a division into battle and the rest, save one, were professional soldiers. A high percentage of these divisional commanders—65% eventually rose to corps command and one would command the army.

The situation was quite different at the brigade level, where 34 of the 44 infantry commanders were led by non-professionals. Thirteen would rise to lead divisions and four later became corps commanders.

Attrition, resignations, and court marshals had rid McClellan's army of many of its initial incompetent officers. Those who remained were certainly better than those he took down to the Virginia Peninsula. However, the new regiments usually brought equally green commanders. The new recruits and their officers did not know how to maneuver or move from column to line of battle, and those who had some training, attained it a mere days before the battle. Division commander, Alpheus Williams wrote home, "The men were of excellent stamp, ready and willing, but neither officers nor men knew anything, and there was an absence of mutual confidence which drill begets. Standing still, they fought bravely." He also explained how he used "a fence to align it" from column into battle line.[54]

Lee benefited by having two effective senior or "wing" officers who he explicitly trusted: Stonewall Jackson and James Longstreet. Both were West Pointers who had begun the war in command of brigades, but quickly rose to their current positions. Although separated by only three years of age, they were vastly different in personality and perspectives. Jackson was quiet, secretive, prickly, and moody, but was a superb offensive fighter. Longstreet was more communicative, less difficult to work with, and favored a defensive approach. They provided Lee with a good balance, and he trusted each, frequently soliciting and welcoming their input. Because of this trust, Lee gave them considerable autonomy that relieved him of the tactical details of battle. He once told an aide: "I plan and work with all my might to bring the troops to the right place at the right time; with that I have done my duty." He left the rest up to his two trusted subordinates.

Both of Lee's senior commanders experienced medical issues during the Maryland Campaign. Like Lee, Jackson experienced "horse" issues. An admirer had given Jackson a fine young horse, but it was not quite broken. On September 6, when Jackson could not get the horse to move, he "lightly" touched her flanks with his spurs and she reared, lost her balance and fell backward. Jackson fell flat on his back. The stunned general remained prone for half an hour before relinquishing his command to his second in command, and retired to an ambulance for the remainder of the day. His sore back continued bothering him during the remainder of the campaign. James Longstreet's malady was much milder by comparison. His boot chafed his foot in early September 1862 and when it would not heal, he resorted to wearing a slipper and riding sidesaddle for much of the campaign.[55]

On paper, the nine division commanders were also impressive: Seven were West Point graduates, one graduated from the Virginia Military Institute, and the last was a 15-year veteran of the U.S. Army. Most were also seasoned in commanding their divisions, as six had commanded their units in at least one battle. But strength on paper does not count in battle and most were not as effective as Lee desired. At least four proved to be problematic: Brig. Gens. Alexander Lawton and J. R. Jones in Jackson's command, and Maj. Gen. Richard Anderson and Brig. Gen. John Walker in Longstreet's, were borderline effective leaders at best. Only A. P. Hill, John Hood, D. R. Jones, D. H. Hill, and Lafayette McLaws could be counted on to excel administratively and on the battlefield.

A total of 39 infantry brigades were scattered among the nine divisions. Brig. Gen. Nathan "Shanks" Evans commanded an independent brigade, bringing the number to 40 with 187 regiments. As many as two-thirds of the brigade commanders had some prior military experience—a much higher figure than in McClellan's army. The numbers do not tell the whole story, however, as Lee imbued an intangible in his officers. According to historian

Scott Hartwig, "It began with Lee, who cultivated an aggressive spirit and encouraged initiative in his subordinates."[56]

The Pennsylvania Campaign of 1863

Most of the infantry corps McClellan brought to Antietam would also fight at Gettysburg, but under different commanders. The I Corps, led by Hooker at Antietam, was commanded by Maj. Gen. John Reynolds at Gettysburg. He should have commanded the Pennsylvania Reserve Division at Antietam, but was recalled by Pennsylvania Governor Andrew Curtin to help organize the State's militia. With the assent of Hooker to command of the Army of the Potomac in January 1863, Reynolds assumed command of the I Corps. Maj. Gen. Winfield Hancock commanded the II Corps, which Sumner led at Antietam. Hancock had assumed command of a division when Israel Richardson was wounded at Antietam, and retained command after Richardson passed away. He climbed to command the II Corps upon the resignation of Maj. Gen. Darius Couch, who had replaced Sumner prior to the Fredericksburg fiasco. The III Corps, not at Antietam, was given to a political general, Maj. Gen. Daniel Sickles, who had commanded a division prior to his rise to corps command before the battle of Chancellorsville.

With Fitz John Porter's court martial and subsequent removal from command of the V Corps, Maj. Gen. George Meade was tapped to replace him. Meade's elevation to army command on June 28 caused him to name division commander, Maj. Gen. George Sykes, as temporary V Corps commander. The VI Corps also had a new leader, Maj. Gen. John Sedgwick, whose II Corps division had been mauled in Antietam's West Woods. He returned to the army after recuperating from his wounds and led the VI Corps during the Chancellorsville Campaign and then the Gettysburg Campaign. The XI Corps, also absent at Antietam, was led by Maj. Gen. Oliver Howard who had a remarkable rise to fame. He commanded a brigade at Antietam and replaced Sedgwick in divisional command after the latter was wounded. Howard then rose to command the XI Corps prior to Chancellorsville, and as senior officer on the field at Gettysburg, commanded the Union forces on July 1 after Reynolds was killed. The final corps commander, Maj. Gen. Henry Slocum, assumed command of the XII Corps after Antietam. He had previously commanded a VI Corps division during the Maryland Campaign.

The Army of the Potomac's corps commanders at Gettysburg were experienced and for the most part, effective. All but one was a West Point graduate, and all but two had commanded their corps at Chancellorsville. The situation was similar with the nineteen division commanders. However, only two of them led divisions at both the Maryland and Gettysburg Campaigns (Maj. Gens. Abner Doubleday and Andrew Humphreys), but all but four had led their divisions at Chancellorsville, so were ready for the challenges of Gettysburg.[57]

These 19 Union divisions fielded a total of 51 brigades. Leaders with formal military experience had already been tapped for higher command, so only 11 (22%) were West Point graduates. A number of them had served in the military prior to the war, but lacked formal training. Only about half had commanded anything like the size of a brigade prior to Gettysburg.

Lee was forced to quickly determine how Stonewall Jackson would be replaced after his mortal wounding at Chancellorsville. The two most obvious choices also had the greatest seniority: Maj. Gens. A. P. Hill and Richard Ewell. Both had effectively commanded divisions under Jackson. Hill had shown to be an aggressive and dependable division commander and appeared ready for higher command. Ewell was a bit more problematic, as he had lost a leg during the Second Bull Run Campaign and was only now returning to the army. Lee believed the two corps system was unwieldy, forcing each commander to oversee too many units and men. This, coupled with his uncertainty that either man could command such a large corps, caused him to split the army into three corps, led by Hill, Ewell, and Longstreet. James Longstreet's First Corps' three division commanders (Lafayette McLaws, John Hood, and George Pickett) were the most experienced in leading large numbers of men. Ewell's Second Corps' division commanders were not as experienced, although two had commanded divisions at Chancellorsville. This included Jubal Early, who rose to division command when Alexander Lawton was wounded at Antietam, and Robert Rodes who assumed command of D. H. Hill's division prior to the Chancellorsville Campaign. Maj. Gen. Edward Johnson commanded Ewell's third division. Like Ewell, he had been wounded the year before, but had experience leading a small army in 1861-62, in what is now West Virginia. A.P. Hill's Third Corps division commanders were probably the least experienced. Two, Dorsey Pender and Henry Heth, commanded brigades at Chancellorsville and were elevated to division command when their two units were created. Maj. Gen. Richard Anderson was the most experienced, and had performed well as a brigade commander, but his performance as a division commander was spotty.

Like the Army of the Potomac, Lee's army lacked formally trained brigade commanders. Of the 37 brigades at Gettysburg, only 11 (30%) graduated from a military academy, but what they lacked in education, they made up in experience, as 70% had prior combat experience as brigade commanders prior to Gettysburg.

Comparisons of the Two Campaigns

Both armies' corps/wing commanders during both campaigns were the elite. The proportion of professional soldiers was about the same in the Union army at Antietam and Gettysburg—five of the six at Antietam (83%) and six of the seven corps commanders at Gettysburg (86%). All of the Confederate corps commanders at Antietam and Gettysburg were West Point graduates.

The nine and a half months after Antietam saw two major campaigns pitting the Army of Northern Virginia against the Army of the Potomac. The armies lost 12,653 and 5,377 respectively at Fredericksburg and 12,764 and 17,287 respectively at Chancellorsville. The losses were especially high in both armies' officer corps. Stonewall Jackson's mortal wounding at Chancellorsville changed Lee's army in profound ways. Not only did he lose the services of an aggressive and effective leader, it also forced him to reorganize his army. Gone were two large corps-- replaced by three smaller ones. Lee would march north with two green corps commanders that were found wanting during the Pennsylvania Campaign.

Experience in command is equally important to education and there were some distinct differences in the two campaigns. Whereas two of the corps commanders in the Union army were inexperienced leading such large commands at both Antietam and Gettysburg, both Confederate wing commanders were experienced at Antietam, but only a third of those commanding corps at Gettysburg had experience commanding such large bodies of troops in battle.

At a qualitative level, the Union corps commanders stacked up well against each other during the two campaigns. At Antietam, one was highly effective (Hooker), one a bit rash (Sumner), three somewhat cautious (Porter, Franklin, and Burnside) and one was very new (Mansfield). At Gettysburg, three or four were highly effective (Reynolds, Hancock, Sedgwick, and perhaps Slocum), one could be rash (Sickles), and two were considered unremarkable (Sykes and Howard).

The divisional commanders were a different story. The number of Union officers with formal military training declined from 88% at Antietam to 53% at Gettysburg. The Confederate army actually improved over time: At Antietam, 89% had some formal military education and increased to 100% at Gettysburg. The division commanders in both armies were more seasoned at Gettysburg than at Antietam. As many as 69% of Union army division commanders had commanded a like-sized unit prior to Antietam; this grew to 79% at Gettysburg. Similarly, 66% of Lee's divisional commanders at Antietam had commanded a like-sized unit before the Maryland Campaign, but 78% had this experience during the Pennsylvania Campaign.

While four Confederate generals commanded divisions during both invasions (44%), 22% commanded brigades at Antietam, and three were not even present at Antietam (33%).[58]

On the Union side, only two Union generals (11%) commanded divisions during both battles, 26% were present at Antietam as brigade commanders, and one division commander at Antietam (George Greene) commanded a brigade at Gettysburg. Additionally, a regimental commander (Francis Barlow) and a divisional artillery commander (Romeyn Ayres) at Antietam (11%) handled divisions at Gettysburg. Finally, ten (53%) of Gettysburg divisional commanders were not on the battlefield at Antietam: David Birney, John Geary, Alexander Hays, Albion Howe, Andrew Humphreys, John Robinson, Horatio Wright, Carl Schurz, Adolph von Steinwehr, James Wadsworth.

The only major difference at the brigade level was in the number of Union officers possessing formal military training. During the Maryland Campaign, 41% were West Pointers, compared with only 22% at Gettysburg. All other variables were similar in the two campaigns, where 30% of the Confederate brigade commanders in both campaigns had graduated from a military academy. At the experience level, 43% of the Union commanders at Antietam and 49% at Gettysburg had led a brigade in a prior battle. The numbers are even more impressive for the Confederates, where 70% of the brigade commanders had prior experience in leading a brigade in both campaigns.

Table 8: Comparison of the Size and Experience of the Infantry

Issue	Maryland Campaign	Pennsylvania Campaign
Corps/wing commanders with formal military education	Confederate: 2/2 (100%) Union: 5/6 (83%)	Confederate: 3/3 (100%) Union: 6/7 (86%)
Corps/wing commanders with experience in at least one battle at that level	Confederate: 2/2 (100) Union: 4/6 (66%)	Confederate: 1/3 (33%) Union: 5/7 (71%)
Division commanders with formal military education	Confederate: 8/9 (89%) Union: 14/16 (88%)	Confederate: 9/9 (100%) Union: 10/19 (53%)
Division commanders with experience in at least one battle at that level	Confederate: 6/9 (66%) Union: 11/16 (69%)	Confederate: 7/9 (78%) Union: 15/19 (79%)
Brigade commanders with formal military education	Confederate: 12/40 (30%) Union: 18/44 (41%)	Confederate: 11/37 (30%) Union: 11/51 (22%)
Brigade commanders with prior experience	Confederate: 28/40 (70%) Union: 19/44 (43%)	Confederate: 26/37 (70%) Union: 25/51 (49%)

Chapter 4: Supplies, Morale, and the Men's Condition

Supplies

The Maryland Campaign of 1862

The onset of the Maryland Campaign found Lee fretting about the condition of his army, which was plagued by all sorts of shortages. A lack of shoes for the men, and inadequate food, horses, and men alike, were among his greatest concerns. Col. Edward McCrady of the 1st South Carolina recalled that fully a third of his men were barefoot at the beginning of the Maryland Campaign. Division commander, Gen. Lafayette McLaws, complained to his wife about his men's condition as they marched north to join Lee's army prior to the Maryland Campaign: "Many of our men are without shoes and all of them are very ragged, in addition we have been marching for the last three days with nothing to east but fresh meat and green corn ... One day there was nothing to eat."[1]

Lee had few options. The army occupied Fairfax County after the Second Bull Run Campaign, but it was stripped of anything usable and the railroads (Orange & Alexandria and the Virginia Central) were inadequate in delivering supplies. He considered dividing his army so each portion could forage off the land, but quickly discounted this idea as "it would be folly" particularly in the face of a powerful Union army. Henry Heth, commander of a brigade at Chancellorsville and a division at Gettysburg, was one of few on a first-name basis with Lee. In a letter after the war, he described a conversation with Lee in 1864 about the Maryland Campaign: "I considered the problem in every possible phase, and to my mind, it resolved itself into a choice of one of two things—either to retire to Richmond and stand a siege, which must ultimately have ended in surrender, or to invade Pennsylvania."[2]

Issues relating to supply can also be seen in the Confederate uniforms. Unlike their Union counterparts, Lee's men were not attired in the same type of clothes, but wore a mix of gray and butternut of a variety of styles, all because of the South's inability to provide consistent uniforms to the men. They were therefore forced to improvise, receiving uniforms from home or grabbing them from dead Yanks on the battlefield. This often led to confusion when Southern troops wore blue blouses, or trousers. They tried not to wear an entire blue uniform, for obvious reasons. The same lack of conformity was true of their hats which could be found in a wild variety of styles and colors. The men traveled light. A young Virginian recalled how he carried, "a musket, cartridge box with forty rounds of cartridges, cloth haversack, blanket and canteen."[3]

Although not in as desperate straits as Lee's army, McClellan's men also experienced supply problems at the end of the Second Bull Run Campaign. The issue was most profound in the original units of the Army of the Potomac who had moved north to help defend Washington from Lee's onslaught. Chief Quartermaster, Col. Rufus Ingalls explained how it took a full month to transport the army to the Peninsula in April, so it could not be "brought back in a day." Shortages were not restricted to these units. Brig. Gen. Abner Doubleday who commanded a brigade in the III Corps of the Army of Virginia, requested equipment and clothing replacements for his men after Second Bull Run, but "owing to the great number making requisitions, mine were not filled and we were soon obliged to take the field deficient in everything." An officer in the IX Corps wrote home on September 5, that his men "looked very bad ... Almost naked & worn out."[4]

The muskets in both armies remained a problem, as arming such growing armies put a tremendous strain on both governments, forcing them to look abroad for assistance. Many unscrupulous manufacturers took advantage of the opportunity by unloading their least effective weapons. For example, the rookie 118th Pennsylvania did not realize that when they went into action at Shepherdstown on September 19, fully half of their Enfield rifles were defective. With the Confederates bearing down on them, this was not a time to learn about this issue.

Many units began the war using smoothbore muskets, effective at up to a mere 75 yards. About 90% of the Confederate infantrymen carried these weapons during the early stages of the war, but they were gradually replaced by rifles. By the Maryland Campaign, 70% of Lee's infantry carried rifles that had an effective range of 300-500 yards. Over 80% of the Union troops carried these arms. Rifles were not a panacea, however, for they came from a variety of manufacturers and were of a variety of calibers, including .52, .53, .577, .58, and .69. Uniformity of arms was important in a unit as it made resupply of cartridges less of a nightmare, but an inspection of the 11th

Pennsylvania Reserves on September 8 found the men equipped with five different types of rifles.[5]

The supply issue was compounded by a lack of time to reequip the men as the Maryland Campaign came right on the heels of the Second Bull Run Campaign.

The Pennsylvania Campaign of 1863

Joseph Hooker's ascension to command of the Union army resulted in a plethora of needed supplies flowing to his men of the Army of the Potomac. Those who had been ragged and hungry were well supplied before the Chancellorsville Campaign. The same cannot be said for the Confederates who continued suffering from inadequate quantities of food, clothing, and supplies. Confederate general Carnot Posey wrote home that during the seven days of the Chancellorsville Campaign, he only ate one small meal per day and slept a total of twelve hours.[6]

Gen. Henry Heth wrote after the war, "It is very difficult for anyone not connected with the Army of Northern Virginia to realize how straitened we were for supplies of all kinds, especially food." During the winter of 1862-83, Lee was forced to reduce the men's daily rations to 18 ounces of flour and four ounces of bacon. The resulting 1,800 calories caused active men to lose weight and the dearth of fresh fruits and vegetables led to outbreaks of scurvy. Each regiment was ordered to send out daily details to collect edible weeds, such as sassafras buds, lamb's quarters, and wild onions.

The problem was not a dearth of supplies—there were plenty in the South—it was the inefficient system of collecting and transporting supplies to the soldiers and civilians who needed them. The blame could be placed squarely on Commissary General Lucius Northrup, who despite his incompetence, was protected by his friend and former comrade, Jefferson Davis. The *Official Records* abounds with Lee's desperate pleadings for help in resolving the critical supply issue that consumed so much of his time and worry. The situation became so dire on January 26, 1863 that Lee wrote to Secretary of War James Seddon, "We now have about one week supply of the reduced rations. After that is exhausted I know not whence further supplies can be drawn. The question of provisions is becoming one of greater difficulty every day."[7]

The armies did have time on their side and the men were able to rest for almost a month before embarking on the Pennsylvania Campaign. However, supplies remained a problem. When Meade's assumed command of the Army of the Potomac in June 1863, one of his first meetings was with the army's quartermaster to attempt to speed the flow of needed supplies. Most concerning were the dearth of shoes—as many as a quarter of Meade's men marched with bare feet or were on the verge of it. Because of the army's distance from Washington, Meade established a supply depot around Westminster, about 22 miles from Gettysburg, to speed the movement of goods to his army.

One of Lee's major goals during the Pennsylvania Campaign was securing massive amounts of supplies to feed his army in the future. The farmers were compensated for their wares most of the time, but usually in worthless Confederate script. Even during the four days Lee's army spent at Gettysburg, his quartermasters were combing the region for supplies. Citizens residing near Gettysburg claimed they lost 800 horses, 12 mules, 1,000 heads of cattle, 200 hogs, and 400 sheep, in addition to 100 wagons and 50 carriages. During the retreat, the wagon train carrying booty was 15-20 miles long, carrying many thousands of tons of grain and other eatables.

By Gettysburg, most of remaining troops on both sides sporting smoothbore muskets now carried rifled weapons. Some still persisted in retaining their short-ranged muskets, such as the Irish Brigade and the 12th New Jersey.[8]

Morale & Straggling

The Maryland Campaign of 1862

With its constant setbacks, hard marches, and often a scarcity of edible food and supplies, it is not surprising that morale in the Union army was at a low point at the start of the Maryland Campaign. Division commander Brig. Gen. Alpheus Williams wrote home, "[f]or over three weeks we have been scarcely a day without marching—for at least seven days without rations." This only exacerbated the men's morale issues. Excessive consumption of alcohol remained an issue, and too many officers spent their days in a drunken stupor. The low morale among the men manifested itself in desertions, illness, and insubordination. The officers' poor leadership also allowed many of the foot soldiers to straggle excessively, sapping the strength of McClellan's army. McClellan became so concerned about the level of straggling that he issued the following circular on September 9:

> The general commanding has observed the frequent absence from their commands while in camp, and from their columns on the march, of superior officers. These laxities must be remedied. Inattention and carelessness on the part of those high in rank has been one fertile source of the straggling and want of discipline which now obtain in the various corps. The safety of the country depends upon what this army shall now achieve; it cannot be successful if its soldiers are one-half skulking to the rear, while the brunt of battle is borne by the other half, and its officers inattentive to observe and correct the grossest evils which are daily occurring under their eyes. The general commanding entreats all general officers to lend every energy to the eradication of the military vice of straggling. He feels assured that their united determination can break up the practice in a single week.

McClellan followed up on the circular with General Orders No. 155 the same day. It dealt specifically with reducing straggling and included roll calls before each march, at each halt, and at the end of each march. Lists of missing men were to be sent to the regiment's adjutant who was to affix the term "straggler" and date to their record. Retribution included loss of pay for the time absent and physical punishment. Officers who did not comply would be reported and possibly brought to trial. Each regiment would establish a strong rearguard and flankers to collect stragglers and return them to the ranks. "The bayonet must be used to insure obedience to these orders," McClellan wrote. Some officers deployed these requirements more strenuously than others and enjoyed a much lower straggling rate, but often earned the enmity of their men.[9]

Straggling was only one cause for the excessive number of soldiers missing from their units. Sickness also took its toll on the men, as did, of course, losses in battle. These sapped a unit's strength by as much as a half. For example, Brig. Gen. Samuel Crawford's XII Corps brigade was down to 629 effectives on September 9, causing him to write to his superiors in a manner that underscored his training as a doctor: "There are many men belonging to the command who cannot, from absolute want of muscular tone, follow in its marches. Men never known to fall behind, upon previous marches, do so now . . . There is nothing which keeps them together but the common interest and association, and I have no hesitation in saying that unless some opportunity is afforded these regiments to rest and to reorganize, their regimental character will cease to exist."[10]

The army did have one factor counteracting its low morale-- the wildly popular McClellan. A soldier in the 9th New York Infantry noted on September 10: "McClellan seems to have put new life into everything, and I hope we will only get a fair shake at the enemy."[11]

After almost continual campaigning for three months, Lee's army was exhausted. According to Brig. Gen. John Walker, a division commander, Lee intended to rest his men for several days at Frederick, Maryland, so they could rest and prepare for the rest of the invasion, but events at Harpers Ferry would mitigate this opportunity.

Many men also straggled in Lee's army, despite their high morale. Maj. Gen. Lafayette McLaws reported his division mustered 7,188 on July 20, but after extensive marching without fighting, the numbers fell by nearly fifty percent to 3,700 men. Straggling had many causes. Trying to walk long distances without shoes is all but impossible and many men lagged behind their comrades. Not having enough to eat sapped their energy, so many could not keep up. The rich supplies Lee hoped to secure did not materialize. The wheat had not yet been harvested and most herds of cattle had been driven north, out of their reach. Lee could not afford to force the Marylanders to surrender food to his army as it could earn their enmity. As a result, most of the men's diet consisted of green apples and corn, which often wreaked havoc on their digestive systems, forcing many to fall from the ranks.

Some Southerners fell from the ranks when ordered to cross the Potomac River and enter Union territory. These soldiers believed they were fighting to protect their homeland, not invade the North. Effective officers could dramatically reduce the incidence of straggling, but were counteracted by the Conscription Act which required all regiments to reelect their officers. This led to elections of more lenient officers, replacing the more effective ones who had been tough and made their men toe the line. Charles Marshall, one of Lee's staff officers noted, the "worst consequences anticipated by the opponents of the elective system were realized." The impact was immediate. Brig. Gen. Cadmus Wilcox explained, "[w]e have no discipline in our army, it is but little better than an armed mob."[12]

Lee's General Orders No. 94 was similar to McClellan's General Orders No. 155 in attempting to reduce straggling. The August 11, 1862 order created a provost guard to march behind each division, accompanied by a surgeon. Those judged ill were transported to the rear; the others were pushed forward to rejoin their units. The order was spotty in its enforcement, so excess straggling continued. Lee followed up with General Orders No. 102 on the eve of the invasion (September 4, 1862), appointing Brig. Gen. Lewis Armistead to oversee the provost guard. Lee's wording was especially harsh in this order: "Stragglers are usually those who desert their comrades in peril. Such characters are better absent from the army on such momentous occasions as those about to be entered upon. They will, as bringing discredit upon our cause, as useless members of the service . . . and be considered as unworthy members of an army which has immortalized itself in the recent glorious and successful engagements against the enemy, and will be brought before a military commission to receive the punishment due to their misconduct . . . The gallant soldiers who have so nobly sustained our cause by heroism in battle will assist the commanding general in securing success by aiding their officers in checking the desire for straggling among their comrades." Lee understood peer pressure and used it to help reduce the incidence of straggling.[13]

The order was apparently not having the desired impact, for Lee wrote to Jefferson Davis on September 7: "…there are individuals who, from their backwardness in duty, tardiness of movement, and neglect of orders, do it [the army] no credit. These, if possible, should be removed from its rolls if they cannot be improved by correction." Lee further explained his concerns about the tardiness of the court martial process: "We require more promptness and certainty of punishment."[14]

What Lee's army lacked in numbers, it more than made up for in morale, particularly because most of the malcontents had been left behind in Virginia. Artillery officer, Porter Alexander recalled that by the time of the Maryland Campaign, the army "had acquired that magnificent morale which made them equal to twice their numbers." A young Marylander watching Lee's soldiers pass by, noted, "they were the dirtiest men I ever saw, a most ragged, lean and hungry set of wolves. Yet there was a dash about them that Northern men lacked. They rode like circus riders. Many of them were from the far South and spoke a dialect I could scarcely understand. They were profane beyond belief and talked incessantly."[15]

The Pennsylvania Campaign of 1863

Morale among the Confederates was probably at an all-time high when the Army of Northern Virginia embarked on the Pennsylvania Campaign. Staff officer Dudley Pendleton wrote, "Our army [is] in the finest spirits & health." The men had bested the Union army, or at least they did in their own minds, on most every battlefield and their belief in Lee almost became God-like. Another staff officer wrote home to his mother that he and the army "will go any where with Genl Lee & its comdrs." The men worried about the loss of Stonewall Jackson, but artillerist William Pegram wrote, "His death will not have the effect of making our troops fight any worse." William Ballinger probably summed it up best: "What a glorious army that of Lee is." Many men continued wearing rags for uniforms and many men remained shoeless or almost so, but these took a back seat to the feeling that total victory would soon be achieved.[16]

The opposite was true of the men in blue. Despite a long string of losses and a borderline victory, the men became more optimistic after Joseph Hooker was installed as commander of the Army of the Potomac during the winter of 1862-1863. He quickly moved to restore discipline, resupply the troops, and provide them with good things to eat, like fresh bread. The Army of the Potomac embarked on the Chancellorsville Campaign with higher spirits than at any time since the beginning of the war. Their hopes were dashed, however, by their devastating loss at Chancellorsville, driving them back to despair about the prospects for victory. A soldier in the II Corps explained, "There is only one real reason [for our defeat at Chancellorsville], and that the simplest possible, -- our army didn't fight as well as that of our enemies. We had every possible advantage . . . They beat us easily." An officer in the Iron Brigade exclaimed, "What an unfortunate set of fellows we are, and have been." Yet, an indomitable spirit remained, as another officer noted, his troops possessed "something of the English bulldog . . . You can whip them time and again, but the next fight they go into, they are in good spirits, and as full of pluck as ever. They are used to being whipped, and no longer mind it. Some day or other we shall have our turn."[17]

They would have something in their favor, however—they were fighting on their own soil and that would make all the difference in the world.

The Men's Condition

The Maryland Campaign of 1862

The North enjoyed a number of advantages over its adversary, such as in the availability of food and supplies. Another was in the Union's medical service, which was vastly superior. They also may have had more competent medical leaders, such as Dr. Jonathan Letterman. A 38-year old career soldier who had never married, Letterman was thrust into the position of the Army of the Potomac's medical director on June 19, 1862. He found an army suffering from scurvy, resulting from a poor diet, unhealthy sanitary conditions, and inadequate medical care. He quickly went to work improving matters. He gained a strong ally in George McClellan, who drafted several orders addressing Letterman's concerns (Special Order No. 197, General Orders No. 139, 147, and 150). Letterman's biographer noted that in Letterman's appointment letter, he was given "widespread authority, coupled with autonomy moderated solely by the requirement that Letterman keep him advised of actions taken and submit requests for necessary supplies." The biographer went on to claim, "No medical director in the history of the United States Army has been given such widespread authority."[18]

Letterman's orders (through McClellan) affected many aspects of each soldier's life. Letterman knew the importance of a healthy diet to promote well being, so he insisted that every company would designate two men as cooks. Scurvy was a problem, so Letterman ensured adequate amounts of fruits and vegetables in the diet. Tents should be provided and periodically moved to promote sanitation, he insisted. Drills were to be limited to two, 45-minute sessions each day. He directed how outhouses were to be constructed and placed and the proper disposal of kitchen wastes. He also mandated a 15-minute bath each week. The impact was almost immediate, for by August, the number of men experiencing illness had declined by a third.[19]

Letterman also turned his attention to the wounded. He created an ambulance corps, staffed with soldiers trained to care for the wounded. Letterman also used a rolling system for the wounded. He identified field hospitals near the battlefields and then, when the men were able to travel, sent them to larger military hospitals that tended to be in cities. He also used a triage system to determine which soldiers should receive priority treatment, those that could wait, and those that were beyond medical assistance.

A member of the Sanitary Commission found Letterman to be an incessant smoker and "dry, taciturn, and impenetrable." Yet, "Out of confusion…[Letterman] fashioned order and a system."[20]

These modernizations were being put into place as the Army of the Potomac marched through Maryland in September 1862. He had the added challenge of trying to train the medical staff of the 36 rookie regiments who had recently joined the army. He also found time to order up 200 wagons and 100 ambulances and established a large hospital in Frederick to receive the wounded. As the army converged on Sharpsburg, Letterman established large hospitals at Keedysville and Smoketown and sent his aides to establish hospitals within five miles of the projected battlefield. He told them to "choose barns well provided with hay and straw, as preferable to houses, since they are better ventilated, and enabled Medical officers to attend a greater number of wounded." He also sent medical supplies to each of these hospitals."

The Maryland Campaign became the test of Letterman's medical advancements and all worked well. His newly formed ambulance corps operated effectively and efficiently during the South Mountain battles on September 14. As the battle raged and men were receiving medical attention, Letterman turned his attention to ensuring an abundant flow of supplies to each hospital.[21]

Dr. Lafayette Guild was the Army of Northern Virginia's medical director. He and Jonathan Lettermen shared many similarities. Both graduated from the Jefferson Medical College in Philadelphia and then entered the U.S. Army's Medical Corps. Guild was dismissed from the Union army at the start of the war for not taking the oath of allegiance and traveled south to join the

Confederate army. Both were appointed to the top medical director positions of their respective armies during the Peninsula/Seven Days Campaign when they were in their late 30's. Without the basic necessities, such as adequate numbers of medical personnel, medical equipment, supplies, and wagons, Guild was forced to perform the basics of caring for the men and the wounded without the ability to innovate. He was, however, able to establish a variety of protocols that prevented the spread of venereal disease.

Confederate hospitals were an onerous sight. Descriptions of "a deplorable want of cleanliness" and the "most extreme filth and positive indications of neglect" were commonplace. However, Guild adamantly required all divisional wagons to carry spare clothing for the wounded so they would not be required to lie in blood soaked garments.

While Letterman and his assistants actively prepared for the large battle in Maryland, it appears that Guild was still caring for the wounded of the Second Bull Run Campaign in Virginia. In a letter to Jefferson Davis on September 13, Lee wrote, "Dr. Guild, the Medical Director, with detachments from each brigade, was left upon the field, and all the wounded committed to his care. All the means of transportation at our command were given to him, including the wagons, with directions that they were ordered to be forwarded thence to Gordonsville, as fast as possible." It is unclear how many wagons actually reached Lee's army in time to transport the wounded. This may have been the reason why Guild failed to file a report after the campaign.[22]

The Pennsylvania Campaign of 1863

Dr. Letterman continued perfecting his medical systems during the Fredericksburg and Chancellorsville Campaigns, so by Gettysburg, the army's medical corps was operating efficiently and effectively. He learned how railroads could be used during these campaigns to transport the wounded to larger medical facilities. As the armies converged on Gettysburg, Letterman established a supply depot at Westminster, about 25 miles away and began bulking up on materials the hospitals would require.

As the battle raged on July 1, Letterman and his staff identified field hospitals near the fighting and moved surgeons and supplies to each. Despite his planning, Letterman was unable to get enough supplies to the hospitals during the battle. Another, more pressing issue arose when some of his designated field hospitals came under enemy fire, forcing their evacuation and relocation.

One of his greatest achievements at Gettysburg was the establishment of the large Camp Letterman field hospital outside of the town. This large tent-city allowed most of the smaller hospitals in barns and homes to close and send their patients to a consolidated medical center.[23]

Lafayette Guild appears to have been present at Gettysburg. Most of his report of the actions of his medical department centered on trying to get the wounded back to Virginia in the face of ongoing enemy attacks and inadequate supplies.[24]

Comparisons of the Two Campaigns

The two campaigns differed dramatically in the length of time the men could rest after the prior campaign. There was virtually no rest for the Confederates between the end of the Second Bull Run Campaign and the start of the Maryland Campaign. The Union troops had a bit more than a week to partially recuperate. The armies had the luxury of almost a month to rest after the battle of Chancellorsville, so when the Pennsylvania Campaign began, both were in better shape for long marches.

The short span between the Second Bull Run Campaign and the Maryland Campaign caused a supply issue for both armies. Although the longer inactive period prior to the Pennsylvania Campaign could potentially allow each army to be resupplied and reequipped, such was not the case, as Meade complained about lack of shoes and other needed supplies shortly after he assumed command of the army.

Probably because of the short duration of the 1862 invasion, Lee's quartermasters collected far fewer supplies than during the much longer Pennsylvania Campaign. Lee may have lost the Battle of Gettysburg, but he returned to Virginia with tons of grain and thousands of livestock.

Straggling was a major issue for both armies during the Maryland Campaign because the men were ill-clothed, ill-equipped, and exhausted by the constant campaigning. The rest at the beginning of the Pennsylvania Campaign was a Godsend for both armies and may have worked to reduce the incidence of straggling. The men, especially the Union soldiers, were also more proficient at marching than perhaps they were during the Maryland Campaign.

Morale was high for the Confederate army during both campaigns and uniformly low for the Union army.

Table 9: Comparison of Supplies and Morale

Issue	Maryland Campaign	Pennsylvania Campaign
Length of time to rest/refit men	Less than a week	At least a month
Supplies	**Confederate:** Deficient **Union:** Deficient	**Confederate:** Deficient **Union:** Adequate
Morale	**Confederate:** High **Union:** Low	**Confederate:** High **Union:** Low
Straggling	**Confederate:** Yes **Union:** Yes	**Confederate:** Yes **Union:** Yes
Special Orders against straggling	Issued by both armies	Not issued by either army
Medical Departments	**Confederates:** Undersupplied **Union:** Well-supplied and innovative	**Confederates:** Undersupplied **Union:** Well-supplied

PART 2: GETTING TO THE BATTLEFIELD

Chapter 5: Intelligence Gathering

A variety of resources were available to both armies for ascertaining the size and movements of the enemy, including: the Provost Marshal, Signal Corps, Military Telegraph and, potentially, the cavalry. The Union army often used balloons, however, U. S. Balloon Corps, the brainchild of Professor Thaddeus Lowe, was grounded during the Maryland Campaign for a lack of transportation, so its balloons and attendants languished in Washington.[1]

Military Intelligence

The Maryland Campaign of 1862

The Union's military intelligence apparatus was still in its infancy during the Maryland Campaign and the Confederate's would not come into being until 1864. Early in his tenure as commander of the Army of the Potomac, McClellan tapped Allen Pinkerton to head up his military intelligence operation. While Pinkerton had developed somewhat of a network of dependable spies in Virginia, although he regularly inflated the strength of the enemy, it did not extend into Maryland, so he could provide even less accurate information during the Maryland Campaign. Pinkerton also operated with about half his normal complement of aides during the campaign, as he left a number behind in Washington. Whatever Pinkerton learned was sent directly to McClellan's headquarters with little or no analysis or interpretation. The information was often wrong, for whether in Virginia or Maryland, Pinkerton regularly overestimated the size of Lee's army. Some have opined that Pinkerton intentionally exploded the enemy's numbers to keep in line with McClellan's thinking. Now in largely friendly territory, with additional sources available, McClellan was presented with a wealth of information, of mixed veracity. One of his sources of information was Pennsylvania Governor Andrew Curtin, who was running his own ring of spies. Curtin also sent inflated numbers of the size of Lee's army that was beyond even Pinkerton's most extreme estimations. The often conflicting information, coupled with not having a mechanism to sort through it to find patterns, caused McClellan some hesitancy. He wrote General-in-Chief Henry Halleck on the evening of September 8: "Our information is still entirely too indefinite to justify definite action . . . As soon as I find out where to strike, I will be after them without an hour's delay." He also wired Curtin, "My information about the enemy comes from unreliable sources, and it is vague and conflicting."

The Lincoln administration demanded continual information about Lee, forcing McClellan to send a stream of wildly conflicting reports to Washington. McClellan informed Halleck on September 9, "From such information as can be obtained, Jackson and Longstreet have about 110,000 men of arms near Frederick." Earlier in the day the *New York Herald* reported Lee's army numbering no less than 150,000, when in actuality, he probably had fewer than 50,000 men at that time. Those reports put too much reliance on the statements of deserters and captured enemy soldiers, some of the inflated numbers resulted from the untrained eye of civilians observers, and quite a bit came from an active disinformation campaign the Confederates were conducting to deceive the enemy.[2]

Not only were there disparities in the estimates of Lee's army's strength, the situation was not much better in discerning Lee's location and intentions. The wealth of information emanating from Frederick, beginning on September 7, suggested Lee was concentrating his army there. By September 9, McClellan could confidently inform Halleck, "I am now in condition to watch him closely." However, McClellan became confused when reports began arriving on September 10, (which proved accurate), of observations of large bodies of Lee's men marching back *toward* the Potomac River—actually two-thirds of the enemy army. The movement did not portend the end of the invasion, as many in Washington hoped, but the movement to capture the Harpers Ferry garrison. McClellan attempted to reassure Lincoln by informing him, "I have scouts and spies pushed forward in every direction, and shall soon be in possession of reliable and definite information."[3]

While Lee may have received information from loyal Marylanders, his major sources of information emanated from his cavalry. As we will see, this information was largely accurate, but lapses caused major issues during the campaign.

Counter-intelligence operations were almost as important as intelligence gathering during both campaigns, and comprised of: "activities conducted to identify, deceive, exploit, disrupt, or protect against enemy intelligence." During the Maryland Campaign, Southern officers regularly spread disinformation. For example, Stonewall Jackson helped spread word that Lee's ultimate destination was Pennsylvania. It may have been down the road, but not when he made these remarks to Maryland civilians. Ongoing reports that Lee's destination was Washington early in the campaign helped freeze McClellan from following the enemy army moving north. Deserters and prisoners regularly passed intentionally incorrect information about Lee's numbers and locations to their captors. The Northern press was an active consumer of this misinformation and spread these rumors throughout their readership. Perhaps the best example of intentional misinformation was when Lee sent his cavalry toward Falls Church and Alexandria as the rest of his army trudged north to Leesburg.[4]

Whether intentional counterintelligence or not, McClellan also received a stream of reports suggesting that Lee was about to be reinforced by strong Rebel armies: Braxton Bragg from the west with 40,000 men moving down the Shenandoah Valley, and Joseph Johnston from the south. These communications proved false, but raised the specter of McClellan being crushed by two or three converging armies.[5]

The Pennsylvania Campaign of 1863

By the start of the Pennsylvania Campaign, the Army of the Potomac had dramatically improved its ability to collect, analyze, and use intelligence about the enemy's strength, their movements, and in some cases, intentions. The Confederates, on the other hand, performed poorly, resulting, in large part, to the collision with the Union army at Gettysburg.

Allen Pinkerton and his staff of operatives left the army after McClellan was removed from command in November 1862. He was replaced by teams of scouts and spies called "operatives." The Provost Marshal's office under Brig. Gen. Marsena Patrick also interrogated prisoners, deserters, and runaway slaves. In exchange for useful information, Confederate soldiers were rewarded with no or reduced prison time, release to home (if within Union hands) and free passage into the North, where they could work for a living. Patrick and his men also arrested suspected enemy spies.

During the early part of 1863, newly minted commander of the Army of the Potomac, Joseph Hooker, ordered Patrick to establish a dedicated military intelligence unit within his department, which became known as the Bureau of Military Intelligence (BMI). Information from the operatives, the Signal Corps, cavalry, and others was sent to the BMI, who had special agents skilled at piecing together the often disparate information into a clearer picture of the enemy's movements and numbers. Col. George Sharpe was placed in charge of the BMI and he created an effective unit that sent streams of accurate information to the army commander. According to one expert, "The management of the secret service of an army requires a profound insight into human nature, and an ability to estimate at once the military worth of the information brought in." The BMI almost immediately went to work recruiting and creating a spy network that would serve it well during the Pennsylvania Campaign.

The South did not create a military intelligence arm until 1864 and it never came close to the effectiveness of the North's. Lee's army collected information when it could, through interrogation of prisoners and the use of spies, such as "Harrison" who was employed by James Longstreet. Lee retained a small staff and he was the only one who regularly pieced together seemingly conflicting pieces of intelligence to form a picture of the size and location of the enemy. Lee became quite adept at this vital task, but it took him away from other important duties.

The Signal Corps

The Signal Corps was another important tool for detecting enemy movements and reporting them to the army's high command. The system was developed by army surgeon, Maj. Albert Myer, and was adopted by the military in 1860. The tools of the trade included the ubiquitous flags and torches that used ciphers with prearranged keywords to ensure the enemy could not translate the messages. One of Myer's assistants prior to the war, Lt. Edward Porter Alexander, joined the Confederacy when the war began and used his experiences to organize a Confederate counterpart. It was Porter and his fellow signalmen who transmitted the Union flanking movement at First Bull Run. Lee eschewed maintaining an officer on his staff to direct signal operations, so it became less of an important information source to him.

The Maryland Campaign of 1862

Both armies utilized several signal stations during the Maryland Campaign to report enemy movements. Lee's initial movements into Maryland were reported by Union signal stations on Sugar Loaf Mountain and at Point of Rocks. Because they did not have a telegraph link, information was sent to Poolesville and Harpers Ferry, respectively, significantly slowing the transmission of information. Sugar Loaf Mountain, just west of Hyattstown, looming 1,281 feet above sea level, was of special importance to both armies as it held a "range of vision unequaled by that from any other in Maryland." It was initially held by the Union signal corps at the start of the invasion and its commander, Lt. Brinkerhoff Miner, signaled Poolesville at 4:00 p.m. on September 4 with information of a large wagon train near Leesburg, Virginia moving toward the Potomac River, shelling of the Monocacy Aqueduct, and he predicted the enemy "are attempting to cross [the Potomac River]." He was correct, and by September 6, the enemy was so close that Miner and his signalman abandoned the high vantage point and made their way to safety. They were captured by enemy cavalry and Confederate signalmen soon scaled the heights to watch the Union army. Sugar Loaf Mountain was so important to McClellan that he sent several cavalry forays to retake it and when they failed, sent a strong infantry contingent on September 11, which recaptured it. If the mountain had been captured the day before, the signalmen would have seen long lines of Lee's men leaving Frederick, moving northwest.

During the battle of Antietam, Elk Mountain (Red Hill) housed the major Union station, under the command of Lt. Joseph Gloskoski. He noted in his report: "The point chosen for observations was an excellent one, and messages sent from it very important. From there we had full view of the enemy's lines. We have reported immediately the positions and each change of position of all their batteries and their forces." Gloskoski's men communicated the information to five stations located on the battlefield, including McClellan's, Burnside's and Hooker's headquarters and "two in the center of our lines." Gloskoski transmitted messages throughout the battle and informed Burnside of A. P. Hill's division's approach to the battlefield during the late afternoon: "Look well to your left. The enemy are moving a strong force in that direction." The locations of the Confederate stations are poorly known. The cupola of Sharpsburg's Lutheran Church served as one, and another may have been located behind the West Woods.[6]

The Pennsylvania Campaign of 1863

Both sides used signal stations, but the North's was vastly more extensive and effective during the Pennsylvania Campaign. For example, a Union signal station atop Maryland Heights, complete with a well-functioning telegraph line, sent a stream of information about Lee's movements north through Maryland during the campaign. The observation post could scan an area northward, from Martinsburg to Williamsport. It could not, however, accurately predict Lee's destination.[7]

The first indication of Lee's possible "mischief" came from balloonists' observations. A balloon that ascended from Bank's Ford on the Rappahannock River and another at White Oak Church observed empty Confederate camps on June 4. However, the usefulness of this avenue faded because of inadequate care of the balloons leading to their grounding for safety reasons.[8]

The Bureau of Military Intelligence also played an outsized role in obtaining information on Lee's movements.[9]

The Cavalry

The cavalry had great potential to collect information on enemy troop whereabouts and numbers. According to an expert on military intelligence, the cavalry should "gain and keep contact with the enemy, and in their movements everything should be subordinated to the one object of gaining information." The Confederate cavalry learned the importance of this function early in the war and became very good at it, sending a stream of information back to the army commander. This was not true of the Union army, at least during the spring and summer of 1862, when Maj. Gen. Daniel Butterfield claimed to Congress, "We were almost as ignorant of the enemy in our immediate front as if they had been in China."[10]

The Maryland Campaign of 1862

The underpinnings of the Union cavalry's failure to effectively perform this function were laid prior to the Maryland Campaign. McClellan put little emphasis on creating an effective cavalry arm, instead, as we have seen, distributing regiments and companies to infantry, whose commanders usually misused them for mundane activities such as delivering messages and protecting resources. It also did not help that cavalry officers were not trained in ways of collecting and interpreting information. Another issue was the limited number and poor quality of horses provided by the War Department that often broke down after even limited use.[11]

Despite these limitations, Pleasonton's cavalry did a fairly credible job of detecting enemy movements early in the Maryland Campaign. He sent pickets to the Potomac River fords on September 5 and notified McClellan that Lee's army was crossing the river into Maryland, and reported another 50,000 men in the vicinity of Dranesville. Where conditions lent themselves, Pleasonton's men engaged Jeb Stuart's who were screening Lee's army. As early as September 7 and 8, Pleasonton's men pushed persistent probes, resulting in sharp skirmishing with Stuart's troopers. Because of the limitations of Pinkerton's operations in Maryland, more responsibility fell on Pleasonton, but he didn't have the troops to carry out this critical mission and those he did have were often dispersed. Bouts of illness among the horses did not help matters. Stuart's cavalry, at least early in the campaign, did a much better job of keeping Lee informed of McClellan's movements. They also did a very good job of spreading disinformation among the civilians which found its way to the Union high command.[12]

A cavalry historian summed up the effectiveness of the two army's cavalry arm: "Pleasonton's cavalry performance, compared to Stuart's shows that Pleasonton, for the most part gave McClellan poorer quality intelligence than Stuart gave Lee." We will see, however, that Stuart often erred in sending adequate and important information to Lee and his generals later in the campaign.[13]

The Pennsylvania Campaign of 1863

The Union cavalry continued frustrating the army commander during the Pennsylvania Campaign with often incomplete and inaccurate information.

Hooker desperately sought information on Lee's movements in central Virginia during June 1863, and Pleasonton was not providing it. Frustrated by Pleasonton's scant intelligence, most of which came from deserters and fugitive slaves, Hooker wrote: "The commanding general relies on you to give him information of where the enemy is, his force, and his movements. You have a sufficient cavalry force to do this. Drive in pickets, if necessary, and get us information. It is better that we should lose men than to be without knowledge of the rebel army, as we now seem to be." Hooker's directive, concluded one historian, implied "a lack of confidence in Pleasonton's grasp of the most elementary duties of his post, which he [Pleasonton] would have had every right to resent." Military intelligence expert Thomas Ryan believed Pleasonton "displayed a distaste for the grueling work of reconnaissance," and "[I]nstead of trained intelligence operatives, Pleasonton forwarded the notoriously unreliable estimates of location inhabitants, which was often based on hearsay, and the word of a single prisoner." He concluded, "Were it not for alternate sources of intelligence, Hooker would have had considerable difficulty tracking Lee's march toward Pennsylvania."[14]

As we will see, Pleasonton tried to force his way through Jeb Stuart's screen in front of the Blue Ridge Mountain gaps to determine if Lee's army was marching north in the Shenandoah Valley. These efforts were largely unsuccessful. Any information forwarded to Hooker was usually old or incorrect. When Lee's army headed across the Potomac River, Pleasonton's cavalry primarily shifted to screening Hooker's infantry moving north. Kilpatrick's cavalry division, forming the center of Pleasonton's net, was also tasked with finding and destroying Jeb Stuart's wayward cavalry division.[15]

Much has been written about Jeb Stuart's ill-advised raid into Pennsylvania that left Lee blind to the movements of the Union army. As we will see in Chapters 8 and 10, Lee allowed the bulk of his cavalry to ride off on a raid, resulting in the collision at Gettysburg. Lee has been blamed for not giving Stuart explicit orders including routes and timelines. Stuart left two brigades behind (Brig. Gen. William "Grumble" Jones' and Brig. Gen. Beverly Robertson's), who were to guard the Blue Ridge passes and then ride north to assist Lee. However, Lee did not effectively use these units in screening his army and collecting valuable information on the enemy's whereabouts.[16]

Happy/Unhappy Accidents

Sometimes vital information just drops into a commander's lap by accident. Such was the situation on September 13 when several Indiana soldiers found three cigars wrapped with Lee's Special Orders 191. The orders, which will be discussed later, described Lee's plans for dividing his army and sending most of it to capture Harpers Ferry.

Comparison of the Two Campaigns

The army commanders were in desperate need of accurate information about the enemy in both campaigns and both struggled to acquire the intelligence they needed. The Union army's signal corps was effective in both campaigns; the Confederate army's less so. The development of the Union's Bureau of Military Intelligence prior to the Gettysburg Campaign was a game changer that was not matched by the Confederates. Cavalry was potentially a primary source of information about enemy numbers and movements. Alfred Pleasonton commanded the Union cavalry in both campaigns and did a poor job during the Maryland Campaign, and was only marginally more effective during the Pennsylvania Campaign, as he put much reliance on deserters, prisoners, and runaway slaves who often provided inaccurate information. Likewise, Jeb Stuart commanded the Confederate cavalry during both campaigns, which was more effective in collecting information and preventing the enemy from learning about Lee's army, but at times provided scant information, and during the Pennsylvania Campaign, did not communicate with Lee at all because it was away on a raid. Overall, both armies operated partially blind in both campaigns.

Table 10: Comparison of Intelligence Gathering

Issue	Maryland Campaign	Pennsylvania Campaign
Signal Corps	**Confederate:** Moderately developed **Union:** Well-developed	**Confederate:** Moderately developed **Union:** Well-developed
Well-organized military intelligence wing	**Confederate:** No **Union:** No	**Confederate:** No **Union:** Yes
Effectiveness of cavalry	**Confederate:** Mixed **Union:** Inadequate	**Confederate:** Mixed; adequate early in campaign; poor later **Union:** Somewhat better

Chapter 6: The Two Campaigns Begin (September 4–8, 1862 and June 3–12, 1863)

For ease of comparison, each army's travels are divided into thirds. For the Maryland Campaign: Beginning (September 3–8); Middle (September 9–12); End (September 13-17). For the Pennsylvania Campaign: Beginning (June 3–12); Middle (June 13–21); End (June 22–July 2).

The Maryland Campaign of 1862 (September 3-8, 1862)

The Maryland Campaign began almost on the heels of the Second Bull Run Campaign, which ended on September 1, with the battle of Chantilly. Lee sent his army twenty miles north to Leesburg, Virginia, beginning on September 3, in hopes of finding food for the men and forage for the horses. Meanwhile, the Union army retreated to the protection of the Washington defenses. Units of both armies were exhausted from their hard marches and fighting it out during the Second Bull Run Campaign. All savored the prospect of rest and resupply. This would not be the case, at least not for the Confederate army. Lee wrote to Jefferson Davis on September 3: "The present seems to be the most propitious time since the commencement of the war for the Confederate Army to enter Maryland." Davis responded quickly, but the communication has not been found. Given the time it took for messages to flow between the two leaders, Lee planned to invade even without Davis' blessing, although it is possible they discussed a strike earlier, perhaps when Lee was fighting around Richmond.[1]

The Confederate army's route to Leesburg was not a direct one. Jackson's wing, in the van, headed 12 miles east to Dranesville, Virginia on September 3 to threaten Washington. This aggressive act weighed heavily on Lincoln and the army's high command, and they worried about Lee's next move. Confederate cavalry details were thrown south toward Falls Church and Alexandria to further confuse the Union high command. The misdirection did not completely work, as Union cavalry commander Alfred Pleasonton concluded, "the enemy is only making a show of force to conceal his movements on the Upper Potomac." Lee's army was again on the march to Leesburg on September 4. Excessive straggling occurred, as many of the men were bare-footed and hundreds fell out of the ranks, and many did the same to scavenge for food.[2]

As Lee prepared for the invasion, he issued General Orders No. 102 on September 4: Wheeled vehicles were to be kept to a minimum with only the "absolute necessaries of a regiment," an inspection was to be made of the horses and those "too much reduced for service" were to be left behind. Brig. Gen. William Pendleton conducted a quick perusal of the army's batteries and designated a number unfit for action. Good horses and men were pulled from these batteries and sent to those making the trip; the remainder stayed behind at Leesburg. The order also made it clear that cannoneers were "positively prohibited from riding on the ammunition chests or guns." The order explicitly outlawed scavenging by the army. Lee worried that "any excesses committed will exasperate the people, lead to disastrous results, and enlist the populace on the side of the Federal forces in hostility to our own." Instead, quartermasters and commissaries would collect supplies and distribute them to the troops, as needed. The order also addressed stragglers, noting that a provost guard would march behind the army, collecting men who had fallen out of the ranks.[3]

Brig. Gen. Robert Rodes' brigade (D. H. Hill's division) crossed the Potomac River first. It splashed across the 3-4 foot deep river at Cheek's Ford, opposite the mouth of the Monocacy River, at about 4:00 p.m. on September 4. The men first stripped off their shoes, socks (if they had any), and pants. Stonewall Jackson's command reached Leesburg about the same time and James Longstreet's troops camped about two miles south, at Newton Hall. Lee, riding in his ambulance, reached Leesburg about noon.[4]

Lee had apparently not determined exactly where the army would cross the Potomac River when he reached Leesburg. Jackson had agitated for a move into the lower Shenandoah Valley since September 2. Such a move could clear the Valley of the enemy before the army crossed at or near Harpers Ferry, he argued. Lee, however, realized he needed to balance being near enough to Washington to lure the Army of the Potomac from its protective lair with his need to protect Richmond. A move into Frederick County, Maryland would achieve both goals and might also hasten the departure of the Harpers Ferry garrison. Sometime between the evening of September 4 and the next morning, Lee decided the army would cross at White's Ford. He realized the campaign's success depended on two factors: Union troops quickly vacating Harpers Ferry and the Shenandoah Valley and the commander of the Union army, John Pope, as Lee did not learn of his dismissal until later, would move slowly, giving him an opportunity for maneuver. Both hopes were not realized.[5]

Across the Potomac River, Lincoln and Halleck attempted to discern Lee's movements and intentions. On September 1, Lincoln placed George McClellan in charge of the Washington "works and their garrison … [but] prohibiting me from exercising any control over the troops actively engaged in front under General Pope." Lincoln had a change of heart the following day, and in the words of McClellan, he "was to assume command of General Pope's troops (including my own Army of the Potomac) as soon as they approached the vicinity of Washington; to go out and meet them, and to post them as I deemed best to repulse the enemy and insure the safety of the city." McClellan immediately went to work integrating the two armies into one.

Information began trickling into Washington of enemy troops crossing the Potomac River near Leesburg on September 4. The most important intelligence may have come from the Sugar Loaf Mountain signal station, which observed large-scale movements in and around Leesburg, Virginia and a long wagon train heading east, toward the Potomac River. To counter a possible attack on Washington from the north, McClellan mobilized the XII Corps and sent it to Tennallytown (now part of N.W. Washington) to join the II Corps already stationed there. Maj. Gen. Darius Couch's division (IV Corps) was sent to Fort Ethan Allen to help counter an enemy attempt to cross the Chain Bridge. Some of Pleasonton's cavalry headed toward Falls Church, Virginia to reconnoiter. The cavalryman accurately reported evidence of the main Confederate army moving north toward Leesburg. Pleasonton was now ordered to cross the Potomac River and head north toward Muddy Branch, Maryland. Until McClellan received a clearer indication of Lee's intentions, he decided to do nothing more, but he expressed concern when the Sugar Loaf Mountain signal station reported an enemy troop buildup around Leesburg, Virginia.[6]

Most of Jeb Stuart's Confederate cavalry splashed across the Potomac River on September 5. Fitz Lee's brigade crossed first and it immediately rode to Poolesville, where it encountered a portion of the 1st Massachusetts Cavalry, just off the boat from South Carolina. The brigade made short work of the Bay Staters, aided by Southern-leaning civilians, who placed obstructions behind them. All was chaos when the Massachusetts troopers' horses fell over the piles of rock and stone, causing over 30 to be captured. Stuart's cavalry then rode east to protect Lee's army's right flank as it crossed the Potomac River. By the morning of September 7, Stuart's cavalry formed a 30-mile screen from near Liberty on the Westminster Pike to the northeast, southwest to Barnsville, near the Potomac River.[7]

Jackson began crossing the Potomac River in earnest by midmorning on September 5. The crossing took on a bow-shaped route as the men forded the half-mile wide river. The column veered to the right to a sandy strip in the middle of the river, then moved left again to complete the journey. Bands played and men cheered while crossing the chest-high water. The banks of the ford proved to be too steep for wagons and artillery, so engineers were deployed to provide a gentler slope. Jackson was behind schedule as he intended to make the 15-mile march to the B&O Railroad Bridge over the Monocacy River by nightfall.

While some of the men refused to cross the river because it violated their beliefs that they were merely defending their homeland, most cheerfully splashed across One soldier described the crossing: "The weather was fine, and on these splendid summer days when the crossing was effected, the broad and placid river, with the long columns of wading infantry, and the lines of artillery and wagons making their way through it, and the men shouting and singing, 'Maryland, My Maryland,' to give vent to their noisy delight, made a picturesque and animated scene."

After crossing the Potomac River, the column marched along the C&O Canal and crossed at the locks. After fording the Monocacy River, Jackson's men forged on, well after nightfall, finally reaching Three Springs, near Buckeystown, three miles shy of their destination, and still nine miles from Frederick. Stuart, who was to help screen the march, had not yet arrived and this also slowed the column's progress. D. H. Hill's division, which had crossed the day before and was engaged in attempting to destroy the canal and railroad bridge, joined the march, falling in behind Jackson's column. By the end of September 5, four of Lee's nine divisions were in Maryland. Longstreet's command was close to the river, marching through Leesburg and camping at Jackson's former bivouac site, Big Spring.[8]

Map 1: The Road to Antietam (September 4, 1862)

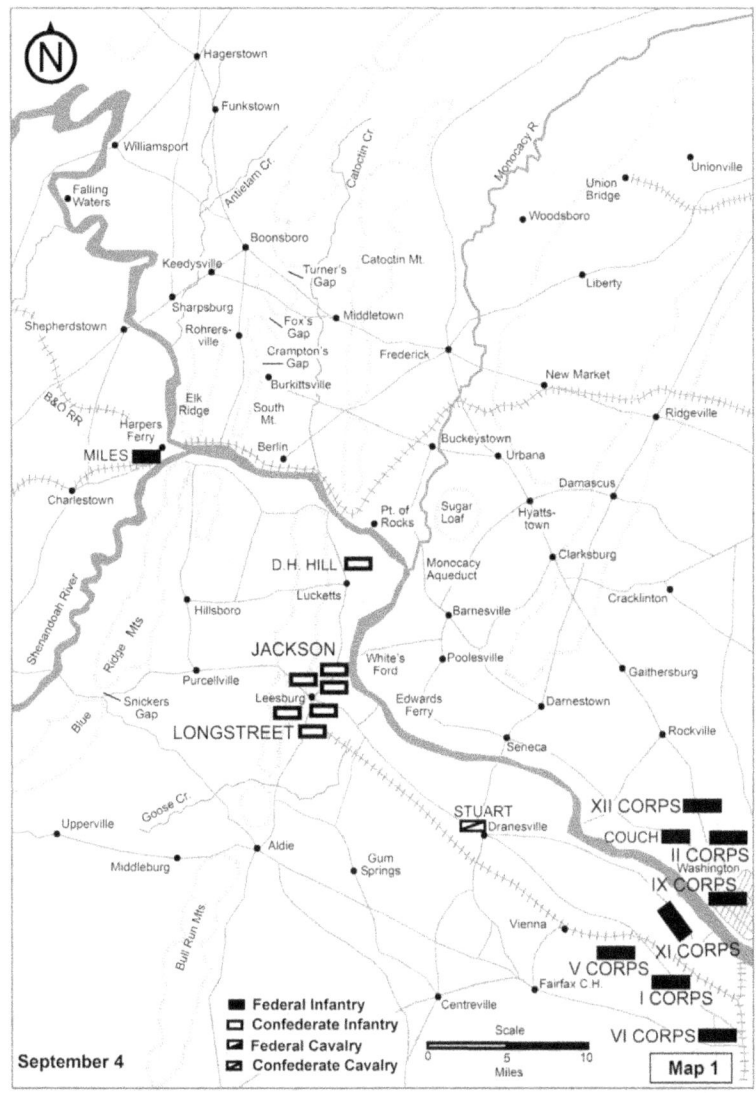

Lee spent much of September 5 drafting communications. Special Orders No. 188 clarified his position on straggling, specifically ordering the provost guard to arrest soldiers from all units. He also wrote yet another communication to Jefferson Davis—his fourth in three days. Lee kept in contact with his president during the entire campaign. In this communication he informed Davis of his army's entrance into Maryland and reiterated "Whatever success may attend that effort, I hope to annoy and harass the enemy." Lee also informed Davis of his new supply line "by way of Luray & Front Royal from Culpeper Court House to Winchester." This would have a profound impact on the campaign, as it meant that Harpers Ferry could not remain in Federal hands.[9]

McClellan continued reorganizing his enlarged army on September 5, while Pleasonton's cavalry cautiously pushed north of Washington into Maryland to ascertain Lee's movements. The cavalry commander reported Lee crossing the Potomac River into Maryland. Most of the rest of the information from spies and civilians was contradictory: The enemy was either advancing on Frederick or remaining near the canal adjacent to the Potomac River; he had as many as 40,000 in Maryland or only a small cavalry force. Meanwhile, Brig. Gen. Julius White abandoned Winchester, Virginia with his 1,500 men and fell back to Martinsburg, while Col. Dixon Miles held Harpers Ferry with over 10,000 men. Maj. Gen. John Wool, commander of the Middle Department, told both commanders to defend their posts "to the last extremity."[10]

Jackson's men continued their march toward Frederick at 10:00 a.m. on September 6 and reached the railroad outside of town by the afternoon. Resident Jacob Engelbrecht recorded in his diary, "No commotion, or excitement, but all peaceably and quiet the soldiers are around the town purchasing clothing—shoes, caps and eatables." He also noted that many townspeople abandoned the town the evening before. Those who remained looked upon an amazing array of "uniforms." While there was some pilfering, most of the soldiers respected Lee's orders.

The van of Longstreet's wing arrived at White's Ford prior to 7:00 a.m. on September 6. Men halting at the riverbank to remove their pants, shoes, and socks, before crossing the Potomac River, along with long trains of wagons and artillery, quickly created a traffic jam at the ford. An impatient Longstreet ordered Maj. Gen. Lafayette McLaws' division across the river at Cheek's Ford, just upriver.

Lee wrote letters to Jefferson Davis on September 7 and 8, informing him that "all the divisions of the army have crossed the Potomac," and requesting assistance in procuring supplies from Maryland. He also pointed out the need for strict action on malingerers, a suggestion that the time was right for the North to explicitly recognize the Confederacy, and provided an update on the campaign.

The appearance of Lee's men left a lasting impression on the Frederick residents. Dr. Lewis Steiner recalled, a "dirtier, filthier, more unsavory set of human beings never strolled through a town—marching it could not be called without doing violence to the word…Their arms were rusty and in an unsoldierly condition. Their uniforms, or rather multiforms, corresponded only in a slight predominance of gray over butternut, and in the prevalence of filth. Faces looked as if they had not been acquainted with water for weeks; hair, shaggy and unkempt, seemed entirely a stranger to the operations of a brush or comb."[11]

Both Lee and Davis were clear about avoiding any depredations on civilians and the army should pay for all goods taken from them. This posed a problem, as Lee explained to Davis on September 7: "There may be some embarrassment in paying for necessaries for the army, as it is probable that many individuals will hesitate to receive Confederate currency… It is very desirable that the chief quartermaster and commissary should be provided with funds, and that some general arrangement should be made for liquidating the debts that may be incurred to the satisfaction of the people of Maryland, in order that they may willingly furnish us what is wanted." The situation was compounded by fact that most of these Marylanders were staunch Unionists and unwilling to give or even sell needed supplies to the Confederates, and the latter were loath to simply take them and risk alienating the border state.[12]

McClellan continued concentrating his army on September 6. He ordered the I and VI Corps, the Kanawha Division (soon to be attached to the IX Corps) and Sykes' division (V Corps) to leave Virginia by crossing the Potomac River. Many considered the march on September 7 to be the most arduous of the entire campaign. The I Corps headed to Leesborough, Maryland (now Wheaton), where it joined the IX Corps; the VI Corps and Sykes' division (V Corps) marched toward Rockville, which hosted the II and XII Corps after their earlier march from Tennallytown. These moves were certainly defensive in nature, as the troops near Rockville could blunt an attack on Washington from the north and the two corps in Leesborough could protect Baltimore. These movements may have been a direct result of communications McClellan received of Lee's intent to capture Washington or Baltimore. McClellan moved his headquarters to Rockville, about 17 miles northwest of Washington, on the evening of September 7. Pleasonton's troopers continued scouting further north for vital information on the Rebels' whereabouts. They reached Clarksburg and sent dispatches indicating that 30,000 Rebels had crossed the river; Maj. Gen. Edwin Sumner heard from a spy the number was closer to 50,000.[13]

The cavalries of both sides were active as Lee crossed the Potomac and headed north. The Union troopers sought to determine the location of Lee's army and the Confederate horsemen screened its infantry and parried enemy attempts to determine the location and size of Lee's foot soldiers. The two clashed in the small Maryland town of Poolesville, first on September 5, as we have already seen, and then again on September 7 and 8 when elements of Col. John Farnsworth's Union cavalry brigade tangled with portions of Col. Thomas Munford's and Brig. Gen. Fitz Lee's brigades.

Jackson's men spent September 7, 8, and 9 resting. This was a commodity in short supply because of the constant marching and fighting since June. Those camping near the Monocacy River were able to wash their bodies and tattered uniforms; those near Frederick walked around the town buying whatever they could afford. Longstreet's men entered Frederick later on September 7 and 8 and were frustrated that most of the desirable goods had already found new owners. Dr. Steiner found shoe stores to be the most popular among the Confederates as so many were ill-shod. The only money most of them had was "Confederate scrip, or shinplasters issued by banks, corporations, individuals, etc--all of equal value. To use the expression of an old citizen 'the notes depreciated the paper on which they were printed.'" Guards were stationed at each door to limit the number of "shoppers" at a time.

Jackson was feeling a bit better on September 8 after the fall from his horse, so he mounted a new one, but he left D. H. Hill in command of his wing. Perhaps Lee's most important act on September 8 was his proclamation to the people of Maryland that cataloged the wrongs wrought by the U. S. Government and explained how "the people of the South have long wished to aid you in throwing off this foreign yoke, to enable you again to enjoy the inalienable rights of freemen, and restore independence and sovereignty to your State." He went on to explain the goals of the invasion: "our army has come among you, and is prepared to assist you with the power of its arms in regaining the rights of which you have been despoiled . . . It is for you to decide your destiny freely and without constraint."[14]

Lee had already lost some of his optimism by the time he drafted the proclamation. He informed Jefferson Davis on September 7 that finding provisions for his men and horses was not an issue, but the citizens were reluctant to accept Confederate currency for their goods. Most of the populous were "kind" but "I do not anticipate any general rising of the people in our behalf..." Lee was correct, for his proclamation to Marylanders on September 8 was, in the words of Ezra Carman, "received with cold indifference." The proclamation may have intended to calm civilians' worries.

Lee hoped to entice thousands of young Marylanders—as many as 25,000—to enter his ranks but this did not materialize. Ezra Carman described the response as "feebly answered." Those who reached Frederick were usually put off by what they saw and smelled. As few as 200 enlisted, and that number did not come close to filling the ranks of the 800 or so sick soldiers left behind when the army moved off because of illness and being just worn out. The outcome might have been different, had Lee moved into Southern Maryland or the Baltimore area, which were hotbeds of Southern sympathizers.[15]

Pennsylvania governor, Andrew Curtin, kept a close eye on the Confederates through an informal system of spies and citizens' reports. During the latter part of September 7, Curtin sent a concerning telegram to Sec. of War Stanton: "Our information is that Jackson occupied Frederick in force, and is preparing to move north. We are organizing militia and arming to meet him." He requested artillery support, and Stanton responded by telling Curtin to retain a battery in the area and not to worry about the enemy as they "will be struck long before they can reach Harrisburg." Curtin requested "seven hundred carbines, slings, and ammunition, with accouterments" to equip cavalry he wished to use for scouting purposes.[16]

McClellan tried to assuage Curtin's fears on September 8 by writing: "This army is in position to move against the rebels, whatever their plan may be. If they intend to advance toward your State, I shall act with all possible vigor." Curtin informed Stanton, an hour later: "I shall to-morrow, unless otherwise advised by you, call out the militia of the State, and mass as many men as possible here, to operate as may be best." Another communication from Curtin informed Stanton that he had "about five regiments of green troops," and suggested that Washington and Baltimore send troops from their garrisons. He also informed Stanton that Fitz John Porter had arrived in Pennsylvania to provide expert advice. Stanton quickly responded that he had no troops to send and the best avenue was McClellan's army. Curtin was not so sure…[17]

While Lee and his army occupied Frederick and its environs, McClellan made only minor adjustments to his army's deployment on September 8, as he did not wish to stray too far from Washington until he was certain of Lee's location. He continued receiving reports of Lee's intended move on Baltimore—the fruits of Lee's counter-intelligence campaign. As McClellan prepared to march north after Lee, he conferred with Gen. Halleck and the two decided to divide the army into a "wing" structure. The actual reason is unknown, but may have been related to streamlining and coordinating the movement of so many units. The army was divided into three wings: The Right Wing consisted of the I and IX Corps and was commanded by Maj. Gen. Ambrose Burnside; the Left Wing consisted of the II and XII Corps and was headed by Maj. Gen. Edwin Sumner; the Reserve Wing was composed of the VI Corps and Couch's division (IV Corps) and commanded by Maj. Gen. William Franklin.[18]

That night, McClellan wrote to Halleck, "I have ordered reconnaissances in all directions to-morrow, including one well to the north and northwest. I think that we are now in position to prevent any attack in force on Baltimore, while we cover Washington on this side." Halleck was probably relieved to read these words and the following: "We are prepared to attack anything that crosses the Potomac this side of the Monocacy." However, the uncertainty of the following sentence probably unnerved him: "I am by no means satisfied yet that the enemy has crossed the river in any large force. Our information is still entirely too indefinite to justify definite action." McClellan ended the communication with: "As soon as I find out where to strike, I will be after them without an hour's delay." Could Halleck trust that the methodical McClellan would keep his word?[19]

Lee almost lost a chunk of his cavalry that night. Jeb Stuart, following his well-known penchant for "frolic and female attention," was hosting a large "Sabers and Roses Ball," with his officers and local ladies in Urbana. The hall was bedecked with Mississippi battle flags and the music was supplied by the 18th Mississippi Infantry band. Five companies of the 1st U.S. Cavalry dashed into Hyattstown on a reconnaissance, about three miles from Urbana, driving back the Confederate troopers and forcing Stuart to halt his festivities and gallop to the front. After driving the enemy away, Stuart returned to the festivities at 1:00 a.m. on September 9.[20]

The first phase of the Maryland Campaign can be summarized as massive Confederate movements first to Leesburg, Virginia, northwest of Washington. Lee then sent his army across the Potomac River to Frederick, beginning on September 4. The Confederates destroyed government property, including portions of the B & O Railroad and the C & O Canal and collected supplies. Lee also issued several important orders during this period, including prohibiting his men from stealing supplies from civilians, preventing straggling, and a call for Marylanders to join his cause; none resonated with their intended audiences. On the Union side, McClellan was placed in charge of all of the forces in and around Washington on September 1, and immediately began the process of consolidating the two armies he inherited. With Lee on the move in Maryland, McClellan did not have the luxury to wait, so he began reposition his army about to counter Lee. By September 7, McClellan was pushing many of his infantry units into a protective ring around Washington. The men were exhausted from long marches and straggling was excessive, but by the last day of this phase (September 8), he disseminated marching orders for the following day that would begin the pursuit of Lee's army. More importantly, the vanguard of the Army of the Potomac made first contact with Stuart's Confederate cavalry on September 8.

The Pennsylvania Campaign of 1863 (June 3 – 12)

The armies eyed each other on opposite sides of the Rappahannock River near Fredericksburg at the start of the campaign. Since the two armies were relatively close to Richmond, Lee needed to rely on stealth to invade the North. He decided to begin moving his troops to Culpeper Court House, about 35 miles to the northwest. Once there, he could decide to continue the invasion or speed south to protect Richmond. The invasion began on the morning of June 3, 1863, when Lafayette McLaws' division broke camp and headed southwest about seven miles and camped near the Chancellorsville battleground. Three divisions, two from Longstreet's First Corps, and one from Richard Ewell's Second Corps, were on the move the following day. Lee chose an invasion route northward through the Shenandoah Valley, using the Blue Ridge Mountains to hide his movements from the enemy's prying eyes. Hooker was aware that something was up, as his balloon corps reported empty Rebel camps and clouds of dust in the distance.

By June 5, all of Longstreet's and Ewell's Corps were on the march, leaving Ambrose Powel Hill's Third Corps behind to guard the approaches to Richmond. Hill's orders were to "deceive the enemy, and keep him in ignorance of any change in the disposition of the army." Hill stretched his line, hoping to bluff the enemy into thinking Lee's entire army was still ensconced behind the Rappahannock River. It was a bold move by Lee, for if Hooker drove south, he could easily push Hill's men aside and make a dash for Richmond. That morning, Hooker accurately predicted "the head of his column will probably be headed toward the Potomac, via Gordonsville or Culpeper, while the rear will rest on Fredericksburg. After giving the subject my best reflection, I am of opinion that it is my duty to pitch into his rear, although in so doing the head of his column may reach Warrenton before I can return. Will it be within the spirit of my instructions to do so?" This was Hooker's first, in what became almost daily requests, to cross the Rappahannock and drive south. To each and all, Lincoln or Halleck replied, "no," worrying they would merely be "swapping queens" if both capitals fell.[21]

The departure of Lee's army may have been delayed a few days by the Union activities of Maj. Gen. John Dix and his 32,000 men scattered along

Map 2: The Road to Antietam (September 7-9, 1862)

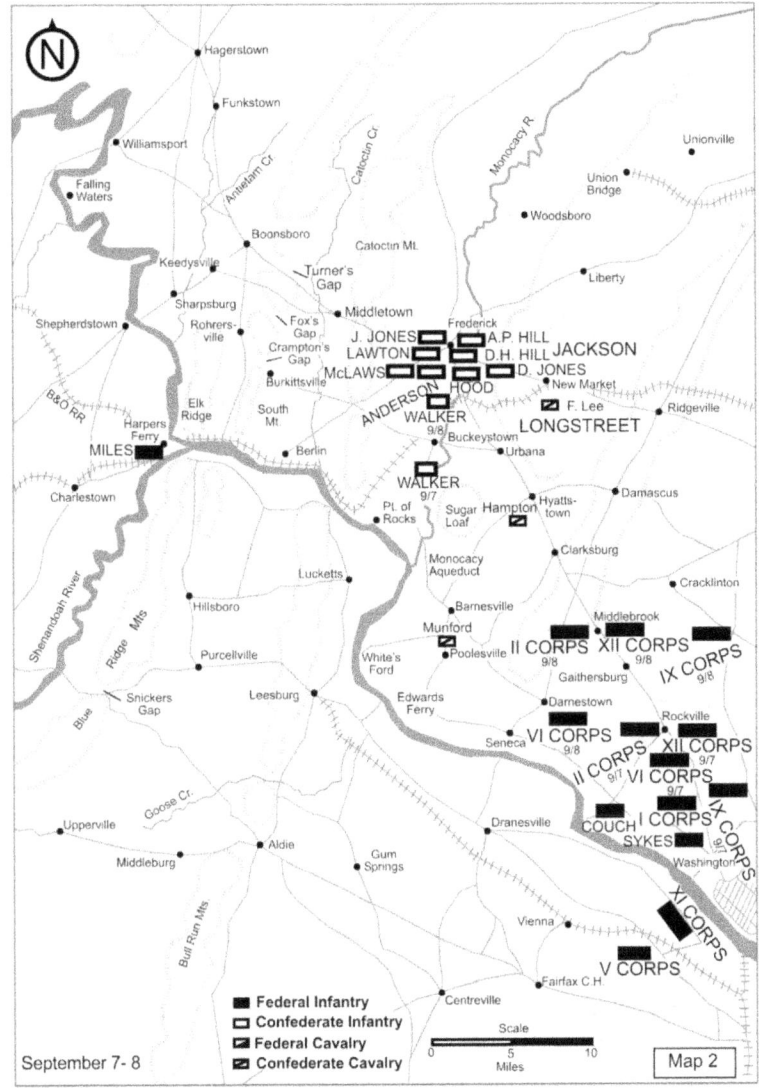

the Virginia Peninsula below Richmond. Both Halleck and Hooker thought a drive north, even if a feign, could cause Lee to abort any notion of an invasion. Dix warned Hooker on June 4 that little should be expected of him, except perhaps a diversion, because of his small force. Still, he planned an expedition northward in mid-June, but because of logistical issues, the move would not begin until June 25, and did not amount to much.[22]

Lee's movements abruptly ended on June 6, as Lee's worst nightmare materialized—Hooker thrust troops across the Rappahannock River. Lee did not know it was only one division of the VI Corps with a two-fold mission: conduct a reconnaissance to determine if Lee had indeed pulled his army from its positions, and show Lincoln and Halleck the road to Richmond was open. Hooker did little more than gain a toe-hold on the south side of the Rappahannock River and was content to rotate his divisions until he pulled them back across the river on June 12. Halleck and Lincoln were unimpressed with Hooker's requests to launch an offensive across the river. Lincoln told Hooker, "In one word, I would not take any risk of being entangled upon the river, like an ox jumped half over a fence and liable to be torn by dogs front and rear, without a fair chance to gore one way or kick the other. If Lee would come to my side of the river, I would keep on the same side, and fight him or act on the defense."[23]

After determining the VI Corps' crossing was merely a feint, Lee again put his troops in motion. Ewell's men continued their march toward Culpeper Court House; Longstreet's men halted at Stevensburg, about seven miles away. By the end of June 7, five of Lee's nine divisions were at or near Culpeper Court House—the first leg of the journey north. Lee continued his attempts to swell his army with reinforcements. He expected additional troops from the Carolinas but a Union incursion there halted the effort. "I think our southern coast might be held during the sickly season by local troops, aided by a small organized force, and the predatory excursions of the enemy be repressed…"

Hooker kept his men in camp as he continued sorting through information about Lee's location. Pleasonton's cavalry was not providing the intelligence he needed. Hooker knew Stuart was concentrating his cavalry near Culpeper Court House and it concerned him. Worst-case scenario, Hooker believed,

Map 3: The Road to Gettysburg (June 3-4, 1863)

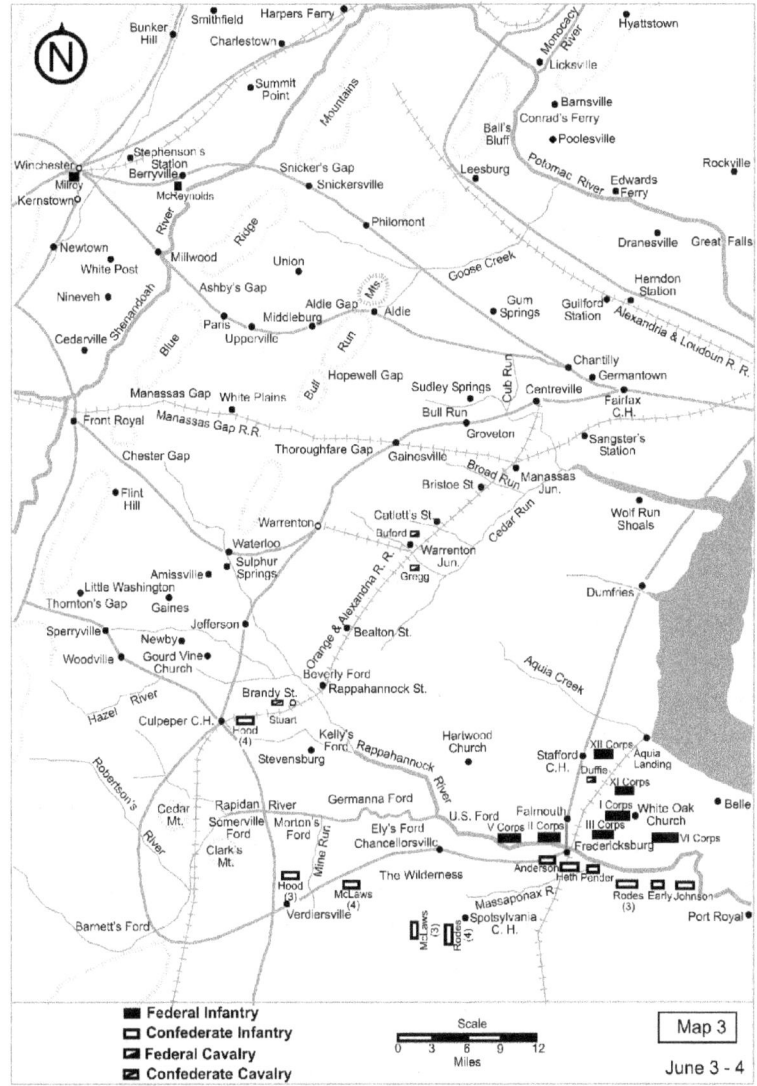

would be a full-scale enemy cavalry raid. He wrote to Halleck on June 6: "As the accumulation of the heavy rebel force of cavalry about Culpeper may mean mischief, I am determined, if practicable, to break it up in its incipiency. I shall send all my cavalry against them, stiffened by about 3,000 infantry" and had them on the road the following day. This resulted in the great cavalry battle at Brandy Station on June 9. Stuart's dispersed deployment of his cavalry almost led to his defeat (see Chapter 10).[24]

Although not a decisive Union victory, Hooker informed Lincoln of the cavalry battle at Brandy Station the following day, that "resulted in crippling him [Jeb Stuart] so much that he will have to abandon his contemplated raid into Maryland, which was to have started this morning. I am not so certain that the raid will be abandoned from this cause. It may delay the departure a few days." This was not the case, as Stuart was simply preparing to screen the Confederate advance as it moved into Maryland and Pennsylvania. Hooker believed a maneuver by some of his cavalry and infantry might cause Lee to shift troops and lay open the path to Richmond. Lincoln responded a few hours later: "I think Lee's army, and not Richmond, is your sure objective point." He also told Hooker, "If he comes toward the Upper Potomac, follow on his flank and on his inside track" but not to cross the river.

The battle of Brandy Station rattled Lee, who had halted all movements of his infantry on June 9 and much of June 10 until he sorted out the situation. Satisfied it was merely a cavalry probe blunted by Stuart's troopers, Lee put Ewell's Second Corps on the road between 3:00 – 4:00 p.m. and they marched about 20 miles to Woodville and Gourd Vine Church, close to the Bull Run Mountains. The Second Corps continued its arduous march on June 11. Temperatures soared and thick clouds of dust enveloped the column. A Confederate soldier confided in his diary how the "dust is almost intolerable & that together with the heat make the marching very severe." By the end of the day, its three divisions camped between Flint Hill and Sperryville, on the east side of the Blue Ridge Mountains, after marches of about 15 miles. The other two corps remained in place: Longstreet's First Corps at Culpeper Court House and Hill's Third Corps facing Hooker across the Rappahannock River.

Hooker finally received accurate intelligence on June 10 that Hill was opposite him across the Rappahannock River, Longstreet was at Culpeper Court House and Ewell somewhere north of Fredericksburg. He informed his corps commanders to be ready to march at a moment's notice. This meant leaving excess baggage and other materials behind with the quartermaster. All non-military personnel were also to be expelled. The Union high command was also concerned about the vulnerability of Maj. Gen. Robert Milroy's 5,100-man garrison at Winchester, Virginia. He was ordered to vacate it on June 11, but this was not the first time he received these orders-- others were dated: January 5, March 16, April 30, May 8, May 29, and June 8. Milroy resisted, responding he could "hold it [Winchester] against any force the rebels could afford to bring against it." As a compromise, he loaded up 114 wagons with supplies and sent them to safety. Another 1,800 men were at Berryville under the command of Col. Andrew McReynolds.[25]

Only Ewell's Second Corps marched on June 12, crossing into the Shenandoah Valley through Chester Gap. With his corps so close to Berryville and Winchester, Gen. Ewell began drafting plans to attack the Union garrisons. Early's and Johnson's divisions would march straight north along the Valley Turnpike to attack Milroy at Winchester, while Maj. Gen. Robert Rodes' division, screened by Brig. Gen. Albert Jenkins' mounted infantry brigade, headed toward the Berryville garrison. Rodes would then move north into what is now West Virginia and attack the 3,000-man garrison at Martinsburg.[26]

Hooker finally stirred on June 12. There was too much information about Lee's movements not to begin countering the enemy's thrust. The I and III Corps headed north to Bealton and the XI marched to Catlett's Station along the vital Orange and Alexandria Railroad. The close proximity of the railroad ensured adequate supplies. Hooker also pulled troops from the VI Corps back across the Rappahannock River. Knowing the entire army would soon be on the march, Hooker issued General Orders No. 62, noting the lax enforcement of his orders about the army's "efficiency." The order addressed straggling, restrictions against non-military personnel in the camps, use of animals only for official business and when used, that they should be treated humanely, the use of passes for civilians to visit the camps, and restriction on the use of soldiers as "waiters or servants." The order also addressed the need for drill when troops were not in active operations.[27]

To exercise adequate command and control measures and expedite the movement north after Lee's army, Hooker divided his army into "wings." Maj. Gen. John Reynolds commanded the "Left Wing" composed of his own corps and the III, V, XI, and the Cavalry Corps. The "Right Wing" was composed to the II, VI, and XII Corps under Maj. Gen. John Sedgwick, and the V Corps operated independently. This arrangement was apparently less formal than during the Maryland Campaign.[28]

Perhaps because of prompting by his strong political ally, Pennsylvania Governor Andrew Curtin, Lincoln established the Department of the Susquehanna under the leadership of Maj. Gen. Darius Couch who resigned from his position as commander of the Union II Corps rather than serve any longer under Hooker. Couch had access to many failed Union officers, but few enlisted men, about 1,300, to protect almost 34,000 square miles that included 180 contiguous miles of border with Maryland. Curtin would rectify that by issuing a call for militia to help snuff out an invasion of the Keystone State.

Curtin was especially active on June 12, perhaps because he doubted whether Hooker and the Army of the Potomac could defend his state. He decided to call out the militia, and to maximize the number of troops he secured, he informed Sec. of War Edwin Stanton he was postponing, "for a short period," orders to recruit new three-year regiments "in order to fill up speedily the army corps for General Couch." Stanton was not happy with this communication and shot a telegram back to Curtin: "The Department cannot sanction any postponement of the order for recruiting for three years' service, but earnestly urges you to execute without delay the authority given you for that purpose." Stanton demanded to know if Couch had anything to do with this order. He told Couch, "If Governor Curtin neglects to act under the authority given to him to recruit for three years, that is his own affair. But you are to give his neglect no countenance or assent, but, on the contrary, do everything in your power to promote the three years' recruiting."

Curtin was dead serious about protecting his state and within hours, released his proclamation to the citizens of the Keystone State, informing

Map 4: The Road to Gettysburg (June 9-11, 1863)

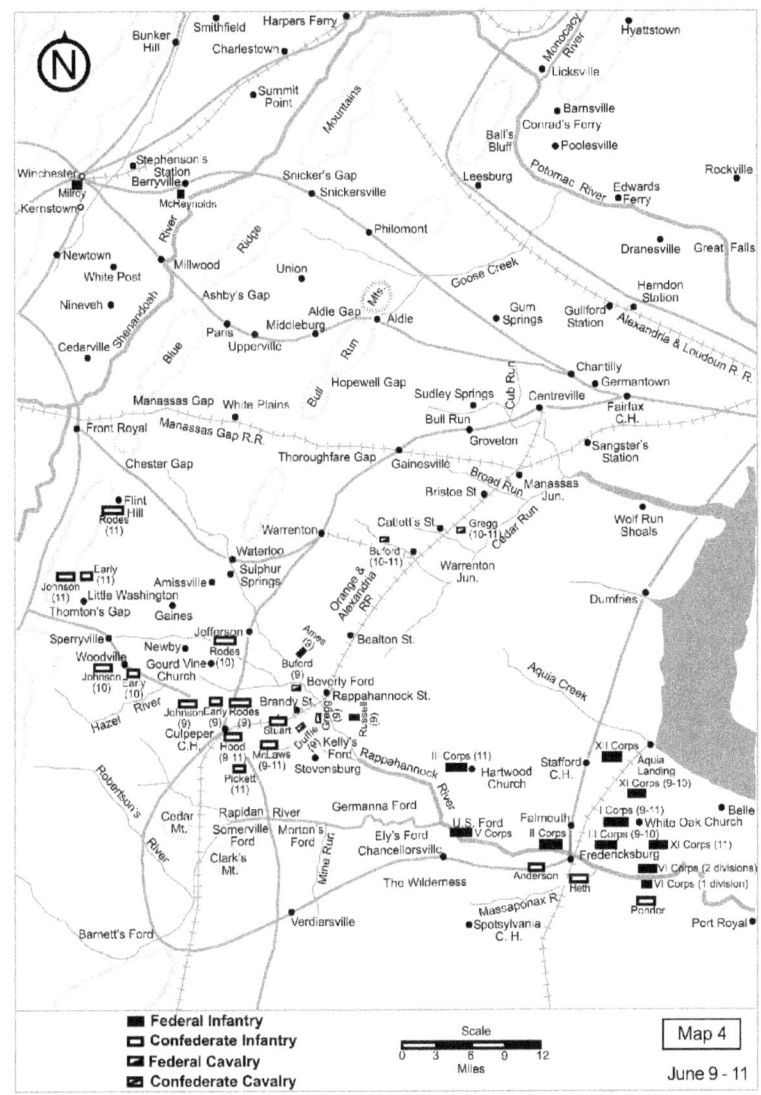

them that a "large rebel force, composed of cavalry, artillery, and mounted infantry, has been prepared for the purpose of making a raid into Pennsylvania" and requested volunteers to "promptly fill the ranks of these corps, the duties of which will be mainly the defense of our own homes, firesides, and property from devastation."[29]

The first phase of the Pennsylvania Campaign can be summarized as being composed of considerable movements and activities by the Confederates; less so among the Federals. Lee began pulling his troops from their lines along the Rappahannock River on June 3, eventually leaving only one corps behind to face the Union army. Lee nevertheless exhibited caution, for while Hill's corps barred Hooker's approach to Richmond and Ewell's Second Corps drove toward Winchester, Lee retained Longstreet's First Corps at Culpeper Court House. If needed, it could sweep southeast to assist Hill, and if not, follow Ewell's footsteps north. Because of conflicting intelligence, a cautious Joseph Hooker, who less than a month ago had been badly defeated by a stunning move by Lee's army, held pat. It was not until the last day of this period (June 12) that he felt he had enough information to get a handle on Lee's movements and began directing his army northward. All but two of Hooker's corps were on the move by the end of June 12. The VI Corps could not march until its detachments across the Rappahannock River returned to it.[30]

With the Confederates sweeping north through the Shenandoah Valley, Pennsylvania Gov. Curtin decided the time was right to begin organizing a militia that could help halt an enemy incursion into Pennsylvania. His approach only alienated Secretary of War Edwin Stanton.

Comparisons of the Two Campaigns

The location of the armies at the onset of each campaign had a profound impact on their first phase. September 1, 1862 found the two armies outside of Washington with a real possibility that Lee could easily maneuver his troops and attack the capital, or at least some of its defenses. Lee understood the folly of such an action, but he feigned a movement toward Washington and crossed the Potomac River close enough to Washington to lure McClellan from its safe confines. The armies were much further south on

June 1, 1863. Astride the Rappahannock River, both capitals were equally vulnerable, but Lincoln worried about the wily Lee moving north, so he prevented Hooker from driving south to capture Richmond. By this point in the war, Lincoln understood the major strategic objective was destroying Lee's army, not capturing Richmond.

Lee's move to Leesburg, Virginia, at the start of the Maryland Campaign was as much to position his army for an invasion as it was to secure needed food and supplies for his men. The Potomac River was an easy five-mile march away. The invasion route was more difficult during the Pennsylvania Campaign as Lee was far from Northern soil and he needed to safeguard Richmond. Therefore, while he crossed the Potomac River over a period of two days during the Maryland Campaign, it would take several weeks for him to do so during the Pennsylvania Campaign.

Straggling was very much on the mind of the army commanders and general orders were disseminated to guard against it, usually at the beginning of the arduous series of marches. Lee issued General Order No. 102 on September 4 as his army moved into Maryland. McClellan did not issue similar orders until the second phase (General Order No. 155 on September 9), when his army was about to move north. While Lee did not issue orders against straggling during the Pennsylvania Campaign, Hooker did on June 12 (General Order No. 62) as his troops were about to abandon Fredericksburg and take up the march toward Washington.

Lee's movements at the beginning of the Maryland Campaign were decisive and swift. After crossing the river, some of his men destroyed public property and then headed for Frederick. The potential loss of Richmond forced Lee to exercise caution during the Pennsylvania Campaign. He boldly left only a third of his army—perhaps 25,000 men to bar Hooker's 100,000-man army's potential thrust toward Richmond. To hedge his bet, Lee left another third of his army, Longstreet's First Corps, at Culpeper Court House, about 35 miles away. Still, the ever-aggressive Lee sent Ewell's Second Corps north into the Shenandoah Valley, where by the end of the first phase of the campaign, it had reached White Post, Virginia, about 75 miles from Fredericksburg, "as the crow flies."

The position and movements of the Union army had little impact on Lee's plans, at least during the initial period, of the Maryland Campaign. Lee believed McClellan would move slowly north, giving him plenty of time to carry out his objectives. The same was not true during the initial phase of the Pennsylvania Campaign. The cavalry action at Brandy Station and the VI Corps' incursion across the Potomac River both stopped Lee in his tracks and he continued pushing his units north only when he ascertained these movements did not pose a threat.

Lee was known as a decisive leader—some would say rash—and this showed itself in the initial period of both campaigns. During the Maryland Campaign, Lee pushed his army north to Leesburg, opening a direct path to Richmond, should McClellan choose to take it. McClellan's orders were to protect Washington and Baltimore and so he did not take advantage of the opportunity. Lee gambled even more during the initial phase of the Pennsylvania Campaign, leaving a third of his available force to face Hooker's large army across the Rappahannock River. Hooker could have pushed A.P. Hill's Third Corps away and driven toward Richmond, and he considered it, but Lincoln and Halleck demanded otherwise. Lee did, however, halt his troops when danger loomed and Longstreet spent considerable time at Culpeper Court House—a position that would allow him to drive south to blunt Hooker's advance on Richmond, should he so choose, or move north.

Lee's aggressiveness and strategic creativity urged caution on the Union high command during both campaigns. The Union army commanders were both hesitant to begin moving their armies after Lee until they had a firmer idea of his strength and intentions. To rashly push forward would put Washington at risk. McClellan began planning his army's move north on the last day of this phase, but no full-scale movements occurred during this period. McClellan was also hamstrung by the need to consolidate his Army of the Potomac with the Army of Virginia. Hooker did not have this chore and could devote his talents elsewhere. He finally had enough information to put his army in motion on the last day of this phase (June 12) when five of his corps broke camp and headed north.

Both armies' cavalry were active during both phases. The Union cavalry under Alfred Pleasonton was tasked with determining Lee's whereabouts during both campaigns, but he failed to do an adequate job in either. Hooker provided much more direction and hostility toward Pleasonton during the Pennsylvania Campaign, than did McClellan a year earlier. The role of the

Confederate cavalry differed in the two campaigns. Jeb Stuart's cavalry did a fairly good job of screening the army as it crossed the Potomac River into Maryland during the Maryland Campaign. Because Lee's invading force was not threatened during the Pennsylvania Campaign, Stuart was able to rest his command. The cavalry clashed during the opening phase of both campaigns, but the small action skirmishes at Poolesville and Hyattstown during the Maryland Campaign pale in relation to the full-blown battle at Brandy Station during the Pennsylvania Campaign. While the results were inconclusive, they boosted the Union cavalry's morale and cast doubts about Stuart's invisibility.

Except as part of cavalry actions during both campaigns, the infantry and artillery did not engage the enemy during the first phase of either.

Gov. Andrew Curtin played an important role during both phases, sending streams of correspondence to the army commanders and Washington. During the Maryland Campaign, he employed spies and actively collected information that he passed on to McClellan and Washington. Curtin was less interested in collecting information on Lee's movements during the Pennsylvania Campaign, concentrating instead on defending his state against a thrust by Lee's army.

Protecting Washington was uppermost in the minds of both McClellan and Hooker, leading to some hesitancy in initiating their early movements in pursuit of Lee. Their comments to Halleck are remarkably similar. McClellan told Halleck on September 8: "Our information is still entirely too indefinite to justify definite action…As soon as I find out where to strike, I will be after them without an hour's delay." Hooker, whose army did not head north until the end of the first phase, later wrote: "As soon as the intentions of the enemy are known to me, I shall be able to advance with rapidity."[31]

Table 11: Comparison of the First Phase of Traveling to the Battlefield (September 4 – 8, 1862 and June 3 – 12, 1863)

Issue	Maryland Campaign	Pennsylvania Campaign
Combat during phase?	No	Cavalry actions
Distance between closest units of armies by end of phase	12 miles	3 miles
Confederates: Army moves to jumping off site?	Yes (Leesburg)	Yes (Culpeper Court House)
Confederates: Army enters Union territory?	Yes	No
Confederates: Enters major Union city?	Yes (Frederick)	No
Confederates: Destruction of Union property?	Yes	No
Confederates: Lee issues special orders?	General Orders Number 102 (September 4): reduce straggling and foraging	No
Confederates: Lee issues proclamation to civilians?	Yes (Marylanders)	No
Confederates: Furthest distance traveled by end of phase	25	75
Confederates: Enemy impacts movements?	No	Yes

Issue	Maryland Campaign	Pennsylvania Campaign
Confederates: Did Lee gamble?	Yes (moves army to Leesburg opening route to Richmond)	Yes (leaves only one corps against entire Union army)
Confederates: Cavalry seeks out enemy?	Yes	Yes
Union: Initial location of army	In and around Washington	In and around Fredericksburg, Virginia
Union: Commander must first reorganize army?	Yes	No
Union: Begins full scale movement after Lee's army?	No	Yes (June 12)
Union: Cavalry seeks out enemy?	Yes	Yes
Union: Wing structure implemented?	Yes	Yes
Union: Army commander issues special orders?	No	General Orders Number 62 on June 12 (straggling)
Union: Nature of movements?	None (except for cavalry)	Conservative
Union: Furthest distance traveled by end of phase	None	25 miles
Pennsylvania Governor Curtin plays a role?	Yes (provides information and calls out militia)	Yes (calls out militia)
Location of armies?	**Confederates:** VA/MD **Union:** VA/MD	**Confederates:** VA **Union:** VA

Chapter 7: The Campaigns in Midstream (September 9-12, 1862 and June 13-21, 1863)

The Maryland Campaign of 1862 (September 9-12, 1862)

McClellan issued General Orders No. 155 on September 9 because straggling had been so severe on September 7. He noted straggling seemed to be occurring, "without the least apparent concern on the part of commanding officers of either the higher or lower grade." McClellan also stated: "straggling is habitually associated with cowardice, marauding, and theft," and as result, he instituted the following system: "The straggler must now be taught that [if] he leaves the ranks without authority and skulks [he will put himself] at the severest risk, even that of death. Commanders of regiments will see that the rolls of every company are called before the regiment starts on the march, at every halt, and at the close of the march. The absentees at these roll-calls will be reported to the regimental adjutant." The adjutant was expected to retain a record of these occurrences. McClellan also called upon corps commanders to "allow rest at proper intervals, that the troops may have an opportunity to adjust their equipments, obey the calls of nature, &c." The order had little impact, and straggling continued. Ezra Carman noted the army "moved slowly to the front, leaving behind a swarm of stragglers, who did more damage to the property of friendly citizens than did the Confederates."[1]

Lee faced a big problem on September 9. He expected the Federals would abandon Harpers Ferry because of its vulnerability. Indeed, even as the invasion was in its infancy, Lee wrote to Jefferson Davis: "I have no doubt that they will leave that section as soon as they learn of the movement across the Potomac." But the garrison remained in place as the invasion unfolded, forcing Lee to act. The garrison interfered with his line of communications through the Shenandoah Valley and threatened his rear as he moved north. Lee intended to move the army to Hagerstown, but that would need to wait. Although Harpers Ferry was a threat, it was also an opportunity for the rich supplies it held. Lee first conferred with James Longstreet about the possibly of dividing his command to capture the garrison there and the smaller one at Martinsburg. Longstreet advised against the move as too hazardous in enemy territory, and when Lee said nothing more about it, he thought the idea was just a passing thought. It was not, for Lee summoned Jackson to his headquarters to discuss the situation and apparently his more aggressive lieutenant approved of the plan. Jackson was the perfect choice to lead the mission because he excelled at independent command and was familiar with the region, having been posted there early in the war. Together they planned a way to reduce the garrison. Jackson advocated turning around to deal with the Army of the Potomac and then going after Harpers Ferry, but Lee disagreed. The two garrisons were relatively small he thought (incorrectly) and could be quickly reduced. The plan that evolved had Jackson with six of Lee's nine divisions (2/3 of his army) marching toward Harpers Ferry, while Longstreet and the remainder of the army headed for Boonsboro.

These discussions led to Special Orders No. 191. The order had ten parts:
I. Prohibited the men from visiting Frederick and posted guards to carry out the order.
II. Major Walter Taylor was to head to Leesburg to arrange for transportation of the ill and those unable to walk to Winchester.
III. Gen. Jackson would leave tomorrow (September 10) along the Hagerstown Road, pass through Middletown, cross the Potomac, and head for Harpers Ferry from the Virginia side.
IV. Gen. Longstreet will head for Boonsbough.
V. Gen. McLaws' division with Gen. Anderson's would follow Gen. Longstreet and then at Middletown, peel off and head for Harpers Ferry, approaching it from the Maryland side.
VI. Gen. Walker with his division would cross the Potomac River at Cheek's Ford, head to Lovettsville and take position on Loudoun Heights.
VII. Gen. D. H. Hill's Division would form the rearguard.
VIII. Gen. Stuart would detach a squadron of cavalry to accompany the major commands and the remainder would form the rearguard.
IX. After the troops involved in attacking Harpers Ferry met with success they would reunite with the main body at Boonsborough or Hagerstown.
X. Each regiment would carry axes for use at their encampments to secure wood.

According to the plan, Jackson's contingent army would undertake a complicated series of marches to encircle Harpers Ferry. The three divisions under his direct control would cross the Potomac River above Harpers Ferry and attack from the west. Lafayette McLaws, in charge of his own division and Richard Anderson's, would march southwest from Frederick, through the Pleasant Valley and at least part of his command would scale Maryland Heights to the east of Harpers Ferry and plant artillery there. The remainder would remain in the Pleasant Valley to ward off any attempt by the Army of the Potomac to save the garrison. John Walker's division would also cross the Potomac River, but further south than Jackson, scale Loudoun Heights to the southeast of Harpers Ferry, and haul guns up its steep sides. Therefore, Jackson's strike force of six divisions would essentially encircle the Federal garrison. While Jackson's contingent headed toward Harpers Ferry, Lee and the remainder of his army under Longstreet, would head for Boonsboro, where it would await the return of Jackson's command.

Historian Scott Hartwig noted how the "plan reflected Lee's boldness and his affinity for doing what was least expected." Lee hoped Jackson's appearance would spell doom for the unprepared garrison at Harpers Ferry and perhaps the smaller Martinsburg garrison, and at the same time, confuse McClellan long enough for the detached troops to complete their mission and return to the army before the Army of the Potomac steamed north. The plan was predicated on the garrisons not standing their ground. Lee actually expected the sudden appearance of McLaws on Maryland Heights east of Harpers Ferry and Walker to the south, to cause the Harpers Ferry garrison to flee to the west—right into the arms of Jackson's three divisions.[2]

Lee was confident of his plan; many of his subordinates less so. They understood the important strategy of "concentration" and Lee was doing just the opposite, especially in enemy territory. Lee believed the mission would be completed by September 12, plenty of time before the typically timid McClellan would bring his large army forward to do battle. The army would then recombine at Boonsboro and Lee could decide his next moves at that point.[3]

On September 9, while Lee planned his moves against Harpers Ferry and his army rested, McClellan worried. He believed at least 110,000 men under Jackson were at Frederick and another army of unknown size was at

Leesburg, Virginia, poised to cross the Potomac River to join Lee or attack Washington. No one seemed to know where Robert E. Lee was and that further concerned McClellan and the high command. McClellan vowed to Washington, "I am now in condition to watch him [the Frederick concentration of the enemy] closely." Parr Ridge loomed ahead of McClellan's army. Running between Frederick and Rockville in a northeast to southwest direction, housing the towns of Ridgeville through Poolesville, it was a good defensive position to thwart Lee's possible moves against Washington and Baltimore. McClellan decided to advance his army to occupy it. The town of Ridgeville was of particular importance, as it sat on where the ridge intersected National Road leading to Baltimore.

McClellan pointed his army north on September 9, screened by Pleasonton's cavalry, to occupy at least a portion of the ridge. Like the spread fingers of one hand, the three wings headed north using different routes. The Right Wing as the name implied, marched on the right of the army, heading for Goshen, Cracklinton, and Brookville, Maryland. The Left Wing was actually the center prong that marched toward Middlebrook. The Reserve Wing marched on the left, closest to the Potomac River, headed for Darnestown. Couch's division (Reserve Wing) sent one of its brigades to Offut's Crossroads (now Potomac, Maryland) on the Potomac River to protect Washington and the other two brigades marched further north, to where Seneca Creek emerges from the Potomac River. By the end of the day, the average corps had marched 10 miles and the Army of the Potomac occupied a 25-mile front from the Potomac River to Brookville, Maryland. While still relatively far from Frederick, it was well positioned to protect both Washington and Baltimore.[4]

Gov. Curtin received incorrect reports on September 9 that the enemy was heading toward Hagerstown, just south of the Pennsylvania border. To counter this threat, he requested the services of "regular cavalry and their officers at Carlisle Barracks" that he would concentrate at the border, near Hagerstown. Although he did not have much by way of militia at this point, he felt more comfortable knowing that two New York regiments were stationed near Harrisburg. This feeling quickly evaporated when Gen. Wool, commanding the Middle Department, ordered them to Washington. The situation only worsened for Curtin the following day (September 10) when

Halleck ordered him to send "all troops possible" to Washington for he did not endorse the idea of "scatter[ing] them in weak parties at several points." This is precisely what Curtin was attempting as a way of delaying Lee's move into Pennsylvania.[5]

September 10 found one army decisively moving toward its goal; the other vacillating. Lee began implementing Special Orders Number 191 when his army left the environs of Frederick. Stonewall Jackson's strike force of 31,600 men divided into three prongs, headed for Harpers Ferry. Jackson personally led his own three divisions, 14 infantry brigades and 31 artillery batteries out of Frederick, followed by McLaws' two divisions, seven brigades, and ten batteries. Walker's division, comprising the third prong, was situated southwest of town. It added two brigades and two batteries to the mix. Longstreet's remaining command of two divisions, plus D. H. Hill's division, followed Jackson out of town, but turned north and headed for Boonsboro. These troops amounted to 17,000 infantry (14 brigades) with 36 batteries and the reserve artillery. The 48,600 men in Lee's army on September 13 would not be the same number fighting at Antietam four days later, as straggling, sickness, desertion, and battle losses would reduce its number of effectives by almost twenty-five percent.[6]

Marching from Frederick at 3:00 a.m., Jackson's force had the furthest to travel of the three columns heading for Harpers Ferry, as he would cross the Potomac River at Williamsport or Shepherdstown and loop around to approach the garrison from the west. Few wagons accompanied the column and the men tossed their knapsacks in a pile so they marched with only the "clothes on their backs." The column reached Middletown at about 10:00 a.m. and finally halted for the night just east of Turner's Gap, after the 18-mile march. Jackson could have gone further, but he needed information about the Martinsburg garrison. If it was still present, he would march through Williamsport; if not, the shorter route through Sharpsburg to Shepherdstown. Although McLaws' two divisions had a long trek to Maryland Heights and Pleasant Valley, they found themselves toward the rear of the line leaving Frederick, and did not clear the town until 4:30 p.m. McLaws mercifully halted the column at Middletown at midnight, knowing his men were exhausted and needed a reprieve.[7]

McClellan received reports, later found to be false, of Stonewall Jackson occupying New Market with a large number of enemy troops. The town was eight miles east of Frederick on the National Road, and a straight shot to Baltimore, only 40 miles away. Federal troops sent to Ridgeville (the current Mt. Airy) could potentially blunt a Confederate advance, so McClellan sat down and drafted orders to his close friend, Ambrose Burnside, for September 10. "No time is to be lost. I regard this movement as decisive, if successful." Burnside was ordered to move in two columns: one via Damascus (directly south of Mt. Airy) and the second via Cooksville. Troops in position at Ridgeville could block Jackson from continuing his march on National Road between Baltimore and Frederick.

McClellan deemed Jackson's threat to Baltimore so dire that he also mobilized Sumner's Right Wing to support Burnside's movement. The II Corps would head to Clarksburg and the XII Corps to Damascus. This would put four large Union corps within striking distance of Jackson's phantom threat. The Reserve Wing would march to Barnesville, still considerably south of the other two corps, but in a position to protect Washington. McClellan positioned his troops to ensure most occupied Parr's Ridge. McClellan halted these movements before they were completed for some unknown reason, possibly because he desired additional intelligence about the enemy's position. Instead of a full-scale movement, only a portion of the Right Wing was sent out on a reconnaissance in force toward Ridgeville and Damascus.[8]

September 11 would be another eventful day for both armies. Jackson's men were not marching east toward Baltimore as McClellan thought—but northwest toward the Potomac River. Because the Martinsburg garrison remained in place, Jackson marched his three divisions toward Williamsport. Reveille sounded at 3:00 a.m. and the troops were on the road an hour later in the darkness of Western Maryland. The column crossed the Potomac River and continued toward Martinsburg, hoping to bag Brig. Gen. White's garrison there. In all, Jackson's men covered between 17 and 23 miles that day and were in position to attack Martinsburg the following day. McLaws' column was also on the road, but a bit later that morning, and after passing through Middletown, turned southwest toward Burkittsville. McLaws crossed

South Mountain at Brownsville Pass under the watchful eyes of the Union troops of the Harpers Ferry garrison up on Maryland Heights.[9]

Learning of a large supply of flour in Hagerstown, Maryland being transported to Pennsylvania for safekeeping and a report of a large enemy force marching south from Chambersburg, Lee decided to leave D. H. Hill's division at Boonsboro and send Longstreet north to Hagerstown with two divisions, thus further dividing his command. Longstreet's men reached the outskirts of Hagerstown the following day. Jackson's columns were also making good progress toward Harpers Ferry: Walker's division was near Loudoun Heights, McLaws' two divisions were all the way down in the Pleasant Valley, at the base of Maryland Heights, and Jackson's three divisions were closing in on Martinsburg. Lee later explained he felt comfortable dividing his army because the "advance of the Federal Army was so slow at the time we left Fredericktown as to justify the belief that the reduction of Harpers Ferry would be accomplished and our troops concentrated before they would be called upon to meet it."[10]

Pleasonton continued providing faulty information on the location of Lee's army, and McClellan was beginning to receive reports from other sources of Confederates heading toward Hagerstown, so was Pennsylvania their destination? Other reports had the Confederates moving west, back to the Potomac River, so was Lee abandoning the invasion? During the afternoon of September 11, McClellan reported to Halleck, "almost the entire rebel army in Virginia, amounting to not less than 120,000 men, is in the vicinity of Frederick City." Because McClellan believed he was outnumbered by "at least 25 percent" he requested reinforcements from Washington's garrison. He explained to Halleck that because Lee's intentions were not known earlier in the campaign, "I left what I conceived to be a sufficient force to defend the city against any army they could bring against it from the Virginia side of the Potomac. This uncertainty, in my judgment, exists no longer." McClellan now wanted some of those troops left behind. He hoped for a second division from the IV Corps, but its arrival from the Peninsula was delayed, so he received instead a 1,800-man brigade under Brig. Gen. Max Weber that had been pulling garrison duty in Virginia. Although he also wanted several corps from Washington, he was pleased to hear the remainder of Fitz John Porter's V Corps was being released for his use.[11]

Map 5: The Road to Antietam (September 10, 1862)

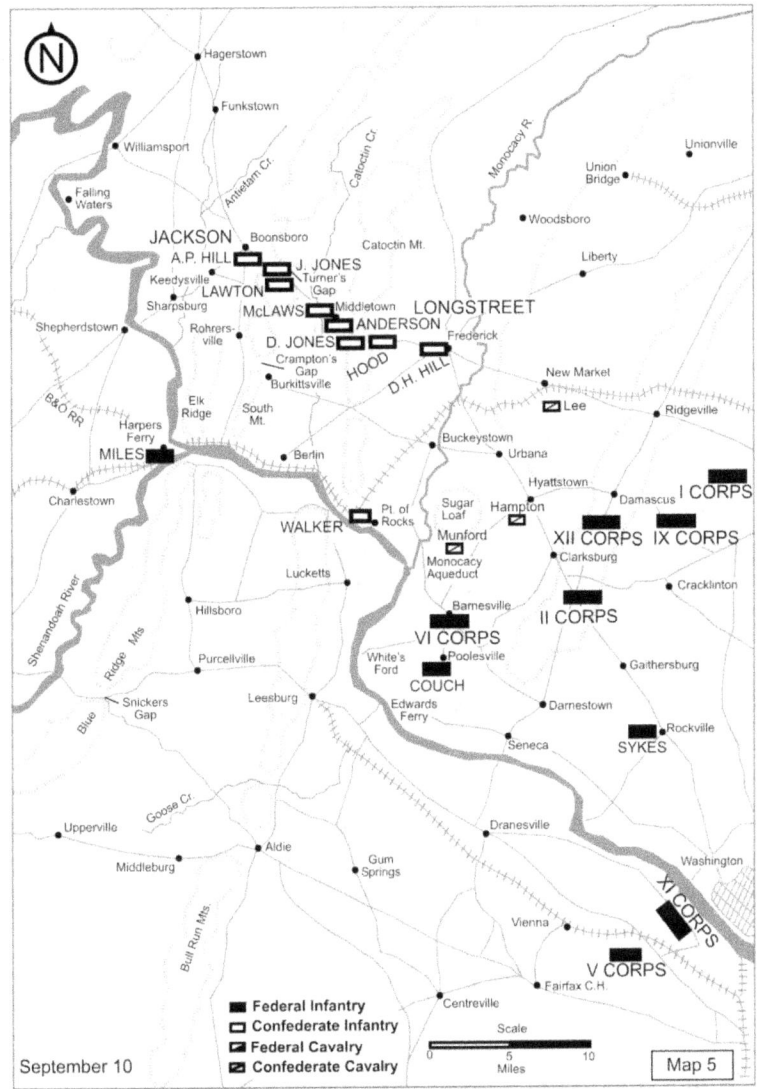

McClellan also sought troops from other sectors. He wrote Halleck the day before, "Colonel Miles is at or near Harper's Ferry, as I understand, with 9,000 troops. He can do nothing where he is, but could be of great service if ordered to join me." Halleck shot down the idea, but left open a tantalizing possibility: when "you can open communications with him…he will be subject to your orders." Neither general could know the importance of Harpers Ferry in stopping the Northern invasion in its tracks. The relief of the garrison became one of McClellan's priorities, but as we will see, was too little too late.[12]

McClellan decided to push his men gingerly north on September 11. The Right Wing's IX Corps marched toward Ridgeville, 15 miles east of Frederick. Two divisions reached it by nightfall; the others were between it and Damascus (six miles to the south). The I Corps was also heading for Ridgeville, but it marched through Cooksville and then headed for Lisbon, halting about half-way between the two towns, and about 12 miles from its ultimate destination. Sumner's Left Wing reached Clarksburg about 16 miles south of Frederick. Sumner sent a division of the II Corps three miles north toward Hyattstown while spinning off the XII Corps to occupy Damascus, about six miles to the northwest.[13]

McClellan craved Sugar Loaf Mountain for its superior view of the countryside and ability to discern Lee's troop movements. The mounted arm of both armies battled for control of the mountain for a few days before Pleasonton threw up his arms on September 10 and told McClellan he needed infantry support to complete his mission. Union infantry from Franklin's Reserve Wing moved forward on September 11 to support Pleasonton's drive against perhaps 800 Virginia troopers. It was now a mismatch and Pleasonton easily captured the mountain, allowing the Union signalmen to quickly scramble up the side of the hill. Had Franklin immediately taken the hill on September 10, his men would have seen Confederate columns moving out of Frederick that day. Even without this valuable outpost, accumulating evidence strongly suggested Lee was leaving Frederick and heading north and west.

The lush surroundings of Maryland heightened the morale of both armies. A young Union lieutenant observed Maryland's countryside to be a "paradise compared to Virginia." Their hearty welcome from the civilians they passed also buoyed their spirits. A Pennsylvanian noted, "it cheered our hearts to see the smiles of welcome bearing on us from every house by the way."[14]

The Confederate invaders were, however, becoming desperate because food was scarce and they brought few provisions with them. Many local farmers had driven their cattle into Pennsylvania, the wheat had not yet been threshed, and local citizens would not sell them food. "If we stay in this part of Maryland we will soon starve, unless the system of impressments is resorted to," wrote an artilleryman. He noted "I visited nearly a hundred farm houses during the day and did not succeed in securing a pound of meat or a bushel of corn." A soldier in McLaws' division marveled at the ripe fruit in the orchards but, according to one soldier, the orchards "are always strictly guarded."[15]

With large numbers of Rebels actually occupying Hagerstown, just a handful of miles from the Pennsylvania border, Gov. Curtin became even more concerned. He realized the northern Maryland town was the gateway to Pennsylvania's Cumberland Valley, and from there the enemy columns could easily march on Harrisburg and even Philadelphia. Curtin demanded assistance from Lincoln, requesting "not less than 80,000 disciplined forces, and order from New York and States east all available forces to concentrate here at once." He begged McClellan for "a large portion of your column in this valley [Cumberland] to save us from utter destruction." Curtin called out his militia and was relieved when Lincoln informed him that he would "receive them into the service and pay of the United States to the extent they can be armed, equipped, and usefully employed."

Curtin felt a need for an experienced officer to command his militia. He wrote to Washington, "I deem it my duty to ask for the immediate presence of an officer of high rank, clothed with full powers to act for the Government, as I design to call out the militia of the State for its defense tomorrow," particularly "an active, energetic officer . . . and one that could rally Pennsylvanians around him." Curtin wanted Brig. Gen. John Reynolds, commander of the Pennsylvania Reserve Division of the I Corps and he got him. McClellan was not so sure Pennsylvania was Lee's intended landing spot, and with the temptation of the Federal garrisons at Martinsburg and Harpers Ferry, he thought an attack on them was more logical. Sending Reynolds to Pennsylvania placated Gov. Curtin, so he dropped the request for thousands of troops, but it did not sit well with Maj. Gen. Joe Hooker who commanded the I Corps, which contained the Pennsylvania Reserve Division. He protested to McClellan: "A scared governor ought not to be permitted to destroy the usefulness of an entire division of the army, on the eve of important operations. . . It is satisfactory to my mind that the rebels have no more intention of going to Harrisburg than they have of going to heaven. It is only in the United States that atrocities likes this are entertained."[16]

A report that Jackson's entire wing was approaching Hagerstown sent Curtin back to the telegraph, frantically writing to Lincoln, "[t]he enemy will bring against us not less than 120,000, with large amount of artillery. The time for decided action by the National Government has arrived. What may we expect?" To McClellan he wrote, "We shall need a large portion of your column in this valley to save us from utter destruction." McClellan responded: "This army is not sufficiently strong to divide it, but I rely upon your troops to hold the enemy in check until I can overtake him."[17]

September 12 was a seminal day in Stonewall Jackson's operation against Harpers Ferry, as all three prongs maneuvered toward their assigned positions. In Martinsburg, Gen. White closely monitored Stonewall Jackson's approach and was in a quandary. According to Gen. Wool, "the place should be held to the last extremity," but he realized, "with the small force at my disposal the position could not [sic] longer be held." So, the garrison was ordered withdrawal to Harpers Ferry at 2:00 a.m. on September 12. White and his men reached their destination about 4:00 p.m. that afternoon. His timing was perfect, for Jackson's troops entered Martinsburg beginning at midday. The Confederates scooped up much needed supplies for three hours, and then Jackson put his men back on the march toward Harpers Ferry. With his division making good progress in approaching Loudoun Heights, Walker hesitated as he did not wish the enemy to observe his movements. He decided on a detour through Hillsborough, which would mask his approach. He camped for the night, ready to take the mountain the following day. McLaws was also preparing for the attack on Harpers Ferry by pushing two of his brigades toward Maryland Heights for an attack the following day.[18]

On September 12, with confirmed reports of the enemy vacating Frederick, McClellan began concentrating his army away from the Potomac

River and prepared to enter the town from two directions. To the east, Burnside's wing pushed toward Frederick from Ridgeville along National Pike, keeping flankers on his right to guard against a surprise attack. Sumner's wing advanced north to Urbana and spun off the XII Corps to Ijamsville to the right, only 7 miles from Frederick. Franklin's wing, closer to the Potomac River, also headed north from Sugar Loaf Mountain and formed on Sumner's left flank, so the army was concentrated east of the Monocacy River in a small area from west near Urbana to the east near National Road. This gave McClellan the option to move rapidly north or stand and defend his position with the Monocacy River between him and the enemy. A cavalry skirmish took place in Frederick between the Confederate rearguard and Cox's division of the IX Corps entering the town.

Frederick was finally back in Union hands, but it had taken McClellan six days to march the 45 miles from Washington to accomplish this, which provided McClellan's critics with a rich source of fodder, but in reality, he was operating under a very difficult environment. He noted in his report of the campaign, filed in October: "During these movements I had not imposed long marches on the columns. The absolute necessity of refitting and giving some little rest to troops worn down by previous long-continued marching and severe fighting, together with the uncertainty as to the actual position, strength, and intentions of the enemy, rendered it incumbent upon me to move slowly and cautiously until the headquarters reached Urbana where I first obtained reliable information [see next section on September 13] that the enemy's object was to move upon Harper's Ferry and the Cumberland Valley, and not upon Baltimore, Washington, or Harrisburg." Nevertheless, McClellan had successfully performed his first task: defending Washington against attack and was now about to move north to protect Pennsylvania. But, Lincoln continued being frustrated by McClellan's inability to provide a concise picture of Lee's movements. The president wrote to Curtin with the plea: "Please tell me at once what is your latest news from or toward Hagerstown." He learned that rebel cavalry occupied Hagerstown, but that was the extent of his information. Lincoln gleaned enough information from other sources to inform McClellan at 5:45 p.m. that Jackson was crossing the Potomac at Williamsport and "probably the whole rebel army will be drawn from Maryland." The President ended this correspondence by writing: "Please do not let him let off without being hurt."[19]

Lee was beginning to worry about the vulnerability of his far-flung troops on September 12. The operation against Harpers Ferry was behind schedule and McClellan was entering Frederick—uncomfortably close to his dispersed army. Lee was most concerned about McLaws' vulnerable command as he had not heard anything from him. During this period, Col. Munford's cavalry brigade on the right was pushed away from Sugar Loaf Mountain and was pursued most of the way to Crampton's Gap in South Mountain, where the enemy could attempt to force its way through to relieve the Harpers Ferry garrison. Brig. Gen. Fitz Lee's brigade was on Lee's army's left and it scouted the Union army's location and strength during this period. Brig. Gen. Wade Hampton's brigade was in the center at Frederick covering the army's move out of the town in compliance with Special Orders Number 191.

Curtin received Lincoln's rejection of his September 11 request for 80,000 "disciplined troops" in good humor as he learned that Jackson was actually crossing the Potomac at Williamsport and was no longer a threat to Pennsylvania.[20]

To summarize the middle section of the campaign, the Army of Northern Virginia left Frederick, Maryland on September 10 after Lee drafted and disseminated Special Orders No. 191. The order split the army into several pieces, sending most toward Harpers Ferry to reduce the garrison in Lee's rear that posed a threat to his future operations. Lee expected the operation to be completed by the end of this phase—the 12th—and then he intended to recombine his army and continue north. Much of this period was taken up by the movements of each of Lee's columns heading to their designated positions. McClellan, still frustrated by conflicting information on Lee's movements and strength, cautiously pushed his army north toward Frederick in a manner to protect both Washington and Baltimore. His troops began entering Frederick on the last day of this period. Pennsylvania governor Andrew Curtin heated up the telegraph wires with pleas for troops to protect his state. He also took action to call out the militia, however, few probably actually arrived in Harrisburg as the end of the campaign was near.

Map 6: The Road to Antietam (September 12, 1862)

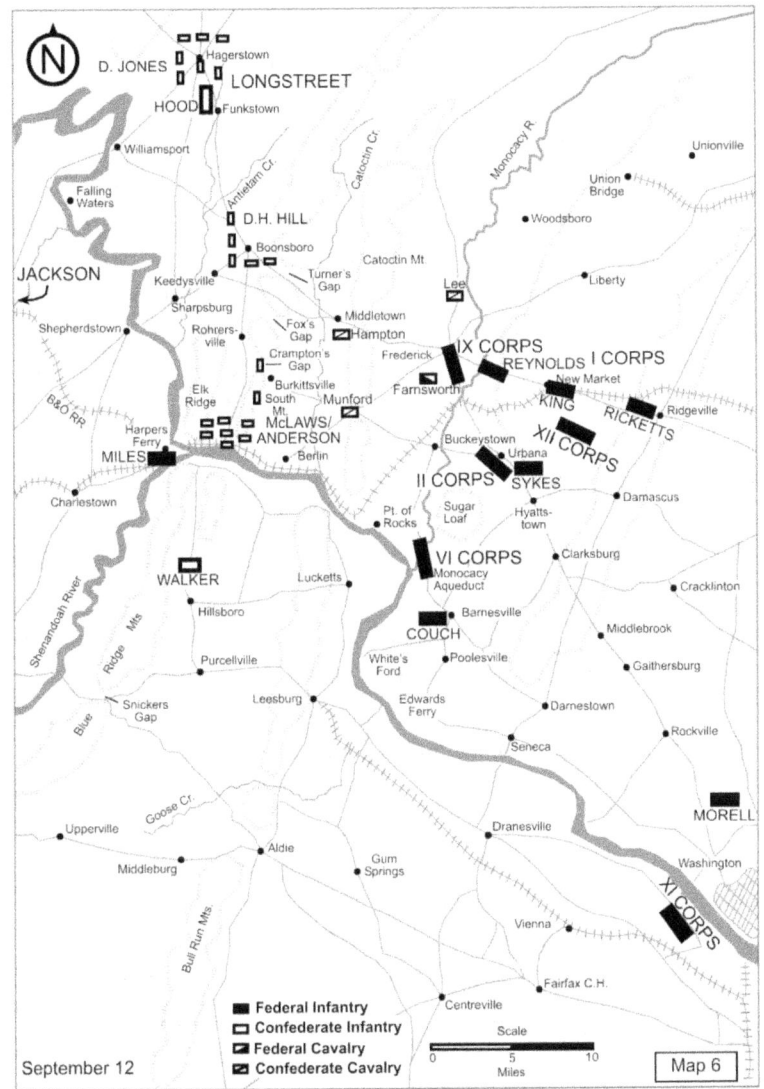

The Pennsylvania Campaign of 1863 (June 13-21, 1863)

The myriad reports of enemy troops moving north in the Shenandoah Valley could no longer be ignored by Hooker, so he ordered his army north to protect both Washington and Harpers Ferry, and moved his base of operations to Centreville on the Orange and Alexandria Railroad. The Right Wing, composed of the I, III, V, and XI Corps was ordered to rendezvous at Manassas Junction, marching through a number of small towns with fancy names. A Michigan soldier related, "what they lacked in size they made up with their names." The Left Wing, composed of the II, VI, and XII Corps remained at Fredericksburg to cover the removal of Federal property, before heading to Dumfries. All but the II and III Corps were on the road for at least part of the day. While Union troop movements dominated June 13, Gen. Richard Ewell's Second Corps approached Berryville and Winchester. The latter actions will be described in fuller detail in Chapter 10.

The majority of both armies were in motion on June 14. By the end of a long march, the Army of the Potomac was concentrated in two areas. Most units (I, III, V, and XI Corps) were between Centreville and Catlett's Station along the Orange and Alexandria Railroad. Adequate water was a severe problem and many men filled their canteens with contaminated water, only to suffer from severe diarrhea. The thick dust caked their uniforms, making them appear brown. Some units halted for the day between 6:00 and 7:00 p.m., but others marched into the night, not halting until near midnight. A second group (VI and XII Corps) marched north from Fredericksburg, so they had some catching up to do. The XII Corps marched all through the night of June 13-14 and reached Dumfries, about 20 miles east of the railroad, in the morning, and were permitted to rest the remainder of the day and night. The widely dispersed VI Corps assembled at Stafford Court House, just north of Fredericksburg during the early morning hours. After a long rest, the men were put back on the road between 9:00 and 10:00 p.m.

The II Corps remained in position near Fredericksburg assisting the quartermaster relocate the army's supplies and to deceive the enemy into thinking the army still occupied its former positions. The men packed up their belongings after dark and marched a couple of hours before going into camp. Hooker felt safe to relocate his headquarters from Falmouth to Dumfries. Lincoln sent ominous news that ended with a request of Hooker:

"The enemy have Milroy surrounded at Winchester and Tyler at Martinsburg. If they could hold out a few days, could you help them?" Lincoln went on to give an apt analogy: "If the head of Lee's army is at Martinsburg and the tail of it on the Plank Road between Fredericksburg and Chancellorsville, the animal must be very slim somewhere. Could you not break him?" Hooker's response may have touched a nerve with Lincoln, when he wrote, "I do not feel like making a move for an enemy until I am satisfied as to his whereabouts. To proceed to Winchester and have him make his appearance elsewhere, would subject me to ridicule." Lincoln responded that "I really fear, almost believe" that Winchester was surrounded and needed Hooker's assistance. However, he would not order Hooker north.

The Confederate commanders received daily reports of the Union army's activities and when Lee learned Hooker's men were pulling out from their positions on June 13, he ordered A. P. Hill Third Corps to prepare to rejoin the rest of the army. Richard Anderson's division began its march to Culpeper Court House on the 14th; the other two divisions prepared to follow the following day. Longstreet ordered his three First Corps division commanders to also prepare to continue their march on June 14, while Ewell's Second Corps was about to engage the isolated enemy garrisons at Berryville and Winchester.[21]

Union commanders always seemed to overestimate the size of Lee's army and Hooker was no exception. He wrote to Lincoln on the evening of September 14: "The enemy has in this column not less than between 70,000 and 80,000 men. A. P. Hill's corps, of about 30,000, is still on the south side of the Rappahannock." That would put Lee's army at between 100,000 and 110,000 men—much larger than the 70,000 or so that Lee actually had with him during the invasion.[22]

June 15 again found both armies on the march. The Federal I, III, VI, and XI Corps continued moving up the Orange and Alexandria Railroad toward Washington, reaching their concentrating position at Manassas/Centreville. The other three corps made good progress in catching up with the remainder of the army. The II Corps began its march from the Fredericksburg area, reaching Dumfries by nightfall, the VI Corps, which had been at Dumfries, marched about eight miles north to Wolf Run Shoals and the XII ended the day at Fairfax Court House, just seven miles to the east of the rest of the army. Because his troops had made such good progress, Hooker moved his headquarters again, this time to Fairfax Station. Hooker sent a telegram to Lincoln at the end of June 15, that was both anticlimactic and cautionary: "It seems to disclose the intentions of the enemy to make an invasion, and, if so, it is not in my power to prevent it. I can, however, make an effort to check him until he has concentrated all his forces. I may possibly be able to prevent the junction, and commence the movement during to-morrow."

While the Union army moved north, Pleasonton's cavalry picketed the Rappahannock River, collecting information and guarding against an attack on Hooker's rear. The Union cavalry commander sent a slew of "confusing, inaccurate, and misleading" information to Hooker, according to historian Thomas Ryan. He misrepresented Longstreet's position, overestimated the enemy's numbers, noted that Ewell's corps was south of the Rappahannock River (not near Winchester), and believed Stuart was heading for Maryland. Hooker often passed along bits of information to Washington, leading Halleck to throw up his arms and acidly write about Pleasonton's information: "They are very contradictory . . . and very unsatisfactory." He reminded Hooker that "Your army is entirely free to operate as you desire against Lee's army, so long as you keep his army from Washington."[23]

Lee was also frustrated about the lack of clarity of the enemy's intentions, but not enough to abort his invasion. All of Longstreet's and Hill's men were put on the road on June 15. They were still on the east side of the Blue Ridge Mountains, so long marches were in their futures just to reach the Shenandoah Valley. They were still widely separated from Ewell's Second Corps, which was outside of Winchester. Gen. Milroy finally saw the handwriting on the wall and decided to abandon Winchester during the early morning hours of June 15. Milroy's troops were shocked when they ran into Ewell's men, who anticipated Milroy's nocturnal movement, and made a looping movement around Winchester, to take position at Stephenson's Depot. Milroy engaged them as the day brightened, but was unable to escape and was forced to surrender a large portion of his command (see Chapter 10). Further north, Gen. Robert Rodes' division began crossing the Potomac River into Maryland. This meant that Lee's army was stretched an incredible 130 miles, with one corps in the Lower Shenandoah Valley and the other two spread on either side of Culpeper, Virginia.[24]

June 15 ended on a dramatic note when Brig. Gen. Albert Jenkins led his 2,000 mounted infantry galloping into Chambersburg, Pennsylvania at 11:30 p.m. after a long ride from Williamsport, Maryland. The raiders remained here, collecting supplies and creating distress, until June 17, when they returned to Maryland. Along the way, Jenkins spun off cavalry to collect supplies at McConnellsburg and Mercersburg, Pennsylvania.

Pennsylvania Governor Andrew Curtin may have had an inkling of things to come when he asked Henry Halleck on June 13 if the Union cavalry would pursue rebel horsemen, should they cross the Potomac River. Halleck, characteristically deflected the question to Stanton and Lincoln. This lack of clarity pushed Curtin to send Col. T. A. Scott of his staff to discuss a plan to raise 50,000 troops to protect Pennsylvania. Scott met with Stanton on June 15 and was told the "President cannot authorize a call in the form you suggest, the law in express terms prohibiting, but he will make a demand or call upon Pennsylvania, Ohio, Maryland, and West Virginia for 100,000 men, in view of the threatened invasion of Maryland and Pennsylvania, to serve six months…The quota of Pennsylvania under the call of the President will probably be 50,000; Ohio, 30,000; Maryland, 10,000; and West Virginia, 10,000."[25]

Lincoln then crafted a proclamation requesting the 100,000 new recruits. He explained, "arms insurrectionary combinations now existing in several of the States are threatening to make inroads into the States of Maryland, West Virginia, Pennsylvania, and Ohio, requiring immediately an additional force for the service of the United States." Stanton went one step further on June 15 and sent telegrams to the remainder of the governors, noting "It is important to have the largest possible force in the least time, and if other States would furnish militia for a short term, to be credited on the draft, it would greatly advance the object. Will you please inform me immediately what number, in answer to a special call of the President, you can raise and forward of militia or volunteers, without bounty, for six months, unless sooner discharged, and to be credited on the draft of your State?" This was

Map 7: The Road to Gettysburg (June 15, 1863)

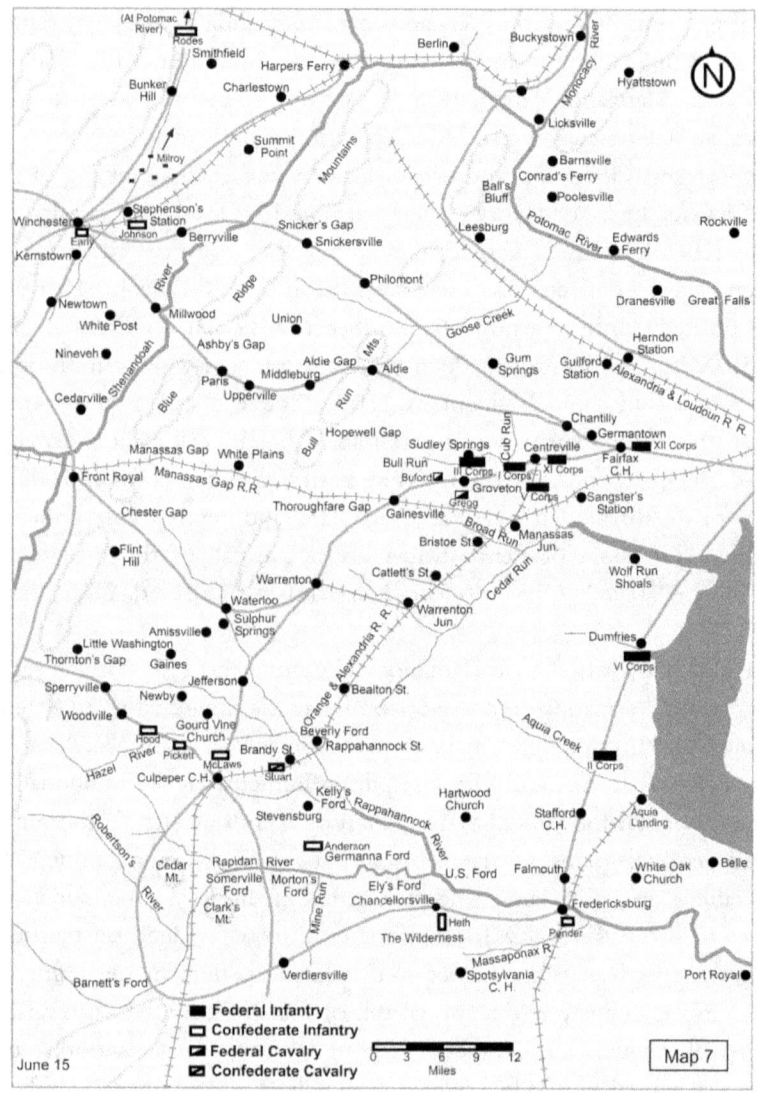

an extraordinary dispatch for it showed in the strongest terms, Lincoln's and Stanton's dire concern about the fate of the Union. They would sacrifice long-term enlistments for quick recruitments that could beef up the size of the force defending Pennsylvania.[26]

Curtin took it upon himself to cast about for support from neighboring states. He wrote to New Jersey Governor, Joel Parker on June 15, "This State is threatened with invasion by a large force, and "we are raising troops as rapidly as possible to resist them. I understand there are three regiments of your troops at Beverly waiting to be mustered out. Could an arrangement be made with you and the authorities at Washington by which the services of those regiments could be had for the present emergency?" Parker reached out to these troops with his own plea on June 17: "It will take time to organize and send other troops to the aid of Pennsylvania. You are already organized and drilled. The hard service you have seen in Virginia has made you veterans, far more efficient than new troops can possibly be. I regret any necessity that may detain you from your homes, but can this appeal from a sister State, in her hour of danger, be disregarded?" The men agreed and New Jersey troops began arriving in Harrisburg at midnight on June 18. Two days later, Parker asked Curtin if he should begin organizing additional units to assist Pennsylvania and Curtin quickly replied in the affirmative.[27]

Stanton's plea to New York's governor, Horatio Seymour, brought an immediate response—within two hours—he would "spare no effort to send you troops at once. I have sent orders to the militia officer of the State." Stanton was ecstatic and quickly telegraphed his thanks and noted, "A strong movement of your city regiments to Philadelphia would be a very encouraging movement, and do great good in giving strength in that State...Can you forward your city regiments speedily?" The state subsequently promised 8,000 to 10,000 men; 2,000 of them were dispatched immediately.[28]

With troops being mobilized for the defense of Pennsylvania, Curtin turned his attention to raising the 50,000 men from his own state. He issued a proclamation indicating the grave situation and ended it with the plea: "call upon the people of Pennsylvania capable of bearing arms to enroll themselves in military organizations, and to encourage all others to give aid and assistance to the efforts which will be put forth for the protection of the State and the salvation of our common country."²⁹

Friction between Hooker and Halleck continued mounting through June 16, causing the army commander to often bypass the general-in-chief and communicate directly with Lincoln. Hooker and Halleck never had a good relationship, but the stress of another invasion caused it to rapidly deteriorate. Hooker wrote to Lincoln at 11:00 a.m.: "You have long been aware, Mr. President, that I have not enjoyed the confidence of the major-general commanding the army [Halleck], and I can assure you so long as this continues we may look in vain for success, especially as future operations will require our relations to be more dependent upon each other than heretofore." Lincoln was not happy that Hooker was bypassing Halleck and sending communications directly to him, so he responded: "To remove all misunderstanding, I now place you in the strict military relation to General Halleck of a commander of one of the armies to the general-in-chief of all the armies. I have not intended differently, but as it seems to be differently understood, I shall direct him to give you orders and you to obey them." These were strong words, underscoring that Hooker was on shaky ground when it came to his continued leadership of the Army of the Potomac. If Hooker thought he would receive guidance from Halleck, he was dead wrong. According to one of Halleck's biographers, "Halleck continued giving general recommendations, but he would not give definitive orders." This frustrated all, including Lincoln, but according to Halleck's biographer, he didn't replace him because he could think of no one better and "he still gave good advice and perhaps that had to suffice for Lincoln for the time being."³⁰

June 16 was a fairly quiet day for Hooker's army as only the two corps to the south, the II and VI Corps, were on the march to join the remainder of the army. The latter corps arrived at Fairfax Station while the II Corps camped at Wolf Run Shoals, still a day's march away from the army. With his army consolidating near Washington, Hooker seemed adrift, as he continued thirsting for information about Lee's activities in the Shenandoah Valley. He knew Ewell was in and around Winchester, but did not know the location of the remainder of the Confederate army. He depended on cavalry chief, Alfred Pleasonton, to provide information on Lee's army's whereabouts, but he was gleaning most of his information from deserters and fugitive slaves, which was of dubious value. Hooker decided to unleash Pleasonton's two cavalry divisions on an operation to breech the Blue Ridge Mountain gaps to discern what Lee was doing in the Valley. Hooker and Pleasonton were unaware that Jeb Stuart, who had been resting his cavalry for almost a week after Brandy Station, had his men in the saddle, heading for the Blue Ridge Mountains to block an enemy incursion through the gaps.

Hooker continued sending contradictory dispatches to Halleck. In one communication he considered moving rapidly north to help defend Harpers Ferry and then sent another a short time later with the idea of interjecting his army between Lee's columns before they could reassemble. There was also a seemingly endless stream of requests for direction. Halleck finally wrote a blunt response to Hooker at 10:15 p.m. on June 16: "You are in command of the Army of the Potomac, and will make the particular dispositions as you deem proper. I shall only indicate the objects to be aimed at." This statement was probably maddening to Hooker, who through the day had been bombarded with communications from Halleck about how the rebels about to capture Harpers Ferry, but he never actually ordered him north to protect it. Halleck would answer questions and make suggestions, but would rarely direct an army commander to undertake a particular action.

The Northern press continued agitating Hooker by publicizing the army's movements. He decided the press could be used for some counterintelligence, and asked Stanton to tell the media his army was moving south to the James River to throw a scare into Lee and perhaps end his movements north. Stanton was in no mood for these antics and caustically responded, "the very demon of lying seems to be about these times, and generals will have to be broken for ignorance before they will take the trouble to find out the truth of the reports."

June 16 found Lee's entire army on the move for the first time in the campaign. With the threat of Hooker crossing the Rappahannock and striking south now past, Lee felt comfortable pushing his columns north. Longstreet's men, who had been the first to move out, had stalled near Culpeper Court House for over a week and were now heading toward the Shenandoah Valley. Ewell's Second Corps, having taken Winchester and captured much of its garrison, was closing in on the Potomac River. The last of Hill's Third Corps, Dorsey Pender's division, finally left the Rappahannock River and headed northwest to Culpeper Court House, where the rest of the corps was also concentrating. Albert Jenkin's mounted infantry brigade remained in Chambersburg, Pennsylvania, scouting and collecting supplies.

Jenkins' presence-- a mere 55 miles from Harrisburg-- set off a panic. Records were removed from the State House, shops were boarded up and merchandise sent to Philadelphia. Hundreds flocked to train stations to escape. Panic spread to other cities and towns and entrenchments were built.[31]

Because Hooker was still in the dark about Lee's location, he sent what little cavalry he still had available to him out toward Winchester and Harpers Ferry. Hooker had much of his army in motion on June 17, some undertaking long, hard marches. Two of Hooker's Corps, the I and XII Corps marched north to positions closer to the Potomac River. The latter stopped at Dranesville; the former at Herndon Station on the Alexandria and Loudoun Railroad, which was less than ten miles from the Potomac River. The II Corps finally reached the Orange and Alexandria Railroad at Sangster's Station, just below Fairfax. Two other corps were pushed northwest. The V Corps headed for Gum Springs (now Arcola) where it could move west to support Pleasonton's cavalry or north to go after Lee. The XI Corps marched north toward to Leesburg "at a lively gait," halting at Goose Creek for the night. After concentrating his army, Hooker was again dispersing it to prepare for any eventuality that Lee could throw at him.

The cavalry caused Lee some stressful moments on June 17, as his eyes and ears were failing him. Because Jeb Stuart was doing his best to stop Pleasonton's cavalry corps from pushing through the Blue Ridge Mountain gaps to ascertain the location of his army, he was not able to ride east to ascertain Hooker's position. Lee realized the vulnerability of his army, strung out over 100 miles. Stopping Pleasonton's prying eyes was so important that Lee halted Longstreet's First Corps to protect the Blue Ridge Mountain gaps rather than follow Ewell's Second Corps. However, Lee wrote to Longstreet on June 17: "I have heard nothing of the movements of General Hooker either from General Stuart or yourself, and therefore, can form no opinion of the best move against him."

Most of Lee's army was still on the march on June 17. Hill's Third Corps continued making arduous marches in the intense heat to reach Culpeper, and all of Ewell's divisions were close to the Potomac River. One had already crossed into Maryland, another rested near Winchester, Virginia, and a third was marching toward Shepherdstown, in what is now West Virginia. With his men so near the Potomac River, Lee wrote to Ewell, "repress marauding. Take what is necessary for the army, and give citizens of Maryland Confederate money or certificates."

The first cavalry fight for the Blue Ridge Mountain gaps occurred on June 17, when Brig. Gen. Judson Kilpatrick's brigade (Brig. Gen. David Gregg's cavalry division) tangled with Col. Tom Munford's brigade outside of Aldie. The fight ended in a stalemate, denying Pleasonton the opportunity of peeking into the Shenandoah Valley.

Hooker rested most of his army on June 18. Only the XII Corps made an extensive 20-mile march north to Leesburg, in northern Virginia to counter Confederate cavalry who were destroying railroad stock on the Maryland side of the Potomac River. Although Hooker was explicitly told by Lincoln to report directly to the General-in-Chief, the latter also informed him that "All telegrams from you or to you are subject to the hourly inspection of the Secretary of War and the President. No important instructions have or will be sent to you without their knowledge." Lincoln still had his hands in the campaign.[32]

Halleck was becoming increasingly frustrated by the lack of clarity on Lee's location and movements, as most of Hooker's information was of dubious value because of its source. Halleck wrote to Hooker on June 18: "Officers and citizens are on a big stampede. They are asking me why does not General Hooker tell where Lee's army is; he is nearest to it. There are numerous suppositions and theories, but all is yet mere conjecture. I only hope for positive information from your front."

Lee's army was on the move on June 18, with Hood's and McLaws' divisions (First Corps) entering the Shenandoah Valley and marching north, struggling along the dusty roads. Edward Johnson's division (Second Corps) was the second division to cross the Potomac River into Maryland, halting near Sharpsburg. Rodes' division was already across the river, leaving only Early's division still in Virginia. The Third Corps was also marching north, heading for the Shenandoah Valley.

June 18 was not a good day for Pleasonton's cavalry, as one of its regiments, the 280-man 1st Rhode Island Cavalry, was virtually surrounded at Middleburg, Virginia, just down the road from Aldie, and almost destroyed. Gen. Pleasonton sent reinforcements to save the command, but they arrived too late. Frustrated by Pleasonton's lack of accountability, Hooker turned to Gen. Julius Stahel's division, part of the Washington defense force, to send a couple of regiments west to see what was going on at Warrenton, Virginia. The troopers encountered a Confederate cavalry brigade there and quickly withdrew. Pleasonton's timidity may have been at least partially caused by the capture of a courier carrying messages from Hooker to Pleasonton stating the size and disposition of the Union army.

Both commanders moved their pieces around the landscape like a game of chess on June 19. The cavalry continued fighting it out just east of the Blue Ridge Mountain gaps, and Pleasonton called for infantry support. The V Corps provided that assistance, and it marched to the small town of Aldie, where it was in a position to aid the cavalry. Their position at Gum Springs was taken by the III Corps. The men began their ten-mile march at about 2:00 p.m. but rain began falling at dusk. The night was so dark the men could remain in the ranks "only by continually shouting." The II Corps made a short march from Sangster's Station to Centreville to recombine with Hooker's main body. The other four corps remained in camp. Although Hooker was experiencing difficulty ascertaining Lee's movements, apparently Lee only had to read Northern newspapers to learn of Hooker's. The Union army commander wrote to Halleck on June 19: "I have just been furnished with an extract from the *New York Herald* of yesterday concerning the late movements of this army. So long as the newspapers continue to give publicity to our movements, we must not expect to gain any advantage over our adversaries. Is there no way of stopping it?" While Halleck sympathized with Hooker's plight, he threw it back in his lap: "I see no way of preventing it as long as reporters are permitted in our camps. I expelled them all from our lines in Mississippi. Every general must decide for himself what persons he will permit in his camps."

Hooker reported the location of his troops by the end of June 19. Those two corps who got a late start in rejoining the army (II and VI Corps), rested in camp, just north of the Orange and Alexandria Railroad. Three others were further north and east, closer to the Potomac River (XII Corps at Leesburg, I Corps at Guilford Station, and XI Corps at Goose Creek). The V Corps was further west supporting the cavalry and the III Corps was just to the east at Gum Springs, where it could move in any direction to support its brother corps, should the need arise. Hooker had effectively arranged his troops to protect Washington or move north after Lee.

The Confederates were becoming less dispersed by the day. June 19 found Ewell's Second Corps continuing to straddle the Potomac River, Hill's Third Corps reaching the Shenandoah Valley and Longstreet's First Corps was in between, still guarding the Blue Ridge Mountain passes. The two cavalry forces tangled near Middleburg, Virginia for control of Ashby's Gap through the Blue Ridge Mountains to the west, but Stuart was able to again halt Pleasonton's probes.[33]

Albert Jenkins, whose men were resting at Williamsport after their ride to Chambersburg, was ordered back toward that Pennsylvania town on June 19. This time his mission was to screen Ewell's Second Corps as it moved north into Pennsylvania.

June 20 was a quiet day for both armies. Hancock's II Corps left Centreville and headed toward Thoroughfare Gap in the Bull Run Mountains to better support the cavalry, and a VI Corps division marched to Bristoe. Only Lee's Third Corps was on the march. Some of its units entered the Shenandoah Valley; others camped for the night just in front of the gaps leading to it. Confederate raiders entered McConnellsburg, Pennsylvania, seeking supplies and terrifying the natives.

Lee hoped to put Longstreet's men on the march northward in the Shenandoah Valley toward the Potomac River on June 21, but Pleasonton's aggressive thrusts toward the Blue Ridge Mountain gaps forced a deferral of these plans. Pleasonton sought a knockout punch against Stuart and told Hooker on June 20, he was planning to "take my whole corps to-morrow morning and throw it at once upon Stuart's whole force, and cripple it up." However, to accomplish this goal, he needed "a couple of large brigades or a division of infantry." Several V Corps infantry brigades arrived to take part in the resulting fight at Upperville, a mere five miles from Ashby's Gap, on June 21.

Col. Strong Vincent's brigade participated in the attack on Stuart's position, and he wrote in his report, the "triumphant strains of the bands, as squadron after squadron hurled the enemy in his flight up the hills…gave us a feeling of regret that we, too, were not mounted and count not join in the chase." Stuart again prevailed and turned back the Union horsemen. They would not see what was going on in the Shenandoah Valley, as Pleasonton finally gave up the attempts after still another setback.[34]

Only Hill's Third Corps made progress toward linking with the rest of Lee's units. Anderson's and Heth's divisions drove all the way to Berryville, Virginia, after long marches, actually passing Longstreet's men. Pender's division, bringing up the rear, entered the Valley, passed through Front Royal, and spent the night near White Post, Virginia.

Hooker's men were also fairly inactive, except for a division of the V Corps (James Barnes') that cooperated with Pleasonton's cavalry in battling Jeb Stuart for control of the Blue Ridge Mountain passes. Stuart was doing a superb job of hampering Pleasonton's attempt to cast a prying eye on the Shenandoah Valley. Hooker wrote to Lincoln that day: "This cavalry force [Stuart's] has hitherto prevented me from obtaining satisfactory information as to the whereabouts of the enemy. They have masked all of their movements." Meanwhile, needing to move quickly, Hooker's engineers threw a 1,340 foot pontoon bridge over the Potomac River at Edward's Ferry in preparation of the army's crossing into Maryland.

Lee issued General Orders No. 71 on June 21, regulating the men's behavior as they entered the North. Composed of six parts, the order explicitly stated no private property could be "injured or destroyed," that the commissary/quartermaster/ordnance chiefs were the only parties that could make requisitions upon the civilians or local authorities, if requests for goods were denied, the chiefs could take them and provide a receipt. The men were most unhappy with this order. A Virginian recalled, "when we crossed the Potomac we thought we would have fine time plundering in the enemy's country, and live fine . . . orders were read out that we were not to molest any of the citizens or take any private property, and any soldier caught plundering would be shot."[35]

Map 8: The Road to Gettysburg (June 19-20, 1863)

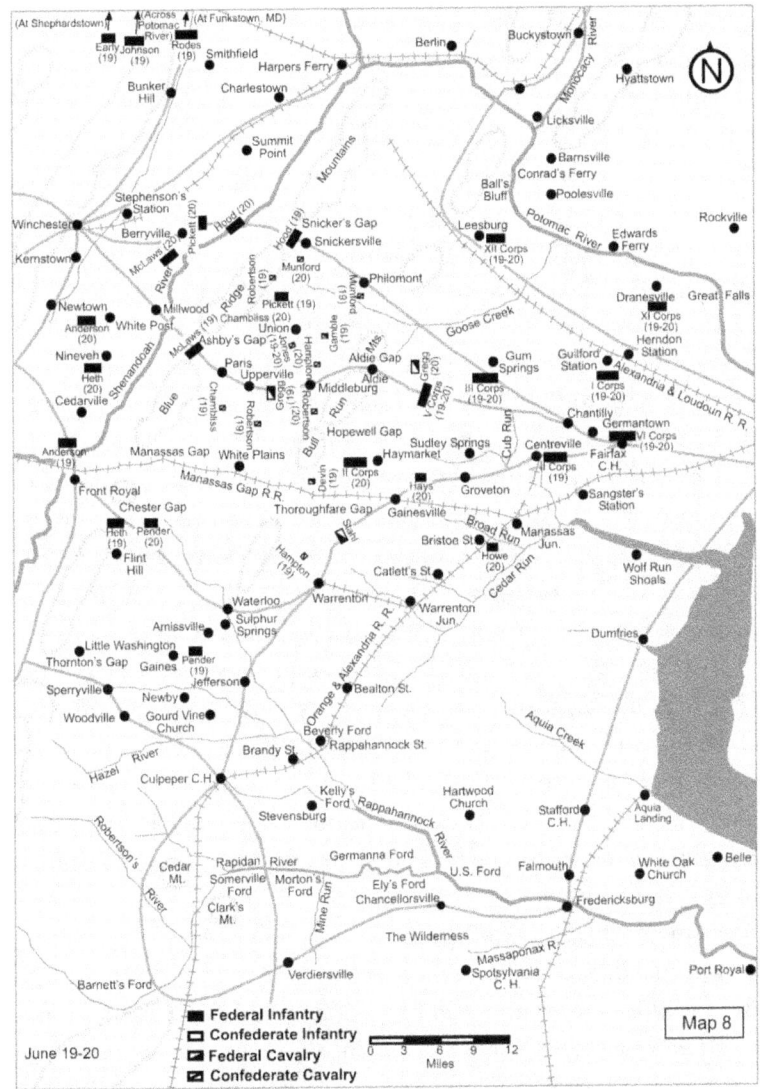

The middle period of the campaign can be summarized as movements in fits and starts northward by both armies. Lee's vanguard, composed of Richard Ewell's Second Corps, captured Winchester and then bagged most of Robert Milroy's army at Stephenson's Depot. Lee's entire army was committed to the invasion, with Ewell's Corps ending the phase straddling the Potomac River and the other two corps either in, or approaching, the Shenandoah Valley. Lee issued General Orders No. 71 which restricted pillaging/stealing as Confederate raiders entered Chambersburg. Hooker effectively moved his army north through long marches, first to their rendezvous along the Orange and Alexandria Railroad just west of Washington. By the end of this period, Hooker's army occupied a box from the Centreville area to the south to Leesburg to the north (25 miles) and from Herndon Station on the east to Thoroughfare Gap to the west (35 miles). Hooker's cavalry under Alfred Pleasonton desperately tried to force its way through the Blue Ridge Mountain gaps to see what Lee was up to, but Jeb Stuart's cavalry, supported by Longstreet's First Corps, stood in his way, resulting in a number of fights east of the mountain. Although Pleasonton never pierced Stuart's and Longstreet's barrier, he effectively delayed Lee's invasion. While Lee's army was on the march most days, Hooker's army marched, then halted, then marched again. It moved quickly and decisively north from June 13-15, took a rest on the 16th, moved a bit on the 17th, then was mostly quiet from June 18–21. This was a period when Hooker sought more accurate intelligence on Lee's whereabouts and was reluctant to commit his army to an aggressive move east or north without additional information.

Comparisons of the Two Campaigns

The commanders of the Union army during each campaign spent considerable time during the middle period of the invasion attempting to ascertain Lee's position. This was potentially easier during the Maryland Campaign as Lee's army was operating in Maryland, closer to Washington, and a stream of information arrived from loyal civilians. The situation was more difficult for Hooker during the Pennsylvania Campaign. Not only was Lee still moving through mostly friendly territory in Virginia, at least during most of this period, his position was screened by the Blue Ridge Mountains.

During both campaigns, the Union army attempted to place itself between Lee's army and Washington and Baltimore.

The Union cavalry was tasked with providing accurate information about Lee's location in both campaigns, and was found wanting in both. The cavalry was poorly organized during the Maryland Campaign and most units operated independently of each other. Pleasonton's organization was perfected by the Pennsylvania Campaign and all of his units were available, but he came up short against Jeb Stuart's determined cavalry (backed up by James Longstreet's First Corps) who stood between the Union troopers and the Blue Ridge Mountain gaps, resulting in three pitched cavalry battles. The Confederate cavalry operated effectively in both campaigns, screening Lee's army and protecting it from Pleasonton's men.

Lee was not overly concerned about McClellan's movements during the second phase of the Maryland Campaign, probably because he continued believing McClellan would exhibit an abundance of caution as he moved north. He was more concerned about Hooker's movements during the Pennsylvania Campaign, possibly because Stuart was not able to provide intelligence because he was preoccupied with stopping Pleasonton from getting into the Shenandoah Valley.

Union garrisons surprised Lee during both campaigns, thinking Harpers Ferry during the Maryland Campaign and Winchester during the Pennsylvania Campaign would both be evacuated as his army moved north. Neither was, and Lee moved to neutralize the threat in both campaigns. The feat was much easier during the Pennsylvania Campaign for a variety of reasons. First, Winchester lay directly in the path of Gen. Richard Ewell's Second Corps; Harpers Ferry required a complex movement that forced Lee to divide his army—always a hazard when in enemy territory. Second, while Winchester was protected by forts, they were easier to defend than the mountains surrounding Harpers Ferry. The Confederates expended valuable time in maneuvering into position and when they were, two three prongs were isolated and in potential danger. Ewell's men during the Pennsylvania Campaign were never in danger of being cut off and defeated.

The second phase of both campaigns was characterized by long marches by the armies. McClellan felt comfortable moving north during the beginning of the second phase of the Maryland Campaign. He moved his army 30-some miles from the environs of Rockville to Frederick between September 9 and 12. McClellan's cautious movements reflected his uncertainty of Lee's numbers and location, complicated by his orders to protect both Washington and Baltimore. Using a wing structure, McClellan effectively moved north over a wide front to detect and engage any enemy unit his corps might encounter. Hooker was more cautious during the early portion of the Pennsylvania Campaign. He was willing to risk Lincoln's wrath by waiting until he had a better understanding of Lee's movements, rather than blunder north and risk the loss of strategic territory or being pulled into an unwanted battle in the open. By the beginning of the second phase, Hooker had enough information to begin moving his army north to counter Lee and protect Washington. In both campaigns, the Union army made the defense of Washington a priority, but they accomplished this mission in different ways. While McClellan fanned his units out over a wide front during the Maryland Campaign, Hooker had to first reach Washington to defend it and this took up much of the time when the army was in motion. Hooker used the Orange and Alexandria Railroad to guide his army toward Centreville. With Washington protected, Hooker was able to disperse his army toward the end of this phase, so some units were close to Leesburg, where they could rapidly move north to counter Lee's movements, some units moved further west to support Pleasonton, and a considerable number of units were retained close to Washington for its protection. By the end of this phase, McClellan was in, or approaching Frederick, Maryland, while Hooker was dispersed around northern Virginia, ready to move as Lee's movements dictated.

The types of movements were also somewhat different. During the Maryland Campaign, Lee spent some of this period resting his tired men in and around Frederick. This was not the case with McClellan, who pushed his troops north on most days. The Pennsylvania Campaign differed, in that both Lee and Hooker kept their men in camp for several days, usually to determine what their adversary was up to. For example, after rendezvousing near Centreville in mid-June, the Union army was largely inactive on June 16, 18, 19, 20, and 21.

The army commanders issued General Orders regulating the men's behavior during the second phase of the campaign. McClellan issued General Orders No. 155 on September 9 to prevent straggling as the men embarked on their journey north. Lee had already issued such orders during the first phase of the move north. Similarly, Hooker had already issued orders against straggling on June 12 (first phase), but Lee issued General Orders No. 71 that prohibited foraging during the second phase.

Pennsylvania governor, Andrew Curtin, devoted much of his time during the middle portion of both campaigns to concentrating troops for the defense of his state. His tactics differed, however. During the Maryland Campaign, he urgently petitioned for troops to be detached from the Army of the Potomac and sent to Pennsylvania for its defense. He probably had learned the folly of such requests during the Pennsylvania Campaign and concentrated on getting recruits from neighboring states to provide manpower. He also called upon his own citizens to answer the call to raise his quota of 50,000 men.

Table 12: Comparison of the Second Phase of Traveling to the Battlefield (September 9-12, 1862 and June 13-21, 1863)

Issue	Maryland Campaign	Pennsylvania Campaign
Infantry combat	No	No
Cavalry combat	Skirmishes	Three large-scale battles
Location of armies?	**Confederates:** MD **Union:** MD	**Confederates:** VA/MD **Union:** VA
Distance between closest units of armies by end of phase	12 miles	17 miles
Commander issues special/general orders?	**Confederates:** No xx**Union:** General Orders No. 155-- straggling	**Confederate:** General Order 71-- foraging **Union:** No
Furthest distance traveled by end of phase ("as crow flies")	**Confederates:** About 21 miles **Union:** About 30 miles	**Confederates:** About 85 miles **Union:** About 45 miles
Nature of movements	**Confederates:** Interspersed with periods of rest **Union:** Continual movements north	**Confederates:** Interspersed with periods of rest **Union:** Interspersed with periods of rest
Miles army dispersed?	**Confederates:** 25 miles **Union:** 16 miles	**Confederates:** about 100 miles **Union:** 15 miles
Confederates: Movements impacted by Union army?	No	Yes
Confederates: Did Lee gamble?	Yes—divides army	Yes—divides army
Union: Army moving north?	Yes	Yes
Union: Cavalry seeks out enemy location?	Yes	Yes

Chapter 8: The Two Armies Approach the Battlefield (September 13-17, 1862 and June 22-July 2, 1863)

The Maryland Campaign of 1862 (September 13 – 17)

George McClellan rode into Frederick to a hero's welcome at 10:00 a.m. on September 13. One of his staff members recalled the "whole city was fluttering with national flags, while the sidewalks to the housetops, shone with happy human faces. It seemed as if the whole population had turned out, wild with joy." As the townspeople celebrated and the rest of McClellan's army marched on Frederick, eight of Pleasonton's cavalry regiments fanned out in search of Lee's army.[1]

Good fortune smiled on McClellan when he received a copy of Lee's Special Orders No. 191 found outside of Frederick on September 13. Wrapped around cigars, it was stumbled upon by Indiana troops and it soon found its way to McClellan. How the orders were lost has been debated for years. We know Stonewall Jackson had the orders transcribed, leaving out the first two portions, and sent it to D. H. Hill, who acknowledged receiving this copy. A second copy was sent directly to him from Lee's headquarters, and this copy was apparently the one found by Union soldiers.

McClellan finally had definitive answers to his questions about Lee's intentions. Upon receiving the communication, he purportedly threw up his arms and said "Now I know what to do!" There remained a number of questions, including whether the order was authentic or just a ruse? The order was dated September 9—four days prior to McClellan receiving it. Had Lee modified his plans in that time? The order also specified "commands," but McClellan had no idea what that meant—probably more than a division, but he wasn't sure. There were also some inconsistencies. For example, McClellan knew there were considerable numbers of enemy troops at Hagerstown, but the order did not mention the town as a destination for any of the units.

After verifying the authenticity of the order, McClellan carefully weighed his options: go after the enemy force in Hagerstown/ Boonsboro, but that would mean the sure loss of Harpers Ferry, or head straight for Harpers Ferry, but that would ignore a sizable enemy force operating in his rear. Either approach was unacceptable, so McClellan decided on a two-pronged operation. One column would march along National Road, through Turner's Gap at South Mountain and continue to Hagerstown to crush the Confederates there. The other column would head toward Jefferson and Burkittsville, cross South Mountain at Crampton's Gap, and move south in the Pleasant Valley, where it could pin McLaws' two divisions against the Potomac River and relieve the Harpers Ferry garrison. The two prongs were only five miles apart, so each could conceivably support the other.[2]

McClellan's reports suggested more Rebel troops at Boonsboro/Hagerstown than on the Maryland side facing Harpers Ferry, so he sent most of his army along National Road—the I, II, IX, XII Corps and Sykes' division—about 50,000 men—through South Mountain at Turner's Gap where they could take on Longstreet's men at Hagerstown and D. H. Hill's at Boonsboro. He next decided to send Maj. Gen. William Franklin's 12,000-man VI Corps south toward Harpers Ferry. Couch's 6,000-man division (IV Corps) was tasked with supporting him, but would probably not arrive until after September 14. Both units were to cross South Mountain at Crampton's Gap and drive south in the Pleasant Valley to relieve the Harpers Ferry garrison. If Franklin was successful, he could add Miles' garrison to his command and head north to help destroy the Confederates at Hagerstown.[3]

Historian Scott Hartwig complimented McClellan's plan for containing several important components, such as seizing the initiative, achieving mass by concentrating troops against Lee's weaker numbers, promoting flexibility and cooperation among his troops, unity of effort in splitting Lee's army and defeating it piecemeal, and for being simple and straightforward. It received lower grades in the area of logistics and surprise.

To get to Lee's army, McClellan's men were first required to cross Catoctin Mountain and South Mountain. He kicked off the movement on September 13 when Pleasonton's cavalry left Frederick and knocked Brig. Gen. Wade Hampton's cavalry brigade from Hagan's Gap in Catoctin Mountain. Hampton retreated west and the two sides tangled again near Middletown between Catoctin Mountain and South Mountain. Hampton was ordered to leave the area and head toward Crampton's Gap in South Mountain, leaving the road to Turner's Gap open. Meanwhile, Col. Thomas Munford's Confederate cavalry brigade rode to Crampton's Gap to aid in its defense.[4]

Gov. Curtin continued stewing in Harrisburg on September 13. Jackson was less of a threat, but he still wanted an officer to help organize his militia and Pennsylvanian John Reynolds fit the bill. He had not yet arrived and this caused Curtin to continue badgering McClellan, telegraphing him, "Services needed immediately." Halleck, who also received the transmittal, patiently explained: "Two orders have been sent to General Reynolds, but his movements in the field may have delayed their reaching him. He was expected to leave for Harrisburg last night." Reynolds arrived in Harrisburg before the day ended and probably conferred with Curtin. Before the day ended, Reynolds shot Halleck a telegram, requesting that his Pennsylvania Reserve Division be sent home to help in its defense. He was savvy enough to realize that "I have no hope that this request will meet with favor from the commanding general of the troops, yet I cannot but think that it would prove a judicious move in the end."5

Information reaching Lee on September 13 gave him pause. First, Stuart reported being pushed back toward South Mountain and then a few minutes later, D. H. Hill atop South Mountain reported thousands of enemy campfires visible in the Middletown Valley. He also learned from a southern sympathizer that McClellan possessed a copy of Special Orders No. 191, so Lee prepared to fight a holding action until his army could be reunited. His reasoning may have been based on his experience with McClellan on the Peninsula, but his adversary had learned some lessons and was considerably more dangerous than Lee imagined. Longstreet later wrote, "[t]he hallucination that McClellan was not capable of serious work seemed to pervade our army, even to this moment of dreadful threatening."6

September 14 was a pivotal day in the Maryland Campaign as several South Mountain passes blazed with gunfire as McClellan attempted to implement his plan by first bullying his way to the west side of the mountain. These battles will be discussed in Chapter 10. Lee and Longstreet, with his two divisions, left Hagerstown and moved quickly south to assist D. H. Hill's defense at South Mountain passes of Fox's Gap and Turner's Gap. Further south, some troops from Lafayette McLaws' division attempted to stop the Union VI Corps from crashing through Crampton's Gap into the Pleasant Valley and a straight shot to Harpers Ferry. The two army commanders had different emotions as September 14 came to a close.

Lee had rarely experienced such a stressful night as he did on September 14-15. The enemy was about to cross South Mountain, putting his army in grave danger. Lee was especially concerned about the fate of McLaws' and Anderson's divisions because Franklin's VI Corps had taken Crampton's Gap and nothing stopped him from entering the Pleasant Valley in McLaws' rear and pinning him against the Potomac River. There was little left to do but end the invasion, so he sent off messages to McLaws and Jackson to break off the attack on Harpers Ferry. Jackson was to march toward Shepherdstown to support the rest of the army's crossing at the ford there.

While Lee pondered his options that night, Longstreet and two division commanders appeared. They recommended a full retreat, but Lee did not play his hand. Another messenger arrived, this one from Stonewall Jackson. The communication read: "Through God's blessing, the advance, which commenced this evening [September 14], has been successful thus far, and I look to Him for complete success to-morrow." The message lifted Lee's spirits and provided hope the campaign might indeed be resumed, despite the setbacks on September 14. There were many factors that could go against Lee, such as an energetic approach by McClellan and/or a delay in Jackson taking Harpers Ferry, but he was a gambler and decided to make a stand. At first he selected Keedysville, but then deemed Sharpsburg to be a better spot for the rendezvous with McLaws, as the terrain was more conducive to a defensive action, if necessary. However, Lee had only enough men to cover the Lower Bridge over Antietam Creek, leaving other crossing points unprotected. The route McLaws might take to the battlefield may have helped Lee determine how to deploy his scant forces.[7]

The Confederates had held McClellan's troops at bay through September 14, and although ultimately defeated, they delayed their enemy's planned movements. The Union troops were content to hunker down and sleep at the end of the day, many without dinner as campfires were prohibited. The three Confederate divisions fighting at Fox's and Turner's Gaps made their way down the mountain toward Boonsboro after dark. The march was exceedingly difficult, particularly for those men in D. H. Hill's division who had fought all day, and Longstreet's men who had marched almost 16 miles and then were engaged in combat for several hours. Using back roads, farm lanes, and fields, the defeated Confederates made their way to Boonsboro, and then on to Keedysville, where the first of D. H. Hill's men arrived at 1:00 a.m. on September 15. The men were permitted to rest there before moving on to Sharpsburg. The remainder of the division arrived in Sharpsburg a few hours later. Some of the troops, particularly those of D. R. Jones' division were demoralized and jaded. They had marched hard from Hagerstown, only to be whipped at the South Mountain passes. Straggling was severe that night. One of Stuart's cavalry brigades, Brig. Gen. Fitz Lee's, was tasked with slowing the Union pursuit on the morning of September 15, but it was thrashed in a sharp encounter in the streets of Boonsboro and forced to beat a hasty retreat back to Lee's army.[8]

Lee expected McClellan to actively push his men after him, and the Union army commander did not disappoint. He ordered Gen. Sumner at 8:45 a.m. on September 15 to break camp at Bolivar and march the II and XII Corps up South Mountain, through Turner's Gap, toward Boonsboro. Richardson's division of the II Corps was already on the road. Joseph Hooker's I Corps, which had fought so effectively at Turner's Gap and Frosttown Plateau, was to draw rations and then fall in behind Sumner's column. The van of the column reached Keedysville at 3:00 p.m. that afternoon. Burnside's IX Corps at Fox's Gap was to be on the road early, but when George Sykes' division approached at about 12:30 p.m., the men were still in bivouac—about three hours after the time they were to move out. Sykes' corps commander, Fitz John Porter, sought and received permission to take the lead. Burnside would later explain that his men were exhausted from the previous day's fight and needed to await the arrival of rations. The delay angered McClellan and he demanded an "explanation of these failures on your part to comply with the orders given you…"[9]

To the south, after claiming Crampton's Gap, Franklin's VI Corps was to enter Pleasant Valley, sweep south toward Harpers Ferry and attack McLaws' two divisions, hopefully pinning them against the Potomac River. However, McLaws quickly brought up several brigades and spread them across the valley floor. Rather than pushing forward, Franklin chose to await Couch's division's arrival, thus squandering an opportunity to potentially crush the two Confederate divisions, although he barely outnumbered them. Back at Boonsboro, Richardson's division led the Union advance. Behind it, the roads were jammed with all manner of infantry, wagons, and artillery.

Map 9: The Road to Antietam (September 14, 1862)

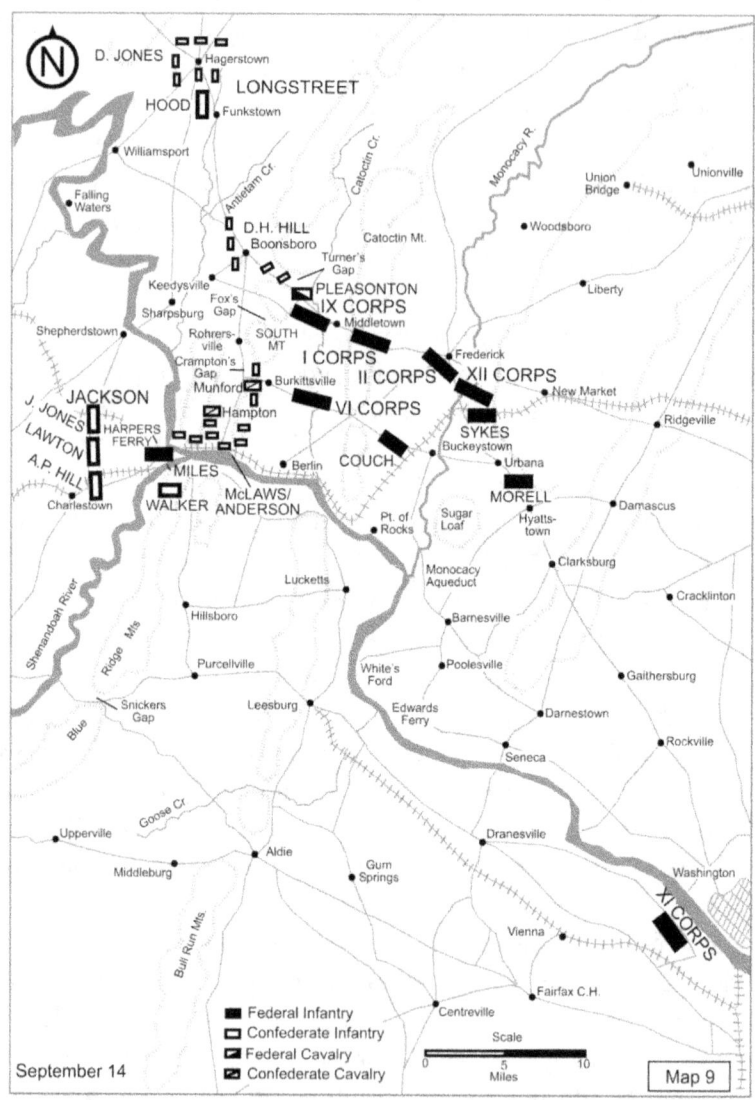

McClellan rode into Boonsboro at 1:00 p.m. on September 15 and planned his next moves. A signal station near Turner's Gap reported the Confederate forces in position behind Antietam Creek. McClellan believed the enemy was whipped and this was merely a rearguard—Lee's main army had to be crossing the Potomac River. Indeed, another signal station reported large numbers of enemy artillery crossing the Potomac River into Virginia.[10]

Earlier in the day, Lee was buoyed by a message from Stonewall Jackson: "Through God's blessing, Harper's Ferry and its garrison are to be surrendered." Equally important to Lee, Jackson wrote that the majority of his command "can move off this evening so soon as they get their rations." Lee received this dispatch about noon and decided he would hold at Sharpsburg, hoping reinforcements would arrive before McClellan attacked. The green fields of Pennsylvania awaited him.[11]

Jackson had bagged all of the Harper Ferry infantry and artillery forming its garrison, but not its cavalry. Lt. Col. Benjamin "Grimes" Davis helped command the garrison's cavalry component, numbering about 1,500 horsemen. Davis saw the handwriting on the wall and began lobbying Miles for permission to break out of the beleaguered town. Miles initially balked at the idea, but finally relented when Davis told him that he was leaving with or without his permission. "Although the enemy was believed to be in strong force on the road chosen and there were unknown dangers to be met in the darkness of night," explained a cavalryman, "it was an immense relief to be once more in motion with a chance for victory." Davis led his men across the Potomac River after dark on the night of September 14-15 and headed north. The column reached Sharpsburg about midnight. When he learned of Confederate troops at Keedysville and Hagerstown, Davis continued north toward Williamsport. While approaching the town, the troopers heard the low rumbling of wagons constituting James Longstreet's ordnance train. Davis' men fell on them, capturing anywhere from 40 to 96, depending on the source. Afterward, Davis' men quickly rode north into Pennsylvania, where they were finally able to rest.[12]

The troops' experiences during the final march to the battlefield varied. For those fighting at Turner's and Fox's Gaps, the distance to Keedysville was less than five miles. Lee's men guarding the gaps did it through the night of September 14-15, and rested on the future battlefield. McClellan's units spent that evening bivouacked around Fox's and Turner's Gap so they were more rested on the morning of September 15. Stonewall Jackson's trek was more difficult. Two of his three divisions left Harpers Ferry during the evening of September 15 and marched all night to reach Sharpsburg the following morning. McLaws' two divisions spent September 15 watching the VI Corps in the Pleasant Valley and did not begin their march to Sharpsburg until the night of September 16. They finally arrived on the battlefield on the morning of the battle after marching all night. Walker's division arrived on the battlefield on September 16. Two units did not begin their march until the morning of the battle: The Union VI Corps in Pleasant Valley, which reached the battlefield about noon and A. P. Hill's division, left behind at Harpers Ferry, did not arrive until mid-afternoon after its long 17-mile march to the battlefield.

As Gov. Curtin monitored the situation, his rhetoric shifted from protecting Pennsylvania to helping defeat Lee. He wrote to Lincoln on September 16, "We have no infantry or artillery sufficiently well organized to march into Maryland to support McClellan, but a force of ten or fifteen good regiments, with some artillery, thrown on the flank and rear of the enemy by to-morrow night might be of immense service." Even when the two armies engaged in deadly combat on September 17, Curtin sought supplies from Brig. Gen. James Ripley, Chief of Ordnance: "Send immediately two millions more & buck and ball, .69 caliber, and one million .58 caliber. They are needed, in addition to previous orders. Can you send us ten thousand stands of muskets, with accouterments?"[13]

The final phase of the march to the battlefield during the Maryland Campaign can be summarized as a period of great excitement for the commanders of both armies. For Lee, it was a period of grave anxiety. Stonewall Jackson was behind schedule in taking Harpers Ferry and the discovery of Lee's Special Order No. 191 gave McClellan new confidence as he forced his way across three South Mountain gaps on September 14. Lee seriously considered aborting the invasion that evening, but word from Stonewall Jackson on the morning of September 15 strengthened his resolve to continue the invasion. The period witnessed two seminal combat events:

Map 10: The Road to Antietam (September 15-16, 1862)

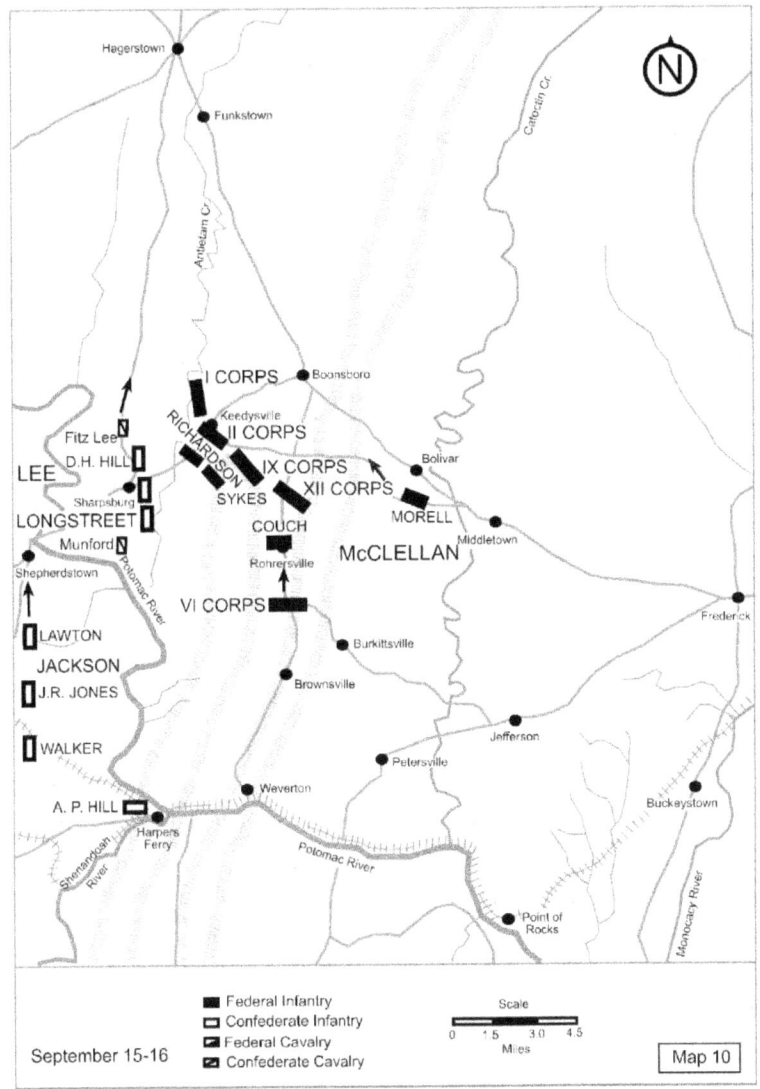

the fight for the South Mountain gaps on September 14 and the siege of Harpers Ferry that ended on September 15.

The Pennsylvania Campaign of 1863 (June 22-July 2, 1863)

The third and final phase of the march to Gettysburg opened on June 22, with the end of the battle for control of the Blue Ridge Mountain passes finally over. Pleasonton could never breach the passes, so he turned his attention to screening the army's movements and obtaining information on Lee's position and activities in other ways. The fight for the passes achieved little, except to freeze several of Lee's divisions in the Shenandoah Valley, thus delaying the invasion's progress. Stuart was already thinking of grander actions beyond holding the Blue Ridge Mountain gaps, especially since all of the Confederate infantry was now further north. He suggested a raid to Lee, who responded with a question: "Do you know where he [Hooker] is and what he is doing? I fear he will steal a march on us, and get across the Potomac before we are aware." Lee reluctantly agreed to Stuart's idea to strike north on a raid into enemy territory. However, Lee's permission came with the stipulation that Stuart "take position on General Ewell's right, place yourself in communication with him, guard his flank, keep him informed of the enemy's movements, and collect all the supplies you can for the use of the army." This raid will be discussed in greater detail in Chapter 10.

June 22 dawned with Ewell's headquarters at Hagerstown and two of his Second Corps divisions already in Maryland and a third poised to enter. Lee suggested routes through Emmitsburg, Chambersburg, and McConnellsburg. "Your progress and direction will, of course, depend upon the development of circumstances. If Harrisburg comes within your means, capture it," he told Ewell. During the day, Rodes' division, the furthest unit north, marched into Pennsylvania and camped at Greencastle. Early's division in the rear, crossed the Potomac River and marched through Sharpsburg and Boonsboro where it linked with Johnson's division. Hood's division (Longstreet's First Corps) was on the move toward Winchester, while the other two divisions prepared for long marches north. Hill's Third Corps, between Ewell and Longstreet, concentrated near Charlestown and Berryville.[14]

Hooker, who had been agitating for additional troops, must have been pleased when Halleck wrote that the portion of Milroy's VIII Corps east of

Cumberland, Maryland was being placed under his command. His army spent the day resting in their camps in Virginia, far south of Lee's army, as they had for the past several days.[15]

Department of the Susquehanna commander, Darius Couch, could write to Stanton on June 22 that short-term regiments were being deployed. He had two New York regiments, numbering about 800 men at Carlisle and a Pennsylvania regiment near Gettysburg to "harass the enemy, and, if possible, to hold the mountains there." The remnants of Milroy's division, about 2,800 men, were at Bedford, Pennsylvania, with an additional 1,000 militia, blocking "any advance in this direction [Harrisburg] from Chambersburg." Although his force was growing, Couch was pessimistic of his ability to do much beyond wave at Lee's veterans. "The New York troops look very well, but are without much confidence in themselves. My little artillery is all raw; my cavalry the same…I speak of the quality and condition of my troops, in order that you may not wonder why I do not boldly face them against the rebels in the Cumberland Valley." Couch sent Gen. Joseph Knipe's New York militia brigade to Chambersburg, to the immense relief of its citizenry. Couch also hoped to have access to New Jersey troops, but told Stanton, "[I]t will require your order authorizing them to report here."[16]

Lee sought to bulk up his army to deliver a knockout punch when he wrote to Jefferson Davis on June 23 about transferring troops to his army from the coastline "during the unhealthy months of the summer and autumn." These new additions, together with troops in North Carolina could be put to better use in Virginia, he thought. Imagine, he told Davis, if a large force under Gen. Beauregard could arrive at Culpeper Court House and drive toward Washington. It could relieve Richmond of any worry of an attack and at the same time drain troops that would otherwise be sent to stop Lee's invasion. He also pointed out that like the prior summer, a threatening move toward Washington could cause the Lincoln administration to scour troops from the south and rush them north to defend the capital. The plan had logistical shortcomings, but was an interesting concept.[17]

While Longstreet's First Corps rested in its camps on June 23, the rest of Lee's army moved deeper into Northern territory. Ewell's three divisions made good progress: Johnson's division reached Hagerstown in the morning and then marched another five miles north, almost to the Pennsylvania border, Jubal Early's bypassed Hagerstown and marched through Cavetown and Smithburg, Maryland, and finally entered Pennsylvania at Waynesboro, and Rodes' division, already in Pennsylvania, rested in its camps at Greencastle. Two of A. P. Hill's divisions, Anderson's and Heth's, reached Charlestown as Pender's division continued bringing up the army's rear—ending its march just beyond Berryville.

While more and more of Lee's units were in, or poised to enter, Pennsylvania, Hooker's men remained in camp on June 23, well to the south, in Virginia. The Union army commander remained glued in place from Manassas north to Leesburg to shield the capital as Hooker did not know whether Lee's destination was Washington, Baltimore, or Pennsylvania.[18]

June 24 was another pivotal day for the Confederates who were making good progress in moving north. Ewell's Second Corps was in the lead and all of its divisions were in Pennsylvania by the end of the day: Johnson's division, which began the day behind the others just north of Hagerstown, crossed the Pennsylvania line and marched to Greencastle and then toward Chambersburg, throwing out a brigade to the west toward Mercersburg and McConnellsburg to collect supplies. Early's division left Waynesboro, Pennsylvania and headed north to Greenwood, just east of Chambersburg, and Rodes' division found its way to Chambersburg and camped three miles north of it. Brig. Gen. Albert Jenkins' mounted brigade screened the Second Corps as it moved north. Ewell rode into Chambersburg and met its town's leaders, demanding supplies: 5,000 suits of clothing, 100 saddles and bridles, 10,000 pounds of leather, 5,000 bushels of grain, 50,000 pounds of bread, 500 barrels of flour and other items. The request astonished the politicians who told Ewell they could not possibly supply that amount of goods in the short time allocated, so they collected what they could. Ewell sent Jenkins' brigade on another raid, this time to Carlisle by way of Shippensburg. A. P. Hill's Third Corps followed Ewell's path. Farther south, Anderson's division crossed the Potomac River and marched to Sharpsburg, Maryland, and Pender's division caught up to Heth's at Shepherdstown, where they both bivouacked for the night. Longstreet's First Corps, bringing up the rear, was still in Virginia.

Hooker was now aware of the approximate location of Lee's still far-flung troops and made preparations to cross the Potomac River. Only the XI

Map 11: The Road to Gettysburg (June 23-24, 1863)

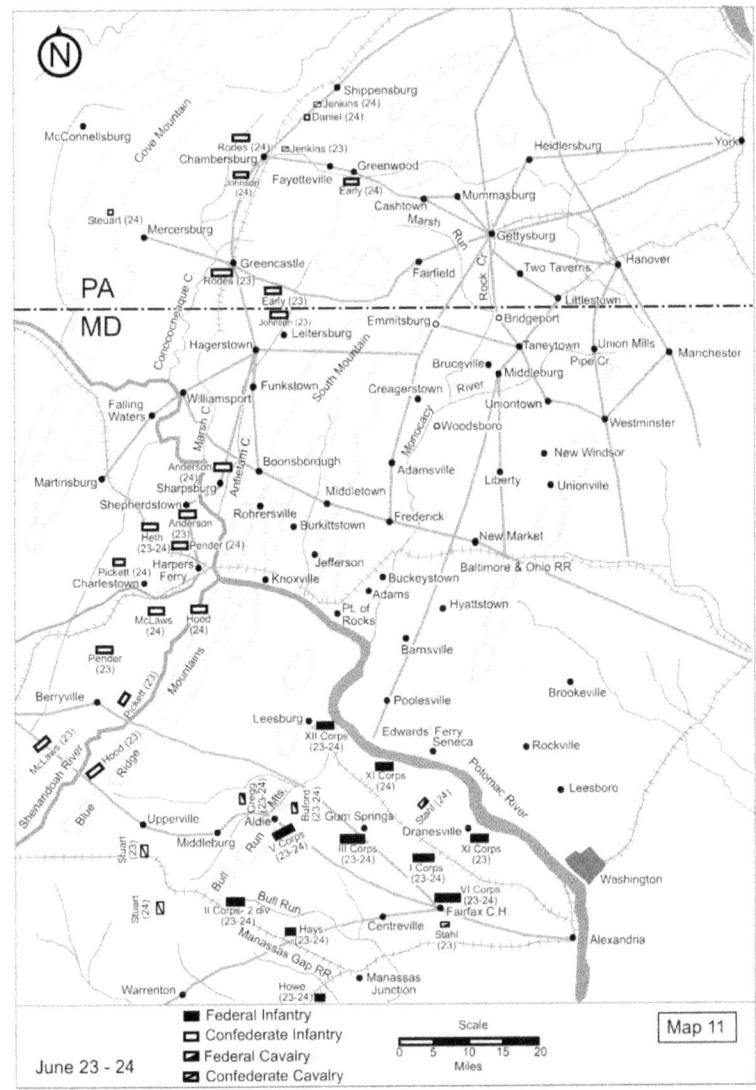

Corps was in motion on June 24, marching from Goose Creek to Edward's Ferry on the Potomac River. Hooker apparently underestimated the progress of Ewell's column, concluding "[I]t is over the river, and now is up the country, I suppose for the purposes of plunder." His next statement was a surprise: "The yeomanry of that district should be able to check any extended advance of that column, and protect themselves from their aggression." How these civilians would be able to halt the Confederate advance is anyone's guess. If Hooker meant Couch's troops, he was also mistaken as they were few in number, raw, undisciplined, and no match for Lee's veterans. In preparation for his move into Maryland, Hooker ordered his engineers to build a second pontoon bridge across the Potomac River. Halleck was not so sure that Washington was not the target for at least a raid, so he armed clerks and sent them to guard warehouses.[19]

The worst possible news reached President Jefferson Davis on June 25: 17 Union gunboats were steaming up the York River toward White House, Virginia, about 25 miles from Richmond. They had purportedly disembarked 6,000 infantry. Thousands more were marching from Fortress Monroe, under command of Maj. Gen. John Dix, at the southernmost tip of the peninsula. It turned out to be a groundless rumor, but made for some stressful hours that day and highlighted the risk of having the Army of Northern Virginia so far from the Confederate capital.

June 25 saw Longstreet's First Corps, now forming Lee's rearguard, heading toward the Potomac River. Hood's and McLaws' divisions bypassed Martinsburg and camped near the Potomac River; Pickett's division was further downstream, and crossed the Potomac near Falling Waters. Hill's Third Corps was also on the move into Maryland: Heth's and Pender's divisions crossed the Potomac River at Blackford's Ford near Shepherdstown and continued past Sharpsburg to within eight miles of Hagerstown. Anderson's division was up ahead, having passed through Hagerstown and camped within a stone's throw of the Pennsylvania line. Ewell's Second Corps, already in Pennsylvania, rested. Johnson's and Rodes' divisions were near Chambersburg and Early's division was at Greenwood (east of Chambersburg). Jubal Early rode over to meet with Ewell at Chambersburg and received orders to march on York, Pennsylvania, destroy portions of the

Northern Central Railroad and the Wrightsville/Columbia Bridge over the Susquehanna River, before rejoining the corps at Carlisle.

Hooker realized he was well behind Lee's army and needed to make progress if he was to stop his adversary from capturing Harrisburg and possibly Philadelphia. He put five of his corps on the road on June 25: I, II, III, VI and XI Corps; the remainder remained in camp, preparing for the march. The XI Corps was up early, around 3:00 a.m. and the men quickly packed their gear and formed into line. Already near Edward's Ferry, they crossed the pontoon bridge over the Potomac River—the first Union troops to step foot on Maryland soil during the Pennsylvania Campaign. The first Confederate division to cross, Rodes', did so on June 15 or ten days earlier. A private wrote, "[w]e have left the deserted fields of Virginia and come to the smiling, happy, thrifty land, to Maryland." The column marched 24 grueling miles that day, through Poolesville and then continued north. The III Corps reached Edward's Ferry at about 11:00 a.m. and after a short break, followed the XI Corps across the Potomac River. Once across, the men marched north along the Chesapeake and Ohio Canal to the Monocacy Aqueduct, where they halted after a 25-mile march. The I Corps approached the river next, arriving at 2:00 p.m., but their journey was delayed by a wagon train rumbling across the bridge. Their 15-mile march brought the men to Barnesville, Maryland, where they bivouacked.

The other two Union corps on the march on June 25 were further inland and it would take longer to cross the Potomac. The II Corps, at Thoroughfare Gap, marched 23-miles to Gum Springs, still about 15 miles from Edward's Ferry. The VI Corps had a relatively short march from Bristoe Station to Centreville—about 15 miles—but it did not begin until 7:00 p.m. so the men marched through the night. The Union army's journey toward and into Maryland was also hampered by heavy rains which turned the roads into quagmires in many places.[20]

Stuart began his fateful raid on June 25. Lee gave him two options: move north, where he could stay in contact with Ewell's divisions, or move south to the Orange and Alexandria Railroad and then strike north, crossing the Potomac River near Edward's Ferry. He chose the latter route, which put him further away from Lee's army. Stuart was on a tight timetable, and he almost immediately lost valuable time when a portion of the Union army inconveniently cut off his intended route, forcing a time-consuming detour. He made other miscalculations. For example, Lee wanted him to leave some of his cavalry behind, so he selected his two worst brigades (Brig. Gen. William "Grumble" Jones' and Brig. Gen. Beverly Robertson's) and rode north with the cream of his cavalry (Brig. Gen. Wade Hampton's brigade, Brig. Gen. Fitz Lee's brigade, Col. John Chambliss' brigade). This would have profound implications in the future. Perhaps worst of all, Stuart received reports of the entire Union army in motion north to the Potomac River which he conveyed to Lee, but the courier never reached him, so Lee remained unaware of this critical intelligence.

The Confederate infantry, well north of any of Hooker's troops, were not resting on June 26. Ewell's Second Corps' movement was probably the most significant as it struck deep into Pennsylvania. Rodes' and Johnson's divisions left Chambersburg and headed for Carlisle. The first day out was a fairly easy one, as the column only marched eleven miles, halting just beyond Shippensburg. After destroying Thaddeus Stevens' Caledonia Iron Works near Greenwood, Pennsylvania, Early's division headed toward Gettysburg, where it encountered the 26th Pennsylvania Emergency Infantry Regiment along Chambersburg Pike. The militia unit was primarily composed of civilians recruited from central Pennsylvania and sent to Harrisburg for a week of training before being turned loose to face Lee's veterans. It was not a pretty sight when the regiment encountered Early's veterans. Militiaman Henry Shriver noted, "[s]uch confusion I never saw—everyone gave orders and no one obeyed—we were all green and knew nothing about regular forming." The Pennsylvanians quickly scattered and Early continued his march to Gettysburg, where his men spent the rest of the day collecting supplies from the stunned townspeople. The latter had heard rumors about an invasion for many months, learned of Jenkins' mounted infantry's incursion into Chambersburg on June 15, and now the threat had materialized.

Pickett's division led Longstreet's First Corps north. On the road before 6:00 a.m., the men marched through Hagerstown where many townspeople gave them a warm welcome, and then crossed into Pennsylvania, camping about a mile from Greencastle. The corps' remaining two divisions prepared to cross the Potomac River near Williamsport. The going was slow as the rain created muddy roads. One of Hood's men stated, "[W]e had breakfasted in Virginia, dined and wined in Maryland, and taken supper in Pennsylvania." Because they had been issued a whisky ration, another soldier wrote, "[W]e were in four states that day, the fourth being in a state of intoxication." One of A. P. Hill's Third Corps divisions also crossed into Pennsylvania in front of the First Corps and halted its march north of Greencastle. His remaining two divisions brought up the army's rear, halting for the night just south of Hagerstown.[21]

Unlike the Confederates who used two crossing points across the Potomac River, Hooker was content to centralize his crossing at Edward's Ferry using two pontoon bridges. He carefully mapped each corps' route once in Maryland and launched them on June 26. The day also saw activity from the militia units rushed into service, including the ill-fated 26th Pennsylvania Emergency Infantry Regiment at Gettysburg and two New York militia regiments under Brig. Gen. Joseph Knipe, who spent much of the day building barricades at Carlisle.

This was a day of easy marching for most of the Union soldiers, particularly those who had made over 20-mile treks the day before. The three Union corps who had crossed the Potomac River on June 25 continued deeper into Maryland. The XI Corps, who had crossed the river first, made its way to Middletown on the east side of the South Mountains after marching only seven miles. The III Corps made a six-mile hike to Point of Rocks. The I Corps, which had only marched about 15 miles the day before, clocked 18 miles more on the June 26, halting for the night at Jefferson, only nine miles east of Frederick. Three additional corps crossed the Potomac River that day: the V Corps crossed the Potomac River at 6:00 p.m. and continued another four miles to Poolesville, the XII Corps, which did not begin its march until 4:00 p.m., marched 15 miles to the Monocacy Aqueduct, and the II Corps, crossed the river after 10:00 p.m. and continued inland for another couple of miles. Only the VI Corps—the army's rearguard—remained in Virginia. It halted for the night at Dranesville, still 20 miles from the pontoon bridges.[22]

By the end of June 26, the Union army was indeed moving north, but remained dispersed—about 45 miles separated the most far-flung units. Lee's

Map 12: The Road to Gettysburg (June 26, 1863)

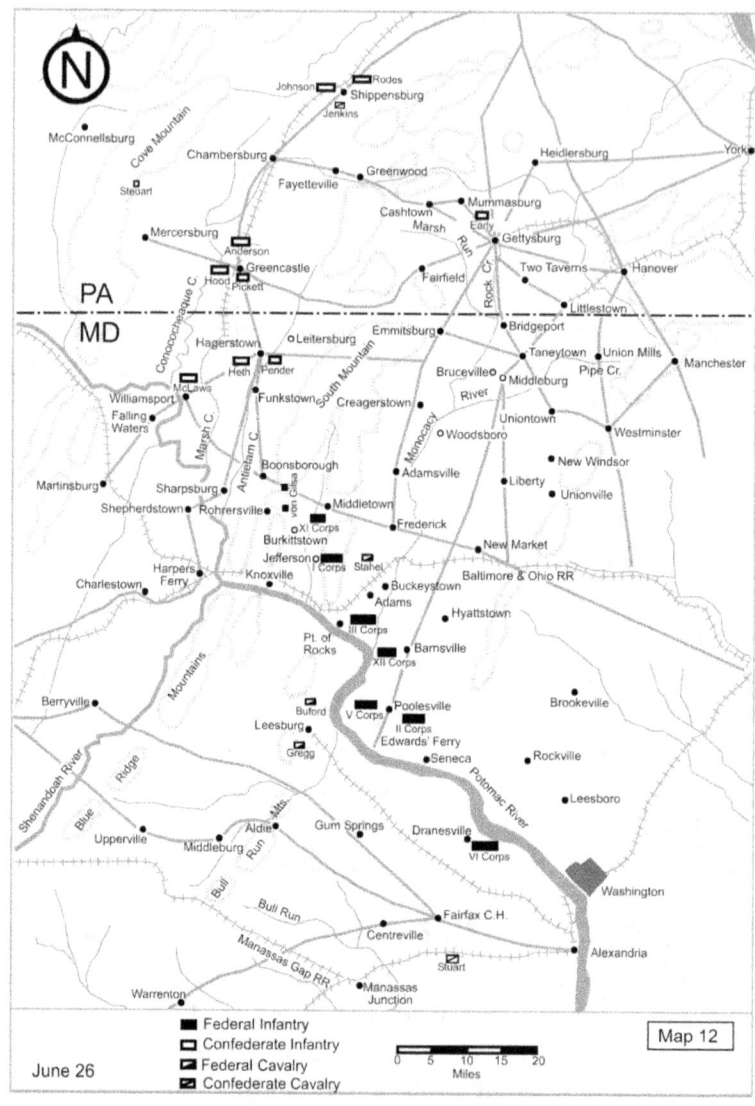

army was also dispersed as its men were spread from Hagerstown to Shippensburg, over 35 miles. Most interestingly, the distance between Hooker's northernmost unit (XI Corps) and Lee's most southern (Pender's and Heth's divisions) was only 21 miles.

Back in Washington, employees of the Quartermaster and Commissary Departments were being armed and drilled to defend the capital. With expected short-term enlistments lagging, Pennsylvania governor Andrew Curtin again took up his pen and crafted yet another proclamation to the citizens of his state. He opened with, "The enemy is advancing in force into Pennsylvania. He has a strong column within 33 miles of Harrisburg, and other columns are moving by Fulton and Adams Counties, and it can no longer be doubted that a formidable invasion of our State is in actual progress. The calls already made for volunteer militia in the exigency have not been met as fully as the crisis requires," so he issued another plea: "You owe to your country your prompt and zealous services and efforts. The time has now come when we must all stand or fall together in defense of our State-and in support of our Government." He called for 60,000 men to come forward to defend the mother state. "I will not insult you by inflammatory appeals" and then went on to state "A people who want the heart to defend their soil, their families, and their firesides, are not worthy to be accounted men."[23]

Lee continued concentrating most of his army around Chambersburg on June 27, while throwing Ewell's Second Corps on a raid north. Rodes' and Johnson's divisions reached Carlisle—the furthest north any of Lee's infantry would travel; Early's division left Gettysburg and camped at Big Mount (York County) to the north. Gordon's brigade was spun off and sent to the Susquehanna River, camping near Farmers (York County). The remainder of Lee's army left Maryland and was in Pennsylvania by the end of the day.

While two-thirds of his army was in or near Chambersburg, Pennsylvania on June 27, Lee decided to augment his General Orders No. 71 with General Orders No. 73, which expressed his satisfaction with how well his prior directives were being obeyed. "No troops could have displayed greater fortitude or better performed the arduous marches of the past ten days." He did note some instances of "forgetfulness, on the part of some." He got to his philosophy in the middle of the order:

> The commanding general considers that no greater disgrace could befall the army, and through it our whole people, than the perpetration of the barbarous outrages upon the unarmed and defenseless and the wanton destruction of private property, that have marked the course of the enemy in our own country. Such proceedings not only degrade the perpetrators and all connected with them, but are subversive of the discipline and efficiency of the army, and destructive of the ends of our present movement. It must be remembered that we make war only upon armed men, and that we cannot take vengeance for the wrongs our people have suffered without lowering ourselves in the eyes of all whose abhorrence has been excited by the atrocities of our enemies . . .

Although the North's philosophy of "total war" was not implemented as yet, most of the men could look to the destruction of the town of Fredericksburg in mid-December, 1862 as an example of Northern atrocities. Charles Bachelor of the 2nd Louisiana Infantry probably best summed up the men's reaction to these orders: "It makes my blood boil to hear the many depredations committed by Yankees—and just to think we invaded their country passing into Pennsylvania almost to Harrisburg…without doing them the least harm and whenever it was necessary for us to take anything they were paid for its true value."

Stuart finally crossed the Potomac River at little known Rowser's Ford. Although undefended, it was not a good choice as it was deep with swift currents, tiring men and horses. Although behind schedule, Stuart was forced to rest his command before continuing north. As they did so, they continued taking time out from their travels to destroy railroad stock and tracks.

The entire Union army was finally across the Potomac River on June 27 and moving rapidly north. The VI Corps marched to Edward's Ferry and crossed the river at about 4:30 p.m., camping between it and Poolesville. The units comprising the Left Wing (I, III, and XI) had fairly easy marches to areas just east of South Mountain, screened by Brig. Gen. John Buford's cavalry division. The II and V Corps were just to the east, in Frederick, and south at Buckeystown. Brig. Gen. David Gregg's cavalry division arrived in Frederick, where it joined Brig. Gen. Judson Kilpatrick's new cavalry division. The division had been Julius Stahel's but he was removed in an anti-immigrant purge and the unit was added to the rolls of the Army of the Potomac. Far to the south, XII Corps moved north from the Monocacy Aqueduct as the VI Corps crossed the river—the last unit to do so.

Hooker continued worrying about the inadequacy of his army against Lee's, which he believed dwarfed his in size. Since his telegrams were not bringing additional reinforcements, Hooker sent his Chief of Staff, Maj. Gen. Daniel Butterfield, to Washington on June 25-26. Butterfield met first with Halleck who rejected his request for troops from the Washington garrison. Unhappy with this response, Butterfield next visited Lincoln who backed his general-in-chief. Butterfield returned to the army with only one inexperienced brigade from Maj. Gen. Robert Schenck's VIII Corps (Brig. Gen. Henry Lockwood's, which was assigned to the XII Corps). Hooker would also receive the services of two brigades of the Pennsylvania Reserve Division, and two brigades from Brig. Gen. John Abercrombie's division.

Halleck could not have been happy when Hooker informed him on June 27 that his 105,000 men were not up to the task of defending Pennsylvania. Hooker ventured to Harpers Ferry that day and wrote to Halleck later that afternoon: "I find 10,000 men here, in condition to take the field. Here they are of no earthly account." He added "Now they are but bait for the rebels, should they return."

Hooker sent a seminal telegram to Halleck five minutes later: "My original instructions require me to cover Harper's Ferry and Washington. I have now imposed upon me, in addition, an enemy in my front of more than my number. I beg to be understood, respectfully, but firmly, that I am unable to comply with this condition with the means at my disposal, and earnestly request that I may at once be relieved from the position I occupy." Whether this was a bluff to get the garrison or an honest representation of his inability to perform his duties without reinforcements, is unknown. However, it played into Lincoln's hands, as Hooker could not be removed because of his strong political connections with the Radical Republicans, but he could now merely honor Hooker's wishes to be removed.[24]

In a campaign filled with "pivotal days," June 28 may have been the most important for both sides. George Meade, commander of the Union V Corps, was asleep in his tent during the early morning hours when Col. James Hardie of Halleck's staff arrived with important news. A groggy Meade initially thought he was being removed from command of his corps. Meade probably read the first line several times before it sunk in: "You will receive with this the order of the President placing you in command of the Army of the Potomac. Considering the circumstances, no one ever received a more important command; and I cannot doubt that you will fully justify the confidence which the Government has reposed in you." Because he was to protect both Baltimore and Washington, "Harper's Ferry and its garrison are under your direct orders." What Hooker could not get, was now handed to Meade. He purportedly quipped, "Well, I've been tried and condemned without a hearing, and I suppose I shall have to go to execution." Lincoln enthusiastically endorsed Meade, saying "I tell you I think a great deal of that fine fellow Meade . . . [he] will fight well on his own dunghill."

Meade and Hardie ventured over to Hooker's tent, where Hardie handed him a communication accepting his resignation. The new and now former army commanders huddled over a map showing the location of the various army corps. Hardie remained in camp for awhile to gauge the men's reaction to the change in command and then headed back to Washington. Meade sat down at 7:00 a.m. and drafted a message to Halleck, accepting the appointment and informing him of his plans to move toward the Susquehanna River. He also promised to keep Washington and Baltimore well covered. Hooker was gracious about his removal and issued General Orders Number 66 informing the army of the command change. Meade immediately followed with his own General Orders—Number 67, providing a pep talk to an army on the move. Sorting through various intelligence reports, Meade posited that Lee was spread out over 50 miles with an army that may have numbered as few as 60,000 or more than 100,000. He carefully charted out the best routes for his army to counter Lee.[25]

The condition of the army posed a grave concern. As much as a quarter of the army was deficient in shoes, uniforms, and supplies. One of Meade's first meetings was with Brig. Gen. Rufus Ingalls, the army's quartermaster-general to press for a stronger flow of needed materials.

By the end of June 28, the entire Army of the Potomac had congregated around Frederick, poised to strike north to head off Lee's army. Only the VI Corps was some distance away, at Hyattstown, Maryland, about ten miles south. Meade later testified that he planned to move the army rapidly from

Frederick toward Harrisburg, "extending the wings of the army on both sides of the line as far as safety would permit." The movement would continue until it encountered the enemy. Meade believed such a move would force Lee to abandon the area around the Susquehanna River and the Union army commander would "give battle wherever and as soon as he could possibly find the enemy."

The day was a quiet one for most of Lee's men, in and around the Chambersburg area, far to the Union's north (55 miles), but Ewell's Second Corps was on the road. Two of his divisions, Rodes' and Johnson's, were at Carlisle, scooping up supplies and destroying government property. Early's division captured York and immediately requisitioned a large number of items. Brig. Gen. John Gordon's brigade headed for the Susquehanna River to secure the bridge between Columbia and Wrightsville. With the bridge in Confederate hands it was a straight shot to Harrisburg, but the Union militia got there first and fired the bridge, denying Early's access to the opposite side of the broad river. Lee drafted seminal orders for his senior officers to be carried out on June 29: Ewell was to march on, and capture Harrisburg, supported by a rapidly marching Longstreet while Hill was to cross the Susquehanna River downstream, and with Early's division, seize the railroad between Harrisburg and Philadelphia. This was predicated on the Union army being far to the south, but Lee did not know exactly where they were.

Stuart's column reached Rockville and spied a long enemy wagon train pulled by strong, healthy mules. The men swooped in and captured about 125 of the wagons filled with supplies, but they soon became an albatross preventing Stuart from making the haste he needed to rejoin Lee's army.

June 28 ended badly for Lee. A spy employed by Lt. Gen. James Longstreet, Harrison, brought troubling news at 10:00 p.m.: Meade was now in command of the Army of the Potomac and it was moving rapidly north to face Lee's army. After interviewing Harrison to ascertain his veracity, Lee sat down to consider his plight. His army was spread over a 65-mile arc from Chambersburg to Carlisle to York and he realized he must immediately pull Ewell's Corps back to the fold. He sent a message to him on the morning of June 29, explaining the changing dynamics of the campaign and the need to quickly move south to join the remainder of the army. Ewell was to "keep on the east side of the mountains. When you come to Heidlersburg, you can either move directly on Gettysburg or turn down to Cashtown." Stuart was unable to provide any information on the Union army's movements because he was frantically searching for Lee's army. The large wagon train he captured was retarding his progress in recombining with the Confederate army. Lee admitted in his report, the "march toward Gettysburg was conducted more slowly than it would have been had the movements of the Federal Army been known."[26]

A day more and Ewell may well have captured Harrisburg. Jenkins' mounted infantry brigade was already in Mechanicsburg on June 29, a mere eight miles from the state capital and was heading in that direction when ordered to pull back. He received the order when skirmishing with New York and Pennsylvania militia units a mere four miles from Harrisburg. Johnson's division left Carlisle at 3:00 p.m., heading for Chambersburg, but a messenger arrived later with orders to concentrate at Gettysburg or Cashtown. It was too late for Johnson to take a direct route, so he turned toward Greenwood, just east of Chambersburg and would arrive at the battlefield via Chambersburg Pike, unlike the remainder of the corps, which arrived from the north. Rodes' division at Carlisle and Early's at York did not begin their march until June 30. The First and most of the Third Corps remained in camp, but Heth's division was on the road by 4:30 a.m. marching toward Cashtown.

Stuart was unable to provide any intelligence to Lee because he was still looking for him. He pushed on to Westminster, Maryland, where he was attacked by a couple of companies of the 1st Delaware Cavalry. Although the latter lost two-thirds of its men, it delayed Stuart's ride north. Stuart finally camped at Union Mills, only five miles from the Mason-Dixon Line.

Meade had high expectations about the distance his seven corps could travel on June 29 and most did not disappoint. The troops moved north in two bands in the pouring rain: one moving due north; the other northeast from Frederick and then north. The two wings were then to move parallel to each other toward Gettysburg. The ten roads leading into and out of Gettysburg heightened the probability of the armies meeting there. On the left, the I Corps was in the lead, camping at Emmitsburg, Maryland, by the end of June 29. It was joined by the XI Corps. Both units had marched 30 grueling miles that day. The XII Corps camped a few miles south in

Bruceville after its 20-mile march. The units marching on the right were led by the III Corps, which reached Taneytown, Maryland, a mere four miles from the Pennsylvania state line. The II Corps marching behind them, in Bruceville after its 20-mile march. The units marching on the right were led by the III Corps, which reached Taneytown, Maryland, a mere four miles from the Pennsylvania state line. The II Corps marching behind them, camped a mile beyond Uniontown, Maryland, after a grueling 35-mile march. The VI Corps made a 28-mile march to near New Windsor, almost ten miles south of Taneytown. The V Corps, which began its march outside Frederick and had to march three miles to reach it, and then marched to Liberty. It was the furthest unit from Gettysburg--over 30 miles from the Pennsylvania border. Although the army was making good progress, Meade fretted that the army stretched 30 miles, placing it in a vulnerable position.

Pleasonton's cavalry was now actively screening the army as it moved north and sought out Lee's army. Buford's division formed the west column, protecting the army's left flank, marching along the base of South Mountain. It passed through Middletown, Monterey Pass, Fairfield, and then Emmitsburg. Gregg's division rode north on the far right of the army, passing through New Windsor, and Manchester, and Kilpatrick was in the middle, riding through Taneytown and Littlestown.

Now in command of the Harpers Ferry garrison, on the afternoon of June 29, Meade ordered its commander, Maj. Gen. William French, to put no more than 3,000 men to work collecting supplies and transporting them to Washington, and to march the rest to join his army.

Panic again visited the North. Gen. Couch worried that his 15,000-man militia would be no match for the Confederate army. Most of these men, about 11,500, were concentrated near Harrisburg. New York had 12 regiments there, comprising 8,000 of the men guarding the capital. By the end of the invasion, 36,730 Pennsylvanians would answer the call to protect their homeland.

Former Sec. of War Simon Cameron raised the concern of what would happen if Lee crossed the Susquehanna River within the next 48 hours, which seemed a distinct possibility. "If Lee gets his army across the Susquehanna, and puts our armies on the defensive of that line, you will readily comprehend the disastrous results that must follow to the country,"

Map 13: The Road to Gettysburg (June 29, 1863)

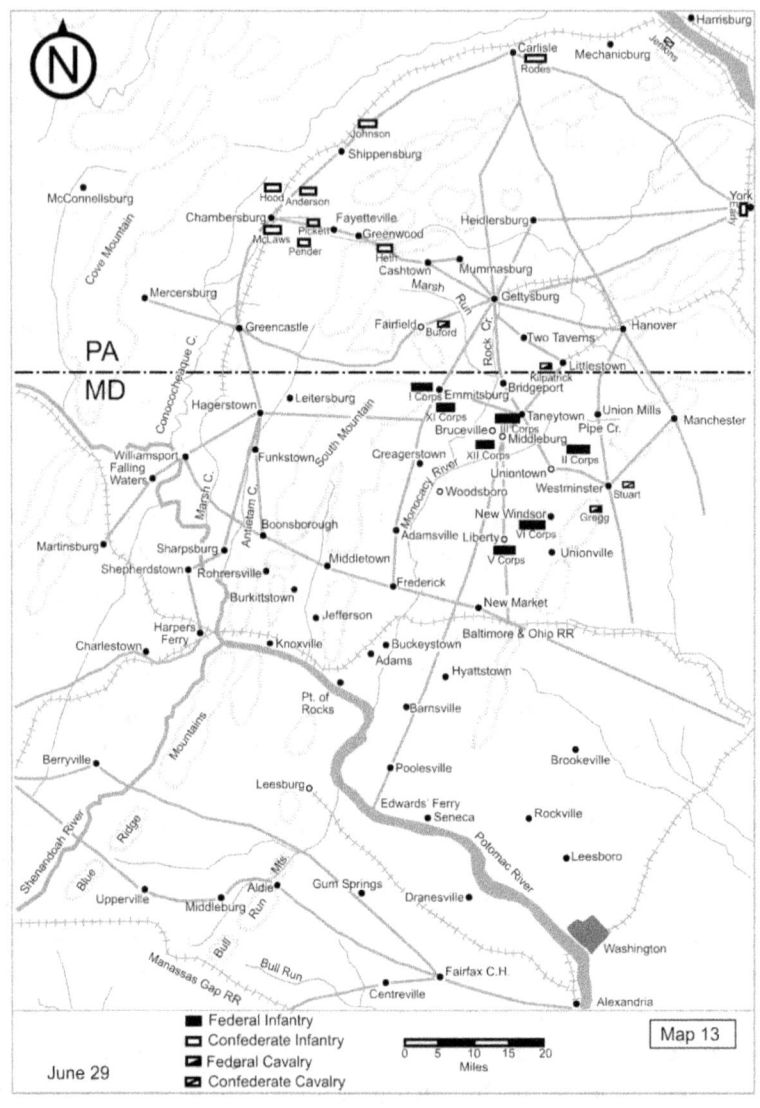

he wrote to Lincoln. In Pittsburgh, 14,000 citizens were manning the trenches. Rumblings began for McClellan to be returned to grace, either replacing Halleck or again commanding the Army of the Potomac.[27]

The Confederate government could finally stop worrying about John Dix's excursion up the Virginia Peninsula toward Richmond. Dix had convened a council of war and all decided to abort the movement.

June 30 found the two armies on a collision course at Gettysburg. Hood's and McLaws' divisions were on the road leading to that small town in the morning, marching about 11 miles before going into camp. Pickett's division was sent south to destroy portions of the Cumberland Valley Railroad. Only James Pettigrew's brigade (Heth's division) of the Third Corps was on the road, marching to Gettysburg, while the rest of the division was camped near Cashtown. Pettigrew's Tar Heels saw the vanguard of John Buford's cavalry division entering the town and decided to retrace its steps back to the division. The Confederate Second Corps was also in motion early, about 5:00 a.m., for the long march toward Gettysburg. These were 20-plus mile marches, for their commanders knew these troops were urgently needed.

Meade's entire army was moving north on June 30. Reynolds' left wing was making good progress. The I and XI Corps were north of Emmitsburg—a relatively short march to Gettysburg. Historian Kent Brown believed it was no coincidence that John Reynolds' I Corps, probably the most dependable leader and unit, led the advance and would probably begin the fight. The III Corps started its march in the afternoon and reached Emmitsburg by the end of the day. To the east, the XII Corps crossed into Pennsylvania and camped between Littlestown and Hanover. The II Corps was given a well-deserved rest at Uniontown after its strenuous march the previous day. This was not the case of for two other Union corps, who had made long marches on June 29, but were still far to the south: the VI Corps trekked another 20 miles to Manchester, Maryland, while the V Corps marched 25 miles, finally halting at Union Mills, Maryland, a mere three miles from Pennsylvania. Meade believed the enlisted men needed another pep talk and ordered his officers to "address their troops, explaining to them briefly the immense issues involved in the struggle." Furthermore, the men need to be reminded of the enemy's presence "on our soil" and that "the country now looks anxiously to this army to deliver it from the presence of the foe," adding "Homes, firesides, and domestic alters are involved."[28]

Meanwhile, Stuart continued his desperate search for Lee's army. He rode to Hanover, Pennsylvania on June 30 and encountered Kilpatrick's division's rearguard as he entered the town. Stuart could not resist attacking the isolated Yanks, but Kilpatrick turned his men around and a fight ensued in the streets and surrounding fields. It was essentially a standoff, but Stuart wasted precious hours he could have used to find some trace of Lee's army. He pulled his men out of Hanover after dark and continued north, first through York County to Dillsburg, where he learned of Confederate infantry in Carlisle, so he headed there, not realizing they had already vacated the town and were moving south toward Gettysburg.

July 1 brought on the initial fighting at Gettysburg. Four of Lee's nine divisions reached the battlefield and fought on the first day: Heth's and Pender's divisions (Third Corps), arriving from the west, and Early's and Rodes' divisions (Second Corps), arriving from the north. Most of the other Confederate troops were close to the battlefield by the end of the day, including Johnson's and Anderson's divisions, which arrived late in the afternoon/early evening, when the action was all but over. McLaws' and Hood's divisions (First Corps) marched behind them. They were not put in motion until 4:00 p.m. because the road was clogged with the two infantry divisions, plus Ewell's wagon train. Longstreet's men were forced to march through the night, not halting until midnight when two miles from the battlefield. Only Pickett's division was far from the battlefield, still near Chambersburg.

So much rode on Meade's shoulders. He could not afford to sustain a loss on Northern soil, yet he was inexperienced in army command. The best approach was caution. Not certain Gettysburg was the best defensive position for his army, he unveiled the "Pipe Creek Circular" on July 1. The directive began by noting how the army had prevented Lee from attacking Harrisburg and Philadelphia. It went on to read; if Lee should attack the Army of the Potomac it was to fall back into Maryland with its left flank resting near Middleburg and its right at Manchester, along Pipe Creek. The circular provided specific instructions on the position of each corps, should implementation prove desirable. The collision at Gettysburg put the plan on hold, but Meade kept it in his back pocket, just in case the events turned against him. Detractors would use the document against Meade to claim his timidity in facing Lee, but artilleryman Henry Hunt had a different perspective. He believed the position provided "perfect liberty of action in all directions," as good roads emanated from the defensive position, allowing Meade to advance or retreat, as conditions warranted. The position, according to Hunt would force Lee to either "attack Mead in the chosen position, or to retreat without a battle. The latter, neither the temper of [Lee's] army nor that of his government would probably permit."

Only two Union corps saw action on July 1: the I and XI Corps. Several others arrived after the action ended. The III Corps was near Emmitsburg at daybreak and began its march to the battlefield only after noon. David Birney's division arrived at about 5:30 p.m. but Andrew Humphreys would not approach for another seven hours as it was sent by way of Black Horse Tavern, and then backtracked when it almost ran into enemy troops. Finally, the XII Corps arrived behind the Union battle line at Rock Creek on Baltimore Pike at about 4:00 p.m. after its eight-mile march from the Two Taverns area. The remaining three corps had longer treks. The II Corps at Uniontown, Maryland, about 23 miles from Gettysburg, broke camp before 8:00 a.m. and endured a forced march through the day, finally halting three miles from the battlefield at 9:00 p.m. The leading elements camped behind Little Round Top on Taneytown Road. The other two corps were even farther away. The V Corps left Union Mills in the morning and reached Hanover, Pennsylvania, at 3:00 p.m. after a ten-mile march. The march continued to Bonneauville, where the men were given a rest at midnight. They were up again and on the road at 3:00 a.m. on July 2. The exhausted men of the VI remained in camp for most of the day around Manchester, when at 8:00 p.m., they were ordered to fall in and complete the march to Gettysburg. Breaks were few and short as the men were desperately needed at Gettysburg.[29]

The residents of Carlisle were in no mood to welcome Jeb Stuart and his Confederate horsemen on July 1. They had already been visited by Jenkins' mounted infantry and later by two Confederate infantry divisions. A militia infantry brigade arrived so the town's surrender was not a foregone conclusion. Stuart threatened to open fire with his artillery if the town did not capitulate. It would not, and Stuart began lobbing shells, creating pandemonium among the civilians. About 1:00 a.m. on July 2, Stuart finally received the news he was craving—Lee's army was in Gettysburg, so he turned his horsemen around and began the long march south.

The last infantry units of both armies arrived on July 2. Two of Longstreet's First Corps divisions, McLaws' and Hood's, had halted near Marsh Creek about four miles from the battlefield during the early morning hours of July 2. They were back on the road at 4:00 a.m. and took a circuitous route from Chambersburg Pike to reach their pre-attack jumping off points on Warfield and Seminary Ridges. Longstreet's third division, Pickett's, still at Chambersburg, was relieved by Brig. Gen. John Imboden's cavalry brigade at 2:00 a.m. on July 2 and began its march to Gettysburg. It arrived about 2:30 p.m. after its 23-mile march. Brig. Gen. Evander Law's brigade (Hood's division) had been sent to New Guilford on June 30 to watch for a Federal thrust from that direction. It finally arrived on the battlefield on the afternoon after its 28-mile march, which James Longstreet called, "the best marching done in either army to reach the field of Gettysburg."

As July 2 dawned, the Federal I, III, XI, and XII Corps were on the battlefield. The II Corps slid into position along Cemetery Ridge during the morning after getting back on the road between 3:00 and 4:00 a.m. The V Corps, which was south of Hanover when the day began, was on the road at about 3:00 a.m. and reached the battlefield a couple of hours later. The final unit to reach the battlefield, the VI Corps had marched all night. The men were permitted a longer rest about dawn. The column had crossed the Pennsylvania State Line in the morning and marched through Littlestown. The head of the column finally reached Gettysburg between 2:00 and 3:00 p.m. after an epic 18-hour, 36-mile march.[30]

Stuart's men approached Gettysburg from the northeast late on the afternoon of July 2 where they encountered a portion of Gen. David Gregg's cavalry division. Stuart had already tangled with Judson Kilpatrick's division at Hunterstown, six miles from Gettysburg when the Union troopers encountered Stuart's rearguard. By the end of July 2, virtually all of the cavalry of both armies was within five miles of the battlefield.

The final phase of the approach to the battlefield during the Pennsylvania Campaign can be summarized as Lee reaching Chambersburg, Pennsylvania and while retaining most of his army there, he unleashed Ewell's Second Corps on a raid deeper into Pennsylvania that included the capture of Carlisle and York, and an attempt to take Harrisburg. The attack on the Pennsylvania capital had to wait when Lee learned George Meade was the new commander of the Union army, and its units were moving rapidly north. Meade skillfully dispersed his infantry and cavalry to maximize his ability to find Lee's army and engage it. The third phase, which began with Hooker allowing his men to rest on June 22, 23, and 24 as Lee pushed north, ended with strenuous marches to the battlefield.

Comparisons of the Two Campaigns

Lee gambled during both campaigns when he decided to disperse his army. During the final portion of the Maryland Campaign, Lee's divisions occupied Hagerstown, Boonsboro, the outskirts of Harpers Ferry, Maryland Heights and Loudoun Heights. At the furthest extremes, Hagerstown to Harpers Ferry, the distance was about 30 miles. Lee felt fully justified dividing his army during the Maryland Campaign because he felt the Harpers Ferry garrison could not be permitted to pose a threat to his rear and he did not believe McClellan would move north as rapidly. The situation was somewhat similar during the Pennsylvania Campaign. Between July 22 and June 29, Lee's army occupied York, Carlisle, and Chambersburg, a distance of about 65 miles. While there were other phases of the campaign where the distances were greater, they occurred when the Union army was not a threat. Unlike the Maryland Campaign, where cavalry commander Jeb Stuart kept Lee apprised of the Union army's position, this was not the case during the Pennsylvania Campaign, so Lee was blissfully unaware of his danger until the evening of June 28. In both campaigns, Lee quickly reassembled his army before the culminating battle, but it was touch and go and the unit's piecemeal arrival on the battlefield prevented Lee from marshalling the mass of troops required for success.

The Army of the Potomac played "catch-up" during both campaigns during the final phase of the approach to the battlefield. McClellan may have had a leg up on knowing Lee's location with the discovery of Special Order 191 during the Maryland Campaign, but he was already on the move when the directive was found. His movements, for the most part, were continuous with few days of rest. Hooker's movements during the Pennsylvania Campaign were more irregular. After long marches, and still desiring additional information on Lee's whereabouts, Hooker rested most of his army on June 22-24. When the men were back on the road, it usually involved long grueling marches on dusty roads in extreme heat. Putting the various wings/corps on parallel roads reduced the possibility of traffic jams and enhanced the possibility of encountering some of Lee's units during the Pennsylvania Campaign. The road system during the Maryland Campaign did not permit the use of many alternate roads, resulting in traffic jams. The area around Frederick became an important gathering area for the Union army during both campaigns, although the units were more scattered during the Pennsylvania Campaign. While most of McClellan's army was on the field by the beginning of the battle of Antietam, Meade's army arrived piecemeal at Gettysburg.

The proximity of the armies to each other was dramatically different during the two campaigns. During the Maryland Campaign, the final phase began with the two armies still fairly close to one another. Most of McClellan's army occupied Frederick, while Lee's furthest unit was at Hagerstown, about 25 miles away. This was quite different from the Pennsylvania Campaign. The onset of this phase found Hooker's entire army still in Virginia and at rest, while Lee's army had crossed into Maryland and was heading north. By the time Hooker put his army in motion and crossed the Potomac River into Maryland, Lee's Second Corps was already in and near Chambersburg, Pennsylvania. With Hooker's northernmost units around Leesburg, the distance was about 75 miles away.

No preliminary fights, except some cavalry clashes, occurred during the final march to the battlefield during the Pennsylvania Campaign. The situation was different for the Maryland Campaign, as the major preliminary fights occurred just a few days before the big battle at Antietam. This included the fight for the South Mountain gaps on September 14 and siege of Harpers Ferry which concluded on the following day.

The cavalry captured a significant number of enemy wagons during each campaign. Col. Grimes Davis, who broke out of the Harpers Ferry and rode north, captured as many as 96 wagons from Longstreet's ordnance trains near

Hagerstown and Jeb Stuart captured a wagon train of over 125 wagons near Rockville, Maryland.

Probably because the armies were so close and a battle imminent, neither army issued any general orders during the final phase of the Maryland Campaign. Both army commanders did issue orders during the Pennsylvania Campaign. For Lee's army, it was General Order No. 73 reminding the men about foraging. Both Hooker and Meade crafted general orders upon the former's removal from command.

Lee's troops never made it into Pennsylvania during the Maryland Campaign and were not about to ransom Maryland towns since he was hoping to shift their allegiance. This was certainly not the case during the Pennsylvania Campaign when several Keystone towns were required to provide goods and money lest they be put to the torch.

At the start of each battle, both armies had significant percentages of their forces still on the road. At Antietam, this amounted to three divisions, or a third of Lee's army, and two of McClellan's six corps were not on the field when the guns exploded into action on the morning of September 17— also about a third. During the Pennsylvania Campaign, only four of Lee's nine divisions (44%) were close enough to be engaged during the initial phase of the battle; Meade had only two of his seven corps engaged on the first day (29%).

Table 13: Comparison of the Final Phase of Traveling to the Battlefield
(September 13-17, 1862 and June 22-July 2, 1863)

Issue	Maryland Campaign	Pennsylvania Campaign
Infantry combat?	Yes (South Mountain and Harpers Ferry)	No
Cavalry combat?	Yes	Yes
Commander issues special/general orders	**Confederates:** No xxxx **Union:** No	**Confederates:** G.O. 73-- foraging **Union:** G.O. 65/66 (Command change)
Furthest distance traveled by end of phase ("as crow flies")	**Confederates:** About 23 miles (Longstreet's wing) **Union:** About 27 miles (VI Corps)	**Confederates:** About 90 miles (Johnson's division) **Union:** About 125 miles (VI Corps)
Nature of movements	**Confederates:** Sustained **Union:** Sustained	**Confederates:** Sustained **Union:** Sustained
Location of armies?	**Confederates:** MD **Union:** MD	**Confederates:** PA **Union:** MD/PA
Army Dispersed?	**Confederates:** Yes **Union:** Yes	**Confederates:** Yes **Union:** Yes
Completeness of the armies at the beginning of the battle	**Confederates:** 67% of divisions **Union:** 66%	**Confederates:** 44% **Union:** 29%
Cavalry capture enemy wagons?	**Confederates:** No **Union:** Yes (Grimes Davis)	**Confederates:** Yes (Jeb Stuart) **Union:** No

Issue	Maryland Campaign	Pennsylvania Campaign
Effectiveness of the cavalry?	**Confederates:** Yes **Union:** Mixed	**Confederates:** Mixed **Union:** Yes
Confederates: Movements impacted by Union army?	Yes	Yes
Confederates: Did Lee gamble?	Yes (Harpers Ferry expedition)	Yes (Continues to disperse army)
Confederates: Army mostly intact by the start of the battle?	No	No
Union: Army moving north?	Yes	Yes
Union: Traffic jams?	Yes	No
Union: Cavalry seeks out enemy location?	Yes	Yes
Union: Army mostly intact by the start of the battle?	Yes	No

Chapter 9: A Comparison of How the Armies Reached the Battlefield

This chapter summarizes how the armies arrived at the major battlefields, outlining the differences and similarities.

Distances Traveled and Duration

The armies' starting points had a tremendous impact on the subsequent actions during each campaign. During the Maryland Campaign, both armies were close to Washington; during the Pennsylvania Campaign, they were almost 50 miles farther south, near Fredericksburg, Virginia.

Not only were the armies further south during the Pennsylvania Campaign, compared with the Maryland Campaign, their ultimate destinations were farther away. Using the most direct routes between the starting and ending points, the Confederates marched about 35 miles to reach Sharpsburg; the Union army about 50 miles. During the Pennsylvania Campaign, because Lee used the Shenandoah Valley to screen his troops, his march took over 200 miles, compared with the approximately 130 miles marched by the Union troops. These figures do not include side trips taken by both sides.

Because of the distances involved, the duration of the marches to the battlefields differed significantly. If the clock begins with the date the Confederates began breaking camp and moving north (September 4, 1862 and June 3, 1863), the time to the major battle was 13 days during the Maryland Campaign and 28 days for the Pennsylvania Campaign. It took less time for the Union army to reach the battlefield. If we use September 8 for the initiation of movement during the Maryland Campaign and June 12 for the Pennsylvania Campaign, the number of days is 9 for the Maryland Campaign and 19 days for the Pennsylvania Campaign.

The Union army's move to each of the battlefields was affected by a lack of intelligence about the size and location of Lee's forces, which froze the army command during both campaigns. The Union army was also glued in place during the Maryland Campaign because McClellan had to first forge two armies into one. Once the Union army began its movements, it took less time to reach its final destination. In both campaigns, Lee sent his troops on side trips, delaying his movement to the battlefield.

The Nature of the Marches

Lee audaciously divided his army during both campaigns, sending pieces far afield on a variety of missions. During the Maryland Campaign, Special Orders 191 divided the army into several parts; most heading toward Harpers Ferry. The rest were sent north to Boonsboro and Hagerstown. A year later, Lee also divided his army again, sending a third of it north to raid as far as Carlisle, Pennsylvania. In both cases, Lee miscalculated the enemy's subsequent reactions. He thought McClellan would show more hesitancy than he did during the Maryland Campaign, and during the Pennsylvania Campaign, he didn't know where the Union army was located.

In both campaigns, Lee was forced to quickly consolidate his forces. Generally, the marches were less strenuous during the Maryland Campaign, as most of his troops were only slightly more than 15 miles away from the battlefield after being dispersed. Recombining the army was more difficult during the Pennsylvania Campaign, as the Second Corps was more than double that distance away.

Both McClellan and Hooker dispersed their corps during the march to facilitate rapid movement and enhance the probability of finding Lee's army. In the Maryland Campaign, McClellan had the added responsibility of ensuring the protection of Washington and Baltimore. Hooker/Meade were less concerned about the safety of these cities, as Lee crossed into Maryland further north, and then into Pennsylvania. However, Lee posed a threat to other important northern cities, such as Harrisburg and Philadelphia.

Lee used different routes during the invasions. During the Maryland Campaign, his troops crossed the Potomac River relatively close to Washington, which he knew would have an impact on McClellan's subsequent movements. This approach, however, put Harpers Ferry in his rear. However, he believed all along that the Union high command would evacuate the garrison. A year later, Lee used the Blue Ridge Mountains as a shield, possibly because he was so far from Washington, and moved north within the Shenandoah Valley. This had him crossing the Potomac River further north, and therefore Harpers Ferry, whether intact or not, posed less of a threat.

The intensity of the marches varied. Lee rested at least some of his commands prior to the big battles in both campaigns. During the Maryland Campaign, he rested his men for a short period outside of Frederick and then Longstreet's three divisions rested at Sharpsburg from September 15 to the start of the battle. Stonewall Jackson's divisions arriving on September 16 had almost 24 hours of rest. There were more periods of rest during the Pennsylvania Campaign. During the early part of the campaign, several of Lee's units rested around Culpeper Court House, probably to give him time to ascertain Hooker's next moves. The Second Corps, which led the movement north, had periods of rest during the middle of the campaign while the rest of the army caught up. During the latter part of the campaign, Lee allowed two of his corps to rest in the Chambersburg, Pennsylvania area for several days while the Second Corps undertook its raid deep into the Keystone State.

The Union army's movements differed during the two campaigns. Once McClellan completed reorganizing his army, he began moving it north, and except for an occasional day of rest, he continued pushing after Lee. Hooker was probably more hamstrung by not knowing Lee's position as his adversary was using the Shenandoah Valley to move north and since it was in "enemy" territory, he was receiving fewer intelligence reports. Therefore, it took him over a week to begin moving north (on June 12) and then he allowed his men to rest for several days near Washington as he continued collecting information on Lee's army.

Concentrating the Armies

During the two campaigns, both armies were fairly far flung during their movements to the battlefields and were forced to quickly reassemble from two directions. During the final phase of the Maryland Campaign, Lee's army was centered in four major areas: (Hagerstown/Boonsboro, Maryland Heights/Pleasant Valley, Harpers Ferry, Loudoun Heights) and used two avenues to the battlefield: Those fighting it out at South Mountain arrived from the east, marching along Boonsboro Pike, crossing the Middle Bridge over Antietam Creek to reach Sharpsburg. Those investing Harpers Ferry crossed the Potomac River at the Shepherdstown ford to the west. During the Gettysburg Campaign, Lee's troops also approached from two directions.

Two of Ewell's divisions (Rodes' and Early's) approached from the north; the rest of Lee's army approached on Chambersburg Road from the west.

During the Maryland Campaign, most of McClellan's army marched through the South Mountain Gaps and then headed south on Boonsboro Road. The VI Corps, which fought at Crampton's Gap and settled in at Pleasant Valley, marched north to reach the battlefield. The Union army during the Pennsylvania Campaign was more dispersed and used several roads approaching Gettysburg from the east and south.

Whether or not major fighting occurred prior to the battle determined how closely the Union army followed its Confederate counterpart. The fight for the South Mountain gaps three days prior to the battle of Antietam permitted the Union troops to closely follow the Confederates to the battlefield. During the Pennsylvania Campaign, the two armies arrived from completely different directions.

Location of the Armies at Beginning of Battle

The locations of the troops when the first shots of the battles were fired also differed. During the Maryland Campaign, Lee had six of his nine divisions on the battlefield the evening before the battle and another two arrived the morning of the battle. Only A. P. Hill's division arrived late in the afternoon to stabilize Lee's line. During the Pennsylvania Campaign, none of Lee's troops were initially on the battlefield, instead arriving piecemeal during the first two days of the battle. Four of his divisions were, however, close enough to participate in the first day's battle (44%).

McClellan, like Lee, had most of his men close to Antietam Creek when the guns fired to open the battle. Only the VI Corps arrived during the middle of the battle. At Gettysburg, none of the infantry were present during the initial phase of the battle. Instead, a constant stream of units approached the battlefield during its first two days. Two of Meade's corps were close enough, however, to participate in the first day's battle (29%).

Traffic jams hindered the movements of both armies to the battlefield. During the Maryland Campaign, a congested Boonsboro Pike prevented McClellan's troops from reaching the battlefield earlier on September 15. Similarly, a traffic jam along Chambersburg Pike during the Pennsylvania

Campaign halted McLaws' and Hood's divisions (Longstreet's Corps from reaching the battlefield on July 1.

Preliminary Fights

Lee felt compelled to reduce garrisons he deemed too dangerous to leave in his rear during both campaigns. The impact was far greater during the Maryland Campaign, for Lee detached two-thirds of his army on September 10 and these units would not begin returning to the army until September 16. The breakup of his army had a profound impact on Lee's plans to take the initiative against McClellan's army and ultimately forced him to fight a defensive battle. It also put Lee's army in grave danger, as three of his divisions were isolated at Boonsboro and Hagerstown and could have been defeated piecemeal. The same is true of two other divisions (McLaws' and Anderson's) down in the Pleasant Valley participating in the siege of Harpers Ferry. The fight for the South Mountain gaps pitted Lee's outnumbered and outgunned men trying desperately to keep McClellan from crossing and potentially destroying Lee's army. The impact was much less dramatic during the Pennsylvania Campaign, where Richard Ewell's Second Corps reduced the Winchester garrison while its men trudged north through the Shenandoah Valley.

The cavalry was involved in some fights during both campaigns; they amounted to mere skirmishes during the Maryland Campaign, but were much larger and bloodier during the Pennsylvania Campaign. The fights during the latter campaign began with the pitched cavalry battle at Brandy Station, continued just east of the Blue Ridge Mountain gaps, and ended with fights at Westminster, Hanover, and Hunterstown during the move north. These are covered in Chapter 10.

Condition of the Armies

The length of the campaign and the distances traveled certainly had an impact on the condition of the troops when they arrived on the battlefield. They were both shorter during the preliminary movements of the Maryland Campaign. Both armies had recently emerged from a major battle and needed rest and resupply. Occasional arduous marches also left many men by the sides of roads. During the Pennsylvania Campaign, the men had almost a month of rest since the last major battle and most of the movements were interspersed with periods of rest, at least during the first two phases of the campaign. The Union army undertook some strenuous marches during the last phase of the campaign and the same was true of Richard Ewell's Second Corps, which had reached Carlisle and the outskirts of Harrisburg.

Collecting Supplies

Lee made sure during both campaigns that his men respected private property. This was especially important during the first invasion, when Lee attempted to curry the favor of Marylanders. He didn't want his men doing anything that would prevent the border state from throwing its lot with the Confederacy. The Confederates spent less time in Maryland during the march to Gettysburg during the Pennsylvania Campaign. The troops attempted to ransom Chambersburg, Gettysburg, and other Pennsylvania towns as a way of attaining supplies. These activities were anathema during the Maryland Campaign.

Command Changes

Robert E. Lee was the only constant during the two campaigns. The Union army experienced a command change in mid-campaign during one of Lee's invasions. That occurred during toward the middle of the Pennsylvania Campaign, when politically connected Joseph Hooker, who could not be removed until he actually resigned, finally did so on June 27. Lincoln quickly accepted the resignation and elevated George Meade to command the Army of the Potomac. Earlier, during the Maryland Campaign, George McClellan assumed oversight of the Army of Virginia and the Army of the Potomac *before* the campaign began, and it took him several days to consolidate the armies before he could move north.

General Orders

Both armies received general orders during the campaign. Because the men were exhausted after the Second Bull Run campaign and their long journeys from the Virginia Peninsula, both Lee and McClellan issued orders against straggling. Hooker repeated these orders during the Pennsylvania Campaign.

This was less of an issue for Lee in 1863 and instead he concentrated on two general orders relating to foraging and procuring private property.

Table 14: Comparison of Getting to the Major Battlefield

Issue	Maryland Campaign	Pennsylvania Campaign
Distance to battlefield	**Confederates:** 35 miles **Union:** 50 miles	**Confederates:** 216 miles **Union:** 129 miles
Time to reach the battlefield	**Confederates:** 13 days **Union:** 9 days	**Confederates:** 28 days **Union:** 19 days
Types of movements	**Confederates:** Some rests between marches **Union:** Almost continuous marches	**Confederates:** Some rests between marches **Union:** Some rests between marches
Troops arrived from how many directions?	**Confederates:** Two (west & east) **Union:** One (east)	**Confederates:** Two (north & west) **Union:** Two (south & east)
Preliminary fights	Harpers Ferry South Mountain passes	Winchester Stephenson's Depot Large cavalry fights
Ransoming of towns by Confederates	No	Yes
Movement of the armies	**Confederates:** Some rests between marches **Union:** Almost continual marches	**Confederates:** Confederates: Some rests between marches **Union:** Confederates: Some rests between marches
Command changes during campaign	**Confederates:** No **Union:** No	**Confederates:** No **Union:** Yes

Issue	Maryland Campaign	Pennsylvania Campaign
Number of days before the battle that initial units arrived	**Confederates**: 2 (September 15) **Union:** 2 (September 15)	**Confederates:** 0 (arrived on day of battle) **Union:** 0 (arrived on day of battle)
When the armies completed assembling on the battlefield	**Confederates:** Late afternoon of battle **Union:** Midday of battle	**Confederates:** Early morning of July 3 **Union:** Afternoon of July 2

Chapter 10: The Preliminary Fights

The Maryland Campaign of 1862

Robert E. Lee and the Army of Northern Virginia fought a series of battles on September 14 and conducted a siege during the same period. Neither of these events was expected when Lee crossed the Potomac River and may have contributed to Lee's ultimate decision to fight the major battle at Antietam, and after it concluded, to end the invasion.

Harpers Ferry

Harpers Ferry, nestled at the junction of the Potomac and Shenandoah Rivers, was surrounded by high mountains that dominated the town. Across the Potomac River, to the northeast, Maryland Heights, the southern terminus of Elk Ridge, rose to a height of 1,380 feet. The slightly shorter (1,200 feet) Loudoun Heights rose to the southeast, across the Shenandoah River. Bolivar Heights, about a mile west of town, was only 700 feet tall at its highest elevation. The town had a rich history even before Stonewall Jackson arrived in mid-September 1862. Settled in 1733, it first functioned as a ferry and facilitated the passage of thousands of wayfarers. The fledgling United States Government established one of its first arsenals there and was the prime reason why John Brown selected the town for his raid in 1859. At one time, Harpers Ferry boasted the only railroad bridge across the Potomac River, built in 1836-37. The town was almost impossible to defend, as the rivers cut the defenses into three distinct sectors with a perimeter of almost seven miles. This resulted in the town changing hands at least eight times during the Civil War.[1]

A garrison of 8,860 infantry, 1,022 cavalry and 585 artillerymen men defended Harpers Ferry at the start of the Maryland Campaign, under the command of Col. Dixon Miles. Lee intended to use the Shenandoah Valley as his line of communications and Harpers Ferry blocked the flow of information and supplies. Lee was also concerned the large garrison would be in his rear as he moved north. He assumed the almost indefensible garrison and town would be evacuated soon after he crossed the Potomac River and moved north. He was wrong, for although McClellan expressed concern about the well being of the garrison, General-in-Chief Henry Halleck would not consider abandoning the post. The word passed down to Middle District commander, Maj. Gen. John Wool, who telegraphed Miles, "There must be no abandoning of post, and shoot the first man that thinks of it."

When Lee's army began moving north to Leesburg, Virginia, Halleck ordered the Winchester's garrison abandoned. The 3,000 men under Brig. Gen. Julius White were ordered to march to Harpers Ferry, giving Miles almost 14,000 to guard the town. Sending White to Harpers Ferry created problems because he outranked Miles and, by the rules of seniority, he should assume command of the garrison. District commander Wool, solved this dilemma by sending White to Martinsburg. Miles was, at least theoretically, the perfect combination of experienced officer who had extensive knowledge of Harpers Ferry's terrain and its strategic position. If Harpers Ferry was to be defended, a significant force must occupy Maryland Heights, so thought Wool, Halleck, and others. Halleck wrote directly to Miles on September 7: "Our army is in motion. It is important that Harper's Ferry be held to the latest moment. The Government has the utmost confidence in you, and is ready to give you full credit for the defense it expects you to make."[2]

The die was now cast for a dramatic confrontation at Harpers Ferry. With firm orders to hold Harpers Ferry at all costs, Miles went to work organizing his infantry. He divided them into four brigades and because he had just three regiments with any experience, he placed one in each of the first three brigades. Miles decided to center his defense on two high points: Maryland Heights and Bolivar Heights. He sent Col. Thomas Ford's brigade to the former. Although Wool ordered the defenses on this high point strengthened, Miles all but ignored him. Ford and his unit were not the best choice for this important mission. Ford had only recently returned to the army after having a fistula removed from his buttocks and he was still unable to walk or ride a horse because of the inflamed area. At only 1,150 men, Ford's unit was among the smallest of Miles' brigades. However, Ford quickly realized the need to strengthen his position. He wanted to establish his first line of defense at Solomon's Gap, about six miles north of Maryland Heights, which provided the enemy with access to the heights from the Pleasant Valley to the east. Miles' request for artillery was denied, and the gap was never strengthened nor was a blockhouse built on Maryland Heights which could have helped stave off an attack. Ford took it upon himself to do what he could to strengthen the heights, building breastworks across the ridgeline with a thick abatis of fallen timber about 80 yards in front.

Miles believed the major attack on Harpers Ferry would be via Bolivar Heights to the west, so he sent Col. Frederick D'Utassy's and Col. William Trimble's brigades, totaling 5,411 men, to this important ridge. Miles' last brigade, under Col. William Ward, occupied Camp Hill, on the north side of the town, presumably to protect the pontoon and railroad bridges over the Potomac River. It could also easily reinforce Bolivar Heights, if needed.[3]

Three Confederate columns under the command of Stonewall Jackson converged on the garrison. According to Special Orders 191, Jackson had immediate control of three divisions, which had the longest march, as he headed back to the Potomac River, crossed at Light's Ford, near Williamsport, Maryland, and then looped around to approach Bolivar Heights from the west. He chose this route because he wanted to capture Martinsburg first. Knapsacks were discarded and wagons limited as lightness meant speed. A second column composed of Lafayette McLaws' and Richard Anderson's divisions, drove through South Mountain, into the Pleasant Valley and then south toward the Potomac River to claim Maryland Heights. Brig. Gen. John Walker's division comprised the last column. It never entered Frederick, but remained along the Monocacy River, destroying government property. It crossed the Potomac River at Point of Rocks and headed for Loudoun Heights by way of Lovettsville, Virginia. Jackson's plan had the six Confederate divisions ringing the Harpers Ferry garrison. It was a good plan, but Lee miscalculated how long it would take for the three columns to get into position.

Jackson's hopes of bagging White and his Martinsburg garrison were dashed when both fled to Harpers Ferry, arriving there on the afternoon of September 12. A disappointed Jackson continued his three divisions' march to Halltown, Virginia, about two miles from Bolivar Heights, on September 13. Walker's division crossed the Potomac River at 7:00 a.m. on September 12. Rather than risk being seen by the enemy, Walker modified his route, taking a longer path via Hillsborough, Virginia. He decided to halt at the latter town and get a fresh start in the morning. Because the roads were so congested out of Frederick, McLaws' column did not leave Frederick until noon on September 10 and reached Pleasant Valley the following day.[4]

The fight for Maryland Heights began on September 12 when Kershaw's South Carolinians scaled South Mountain at Solomon's Gap and exchanged volleys with some of Ford's pickets. Brig. Gen. Joseph Kershaw's brigade's skirmishers slowly pushed Ford's men back through the tangles toward Maryland Heights. Thick mountain laurel and other vegetation hampered their movements. Nightfall ended the preliminary action. Kershaw continued his advance between 6:30 and 7:00 a.m. the following morning, sending two of his regiments forward, supported by his other two. The South Carolinians spied abatis up ahead with breastworks beyond it. Meanwhile, William Barksdale's Mississippi brigade marched on the eastern side of Elk Ridge and then began the arduous climb toward its summit. Ford saw these movements and sent Miles a stream of pleas for reinforcements. His men behind the breastworks held their own against Kershaw's mounting pressure as Union reinforcements arrived to shore up the defense. By 10:00 a.m., the van of Barksdale's brigade had clawed their way up the mountainside and began firing into Ford's right flank. Ford was not present on the top of the hill, though, as he was again ill, so he sent up Maj. Sylvester Hewitt, a physician with no prior military experience, to assume command of the brigade. Hewitt panicked and ordered the men to withdraw from the barricade. Ford and Miles down in Harpers Ferry received word of the withdrawal and immediately sent orders for the men to reoccupy the breastworks, and then the two officers crossed the river to see what was happening. It was too late, as the Confederates had already surged forward and occupied the breastworks. The two leaders cobbled together a defensive line further south of the barricade and then Miles returned to Harpers Ferry, leaving Ford in charge of the defense of Maryland Heights as additional Union reinforcements climbed the mountain to assist. Ford now outnumbered his foe by a factor of 3-2, but his green troops were no match for the battle-hardened veteran Confederates. By 3:30 p.m., the Mississippians were lapping around Ford's right flank while Kershaw's men were hitting his front. Ford was under the impression he had discretionary orders to abandon the heights, and he exercised them. Miles could not believe his eyes: "God Almighty!" he yelled, "They are coming down! Hell and damnation!"[5]

Meanwhile, the other components of Jackson's trap were also moving into position on September 13. Walker's Confederate division reached the base of

Loudoun Heights at 10:00 a.m. and two of its regiments scaled the steep slope. They periodically left the road to hack a path through the vegetation so their presence would not be revealed to the Harpers Ferry garrison. The men finally gained the summit by 5:00 p.m. Jackson's three divisions were about 13 miles away when they began their march. The roads and weather were conducive to a rapid march, so the van of the column reached Halltown, about two miles from Bolivar Heights at about 11:00 a.m. Miles realized his only hope was strong reinforcements, so he ordered Capt. Charles Russell of the 1st Maryland Cavalry to break through the enemy lines with a handful of men to "try to reach somebody . . . anybody . . . [about] the condition of Harpers Ferry." Miles thought he could hold out for another 48 hours, but no more. Russell successfully eluded the Confederates and delivered his message to Maj. Gen. Jesse Reno, commander of the Federal IX Corps who gave him a fresh horse and sent him on to McClellan at 9:00 a.m. McClellan sent three different couriers to Miles with word that help was on the way.[6]

September 14 was a seminal day for the men in and around Harpers Ferry. Miles continued developing his defense and fretting about his ability to hold out until promised reinforcements arrived. He worried most about his defensive line on Bolivar Heights and the enemy on Maryland Heights. Loudoun Heights was less of a concern, as he considering it too far for effective small arms fire and its slopes too steep to allow cannon to reach its summit. He was wrong about the latter, for by 8:00 a.m., the crest contained five rifled guns frowning down on Harpers Ferry. Walker asked Jackson for permission to immediately open fire, but he was told to wait until the rest of the besieging force, particularly McLaws' on Maryland Heights, was in position and ready for action. McLaws' men were hard at work pulling cannon up the side of the mountain. It took 200 men pulling heavy ropes to manhandle each cannon up to the summit. By 2:00 p.m., two rifled cannon were in place and others would soon follow.

Jackson sent McLaws a dispatch on September 14 laying out his plans: "So soon as you get your batteries all planted, let me know, as I desire, after yourself, Walker, and myself have our batteries ready to open, to send in a flag of truce, for the purpose of getting out the non-combatants, should the commanding officer refuse to surrender. Should we have to attack, let the work be done thoroughly; fire on the houses when necessary. The citizens

Map 14: The Preliminary Antietam Battles
A= Harpers Ferry
B= Fox's Gap

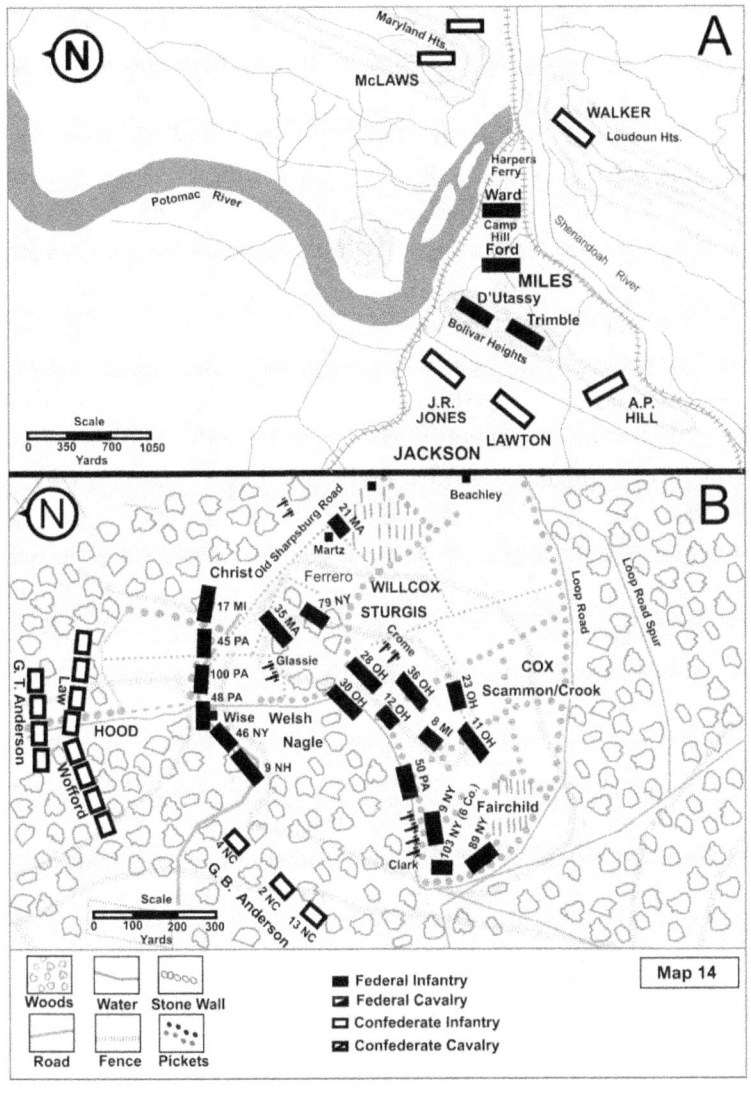

can keep out of harm's way from your artillery. Demolish the place if it is occupied by the enemy, and does not surrender."[7]

Jackson knew the threat to his command posed by McClellan's advance toward the South Mountain gaps, and felt the pressure to neutralize Harpers Ferry quickly. Meanwhile, Miles perfected his defensive position on Bolivar Heights which he knew would be the focal point of the enemy's attack. He did not position more than a skirmish line on the left of his line because he did not think the enemy could climb the high bluffs along the Shenandoah River. He was again wrong. Jackson sent A. P. Hill's division toward that flank at 3:00 p.m. on September 14 as the guns on Loudoun Heights and Maryland Heights burst into action. Miles quickly scrambled troops over to cover his left flank to counter the threat. Darkness gave the beleaguered Harpers Ferry a reprieve. Jackson wrote to Lee that night, "the advance which commenced this evening has been successful thus far, and I look to Him for complete success tomorrow."[8]

The night of September 14-15 found Col. Miles arguing with his senior officers. Some wanted to evacuate the town; others to attempt a recapture of Maryland Heights. An impatient Miles finally blurted out, "I am ordered to hold this place and God damn my soul to hell if I don't." Seeing the handwriting on the wall, cavalry commander, Col. Benjamin "Grimes" Davis, lobbied Miles to allow him to attempt a breakout with his troopers. Miles reluctantly agreed and Davis' 1,500 men slipped away (see Chapter 8). Miles spent the night repositioning his regiments on Bolivar Heights into a defensive line resembling a "V" to combat A. P. Hill's division approaching from along the Shenandoah River and Jackson's two other divisions on its left. He also repositioned his cannon and awaited the dawn of September 15. Jackson was also active, repositioning his infantry and bringing up additional artillery.

Seventy Confederate cannon ringing Harpers Ferry opened fire at 6:00 a.m. on September 15 and pounded Harpers Ferry and Bolivar Heights for an hour. The Union guns responded, but they could not reach Maryland or Loudoun Heights and were running out of ammunition, so they fell silent. The Confederate guns also ceased firing as the Confederate infantry began their final push against Bolivar Heights. They had not traveled far before white flags could be seen fluttering along the Federal positions. Intermittent Confederate artillery fire claimed Miles' life, as one exploded within a few feet of him. He would die the following day, unable to defend himself from the onslaught of future recriminations. The captured booty was immense: 13,000 small arms, 73 cannon, and over 200 wagons. The more than 12,000 men captured stood as the largest number of Americans surrendered in a single battle in U. S. history until World War II. Jackson's men "fared sumptuously. In addition to meat, crackers, sugar, coffee, shoes, blankets, underclothing, &c ... The ragged, forlorn appearance of our men excited the combined merriment and admiration of our prisoners."

Jackson did not have time to savor his victory, as he knew he needed to get his men on the road as quickly as possible to reinforce the rest of Lee's army at Sharpsburg. He began the march that night, leaving Hill's division behind to process the prisoners' paroles and secure captured supplies/equipment.[9]

South Mountain

After reviewing Lee's Special Order No. 191 and validating its authenticity, McClellan established a two-pronged approach to take on the enemy's dispersed army. His VI Corps, followed at a distance by Couch's division would force its way through Crampton's Gap, enter the Pleasant Valley, drive south and hit McLaws' and Anderson's divisions in their rear, pinning them against the Potomac River, and then break the Harpers Ferry siege. Another column, led by the IX Corps with support by the I Corps would force its way through Turner's Gap, and attack the fragment of Lee's army at Boonsboro and Hagerstown. Several other army corps marched behind them. These orders would result in fights at four locations on September 14, 1862.[10]

Lee was ill prepared to halt this deadly Union thrust. Only D. H. Hill's 8,000-man division blocked the path of McClellan's I, II, V, IX, and XII Corps' path through South Mountain at Turner's Gap (and later Fox's Gap). Hill, outnumbered by over 6 to 1, could not hope to prevent McClellan's thrust. His only salvation was Longstreet's two divisions near Hagerstown. Could they arrive in time to assist? The men began their march late morning of September 14, as the fighting at Fox's Gap was in full bloom. Longstreet set a killing pace, causing as many as half of his men to fall from the ranks during the 13-mile march. An infantry officer recalled, the "march was very rapid and at times a double-quick step was kept up for 2 or 3 miles together. Men exhausted by the rapid march and overcome by the dust and heat, fell out of ranks and were left along the roadside by dozens, yet on swept the column at a tremendous pace." Longstreet estimated that only 4,000 muskets were available when the column finally reached Turner's Gap, beginning at 2:30 p.m. [11]

Fox's Gap

September 14 dawned bright and increasingly hot as the men of the IX Corps broke camp west of Middletown, Maryland, after a chilly night. Corps commander Maj. Gen. Jesse Reno sent Col. Eliakim Scammon's brigade (Brig. Gen. Jacob Cox's division) along the National Road toward Turner's Gap. Some units of Brig. Gen. Alfred Pleasonton's division rode ahead with orders to clear the gap. The cavalry commander did not expect much resistance, however, a chance meeting with a recently paroled Union officer making his way east changed everyone's mind, as it appeared the gap was defended. The officer, Col. Augustus Moor, blurted out "My God! Be Careful!" The troops the officer saw were two brigades from Maj. Gen. D. H. Hill's division (Col. Alfred Colquitt's and Brig. Gen. Samuel Garland's), sent to Turner's Gap, where the National Road crosses South Mountain. Lee sent Hill orders to defend the gap, so the irascible division commander was on his horse at about 4:00 a.m., riding from his headquarters in Boonsboro to Turner's Gap. He saw Garland's brigade at the top of the mountain and Colquitt's further down the east face of the slope. After repositioning the latter's brigade, Hill decided to ride south and learned of the presence of Fox's Gap, defended by only 200 dismounted cavalrymen and a couple of horse artillery pieces.

Cox decided to heed the paroled officer's advice and avoid a direct confrontation at Turner's Gap. He detoured his division southwest to Fox's Gap. He planned to cross South Mountain there, then swing north and take Turner's Gap from the rear. No one knew Longstreet and his remaining two divisions had left Hagerstown and were heading south to Boonsboro under Lee's orders.[12]

Scammon's brigade skirmished with a handful of Confederate cavalrymen from the 5th Virginia Cavalry at Fox's Gap until Hill sent Garland's 1,100-

man brigade south to reinforce them. Hill later wrote, "He went off in high spirits and I never saw him again." The single Union and Confederate brigades slugged it out beginning at 9:00 a.m. Among the combatants was future president Rutherford Hayes, who commanded the 23rd Ohio. Hayes was severely wounded in the arm and did not participate in the battle of Antietam. Cox brought up Col. George Crook's brigade and the two Union brigades successfully pushed the outnumbered Confederate infantry back from their defensive line behind stout stone walls. Garland fell mortally wounded during the fray and his brigade was forced to flee. Garland's replacement explained, the enemy "with a long-extended yell, burst upon our line . . . the enemy's strength was overpowering, and could not be resisted." The commander of the 20th North Carolina reported, "[T]here was nothing to do but get away or surrender."

Help was on the way for both sides. Hill sent Brig. Gen. George B. Anderson's brigade to help the outgunned Tar Heels, and after a lull in the action between noon and 2:00 p.m., Brig. Gen. Orlando Willcox's division of the IX Corps arrived and entered the fight. Longstreet's units also arrived in the afternoon, but the strenuous forced march caused his brigades to arrive piecemeal and exhausted. Hill sent three brigades from his and Maj. Gen. D. R. Jones' division, Col. G. T. Anderson's, Brig. Gen. Roswell Ripley's and Brig. Gen. Thomas Drayton's, south to assist Anderson. These brigades, with G. B. Anderson's, were to march down Old Sharpsburg Road, halt and then wheel to the left and attack the growing host of Union units in and around Fox's Gap. Hill put Ripley in charge of the mission, but the latter erred badly by marching too far down Old Sharpsburg Road, leaving a gap with Drayton's brigade, marching at the end of the column. A soldier in Ripley's brigade recalled how the men "marched forward and backward across the mountain and were marched to the top of it by the left flank in a line of battle, waited there till near sundown, then back again." Ripley defended his actions in his report: "The natural difficulties of the ground and the condition of the troops prevented these movements from being made with the rapidity which was desirable, and the enemy forced his way ... between General Drayton's force and my own." Hill still remained angry with Ripley 25 years after the battle, writing how he was "sent for in hot haste . . . but he was a coward and did nothing."

Two Union divisions against a single Confederate brigade was a recipe for disaster and Drayton's unit was thrashed. Meanwhile, Reno's third division arrived, tipping the balance even further to the Union side. The IX Corps captured the top of Fox's Gap as night descended on the battlefield, but Brig. Gen. John Hood's division (Longstreet's command) arrived and slid into position, barring the IX Corps from reaching Pleasant Valley on the west side of South Mountain. The fighting continued until just after 7:00 p.m. with the IX Corps holding the gap, but the Confederates blocking the road. The IX Corps lost 889 men in this fight; the Confederates suffered about 869 killed and wounded. These losses may not include many of those who were captured. Among the mortally wounded was Jesse Reno, commander of the IX Corps. He had ridden forward in the growing darkness and was shot near the front lines. He encountered Brig. Gen. Samuel Sturgis as he was being carried to the rear. Sturgis recalled how Reno called out to him "in his characteristic cheerful manner—'Hallo. Sam, I'm dead!'" The strong and cheerful response caused Sturgis to disagree with the statement and he said, "Oh, no, General, not so bad as that, I hope." Reno simply responded, "Yes, yes, I'm dead—good bye," and died moments later under a large tree in the rear.

The Confederates pulled out of their positions later that night, leaving the roads to and from Fox's Gap in the IX Corps' hands. Burnside rested his men after their long ordeal.[13]

Frosttown Gap/Plateau

While the IX Corps attempted to ram its way through Fox's Gap for the better part of September 14, the I Corps approached Turner's Gap that afternoon. If all the pieces fell in place, both gaps could well be in Union hands well before the end of the day.

The men of Joseph Hooker's 14,000-man I Corps were up at 3:00 a.m. on September 14, munching on hardtack and drinking coffee south of Frederick. They hit the road by 6:30 a.m., reached Frederick by 8:00 a.m. and then headed to Middletown, where they halted at 1:00 p.m. The column then marched a bit further and turned right onto Old Tabor Road at Bolivar and was almost immediately hit by Confederate artillery fire. By about 4:00 p.m., Brig. Gen. George Meade's division of Pennsylvania Reserves deployed for action at the base of the mountain. Up against Meade's 4,000 men was a mere a brigade of 1,200 Alabamians under Brig. Gen. Robert Rodes stretched to cover as much of the Frosttown Plateau as possible. Meade's three brigades quickly lost sight of each other and advanced at different speeds given the varying mountain terrain. Brig. Gen. Truman Seymour, the commander of one of Meade's brigades, told a regimental commander, "Put your regiment into that corn-field and hurt somebody!" Rodes' men fought tenaciously, hoping to hold out until nightfall ended the fighting, but they were soon overwhelmed and forced up the mountainside. Historian Ezra Carman described the action: "Meade's men were very persistent...they followed them [Rodes' men] closely up the mountainside, pushed them from every point of vantage...penetrated their thin and broken line, working in and on their flanks, and continued swinging around their left."

A small brigade of South Carolinians arrived just as Rodes' men were vacating their positions, but it was quickly flanked and joined the retreat up the side of the mountain. Meade was justifiably proud of his men's performance. He noted in his report, "Steadily the line advanced up the mountain side, where the enemy was posted behind trees and rocks, from whence he was slowly, but gradually, dislodged..."

Other I Corps units were also slugging it out to the left of Meade's division. Two small Virginia brigades under generals who would gain lasting fame at Gettysburg, Brig. Gen. Richard Garnett and Brig. Gen. James Kemper, fought Brig. Gen. John Hatch's division (I Corps). During the difficult journey up the side of the mountain, the Union troops encountered an elderly woman who emphatically told them, "Don't go up there. There are hundreds of 'em up there...Some of you might get hurt." The men just smiled and continued picking their way up the slope. D. H. Hill watched the Union troops move up the mountainside with a mixture of awe and dread. "His colors were all flying, and the alignment of his men seemed perfectly preserved. From the top of the mountain the sight was grand and sublime." The subsequent fight was a numerical mismatch, and the Virginians were driven up the side of the mountain. By nightfall, two I Corps divisions had driven four small Confederate brigades from their defensive positions at a cost of 639 men. The Confederates lost 941.[14]

Turner's Gap

While three of Hatch's brigades clobbered the Confederate defenders on the Frosttown Plateau, a fourth brigade under Brig. Gen. John Gibbon marched straight up the National Road. The future "Iron Brigade" encountered Col. Alfred Colquitt's brigade on the side of the mountain and the two sides battled until night enveloped the area. Colquitt described the action in his report: "Confident in their superior numbers, the enemy's forces advanced to a short distance of our own lines, when, raising a shout, they came to a charge…they were met by a terrific musketry…this gave a sudden check to their advance. They rallied under cover of the uneven ground, and the fight opened in earnest. They made still another effort to advance, but were kept back by the study fire of our men."

Colquitt's men accomplished their task of holding the enemy at bay and then joined the other Confederate brigades who had been bested on the plateau in retreating up the mountainside. By midnight, the Confederates had abandoned Turner's Gap and were streaming through Boonsboro on their way to Antietam Creek. The I Corps, so thoroughly thrashed at Second Bull Run when it was part of the Army of Virginia (designated then as the III Corps), could spend a night on the battlefield as victors. They would march the next day to Boonsboro or Keedysville to take on Longstreet's wing of Lee's army, or so they thought. Gibbon's men lost 318 men on the slopes of South Mountain with little to show for it; Colquitt's Confederates lost 109. Colquitt noted in his report, "Not an inch of ground was yielded. The ammunition of many of the men was exhausted, but they stood with bayonets fixed."[15]

Crampton's Gap

McClellan provided clear orders to VI Corps commander, Maj. Gen. William Franklin, at 6:20 p.m. on September 13: "Having gained the pass, your duty will be first to cut off, destroy, or capture McLaws's command and relieve Colonel Miles [and the Harpers Ferry garrison]." So, while the I and IX Corps were tasked with battling Longstreet's wing, McClellan wanted the VI Corps, with assistance from Couch's division, to relieve the siege on Harpers Ferry. South Mountain stood in their way, so they needed to cross at one of the gaps. There were several, but Franklin selected Crampton's Gap

Map 15: The Preliminary Antietam Campaign Battles
A= Frosttown Plateau/Turner's Gap
B= Crampton's Gap

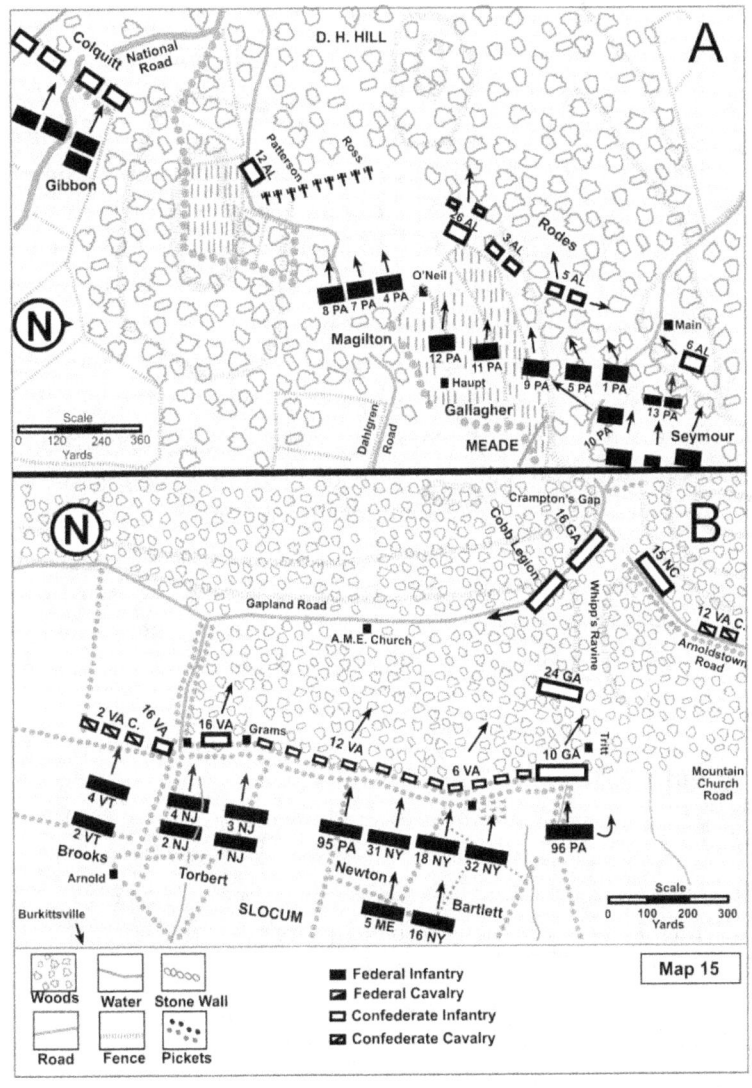

because it was not excessively steep, had good roads leading to and from it, and would place the men in close proximity to McLaws' and Anderson's divisions in the Pleasant Valley.[16]

Franklin's men camped at Buckeystown, Maryland, the night before, so it was a 14-mile trek to Crampton's Gap. The column moved out at 6:00 a.m. on September 14 and halted just beyond Jefferson, waiting for Couch's division to appear. When it didn't, Gen. Franklin again put his command on the road sometime between 10:00 and 10:30 a.m. Only three Confederate brigades under Brig. Gen. Paul Semmes opposed Franklin. He was responsible for defending both Brownsville Pass and Crampton's Gap, but with too few men to guard either, he gambled the enemy would attempt to force its way through the former and put most of his troops there. He sent Col. William Parham's tiny Virginia brigade to Crampton's Gap where it joined some cavalry units and eight companies of the 10th Georgia (Semmes' brigade). Parham had at most 1,000 men to defend the gap against as many as 12,000 enemy troops in the VI Corps. While Franklin again rested his command at midday, the Confederate defenders deployed for action. Col. William Munford, commander of the 2nd Virginia Cavalry, was first on the field, and Col. Parham wisely allowed him to command the sector after the infantry arrived. Rather than deploying his men at the top of South Mountain, Munford deployed the three infantry regiments and one cavalry regiment at its base.[17]

Maj. Gen. Henry Slocum's division led the VI Corps to Crampton's Gap, entering Burkittsville at the base of the mountain, sometime between 3:30 and 4:00 p.m. Brig. Gen. Alfred Torbert's brigade formed on the left of the attacking line, Col. Joseph Bartlett's on the right and Brig. Gen. John Newton's in reserve behind it. Brig. Gen. W. T. Brooks' brigade (Maj. Gen. William Smith's division) arrived and deployed on the left of Torbert's brigade. The Union brigade commanders conferred and realized "nothing but a united charge would dislodge the enemy and win the battle," so the attack began. Yelling "Remember Manassas and Gaines' Mill," the Union soldiers, who had never tasted victory in battle, sprinted toward the Virginians and Georgians behind the stone wall at the base of the mountain. The defenders knew a mismatch when they saw one, abandoned their posts and sprinted up the side of the hill with the Union soldiers in close pursuit.

Confederate reinforcements from Brig. Gen. Howell Cobb's brigade rushed to the scene. Cobb probably thought about his orders from division commander, McLaws: "Hold the gap if it cost the life of every man in [your] command." Cobb's men arrived too late to be of much help, for as soon as they appeared and began moving into position about halfway down the mountainside, Slocum's men were already scaling the heights. Cobb's Legion, a small infantry battalion under Lt. Col. Jefferson Lamar, was hit just as it deployed. It could have escaped, but its commander decided to remain in place and attempt to hold back the enemy to allow the retreating Southern soldiers to gain freedom. It was a mistake, as the unit lost 80% of its men in a short time, including its commander. The victorious Union soldiers continued clawing their way up to the summit where Cobb rallied some survivors to make a last ditch effort. It was too little, too late, and they were swept away. The Confederates lost 962 men in the desperate fighting at Crampton's Gap; the Federals lost 533.[18]

The VI Corps now occupied Crampton's Gap and nothing stood between it and the rear of McLaws' command in Pleasant Valley. Darkness had fallen and Franklin decided to rest his men. McClellan was jubilant when he learned of the victory at 1:00 a.m., and ordered Franklin to move into the Valley. McClellan spent time laying plans for Franklin to relieve the siege, combine with Miles' garrison, and then march up to Boonsboro to join the rest of the army in destroying Lee. But during the night, McLaws brought up six brigades and spread them across the width of Pleasant Valley to prevent a Union movement toward Harpers Ferry. A disturbed Franklin chose to wait for Couch's division to join him. The great battle in Pleasant Valley and the relief of Harpers Ferry never occurred, as the garrison surrendered that morning.[19]

September 14, which began with such high hopes for McClellan, ended with disappointment. While the Confederates were forced from all of their defensive positions, nightfall put an end to the pursuit, allowing Lee's men to march to Antietam Creek and Sharpsburg beyond.

The Pennsylvania Campaign of 1863

Winchester

Lt. Gen. Richard Ewell's Second Corps made good progress moving north in the Shenandoah Valley in mid-June 1863. The Blue Ridge Mountains shielded Lee's invading columns from being seen by Union spies, but enemy troops occupied part of the Valley, particularly at Berryville, Martinsburg, and Winchester. Maj. Gen. Robert Rodes' division, with support from Brig. Gen. Alfred Jenkins' brigade of mounted infantry, was ordered to Berryville, occupied by a 1,800-man Union brigade under Col. Andrew McReynolds. After successfully capturing or driving away the garrison there, the two units were to next turn their attention to Martinsburg, where Col. Benjamin Smith's 1,300 men guarded the Baltimore & Ohio Railroad. Ewell's other two divisions were to head directly for Winchester, where Maj. Gen. Robert Milroy was holed up with about 8,000 men. Maj. Gen. Edward Johnson's division would advance straight from the south to distract Milroy, while Maj. Gen. Jubal Early's division looped around to the left and take Winchester from the west. Ewell reported "The fortifications of Winchester were only assailable from the west and northwest." He decided to use the same successful tactics Stonewall Jackson employed a year earlier, putting Milroy in a difficult position. Milroy had been warned multiple times to evacuate the town over the past six months, but ignored the orders, believing his strongly fortified position could halt any Confederate attack against it.

The initial encounter took place on the morning of June 12 when a Union cavalry patrol encountered Johnson's division south of Winchester. Milroy remained in denial. "I deemed it impossible that Lee's army with its immense artillery and baggage trains, could have escaped from the Army of the Potomac, and crossed the Blue Ridge." However, Milroy took no chances and began deploying his men. June 13 found Ewell's two divisions moving into position. Early's division arrived first and headed straight for Winchester, encountering several of Milroy's troops south of town. A well-timed counterattack drove Early's men backward. Nightfall ended the fighting.

Rodes' division was also stymied from capturing a Union garrison on June 13. He pointed his division toward Millwood, south of Berryville, using back roads to avoid detection, but it didn't work, as Union cavalry observed the movement and hastened to Berryville to warn the garrison there. Jenkins' mounted men were supposed to screen the division's movement, but did a poor job of it, causing Rodes to complain his column would not have been seen if "General Jenkins occupied Millwood during the night before, as he was ordered to do." Rodes decided to immediately push on to Berryville, hoping to engage and defeat the garrison there. He quickly deployed his men and looped some around the town, only to find that the "birds had flown." Jenkins' brigade, who rode ahead of Rodes' division, again failed, this time to pin the enemy in place at Berryville. In the absence of orders from Ewell, Rodes continued his march to Martinsburg on June 14. With Jenkins' brigade again riding ahead, the enemy evacuated the town unscathed. Two garrisons had eluding Rodes' grasp and he blamed Jenkins for both.

The Confederates in siege formations outside of Winchester were also frustrated by their lack of progress on June 14. While Johnson's division remained south of Winchester, Early sent three of his brigades with 20 cannon on a circuitous march around to the west, where they drove some of Milroy's men from West Fort, but night again put an end to the fighting.[20]

Milroy assembled his brigade commanders at 9:00 p.m. that night to discuss options. He knew a retreat now would provide credence to all of the orders he had received over the past six months to vacate the town, and he did not wish to admit he was wrong. With the enemy encircling the town, he felt he no choice but to attempt a night escape. Milroy put his division on Martinsburg Pike between 1:00 and 2:00 a.m. on June 15. Stealth was the order of the night as accoutrements were muffled as the men slipped out of town. Wagons would be too noisy and were left behind, as were the cannons, which were spiked before being abandoned. Excess ammunition that could not be carried was dumped in wells. The moonless night helped cover the movement and the noise was overshadowed by the sound of Early's men busily digging entrenchments prior to the next day's battle.[21]

Stephenson's Depot

Milroy was feeling increasingly confident about successfully slipping away as the hours passed and the sky brightened. Then he heard a smattering of musket fire up ahead toward the van of his column and began feeling a bit uneasy. He could not have known that Ewell anticipated his breakout. While Milroy was meeting with his senior officers at 9:00 p.m., Johnson's division left its position south of Winchester, looped to the northeast, and took up a position south of Martinsburg Pike at a small hamlet called Stephenson's Depot. Two of Johnson's brigades were sliding into position just as Milroy's column approached and the night began giving way to day. Brig. Gen. Washington Elliott immediately brought up his Union brigade, quickly deployed it for action, and then attacked the unknown foe to the right of the road. He was unaware that two Confederate brigades were deployed along the railroad cut of the Winchester & Potomac Railroad, who quickly cut down Elliott's men. Col. William Ely's Union brigade arrived next and it too deployed for action. Ely's brigade attacked and its men were also knocked about by the unseen enemy behind the railroad embankment as a second attack by Elliott's brigade met the same fate.

The Stonewall Brigade arrived to reinforce the two Confederate brigades behind the railroad embankment. With the enemy in obvious disarray after its unsuccessful attacks, the Virginians were launched toward the road. A couple of regiments looped to the right and formed perpendicular to Martinsburg Road, thus cutting off an escape in that direction. Brig. Gen. James Walker, the Stonewall Brigade's commander, reported the "enemy gave way, and retreated back from the pike in disorder at the first fire, returning only a straggling and inaccurate fire…they made no stand, but hoisted a white flag, and surrendered to the two regiments [2nd and 5th Virginia] before the others came up."

While the Stonewall Brigade was fighting it out with Milroy's troops along the Martinsburg Pike, Col. Andrew McReynolds' Union brigade arrived. Milroy quickly ordered it into action, but rather than launching a futile frontal attack against the main Confederate line, he ordered the brigade to take on the enemy's left flank. It was a good tactic, but the Confederates saw it coming and shifted some regiments to face it, ending the ardent attempt to drive the Confederates away, clear the road, and allow Milroy's men to make their way to safety. Many of Milroy's men threw up their hands as they feared escape was not an option. Milroy lost half of his men at Stephenson's Depot—about 4,500 or so. Most, about 3,900, were captured, the rest of Milroy's command scattered. The Confederates lost only about 270 men. The

Map 16: The Preliminary Gettysburg Campaign Battles
A= Winchester
B= Stephenson's Depot

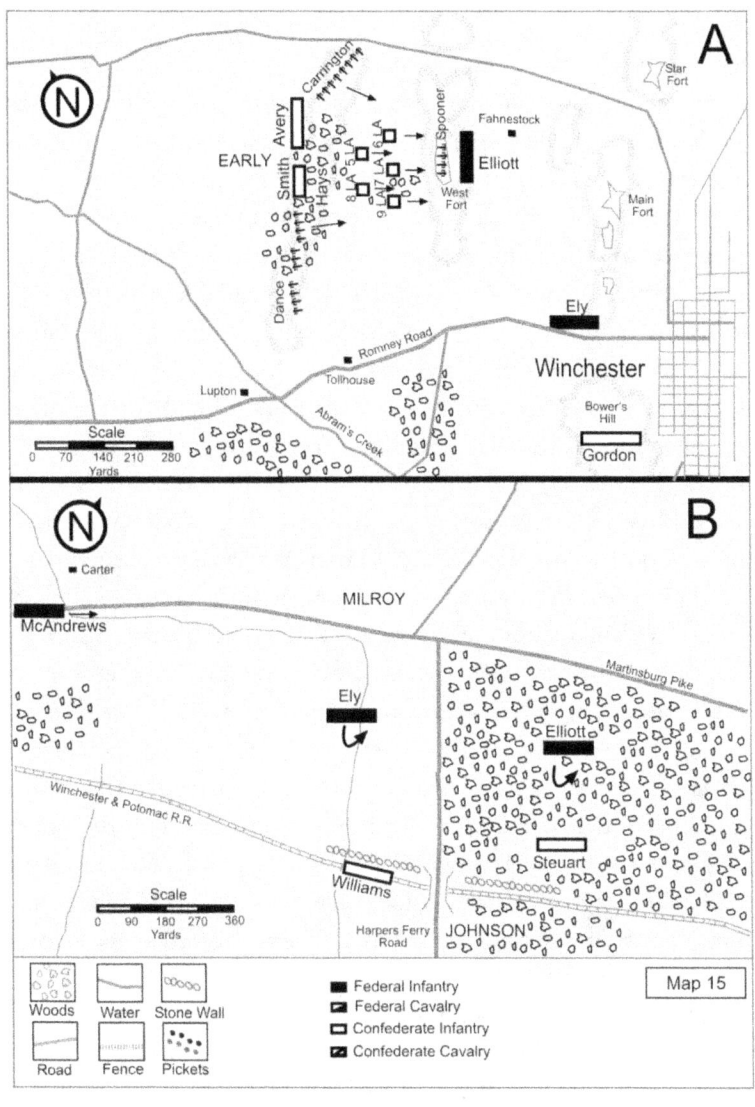

haul at Winchester brought the Confederates 200,000 rounds of ammunition, 300 loaded wagons, 23 cannon, over 300 hundred horses/mules, and a large quantity of supplies.[22]

Cavalry Battles

Cavalry actions, large and small, characterized the Pennsylvania Campaign. Early in the campaign, on June 9, 1863, Pleasonton launched a surprise attack on Jeb Stuart's division, whom he believed to be concentrated around Culpeper Court House, Virginia. Hooker thought the venerable Confederate cavalry leader was planning yet another raid into Northern territory and decided a surprise attack could staunch Jeb Stuart's urges. The battle of Brandy Station began at daylight with a complex pincer movement involving Pleasonton's three divisions. Stuart was not, however, at Culpeper, as his troops were scattered about, most were at or near Brandy Station, closer to the Rappahannock River. This resulted in a disjointed cavalry fight that became the largest on American soil. Brig. Gen. John Buford's division splashed across the river first and attacked Brig. Gen. William Jones' unprepared Confederate brigade. His Virginians were dispersed and so were many of the horses, so those few still able to jump on their mounts, did so shirtless or shoeless, or both. They were able to hold Buford at bay, despite desperate mounted charges around St. James Church. Other units arrived to reinforce Jones' men, as Buford opened a new front near Yew Ridge. Brig. Gen. David Gregg's Union division, which was on its way to Culpeper Court House, was ordered to abort its mission and head to Brandy Station. Its route put it on Stuart's right flank and rear. Jones again saved the day by shoving some of his units toward Fleetwood Hill, which stood between Stuart and Gregg. The resulting charge and counter-charge occupied Gregg's attention, preventing him from working in conjunction with Buford's attacks on other parts of Stuart's line.

Although surprised and outnumbered, Stuart was able to hold out until nightfall, when Pleasonton decided to call it quits. Many of Pleasonton's men lost faith in their leader because of the lost opportunity to crush Stuart's dispersed force. Charles Adams, one of Pleasonton's officers claimed, "I am sure a good cavalry officer would have whipped Stuart out of his boots; but

Pleasonton is not and never will be." Despite the shortcomings of Pleasonton and some of his leaders, the Union cavalry showed its mettle against Stuart's formidable mounted force. One of Stuart's aides explained how the battle "made the Federal Cavalry. Up to that time confessedly inferior to the Southern horsemen, they gained on this day that confidence in themselves and their commanders which enabled them to contest so fiercely the subsequent battlefield." Stuart's actions were called into question for the first time in the war.[23]

June 17 – 21 saw extensive cavalry actions just east of the Blue Ridge Mountains. Hooker, in desperate need of information about the location and movements of Lee's army, sent Pleasonton (whose corps was now consolidated into two divisions) west to try to force his way through one of the mountain gaps, where he could see what was happening in the Shenandoah Valley. This resulted in intense cavalry fights at Aldie, Middleburg, and Upperville. With each fight, Pleasonton progressively pushed Stuart back toward the gaps, but was never able to achieve his ultimate goal. The Union commander and his lieutenants showed an alarming propensity to not coordinate movements and attack piecemeal, thus dissipating their strength.[24]

Lee relied on Stuart to accomplish two major tasks: Screen the army's movements and be aware of Hooker's whereabouts. Lee cast these aside when he agreed to Stuart's cavalry raid into Maryland and Pennsylvania. The foray led to several cavalry fights at Westminster, Maryland, and Hanover and Hunterstown, Pennsylvania. The first of these fights, at Westminster, involved a foolhardy charge by two companies of the 1st Delaware Cavalry against the head of Stuart's column. The Blue Hens lost 67 of their 95 men during their several attacks on June 29. However, it delayed Stuart's progress in finding Lee's army. The fight at Hanover was most intense and occurred when Stuart accidently bumped into Brig. Gen. Judson Kilpatrick's division's rearguard. The two sides fought in and around the town until darkness put an end to the fighting. Again, Stuart wasted valuable time he could have been spending looking for Lee's army. The tables were turned on July 2, when Farnsworth encountered Brig. Gen. Wade Hampton's brigade's rearguard at Hunterstown. The sharp little fight accomplished little except to delay both units' arrival on the Gettysburg battlefield.[25]

Comparisons of the Two Campaigns

The two campaigns share several striking similarities. In both cases, a troublesome Federal garrison stood in Lee's path to success. He expected both to evacuate long before his army approached and, when they didn't, decided to reduce them. During the Maryland Campaign, Lee fully expected Harpers Ferry and other nearby garrisons to be abandoned, but General-in-Chief Halleck refused to allow their evacuation. The situation was somewhat different in the Pennsylvania Campaign. Perhaps Halleck had learned his lesson about leaving garrisons vulnerable to attack, so he sent multiple messages over a six-month period to Milroy to evacuate Winchester. Milroy was able to parry these orders and disaster resulted.

The size and complexity of the preliminary operations differed. The siege of Harpers Ferry and the dispersion of Lee's army led to bitter combat on September 14. The fight at Crampton's Gap was a desperate attempt to rescue the Harpers Ferry garrison. While portions of the VI Corps were successful in gaining the gap and driving down into the Pleasant Valley, the Confederate division commander quickly spread six brigades across the valley to blunt any Union attempt to drive south and lift the siege. The parallel fights at Fox's Gap, Turner's Gap, and the Frosttown Plateau all had the goal of punching through South Mountain to attack isolated portions of Lee's army. These actions, while tactically successful, did not achieve their desired goal as Longstreet pulled his units toward Sharpsburg that night.

Reducing several garrisons was also a centerpiece prior to the battle of Gettysburg. While the Confederates drove the Union garrisons from Winchester, Berryville and Martinsburg, they were not able to bag them, and only the fight at Stephenson's Depot resulted in the capture of a large number of prisoners and supplies.

The preliminary actions in both campaigns resulted in a significant number of Union prisoners, supplies and equipment. The surrender of the Harpers Ferry garrison during the Maryland Campaign yielded significantly more prisoners, ammunition, cannon, and supplies. While Ewell's haul was not as great during the Pennsylvania Campaign, the quantities were nevertheless significant and buoyed the spirits of the entire Confederate army, while depressing the Union's.

The Confederate Second Corps played a major role in reducing the garrisons in both campaigns. While the corps structure did not exist during the Maryland Campaign, two of Stonewall Jackson's divisions (under Lawton and J. R. Jones) would go on to play a major role in attacking Winchester (under Early and Johnson) in 1863.

The dates of the campaigns are surprisingly similar. The Confederates began moving into position to capture Harpers Ferry on September 13 and began their push against Winchester on June 13 during the Pennsylvania Campaign. The surrender of the entire Harpers Ferry garrison (Maryland Campaign) occurred on September 15 and a large portion of the Winchester garrison surrendered on June 15 at Stephenson's Depot (Pennsylvania Campaign).

The captures of these garrisons occurred at different periods during the campaign and had vastly different impacts on future events. The capture of Harpers Ferry occurred during the final period of the campaign, just two days before the battle of Antietam, delaying the arrival of Lee's troops. Lee was fortunate McClellan did not launch a full-scale attack on the afternoon of September 15, as none of Jackson's six divisions would have been on the field at that time and McClellan would face only three decimated Confederate divisions. The impact of Stephenson's Depot and the capture of much of the Winchester garrison did not have as great an impact as it occurred during the second phase of the move north, 16 days before the battle of Gettysburg.

The cavalry tangled during both campaigns, but the combat was more extensive during the Pennsylvania Campaign, where large scale fights occurred at Brandy Station, in front of the Blue Ridge Mountain gaps, and at Hanover, Pennsylvania, before the battle of Gettysburg. The less well stocked cavalry did not engage in as much combat during the Maryland Campaign. They were engaged in fighting during the early part of the campaign, but those could be considered little more than skirmishes. Most of the cavalry's activities involved scouting and screening, but little fighting during the 1862 campaign.

Table 15: Comparison of the Preliminary Fights

Issue	Maryland Campaign	Pennsylvania Campaign
Fights	Harpers Ferry South Mountain passes	Winchester Stephenson's Depot Large cavalry battles
Impact on Lee's objectives?	Yes: forced Lee to halt his invasion and wait for Jackson	No: battles occurred while troops were en route to Pennsylvania
Length of time for garrison to fall	Harpers Ferry: three days (September 13-15)	Winchester: three days (June 13-15)
Captured men/material		
- Men	12,700	3,900
- Cannon	47	23
- Small arms	13,000	unknown
- Ammunition	unknown	200,000 rounds
- Horses/mules	unknown	300
- Wagons	200	300

Chapter 11: The Final Marches to the Battlefield

The Maryland Campaign of 1862

The armies converged on the small town of Sharpsburg as early as September 15 when elements of D. H. Hill's division marched along Boonsboro Pike from Keedysville to Antietam Creek, crossing at the Middle Bridge, beginning at daylight. The men had desperately fought to hold the area around the Fox's and Turner's Gaps' sectors for portions of the prior day and had marched all night, so were exhausted and relished a well-deserved rest. The division rested just east of Sharpsburg near the pike until Longstreet's two divisions, D. R. Jones' and John Hood's, arrived later in the day. These troops were probably also at the limit of their endurance. They left Hagerstown during the morning of September 14 and made a forced 13-mile march to reach Turner's Gap. After fighting through the afternoon and into the evening, the men left the South Mountain battlefields later that night and marched to Sharpsburg. Jones' division extended the line south and Hood was sent along Hagerstown Pike to the Dunker Church and West Woods, forming at a 90-degree angle to the rest of the army. These units faced Antietam Creek, the direction of McClellan's arrival on the battlefield.[1]

With the surrender of Harpers Ferry, Stonewall Jackson prepared to put his three divisions on the road for Sharpsburg, but it would take some time, as the men needed three-day's rations. Half of Lawton's division were issued rations from Harpers Ferry and immediately began their march. The other half of the division and J. R. Jones' division were required to wait for theirs and did not begin cooking them until 3:00 p.m. The last two brigades of Lawton's division finally began the 14-mile trek at about 1:00 a.m. on September 16 and overtook the rest of the division, bivouacking near Shepherdstown. The recombined division reached the Potomac River at Shepherdstown (Boteler's) Ford by dawn, splashed across and halted in woods west of Sharpsburg, where they joined J. R. Jones' division, which had passed Lawton's men on the march. The all-night march would be difficult under any circumstances, but Jackson's poorly clad and shod men were exhausted, having been under arms since September 10. Jackson, never known to exaggerate, called the march, "severe."

Jackson invited McLaws and Walker to Harpers Ferry to discuss their movements northward to Sharpsburg soon after the garrison fell. Walker wasted time attempting to find a ford over the Shenandoah River and when he couldn't find one, ordered his men around the mountain to Key's Ford. He finally crossed after dark on September 15 and halted near Halltown, where his men received rations and rested. The men were back on the road at 1:00 a.m. on September 16, reaching the Shepherdstown Ford between daylight and sunrise. McLaws had a more difficult time, as he could not move north because many of his troops blocked the Union VI Corps in Pleasant Valley. When Franklin stood down, McLaws brought his men to the pontoon bridge over the Potomac River linking Maryland with Harpers Ferry. However, a long line of captured prisoners clogged the bridge, forcing McLaws' men to cool their heels until 2:00 a.m. on September 16. They reached Halltown at 8:00 a.m., where the men rested until 3:00 p.m., and then began their tortuous all-night march to within two miles of Shepherdstown. Here, McLaws received an urgent message to come quickly to Sharpsburg. The van of McLaws' column reached Lee's headquarters on the west side of town around sunrise. By 9:00 a.m., all but one of Lee's divisions was on the battlefield.[2]

McClellan expected his troops to converge on Sharpsburg as quickly as possible on September 15, and noted in his report, "Orders were given to corps commanders to press forward the pickets at early dawn. This advance revealed the fact that the enemy had left his position and an immediate pursuit was ordered." McClellan sent the I, II, and XII Corps via National Road to Boonsboro and then toward Keedysville on Boonsboro Pike. Burnside with his IX Corps was to either head toward Brownsville, if Franklin needed help, or Sharpsburg if he didn't. He received the following directive during the morning of September 15: "General McClellan desires to impress upon you the necessity for the utmost vigor in your pursuit." Word of Lee's wholesale movement to escape McClellan's clutches caused headquarters to send another message to Burnside: the Rebels are "retreating in disorder for the Shepherdstown Ferry." If Burnside could corroborate this information, he was to "follow the enemy up by Porterstown and Sharpsburg. Keep open your communications with Sumner, on your right, and Franklin on the left." There was no sign of hesitancy here—McClellan had Lee on the ropes and he was moving in for the kill before he could escape into Virginia.

Burnside received three dispatches from McClellan's headquarters between 8:00 and 9:30 a.m. to move expeditiously. Burnside decided to wait for his troops to be resupplied with food, but the wagons were delayed. Sykes' division (V Corps) arrived at Fox's Gap, fully expecting it to be clear of Burnside's men, as he had been informed four hours earlier to begin his march after Lee's army. Sykes found the gap clogged with Burnside's men and was given permission to march through them and head for Sharpsburg. The delay annoyed McClellan, who ordered an aide to write Burnside: "I am instructed to call upon you for explanations for these failures on your part to comply with the orders given you…the commanding general cannot lightly regard such marked departure from the tenor of his instructions."[3]

Sykes' division (V Corps), with the tardy IX Corps marching behind it, made its way down Old Sharpsburg Road to Boonsboro and then on to Keedysville. Franklin's VI Corps remained near Brownsville, facing six Confederate brigades spread across the Pleasant Valley. The cessation of artillery fire on the morning of September 15 told Franklin the garrison had surrendered.

McClellan informed his commanders on September 15, "If the enemy were overtaken on the march, they should be attacked at once; if found in heavy force and in position, the corps in advance should be placed in position for attack, and await my arrival." When McClellan arrived at Antietam Creek that afternoon, he found only two divisions—Richardson's (II Corps) on the right of Boonsboro Pike and Sykes' (V Corps) on the left side. McClellan pulled out his field glasses and noted the enemy occupying a strong position on the heights on the opposite (west) side of Antietam Creek. Although Lee had fewer than 15,000 men in position, he made sure the 62 battle flags were conspicuously displayed to give the impression of twice their numbers. It worked, for McClellan decided to await the arrival of the rest of his troops, which were involved in a major traffic jam along Boonsboro Pike. James Longstreet watched the Union buildup on the opposite side of the creek and was equally impressed: "The number increased, and larger and larger grew the field of blue until it seemed to stretch as far as the eye could see, and from the tops of the mountains down to the edges of the stream gathered the great army of McClellan. It was an awe inspiring spectacle as this grand force settled down in sight of the Confederates."4

Although McClellan was frustrated by the time it was taking for his army to converge on Sharpsburg, he set about positioning his artillery on the bluffs overlooking Antietam Creek. He also began thinking about a tactical plan to take on Lee. When the I Corps finally arrived as light was fading on September 15, Hooker sent it a mile and a half upstream to bivouac in the fork between Antietam and Little Antietam Creeks.5

September 16 dawned bright, but a ground haze obscured the view. Lee was on Cemetery Hill, refreshed from his first good night's sleep in days. He strained his eyes to see what McClellan was doing across Antietam Creek. Lee had about 10,930 infantrymen and 63 skillfully placed cannon in position that morning. He was feeling a bit more confident when he learned the van of Jackson's column had reached the Potomac River and would soon appear. Lawton's and J. R. Jones' divisions had camped about four miles from Boteler's Ford and were crossing the river by dawn and heading directly to Sharpsburg. McLaws' and Anderson's divisions were on the march and were slated to arrive on the morning of September 17.6

While pacing among his guns on Cemetery Hill on September 16, Lee apparently pondered the possibly of moving north toward Hagerstown as soon as McLaws' and Anderson's divisions reached the battlefield. To this end, he sent Jeb Stuart and three cavalry regiments north to reconnoiter routes. He also sent his spare wagons rumbling back across the Potomac River to lighten his army.7

McClellan had other plans and slammed the door on Lee. Virtually all of McClellan's army were in motion toward Antietam Creek, or already there, on September 16. Halleck could read a map and he expressed concern about Jackson marching up from Harpers Ferry and falling on McClellan's left flank. McClellan decided to leave Franklin's VI Corps in Pleasant Valley and make Burnside aware of the potential dangers to his own left flank. He knew there were three major bridges spanning Antietam Creek that could be used to cross his troops to get to Lee, and he stationed troops in front of each of them. The XII Corps marched to Keedysville during the late morning and massed just west of the village. Morell's division (V Corps) also arrived and settled on the left of Boonsboro Pike near Sykes' division, recombining the V

Corps. The IX Corps came up and moved further south to occupy the area opposite the Lower Bridge and watch for Jackson's possible arrival. The I Corps settled in opposite the Upper Bridge and the II Corps was in between.[8]

With the troops moving into position, the battle was about to begin.

The Pennsylvania Campaign of 1863

Only John Buford's cavalry division occupied Gettysburg on the morning of the battle, having arrived about 11:00 a.m. the day before. While Buford made his headquarters at the Eagle Hotel in Gettysburg, he sent one brigade (Col. William Gamble's) west of town and a second (Col. Thomas Devin's) north to await the enemy's expected arrival. Buford's arrival in town was witnessed by Brig. Gen. James Pettigrew's brigade, which was marching toward Gettysburg from Cashtown. Pettigrew quickly retraced his steps back toward Cashtown.

Troops flowed onto the battlefield during the first two days of the fight. The Confederates began arriving first: Maj. Gen. Henry Heth's division arrived from the west, taking on Gamble's troopers at first light on July 1. The Union I Corps arrived next and Brig. Gen. James Wadsworth's division blocked Heth's path to Gettysburg. Most of the morning involved fighting between these two units. The Union XI Corps arrived next, and it moved north where Maj. Gen. Robert Rodes' men were deploying for action on Oak Hill at about noon. Two additional Confederate divisions arrived: Maj. Gen. Dorsey Pender's (Third Corps) approached from the west during the late morning and Maj. Gen. Jubal Early's division (Second Corps), appeared to the north at about 2:30 p.m. Pender drove the I Corps into Gettysburg from the west and Early's and Rodes' division did the same to the XI Corps north of town later that afternoon.[9]

The remainder of the troops arriving on July 1 did not appear until after the fighting was over for the day. The XII Corps reached Rock Creek at about 4:00 p.m. and the III Corps began arriving at 5:30 p.m. Johnson's Confederate division (Ewell's Second Corps) arrived at 7:00 p.m. after a 25-mile march.

Lee finally arrived on the battlefield on the afternoon of July 1, surveying the situation and chastising Heth for bringing on the engagement. He finally decided to unleash the full fury of his attacks when he realized his troops arriving from the north and west could well trap the enemy in a deadly vise. Meade did not arrive until just after midnight on July 2 (see below).

Several units, from both armies, marched through the night of July 1-2 to arrive during the pre-dawn hours of the second day of the battle, including the Union V Corps and Hood's and McLaws' divisions (First Corps). Two units were still on the march to the battlefield well into July 2: The Union VI Corps completed its epic 18-hour, 36-mile march at 3:00 p.m. and Pickett's division left Chambersburg and marched 23 miles to Gettysburg, arriving about 2:30 p.m. James Bowen of the 37th Massachusetts described the VI Corps' march: "It was a hot, breathless July day. The sun poured down with merciless, unbroken heat, and the dust that rose in great lazy clouds from the highway enveloped man and horse…in its all-embracing mantle of torture…strong men gasped and staggered and fell…"[10]

Comparisons of the Two Campaigns

Although Lee did not wish to fight at Sharpsburg, he had the luxury of occupying the ground for a couple of days before the battle. This permitted his army to get a better understanding of the terrain and develop a defensive strategy. Likewise, McClellan reached the sector on September 15 and had time to survey the battlefield with his field glasses and prepare his offensive plans. The situation was quite different at Gettysburg, where neither commander was on the field at the start of the battle.

By the start of the battle of Antietam, Lee had most of his troops on or very near the battlefield. A. P. Hill's division at Harpers Ferry was the exception and it would not arrive until the battle was almost over. Likewise, most of the Union units that fought at Antietam arrived at least the day before the battle. The VI Corps was the exception, as it arrived about noon on the day of the battle. As at Gettysburg, it was the last Union unit to arrive.

Only Union cavalry were in the Gettysburg area just before the battle and both sides' armies arrived in a piecemeal fashion. Large units were still approaching the battlefield on the second day of the fight and that certainly influenced how the battle was waged.

Table 16: Comparison of the Final Marches to the Battlefield

Issue	Maryland Campaign	Pennsylvania Campaign
Percentage of army present on the morning of the battle	**Confederate:** 67% **Union:** 83%	**Confederate:** None **Union:** Under 3%
Furthest march to get to the battlefield	**Confederate:** about 15 mi. (H. Ferry) **Union:** about 8 mi. (Pleasant Valley)	**Confederate:** about 28 mi. (Carlisle) **Union:** about 36 mi. (Manchester)
When last unit arrived on the battlefield	**Confederate:** About 3:30 p.m. on September 17 **Union:** Noon on September 17	**Confederate:** 2:30 p.m. on July 2 **Union:** 3:00 p.m. on July 2
When army commanders arrived	**Confederate:** September 15 **Union:** September 15	**Confederate:** Afternoon of July 1 **Union:** Night of July 1-2
Last unit to arrive on the battlefield	**Confederate:** A. P. Hill's Division **Union:** VI Corps	**Confederate:** Pickett's Division **Union:** VI Corps

Chapter 12: Battlefield Terrain

Antietam Battlefield

The combat-related portion of the battlefield stretched approximately 2.8 square miles. Antietam Creek, one of its most distinctive features, served as an effective barrier between the two armies. Three narrow bridges and several fords traversed the waterway. The wide Potomac River was a mere three miles to the west. In between the two waterways, the long Sharpsburg Ridge, running roughly in a north-south direction, dominated the landscape. Lee skillfully used this high ground to position his troops and artillery or hide them behind the ridge. He used the highest point, Cemetery Hill, as his observation post for much of the battle.

In the middle to northern part of the battlefield, Sharpsburg Ridge climbs to about 100 feet. The area south of Boonsboro Pike is more rugged with deep ravines and higher ground. For example, the bluff used by Georgia troops defending the Lower Bridge rises almost 200 feet above the span. This is about the same height as Cemetery Hill on which Lee watched much of the fighting. Lee's position also encompassed other high ground, such as Hauser's and Reel Ridges and Nicodemus Heights. All held a multitude of Confederate cannon from time to time. McClellan's army on the east side of the creek also had high ground, slightly higher than Lee's ridgeline, and was a perfect platform for long-range artillery. McClellan took advantage of this feature by placing his long-range "guns of position" there.

Five roads entered Sharpsburg and played important roles in the battle. McClellan's army primarily arrived at Antietam Creek along Boonsboro Pike, as did D. H. Hill's and Longstreet's men who had defended the South Mountain gaps on September 14. Stonewall Jackson's men arrived via Shepherdstown Pike and Miller's Sawmill Road. Once on the battlefield, the troops mostly marched over fields to their assigned positions. There were some exceptions, especially in the northern part of the field, where the Smoketown Road and Hagerstown Pike saw large troop movements at times during the battle.

Many soldiers wrote of the abundant limestone outcroppings they used for cover during the battle. Trees were sparse on the battlefield and were primarily confined to defined woodlots: North Woods, East Woods, and

West Woods. These were open with little to no underbrush because the farmers regularly grazed their livestock there. The area also boasted a number of stone walls used by the soldiers on both sides for protection. The open fields of fire contributed to the large number of casualties and led some historians to label the field as "artillery hell."

The battlefield contained a large number of post-and-rail fences and worm fences, which restricted movements. The numerous cornfields concealed movements until knocked down by artillery and thousands of marching feet. A multitude of plowed fields dotted the terrain.[1]

Gettysburg Battlefield

The combat-related portion of the battlefield stretched approximately 12 square miles. The major defining feature of the Gettysburg battlefield is the high ground. Several ridges run in a north-south orientation, west and south of town. A number of hills, some quite high, also dot the landscape. Meade's right flank rested on Culp's Hill, a rocky and heavily wooded hill just southeast of town. The line continued almost due west to Cemetery Hill (60-80 feet), which, while shorter than Culp's Hill (140 feet), provided a superb artillery platform because of its clear, flat surface. Cemetery Hill tapers to the south to form Cemetery Ridge, which runs for about a mile and a half, where it loses its elevation. The low ground gives rise to Little Round Top (170 feet) further south and about a quarter mile beyond sits Big Round Top (305 feet). The rocky summit of Little Round Top had been logged, so it was fairly open, and although difficult to reach, could provide a good artillery platform for fewer than a dozen Union cannon. The same was not true of Big Round Top which was heavily wooded and steeper, robbing it of any military value. Lee's army enveloped Meade's defensive line and extended from Oak Hill/Ridge to the north, and then ran south along Seminary Ridge, which gives way to Warfield Ridge.

Several small waterways, such as Willoughby Run and Rock Creek were an impediment to Lee's movement, but they did not require bridges or fords to cross. There are also some stone outcroppings in various portions of the terrain that impacted the battle, such as those forming Devil's Den, western side of Little Round Top, and along the Wheatfield. Both armies effectively used these rock outcroppings defensively.

Map 17: Antietam Environs

The battleground was also characterized by an abundance of high-quality roads—ten in number—that entered Gettysburg. Most were in a north-south and east-west orientation, making it easier for the two sides to reach the battlefield. Once present, Meade had the advantage of interior lines, so he could move troops about on Taneytown Road and Baltimore Pike. Lee did not have this luxury as he occupied a larger area utilizing exterior lines.

Much of the battlefield, particularly on the high ground, was wooded, providing shelter for the men of the two armies. However, the area that saw large-scale fighting between Seminary/Warfield Ridge and Cemetery Ridge/Houck's Ridge was fairly open, contributing to a large number of artillery-related casualties.

Because of the region's rocky nature, many stone walls dotted the battlefields. Both sides used these walls to shelter their men and artillery.[2]

Comparisons of the Two Campaigns

The two battlefields boasted commonalities and differences. Given the much larger sizes of the armies, it is not surprising that Gettysburg's battleground was significantly larger than Antietam's. Both battlefields contained high ground, but Gettysburg's tended to be taller and played a more significant role as Lee specifically attempted to capture the high ground on Herr's, McPherson's, and Seminary Ridges on July 1, and Culp's and Cemetery Hills, Little Round Top, and Cemetery Ridge on July 2, and Cemetery Ridge and Culp's Hill on July 3. McClellan at Antietam also tried to capture Lee's high ground, such as around the Dunker Church and Cemetery Hill to neutralize Lee's artillery placed there, and presumably, to place his own in those positions. In both battles, most of the hills were occupied by the army on the defensive: Lee at Antietam; Meade at Gettysburg.

What Antietam did not have in large hills, it made up for in Antietam Creek, which Lee attempted to use as a barrier to the enemy crossing over to his side. Because it was deep, had swift currents, unstable floor, and steep banks, it could only be crossed by means of a few bridges and fords. The results were mixed, however, as Lee did not have enough troops to adequately defend its entire span, and the Union troops initially crossed the creek at its Upper Bridge and nearby fords. The area had another waterway that could have led to Lee's demise. If pushed back by McClellan's troops,

Map 18: Gettysburg Environs

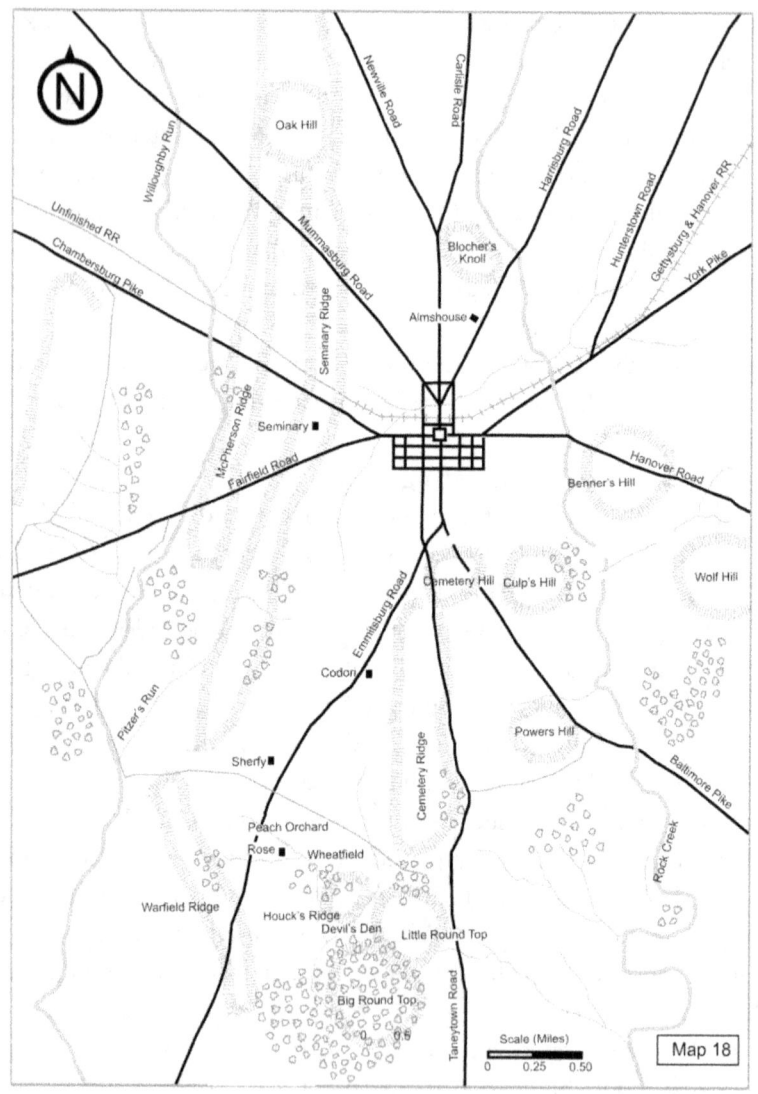

the Potomac River loomed in his rear with few fords and no bridges. Gettysburg had no significant water features.

Both battlefields contained good roads and both Union army commanders used them to move troops around the battlefield. Both battlefields enveloped a town and in both cases the Confederates controlled them during the battle. Both towns were also close to the fighting, but there was actual fighting in the streets of Gettysburg on the evening of the first day's battle and sharpshooter activity occurred between the two sides through the evening of July 3. No Union troops came close enough to the town of Sharpsburg to trigger a fight within it. However, a number of Union artillery shells overshot Lee's positions and caused significant damage in the town.

Both battlefields contained woods, but they tended to be confined to certain areas. Large swaths of the battlegrounds were open, contributing to the deadliness of the artillery. Similarly, both contained stone walls but they were more plentiful on the Gettysburg battlefield. Gettysburg did not have the numerous limestone outcroppings of the Antietam battlefield, however. Finally, because Antietam occurred later in the season, many of the fields had already been harvested.

Table 17: Comparison of the Battlefield Terrain

Issue	Maryland Campaign	Pennsylvania Campaign
Size of the contested areas	2.8 square miles	12 square miles
Roads	Five major roads into town	Ten major roads into town
Hills	Yes, but mostly shorter than Gettysburg's	Yes, but mostly taller than Antietam's
Side occupying town during battle	Confederates	Confederates
Water features that impacted the battle	Yes (Antietam Creek & Potomac River)	Minor role
Abundance of woods	Tended to be confined to certain areas	Tended to be confined to certain areas
Stone structures	Few walls; more outcroppings	More walls; fewer outcroppings
Harvested fields	More	Fewer

Chapter 13: Initial Encounters on the Battlefield Prior to the Battle

The Maryland Campaign of 1862

The two armies had their first encounter the evening before the battle, on the evening of September 16. McClellan ordered Hooker's I Corps across Antietam Creek at 2:00 p.m. to get into position to crush Lee's left flank the following day. Ricketts' and Meade's divisions crossed at the Upper Bridge and Doubleday's splashed across Pry's Ford between 3:00 and 4:00 p.m. Once across, the 10,000 men marched west. When Ricketts' and Doubleday's divisions approached Hagerstown Pike, they turned south through the fields toward the Joseph Poffenberger farm. Meade's division was delayed in crossing the creek, marched west to the Smoketown Road and then followed it south to the Poffenberger farm. McClellan hoped the move would both help identify the location of Lee's left flank and also position the I Corps for the following day's fight. Unbeknownst to McClellan, securing Hagerstown Pike slammed the door on Lee's intended route north. Sending a single corps across Antietam Creek when the rest of the army remained on the east side was risky and McClellan and Hooker both understood it. McClellan attempted to assuage Hooker's fears by sending the XII Corps across Antietam Creek well after dark, and telling him to use these new arrivals as needed.[1]

Lee did not have enough men on September 16 to cover all of the potential Antietam Creek crossings, so he concentrated on the Middle and Lower Bridges and left Fitz Lee's cavalry brigade to patrol along the Upper Bridge on the left flank. These troopers saw Hooker's crossing and immediately sent word to Lee, who was meeting with Jackson and Longstreet at the time. Lee responded by sending Hood's division north, supported by J. R. Jones' and Lawton's divisions, about 8,000 versus Hooker's 18,000.[2]

As Meade's division angled toward its bivouac site during the late afternoon of September 16, Hooker spied high ground just to the south and ordered a brigade into the East Woods. Brig. Gen. Truman Seymour's brigade was in the van, so Meade sent it south. Seymour deployed his 13th Pennsylvania Reserve Regiment as a skirmish line and sent it into the woods in its front. The regiment was dubbed the "Bucktails" because of the distinctive feature worn on the men's hats. Confederate artillery and cavalry opened fire on the Bucktails' steadily advancing line. The Pennsylvanians entered the East Woods and continued south under orders from their commander, Col. Hugh McNeil, to charge and drive the enemy from the woods. He placed himself in front of his men and the unit drove into the East Woods. A volley rang out, and a bullet pierced McNeil's heart, killing him instantly. The line halted about halfway into the woods because of the increasingly heavy fire from the 4th and 5th Texas (Col. William Wofford's brigade, Brig. Gen. John Hood's division) in the cornfield to the west of the East Woods. Hood's other brigade, under Brig. Gen. Evander Law, also advanced to a position just in front of the East Woods and connected with Wofford's right flank, presenting a solid wall against the Bucktails' approach. Seymour brought up the remainder of his brigade and threw them into the lively skirmish. Both sides ordered up artillery, adding to the casualty rolls. The fighting continued for a while in the darkness. "We got mixed up until we hardly knew each other apart in the darkness," recalled Jonathan Stevens of the 5th Texas. The two sides finally broke off their skirmish, the prelude to the following day's battle. Casualties were few, but both sides lost a regimental commander, McNeil and Col. P. Liddell of the 11th Mississippi.[3]

The Pennsylvania Campaign of 1863

Highly educated, intelligent, and wealthy, Brig. Gen. James Pettigrew was new to the Army of Northern Virginia. He and his brigade arrived from North Carolina just prior to the Pennsylvania Campaign, and even though both were combat veterans, Pettigrew had not yet earned the respect of his new superiors and peers. June 30 found Pettigrew and his Tar Heels marching toward Gettysburg from Cashtown at 6:30 a.m. to collect supplies. It is unclear whether Pettigrew or his commander, Maj. Gen. Henry Heth, realized that Maj. Gen. Jubal Early's division had already visited the town on June 26-27, stripping the town of useful supplies. The eight-mile trek in the growing heat ended when Pettigrew and his men approached Seminary Ridge and observed what appeared to be Union cavalry. Some of his men claimed hearing drums beating in the distance, suggesting infantry in the town. Heth's orders to Pettigrew were clear—do not get into a fight with organized enemy

Map 19: The Antietam Battlefield on the Eve of the Battle

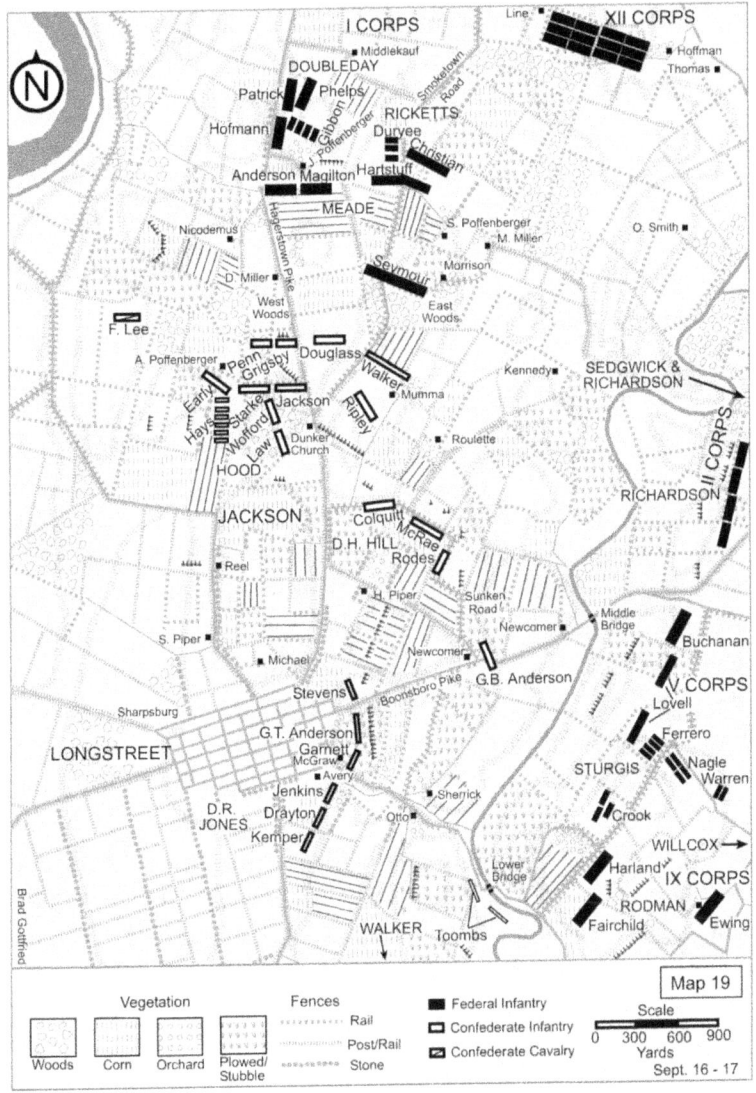

troops, so Pettigrew wisely retraced his steps back to Cashtown. His subsequent interaction with Heth was anything but positive. As Pettigrew gave his report, Third Corps commander, A. P. Hill, rode up and listened. Hill blurted out, the "only force at Gettysburg is cavalry, probably a detachment of observation." He and the rest of Lee's senior officers still believed Meade was far to the south. Heth quickly replied, "If there is no objection, I will take my division tomorrow and go to Gettysburg and get those shoes." Hill replied, "None in the world," and the die was cast.[4]

History would prove Pettigrew correct. A Union cavalry division under Brig. Gen. John Buford had approached Gettysburg from the south. Buford was perhaps the finest cavalry commander in the Union army and he vowed to fight it out against Confederate infantry until his army's infantry arrived and he would do just that the following day. He also knew terrain, and Gettysburg provided an outstanding defensive position for Meade's army.[5]

Comparisons of the Two Campaigns

The two opening interactions could not have been more different. Antietam's began in the late afternoon/early evening and involved heavy skirmishing; Gettysburg's was in the morning and the two forces simply eyeballed each other. Antietam's early interactions involved veteran infantry units that were no stranger to fighting; Gettysburg's warm-up featured the possibility of battle-hardened cavalry against infantry with considerably less combat experience. Both interactions, if used correctly, could have impacted the subsequent battle. This was indeed the case at Antietam, where the interaction served to tell Hooker and McClellan that enemy forces occupied the area near the Cornfield/East Woods and allowed them to plan accordingly. Such was not the case with Gettysburg, as senior Confederate officers discounted the observations of a relatively inexperienced brigade commander and therefore blundered into an unexpected confrontation the following day.

Table 18: Comparison of the Initial Interactions on the Battlefield

Issue	Maryland Campaign	Pennsylvania Campaign
Timing of interaction	Evening before the battle	Morning before the battle
Nature of the combatants	13th Pennsylvania Reserves/Truman Seymour's brigade versus John Hood's division	James Pettigrew's brigade versus John Buford's division
How interactions ended	Night puts an end to the fighting	Pettigrew returns to Cashtown
Impact on subsequent battle	Informs both sides of possible fight the following day	None; the Confederate senior leaders discounted the Pettigrew's observations

PART 3: THE MAJOR BATTLES OF THE CAMPAIGNS

Chapter 14: Battle Plans

The battle of Antietam lasted only a day; Gettysburg three. Historian Ezra Carman wrote, "The battle of Antietam was really three distinct engagements, at different hours of the day, on entirely different parts of the field." Therefore, for comparison purposes the morning phase of Antietam will be compared with July 1 at Gettysburg, the middle phase at Antietam with July 2 at Gettysburg, and the afternoon phase of Antietam with July 3 at Gettysburg.[1]

The Maryland Campaign of 1862

Lee's army became progressively stronger as September 17 approached. Dawn found six of Lee's nine divisions on the fields around Sharpsburg (about 26,000 men), two more were arriving or about to cross the Potomac River (about 7,000 men) and the last was still at Harpers Ferry (about 3,000 men), preparing to begin its march to the battlefield. He correctly predicted "there would not be much fighting on the 16th," believing McClellan would give him another 24 hours to escape the box at Sharpsburg. If McClellan did not attack, Lee strongly considered moving north and giving battle elsewhere. However, the door started closing on Lee's plans to move north on September 16 when the I Corps approached the Joseph Poffenberger farm.[2]

McClellan carefully considered his options when devising his plans to attack Lee's army. The size of Lee's army was still an unknown. Some reliable sources believed it was as large as McClellan's and maybe even much larger. Lee's strong defensive position was also a concern. McClellan called it "one of the strongest to be found in this region of the country, which is well adapted to defensive warfare." He also worried about Stonewall Jackson. Would he move northeast and attack his left flank? It was a distinct possibility as Jackson was known to move fast and boldly. McClellan could not know that Lee told Jackson to get to Sharpsburg using the fastest route possible and that was crossing at the Shepherdstown Ford. Because of this uncertainty, McClellan decided to leave the powerful VI Corps in the Pleasant Valley until the morning of September 17, thus denying a large portion of his army anything more than a supportive role during the battle.[3]

McClellan described his tactical plan in his preliminary report of the battle on October 15, 1862:

> The design was to make the main attack upon the enemy's left—at least to create a diversion in favor of the main attack, with the hope of something more by assailing the enemy's right—and, as soon as one or both of the flank movements were fully successful, to attack their center with any reserve I might then have on hand.[4]

A careful reading of this statement may create some confusion. While it is clear McClellan intended the major attack to be on Lee's left flank, but was the attack a diversion or "something more?"

McClellan elaborated on his plan several months later. Some postulate McClellan framed his statement in light of some of the criticism he was already receiving:

> My plan for impending general engagement was to attack the enemy's left with the corps of Hooker and Mansfield, supported by Sumner's and, if necessary, by Franklin's, and, as soon as matters looked favorably there, to move the corps of Burnside against the enemy's extreme right, upon the ridge running to the south and rear of Sharpsburg, and, having carried their position, to press along the crest toward our right, and, whenever either of these flank movements should be successful, to advance our center with all the forces then disposable.[5]

This statement again clearly indicates the importance of the attack on Lee's left flank, especially since McClellan notes that as many as four full corps might be involved in this effort. This version has Burnside's IX Corps being unleashed, not as a diversion, but a full-scale attack after the fighting to the north was meeting success.

Attacking from the east also posed another complicating factor for McClellan. Because the ridges ran north-south, where Lee skillfully placed his cannon, any attack from the east would likely result in excessive casualties. He therefore chose to initially attack from the north—a direction that would bring him perpendicular to the ridges. This approach was somewhat negated by the high ground around the Dunker Church where Lee placed 19 cannon under Col. Stephen Lee.

Both statements clearly show McClellan wishing to avoid an initial frontal attack on Lee's center or right, partly because McClellan was unsure of Lee's strength—a force that could have equaled or exceeded his own—and partly because of Lee's strong position in and around Sharpsburg. McClellan was also hampered by not being able to see what troops Lee had hiding beyond Sharpsburg Ridge. McClellan had seen the folly of frontal attacks against an enemy with strongly placed artillery on high ground during the prior summer when Lee threw line after line against well-positioned artillery at the battle of Malvern Hill, achieving nothing but heavy casualties.

McClellan therefore decided against a frontal attack in favor of hitting both flanks and, if successful, he could launch a subsequent frontal attack against Lee's middle. Regardless of the size of the Confederate army, McClellan probably expected Lee to move troops about to meet new attacks. The attack on Lee's left could force him to pull troops from other sectors, thus ripening them for subsequent attack. This indeed occurred, as the initial attacks on Lee's left caused him to pull his available reserves from around Sharpsburg and south of the Lower Bridge.

Selecting an initial attack against Lee's left flank also made the most sense, as the Upper Bridge was the only poorly defended crossing over Antietam Creek. As such, McClellan could potentially avoid heavy losses through small arms and artillery fire that would occur by frontal assaults on the Middle or Lower Bridges first. Historian Joseph Harsh believed McClellan reserved the final blow to be against Lee's center, and it would be "expected to crush the Confederate army."[6]

Pennsylvania Campaign of 1863

The two armies collided at Gettysburg on July 1. It was not planned and the leaders did not have the luxury of sitting back and developing tactical approaches to best the other's army. The two widely dispersed armies merely continued travelling along roads converging on Gettysburg. Most of the initial fighting occurred west and north of town because that's the direction from which Lee's troops' arrived on the first day of the battle. Two Confederate divisions, Heth's and Pender's (Third Corps), arrived from the west and two others, Early's and Rodes' (Second Corps) approached from the north. Both Federal Corps (I and XI Corps) arrived from the south that morning and immediately pitched into the Confederates.

Lee was riding behind the troops arriving from the west; Meade was still many miles away when the combat began on the morning of July 1. Lee did not wish to begin a fight when his army was still dispersed over a wide area, particularly because he did not know the strength and exact location of the enemy. Heth's division had engaged the enemy in the morning, but it was quiet when Robert Rodes' division arrived from the north around noon. Lee sent a stream of couriers to Ewell to call off the attack, but the die was cast when he realized Rodes' location was fortuitous as it placed the Union infantry in a vise.

Lee pushed the enemy troops off high ground to the north and west of Gettysburg, but the Union army was establishing itself on formidable high ground south of town, including Cemetery Hill, Culp's Hill, and Cemetery Ridge. Newly arriving troops were also establishing themselves near Little Round Top, which would eventually anchor the Union line. As additional Union troops arrived, they were placed around the battlefield, creating a "fish-hook" alignment. When George Meade finally arrived during the middle of the night of July 1-2, he was informed by trusted officers that the army occupied a strong position. He had the Pipe Creek Circular in his back pocket, but he decided to leave it there and fight it out at Gettysburg.

Lee chose to be the aggressor during the remainder of the battle and he spent considerable time during the evening of July 1 determining the tactics he would use the following day. He was hampered by not knowing the exact number of enemy units and their location—partly because additional Union units were continually arriving from the south and east. He was also without his "eyes and ears," as Stuart and his cavalry were still further north, desperately trying to locate and recombine with Lee's army. Longstreet, Lee's "Warhorse," had provided his view of the campaign being "offensive in strategy, but defensive in tactics." He further elaborated, "after piercing Pennsylvania and menacing Washington, we should choose a strong position, and force the federates to attack us." It could be a repeat of the battle of Fredericksburg, where the Union army bloodied itself by successive attacks on Lee's strong defensive position. Longstreet believed Lee accepted his recommendation and was surprised when on the evening of July 1, the army commander told him, "If the enemy is there tomorrow, we must attack him."[7]

This was a difficult time for Lee. It was his first major battle without his trusted Stonewall Jackson, his normally reliable cavalry chief, Jeb Stuart, had gone missing, and his remaining respected subordinate strongly objected to his plan to attack the enemy. It did not help that both of his two new corps commanders were showing signs of not being up to the demands of leading large numbers of troops in battle.

Lee went to work crafting a battle plan to oust the enemy occupying the high ground. However, without his cavalry, he was hampered by not knowing the enemy's strength and actual positions. Equally vexing, his entire army was not yet on the field. Lee decided an attack against Cemetery Hill early on the morning of July 2 would be a good way to continue the offensive. Riding over to see Ewell, whose troops successfully drove the enemy through the town, Lee carefully explained his plans for July 2.

Division commander Jubal Early was present and immediately disagreed with Lee's plan. The line of attack, he thought, would be against the steepest and most difficult part of Cemetery Hill and would result in heavy losses. Why not attack the opposite end of the Union line? Cemetery Ridge and the Round Tops beyond, if captured, would force the enemy off Cemetery Hill. Lee considered Early's ideas and when he asked if the men could be moved from their current positions on the Union right flank, Early again demurred. He thought moving the Second Corps troops from the ground they had gained through comrades' blood, would cause the combatants to become demoralized, and it would force him to leave many of their badly wounded behind. Ewell said little, appearing to agree with his subordinate. We don't know Early's true motives, but it may have been a desire to protect his battle-weary men from further action while two of Longstreet's fresh divisions approached the battlefield.[8]

A depressed Lee rode back to his headquarters to refine the plan for the following day's offensive. After considering his options, he informed Ewell to move to the enemy's left. This upset Ewell, who rode over to see Lee with news of a reconnaissance on Culp's Hill that revealed it was devoid of troops. He requested permission to stay in position and attack those heights. Lee reluctantly agreed and his plan was more or less set. While Ewell would attack the right of the Union line, Longstreet's two fresh divisions (McLaws' and Hood's) with one of A. P. Hill's not engaged on the first day (Anderson's) would assail the enemy's left and center. Such a plan extended the Confederate line two and a half miles—too long for effective communication and coordination.

With the basic outline in place, Lee went to work fleshing out his plan. He did not know the location of the enemy's left flank, so he sent aide and engineer, Capt. S. R. Johnston, south to reconnoiter just before daylight on July 2. Johnston returned to Lee at about 9:00 a.m. with a report of his ride as far south as Big Round Top, at least that's what he told Lee. No enemy troops were as far south as Little Round Top, he reported—the line ended around the Peach Orchard. Longstreet would launch his attack, find the enemy flank along Emmitsburg Road, and roll up the Union line. Upon hearing Longstreet's attack on the enemy's left flank, Ewell would "make a simultaneous demonstration upon the enemy's right, to be converted into a real attack should opportunity offer."

Lee wanted an attack early on July 2 and this seemed possible as Longstreet's two divisions reached Marsh Creek by midnight. After several hours of resting, a two-and-a-half-hour march, at most, would bring these powerful divisions to Lee's headquarters on Chambersburg Pike. Lee put his faith in two commanders who had their own issues. Longstreet was not pleased about fighting at Gettysburg and Ewell was given discretionary powers to launch an attack, when he really needed firm direction.[9]

After several hours of intense fighting on the afternoon and evening of July 2, both army commanders pondered their army's actions. Lee considered his series of "almosts." His men had almost captured Little Round Top and Cemetery Ridge. They had captured a portion of Cemetery Hill, but were flung back and the only decisive ground his men held was a small portion of Culp's Hill. Because of these successes, Lee decided to concentrate his thrust toward the center of the Union line and expanding his foothold on Culp's Hill. The former attack would begin with a massive artillery barrage to neutralize the defenses there, followed by a large-scale advance of his infantry, spearheaded by Maj. Gen. George Pickett's fresh division. The two thrusts were to be synchronized. Longstreet expressed his concerns about this approach but ultimately supported his commander.[10]

New to command, Meade conducted a council of war with ten of his corps and division commanders at the widow Lydia Leister's house on the evening of July 2. Meade began the meeting by asking each corps commander to report on the condition of his troops. There may have been as few as 58,000 troops remaining to carry on the fight. Meade's chief of staff, Maj. Gen. Daniel Butterfield, asked three questions of the assemblage: 1- Under existing circumstances, it is advisable for this army to remain in is present position, or to retire to another nearer its base of supplies? 2- Should the army remain on the defensive or attack? 3- How long should they wait for an enemy attack? The results of the voting were fairly decisive: the army should remain where it was and fight on the defensive, but not wait more than a day for Lee to attack. Meade was now set for July 3. As the assemblage dispersed, Meade told II Corps division commander, Brig. Gen. John Gibbon, "If Lee attacks tomorrow, it will be on your front." Meade guessed correctly. Historian Kent Brown posited the importance of this particular council of war because the heavy losses and the continual shuffling of troops from place to place demanded that all senior leaders have the opportunity to share their experiences and perspectives.[11]

Comparisons of the Two Campaigns

The tactics of both major battles were influenced by how the armies arrived on the contested ground. Because McClellan and Lee reached the Antietam battlefield a couple of days before the battle, they had the luxury of time to plan. This was not the case during the Pennsylvania Campaign, as both Lee and Meade observed the battlefield for the first time when their troops were already engaged on the first day's battle. The fact that most of the units were on the battlefield during the battle of Antietam, but not at Gettysburg, certainly had an impact on planning subsequent tactics.

Agreement among the senior commanders is an important component of an effective strategy. This was a mixed bag. At Antietam, Lee, Jackson, and Longstreet were on the same page, although they probably wished they occupied a better defensive area. Most of McClellan's corps commanders apparently agreed with his tactical plan, but Joseph Hooker, usually very aggressive in battle, openly complained to McClellan about being tapped to cross Antietam Creek—the first Union corps to do so. He told McClellan that he would be "eaten up" by the enemy.

Gettysburg was slightly different. Meade's senior officers and aides were of one mind that Gettysburg was a good place to fight, rather than the Pipe Creek Line. Lee had initially discussed overall campaign strategy with Longstreet, his most senior and trusted lieutenant, but then chose to adopt a different approach. Longstreet was not wholly supportive of the massive attack Lee planned on July 3. When Lee determined to attack the Union right, Ewell disagreed, so two of his three corps commanders openly disagreed with Lee. Gen. A. P. Hill was the exception, but he was ill, and when he was able to assume command of his troops, he provided poor advice to Lee.

Councils of war were a common way for commanders to solicit advice and information from their senior leaders and make their own intentions clear. Commanders commonly utilized these councils in every campaign. Lee met with both Longstreet and Jackson several times before and after the battle of Antietam. During the battle of Gettysburg, Lee called a meeting with two of his corps commanders, Hill and Longstreet, as well as several division commanders. McClellan also held a council of war on September 15 and Meade met with his senior leaders the evening of July 2.[12]

Meade, at the battle of Gettysburg, enjoyed a strong defensive position on either end of his line: Culp's Hill and Cemetery Hill on his right and Little Round Top on his left. These areas proved to be all but impregnable during the fight. Lee did not have this luxury at Antietam. At the start of the battle, his left was on a meadow, not anchored on any easily defensible landmark, such as a waterway or hill. His right was initially anchored on Antietam Creek by John Walker's division, but it was pulled away from this position to reinforce the troops fighting in the northern part of the field. As a result, both positions were ultimately flanked and Lee's army was almost destroyed in the process.

Although McClellan made limited use of cavalry to scout Lee's position at Antietam, he could see some of the enemy's positions from the high ground near his headquarters and the bluffs on the east side of Antietam Creek. He also received valuable information from signal stations, such as the one on Red Hill. Lee stationed a brigade of cavalry on each flank at Antietam to collect information and try to protect his flank, but could not use cavalry to scout the enemy's positions at Gettysburg, because Stuart was off on his raid. The two brigades left behind, Brig. Gen. William "Grumble" Jones' and Brig. Gen. Beverly Robertson's, were not effectively used by Lee to scout the enemy's positions. Lee did scale the Lutheran Theological Seminary tower and the cupola of Pennsylvania Hall on the Pennsylvania College campus was also used, but they provided only limited effectiveness. Lee was so blind that he sent an engineer from his staff, Capt. R. Johnston, on an extremely dangerous mission to determine the location of the enemy's left flank during the early morning hours of July 2.

There were some similarities in the offensive plans used in each battle. At Antietam, the fighting began to the north; at Gettysburg, first the west and then followed by the north. Subsequent fighting next occurred at the opposite end of the line. Attacking the middle of the line, always a dangerous proposition was left for last in both offensive plans. In both cases, the offensive plan involved a flanking action, which if successful, would roll up the enemy's line.

It is not always unclear what the army taking the offensive planned if successful. For McClellan at Antietam, it was to defend Washington and Baltimore, deny Lee entry into Pennsylvania, and drive him back across the Potomac River. Lincoln preferred another possibility. Because the Potomac River was only three miles in Lee's rear, by driving Lee back from his position near Sharpsburg, he could potentially pin him against the river and destroy his army.

It is unclear what Lee intended to do if he defeated the Union army at Gettysburg. Would he have tried to continue his push toward Harrisburg? We will never know. We do know that Lee seriously considered moving north after Antietam, but was dissuaded by his senior officers and aides.

Table 19: Comparison of the Tactics Used in the Battles

Issue	Maryland Campaign	Pennsylvania Campaign
Armies mostly in place at start of battle	Yes	No
Initial planning for the battle	Begins two days before the battle	No time to plan as the armies collided
Direction of attacks during the first part of the battle	Attack from the north	Attack from the west and north
Direction of attacks during the second part of the battle	Attack from the south	Attack from the west and north
Direction of attacks during the third part of the battle	Attack from the south/central	Attack from the center/north
Were councils of war held	Yes	Yes
Alignment of defensive line	Straight	Fishhook
Experienced senior leaders	Yes	No (Meade, Ewell, and Hill were new)
Major offensive tactic	McClellan: Attack enemy's flanks	Lee: Attack enemy's flanks
Flanking Approach	McClellan: Attack Lee's left flank (early in the morning) then attack right flank (beginning at about 10 a.m.)	Lee: Attack both flanks simultaneously

Chapter 15: The First Phase of the Battles

The Maryland Campaign of 1862

The first phase of the battle occurred in the fields north of the Sunken Road and began at 6:00 a.m. and continued through the late morning. It involved fighting at the David Miller Cornfield and the East and West Woods.

Miller Cornfield/East Woods

McClellan planned an initial thrust against Lee's left flank, north of the Dunker Church, selecting Maj. Gen. Joseph Hooker's I Corps to open the battle with support from Maj. Gen. Joseph Mansfield's XII Corps. The II Corps was positioned across Antietam Creek, ready to provide assistance. McClellan's selection of the two corps initially committed to battle seems a bit odd as both were previously part of the Army of Virginia and new to the Army of the Potomac. Although under Hooker for a mere three weeks, the I Corps performed well three days before when it attacked Turner's Gap. The XII Corps had a checkered past and was loaded with new recruits. Mansfield being placed in command a mere two days before the battle compounded its problems. The II Corps, led by Maj. Gen. Edwin Sumner, was the largest corps in the army and perhaps the most effective, but was initially kept out of harm's way, in favor of two units of unknown fighting capacities. It was, however, positioned in a manner to quickly cross Antietam Creek and lend assistance, if needed. The fight would therefore begin with a unit that had already been bloodied a few days before, with support from two units that had merely stood by.

Hooker's reputation and demeanor may have tipped the balance in his favor. Known for his aggressiveness on the battlefield and strong self-confidence off of it, he may have impressed McClellan as just the person to lead the army into the fight. Hooker was not so sure he relished being placed in command of the initial attacking columns. He subsequently wrote, "I could not know whether I was advancing against a mouse or an elephant," but McClellan assured him, "I was at liberty to call for re-enforcements should I need them." When McClellan crossed Antietam Creek later in the afternoon, a slightly agitated Hooker told him, "the rebels would eat me up." The army commander reassured him by committing to send over the XII Corps, his reserve, to assist Hooker, as needed.

The condition of the XII Corps was quite different from that of the I Corps. Its commander, Joseph Mansfield, was old—almost 60 years old—had not seen combat at all during the Civil War, and only two days before was put in command of the small XII Corps. He had a reputation for not respecting the abilities of volunteers and that's just what he commanded. Hooker probably didn't quibble over Mansfield's selection, as he needed help. He would command over 18,000 men, using his veterans and rookies as he saw fit to roll up Lee's left flank.

Hooker was aware of the approximate location of the enemy's left flank because of the East Woods skirmish that occurred during the evening of September 16. He hoped to drive the enemy from the East Woods and Cornfield to its right and capture the high ground around and beyond the Dunker Church, which became a landmark and destination.[1]

His plan was a fairly simple one. He would send two of his divisions, Brig. Gen. Abner Doubleday's and Brig. Gen. James Ricketts' from their bivouac areas near the Jacob Poffenberger farm, south toward the Dunker Church at first light. Two of Meade's brigades would remain in reserve; his third under Brig. Gen. Truman Seymour remained in close contact with the enemy in the East Woods and would continue engaging them at first light. Hooker knew he could call up the XII Corps as reinforcements
from the rear when needed.[2]

It sounded like a good plan, but it had flaws. The rolling topography made coordination difficult as it was impossible to see one end of the line of a unit from the other and sometimes, even a unit as small as a regiment. Second, it required Hooker's men to traverse open fields for almost half a mile, making them vulnerable to enemy artillery fire. Third, because Mansfield's men were not provided with guides when they crossed Antietam Creek after dark on September 16, they camped too far north. Compounding matters, Hooker did not order them forward at the same time he ordered his own corps' attack. Confederate artillery fire may have caused Hooker to send his men forward almost immediately (see below). As a result, his I Corps would be devastated before help could arrive.

Historian Ezra Carman accurately summarized Hooker's situation as night fell on September 16: "he knew very little more of the enemy's position than when he crossed the Antietam. He had been ordered to turn Lee's left flank, and completed his day's work by posting his own command in such a manner as to secure it from a flank attack of the enemy...not contemplated when he started; he had given Lee complete and reliable information as to McClellan's intentions for the morrow."[3]

Hooker's men had a difficult night as periodic cannon and small arms fire disturbed their sleep and rain made them miserable. Few probably slept, knowing they would be engaged when the sun rose. The men were dismayed when told they could not build fires to boil water for their coffee. They were up and formed into line by 6:00 a.m. and moving forward. Doubleday's division was on the right, with its right flank glued to Hagerstown Pike; Ricketts' was off to its left. Meade's two brigades were in the middle in the North Woods, ready to provide support.

Stuart, Lee's cavalry chief, had placed about 15 cannon on Nicodemus Heights, looming less than half a mile from Hooker's right flank. They were close enough to see and fire into Hooker's men as the early morning mists rose. Equally vexing was Col. Stephen Lee's artillery battalion on the high ground beyond Dunker Church. Its 19 guns put Hooker's men in a deadly crossfire. Division commander Abner Doubleday "came galloping along the line and ordered our brigade be moved from its exposed position," stated Maj. Rufus Dawes of the 6th Wisconsin. One shell exploded within his regiment, killing two and wounding eleven others. The rest of the brigade quickly fell back to the shelter of the nearby Joseph Poffenberger barn.[4]

Hooker quickly responded by bringing up five batteries to blast Nicodemus Heights, with mixed results. He later brought up multiple batteries into and behind the Cornfield to batter the Confederate infantry defending it. McClellan had his own concentration of artillery that tormented the Confederates throughout the battle. His artillery chief, Brig. Gen. Henry Hunt, aligned seven batteries of heavy armament ("guns of position") on the eastern bank of Antietam Creek that could fire on almost any portion of the Confederate lines.

Hooker's six brigades were to quickly traverse the open ground and engage Stonewall Jackson's men. Jackson had portions of two divisions on the front line ready for action on September 17. His former division, the Stonewall Division, now under Brig. Gen. J. R. Jones, was on the west side of Hagerstown Pike in two lines of two brigades each. Their front line, composed of Col. Davidson Penn's and Col. A. J. Grigsby's small brigades, extended from Hagerstown Pike, west, into the northern extension of the West Woods. The division's remaining two brigades were about 250 yards behind them. Maj. Gen. Richard Ewell had lost a leg during the Second Bull Run campaign, so his division was under the command of Brig. Gen. Alexander Lawton. Two of his brigades, Col. Marsellus Douglass' and Col. James Walker's, were in the "hot spots" in front of the Cornfield and East Woods on the east side of Hagerstown Pike. Lawton's remaining two brigades, Brig. Gen. Harry Hays' and Brig. Gen. Jubal Early's, were in reserve in the West Woods, near the Dunker Church, ready to provide support. Brig. Gen. John Hood's division was also in reserve in the same woods. The topography prevented the two divisions on the front lines from seeing each other and each would fight it out independently. Jackson also erred by leaving a 120-yard gap between the left of Douglass' brigade and the right of the Stonewall Division across Hagerstown Pike.

Hooker's men should have rolled over Jackson's without much difficulty, as six of his brigades, numbering 6,600 men, plus Truman Seymour's thousand, were up against Jackson's six brigades numbering 3,650. It did not turn out that way though, as five of the six Union brigades did not immediately attack the Cornfield/East Woods. This fragmented deployment would be the first of many throughout the day. Over on the right, Doubleday's men bore the brunt of Stuart's artillery barrage and this disordered the men and piled up the casualties as they advanced from the Poffenberger farm. The rolling terrain also disrupted the ranks, as did the D. R. Miller farm buildings. Skirmishers from the Stonewall Division across the road also created problems. These all transpired to delay Doubleday's advance.[5]

It was not much better on Ricketts' front. Brig. Gen. George Hartsuff rode ahead of his brigade to reconnoiter and was shot, delaying his unit's advance until his second in command could be located to assume command of the brigade. Over to the left, Col. William Christian led his brigade forward toward the East Woods. John Vautier of the 88th Pennsylvania recalled how the enemy shells were "howling and shrieking as they went on their mad course. Soon the zip, zip, zip, zip of the musket balls sound around our ears." When out in the open, the brigade was hit by a massive crossfire of artillery projectiles, which disordered the ranks. Christian tried to reduce casualties by moving his men in one direction, then another. According to Vautier, "First it was 'forward guide center,' then 'by the right flank,' and then 'Forward guide center' again, then we would oblique to the left and so on." Nothing worked and then the men were horrified to see Christian galloping to the rear, presumably the victim of a nervous breakdown. Like Hartsuff's brigade, it would take time for Christian's second in command to be thrust into his new leadership position.[6]

This left only one brigade, Brig. Gen. Abram Duryee's mixed brigade of Pennsylvanians and New Yorkers, to advance toward the enemy's line. Weathering the intense enemy artillery fire, the brigade entered the Miller Cornfield and headed for Douglass' Georgia brigade deployed for action in a clover field on the opposite side of the corn, with its skirmish line in front of it.

Duryee's skirmish line pushed its counterpart out of the Cornfield just before 6:00 a.m., but the Georgians' battle line was ready. A young soldier recalled how Douglass "ran from regiment to regiment exhorting the men not to fire until the enemy reached the fence and began to get over it – to shoot low and make every bullet count." He urged the men to pick out rows of corn and fire at them. The Georgians rose and sent a volley into Duryee's men as they reached the fence. Some of Walker's men on Duryee's left sent a flank fire into the enemy brigade, further staggering it. A Union soldier recalled his comrades fell like "leaves before an autumn breeze." The two sides fired into each other and the number of casualties multiplied by the minute. Hooker brought up several batteries to fire into the Confederate infantry and the artillery beyond.

Over to Douglass' right, a portion of Walker's brigade battled Seymour's Pennsylvania Reserve brigade which had renewed its advance through the East Woods. The men of the 13th Pennsylvania Reserves were fired up and intent on repaying the Confederates for killing their commander the prior evening. But Duryee's brigade was in trouble, as Douglass' brigade was firing into its front and right flank, and Walker's brigade was firing into its left flank. The killing went on until about 6:30 a.m., when Duryee received a report of enemy troops in the East Woods, threatening his left flank. Feeling isolated, hearing he was being flanked on his left, and with losses mounting— he had already lost more than a third of his men-- Duryee pulled his survivors back through the Cornfield. He would have had company had he waited longer, for the remaining two brigades of Ricketts' division, Hartsuff's and Christian's, each led by its second in command, came charging into the front. Hartsuff's came through the Cornfield and Christian's moved through the East Woods, relieving Seymour's exhausted men.[7]

As Hartsuff's men appeared at the edge of the corn, they were attacked by a fresh brigade of Louisianans under the command of Brig. Gen. Harry Hays. The unit had been in reserve in the West Woods near the Dunker Church and was called into action to help support Douglass' men. Attacking toward the southeast corner of the Cornfield, the men were hit by frontal and right flank fire from Hartsuff's units. "Our brigade had become very small being thinned out so fast that we were in an angle the enemy had formed, they were shooting us from two directions," wrote one of the Louisiana boys. The ill-fated charge left about half of the brigade dead and dying in the open fields without accomplishing anything. Although successful in holding their positions, Hartsuff's and Christian's brigades took heavy losses.[8]

As these two remaining brigades of Ricketts' division fought in the Cornfield and East Woods, three brigades of Doubleday's division also came into action on their right. The Iron Brigade, "westerners" from Indiana and Wisconsin wearing tall Hardee hats, were initially in two lines of regiments, followed by two other brigades. Gunfire suddenly flared from across Hagerstown Pike, hitting the westerners on their vulnerable right flank. The Iron Brigade's commander, Brig. Gen. John Gibbon, quickly responded by sending the two regiments in his second line, the 19th Indiana and 7th Wisconsin, scrambling over the fences lining the road to advance across Hagerstown Pike. Brig. Gen. Marsena Patrick's brigade followed them, while Col. Walter Phelps' brigade followed the 2nd and 6th Wisconsin moving south through the Cornfield. Doubleday's division would therefore fight almost independently on both sides of Hagerstown Pike.

The 2nd and 6th Wisconsin of the Iron Brigade, with Phelps' brigade in tow, made their way toward the southern end of the Cornfield at about 6:45

a.m. Maj. Rufus Dawes of the 6th Wisconsin recalled, "As we appeared at the edge of the corn, a long line of men in butternut and gray rose up from the ground. Simultaneously, the hostile battle lines opened a tremendous fire upon each other. Men, I cannot say fell; they were knocked out of the ranks by dozens. But we jumped over the fence and pushed on, loading, firing, and shouting as we advanced." Phelps' men came up onto the front line, jumbling the lines but still presenting a formidable force.

The new arrivals hit Douglass' brigade in its front and left flank. The Georgians had already lost their commander, about half their men, and ammunition was running low. They could not resist this new Union push, and began making their way to the rear, with the Iron and Phelps' brigades right behind them. Only Walker's brigade held its position in front of the East Woods. Looking ahead, the Union troops could easily see their objective, the high ground around the Dunker Church, less than half a mile up ahead. Hartsuff and Christian's men held their positions while Gibbon's and Phelps' men headed toward their objective.

Meanwhile, the rest of Doubleday's division advanced on the opposite side (west) of Hagerstown Pike. These troops faced a potentially more formidable enemy, as the entire Stonewall Division (under Brig. Gen. J. R. Jones) was deployed in front of them in two lines. It sounded like a strong unit, but in actuality, it fielded fewer than 2,000 worn-out men. Attacking from an angle the 19th Indiana and 7th Wisconsin, with Patrick's brigade in support, smashed into the left flank and rear of J. R. Jones' two brigades in the front line, composed of about 600 men, and sent them packing.[9]

While this occurred, the 2nd and 6th Wisconsin with Phelps' brigade on the opposite (east) side of the road made their way south to take the high ground. A shell exploded over Jones, causing a possible concussion, so Brig. Gen. William Starke assumed command of the division. Seeing the threat on the opposite side of the road, Starke wheeled his two remaining brigades on the second line around to the right to face Hagerstown Pike and the enemy troops beyond. In the confusion, the two brigades slammed into each other as they wheeled to face Hagerstown Pike. There was no time to sort out the commands, so the brigades approached the fence in disarray. Col. Edmund Pendleton of the 15th Louisiana noted, "we found ourselves face to face with the enemy, heavily massed and within close musket range... [the men] charged forward in the face of a murderous fire, which thinned our ranks at every step." Historian Ezra Carman explained, "the two brigades, under a murderous fire, thinning its ranks at every step, reached the high and strong post and rail fence of the road and came face to face with the Wisconsin men [2nd and 6th] across the road, only 30 – 75 yards away." With units from Phelps' brigade filling in the gaps, the Union troops turned and faced the new threat. Some of Starke's men climbed the fence lining the road and headed toward the startled Union troops. The Confederate success was short-lived, for the rest of the Iron Brigade and Patrick's brigade on their side of the pike barreled into their left flank and rear, killing Starke and many of his men, and forcing the rest to flee. Capt. James Campbell's battery of Napoleon cannons also sent deadly canister charges into its flank. Starke was shot several times after grabbing a flag to rally his men, and died within an hour.[10]

It was now 7:00 a.m., and Hooker could be satisfied that two of his I Corps divisions had bested two of the enemy's (except one of the eight brigades) and he still maintained two of Meade's brigades in reserve. Confederate losses were heavy, including both division commanders, virtually all of the brigade commanders and regimental leaders.

With the threat from Starke's men across the road neutralized, the men of the 2nd Wisconsin, 6th Wisconsin and Phelps' brigade saw a clear path to their destination, the high ground around the Dunker Church. Dawes explained what happened next: "A long and steady line of rebel gray…comes sweeping down through the woods around the church. They raise the yell and fire. It is like a scythe running through our line. 'Now save, who can.' It is a race for life as each man runs for the cornfield." The Union troops on the Cornfield side (east) of Hagerstown Pike were now up against Maj. Gen. John Hood's tough Confederate division, composed of two brigades numbering about 2,200 men. These were among Lee's most effective fighters, but on this day they were even more motivated as the Yanks had interrupted their long-awaited breakfast. The division had been deployed in front of the East Woods and Cornfield the evening before and had battled Seymour's brigade. Hood knew his men had not eaten for several days and were nearing the end of their effectiveness, so he petitioned Stonewall Jackson for relief, so they could retire to the West Woods to cook and consume their food. Jackson agreed to replace the troops with Walker's and Douglass' brigades

Map 20: The Cornfield

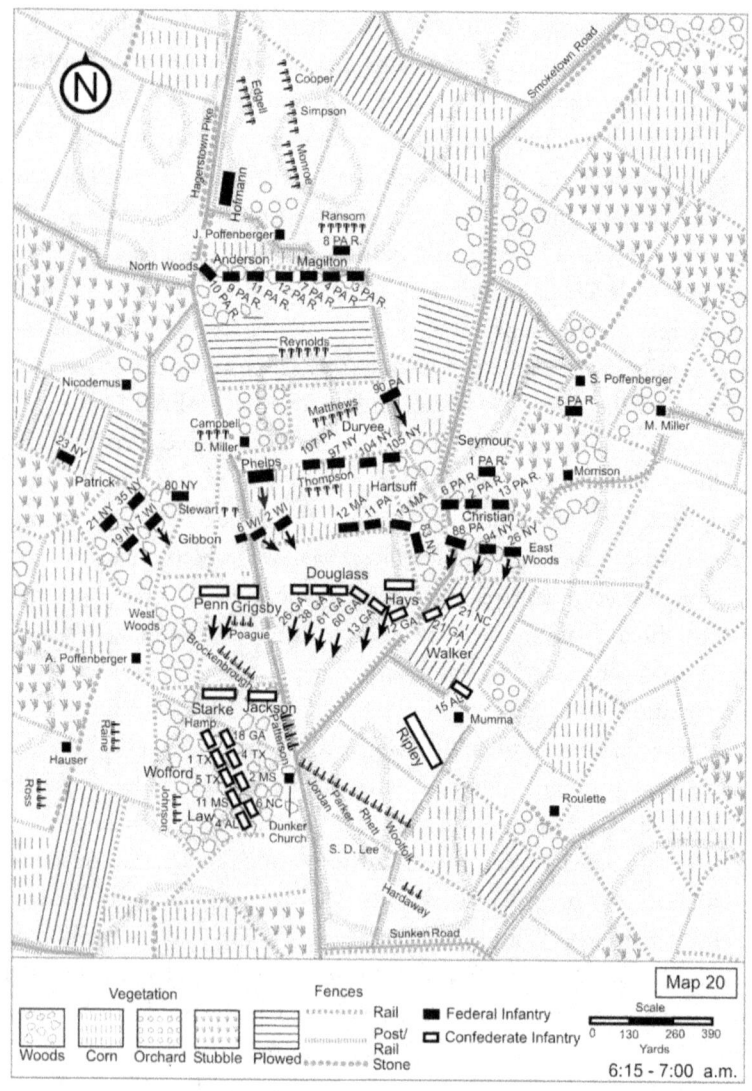

(Lawton's division), but only if Hood promised to help out if needed the following day.

Hood agreed and pulled his men back to the West Woods. The wagons carrying provisions did not arrive until 4:00 a.m. Lt. James Lemon of the 18th Georgia explained, "The wagons did not reach us until just before dawn & were almost assaulted by the men, wild as they were in their hunger...."

The men were still cooking and preparing their breakfasts when Hooker unleashed his attack on the Confederate line. They were furious when ordered to stop their culinary activities, grab their muskets, and prepare for battle. Lemon recalled, "A savage yell went up in response & the men's faces I shall never forget. Wild-eyed & furious, clenched teeth & oaths from every man...They were like savage Devils from the Infernal regions, howling madly & looking for a fight." Their officers told them to reserve their anger for the Yanks, who they would soon encounter. Filing into the meadow adjacent to Smoketown Road, the column faced to the left—directly in the path of half of the Iron Brigade and Phelps' men. The black hats were supposed to generate fear among the enemy, as the Iron Brigade was a formidable foe, but it didn't work on this occasion, as one of Hood's men yelled, "Looky there boys, at them black hats! Let's go knock 'em off!" Hood's men charged directly toward Doubleday's men. Dawes' quote (above) captures the surprise and horror of the Union troops who thought victory was within their grasp.[11]

Col. William Wofford's "Texas Brigade" on the left of the division, drove Doubleday's division, on the east side of Hagerstown Pike through the fields and then into the Cornfield and closely followed them. Col. Evander Law's brigade, on Wofford's right, drove Ricketts' men out of the Cornfield and East Woods and followed them through the corn. Those able to see through the smoke and confusion of fleeing enemy soldiers might have looked ahead and seen a line of fresh Union troops filing behind the fence lining the north edge of the Cornfield. Hooker saw what was transpiring and ordered his last reserve—two brigades of George Meade's Pennsylvania Reserves into action. Many lie prone behind the fence, positioned their muskets on the bottom rung, and opened fire on Hood's approaching men. The surprises continued when an enfilade fire from across Hagerstown Pike blew apart Hood's left flank, held by Wofford's brigade. Unbeknownst to Hood and his men, the two Iron Brigade regiments on the opposite side of Hagerstown Pike (19th Indiana and 7th Wisconsin) and Patrick's brigade who had finished off J. R. Jones'/Starke's division, now turned toward Hagerstown Pike and fired into Hood's troops rushing past on the opposite side of the road. Capt. Joseph Campbell's battery had also come into action, sending deadly canister charges into Hood's flank. Three of Wofford's regiments turned toward Hagerstown Pike and fired into the new arrivals, and the two sides battled within 12 feet of each other in the deadly confrontation. It was probably worse for Hood's men, as Campbell's guns continued to fire deadly canister rounds into the Confederates' right flank. A Texan wrote, "legs, arms, and other parts of human bodies were flying in the air like straw in a whirlwind." J. M. Polk of the 4th Texas said, "the air was full of shot and shell…it seemed almost impossible for a rat to live in such a place." Hit in front by these adversaries, and the right flank by Campbell's battery and the Pennsylvania Reserves further to their right, Wofford's three regiments were forced to retire.[12]

A fourth regiment from Wofford's brigade, the 1st Texas, did not turn to face the threat across the road, but continued through the Cornfield, where it went toe to toe with several regiments from Col. Robert Anderson's brigade of Pennsylvania Reserves lining the northern fence line. Hood described the Texans' wayward action as it "slipped the bridle and got away." Arguably the toughest regiment in Lee's army, the Texans gave as "good as they got," but their ranks melted away. A Pennsylvanian noted, "these brave men were mowed down like the corn surrounding them." With losses quickly mounting and no reinforcements in sight, the Texans realized it was time to retreat. Only 40 of the 226 men that marched into the Cornfield were unharmed—an amazing 82% were casualties. The men would mourn their missing comrades, but they would equally despair over the loss of their beloved flag, which was partially made with the wedding dress of the regiment's original commander's wife.[13]

While Wofford's brigade was being driven from the Cornfield, Hood's other brigade, Evander Law's, occupied Wofford's right. They drove the remnants of Hartsuff's and Christian's brigades back through the Cornfield and East Woods and headed for the fence lining the northern edge of the field, where they battled Col. Albert Magilton's brigade of Pennsylvania Reserves. They initially punched a hole in Magilton's line, driving back the

3rd and 4th Pennsylvania Reserves. "An infantry line appeared on the crest and engaged our line," remembered the 11th Mississippi's Pvt. Love. "The flag of the regiment opposing [us] was shot down or lowered at least a half a dozen times before it disappeared behind a hill." Massed Union cannon in the field just north of the Cornfield opened a withering canister fire, halting Law's move north. "So far, we had been entirely successful and everything promised a decisive victory, reported Law. "It is true that strong support was needed to follow up our success, but this I expected every moment." Losses mounted, and with no reinforcements in sight, Law reluctantly ordered a withdrawal. Hood's entire division was now in retreat, except for the 4th Alabama (Law's brigade), 5th Texas (Wofford's brigade), and 21st Georgia (Walker's brigade) which held steady in the East Woods.

Nothing stood between the Pennsylvania Reserves occupying the Cornfield northern fence and the high ground around the Dunker Church, so they rose and began their advance through what was left of the corn. The 19th Indiana and 7th Wisconsin of the Iron Brigade and portions of Patrick's brigade who had helped destroy Wofford's left flank, also crossed Hagerstown Pike.[14]

Sudden small arms fire from their left caused the victors to halt and look in that direction, where they spied a line of enemy troops moving relentlessly in their direction. These troops were from D. H. Hill's division. As seen in Chapter 10, Hill's division had battled the I and IX Corps at the South Mountain gaps on September 14 and marched all night to arrive at Antietam Creek the following morning. The division was initially deployed around Boonsboro Pike to protect the middle of Lee's line. With the threat to Lee's left flank, Hill was ordered to send three brigades to help staunch the Union thrust toward the Dunker Church. Brig. Gen. Roswell Ripley's brigade led the column. It was not engaged at the battle of Fox's Gap, but the troops marching behind it had been. Col. Alfred Colquitt's brigade, which had battled the Iron Brigade at Turner's Gap, followed Ripley's and Brig. Gen. Samuel Garland's brigade (now under Col. D. K. McRae), severely manhandled by the Union IX Corps at Fox's Gap, brought up the rear.

Ripley's men slammed into the Union troops moving south through the Cornfield. Tired from their previous fights, these Union troops realized they were no match for the new arrivals, so they turned and headed back toward the North Woods. With their departure, the last of Joseph Hooker's I Corps was bested and there were seemingly no additional troops to halt this new Confederate thrust. D. H. Hill's men sensed ultimate victory and the potential to re-secure Lee's initial line. The Confederates were also in bad shape, though. Like their Union foes, three divisions had been defeated and masses of additional enemy troops hove into view; the vanguard of Mansfield's XII Corps, which had been far in the rear of the I Corps at the start of the battle, now approached the contested area. The corps was composed of two divisions; Brig. Gen. Alpheus Williams' was in the lead. Williams deployed his two brigades in the field just north of the Cornfield. This was more difficult than it seemed for several of the regiments were rookies. Williams wrote to his daughters, how he was able to get one of the regiments in line "by having a fence to align on and having got it in this way I ordered the colonel to go forward and open fire the moment he saw the Rebels." Although green, he believed there was hope for the unit, for the "men were of an excellent stamp, ready and willing, but neither officers nor men knew anything, and there was an absence of the mutual confidence which drill begets." Drill would come later—Williams needed to ensure they presented a solid front and did not all get themselves killed.

One of the rookie regiments did not fare so well. Col. Joseph Knipe of the 46th Pennsylvania saw the green 128th Pennsylvania clumped up behind his regiment. He later wrote, "seeing the uselessness of a regiment in that position [behind him] I took the responsibility of getting it into line of battle the best way circumstances would admit," and he led the regiment to a position on the right of his own, behind the fence lining the northern boundary of the Cornfield. Knipe then suggested a charge to the regiment's commander. He readily agreed and the regiment advanced deep into the Cornfield before being forced back by Ripley's killing volleys. The Confederate brigade never entered the Cornfield, contenting itself with repelling the rookies and engaging in long-range skirmishing with the Union troops behind the fence on the opposite side of the field. Its casualties rose, all the same.[15]

Both Hooker and Mansfield shared the common attribute of "leading from the front," as a way of inspiring their volunteers, and both would pay the price at Antietam. Mansfield positioned some of Williams' men into the

East Woods. When members of the 10th Maine saw enemy troops up ahead (remnants of Hood's division), they opened fire. Mansfield was in the sector and he galloped up and ordered the men to cease firing as Union troops occupied the woods, or so he thought. The men calmly showed Mansfield the error or his ways and he allowed them to continue firing, but not before he was shot in the chest. He was taken to the rear, where he died the following day. He was not the only corps commander to be hit by enemy fire. Joseph Hooker was wounded in the foot, but refused to leave the field. When he lost so much blood, however, and was about to pass out, his staff ordered him to the rear for medical attention. Both of Jackson's division commanders were also out of the fight. J. R. Jones, as we have already seen and Alexander Lawton, who suffered a severe leg wound.

Colquitt's brigade now arrived and relieved Ripley's men. Not content to remain on the edge of the Cornfield, the mixed Alabama and Georgia brigade advanced into it in a diagonal fashion. Its right flank reached the intersection of the Cornfield and East Woods; its left never reached the northern fence, instead halting in the middle of the field. The two sides fired into each other's ranks until George Greene's Second Division (XII Corps) arrived in the East Woods and positioned itself on Colquitt's right flank, which hung in the air. It was supposed to be connected to Garland's brigade in the East Woods, but the North Carolinians never advanced. The men, who had lost their commander and many of their comrades at Fox's Gap, thought they were being flanked on the right as an officer panicked and screamed they were in dire straits. According to commander of the 5th North Carolina, Capt. Thomas Garrett, "The men before this were far from being cool, but, when this act of indiscretion occurred, a panic ensued, and, despite the efforts of the file-closers and officers, they began to break and run." The entire brigade followed suit, leaving Colquitt's men with Yanks in their front, right flank, and rear. The 6th Georgia had the misfortune of occupying Colquitt's right flank and was hit in three directions by a storm of bullets. The unit simply disintegrated, losing almost 80 percent of its men in a matter of minutes. As many as 250 men marched into the Cornfield, but only 54 made it out unscathed. With the 6th Georgia gone, the XII Corps now turned its attention to the 27th Georgia, next in line. It did not remain in position very long as Colquitt ordered his entire brigade out of harm's way.[16]

The time was probably about 8:30 a.m. and Lee had no more troops to immediately dispatch to the Cornfield. With its path open, Greene's division swept out of the East Woods and took the high ground in the open fields around Dunker Church, driving Col. Stephen Lee's massed artillery from this area. It took over two and a half hours and two Union corps, but Hooker finally achieved his objective. Greene's men were permitted to rest and were resupplied while receiving a well-deserved rest.

The fight, which began at 6:00 a.m. and ended at 8:30 a.m., involved about 17,100 Union and 10,700 Confederate troops. Hooker lost 4,400 during this period; Stonewall Jackson, 4,300.

The West Woods

A third Union corps, the veteran II Corps, commanded by Maj. Gen. Edwin Sumner, was finally permitted to cross Antietam Creek and make its way to the battlefield. Sumner received orders just prior to 7:30 a.m. and he quickly sent Maj. Gen. John Sedgwick's Second Division across the Creek. A rapid march brought the 5,500 men to the East Woods. All of the Union troops up to this point had advanced in a north to south orientation; Sedgwick arrived from the east and drove west toward the West Woods. It is unclear exactly what Sumner was attempting, but it appears he wanted to clear residual enemy troops from the West Woods, turn left and come up on Greene's right flank. Another of Sumner's divisions, Maj. Gen. William French's Third Division, followed Sedgwick across the creek, but it would turn at the East Woods and advance on Greene's left flank. This would put three divisions in a line which could then move south and crush the rest of Lee's army. It didn't quite happen that way. Some believed that French simply turned left and headed toward the Sunken Road because he saw enemy troops there.

Sumner pushed Sedgwick's large division toward the wooded area in front of him in three lines, each composed of a brigade. The two leaders rode between the first and second lines at about 9:00 a.m. The first line encountered about 200 enemy soldiers—the remnants of the Stonewall Division and eventually swept them away. The quiet was broken when the division was suddenly attacked on its front, left flank, and rear by masses of Confederate troops from Lafayette McLaws' division, which had marched all night from Harpers Ferry and had only just arrived at Sharpsburg. Another division that had participated in the siege of Harpers Ferry, John Walker's, also arrived behind McLaws' men. These two divisions arrived too late to assist in the Cornfield fight, but had the good fortune of encountering Sedgwick's division in a vulnerable position.

Both sides were in for a surprise as neither expected to see enemy troops in the West Woods. As Sedgwick's first brigade, under Brig. Gen. Richard Gorman, marched through the West Woods, it was exposed to a massive bombardment from Confederate cannon deployed on the ridges in front of it. Sgt. Jonathan Stowe of the 15th Massachusetts saw "shells fly past me every few seconds carrying away limbs from trees and scattering limbs around," and concluded, "we had a bad place." Chaos reigned as Gorman attempted to withdraw by marching his men by the right flank and out of harm's way. The full fury of McLaws' attack was then unleashed on Sedgwick's division.

Sumner was near Gorman's brigade when he saw the Confederate onslaught, yelling, "My God, we must get out of this!" He then rode to Brig. Gen. Oliver Howard's Philadelphia Brigade, on the third line, to try to reposition it to withstand the attack. He was too late, and all he could yell to the Pennsylvanians was, "Back boys! For God's sake move back; you are in a bad fix!" The men of the Philadelphia Brigade in the third, or last line, of Sedgwick's division had probably thought they were safe as they were furthest away from danger, so it came as quite a shock when McLaws' screaming men hit their left flank and rear.

It took a mere 20 minutes for Sedgwick's division to lose about 40% of its men (2,210) and its survivors scrambled to the rear. The Confederates lost more than 1,800 men in the bitter fighting. At least one Confederate brigade followed the Union troops all the way to the D. R. Miller house, but the Union artillery mounted a stout defense. During this time, some South Carolina units stormed out of the West Woods to attack Union artillery deployed in front of them, but were bloodily repulsed. The fight in the West Woods was the only portion of the battle where the Confederates outnumbered their Union counterparts: the Confederates numbered approximately 8,100 to Sedgwick's 5,500 men.[17]

Map 21: The West Woods

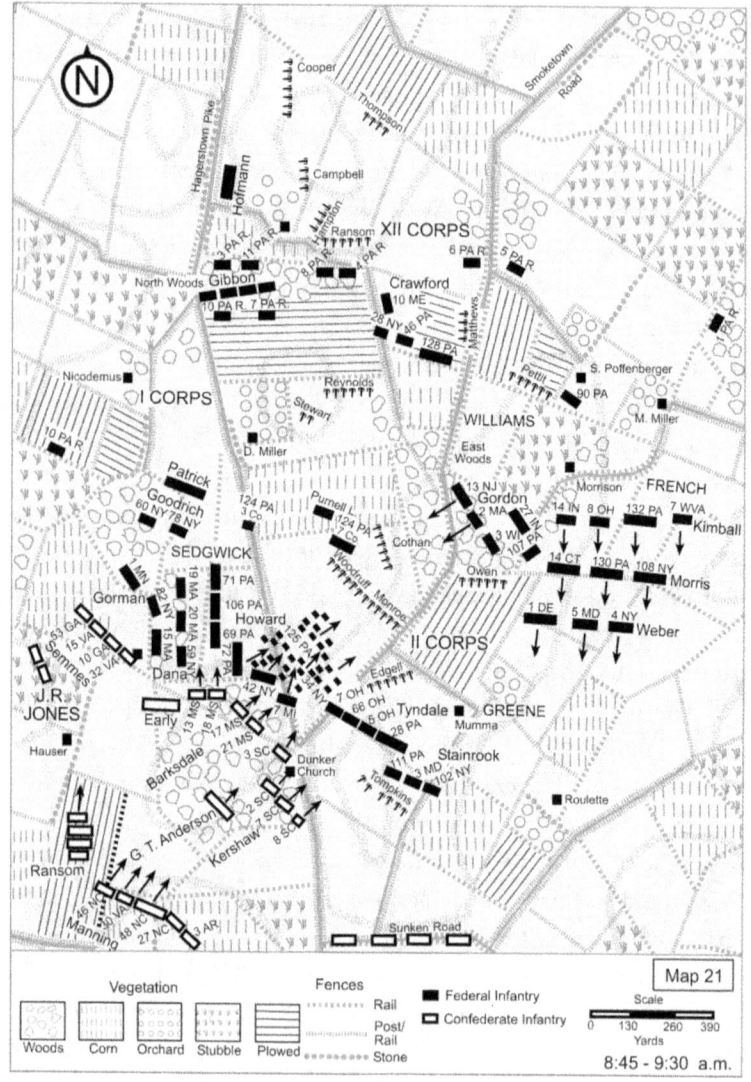

The fighting in the West Woods was not yet over, however. Near 10:30 a.m., several regiments from Greene's division's ventured into the West Woods near the Dunker Church and formed a long line of battle within it. They were reinforced by a couple of regiments from Williams' division. All was quiet until about 12:30 p.m., when portions of Walker's division fell on both flanks and drove the men from the woods. When the Union VI Corps arrived, Col. William Irwin's brigade was sent toward the West Woods, but blazing guns from the Confederates in the West Woods drove them backward.

The bitter fight for the Cornfield, East Woods, and West Woods involved 22,450 Union troops and 18,800 Confederates. The losses were 6,550 (24%) for the Union and 6,200 (33%) for the Confederates. The massed artillery of both armies on high ground north of Sharpsburg, coupled with the open fields, caused a sizable number of casualties to the infantry.[18]

The Pennsylvania Campaign of 1863

Initial Fight for the Ridges West of Town

Gettysburg's first day began very simply--when Henry Heth received permission to take his division to Gettysburg for supplies. One of his brigades had already made the trek from Cashtown the day before, but returned empty-handed when its commander, Brig. Gen. James Pettigrew, saw Union cavalry in and around the town. Heth and Third Corps commander, A. P. Hill, had laughed it off and Heth put his entire division on Chambersburg Pike at 5:00 a.m. He expected to find at worst, enemy militia who were no match for his 7,500-man force. Heth should have heeded Pettigrew's advice, for the division was marching toward John Buford's veteran cavalry division. Buford had spread his 2,200 troopers over a seven-mile arc extending from east, to north, and then west of Gettysburg. Col. Thomas Devin's brigade patrolled the area north and east of town and Col. William Gamble's brigade guarded the western approaches. Although his cavalry were relatively few in numbers, Buford knew that Maj. Gen. John Reynolds' I Corps was marching toward Gettysburg on Emmitsburg Road and would arrive shortly. The XI Corps marched several miles behind

Reynolds, so within a few hours there would be a sizable number of Union infantry in and around the town.

Gettysburg's terrain impressed Buford, so much so, he would sacrifice his men, if necessary, to guard the high ground. A series of ridges ran in a north-south direction west of town. Seminary Ridge was closest to town, and then moving west was: McPherson's, Herr, and Knoxlyn. While none were particularly high, they offered good defensive positions. Gamble's brigade's picket posts initially occupied Knoxlyn Ridge. Gamble deployed a stronger line behind it on Herr Ridge, but most of his men were on McPherson's Ridge. Buford hoped his troopers on each ridge would delay the enemy's advance long enough to buy time for Reynolds' infantry to arrive. Buford also had Lt. John Calef's battery of six cannon, which he spread west of town to give the illusion of additional troops.[19]

Seldom in battle is the "right person at the right time" in place to command a portion of the field. Such was the case of John Buford at Gettysburg. One of Meade's staff officers described Buford as being "cool, calm, and serenely receiving the reports, quietly weighting in his military mind their value, but saying nothing." Buford may have seemed outwardly calm, but inside he was anything but, realizing the enemy might overpower his relatively small cavalry force. He had already told his officers on the evening of June 30, "[t]hey will attack you in the morning and they will come booming—skirmishers three deep. You will have to fight like the devil to hold your own until supports arrive."[20]

The Confederate infantry trudging along Chambersburg Pike, with Marylander Brig. Gen. James Archer's mixed Alabama and Tennessee brigade at the head of the column, encountered Gamble's videttes between 7:00 and 7:30 a.m. Gunshots rang out, so Archer shook out a skirmish line and deployed his brigade for action on the south side of the Chambersburg Pike. Pettigrew had tried to tell Archer what he was up against, but in the words of an aide, "General Archer listened but believed him not." The two sides engaged in long-range fire for about an hour—buying precious time for Buford and his men. Archer was in no hurry, as he did not realize that two powerful Union infantry corps were approaching Gettysburg. Brig. Gen. Joseph Davis' brigade was the second unit in Heth's column and when it arrived, it deployed on the north side of Chambersburg Pike. This also ate up valuable time. Gamble, in the meantime, brought up about 900 troopers to Herr Ridge to contest the enemy's advance. The line held off the infantrymen for about a half hour before being forced back to McPherson's Ridge at about 8:00 a.m. Heth's two brigades scaled Herr Ridge and could easily see Buford's strong defensive line on McPherson's Ridge up ahead. Archer was angry about the turn of events. His brigade had sustained heavy losses at its prior battle—Chancellorsville—and numbered only about 1,200 men. He had earlier complained to Heth that his brigade was too "light to risk" moving forward without adequate support. Heth waved off Archer's concerns and ordered him forward.

Buford's men, running low on ammunition, and exhausted from fighting Heth's infantry all morning, were at the end of their effectiveness, when at about 10:00 a.m., Reynolds arrived. He asked Buford if he could hold out a bit longer until the infantry arrived and the cavalry leader said, "I reckon I can." As Reynolds turned to return to his column, he encountered Gamble who yelled out, "Hurry up, General, hurry up! They are breaking our line!"[21]

Gamble and Buford did not have long to wait, for the head of the I Corps, Brig. Gen. James Wadsworth's division, hove into view at about 10:15 a.m. Brig. Gen. Lysander Cutler's brigade of New Yorkers and Pennsylvanians headed north across Chambersburg Pike to take on Brig. Gen. Joe Davis' men. Behind them marched the Iron Brigade, which had played such a large role at Antietam. The latter brigade slammed into Archer's front and right flank as it crossed Willoughby Run. Pvt. W. Bird of the 13th Alabama, on Archer's right flank, had just crossed Willoughby Run when "all of a sudden a heavy line of battle rose up out of the wheat, and poured a volley [sic] into our ranks, it wavered and they charged us, and we fell back to the ravine again, and before we could rally, it seemed to me there were 20,000 Yanks down in among us hallowing surrender." With the Iron Brigade wrapping around Archer's right flank and rear, hundreds of Confederates threw down their arms and thrust their hands in the air. Archer was among the captured, the first general officer from Lee's army ever to befall such a fate. The rest of the brigade was forced to flee the Iron Brigade's onslaught.[22]

On the opposite side of Chambersburg Pike, Davis' men attacked three regiments of Cutler's brigade. The 55th North Carolina on the left of Davis' line extended far beyond Cutler's line, causing the Union force to retreat toward Gettysburg. Just then, three Union regiments (two from Cutler's brigade and another from the Iron Brigade) from the opposite side of Chambersburg Pike, changed direction and charged across it, approaching Davis' right flank, in the process of following Cutler's fleeing regiments. Davis quickly pivoted his men to face the threat head on. Suddenly, the Southerners just disappeared. As Davis' men approached an unfinished railroad cut, they thought it would be the perfect terrain feature to avoid being exposed to a hail of bullets from the newly arriving Union troops.

Davis' men didn't realize the steepness of its banks, trapping hundreds when the three Union regiments appeared along the edge, overlooking Davis' men below in the railroad cut. A Mississippian bitterly noted, "An order [came] down the line…to lay down in a cut for a rail road nearby. Well we obeyed—& in obeying sacrificed our freedom." Making matters worse, "all the men were jumbled together without regard to regiment or company." Union troops lining the top of the cut began yelling, "Throw down your muskets! Down with your muskets!" rather than fire into the helpless men. Some Union troops jumped into the cut to engage in hand-to-hand combat. The remnants of Davis' brigade either fled to safety or threw up their arms and surrendered.[23]

By the time the fighting ended about 11:15 a.m., Wadsworth's two brigades had decisively thrashed an equal number of Confederate units. Reynolds would not savor the Union victory though, as a Confederate bullet slammed into the back of his head as he turned to encourage his troops entering the battle, killing him instantly.

A lull now settled over the battlefield as the two sides caught their breaths and brought up reinforcements. Between 11:00 a.m. and noon, the Second Division of Reynolds' corps, under Brig. Gen. John Robinson arrived and crossed Chambersburg Pike to settle on Oak Ridge, a continuation of McPherson Ridge. The Third Division, under Brig. Gen. Abner Doubleday, also arrived and formed on both sides of the Iron Brigade. As senior officer, Doubleday assumed command of the I Corps, which stretched over a mile and a quarter in a line from Mummasburg Road on Oak Ridge to the north to almost Fairfield Road to the South.

Both sides deployed individual batteries during the morning battles, but the Confederates upped the ante by bringing up two artillery battalions, Col.

Map 22: The Morning Fight at Gettysburg
A: Davis' Brigade's Fight with Cutler's Brigade
B: The Iron Brigade's Fight with Archer's Brigade

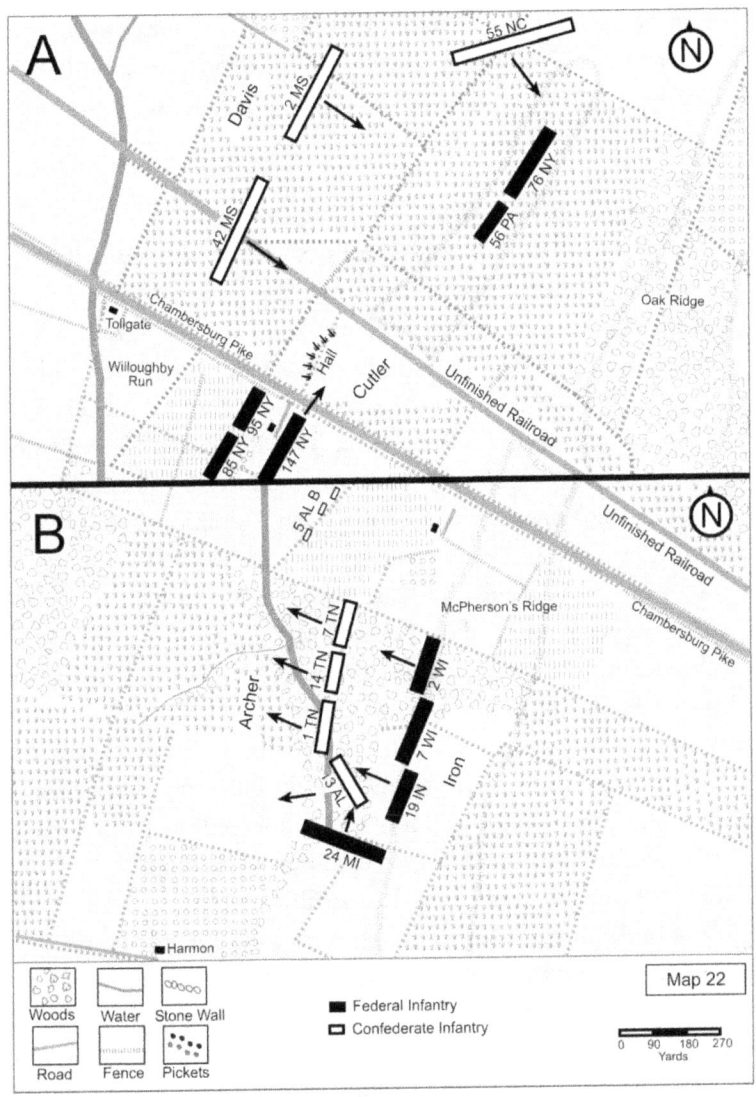

William Pegram's and Col. David McIntosh's, onto McPherson's Ridge, where they opened fire on the enemy in the fields west of the Seminary.

Buford's men would fight later in the afternoon, but their major contribution lie in their tenacious defense during the early morning hours prior to Reynolds' arrival. Because they were outnumbered, Buford used a "defense in depth" tactic, relying on the series of parallel ridges to help delay Heth's entry into Gettysburg.

Initial Fighting North of Town

One-armed Maj. Gen. Oliver Howard's XI Corps arrived in Gettysburg about noon. This was the ill-fated and ill-regarded "German" corps, devastated by Stonewall Jackson's flank attack at Chancellorsville. Two of its three divisions (Brig. Gen. Francis Barlow's and Brig. Gen. Alexander Schimmelfennig's) marched through Gettysburg and into the fields north of town, but did not connect with Brig. Gen. John Robinson's I Corps division on its left. Therefore, both of its flanks floated in the air, vulnerable to enemy flank attacks. A third division, under Brig. Gen. Adolph von Steinwehr, was stationed on Cemetery Hill as a reserve. Howard was now in charge of all Union forces on the battlefield because of Reynolds' death and Maj. Gen. Carl Schurz assumed command of the XI Corps.

The Confederates were also bringing up powerful divisions, including Maj. Gen. Dorsey Pender's (Third Corps), which marched behind Heth's from the west and the first two divisions of Lt. Gen. Richard's Ewell's Second Corps arrived from the north. Maj. Gen. Robert Rodes' division of the latter corps arrived first and settled on Oak Hill, which hovered north of Oak Ridge. Robinson's men had attempted to gain Oak Hill when they reached the field, but Rodes' men arrived there first. Lee finally arrived on the battlefield at about 2:00 p.m. With his troops arriving from both the north and the west, Lee discarded his reluctance to bring on a general battle here and ordered his men to prepare for a more coordinated approach.[24]

After a couple of hours reprieve, the two sides again went into combat. The fighting first shifted to the north, where Rodes' division launched its attack against Union forces on Oak Ridge. At least three of Rodes' brigades were intended to go into action together between 1:30 and 2:00 p.m., to crush the

Union troops on Oak Ridge, but this did not happen. Col. Edward O'Neal launched his brigade prematurely, attacking almost due south. Robinson saw them coming and quickly shifted those regiments facing west to the north and east, and they easily cut down the Alabamians. Rodes reported "the whole brigade . . . was repulsed quickly, and with loss." Brig. Gen. Alfred Iverson was surprised to see O'Neal's men launch their attack before he was in position, so he quickly ordered his troops to their feet and into line of battle, and attacked Oak Ridge from the northwest. Robinson's men, who had already polished off O'Neal's, shifted to the west as Iverson's North Carolinians attacked through an open field.

Robinson ordered his men to hold their fire as Iverson's men approached, the latter seemingly unaware of the danger that lurked before them on the ridge. A Union soldier recalled, "the field in our front was swarming with Confederates who came sweeping on in magnificent order with perfect alignment, guns at right shoulder and colors to the front." Suddenly flames of fire shot out from the hidden Union troops. Few North Carolinians remained standing after the first volley and most of those who survived quickly attempted to take cover in the open field. Realizing the folly of continuing the contest in the open, scores of white flags fluttered in the breeze. Iverson lost 900 of the 1,400 men he sent into battle. A young Confederate artilleryman recalled after the battle: "The feet of these dead men were in a perfectly straight line...They had evidently been killed by one volley of musketry and they had fallen in their tracks without a single struggle." It would have been worse, had another Confederate brigade not arrived to distract and drive back the Union troops trying to kill and capture Iverson's survivors.[25]

Although outnumbered, the Union I Corps was holding its own north and west of Gettysburg. It had already held off uncoordinated attacks from two brigades of Heth's division from the west in the morning and other attacks by Rodes' division from the north in the early afternoon. By 3:00 p.m., the Confederates west and north of town were ready to make another push against the determined I and XI Corps. The XII Corps should have arrived by that time to provide additional firepower. It left Littlestown, Pennsylvania, earlier in the morning and had reached Two Taverns by 11:00 a.m. A five-mile march would have brought these 10,000 men to Gettysburg, but their commander, Maj. Gen. Howard Slocum, ordered the men to rest until 3:00 p.m. Slocum claimed not to hear the sounds of battle up ahead, but some of his men tried to convince him of his error. He later wrote that Meade ordered him to Two Taverns to await further orders. In the absence of those orders, Slocum stayed put and his comrades were soon routed by overwhelming Confederate numbers.[26]

The Confederates Crush the Union Lines

Lee was apparently able to begin coordinating the actions north and west of Gettysburg by 3:00 p.m. To the west, Gen. Heth, whose two brigades had taken a beating in the initial fighting, now brought up his remaining two brigades in an attempt to knock the Iron Brigade from its perch atop McPherson's Ridge. One was none other than Brig. Gen. James Pettigrew's brigade, which had first marched to Gettysburg the day before. It now deployed for action in the center of Heth's line. The largest brigade in Lee's army, at 2,600 men, it had recently joined the army from North Carolina. Col. John Brockenbrough's small Virginia brigade formed on its left and the remnants of Archer's brigade, now under Col. Birkett Fry, formed on its right.

The Iron Brigade also received reinforcements with the arrival of Abner Doubleday's division. One of its brigades, Col. Chapman Biddle's, formed several hundred yards southeast of the Iron Brigade's left flank, but the two units did not link. Doubleday's other brigade, Col. Roy Stone's Pennsylvanians, formed on the right of the Iron Brigade and along Emmitsburg Road.

After perfecting his division's alignment, Heth ordered it forward across Willoughby Run to take on the left of the Union line. Pettigrew's large 26th North Carolina stood toe to toe with a couple of the Iron Brigade's Wisconsin and Michigan regiments, taking and giving punishing volleys. The 24th Michigan and 26th North Carolina engaged in a deadly struggle. The Tar Heels approached to within 50 yards, when the Michiganders let loose a devastating volley. The regiment's commander explained, the Confederate "advance was not checked, and they came on with rapid strides, yelling like demons." The opponents stood toe to toe and might have fought each other to annihilation had not a portion of Pettigrew's right flank not overlapped the

Map 23: The Fighting North of Gettysburg

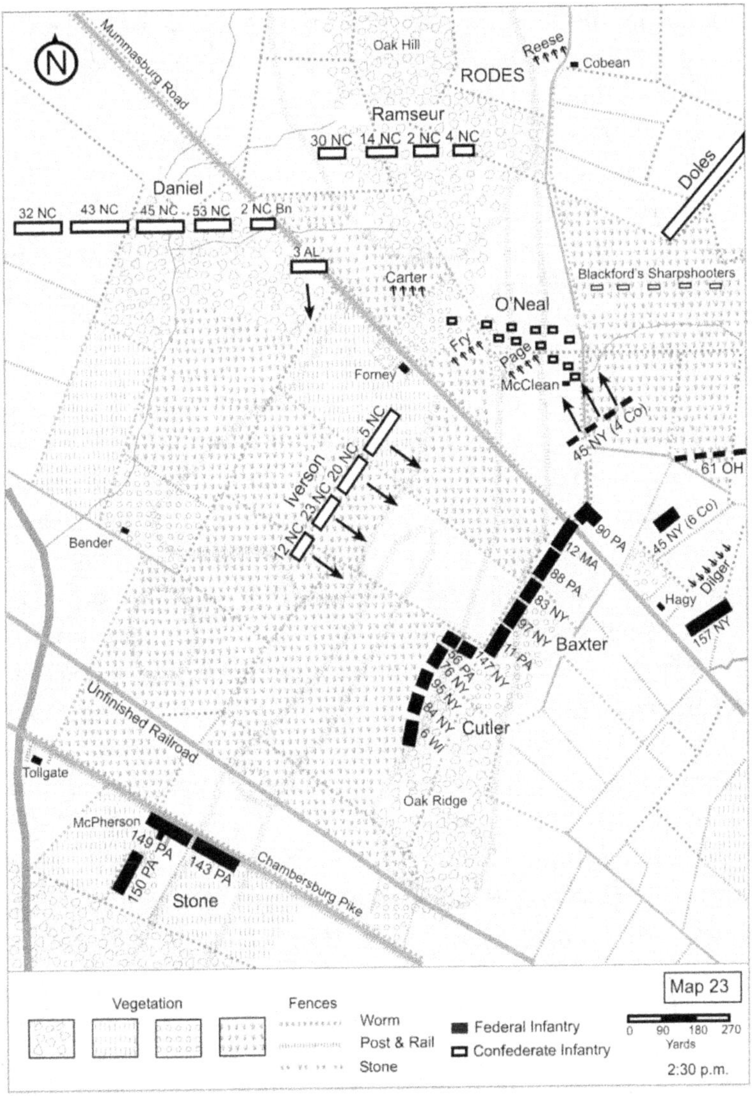

Iron Brigade's left flank, wrapped around it, and threw destructive volleys into its left flank and rear. The tough westerners knew an untenable situation when they saw it, and began pulling back to Seminary Ridge, stopping periodically to fight along the way. Biddle's and Stone's brigades were also attacked, and they too were forced to retreat to Seminary Ridge.[27]

Lee now replaced Heth's worn out division with Pender's, fresh from its march, to finish off the part of the I Corps deployed south of Chambersburg Pike. The situation was not much better north of the pike. While portions of the I Corps continued battling Rodes' division on Oak Ridge, the XI Corps to its right, was attacked by Maj. Gen. Jubal Early's division. Brig. Gen. Francis Barlow's First Division was shelled by Confederate artillery, so he brought up a battery and deployed it on Blocker's Knoll in front of his infantry. Then, without orders, he moved his division forward to occupy the knoll, thinking it was a good defensive position. It was, however, too close to a tree line, which provided protection for Early's men as they approached. Brig. Gen. John Gordon's Georgian brigade attacked the knoll from the north and Brig. Gen. George Doles' Georgians (from Rodes' division) from the west, creating a vise-like situation for Barlow. A Confederate soldier recalled, "Men were being mowed down in great numbers on both sides," but Barlow's position, being attacked in front, left flank, and rear was untenable. He went down with a severe wound and was joined by hundreds of his men and the remainder ran for the safety of the town. The two brigades continued their attack and struck the XI Corps' Third Division under Brig. Gen. Alexander Schimmelfennig out in the open fields. They made short work of the German immigrants, who fled through the town. A Union soldier looking back saw "a regular swath of blue coats as far as I could see along the line. They were piled up in every shape."[28]

Two of Early's brigades, probably numbering fewer than 2,500 men, thrashed the two other XI Corps brigades. Requests for assistance had gone unanswered until finally Col. Charles Coster's small 1,000-man brigade from von Steinwehr's Second Division was sent down from its reserve position on Cemetery Hill and marched through town. It was too little, too late as the rest of the two divisions had already met defeat. Just as Coster deployed his men in the John Kuhn brickyard, it was attacked by two fresh brigades (Brig. Gen.

Harry Hays' and Col. Isaac Avery's). Outnumbering Coster by more than three to one, the Confederates swung around both flanks and got into the enemy's rear. Hundreds of New Yorkers and Pennsylvanians fell or were captured and the rest stampeded back to Cemetery Hill.[29]

Over on Oak Ridge, Rodes had finally cobbled together a semblance of an organized line that hit Oak Ridge from the north and west, causing the entire Union line to flee toward Gettysburg. The 16th Maine was ordered to halt its retreat, and take "a position and hold it as long as there is a single man left," as it would act as a rearguard to buy time for its colleagues to find their way to safety. It was a suicide mission and the men knew it. The regiment's commander merely saluted and told Gen. Robinson, "All right, General, we'll do the best we can" and then gave the command: "About face, fix bayonets, charge." The unit was almost annihilated when it was hit from multiple directions. The men had the presence of mind to tear their precious flag into multiple pieces rather than see it captured. Each man received a small piece of the banner.

Lee launched his knockout punch at about 4:00 p.m. when Dorsey Pender unleashed a vicious charge against Seminary Ridge, west of town. Pender's three brigades (one was kept in reserve) would be forced to march several hundred yards across open fields against the newly formed Union defensive line on Seminary Ridge. The Union troops had run out of ridges to defend. If they lost this one, they would be driven into Gettysburg. The desperate Union soldiers from three infantry brigades, with a host of cannon, lined Seminary Ridge. Gamble's cavalry brigade formed on their left. It was a formidable line. Pender's left-most brigade, Brig. Gen. Alfred Scales's, straddling Chambersburg Pike, was turned back by the massive artillery and small arms fire thrown against it. Over on the right, Brig. Gen. James Lane's brigade saw Gamble's cavalry on its right flank and turned to face this threat, leaving only a South Carolina brigade under the command of Col. Abner Perrin. Only temporarily in command of the brigade, Perrin was told to keep pace with Scales on his left. When Scales turned back, Perrin continued forward. His men's orders were: "Do not fire your guns; give them the bayonet; if they run, then see if they can outrun the bullet." Without support on his right or left, Perrin pointed his men toward the Union line and found a gap between the I Corps infantry and Gamble's cavalry brigade, driving through it, and rolling up the defensive line. The defenders abandoned the ridge and ran through Gettysburg.

It had taken all day, but Lee's men had finally defeated the Union I and XI Corps. The Confederates entered Gettysburg, scooping up prisoners by the hundreds. Those who escaped made their way to Cemetery Hill, where the shattered army units were being reformed.[30]

Lost Opportunities

This was now Lee's supreme moment. The defeated and demoralized men of the I and XI Corps were reforming on Cemetery Hill and with decisive actions, his troops might capture the high ground, potentially ending the battle with a smashing victory. The possibilities were endless. Lee clearly expected such an action. He sent an aide, Col. Armistead Long to reconnoiter the enemy's position and told the chief of his artillery reserve to find good positions along Seminary Ridge to "enfilade the valley between our position and the enemy's batteries next to the town." Lee was clearly thinking of Cemetery Hill and a "flank movement against the enemy in his new position." This would require the acquiescence of Third Corps commander, A. P. Hill.

Lee understood the strategic value of Cemetery Hill, but erred in not explicitly ordering his subordinate to take the hill. Hill was probably a bit gun-shy about launching another attack, perhaps still chastened by not showing adequate caution in the morning leading to the opening fight between Heth's division and Buford's troopers. He was not about to blunder into another confrontation in which he was unprepared. Hill noted in his report, "Prudence led me to be content with what had been gained." He singled out Jeb Stuart's missing troopers for part of his reluctance, noting, "The want of cavalry had been and was again seriously felt." While the men of his two divisions committed to battle on July 1 were exhausted, Hill never mentioned that his third division under Maj. Gen. Richard Anderson was just at the edge of Gettysburg, available and ready for action. Two of Pender's four brigades were still fresh and could have been thrown forward as well. Many of Hill's artillery officers were dismayed that he did not order them up to Seminary Ridge, where they could have blanketed Cemetery Hill with exploding projectiles, which could have, at least theoretically, driven the

Map 24: Final Attack on Seminary Ridge

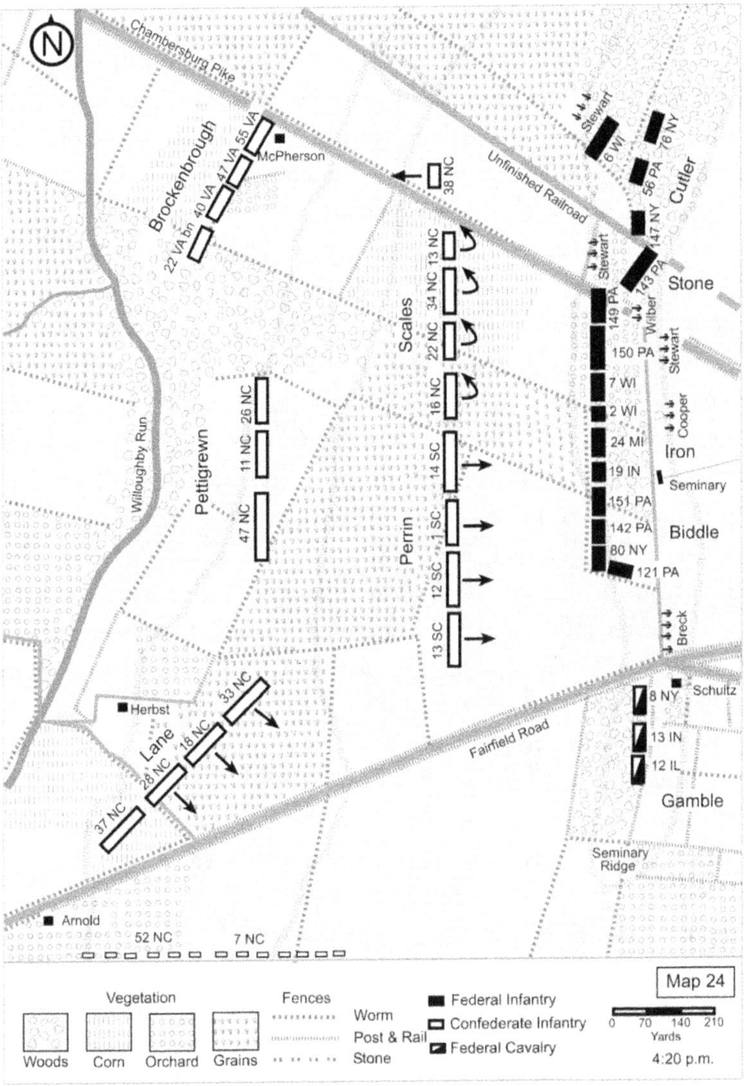

enemy from the exposed area. Artillery officer, Col. David McIntosh, thought it "almost incomprehensible" that cannon were not placed on Seminary Ridge to pound the Union positions.[31]

Ewell's two divisions that had crushed the XI Corps north of town could also have been sent through Gettysburg to capture Cemetery Hill. Ewell seemed interested in taking the high ground but he hesitated for two reasons. First, one of his brigade commanders posted to the left of the line along York Road sent a stream of messages warning Ewell of heavy concentrations of enemy troops in that direction. Secondly, Ewell did not believe he could launch a southward attack when his left flank was vulnerable. He therefore sent another one of his brigades in that direction to investigate, robbing him of half of Early's division's combat units. As Ewell rode through Gettysburg, he also despaired of moving his troops through the narrow streets in view of the enemy batteries on Cemetery Hill. Only a direct order from Lee would light a fire under Hill and Ewell, but this was not his mode of operation. Such an approach worked for Stonewall Jackson and Longstreet, but not for novices like Hill and Ewell.

Lee sent his adjutant, Col. Walter Taylor, to Ewell with orders to "press the enemy . . . secure the heights if practicable." Lee clarified his thinking in his report of the battle: "General Ewell was, therefore, instructed to carry the hill occupied by the enemy, if he found it practicable, but to avoid a general engagement until the arrival of the other divisions of the army, which were ordered to hasten forward." Ewell weighed his options: his men were tired, the trip through the town would be difficult and he expected his third division under Maj. Gen. Edward Johnson to appear momentarily, so he decided to wait. This indecision might have led to thousands of unnecessary casualties on July 2 and 3 on Culp's and Cemetery Hills, and possibly the loss of the battle.[32]

Meade was not yet on the battlefield, but upon learning of Reynolds' death, he ordered trusted lieutenant, Maj. Gen. Winfield Hancock of the II Corps to head to Gettysburg and take command of the troops. Hancock spent the first portion of the trip riding in an ambulance so he could study maps and then mounted his horse and headed for Gettysburg. He arrived on Cemetery Hill between 4:00 and 4:30 p.m. and rearranged some of the troops. His presence was an inspiration for all, but it created a problem Meade had probably not anticipated. The date of appointment to rank was of ultimate importance in determining line of succession and Howard had greater seniority. After reviewing the situation, Hancock mounted his horse and returned to report to Meade, thus ending a sticky situation.[33]

The first day's battle was a decisive Confederate victory. The victors outnumbered the Union defenders, 27,500 to 24,200. The Union losses were about 10,000 (41%), however, some of these occurred on July 2. The number included a sizable number of prisoners—about 3,650.

The Confederate losses are more difficult to ascertain as many of these units also participated in later fighting. The loss on July 1 is therefore estimated to amount to 5,750 (21%). The losses of the two sides would be similar if the number of Union soldiers captured was removed from the calculations.[34]

Comparisons of the Two Campaigns

Units and number of troops involved

During the first phase of Antietam, two Union corps, the I and XII, opened the fighting, although not in tandem. Joseph Hooker brought his I Corps into battle first and then called up the XII Corps, which entered the fighting almost two hours later. Gettysburg saw the I Corps also opening the fight and then joined several hours later by the XI Corps. Unlike Antietam, where the two corps fought for possession of the same fields (Cornfield and East Woods), the two Union corps at Gettysburg fought for different parts of the battlefield. The I Corps fought west of town and northwest of it; the XI Corps fought almost due north.

The Confederates did not have corps structure at Antietam—only "wings" — with Jackson and Longstreet in charge of each. The first phase involved both, although Jackson committed more troops than Longstreet. At Gettysburg, the first day's fight was waged by the Confederate Second (Ewell's) and Third Corps (A. P. Hill's).

After Hooker's men captured the Cornfield and East Woods, the battle shifted to the West Woods where fresh troops made their appearance at about 9:00 a.m. John Sedgwick's division (II Corps) marched into the West Woods and was assailed by McLaws' division with support from Walker's division and the remnants of J. R. Jones' division. At Gettysburg, some might consider the appearance of the XI Corps marching into the fields north of town to be a new front and therefore similar to Antietam in that regard.

McClellan fielded six divisions during the opening phase (three from the I Corps, one from the II Corps, and two from the XII Corps); the same number that battled Lee on the first day at Gettysburg, where the I and XI Corps each fielded three divisions. Not all of the XI Corps' Second division was committed to battle, however, as one brigade remained in reserve on Cemetery Hill and did not see action.

The Confederates opened Antietam with two divisions (J. R. Jones' and Lawton's) in Stonewall Jackson's wing who were joined by two other divisions (Hood's and D. H. Hill's) during the desperate fighting in the Cornfield and East Woods. When the fighting expanded to the West Woods, McLaws and Walker added their divisions to the fray. Therefore, Lee committed six of his nine divisions to protecting his left flank. During the first day of fighting at Gettysburg, only four of Lee's nine divisions (Heth's, Pender's, Early's and Rodes') participated in the fighting and they were able to defeat Meade's six divisions west and north of town. The Confederate units were larger at Gettysburg than Antietam, so number of divisions was not as important a factor (see below).

The first phase of the battle of Antietam saw the Confederates fielding 16 brigades (Lawton, J. R. Jones, and McLaws had four brigades each; Hood and Walker had two). McClellan at Antietam fielded 17 brigades during the first phase (the I Corps had nine brigades; the XII Corps had five; Sedgwick's division had three brigades). The numbers were mixed at Gettysburg: the Union army deployed 11 brigades; Lee had 17 brigades in action.

The number of units on the battlefield at the beginning of combat was one of the biggest differences in the two battles. Lee had about 25,000 men when the attack on his left flank began. Two other divisions would arrive during the morning, but were not in place when Hooker crashed through the Cornfield. McClellan, on the other hand, had all of his units ready for combat, about 49,000, except for the VI Corps, which did not arrive until around noon. Only John Buford's two cavalry brigades were in place at the beginning of Gettysburg. The others were thrown into battle as they arrived.

Approximately 25 percent more troops fought during the first phase of Gettysburg, compared with Antietam. This amounted to 41,300 troops (22,500 Union; 18,800 Confederate) at Antietam and 51,700 troops at Gettysburg on July 1 (24,200 Union; 27,500 Confederate). In both actions, the aggressor fielded the greater number of troops.

Because the armies that fought at Gettysburg were being thrown into battle as they arrived on the first day, only 38% of the Confederate army and 26% of the Union army participated in the first day's fight, compared with 52% (Confederates) and 39% (Union) at Antietam.

Tactics & Leadership

Antietam saw Hooker's I Corps attempting to crush the Confederate left flank and take the high ground beyond it. He was ultimately successful, but it took about two and a half hours to do it. Lee's senior officers also attempted to take the high ground west and north of Gettysburg, but it took almost a day to be successful. However, the proportion of time is nearly similar as Antietam was a shorter battle than Gettysburg.

In both campaigns, the Union army commander placed a subordinate in charge of an important sector during the first phase of the battle. At Antietam, Hooker was placed in charge of his own and the XII Corps' during the early fighting; at Gettysburg, Reynolds was in command of the field. His mortal wounding elevated Howard to command of the field.

The I Corps opened the fighting in both campaigns. It was led by highly respected and competent officers. Hooker, at Antietam, new to corps command, had proven himself to be an aggressive and able fighter at the divisional level; John Reynolds, at Gettysburg, was so well respected that Lincoln offered him command of the Army of the Potomac prior to the campaign. The second units entering the fights were not as well regarded. Like the I Corps at Antietam, the Union XII Corps served with the Army of Virginia under Maj. Gen. John Pope and had only recently been integrated into the Army of the Potomac. It was led by an elderly officer, Maj. Gen. Joseph Mansfield, with virtually no combat experience during the Civil War. Making matters worse, Mansfield had only been in command of his corps for two days. The unit had an inordinate number of new recruits, making its effectiveness even more suspect. Maj. Gen. Edwin Sumner, II Corps commander, was perhaps McClellan's most experienced corps commander, but he did not fare well at Antietam. He was so anxious to join the fight that he rode forward with Maj. Gen. John Sedgwick's division, all but ignoring his other two divisions. Poor reconnaissance may have doomed Sedgwick's division when it was routed in the West Woods.

The XI Corps was the second Union corps to enter the battle at Gettysburg, but it had a cloud hanging over it. Dubbed the "German" Corps because of its large number of immigrants, the unit had been routed by Stonewall Jackson at Chancellorsville, where the men were called the "Flying Dutchmen." Pious, one-armed general, Oliver Howard, was not well regarded by his comrades. Although competent, some considered him sanctimonious. The death of Reynolds took Howard from command of his corps and placed him in charge of the field. This meant that Maj. Gen. Carl Schurz, a political general with little military experience, was thrust in command of the XI Corps. Whether a more seasoned officer could have staved off defeat can only be surmised.

On the Confederate side, while men from both Jackson's and Longstreet's "wings" were present during the opening phase at Antietam, the former commanded the contested sector. Both commanded large bodies of troops in previous battles and were up to the task. Jackson managed to come out of the battle unscathed.

Lee's two new corps commanders at Gettysburg, Ewell and A. P. Hill, showed they were not up to the demands of the position, and both exhibited physical limitations during the battle. Hill was ill, probably with a flare-up of his venereal disease that always seemed to recur when his units went into battle; Ewell had recently returned to the army after losing a leg during the Second Bull Run Campaign. He was not the same aggressive fighter he had been when he led a division. Ewell was now married, had found religion, and his stump gave him all kinds of discomfort during his first battle back with the army. Hill's performance was probably most egregious as he disobeyed Lee's direct orders against bringing on a fight before the army assembled and instead allowed his lead division (Heth's) to blunder into the fight that began the battle of Gettysburg.

The performance of officers at the lower command levels was spotty. During the Maryland Campaign, both armies' division and brigade levels performed fairly effectively. The only clear exceptions were Confederate division commander, J. R. Jones, who abandoned his position after declaring a shell had exploded over his head, and Union brigade commander Col. William Christian who apparently suffered a nervous breakdown during the fight. The leaders of the I Corps at Gettysburg also performed effectively, but this was not the case with the XI Corps, who deployed their troops in open terrain with both flanks exposed, inviting an attack, which the Confederates were all too willing to launch.

The Confederates during the Maryland Campaign were undermanned and understaffed. For example, one of the brigades in the Stonewall Division was commanded by a captain and the division was commanded by a colonel by the end of the battle. With the departure of division commander J. R. Jones, less experienced commander, Brig. Gen. William Starke, was thrust into command. A combination of bad luck, poor command decisions, and a surge of patriotism led to his death and the destruction of much of his division. The brigade commanders, for the most part, performed well under very difficult circumstances.

Effective command decisions were certainly not the hallmark of the Confederates at Gettysburg during the first phase of the battle. The all too eager Heth blundered by marching his division into the opening fight at Gettysburg, despite the warnings of two of his brigade commanders. Rather than marshalling his powerful division, Heth threw two of his brigades forward in the morning. Each fought separately on either side of Chambersburg Pike and both were defeated. Brig. Gen. Joe Davis, a nephew of the president, blundered into the unfinished railroad, thinking it was a good defensive position, and lost hundreds of his men because of it. To the north, Rodes lost control of his division and three of his brigades, which were to attack simultaneously, instead attacked piecemeal, and two of them were badly thrashed as a result. It would not be until later in the afternoon that Lee's men were able to launch a coordinated attack and best the Union defenders.

Coordination

Hooker formulated a good plan on the morning on the morning of the Battle of Antietam to crush Lee's left flank, sending two I Corps divisions against the Confederate left, and leaving Meade's division in reserve. Mansfield's XII Corps could provide relief, if needed. However, the plan was poorly executed. Because of the terrain features, Confederate artillery fire, and the behavior of some brigade commanders, the coordinated attack never materialized and Hooker's two divisions fought almost independently of each other. However, their superior numbers overwhelmed the Confederate defenders. Fate smiled on Hooker when the XII Corps arrived just as the last of his I Corps was being driven to the rear, but he has been criticized for not calling up the large unit sooner. A coordinated attack by two Union corps at the beginning of the battle could have swept the Confederates from the field and possibly achieved total victory for McClellan. However, a case can be made that given the terrain and fog, it would have been difficult to jam any additional troops onto the field of battle. Sumner attempted to coordinate his efforts with the troops already on the field, but by the time he arrived, the fighting had all but ended.

The Confederates' coordination during the morning actions in the northern fields was mixed. Jackson, in command of the forward battle line facing the Cornfield and East Woods allowed both of his flanks to be exposed and his left was easily turned by Doubleday's division. He also permitted a 120-yard gap to yawn between his two front-line divisions. Because the two divisions could not see each other, they fought fairly independently, and that's the way they were beaten. While the two front-line divisions, J. R. Jones' and Alexander Lawton's, and did not coordinate their actions, Lee sent a stream of reinforcements at opportune moments through the early fighting to help blunt the Union thrusts in the Cornfield and East Woods. Only when Lee was unable to bring additional troops into the mix did the Union side prevail and capture both sectors. When Lafayette McLaws' and John Walker's divisions hit Sedgwick's division in the West Woods after 9:00 a.m., it was not because Lee effectively anticipated the Union thrust, as much as he was bringing additional troops to bear in the Cornfield/East Woods fight.

The opening phase of the Gettysburg campaign featured even less coordination by both armies. Possibly because of the early mortal wounding of Reynolds, the I Corps' divisions and brigades under Doubleday rarely coordinated their actions. Terrain and distance certainly played a role. During the opening fight, Wadsworth's two brigades supported each other to some degree, leading to Davis' brigade's ultimate defeat. The rest of the corps fought fairly independently. Robinson's division on Oak Ridge, except for one of Wadsworth's brigades driven back there, fought independently of the rest of the I Corps and when Col. Chapman Biddle's brigade took position on the afternoon of July 1, it did not link up directly with the Iron Brigade's left flank, instead deploying in an open field behind, and to its left, and as a result, both units were flanked and forced from their positions.

The I Corps fought independently of the IX Corps, and the latter's divisions fought fairly independently in the fields north of Gettysburg. Brig. Gen. Alexander Schimmelfennig's division did not link up with the I Corps to its left and Brig. Gen. Francis Barlow's division marched north toward Blocher's Knoll, outpacing its support. As a result, both XI Corps divisions were flanked and defeated.

The situation at Gettysburg, as we have already seen, was worse with the Confederates. Until Lee came up, no one coordinated the actions of Hill's and Ewell's Corps. Even after Lee arrived, he seemed to allow each corps commander to carry on as he wished (see next section). Lee clearly wished Hill and Ewell would take the high ground south of Gettysburg during the late afternoon, but he left it up to his corps commanders, using the phrase, "if practicable."

At the division level, the initial attack by two of Heth's two brigades during the initial advance was uncoordinated, and the same was true with Rodes' initial attack during the early afternoon. This lack of coordination resulted in deadly repulses. It was not until later in the afternoon that Ewell and Rodes mounted coordinated attacks on Oak Ridge, which threw the defenders into retreat. Similarly, to the west, Heth finally committed his entire division to the attack and captured McPherson Ridge. Pender's division's subsequent attack was also coordinated and drove the enemy from Seminary Ridge. Once these attacks were coordinated, they became irresistible.

Pulling Troops from One Sector to Another

At Antietam, Lee initially had fewer than 4,150 troops on his front line when Hooker launched his I Corps toward the Dunker Church. Lee and Jackson skillfully pulled troops from other sectors to counter the hammer blows. Jackson first pulled those troops closest to the action, such as the rest of Lawton's division and then Hood's division from his reserve behind the Dunker Church in the West Woods. After depleting these reserves, Lee called up three brigades from D. H. Hill's division occupying the middle of his line. He was able to pull these troops because this sector was not threatened at the time. The XII Corps only overran the Cornfield and East Woods when Lee could no longer send additional troops to blunt their thrust.

McLaws' division had recently arrived from Harpers Ferry when it was sent to shore up Lee's left, but the XII Corps had finished off the remainder of Jackson's troops before the reinforcements arrived. However, McLaws' troops appeared in time to devastate Sedgwick's division in the West Woods. He was aided by Walker's division, which had been deployed to the south, covering Snavely Ford below the Lower Bridge. Since the Union IX Corps did not appear to be threatening a crossing, Lee felt able to pull Walker's powerful division from its position and send it north.

Gettysburg saw little movement of troops from one sector to aid those in another. Three regiments (two of Cutler's and one from the Iron Brigade) crossed over Chambersburg Pike to pounce on Davis' brigade, which had driven Cutler's troops to the rear. Another example was when Col. Charles Coster's brigade was sent north from its reserve position on Cemetery Hill to assist in blunting the Confederate advance toward Gettysburg.

Duration of combat

Hooker's I and XII Corps battled Stonewall Jackson's men for about two and a half hours during the first phase of Antietam. Sedgwick's defeat in the West Woods took less than half an hour.

The first phase of Gettysburg (July 1) lasted much longer. The morning portion lasted from Buford's first encounter with Heth's division at about 7:00 a.m. and continued to 11:00 a.m. The afternoon fighting lasted from 1:30 p.m. to 5:00 p.m. for a total of seven and a half hours of fighting. If just the infantry is counted, the fighting would be four hours, still longer than the first phase at Antietam. This does not include fighting in the town of Gettysburg as Union troops fled to the safety of Cemetery Hill.

Losses

The Confederates lost 6,118 men (33%) and the Federals lost 6,546 (24%) for a total of 12,664 casualties during the initial phase of Antietam. The Union casualties numbered 9,993 (41%) at Gettysburg; the Confederate losses are estimated to number 5,740 (21%). While the total number of losses was higher at Gettysburg, 15,733 (30%) versus 12,664 during the first phase of Antietam's, the percentages are almost identical-- 31% for Gettysburg and 30% for Antietam. Several generals were killed or mortally wounded, including Union general Joseph Mansfield and Confederate general William Starke at Antietam. Only Union Gen. John Reynolds lost his life during the first phase of Gettysburg and Confederate general James Archer was captured.

Table 20: Comparison of the First Phase of the Battles

Issue	Maryland Campaign	Pennsylvania Campaign
Role of cavalry	Confederates/Union: Minor: guard flanks/screening/ reconnaissance	Union: Buford played major role Confederates: Cavalry on raid; did not assist
Large units that opened the fight	Confederates: Jackson's Wing Union: I Corps	Confederates: Heth's division (Third Corps) Union: Wadsworth's division (I Corps)
Other large units fighting during the opening phase	Confederates: Longstreet's Wing Union: XII Corps and Sedgwick's division (II Corps)	Confederates: Pender's division (Third Corps); Rodes & Early's divisions (Second Corps) Union: Remainder of I Corps and two divisions of XI Corps
Number of infantry divisions engaged	Confederate: 6 (67%) Union: 6 (38%)	Confederate: 4 (44%) Union: 6 (32%)
Number of brigades engaged	Confederates: 16 (40%) Union: 17 (39%)	Confederates: 11 (30%) Union: 17 (33%)
Number of troops engaged (in relation to size of army)	Confederates: 18,800 (52%) Union: 22,450 (39%) Total: 41,250	Confederates: 27,500 (38%) Union: 24,200 (26%) Total: 51,700
Leader directing initial action wounded/killed?	Confederates: No Union: Yes (Hooker)	Confederates: Yes (Heth) Union: Yes (Reynolds)
Second in command takes over the field	Confederates: No Union: No	Confederates: Yes Union: Yes
Major goal	Take high ground	Take high ground
Duration of the fighting	3.0 hours	7.5 hours

Issue	Maryland Campaign	Pennsylvania Campaign
Pulling troops from other sectors	**Confederates:** Yes **Union:** Yes	**Confederates:** No **Union:** No
Direction of major initial attack	North to south	West to east
Direction of second attack	East to west	North to south
Dubious deployment and coordination of troops	**Confederates:** Yes **Union:** Yes	**Confederates:** Yes **Union:** Yes
Time of initial movement toward the enemy	6:00 a.m.	5:00 a.m.
Number of troops on battlefield before the start of combat	**Confederates:** 25,000 (69% of army) **Union:** 49,000 (85% of army)	**Confederates:** 0 **Union:** 4,000 (4% of army)
Number of casualties	**Confederates:** 6,200 (33%) **Union:** 6,550 (24%) Total: 12,700	**Confederates:** 5,740 (21%) **Union:** 10,000 (41%) Total: 15,740

Chapter 16: The Second Phase of the Battles

The Maryland Campaign of 1862

The major portion of the second phase of the battle of Antietam involved fighting in the middle of the battlefield occurring between 9:15 a.m. and 1:00 p.m.

Sunken Road

The center of Lee's line was initially held by D. H. Hill's division, which had seen significant action atop South Mountain on September 14. Now its 6,000 men occupied the area around Boonsboro Pike. Three of its five brigades were sent north earlier in the morning to help counter the I Corps thrust through the Cornfield and East Woods, leaving only Brig. Gen. Robert Rodes' Alabamians and Brig. Gen. G. B. Anderson's North Carolinians in this sector. The two brigades were ordered forward to assist their brother brigades, but according to Gen. Rodes, "I had hardly begun the movement before it was evident that the two latter [Colquitt's and Garland's] had met with a reverse, and that the best service I could render them and the field generally would be to form a line in rear of them and endeavor to rally them before attacking or being attacked." Hill had the same notion and ordered Rodes' and Anderson's brigades into a road that was sunken that snaked between Hagerstown and Boonsboro Pikes. Erosion and the travel of hundreds of wagons through the years had caused the road to sink, making it a naturally strong defensive position. Rodes' brigade formed from the Mumma farm lane to where the Sunken Road bent to the right. Anderson's brigade extended the line eastward from there. Portions of Cobb's and Colquitt's brigades formed on Rodes' left, extending the line to Hagerstown Pike.

The men did not have long to wait before Brig. Gen. William French's powerful 6,000-man Union division appeared before them. The division crossed Antietam Creek behind Sedgwick's division, but because so many of its men were rookies, it could not keep pace. French wrote in his report, "When my left flank had cleared the ford a mile, the division faced to the left, forming three lines of battle adjacent to and contiguous with Sedgwick's, and immediately moved to the front." This is an odd and incorrect statement.

When French reached the East Woods, Sumner was nowhere to be found, as he had ridden ahead with Sedgwick's men. French was unsure of what to do, but when he saw large numbers of Union soldiers around the Dunker Church and Rebels beyond them near the Sunken Road, he decided to turn left and march south. The move put his division on Greene's division's left flank. If Sedgwick was able to swing around to Greene's right flank, three divisions numbering 13,600 men would appear opposite what was now the left flank of Lee's line. Lee had few reinforcements at this time—only Maj. Gen. Richard Anderson's newly arrived division. Further south, Brig. Gen. D. R. Jones had another 2,500 men for a total of perhaps 8,000 men (with D. H. Hill's two brigades). This could have been a desperate time for Lee, but as seen earlier, Sedgwick's division was routed in the West Woods and Greene's division stayed put near the Dunker Church after helping rout the Confederates in the Cornfield/East Woods. French's division continued south on its own, past the burning Mumma farm buildings and the Roulette farm, on a collision course with the Confederates deployed along the Sunken Road.

French's division was not the optimal choice for opening a new front. The Third Division officially formed a mere week before, on September 10, 1862. One brigade, under Brig. Gen. Nathan Kimball, was an experienced unit but the other two were inexperienced. Col. Dwight Morris' three regiments were completely green and Brig. Gen. Max Weber's brigade had seen service on garrison and outpost duty, but its men had not seen actual combat. According to historian Ezra Carman, "The three brigades were strangers to each other and had been thrown together as a division but the day before."[1]

According to military parlance of the time, the inexperience brigades were thrown into battle first; the most experienced occupied the last line. This approach would sacrifice the novice troops, but the veterans in the rear could prevent a stampede. If victory was achieved by the inexperienced troops, the veterans could deliver the knockout punch. French took a modified approach, keeping Kimball's most experienced men in the last rank, but retaining Morris' novice troops in the second line, so Weber's semi-experienced troops took the lead.

Rodes watched the Union troops' advance at about 9:15 a.m.: "Their advance was beautiful in the extreme and great regularity marked their columns and this precision of movement was preserved." As Weber's brigade appeared at the top of the hill in front of the sunken road, Rodes' "entire brigade rose & delivered its volley at a distance of no more than 80 yards." Col. John Gordon of the 6th Alabama on the right of Rodes' line recalled his men's first volley: "The effect was appalling. The entire front line, with few exceptions went down in the consuming blast." A soldier in Weber's brigade recalled how the men were "met by a murderous fire, which made the bravest shrink for a moment." Morris' brigade formed behind Weber's men to provide support. However, in the confusion, "new levies... instead of supporting our advance, fired into our rear," reported the commander of the 1st Delaware. After only a few minutes at the top of the hill, Weber's men quickly fell back in disorder.[2]

Morris' fresh regiments now advanced to replace Weber's stunned men and they suffered the same fate. Around this time, sector-commander Longstreet launched a counterattack against French's wavering enemy line, sending forward Rodes' brigade and the remnants of Cobb's and Colquitt's brigades. The move was poorly coordinated, as some regiments made a sincere effort to drive the enemy away, while others, like the 6th Alabama, did not budge, claiming not to hear the order to charge. Cobb's brigade and other troops on Rodes' left made a half-hearted effort. The casualties were high in those regiments making a determined attack.

Ezra Carman explained the condition of French's first two brigades making attacks on the Sunken Road: "The two brigades of Weber and Morris had made spirited efforts to drive the enemy but were brought to a stand; had lost heavily and, being new troops, had become confused and much broken; many of the men had gone to the rear, but enough of them remained on the firing line to resist the enemy, though without sufficient aggressive force to advance." Additional manpower would appear with the entry of Kimball's veterans into the fray. A messenger from Sumner approached French with orders to take the Sunken Road once and for all, as a diversion was needed to pull enemy troops from attacking Sedgwick's division in the West Woods. French complied by bringing up his last brigade. Kimball yelled to his men, "Boys we are going in now to lick the rebels, and we will stay with them, all day if necessary." The veterans fingered their weapons and advanced toward the top of the hill overlooking the Sunken Road, however, as Kimball later related, "As my line advanced to the crest of the hill, a murderous fire was opened upon it from the entire force in front. My advance further was checked."³

French had committed his three lines of infantry in tandem, but the Confederates were also being reinforced. Richard Anderson's division, numbering 3-4,000 men, arrived after McLaws' division in the morning from its all-night march from Harpers Ferry. After a short rest near Sharpsburg, the division was rushed to reinforce what had been the center of Lee's line at the Sunken Road. Anderson was almost immediately wounded by an artillery projectile, thrusting his second in command, Brig. Gen. Roger Pryor, into the hot seat. Pryor, an attorney and newspaper editor prior to the war, certainly did not have the military experience or personality to effectively function during this troubled time. He also had not a clue of what he was supposed to do. The division broke apart, as each of its six brigades independently attempted to make its way toward the Sunken Road. Therefore, the fresh division's immense power was dissipated before it reached the contested road. Union "guns of position" on high ground across the river and a battery near the Mumma farm pounded the Confederates as they advanced through a cornfield and casualties mounted as the men desperately made their way to the protection of the Sunken Road. Some simply turned back rather than risk injury, others fell to the ground and made themselves small, and those who advanced, jumped wildly into the road. "They came up opposite us & sink out of sight in the Sunken Lane. It is a mystery that so many men could crowd into so small a space," noted a soldier in the 8th Ohio. Some of these men did not stop at the road, but surged up and over it to engage the enemy attempting to attack the road. They were quickly repulsed with heavy losses.⁴

Maj. Gen. Israel Richardson's division of the II Corps arrived at the Sunken Road sector at about 11:00 a.m. Sumner's last division had been guarding Union artillery when it was finally relieved by Morrell's division and quickly crossed Antietam Creek. Its three brigades followed the path of French's division and came up on its left flank, across the Roulette farm lane. Like French's attacks, Richardson launched his men piecemeal, one brigade at a time. The venerable Irish Brigade formed the first line and it steadily advanced. Unlike most of the troops in the Union army, most of the brigade was armed with smoothbore muskets, effective at less than 75 yards. Most of

Map 25: The Sunken Road
A: French's Attack
B: Richardson's Attack

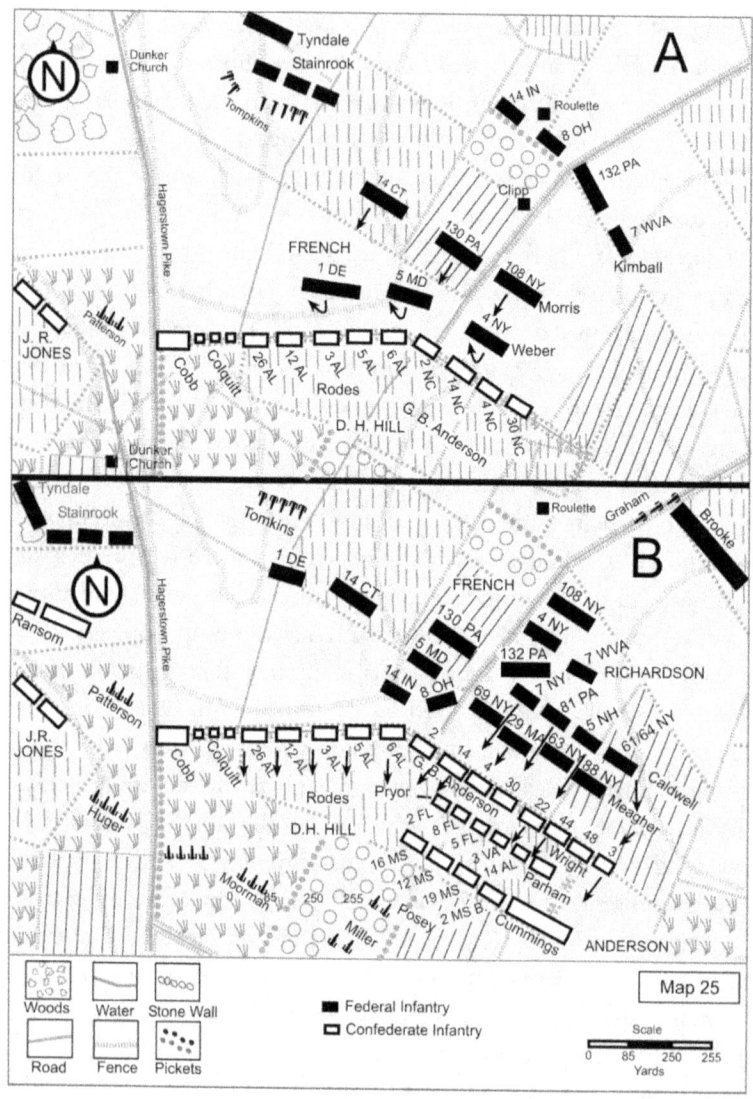

the Confederates in the sunken road had muskets, they were forced to watch the Irishmen close on their positions before the two sides could fire. According to the brigade's commander, Brig. Gen. Thomas Meagher, the enemy bullets "literally cut lanes through our approaching line." Above the din of battle came the Irish cry "Faugh-a-Ballagh" (Gaelic for "clear the way"). Some regiments lost over half of their men in this desperate charge, but raw courage was not enough to drive the enemy from the Sunken Road. The brigade would make a similar charge at Fredericksburg a few months later with similar grisly results.[5]

Casualties were also mounting among the Confederate troops in the Sunken Road, making movement difficult and dissipating their effectiveness. The losses were especially significant among the officers. Brigade commander G. B. Anderson went down with an ankle wound, and one by one, the brigade's next in command were also shot down. The officers in Rodes' brigade were also being struck down.

It was now getting close to noon and the defenders' time was running out. Ammunition was becoming scarce as was their manpower. Trouble was brewing on the right side of Rodes' brigade when the 6th Alabama's acting regimental commander, Lt. Col. James Lightfoot, sought out Gen. Rodes because his regiment was being enfiladed from the right. Rodes told him to turn the right of his regiment to better alleviate the flank fire, and then left the sector to assist a wounded aide. He was shocked when he returned to see his entire line retreating. The acting commander apparently misinterpreted Rodes' orders and gave the command, "About face, forward march." When the commander of the 5th Alabama on the left of the 6th asked if the order was for the entire brigade, Lightfoot said "yes" and eventually the entire brigade marched out of the sunken road. Rodes returned too late to reverse the movement.

The right side of the Sunken Road defensive line was also in danger of collapse. Gen. Richardson sent in his second brigade under Brig. Gen. John Caldwell to relieve the Irish Brigade. Col. Francis Barlow, commanding the 61st/64th New York on the left of Caldwell's line advanced against the Sunken Road. Barlow later reported, "Our position giving us peculiar advantages for attacking in flank this part of the enemy's line, my regiments advanced and obtained an enfilading fire upon the enemy." This caused the defenders on the right side of the Sunken Road to abandon their positions. At around the same time, the 29th Massachusetts, the "Plymouth Rock Presbyterians," who were brigaded with the Irish regiments in Meagher's Irish Brigade, but not called upon to attack the enemy line, left their protected positions behind the hill and launched a determined attack against the center of George Anderson's line. This attack, coupled with Barlow's caused the Sunken Road defensive line to crumble. The surging Yanks captured almost 300 men and two sets of colors.

French's and Richardson's division's fight for the possession of the Sunken Road was finally over after two and a half hours of combat.[6]

Piper Farm

The goal of French's and Richardson's divisions was never to simply capture the Sunken Road, it was to drive hard against Lee's center, capture Sharpsburg and force him to retreat toward the Potomac River, which was only a couple of miles away. The move would cut off the direct retreat route to the Shepherdstown Ford and possibly cause the capture of a chunk of Lee's army. The Confederates pushed out of the Sunken Road were still full of fight, and combat now shifted to the south in the fields around the Henry Piper farmstead. The fighting was desperate there as can be seen by the actions of their leaders. D. H. Hill, who before the campaign commanded a division of as many as 8,000 men, grabbed a musket and led a band of 200 men against the surging Union troops. Longstreet and his staff helped man Miller's battery near the Piper orchard as combat had thinned their ranks. Longstreet ordered his staff members to man the cannons while he held the reins of their horses. Some of the fighting also involved still-organized Confederate regiments, but all were driven back. Masses of Confederate artillery on Reel Ridge to the west, helped blunt the Union advance.

If the surge of the XII Corps toward and beyond Dunker Church caused Lee anxiety earlier in the morning, the fighting in and around the Sunken Road created even more concern, for while Greene's men halted near the Church, Richardson's continued surging toward the village. The Union advance suddenly stopped and then receded back to and beyond the Sunken Road. Richardson apparently realized he needed to pull his men back to reorganize and resupply them, but an artillery shell wounded him as he attempted to reposition a battery to have a greater impact on the enemy. These events caused a pause in the action, but it was never continued and the Union army squandered yet another opportunity to crush Lee's army.

The fighting during the middle phase of the battle lasted from about 9:30 a.m. to 1:00 p.m. In that time, 17,650 troops (11,450 Union; 6,200 Confederates) desperately battled for the Sunken Road and the Piper farm fields. The losses totaled 5,150 (3,050 for the Union or 27%; 2,100 for the Confederates or 34%).[7]

The Pennsylvania Campaign of 1863

The Strong Union Defensive Line

Additional Union army forces arrived during the night of July 1-2 and during the latter day, so the second day's battle saw the heaviest fighting with the largest numbers of troops. By the morning of July 2, the Union line was deployed in the form of a fish hook. The XII Corps formed the right flank on Culp's Hill, south of Gettysburg. It occupied a very strong position, made even more so when the men worked through the night chopping down trees to construct an almost impregnable breastwork. The defensive line stretched west toward Cemetery Hill, where the battered I Corps was placed on the left of the XII Corps and the equally decimated XI Corps was on its left, on, and at the base of, Cemetery Hill. While the hill teemed with artillery and was a strong defensive position, it was probably not the best place to locate the demoralized and under-manned remnant of the XI Corps. The line then bent south to Cemetery Ridge, where the powerful II Corps extended the line south toward Little Round Top. The III Corps continued the line south, extending from the end of Cemetery Ridge to the Round Tops. The V Corps arrived during the morning of July 2 after marching over 60 miles in three days, 26 of them since the morning of July 1. They were a tired bunch when they reached the battlefield. The VI Corps' march was even more difficult, and would not reach the battlefield until later in the afternoon after marching 36 miles in 18 hours from Manchester, Maryland.

Meade finally arrived at the Evergreen Cemetery gatehouse at about 1:00 a.m. on July 2, looking haggard and careworn. Maj. Gen. Carl Schurz, who had commanded the XI Corps on July 1, watched him arrive with a single aide and an orderly and recalled he had "nothing in his appearance or his bearing—not a smile not a sympathetic word addressed to those around him—that might have made the...soldiers warm to him." Three corps commanders, Maj. Oliver Howard (XI Corps), Maj. Gen. Howard Slocum (XII Corps), and Maj. Gen. Daniel Sickles (III Corps), joined him at the gatehouse in an impromptu meeting and all sang the praises of the army's position, particularly Cemetery Hill. Meade purportedly asked, "Well, Howard, what do you think, is this the place to fight the battle?" Howard replied in the affirmative. He believed Cemetery Hill could be held, especially if its flanks were secured by the newly arriving troops. Slocum agreed. Meade quietly took it all in and finally said, "I am glad to hear you so, gentlemen, for it is too late to leave it." He later murmured, "We may fight it out here as well as anywhere else." When asked how many soldiers he could muster, Meade replied about 95,000. "Enough, I guess for this business." Meade then set off to examine his army's position and make necessary adjustments. Two of his corps (I and XI Corps) were wrecked and in no shape for further action, three (II, III, and XII Corps) were fresh and ready for action and two more (V and VI Corps) were expected sometime during July 2. Meade considered a bold move against Lee's left flank by the V, VI, and XII Corps, but it would need to await the former two corps' arrival and deployment. In the meantime, Meade realized he was not strong enough to initiate offensive action, so he decided to merely wait and hope to fend off Lee's attacks until help arrived.[8]

Lee Takes Position

As seen earlier, Lee wanted to attack the enemy's right flank on Cemetery and Culp's Hills at first light but was dissuaded by Ewell, commander of the Confederate Second Corps, and one of his vocal subordinates, division commander Jubal Early. Lee next shifted his focus to the enemy's left flank using Longstreet's two fresh divisions and one of A. P. Hill's divisions that reached the battlefield too late to join the fight on July 1. Lee settled on an *en echelon* strategy to knock Meade off the high ground. This approach envisioned finding Meade's left flank along Emmitsburg Road, and launching the brigades, one after the other, like a row of dominos. This type of attack was designed to force the move of enemy units not under attack to reinforce areas that were, thus weakening parts of the enemy's line that would soon be under attack. Such a broad approach could also detect weak spots in the enemy line, but unless there were adequate reserves, the breach could not be exploited. This was indeed the case. Maj. Gen. John Hood's division on Warfield Ridge to the south would begin the attack. Its right flank faced the Round Tops. It would attack along Emmitsburg Road, rolling up the enemy's flank. After Hood launched each of his brigades, Maj. Gen. Lafayette McLaws' division would take up the attack. When Ewell heard Longstreet's artillery, he was to launch his attack against Culp's and Cemetery Hills.[9]

If Meade looked rumpled and concerned, Lee was regally dressed and optimistic, but still given to deep introspection. After disseminating his plan, Longstreet objected. "I never like to go into battle with one boot off," he remarked to a subordinate. He had 11 brigades in his three divisions, but Pickett's three were still on the road from Chambersburg and a fourth, Brig. Gen. Evander Law's (Hood's division) was on the march to the battlefield from a scouting mission, leaving him with seven brigades. Lee told Longstreet not to worry, for he could use the five brigades of Maj. Gen. Richard Anderson's fresh division (Third Corps) to roll up the enemy's line. This would exactly compensate for his missing brigades. As Hood advanced he would reach Emmitsburg Road, turn left and drive north on Meade's left while McLaws' and Anderson's divisions attacked the enemy's front. The vise-like attack would surely roll up Meade's flank and force him from the field.

All agreed to the plan, but Longstreet added one proviso—he did not want a repeat of the battle of Chancellorsville, where the enemy saw the attack columns as they moved into position. Fortunately, the observers did not believe what they were seeing at that battle. Longstreet advocated for a less direct, but more concealed route. It would take five miles and a couple of hours to complete. The group next conferred with Capt. Samuel Johnston who claimed he rode all the way south to Little Round Top early that morning, scaled it, and returned without seeing any enemy troops. With all in agreement, the conference broke up, but Longstreet had one last request for Lee—could he await the return of Evander Law's brigade, which was slated to arrive any moment? Lee agreed, but it did not arrive until shortly before noon, when Longstreet began his circuitous movement.

Hindsight suggests that a morning start of the fight might have yielded far different results, as the V Corps, which bore so much of the fighting later in the day, had not yet arrived on the battlefield from its long march.

All was proceeding smoothly when McLaws, whose division was leading the column south, noticed Little Round Top to his left. If he could see the hill, the enemy on it could also see him. Longstreet reluctantly turned the column around and retraced his steps, wasting further time as the V Corps was approaching the battlefield and the VI Corps was only a couple of hours away. As the Confederate line moved into position, the commanders quickly realized Capt. Johnston's mistake. The Union line did not end at the Peach Orchard—it extended all the way south toward Little Round Top.[10]

An Unhappy Dan Sickles

Longstreet was not the only person stewing about his position. Sickles, commander of the Union III Corps, was also unhappy. He did not like his assigned position along the low ground south of Cemetery Ridge and asked Meade to venture south to look at his position and make changes as necessary. Sickles had already seen the impact of a devastating enemy flank movement just two months earlier at Chancellorsville and did not wish to invite another decisive defeat. At that battle, Sickles learned the importance of high ground and the "low marshy swale" most of his troops now occupied greatly concerned him. He sent a reconnaissance in force consisting of several regiments across the fields to the Pitzer's Woods on Seminary Ridge opposite his position, and upon entering it, they saw row upon row of enemy infantry poised for battle. His men quickly retraced their steps to Sickles' line with the bad news, but not before engaging in a sharp skirmish. Meade believed the attack would be from the north, so he worried less about one from the west. Frustrated, Sickles rode to Meade's headquarters at the widow Lydia Leister house to plead his case. He was merely told to tie his right flank to the II Corps on Cemetery Ridge and his left to the Round Tops. Meade remained glued to his headquarters and would not personally inspect Sickles' position. Signalmen on Little Round Top also reported enemy activity from the west, but Meade would still not budge. Sickles decided to act on his own, moving his line forward over half a mile to occupy the high ground along Emmitsburg Road, and then angling it back toward the Round Tops. While

Map 26: The Armies on the Eve of the Fighting on July 2

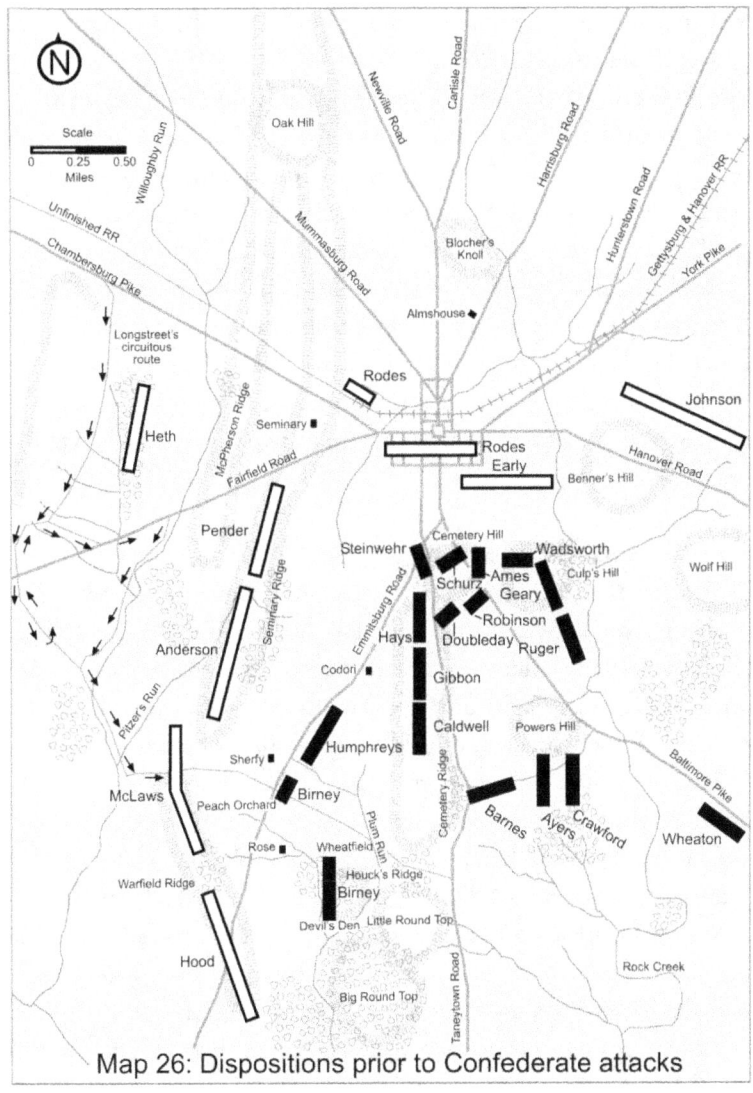

Map 26: Dispositions prior to Confederate attacks

the initial position contained one vulnerable flank, the new one created three, including a salient at the Peach Orchard. Sickles did not have enough infantrymen to man the entire position, but believed he could adequately compensate with massed artillery.[11]

Meade was one of the last to hear about Sickles' redeployment and he demanded a visit by his wayward commander. Sickles reluctantly complied, although his line was now being peppered by enemy artillery fire. Meade immediately called up the V Corps, which was resting northwest of the battlefield, near Powers' Hill, and then rode with Sickles to his disputed sector. Meade did not like it and asked Sickles if he could defend it. He could, replied Sickles, perhaps with tongue in cheek. Meade continued pressing his subordinate until Sickles finally told him that he would be "happy to modify" his position, but the army commander muttered, "I wish to God you could, but the enemy won't let you!" Sickles would stay put and Meade would bring up support.[12]

Longstreet Launches His Attack

Lee's patience with Longstreet's delay in launching his two divisions against the Union left flank was running out. When Hood deployed his division on the attack column's right flank, he believed he should be facing only air, because his command was supposed to be positioned beyond Meade's left flank. He quickly realized the error of the scouting reports, as he actually faced enemy troops in front of him. There would be no turning left on Emmitsburg Road and rolling up the enemy's flank unless Hood could drive the enemy from the heights in front. Hood pleaded with Longstreet to allow him to move further to the right to get on the flank, but Longstreet realized he could delay no longer and waved off the protests. Hood kicked off his attack at 4:00 p.m. with Brig. Gen. Evander Law's and Brig. Gen. Jerome Robertson's brigades at the far right end of his division.

The Army of the Potomac's Chief Engineer, Brig. Gen. Gouverneur Warren, rode up Little Round Top, devoid of Union troops, except for a signal station. He spied the glint of steel in the distance and his stomach knotted as he knew trouble was brewing. He quickly rode down the hill to mobilize troops to defend the high ground, with good reason, as the remainder of the afternoon would see fighting at Little Round Top, Devil's

Den/Houck's Ridge, Wheatfield, Peach Orchard, and along Emmitsburg Road. All involved the III and V Corps, up against Longstreet's two divisions and parts of Anderson's division.[13]

Houck's Ridge, Devil's Den, and the Slaughter Pen

Hood's attack went awry almost from the start when Capt. James Smith's Union battery on Houck's Ridge blistered his line with well-aimed artillery shells. One exploded above Hood and a fragment tore into his arm, removing him from command at the most important point in his career. He would later lose the use of the arm. The artillery fire unnerved Law, commanding Hood's right-most brigade, causing him to peel off two regiments and send them to Houck's Ridge to silence the battery. This denied hundreds of men from the subsequent attack on Little Round Top. As the 44th and 48th Alabama regiments approached Houck's Ridge from the southwest, a portion of Robertson's brigade approached from the west.

Up on Houck's Ridge, Brig. Gen. Hobart Ward deployed his brigade (III Corps) for the coming shock. Ward was especially worried about the low area to his left; so he sent the 4th Maine down to protect his flank. Its commander was in no mood to accept his orders, as he understood the vulnerability of the position, in what would later be called "The Slaughter Pen." He finally obeyed, and after a tough fight, the Alabamians captured the area, driving the rugged Maine soldiers back onto Houck's Ridge. They arrived in time to attempt to save Smith's guns, which were under heavy attack. The 3rd Arkansas and the 1st Texas of Robertson's brigade had earlier approached Houck's Ridge. The former regiment attacked the far right of Ward's line, composed of the 99th Pennsylvania and 20th Indiana. Despite several determined charges, the Razorbacks were unable to throw the Yanks off the ridge. The sounds of battle were so earsplitting, the regiment's colonel was forced to yell orders into the ears of his officers and literally push his men into position. The 1st Texas approached further to their right, but came under Smith's destructive artillery barrage. As they continued closing the distance to Houck's Ridge, the Texans were stunned by an audacious charge of the 124th New York, the "Orange Blossoms," who pushed them back a considerable distance. The New Yorkers' commander, Col. A. Van Horne Ellis, yelled for his men to "Charge bayonets! Forward; double-quick—

March!" The New Yorkers did not have long to savor their victory, for the Texans counterattacked, killing and wounding scores of New Yorkers, including all of their field officers.

Help was on the way for both sides. Brig. Gen. Henry Benning's Georgia brigade threw its weight into the fray. With Robertson's two regiments, they forced Ward's men from the ridge and captured three of Smith's cannons. Additional Union regiments were rushed to the sector, but they were too few to stop the Confederate onslaught. The Confederates now held Houck's Ridge and the Slaughter Pen to its right. Alas, they had little to no strategic value—the prize was Little Round Top, which loomed just ahead. However, Benning believed his men had seen enough fighting for the day and did not add his weight to the attempt to take the heights. He later reported, the "ground was difficult—rocks in many places presenting, by their precipitous sides, insurmountable obstacles, while the fire of the enemy was very heavy and very deadly. The progress was, therefore, not very rapid, but it was regular and uninterrupted."[14]

Little Round Top

While two of Law's regiments tangled with Ward's men in the Slaughter Pen, two others, the 15th and 47th Alabama, headed directly for Big Round Top. The Alabamians drove up the side of the steep hill and upon reaching its summit, thought this would be a fine spot for bringing up artillery to pound the Union lines. The divisional and corps commanders disagreed and ordered them down the north face of the hill, toward a spur of Little Round Top where they came face to face with the 20th Maine of Col. Strong Vincent's brigade (V Corps). Vincent's brigade was on its way to the Wheatfield when it was waylaid by Brig. Gen. Warren who understood the hill's importance. The brigade headed up the side of the hill on the "double quick." The Alabamians venturing down Big Round Top were in bad shape as they did not have water on this hot day and many had fainted. Those who carried on came face to face with the 20th Maine, forming the left flank of not only Vincent's brigade, but also of the entire army.

While they battled it out, two Texas regiments of Robertson's brigade and an Alabama regiment from Law's attacked Vincent's main body from the west. The slope was steep and covered with large rocks and bramble bushes.

Lt. Col. K. Bryan of the 5th Texas reported, "The huge rocks form[ed] defiles through which not more than 3 or 4 men could pass abreast, thus breaking up our alignment and rendering its reformation impossible." Another Texan recalled the slope so steep "a mountain goat would have reveled" in them.

The first attack was repulsed and then the second. The 48th Alabama, fresh from its victory over the 4th Maine in the Slaughter Pen arrived and fastened itself to the left of the Confederate line. The now-longer Confederate line attacked Little Round Top for a third time, lapping around Vincent's right flank. Disaster was in the air for Vincent's brigade, but Warren had spied Col. Patrick O'Rorke's 140th New York (Brig. Gen. Stephen Weed's brigade, V Corps) heading west to support the III Corps and told the young officer to head up the side of Little Round Top. When O'Rorke balked because it violated Weed's direct orders, Warren yelled out, "Never mind that, Paddy, bring them up on the double quick—don't stop for aligning. I will take the responsibility." O'Rorke complied, and with a handful of companies, smashed into the Confederates just reaching the top of Little Round Top. They halted the Confederate attack, but young O'Rorke was mortally wounded. Lt. Charles Hazlett's battery also made its way up the steep hill, but its barrels could not be sufficiently depressed to hit the advancing Confederates. Still, they opened fire to provide emotional support to the beleaguered infantry defenders. Vincent's brigade was battered and bruised, but the line held. Vincent gave his life for the cause, as did Weed and Hazlett later that evening.[15]

Wheatfield/Stony Hill/Rose Woods

Brig. Gen. Tige Anderson's brigade formed the left flank of Hood's division and therefore was the last of the brigades to attack. When launched, it headed for the Rose farm's Wheatfield. The sector was defended by Col. Regis de Trobriand's brigade (Maj. Gen. David Birney's division, III Corps), whose left flank was held by the 17th Maine, using a stone wall for protection. The line then ran to the right (northwest) up Stony Hill in the Rose Woods. Some of the regiments were from Col. George Burling's brigade. The Georgians first traversed a wide-open area, were pounded by massed Union batteries in the Peach Orchard to the northwest and losses

Map 27: Gettysburg—July 2
A: Little Round Top
B: Houck's Ridge/Slaughter Pen

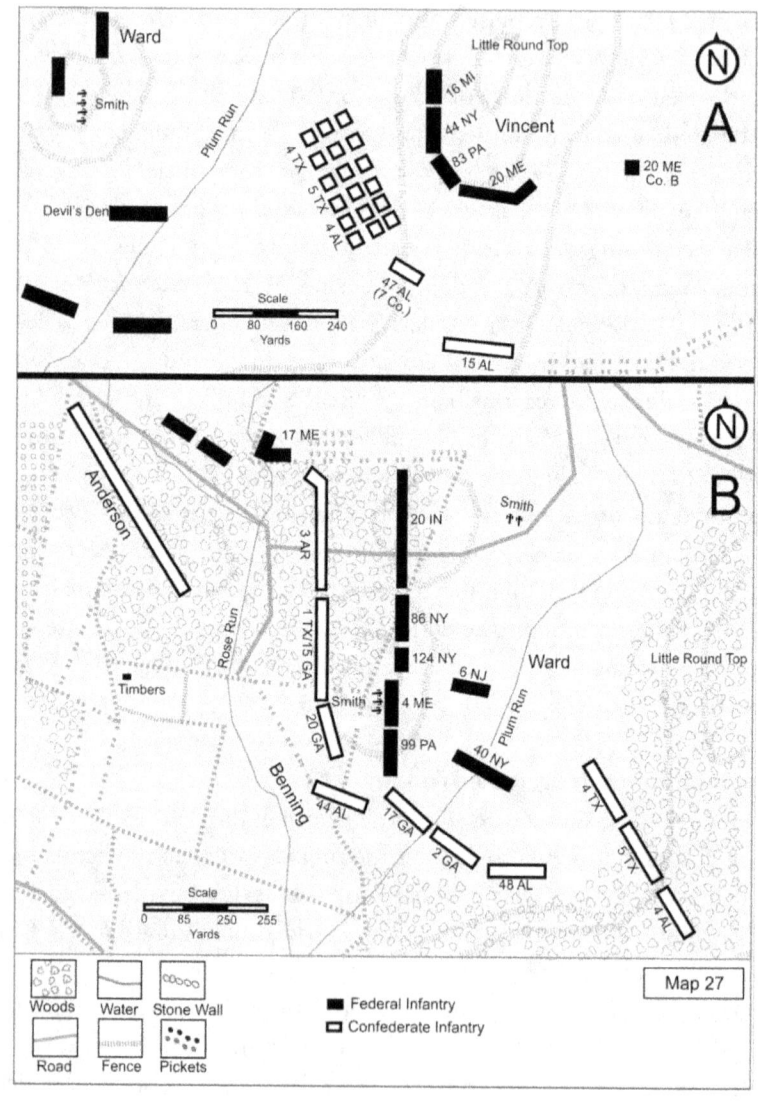

mounted by the moment. The five Union regiments held firm against Anderson's attacks. He only had three regiments as a forth wandered over to fight for Houck's Ridge to the right.

Both sides received reinforcements to continue the deadly combat. De Trobriand was reinforced by Col. William Tilton's and Col. Jacob Sweitzer's brigades, which pulled up behind the defenders. Brig. Gen. Joseph Kershaw's South Carolinian brigade, the first of Maj. Gen. Lafayette McLaws' division, advanced toward Stony Hill, but the intense artillery fire from the Union artillery in the Peach Orchard caused the three left regiments to peel off to neutralize the guns. That left only two regiments, the 3rd and 7th South Carolina who drove against the Rose Woods and Stony Hill from the west, while Anderson resumed his charge from the south. A defender watched as Kershaw's men approached, "moving with a shout, shriek, curse and yell…loading and firing with deliberation as they advanced, begrimed and dirty looking fellows, in all sorts of garb, some without hats, others without coats, and none apparently in the real dress or uniform of a soldier." They may not have looked like soldiers, but they knew how to fight. A soldier in the 1st Michigan later wrote, "Shot, shell and bullets flying pretty thick here. Men are dropping pretty fast… We were outflanked both right and left and fall back." Division commander Brig. Gen. James Barnes, ordered Tilton to withdraw, forcing de Trobriand to follow suit. Over to the left, the 17th Maine was finally forced from its perch behind the stone wall. The Confederates surged forward and captured Stony Hill and the stone wall.[16]

This was a desperate time for the Union defenders as their center was in danger of being pierced by the enemy who could continue moving forward to expand the breach. Fortunately, Brig. Gen. John Caldwell's division (II Corps) approached along Wheatfield Road, deployed for action and advanced through the Rose Woods and the Wheatfield. Col. Edward Cross' brigade, on the left of the division charged through the Wheatfield as Brig. Gen. Samuel Zook's brigade and the venerable Irish Brigade attacked Stony Hill. They all took heavy losses, but they drove Anderson's and Kershaw's men from the Wheatfield and Stony Hill. An officer in Zook's brigade explained how the men "pressed steadily forward" through fields and over fences under a "murderous fire [that] was poured upon us as we advanced, but without avail, as nothing could stop the impetuosity of our men." Caldwell's reserve brigade, Col. John Brooke's, was unleashed and drove beyond its brother brigades and attacked another of McLaws' brigades, Brig. Gen. Paul Semmes', that was about to add its weight to the Wheatfield/Stony Hill fight. Brooke's men mortally wounded Semmes and defeated his Georgians. Caldwell's men had also sustained heavy losses, including the mortal wounding of two of its four brigade commanders, Brig. Gen. Zook and Col. Cross.[17]

Caldwell's division rested on its hard fought ground as the Confederates regrouped. Up to this time, all of the Confederate attacks had been fairly uncoordinated, but now four Confederate brigades reformed and advanced against Caldwell's exhausted troops, forcing them to retreat from Stony Hill and the Wheatfield. If an entire division could not hold the Wheatfield/Stony Hill sector, senior V Corps officers decided that a single brigade could and they sent in Col. Jacob Sweitzer's lone brigade (Brig. Gen. James Barnes' division, V Corps). It was immediately attacked in its front and both flanks by the surging Confederates, and forced to flee. The Union high command was not willing to cede victory to the Confederates, so the U. S. Regulars Division (V Corps) moved forward into the Wheatfield and it was also forced to retreat without tasting victory. Without additional Union troops to feed into the fray, the fighting finally died down in the Wheatfield. The Confederates then continued their drive toward Little Round Top (see below).[18]

Peach Orchard/Along Emmitsburg Road

The Peach Orchard came under attack while the fighting raged in the Wheatfield/Stony Hill sector. Because of Sickles' advance from his assigned position, a salient formed at the Peach Orchard. This meant that some of his units lined Emmitsburg Road and then bent back 90 degrees along Wheatfield Road. Sickles did not have enough infantry to defend this area so it bristled with cannon—nine batteries—most along Wheatfield Road. Kershaw's brigade's three left regiments attacked the Peach Orchard salient from the south, but were decimated by the concentrated Union artillery fire. Col. John Kennedy of the 2nd South Carolina wrote about the horrific carnage caused by the Union artillery: "We were in ten minutes or less, terribly butchered," he wrote. "I saw half a dozen at a time knocked up and

Map 28: Gettysburg—July 2
A: The Wheatfield
B: The Peach Orchard

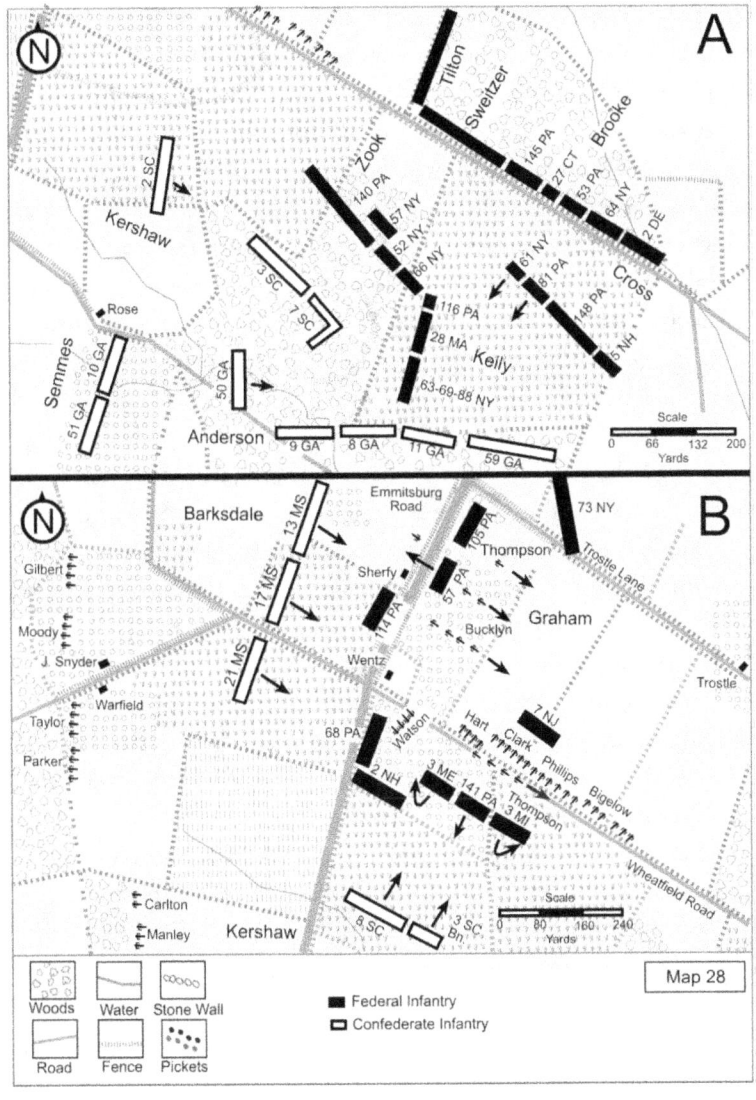

flung to the ground like trifles ... there were familiar forms and faces with parts of their heads shot away, legs shattered, arms torn off, etc."

The Union defensive line was manned by Brig. Gen. Charles Graham's brigade with support from some regiments from other brigades, and during Kershaw's initial charge, pushed out the 2nd New Hampshire to meet it. This unexpected turn of events caused the South Carolinians to do "what any other body of troops would have done under like circumstances—about-faced and went back as fast as they could run, for a new start." Kershaw's men regrouped and tried it again with the same result.[19]

Just then, another of McLaws' brigades, Brig. Gen. William Barksdale's, was launched from Seminary Ridge. Barksdale, an aggressive fire-eater from Mississippi, was chomping at the bit to gain permission to attack the enemy. When finally granted, the brigade sped rapidly across the fields from Seminary Ridge toward the Sherfy house. At the same time, several of Graham's Pennsylvania regiments had crossed the road to the Sherfy house on the west side of Emmitsburg Road, as Barksdale's men advanced on them. Danger to Graham's line also appeared from the west as Kershaw's Carolinians renewed their charge. Caught in a vice between these two charges, the Union line collapsed. The artillery along Wheatfield Road limbered up and scattered and the infantry along Emmitsburg Road were rolled up and retreated northward. "So deadly and unexpected was our assault that the enemy halted, reeled, and staggered like drunken men, then scattered and ran in every direction like a flock of frightened sheep," one of the Carolinians wrote. "We gave several rousing cheers and felt decidedly good." The dead and wounded littered the field. Many were captured, including Graham.

Col. William Brewster's brigade (Maj. Gen. Andrew Humphreys' division, III Corps) was to the right of Graham's brigade along Emmitsburg Road with its left flank on the Trostle Lane. After Graham's defeat, Brewster pulled his brigade back from Emmitsburg Road to face Barksdale's men. Although a formidable line with five regiments, including one from Brig. Gen. Joseph Carr's brigade, the Union line melted away in the face of Barksdale's determined charge.[20]

The remainder of Carr's brigade, five regiments, held their positions along Emmitsburg Road to the right of what had been Brewster's line. Barksdale's men turned east and headed for Cemetery Ridge, so they were not a threat to Carr. However, the first two brigades of Maj. Gen. Richard Anderson's division (Third Corps) headed straight for them. Brig. Gen. Cadmus Wilcox' Alabama brigade was on the right and Col. David Lang's small Florida brigade was on the left. Driving forward from Seminary Ridge, the two brigades' attack looked overwhelming. Sickles had been wounded and his replacement, Maj. Gen. David Birney, ordered Humphreys' division back to Cemetery Ridge. Humphreys believed he could hold his position, but Birney was adamant, so Carr's and what was left of Brewster's brigades "changed fronts to the rear." The right of Carr's line may not have received the orders and maintained its position until forced to withdraw by the Confederate onslaught. Humphreys lost almost 40% of his men during the fairly short time his division was in action.[21]

Plum Run

Although Hood's division appeared stymied in its attempts to take the high ground, Barksdale's brigade and half of Anderson's division (Brig. Gen. Cadmus Wilcox's and Col. David Lang's brigades) successfully extracted the enemy from Emmitsburg Road and were now driving inward toward Cemetery Ridge. Flushed with victory, there was no time to halt to dress their lines. High ground loomed before them and they were going to take it. The entire Union III Corps was thrashed by this time and fresh troops were desperately needed. Maj. Gen. Winfield Hancock's II Corps occupied the sector to the north (right) of Sickles. One of its three divisions, Caldwell's had already been engaged in the Wheatfield, while Brig. Gen. John Gibbon's division stood ready for action. He sent the small (360 man) 19th Massachusetts and 42nd New York (Col. Norman Hall's brigade) south to support Humphreys' troops, where they encountered Wilcox's 1,500 men. They could slow Wilcox's advance, but not stop it and were forced to slide to the rear with the Alabamians behind them. Further north, the 19th Maine from Brig. Gen. William Harrow's brigade, supported by Capt. Gulien Weir's battery, were directly in the path of Lang's advancing Floridians. Although a mistake in communication caused the rugged men from Maine to fall back about 20 yards, they held their position. A Union soldier recalled the

Floridians advance as "snail-like," but Lang was merely reorganizing his ranks for the final push.[22]

The stuff of legends, so common at Gettysburg, now occurred as three Confederate brigades pointed their advance at the Union center. This was a desperate time for Hancock, Meade, and the Union army. Hancock rode about frantically in search of units to help plug the hole. He encountered Col. William Colvill's 1st Minnesota, 262 strong, and ordered it forward to stop Wilcox's thrust. He yelled out, "Advance and take those colors!" A soldier recalled he "never felt so bad in my life. I thought sure the day was gone for us." Bullets whistled around the men as they advanced steadily against the Alabamians, and then Colvill ordered a charge, which startled Wilcox's men. The Minnesotans reached the small waterway called "Plum Run," where they exchanged gunfire with the enemy. They could easily see Wilcox's long line stretching far beyond each of their flanks. Scattered bands of men from Humphreys' division fired into Wilcox's right flank and the pesky Minnesotans stood strong in his front. Wilcox sent several aides requesting reinforcements, but none appeared, and in a fit of frustration, he ordered his men to break off the advance and pull back. He lamented after the war, "With a second supporting line, the heights could have been carried." Over to Wilcox's left, Col. Lang received news of the Alabamians' withdrawal and then learned the enemy was approaching his left flank and rear. With the 400-man 19th Maine in his front and the potential of being flanked, Lang reluctantly gave orders to withdraw.

Only Barksdale's Mississippians continued their victorious advance in what one soldier called "the greatest charge of the war." The ranks were disordered and the men tired as they approached Plum Run. They did not realize that Col. George Willard's brigade (Alexander Hays' division, II Corps) was approaching the opposite side of the Run. It was a hard-luck brigade that had recently returned to the army after surrendering *en mass* at Harpers Ferry the prior September. Now called the "Harpers Ferry Cowards," the men had something to prove and they would do so on the afternoon of July 2. Charging with bayonets fixed and yelling "Remember Harpers Ferry," they burst through the underbrush lining Plum Run and hit Barksdale's brigade, which was spent after its long charge. Barksdale was hit several times and, mortally wounded, slid off his horse and the rest of his Mississippians headed

Map 29: Gettysburg—July 2
A: Plum Run
B: Cemetery Ridge

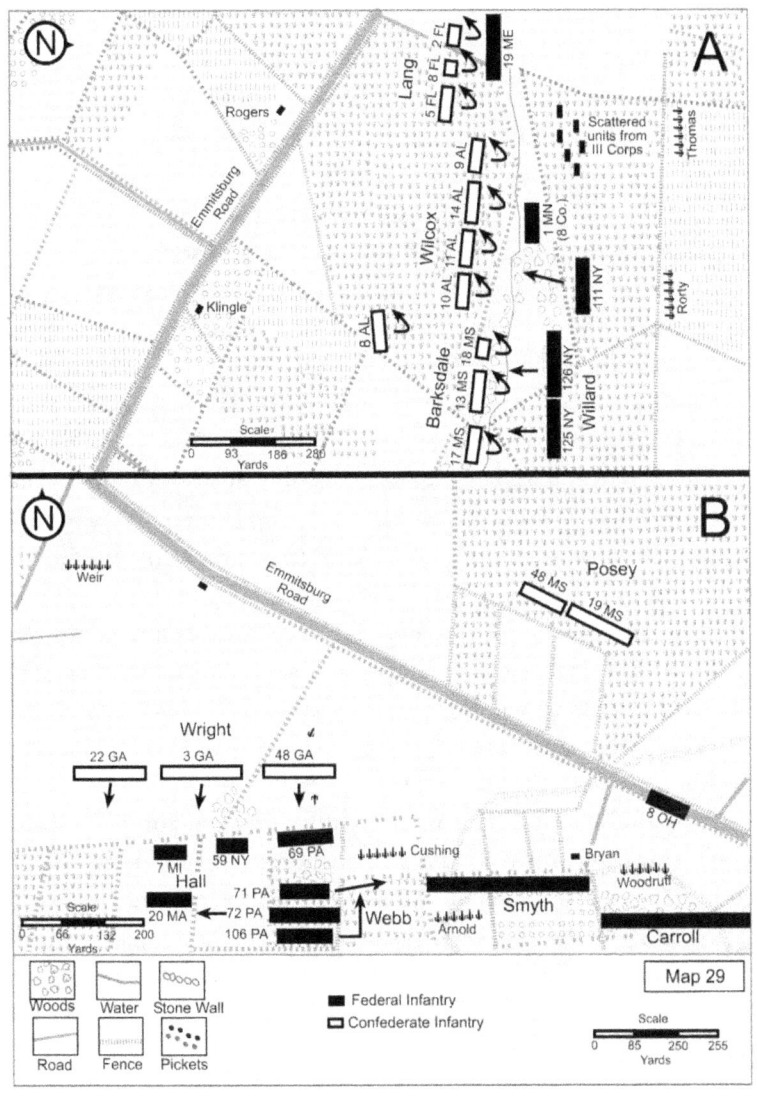

for the rear with Willard's men right behind them. Willard would not live long enough to gather laurels for his brigade's actions, as the Confederate artillery opened on his men and a shell burst nearby, taking away most of his head.[23]

Cemetery Ridge

The situation was decidedly grim for Meade and the Army of the Potomac. Devil's Den/Houck's Ridge, the Wheatfield, and the Peach Orchard were in Confederate possession and the attacks kept coming. Between 6:15 and 6:30 p.m., and after Wilcox and Lang began their charges toward Cemetery Ridge, Anderson released his third brigade, Brig. Gen. Ambrose Wright's, aiming for a "copse of trees" in the center of the Union line on Cemetery Ridge. Only the 600 men of the 15th Massachusetts and 82nd New York (Harrow's brigade) stood firm between the two ridges. They fired "one of the most destructive volleys I ever witnessed ... they [the Confederates] hesitated, then reeled, they staggered and wavered slightly, yet there was no panic," according to a Bay Stater. The Georgians continued forward, overwhelming the two regiments. A soldier recalled, we "retired in some disorder, being pressed so closely that we lost quite a number of prisoners, captured by the enemy."

The Georgians were now up against the tough Philadelphia Brigade (Brig. Gen. John Gibbon's division, II Corps) and some units from Col. Norman Hall's brigade. Wright's men drove all the way to the base of Cemetery Ridge where the Philadelphians were in position behind a stone wall. The attacker's line was ripped and torn by Union artillery shells, but it continued on, only to be halted by concentrated volleys from the Union infantry. A portion of Wright's men found a gap in the line and drove up Cemetery Ridge and planted their flag on the summit before being forced to retreat by the timely approach of Brig. Gen. George Stannard's brigade (Maj. Gen. Abner Doubleday's division; I Corps). These 9-month Vermont troops would play another important role the following day as well. Wright lost over half his men with little to show for it.

The Confederate attack was to keep rolling north. Brig. Gen. Carnot Posey's brigade was to attack next, and while a regiment or two may have attacked with Wright, the rest did not budge from their positions on

Seminary Ridge, ending the en echelon attack against Meade's defensive line.[24]

Valley of Death

The remnants of four Confederate brigades that captured the Wheatfield were not satisfied with their gains and approached Little Round Top. The Pennsylvania Reserve Division (V Corps) was on Little Round Top and watched the Confederate approach with some trepidation. The division's commander, Brig. Gen. Samuel Crawford, ordered Col. William McCandless to charge down the hill and into what is now called the "Valley of Death." A newly arrived VI Corps brigade under Col. David Nevin also slid into position and then charged the approaching enemy troops, whose lines were in disarray. The Confederates saw masses of enemy heading in their direction and decided they had seen enough fighting for the day and pulled back.[25]

The fighting was now over, from Cemetery Ridge south to Little Round Top. Meade's troops had prevailed. While the Confederates had captured some areas, such as Devil's Den, Houck's Ridge, the Slaughter Pen, the Wheatfield and the Peach Orchard, they had little tactical value. The all-important high ground—Little Round Top and Cemetery Ridge—were still in Union hands.

Cemetery and Culp's Hills

Lee craved two other hills occupied by Meade's men: Cemetery Hill and Culp's Hill, and he visited Ewell during the afternoon of July 2 to discuss how the Second Corps could take them. When Lee left Ewell at about 2:00 p.m., he believed all understood that Ewell would launch his attack upon hearing Longstreet's opening guns to the south. Maj. Gen. Edward Johnson's fresh division would climb Culp's Hill and two lightly used brigades from Maj. Gen. Jubal Early's division would advance against Cemetery Hill. The latter were to be assisted by Maj. Gen. Robert Rodes' division which was to move through the town of Gettysburg and attack from the west, while Early attacked from the north.

Despite Lee's wishes, Ewell's attacks were not coordinated with Longstreet's. Instead, they began as daylight was fading and the latter's

Map 30: Gettysburg—July 2
A: Culp's Hill
B: Cemetery Hill

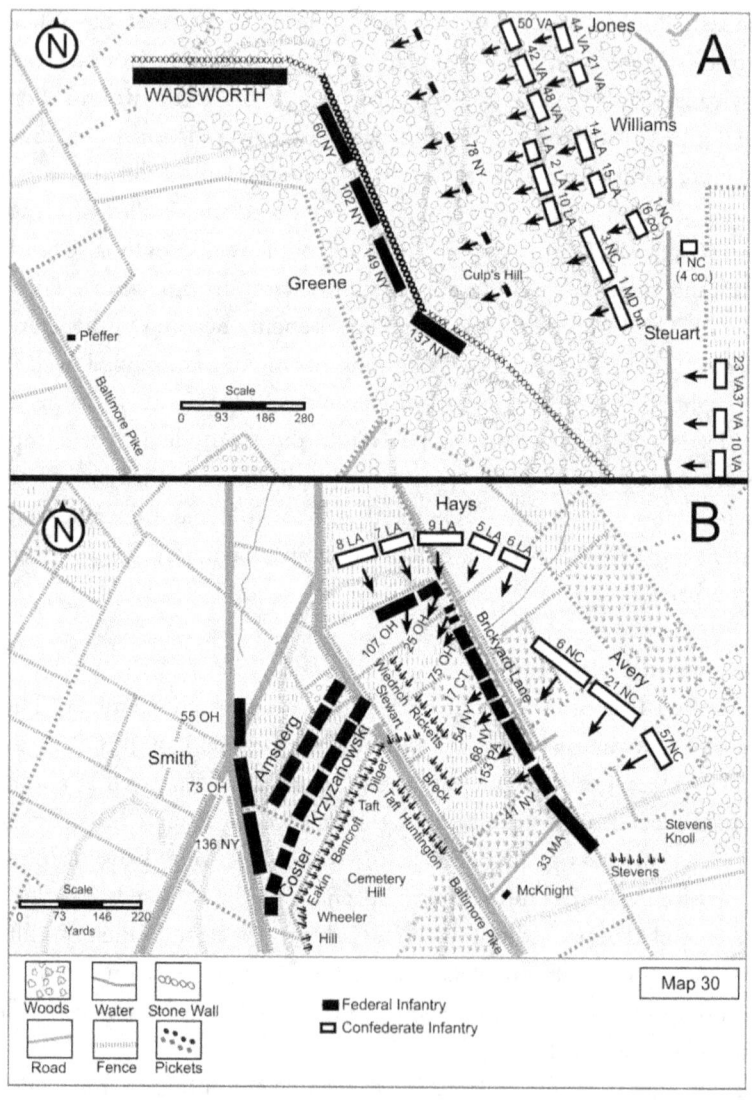

318

attacks were losing steam. Cemetery Hill bristled with Union artillery pieces, but down below at the base of the hill, facing northeast, the already-defeated members of Barlow's division (XI Corps) waited behind a stone wall. There were not enough defenders to protect the entire line so gaps dotted the line. Brig. Gen. Harry Hays' and Col. Isaac Avery's brigades suddenly emerged from the right side of town and headed in their direction. The Union artillery immediately pounded the Southern infantrymen, who were protected by the undulations of the ground. A Louisiana officer explained, "[W]e are too quick for them, and are down in the valley in a trice, while the Yankee missiles are hissing, screaming & hurtling over our heads, doing but little damage." They also quickly traversed the open ground to reduce their exposure. Hand to hand fighting erupted at the wall at the base of Cemetery Hill. A Confederate soldier wrote, the enemy "did not want to leave…with bayonets & clubbed guns we drove them back." The Union soldiers sprinted back up the hill with Louisianans and North Carolinians behind them. More hand to hand fighting raged at the top of the hill between the cannoneers and Confederate troops and several cannon fell into the enemy's hands. The cannoneers would not submit easily, fighting "with ramrods, wielding them like ball bats."

It was dark now and the Confederates atop the hill could hear the steady tramp, tramp, tramp of approaching troops, praying it was their own reinforcements. It was not. Col. Samuel Carroll's Gibraltar Brigade (Brig. Gen. Alexander Hays' division, II Corps) marched through the Evergreen Cemetery archway and headed for the Confederates atop the hill. The two sides exchanged gunfire, but neither side could see the other in the darkness. Only the flashes of rifle discharges indicated the combatants' positions. The Confederates realized they were outnumbered and alone on the hill, so they pulled back. Rodes' division, which was to attack from the west, never approached, as their leaders misjudged how long it would take to move through Gettysburg and aborted the mission as they thought it was too late.[26]

Maj. Gen. Johnson launched his division's attack against Culp's Hill at about the same time. This was a suicide mission if there ever was one. The entire Union XII Corps had occupied the entire tall, steep hill, and had spent much of the night before and July 2 fortifying its positions with breastworks that completely covered the defenders. When the Confederates did not launch attacks against Culp's Hill earlier that afternoon, Meade pulled all but one brigade from the hill and sent them to help staunch Longstreet's hammer blows to the south. Only Brig. Gen. George Greene's brigade was left to man the works and he stretched his New Yorkers in a thin line to cover as much of the barricades as possible. Johnson's men launched their attacks in the darkness. Night fighting was rare during the Civil War and this was one of the exceptions. The New Yorkers watched their skirmish line "came running back followed by a Confederate line of battle, yelping and howling in its particular manner," according to George Carr of the 149th New York. Greene's troops knew they were to hold out to the last and it showed on the men with their, "pale faced, staring eye-balls, and nervous hands grasping loaded muskets," but they held their own. Union regiments appeared in the darkness to reinforce Greene, but some became disoriented in the darkness and were of little help. While most of the Confederate attacks were blunted, Brig. Gen. George Steuart's brigade, on the left of Johnson's attackers, stretched beyond the New Yorkers' right flank and rolled it up. By the time the fighting ended for the night, some of Steuart's men occupied the heights. Johnson would renew his attacks the following day and try to take the entire hill.[27]

The middle part of the battle, July 2, proved to be a frustrating time for Lee. His subordinates thwarted his aggressive instincts and the attacks were launched later than he desired. He was severely hampered by not knowing which enemy units were on the battlefield and which were still approaching. He probably realized the longer he delayed making his attack, the more time for the enemy units to arrive on the battlefield. When the fighting finally began, it raged over almost the entire Confederate line and while there were some "almosts," Meade's line held. Meade benefited by the delay in Lee's attack, allowing him to get the V Corps into place and have the VI Corps ready for action by the end of the day. Because Ewell did not attack Culp's Hill until later, Meade was able to shift troops from Culp's Hill to other sectors under attack. In any other battle, this may have been a fatal error on Meade's part, but the Culp's Hill defenses were so impregnable that a mere brigade could hold out against over three times its number.

This ended one of the bloodiest days of the Civil War. The Confederates threw Hood's, McLaws', Johnson's, and portions of Anderson's and Early's divisions into the fray, numbering 27,700. On the Union side, all of the III and V Corps, most of the II Corps and portions of the XI and XII Corps participated in the July 2 fight, numbering 34,500.

The losses are difficult to ascertain, as many units fought on multiple days. Taking this into account, it appears Meade lost 10,500 men (30%); the Confederates 7,500 (27%).

Comparisons of the Two Campaigns

Units and Number of Troops Involved

A comparison of the second phase of the two battles is difficult, as the scope differed so dramatically. The middle phase of Antietam merely involved the fight for the Sunken Road, where two Union II Corps divisions attempting to drive into Sharpsburg were first confronted with a handful of brigades from D. H. Hill's division and Richard Anderson's newly arrived division and the subsequent desperate fighting around the Piper farm.

The fight on July 2 at Gettysburg was among the most complex one-day fights in the entire Civil War. The day involved several major fights for the high ground south of town, where Longstreet's First Corps (with support from Richard Anderson's division) fought for control of Cemetery Ridge and the high ground to the south (Little Round Top, Slaughter Pen, Houck's Ridge/Devil's Den, Wheatfield, Peach Orchard, and along Emmitsburg Road). Ewell's Second Corps also fought for high ground to the north: Culp's Hill and Cemetery Hill.

The number of units on the battlefield at the start of the second phase played a major role in both battles. At Antietam, 78% of Lee's army was on the field, but Richard Anderson's division would soon arrive. McClellan's VI Corps had not yet arrived, so he had only 85% of his army available for combat. Gettysburg saw massive increases in troop numbers, compared with just before dawn on July 1. Only Pickett's division had not yet joined the army, allowing Lee to have 90% of his forces available for action. On the Federal side, Meade still awaited the arrival of his V and VI Corps, so he only had 73% of his army ready for action. However, the two corps would arrive during the day.

At Gettysburg, Longstreet used two full divisions (Hood's and McLaws'), and A. P. Hill contributed one of his divisions (Anderson's); Ewell used parts of two other divisions, so 56% of his divisions were engaged). Portions of six Union corps were directly involved in the fighting. Four corps fought for Cemetery Ridge and the high ground south of it: I Corps (one brigade); II (two divisions), III (two divisions), and V (three divisions). Only one brigade (Greene's) of the XII Corps held Culp's Hill during the evening attack and another (Brig. Gen. Henry Lockwood's) helped repulse part of Longstreet's attack. The fight for Cemetery Hill involved part of the XI Corps and a brigade of the II Corps (Col. Samuel Carroll's Gibraltar Brigade). Therefore, five of Meade's seven infantry corps battled on July 2, with all or part of 12 divisions (63%) participating in the fighting.

The fighting during the middle period of the battle of Antietam involved 17,650 troops. Although the numbers appear lopsided: Union: 11,450; Confederates: 6,200, the percentage of each army was similar (Union: 20%; Confederates: 17%). These numbers pale in relation to those in action during Gettysburg's second day. Both sides threw 61,800 men into the fight (Union: 34,100; Confederates: 27,700). However, the percentage of the total army engaged was much higher than at Antietam (Union: 36%; Confederates: 38%). Outnumbered and outgunned, Lee nevertheless attempted to take the high ground on July 2.

Conventional military tactics dictated that the aggressors bring more troops into battle, and this did indeed occur at Antietam, where Union troops outnumbered the Confederates by a factor of almost two to one. This was not the case at Gettysburg, where Lee's numbers were inferior to those of Meade's.

Tactics

During the second phase of Antietam, two II Corps divisions attempted to capture Sharpsburg, cut the road to the Shepherdstown Ford and finally defeat or better yet, destroy Lee's army. William French's division, although outnumbering the Confederate defenders in the Sunken Road by two to one, was unsuccessful in driving the enemy from its position. French frittered his advantage away by launching his brigades in piecemeal attacks against the strong defensive position. Israel Richardson also employed the same tactic, but was ultimately successful when Confederate resistance in the Sunken Road waned as casualties mounted and devastating flank and frontal attacks finally drove the defenders from the road. Desperate fighting then occurred around the Piper farm fields as the Confederate survivors desperately attempted to staunch the flow of Union troops toward the vital town of Sharpsburg. The exhaustion of the men, coupled with Richardson's wounding, and the unkept promise of reinforcements, ended the fight at 1:00 p.m.

After several conversations with his senior leaders, Lee settled on a plan for July 2 at Gettysburg that featured a coordinated attack on all parts of Meade's army. Ewell would attack from the north, and Longstreet, with support from A. P. Hill, would drive in from the west. Longstreet's attack came later than expected by Lee, but Ewell launched his men even later, losing the opportunity of a coordinated attack on all of Meade's positions. This permitted Meade to effectively move units, especially the XII Corps on Ewell's front, to other areas of the battlefield under heavy attack.

The Confederate attacks on July 2 at Gettysburg were similar to the first phase of Antietam—although it was the Union army attempting to capture the high ground in the latter battle. Ewell's attack on the evening of July 2 was similar to French's and Richardson's divisions' attack on Antietam's Sunken Road—a large-scale attack, sending wave after wave of troops against a strong defensive position. These were, however, not piecemeal attacks. Although most of the attacks against George Greene's lone brigade were beaten back, a portion of Edward Johnson's division captured some Union breastworks.

Longstreet's attacks were to be more nuanced—using a sophisticated *en echelon* attack to find weak portions of the enemy's line. This would theoretically cause Meade to send reinforcements to shore up these vulnerable areas, and then Longstreet's men would attack the newly weakened sector with fresh troops. Longstreet was successful in taking some high ground, most notably Houck's Ridge and the Peach Orchard, but these areas had little tactical value. The real prizes, Little Round Top and Cemetery Hill, came close to falling into Confederate hands, but the Union troops ultimately prevailed.

Leadership

McClellan did not order French's and Richardson's divisions south to the Sunken Road at Antietam and played a minor role during the second phase of Antietam's battle. Meade appears to have played a much larger role at Gettysburg on July 2, moving troops about to threatened areas, but he may have erred by not taking Sickles' concerns about his position seriously. His left flank became vulnerable to defeat because of Sickles' actions.

The initial defensive line, composed of Brig. Gen. Robert Rodes' and Brig. Gen. George Anderson's brigades were not sent to the Sunken Road by Lee, but he did monitor the situation and sent Maj. Gen. Richard Anderson's division to support them.

Lee's decisions on July 2 at Gettysburg have been questioned, almost as soon as the battle was over. He allowed Ewell and Early to dissuade him from attacking the Union right and he all but ignored Longstreet's suggestion about moving around the Union left. Lee also desired an early resumption of the fighting, but allowed his subordinates to delay it until late in the afternoon.

After Lee finally settled on his tactics for the day and informed his commanders, he appeared to take little direct action in overseeing the fighting and apparently did not step in to assure coordination of the First and Second Corps' attacks. This egregious lapse contributed mightily to the lost opportunities at Gettysburg. Lee's ill-health may have played a major role in his passivity at Gettysburg.

The corps and divisional commanders played major roles during the middle phase of the battles. Antietam was a low point for II Corps commander Edwin Sumner. He chose to remain with Sedgwick's doomed division at the West Woods, so was not present during the combat at the Sunken Road, where two-thirds of his corps attempted to drive toward Sharpsburg. French's division attacked first and Richardson's came up later, but it is unclear whether the two discussed coordinating their actions.

At Gettysburg, II Corps commander, Winfield Hancock closely monitored his unit's actions, making effective adjustments as necessary. George Sykes effectively moved his V Corps divisions and brigades around the battlefield, but Daniel Sickles placed his III Corps in an untenable position and was wounded early in the fighting. Henry Slocum was mostly an onlooker during

July 2, as his XII Corps brigades were peeled off from Culp's Hill and sent to other sectors needing reinforcements. It is unclear what role Oliver Howard played when his troops were driven up the side of Cemetery Hill, only to be driven back by a determined advance by Samuel Carroll's Gibralter Brigade.

On the Confederate side, Longstreet's men played a major role during the middle phase of both battles. At Antietam, when his troops manning the left side of the Sunken Road repulsed one of French's charges, Longstreet ordered an ill-advised counterattack, resulting in heavy losses. Later, he gathered troops in the West Woods sector and launched them against French's right flank, which also failed. Longstreet apparently frittered away the potential of victory by misusing Richard Anderson's division, recently arriving on the battlefield after its all-night march from Harpers Ferry. Lee sent this powerful division to reinforce the Sunken Road, but Anderson was wounded as his division left Sharpsburg, leading to considerable confusion. Either Anderson's second in command, Brig. Gen. Roger Pryor, did not know he was in charge, or he was unfit to oversee such a large unit. It was Longstreet's responsibility to ensure the division was ably led. Instead, the division broke apart, its brigades going into action piecemeal, which severely compromised its potential to disrupt the enemy attacks. Longstreet performed better on July 2, continuing to use a hands-on approach by directing when each brigade entered the fray. He was not, however, able to effectively follow up on Confederate successes with additional troops, resulting in lost opportunities.

Richard Ewell, commanding the Second Corps at Gettysburg attacked the high ground of Cemetery and Culp's Hills south of Gettysburg on July 2. The attacks were to be coordinated with Longstreet's, but they occurred too late to take splinter Meade's army. Ewell apparently did little more than order his men forward and let fate intervene. He certainly shared the blame for not ensuring enough time for Rodes' division to march through Gettysburg and get into position to attack Cemetery Hill from the west. The hill bristled with enemy artillery, so Rodes' success may have been problematic anyway.

Lee is usually credited with giving his division and brigade commanders more autonomy than the Union high command. This showed itself at Antietam when one brigade commander, Rodes, took it upon himself to halt his movement north to reinforce his already defeated comrades in the

Cornfield and East Woods, and instead took up a defensive position along the Sunken Road. Sumner also gave his division commanders considerable autonomy, although they were unable to coordinate their attacks.

This autonomy caused problems for Lee at Gettysburg. When Brig. Gen. Henry Benning finally captured Houck's Ridge with his Georgia brigade, he chose not to continue east to assist in capturing Little Round Top. It certainly did not help that his commander, John Hood, was wounded, and his replacement, Evander Law may not have risen to the occasion. Similarly, the *en echelon* attack rolling north essentially ended with Wright's brigade because Brig. Gen. Carnot Posey did not send in his entire brigade forward, and Brig. Gen. William Mahone to his left, failed to move his brigade at all. At times there was no autonomy, as when John Hood realized he was attacking not the enemy's left flank, but a strong position, and was not permitted to move south to find the flank.

There were some examples of autonomy in the Union army. For example Col. Strong Vincent, who took it upon himself to lead his brigade up the side of the undefended Little Round Top and subsequently defended this vital high ground against repeated enemy attacks. Likewise, engineer, Brig. Gen. Gouverneur Warren, sent the 140th New York up the side of Little Round Top to blunt a determined Confederate charge.

Pulling Troops from One Sector to Another

At Antietam, Lee continued pushing additional troops to contested areas when he brought up Anderson's division, which had just recently arrived from Harpers Ferry, and sent it to the Sunken Road. Anderson's untimely wounding frittered away his division's potential in turning the II Corps' flank or at least preventing the enemy from overrunning the Sunken Road.

Meade did a masterful job of moving troops around the battlefield on July 2 to counter the Confederate thrusts. All but one of the XII Corps brigades on Culp's Hill were sent south to help battle Longstreet's divisions and when the V Corps arrived, Meade skillfully moved its various units to parts of the field needing them most. Without these reinforcements, Lee may well have captured the important high ground. Of special note are Col. George Willard's (II Corps) attack that stymied Barksdale's victorious advance along Plum Run, the 1st Minnesota's counterattack on Wilcox's brigade, and the arrival of the Gibraltar Brigade on Cemetery Hill that drove the Confederates from their foothold.

Duration of Combat

The middle phase of the battle of Antietam, primarily the action around the Sunken Road, began at about 9:15 a.m. and continued until about 1:00 p.m. Skirmishing around the Middle Bridge area continued through the afternoon. Gettysburg's action did not begin until late afternoon—about 4:00 p.m.—and continued into the late night hours, between 10 and 11 p.m., when the Confederates finally ended their attack at Culp's Hill. Therefore, the middle phase of Gettysburg lasted for six to seven hours—much longer than the three and three quarter hours of fighting in and around the Sunken Road at Antietam.

Losses

Given the disparity of the number of troops involved and the complexity of the action, it is not surprising that Gettysburg's losses dwarfed those at Antietam. The losses in the Sunken Road and Piper farm sectors during this phase of Antietam were 5,150 (Union: 3,050 or 27%; Confederates: 2,100 or 34%). The casualties resulting from the extensive fighting at Gettysburg during the second day totaled 18,000 (Union: 10,500 or 30%; Confederates: 7,500 or 27%). In both battles, the side on the defense sustained a higher percentage (over 30%) than those on the attack (27%).

Two generals were mortally wounded at Antietam during the second phase: Union Gen. Israel Richardson and Confederate Gen. G. B. Anderson. Both men's wounds were initially thought to be non-life threatening by some, but both died several weeks after the battle. Two Union generals (Samuel Zook and Stephen Weed) were mortally wounded during the second day at Gettysburg and three Confederates (Dorsey Pender, Paul Semmes, and William Barksdale). Three other Union brigade commanders who held the rank of colonel (Strong Vincent, George Willard and Edward Cross) were also mortally wounded. One Confederate brigade commander holding the rank of colonel, Isaac Avery, also died of his wounds. In addition, a Union general, Charles Graham, was captured during the second phase.

Table 21: Comparison of the Second Phase of the Battles

Issue	Maryland Campaign	Pennsylvania Campaign
Role of cavalry	Minor	Minor
Large units that opened the second phase of the battle	**Confederates:** D.H. Hill's Division **Union:** II Corps	**Confederates:** Longstreet's Corps **Union:** III Corps
Other large units fighting during the second phase	**Confederates:** Richard Anderson's Division **Union:** None	**Confederates:** All three of Lee's Corps **Union:** II, V, XI, XII Corps
Number of divisions engaged	**Confederates:** Parts of 2 (22%) **Union:** 2 (13%)	**Confederates:** Portions of 5 (56%) **Union:** Parts of 12 (63%)
Number of brigades engaged	**Confederates:** 9 (23%) **Union:** 6 (38%)	**Confederates:** 17 (46%) **Union:** 26 (51%)
Number of troops engaged	**Confederate:** 6,200 (17%) **Union:** 11,450 (20%) Total: 17,650	**Confederate:** 27,700 (38%) **Union:** 34,100 (36%) Total: 61,800
Leader directing the action wounded/ mortally wounded	**Confederates:** Yes (R. Anderson) **Union:** Yes (Richardson)	**Confederates:** Yes (Hood) **Union:** Yes (Sickles)
Second in command takes over the field	**Confederates:** Maybe **Union:** Eventually	**Confederates:** Yes **Union:** Yes
Major goal	Crush Confederate center & capture Sharpsburg	Take high ground
Duration of the fighting	3.75 hours	6-7 hours
Pulling troops from other sectors	**Confederates:** Yes **Union:** No	**Confederates:** No **Union:** Yes
Direction of major initial attack	North to south	West to east
Direction of second attack	-	North to south

Issue	Maryland Campaign	Pennsylvania Campaign
Dubious deployment/ coordination of troops	**Confederates:** Yes **Union:** Yes	**Confederates:** Yes **Union:** Yes
Time of initial movement toward the enemy	9:15 a.m.	4:00 p.m.
Number of troops on battlefield before the start of combat	**Confederates:** 28,300 (78% of army) **Union:** 49,000 (85% of army)	**Confederates:** 64,500 (90% of army) **Union:** 69,000 (73% of army)
Number of casualties	**Confederates:** 2,099 (34%) **Union:** 3,047 (27%) Total: 5,146	**Confederates:** 7,454 (27%) **Union:** 10,267 (30%) Total: 17,721

Chapter 17: The Third or Final Phase of the Battles

The last phase of both battles featured a grand charge and timely reinforcements helping to blunt the attack.

The Maryland Campaign of 1862

McClellan's original tactical plan involved a two-pronged approach to best Lee's army. First, the I Corps, with immediate assistance from the XII Corps, would attack from the north (North Woods) to capture the high ground around the Dunker Church. Later, the IX Corps would cross Antietam Creek at the Lower Bridge and drive west toward Sharpsburg. It is unclear whether this was to be a major thrust or simply a diversionary tactic. The two sectors were linked somewhat, as the inactivity of the IX Corps on the east side of Antietam Creek allowed Lee to shift Brig. Gen. John Walker's sizable division from near the Lower Bridge to counter the morning thrusts by the XII Corps in the West Woods.

The Lower Bridge

Maj. Gen. Ambrose Burnside's major objective was not merely crossing Antietam Creek; it was to drive west, rolling up Lee's right flank and capturing Sharpsburg.

All of McClellan's other troops had crossed at undefended crossings: the Upper and Middle Bridges and nearby fords. Such was not the case with Burnside's IX Corps which had to cross at the contested Lower Bridge. Getting across Antietam Creek posed a formidable challenge. Everyone who studied the Lower Bridge, measuring 12-feet wide and 125-feet long, realized it would be difficult to send a powerful column across it. The depth and poor substrate of Antietam Creek and its steep slippery banks prevented the men from fording it except at a few places. McClellan sent his chief engineer, Capt. James Duane, to the area to find a ford downstream on the day before the battle. Burnside was to position a strong division at the ford on the morning of the battle, and while he attacked the bridge head-on, the flanking party would cross and then hit the bridge defenders on their right flank and rear. It was a good plan, but poorly executed, for when Duane's engineers reconnoitered downstream, they came under fire from Confederate sharpshooters, hastening their retreat. Instead of actually seeing the ford and perhaps even attempting to cross it, they relied on information provided by locals and by area maps.

An ambiguous command structure also plagued the IX Corps. Burnside had initially been a wing commander, in charge of his own IX Corps and Hooker's I Corps. Maj. Gen. Jesse Reno was placed in charge of the IX Corps, but with his death at Fox's Gap, Brig. Gen. Jacob Cox assumed command. McClellan dissolved the wings on the eve of the battle, but Burnside continued to act as though Cox retained command of the corps. When Burnside received an order from McClellan or his staff, he glanced at it, and then handed it to Cox, who invariably stood or rode next to his commander. Cox repeatedly asked Burnside to assume command of the corps but was waved off each time.

Burnside was ordered to deploy his 10,000 troops at 7:00 a.m. on September 17 and await further orders. He watched the battle to the north from high ground east of the Lower Bridge and cheered his army's apparent victory. Burnside finally received the order to launch his attack at about 10:00 a.m. The message was drafted at 9:10 a.m.—a time when the fights for the East Woods and Cornfield were over, but Sedgwick's division was in the West Woods and French's division was moving south toward the Sunken Road. It made sense to unleash Burnside's attack at this time, as it would put pressure on Lee's left, center, and right. Franklin's VI Corps was within a mile and a half of the battlefield and could be sent to any part of the field needing it most.

Burnside immediately put his men in motion. He first sent a company of the 11th Connecticut forward as a skirmish line to drive the enemy from the bridge and perhaps fire into enemy soldiers on the opposite side of Antietam Creek, causing them to keep their heads down. The Confederate defenders were woefully undermanned and undergunned. Two Georgia regiments, the 2nd and 20th (Brig. Gen. Robert Toombs' brigade; Brig. Gen. D. R. Jones' division; Longstreet's Wing) occupied the bluff above the bridge. Although they numbered about 400 men, their position was exceptionally strong. They occupied several lines along the bluff, including a quarry that protected them while firing into Burnside's troops. The small 50th Georgia (Drayton's brigade) was deployed to their right. The regiment was decimated at Fox's

Gap a few days before and mustered perhaps a hundred men. A company of sharpshooters from Brig. Gen. Micah Jenkins' brigade under Col. Joseph Walker (D. R. Jones' division; Longstreet's Wing) was split in half and deployed on either side of the 50th Georgia. These Georgians and South Carolinians numbering perhaps 120 men were widely spaced as they had to cover over half a mile of creek below the bridge.[1]

The 11th Connecticut headed down to the creek with Col. Henry Kingsbury at its head. The Georgians made short work of the Nutmeggers, killing and wounding a number of them, including Kingsbury who died the following day. Col. George Crook's brigade followed, supported by Brig. Gen. Samuel Sturgis' division. Crook was clearly baffled by his orders. He noted in his memoirs how he believed he was following Sturgis' division, not making the first full-scale charge, and he and his officers were even unaware of the bridge's location. The attack of his three large Ohio regiments was poorly planned and coordinated. One remained in an orchard, Crook broke another in two with half advancing as a skirmish line north of the bridge and the other half charging with Crook's third regiment, but it got lost along the way. So, rather than three large regiments attacking the bridge, only a portion of one actually made the attempt. Its commander later complained his regiment advanced across a plowed field, "The right and left divided, under conflicting orders" moving in different directions and ultimately being turned back by the Georgians' massive firepower.

It was not much better downstream where Brig. Gen. Isaac Rodman's division, fortified with an additional brigade from the Kanawha Division, confidently made its way to the ford across Antietam Creek identified the day before by McClellan's engineers. Rodman quickly realized the banks were too steep for a crossing, so he turned his men southwest to find another ford, purportedly further downstream.[2]

Sturgis was ordered to take the bridge with his division at around 11:00 a.m. He had two brigades and decided to send them forward piecemeal. Crook had attacked from high ground directly opposite the bridge and since that didn't work, the second attack would be made along a road that paralleled the creek. Two regiments of Brig. Gen. James Nagle's brigade would rush down the road in columns of four, supported by two others, turn left to cross the bridge, and drive the Georgians from their perch. The 2nd

Maryland led the attack, followed by the 6th New Hampshire. Before reaching the road, officers dashed ahead to punch a hole in the fence. The attempt went badly.

They only cleared a small section, creating a logjam and the Georgians calmly fired into the bunched up Maryland and New Hampshire troops as though they were shooting fish in a barrel. The historian of the 6th New Hampshire recalled, "Of the first hundred men who passed through the opening in the fence, at least nine tenths were either killed or wounded. Such sweeping destruction checked the advancing column." Sturgis reported how Nagle's men "made a handsome effort to execute this order, but the fire was so heavy on them before they could reach the bridge that they were forced to give way and fall back." Overall, the losses ran as high as 40% as the attack fell apart. Further downstream, Rodman continued searching for the elusive crossing point known as "Snavely Ford."[3]

With Nagle's defeat, Sturgis' second brigade prepared for action just prior to noon. Its commander, Brig. Gen. Edward Ferrero, selected the 51st New York and 51st Pennsylvania and aligned them at the top of the hill facing the Lower Bridge. Sturgis' orders were to "charge with the bayonet." Observing their charge, Sturgis wrote, "They started on their mission of death full of enthusiasm, and taking a route less exposed than the regiments which had made the effort before them." The Confederate artillery fire, so prevalent in ending the prior attacks, again opened fire, as did the Georgians' muskets. The two 51st regiments made it as far as the creek, but could go no further. The 51st Pennsylvania, under Col. John Hartranft, took cover behind a stone wall to the right of the bridge and the New Yorkers, under Col. John Potter, hid behind a fence on the left side. After a few minutes, Potter perceived a lessening of the enemy's fire and asked his Hartranft to try to take the bridge. When Hartranft demurred, Potter returned to his regiment and ordered the men to rise. The Pennsylvanians also rose at the same time and the two regiments quickly crossed the bridge at the same time.

Gallant, it certainly was, but their success was created by several factors that had little to do with the two Union regiments. The Georgians were in trouble. They had been in action for almost three hours and their ammunition was almost expended. The enemy brought up artillery that blasted the hill and with the small arms fire, casualties mounted. According to an officer in the 2nd Georgia, "So many of the men were shot that the officers filled their places & loaded & fired their guns." There were no reinforcements. Finally, the men learned of heavy concentrations of Yanks crossing downstream at Snavely Ford, threatening their right flank and rear. It was time to withdraw, but they did so only reluctantly.[4]

The Final Attack

Nothing now stopped Burnside and Cox from sending the entire IX Corps across Antietam Creek to fulfill its ultimate mission of driving Lee's right flank into Sharpsburg/Potomac River. The large number of troops attempting to cross Antietam Creek on the long, narrow Lower Bridge and nearby fords slowed the process. Once the troops crossed the creek, they scaled steep ridges running in a north-south direction to finally reach their kick-off points. Their front line was about 450 yards from the Lower Bridge, stretching almost a mile wide, beginning a couple of hundred yards south of Boonsboro Pike. Cox placed his lightly used divisions on the front line: Rodman's on the left and Willcox's on the right. He hoped he could avoid using either Sturgis' division, which had been bloodied earlier in the day in attempting to take the bridge, or Scammon's division, which bore the brunt of the early morning fighting at Fox's Gap on September 14 and the initial attack on the Lower Bridge (Crook's brigade).

The final attack was launched at about 3:15 p.m. Lee could only muster a handful of small brigades from D. R. Jones' division—perhaps a couple of thousand men. Burnside probably had 10,000-12,000 men in line to make the attack, so it would be quite a mismatch that boded well for Cox's ultimate success. Willcox's division on the right angled toward the southeast corner of Sharpsburg. Col. Benjamin Christ's brigade on its right had a fairly easy route and it outpaced its brother brigade, Col. Thomas Welsh's, which faced more rugged terrain that retarded its movement. When Christ did not see Welsh's men on his left, he decided to halt his advance. He reported, "I discovered that my support on my left had not come up. Deeming my force alone inadequate for the attack on both artillery and infantry, I was obliged to halt until supported on my left." However, the open terrain provided opportunities for the massed Confederate artillery to batter Christ's men. The Confederate artillery fire commanded Christ's "whole line from left to right,

Map 31: The Bridges During the Third Phase at Antietam
A: The Middle Bridge
B: The Lower Bridge

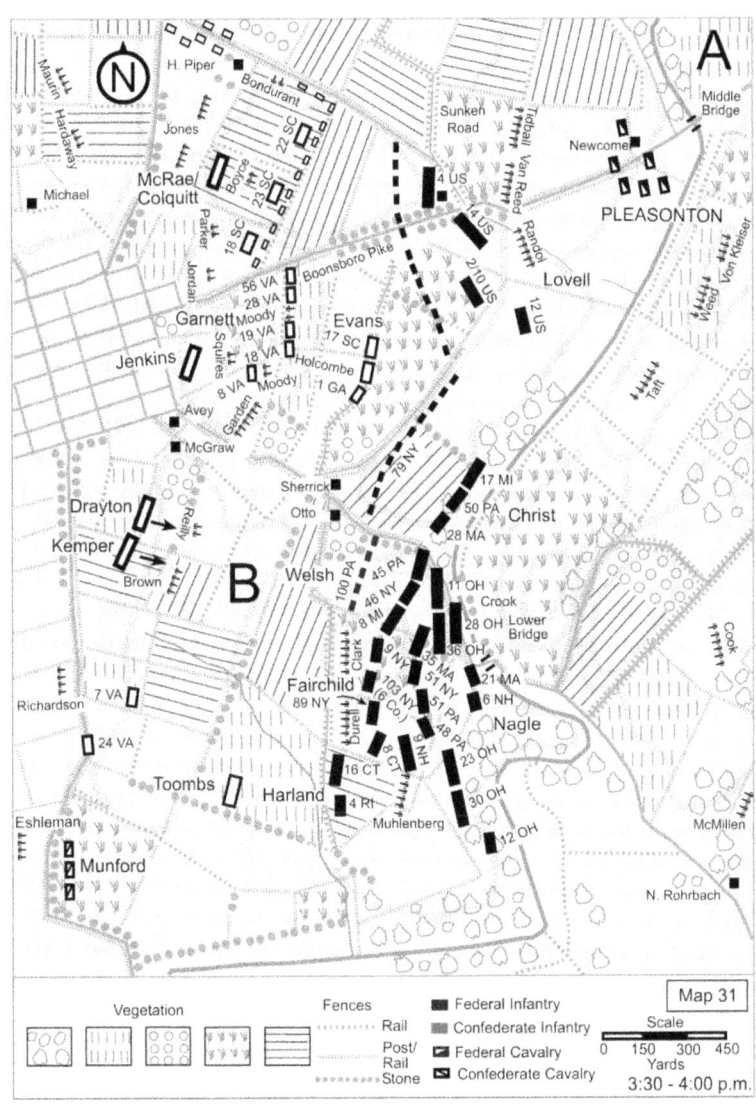

and for thirty minutes we were under a most severe fire of round shot, shell, grape, and canister, and suffered severely." Christ's 244 losses testify to the intensity of the enemy fire. Welsh continued his drive beyond Christ, and pushed a couple of Confederate brigades back to Harpers Ferry Road that led into town. Some exhausted Southern foot soldiers retreated through the town. It was a desperate time for Lee's army.[5]

Rodman's division also attacked south (left) of Willcox's division. Col. Harrison Fairchild's brigade far outpaced Cox's other troops and drove several enemy brigades back to Harpers Ferry Road all the while taking heavy losses from Lee's artillery aligned along the road and on Cemetery Hill to the right. Charles Johnson of the 9th New York wrote the "air was filled with a deluge of bullets, grape, canister and shell," yet the line continued on. The men's orders were to halt, fire a volley, and then charge with fixed bayonets. Confederate artillery fire had already subtracted almost a third of Fairchild's men, but now they advanced at a quick step as if on parade. Alexander Hunter of the 17th Virginia (Kemper's Brigade) recalled his emotions as he watched the "onset of solid ranks of blue," and "felt his heart sink within him and grow faint." The officers yelled, "Men, we are to hold this position at all hazards. Not a man [should] leave his place. If need be, we will die together in this road." The historian of the 17th Virginia described the scene: "The first thing we saw appear was the gilt eagle that surmounted the pole, then the top of the flag, next the flutter of the Stars and Stripes itself slowly mounting—up it rose; then their hats came in sight; still rising, the faces emerged; next a range of curious eyes appeared, then such a hurrah as only the Yankee troops could give broke the stillness, and they surged towards us." The Confederates waited until Fairchild's men were within 50 yards. The enemy continued advancing, forcing the outmanned Confederate defenders to flee.[6]

To the south, Rodman's other brigade, under Col. Edward Harland, moved forward into a 40-acre cornfield. His brigade formed the left side of Cox's line of attack. The 8th Connecticut's (Harland's brigade) persistent advance drove the cannoneers of Capt. David McIntosh's battery from their guns and surged forward to capture them while the 4th Rhode Island and 16th Connecticut remained in the cornfield.

The situation looked bleak for Lee's army, but just then, the leading elements of Lee's last division to reach the battlefield swung into view. Maj. Gen. A. P. Hill's division had been left at Harpers Ferry to process captured Union troops and collect supplies. In response to an urgent plea for help, Hill put his men on the road shortly after 7:00 a.m. that morning. It was a grueling 17-mile march, causing hundreds of men to fall by the wayside. The lead elements approached the Potomac River at 2:30 p.m. Lee would now have about 2,600 new troops, albeit exhausted, to counter Cox's drive. The route of Hill's approach put him directly on the IX Corps' vulnerable left flank.[7]

Hill's first brigade, under Brig. Gen. Maxcy Gregg, drove straight east into the 40-acre cornfield housing a portion of Harland's brigade. The rookie 16th Connecticut was there along with the veteran 4th Rhode Island. Some of the men of the former regiment claimed they loaded their rifles for the first time that day. A couple of Gregg's South Carolina regiments got confused and never entered the battle, but three did and they eventually caught Harland's men in the front, flank, and rear, causing them to stampede to the rear. Sgt. Jacob Bauer told his wife the men accomplished their retreat "in a Bull Run fashion."[8]

A second brigade, under Brig. Gen. Lawrence Branch, arrived next and drove north along Harpers Ferry Road and attacked the 8th Connecticut which had ventured toward the Confederate line by itself because the 16th Connecticut and 4th Rhode Island had not moved out of the 40-acre cornfield. The North Carolinians hit the Nutmeggers' left flank and rear and drove the men to the rear. Rodman had seen the isolated regiment and galloped forward to bring it back to safety, but was mortally wounded in the process. Branch was also killed in this fight.

Burnside brought up Col. Hugh Ewing's brigade (Scammon's division) to try to stop Hill's newly arriving troops from doing additional damage. It formed behind a stone wall and was hit by Gregg's South Carolinians on the left and rear and by a third brigade from Hill's division, Brig. Gen. James Archer's, in the front. After a valiant fight, the Ohioans were forced to give way. What appeared so promising an hour earlier now was becoming a rout. Four of Burnside's brigades were defeated and only nightfall put an end to the fighting. Although the IX Corps dwarfed Hill's division in numbers, his sudden appearance on their flank reinforced the concern that Lee had more troops available than he actually did.[9]

The fighting in this phase involved 16,300 men. The IX Corps numbered 11,700 infantry and D. R. Jones' and A. P. Hill's men numbered about 4,600. The losses totaled 3,550 (Union: 2,350; Confederate: 1,200).[10]

Middle Bridge Sector

McClellan's tactical plan involved an early thrust against the enemy's left flank, and then after awhile, an attack on Lee's right flank and if either was successful, an attack against Lee's center along Boonsboro Pike. Attacking an enemy's center is always fraught with difficulties and should be undertaken only if one or both flanks are in disarray.

McClellan assembled an array of units in the middle part of the field, including Brig. Gen. George Sykes' division (V Corps), a number of cavalry units, and his "guns of position." Brig. Gen. Pleasonton's cavalry with four of its batteries crossed the Middle Bridge at about noon to bolster and protect Sumner's left flank that was fighting near the Sunken Road. It quickly encountered Confederate skirmishers and a lively exchange occurred. Pleasonton called up some of Sykes' U.S. Regulars, who crossed the bridge and with the help of the guns of position, drove the pesky enemy sharpshooters away. Additional U. S. Regular regiments crossed the bridge and added their weight to the battle against Confederate infantry stationed east of Sharpsburg. The Regulars were under the command of Capt. Hiram Dryer, who aggressively pushed his men toward the town. Sykes never liked the look of the situation and when he realized Dryer was exceeding his orders, pulled his command back across Antietam Creek, much to the regret of the Regulars, who believed they could have successfully pushed into Sharpsburg. The losses during this encounter were relatively light: Pleasonton's cavalry lost about 30 men and the Regulars lost almost 100. The Confederates losses are unknown, but probably were at least double the Union's number.

Some soldiers and historians have questioned why McClellan did not send over the bulk of the V Corps to attack Lee's center while Burnside attacked the right. Cavalry commander, Alfred Pleasonton, pressed the issue, but the

Map 32: The Final Actions of the Maryland Campaign
A: The Final Attack at Antietam
B: The Battle of Shepherdstown

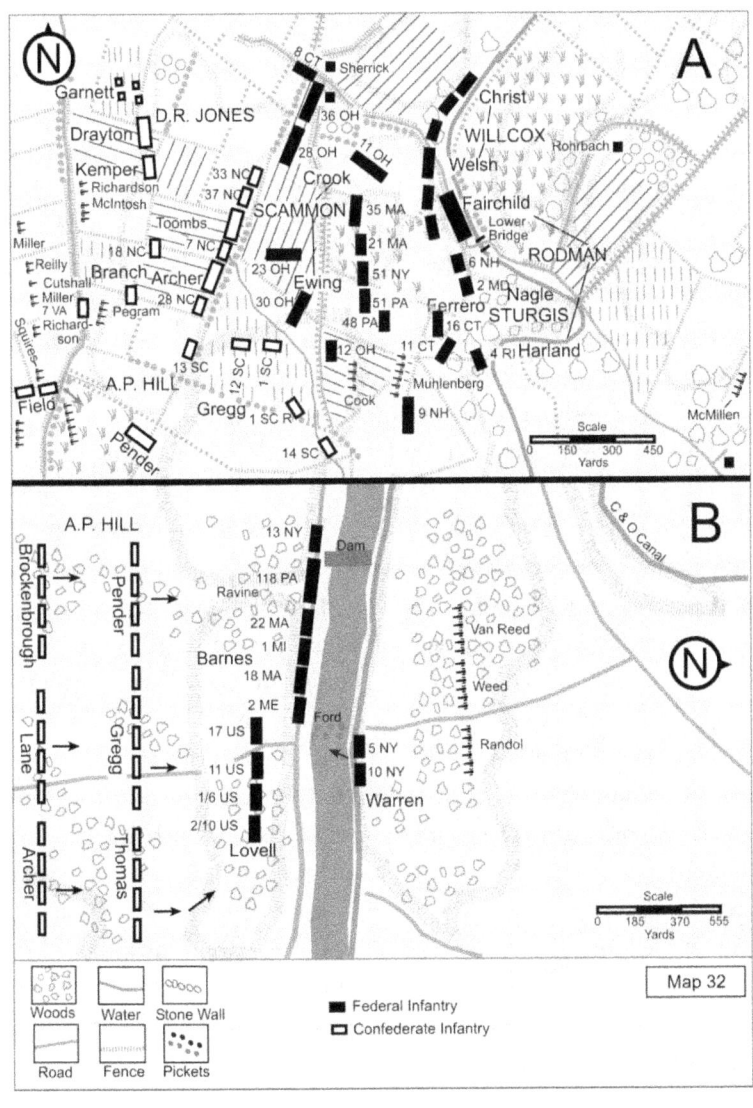

V Corps commander, Fitz John Porter, demurred believing it was too late to have an impact. [11]

The Pennsylvania Campaign of 1863

Lee came close to winning the second phase of the battle of Gettysburg. His men captured and held onto some high ground: Culp's Hill, Peach Orchard, and Houck's Ridge, and briefly held other important high ground: Cemetery Hill and Cemetery Ridge before being hurled back. He wrote in his report: "These partial successes determined me to continue the assault the next day. Pickett, with three of his brigades, joined Longstreet the following morning, and our batteries were moved forward to the positions gained by him the day before. The general plan of attack was unchanged, excepting that one division and two brigades of Hill's corps were ordered to support Longstreet." Curiously, Lee never mentioned Ewell's renewed attack on Culp's Hill—an event that would add thousands of names to the casualty lists.[12]

Lee did not have many fresh troops to make the attack on July 3. Longstreet could commit Pickett's division and A. P. Hill had two brigades on the field, Brig. Gen. Edward Thomas' (Pender's division) and Brig. Gen. William Mahone's (Anderson's division), which were not used in the major attack. Hill instead provided all of Heth's division, two brigades from Pender's (Lane's and Scales') and two brigades from Anderson's (Wilcox's and Lang's). Many of these units had suffered tremendous losses on July 1 or July 2 and were in no shape to be committed to battle so soon. For example, Brig. Gens. Archer's and Davis' brigades had been overwhelmed during the early fighting and lost hundreds of prisoners, including Archer. Pettigrew's and Scales' brigades had sustained heavy losses on July 1, as had Wilcox's and Lang's men on July 2. Only Lane's and Col. John Brockenbrough's brigades were in any shape for an all out charge, but the latter was unsteady because of its loss of officers at Chancellorsville and the questionable abilities of its temporary commander.

Culp's Hill

As Longstreet assembled his men for the charge across almost a mile of open fields toward Cemetery Ridge, the fighting raged in other parts of the battlefield, namely Culp's Hill and around the Bliss Farm between Seminary and Cemetery Ridges. By daylight on July 3, Maj. Gen. Howard Slocum's entire XII Corps had returned to Culp's Hill and was prepared for the coming fight. Slocum also brought up 26 guns to help defend the high ground. Ewell also reinforced his attack column during the night, bringing up two brigades (Brig. Gen. Junius Daniels' and Col. Edward O'Neal's) from Rodes' division and Brig. Gen. William Smith's brigade from Early's division. Ewell now had seven brigades to throw up the slopes of Culp's Hill. One of Ewell's aides recalled Lee's orders on the evening of July 2: "An attack would be renewed at daylight of the third by Longstreet. We were to cooperate, as before, by opening with artillery & engaging the attention of the enemy as far as possible. Also to push out success on the left if practicable."[13]

The Union guns opened fire at first light and Ewell had his men moving up the steep, rock-strewn hill soon after. The Confederate infantrymen attacked and were repulsed, and they did it again and again, each time leaving the side of the hill strewn with additional dead and wounded. Union division commander Brig. Gen. John Geary cycled regiments into and out of the front lines to keep his men fresh and maintain a high level of killing volleys. Some of the Confederates came within feet of the Union defenses before being shot down. Brig. Gen. Junius Daniel summed up the situation when he reported, "the hill in front…was, in my opinion, so strong that it could not have been carried by any force." Brig. Gen. James Walker, whose Stonewall Brigade attacked the middle of the Union line, concluded, that his renewed attacks were "done with equally bad success as our former efforts, and the fire became so destructive that I suffered the brigade to fall back to a more secure position, as it was a useless sacrifice of life to keep them longer under so galling a fire."

Steuart's brigade, which had captured a portion of the Union works the night before, continued its advance to expand its breach, but was met by killing volleys in what was later called, Pardee Field, and pushed from its tentative toehold on Culp's Hill.

Map 33: Culp's Hill (July 3)

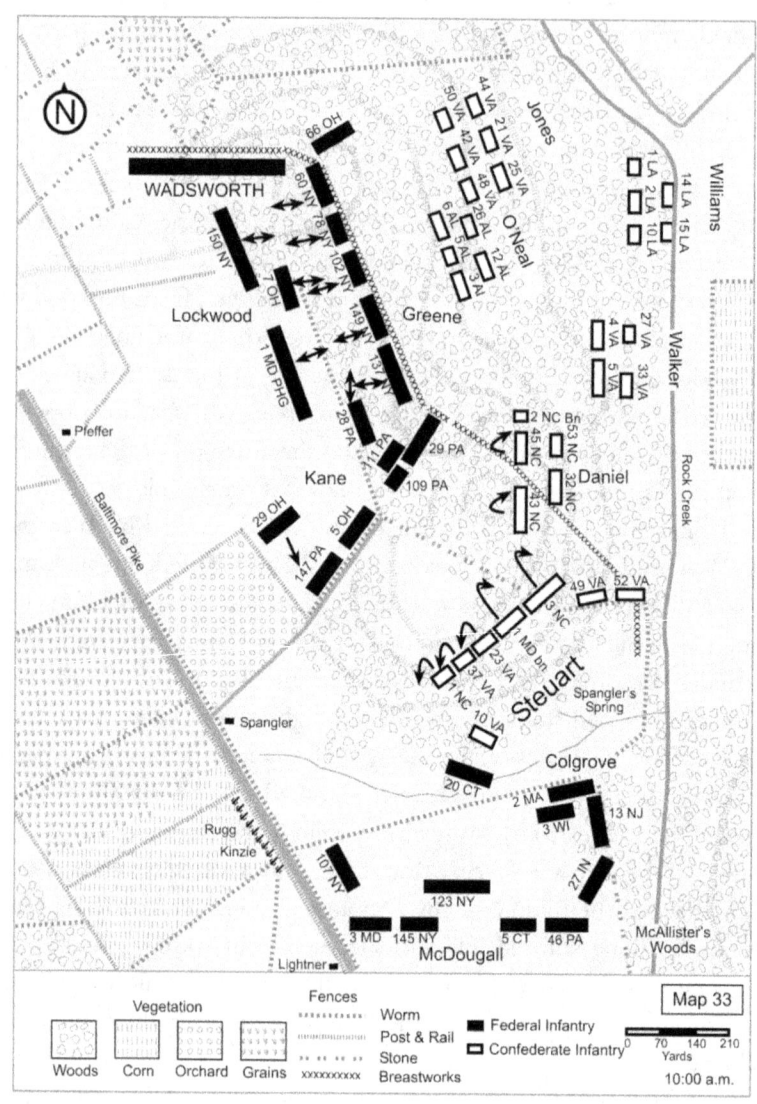

Only Brig. Gen. William Smith's brigade achieved some success at Spangler's Meadow, at the base of Culp's Hill. Ensconced behind a sturdy stone wall, it bloodily stopped an attack by Col. Silas Colgrove's brigade's Indiana and Massachusetts boys. Rather than simply savor the victory, Smith ordered his men to leave the protection of their stone wall and venture into the meadow, where their ranks were torn apart by Colgrove's men.

Thousands of bodies of fallen Confederates lay in clumps, covering Culp's Hill's slopes. Reinforcements from the Union VI Corps arrived to assist by 11:00 a.m., but by then the bloodbath was over. Ascertaining the strength and losses of the combatants is difficult as most of the Confederates had already shed blood on July 1 or July 2. Of the XII Corps, only a few brigades sustained losses on July 2, and of its 9,600 combatants, fewer than 400 were were casualties (4%). Johnson's division and the three brigades from other divisions fielded a similar number of men—9,100 but sustained losses of almost 2,400 (26%).[14]

The Culp's Hill fight is usually regarded as a wasted effort. The Union position was impregnable, but the toehold the Confederates gained the evening before may have convinced Ewell that he could expand his breach. Like the earlier attack on July 2, it was made in isolation and not coordinated with Longstreet's efforts to the south.

The Bliss Farm

While Ewell's men were being slaughtered on the side of Culp's Hill, a smaller affair occurred at the Bliss farmstead in the "no man's land" between Seminary and Cemetery Ridges. Both sides wanted possession of the farm and its outbuildings. The subsequent fight involved Brig. Gen. Carnot Posey's brigade of Mississippians on Seminary Ridge against portions of Brig. Gen. Alexander Hays' division stationed on Cemetery Ridge. Each side took turns occupying the farm buildings until Hays ordered them set ablaze, ending the fighting with neither side in control.[15]

The Pickett-Pettigrew-Trimble Charge

The big event, the one Gettysburg is probably known best for, involved a full-scale attack on Cemetery Ridge by eleven Confederate brigades. Their target was a clump of trees on Cemetery Ridge. Lee was confident of success.

Brig. Gen. Ambrose Wright's brigade, alone and unsupported, had briefly occupied the ridge the day before, so he reasoned an attack by eleven times that number might just take and hold the heights, especially if preceded by a massive artillery barrage. Lee met with Longstreet soon after dawn to explain his plan, but his subordinate did not take it well. Longstreet later explained how he hoped the idea of attacking these heights from the west "had been fully tested the day before." He again believed the most effective approach involved sliding south and hitting Meade's vulnerable left flank. Longstreet even sent scouts to find a way to carry out his ideas, but Lee was not convinced. Pointing "with his fist" toward the high ground, Lee said "the enemy is there; I am going to strike him." Longstreet believed such an attack would require at least 30,000 men for success. Lee envisioned sending fewer than 13,000 men across the open ground.

Lee persisted and Longstreet finally threw his hands in the air and said, "General, I have been a soldier all my life…it is my opinion that no fifteen thousand men ever arrayed for battle can take that position." Lee was unmoved and when Pickett's division arrived, it deployed in the trees on Seminary Ridge. Six brigades from Heth's and Pender's divisions (A. P. Hill's III Corps) formed on his left. Later, two other brigades (Wilcox's and Lang's) from Anderson's division took position further to the right of the line. Many of these troops had fought hard on July 1 or July 2 and were in no shape for a full-scale charge against a strong Union position.[16]

All were concerned about the 1,400 yards of open ground between the two ridges. Caught out in the open, the infantrymen could be torn apart by the Union artillery. Lee placed young Georgian Col. Edward "Porter" Alexander in charge of the counter-artillery fire. Lee provided him with over 150 cannon to neutralize Meade's enemy's artillery and break up his infantry formations. He believed the relatively short, efficient, and effective cannonade could wipe out the enemy's artillery positions. Then, with his artillery's limbers resupplied with ammunition, a number would advance just behind the infantry and blast the last of the enemy from its defenses.

Meade initially thought the major Confederate attack on July 3 would be directed at his center, held by his veteran II Corps. One of its divisions, Brig. Gen. John Caldwell's, was wrecked at the Wheatfield the day before, but Maj. Gen. Winfield Hancock retained two relatively fresh divisions, Brig. Gen.

John Gibbon's and Brig. Gen. Alexander Hays', on Cemetery Ridge. Some units from both divisions had seen action on July 2, helping repel Wright's and Barksdale's charges and assisting in throwing Early's division off Cemetery Hill. The two divisions numbered about 5,200 and were composed of battle hardened veterans who occupied a slight rise in ground populated by several stone walls. The Union troops had the added incentive of defending their home soil. Additionally, artillery commander Brig. Gen. Henry Hunt had 139 guns between Little Round Top and Cemetery Hill and another 95 waiting in reserve. Unless these guns were neutralized, Lee's attack column would have little chance of reaching the Union line, let alone breaking it.

Pickett's men had marched all night to get to the battlefield and were still arriving when the sun rose on July 3. They were probably in no shape to mount a serious charge, but the men knew how close the army was to victory and a successful effort might end the war. A single Confederate cannon fired at 1:00 p.m. and suddenly as many as 150 cannons roared into action. They were to fire until it appeared the Union line was sufficiently pummeled and the enemy artillery neutralized. Then the Confederate infantry would begin their charge. How much time the artillery fired is debatable, but the cannonade lasted for at least an hour and possibly a bit more. The Union response was tepid because Hunt wanted to save his artillery's ammunition for the infantry charge he knew would soon be launched. He came into direct conflict with Hancock, who wanted the artillery near his lines to respond, if only to bolster his infantry's morale. Many of them did and, as Hunt predicted, were out of ammunition when the Southern infantry stepped off.

The Confederate artillery was initially successful in blasting the Union lines, but shells began overshooting the enemy's positions, exploding harmlessly in the rear or simply thudding to the ground without exploding. The dense smoke prevented the cannoneers from seeing the impact of their efforts, so they were essentially firing blindly. Most of the Confederate ordnance, as much as 75%, never exploded because of defective fuses or exploded too late or too soon. Most were from a new manufacturing facility, so were different from what the cannoneers were accustomed to. Nevertheless, the cannonade created many Union casualties and demoralized the men. The historian of the 69th Pennsylvania (Brig. Gen. Alexander Webb's brigade) noted, the "air is filling with the whirling, shrieking, hissing sound of the solid shot and bursting shell; all throw themselves flat upon the ground, behind the little stone wall ... [some of the shells] traveling through the air, high above us, or striking the ground in front and ricocheting over us, to be imbedded in some object in the rear."[17]

When it looked as though the Confederate artillery had sufficiently softened the enemy's line, Longstreet reluctantly called forth his infantry. In reality, the cannonade did not significantly wound the Union artillery and the Confederates may have only seen a swapping of batteries. Pickett's three brigades advanced on the right; Heth's division, now under Pettigrew, advanced on Pickett's left and two brigades of Pender's division (now under Maj. Gen. Isaac Trimble) formed behind Pettigrew. The remaining two brigades of Anderson's division remained in reserve to the right of Pickett's division.

More than the first half of the attack went according to plan, but suddenly, the Union artillery came to life and shattered the Confederate infantry. A dozen cannon that Alexander carefully husbanded for the final attack had disappeared and could not be found. Other pieces were out of ammunition, so only a handful of guns actually advanced.

Still, the Confederates continued their long charge of almost three-quarters of a mile of open, undulating terrain. The Union artillery addressed the well-dressed lines, causing them to melt with each step the men took. The Union infantrymen hunkered down behind the stone wall and awaited orders to stand and fire at the approaching enemy troops. The officers finally ordered their men into action when the Confederates reached Emmitsburg Road. Most of Pickett's attack fell on the part of the line manned by the Philadelphia Brigade. These men had repelled Wright the day before and they had collected two, three, or even more rifles. All were loaded and within easy reach of the defenders. When ordered to open fire, they shot off each gun, creating the illusion of many more men and inflicting many more casualties than would have occurred if each man had only one firearm.[18]

A stout fence lined each side of Emmitsburg Road and many a Southerner was struck while climbing over these barriers. Pickett's men readily navigated the fences, and several hundred reached the stone wall, where hand-to-hand combat erupted. Sgt. William Burns of the 71st Pennsylvania recalled, "the fight soon became awful. We mowed the rebs right and left but still they came on. We had to retreat." The Irishmen of the 69th Pennsylvania to their left, despite all the venom and discrimination heaped upon them because they were foreign born, refused to budge from their positions in front of the copse of trees, but were forced back by the sheer weight of the attack. Some of the other units around them broke for the rear. Pickett's men were at a disadvantage, for as they closed on the wall, several Vermont regiments from Brig. Gen. George Stannard's brigade, the same men who had helped blunt Wright's charge the day before, now rushed forward into the field, wheeled right and crashed into Pickett's right flank. Some of Pickett's men fled to the rear and others turned and faced the Vermonters, preventing them from adding their weight to their comrades' attack on the stone wall.

The situation was also grim to Pickett's left, where six brigades of Pettigrew's and Trimble's brigades headed for Emmitsburg Road. Because of the angle of the road, they were actually closer to the Union line, manned by Hays' division (II Corps). These attacking units were poorly chosen to make the charge for they were still in shock over the loss of so many comrades on July 1. Many reached the fence lining Emmitsburg Road, but decided it was not prudent to continue and turned back; others crossed and were shot down as they approached the wall. The brigade on the left, Col. John Brockenbrough's Virginians, was hit by the same type of flank attack that eviscerated the right wing of Pickett's division. In this case it involved the 8th Ohio. When its commanding officer saw Pettigrew's advance, he pushed his men into the open field, wheeled them to the left and hit Brockenbrough's left flank. It was too much to bear and the Virginians headed for the rear. The Buckeyes now turned their attention to the next unit in line, the Mississippians of Davis' brigade. Many of the latter made it to the Abraham Brian farm buildings, but were under fire from front and left flank.[19]

While perhaps a hundred of Pickett's men breached the defensive line, Union reinforcements swarmed the area, killing, capturing, or driving away the Confederates. Many of the survivors gazed at their starting point and decided to throw down their guns and surrender rather than be shot in the back. Just as Pickett's men were breaching the Union line, two more brigades—Wilcox's and Lang's—from Anderson's Confederate division were launched toward Cemetery Ridge. These units were not behind Pickett's men to help them hold the wall and widen the breach, but to their right. The

Map 34: The Pickett-Pettigrew-Trimble Charge

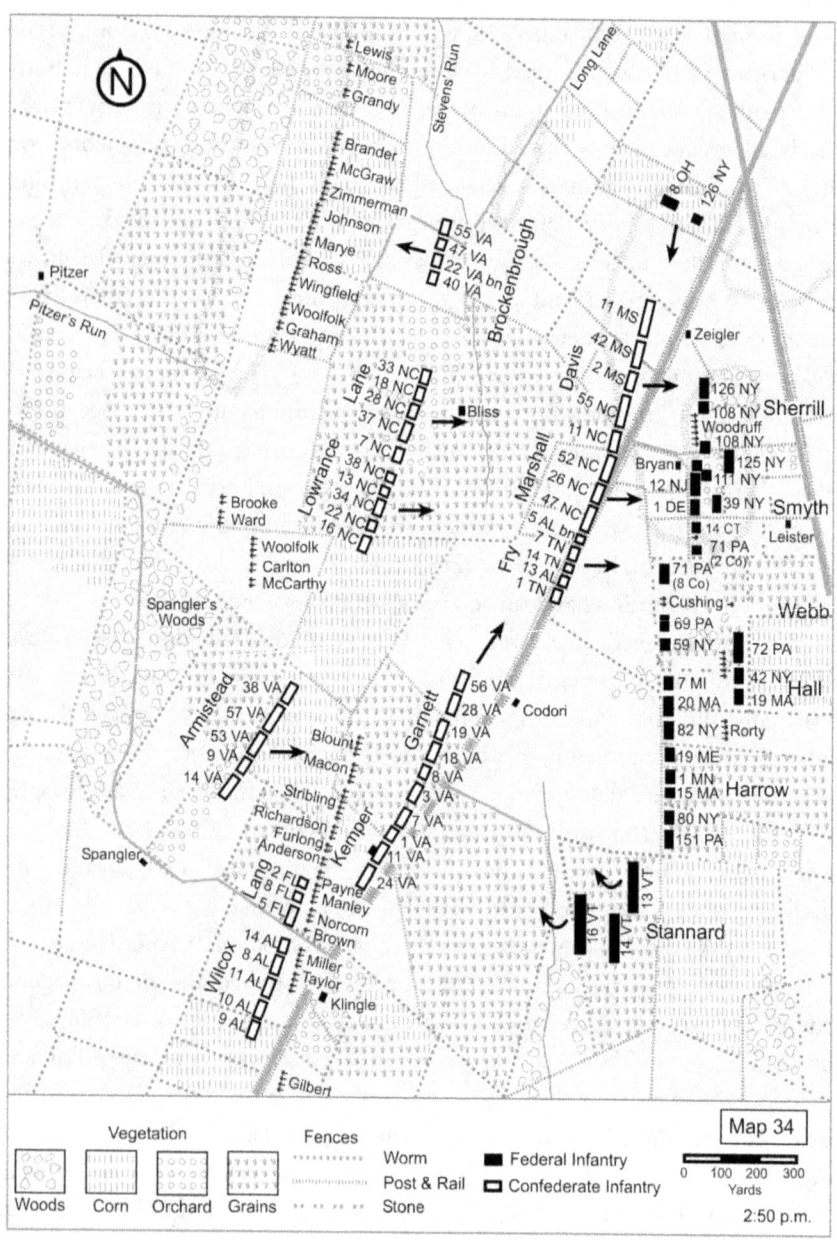

Alabamians and Floridians were hit on the right flank by the same Vermont troops who attacked Pickett's right flank and by II Corps troops in their front, and flung backward with heavy losses. This attack gained nothing but casualties.

As the survivors filtered back to Seminary Ridge, Lee realized the folly of the attack and was heard to say, "It is all my fault!" which was certainly the case.

The number of troops participating in the last phase of the battle is difficult to ascertain, as most of the units had already sustained losses earlier in the battle, so only an approximation is possible. The two divisions of the Union II Corps on Cemetery Ridge numbered about 5,200 on July 3 and with Stannard's brigade, the Union army fielded 7,500 against Lee's 13,000. As expected, the losses were lopsided: The Confederates lost 5,400 (41%) compared with the 1,950 for Meade's army (26%).[20]

Cavalry actions

July 3 also saw several cavalry confrontations northeast and south of Gettysburg. Confederate cavalry commander, Maj. Gen. Jeb Stuart finally reached the northeastern outskirts of Gettysburg and attempted to unite with Lee's army during the afternoon. Brig. Gen. David Gregg's division, augmented by George Custer's brigade (Brig. Gen. Judson Kilpatrick's division) stood in the way and battled Stuart to a standstill that ended when the Confederate horsemen launched a desperate charge that was blunted by attacks against its flanks and front.

To the south, Kilpatrick launched an attack against Lee's right flank. He committed Brig. Gen. Elon Farnsworth's cavalry brigade from his own division, and Brig. Gen. Wesley Merritt's brigade from Brig. Gen. John Buford's division against the enemy infantry and artillery. Cavalry against foot soldiers is never a good idea and these two brigades were up against elements of three Confederate infantry brigades. Kilpatrick's men were quickly repulsed and Merritt's fought to a stalemate.

Further west, reports of a Confederate wagon train near Fairfield caused Merritt to unleash the 6th U. S. Cavalry. They encountered an entire enemy brigade under Brig. Gen. William "Grumble" Jones, who almost destroyed the Regulars.

The Union cavalry outnumbered its Southern counterparts during these engagements: Union: 7,830; Confederate: 7,550. The losses in the three actions were 700 for the Union cavalry (9%) and 440 for the Confederates (6%).[21]

Comparisons of the Two Campaigns

Units and Number of Troops Involved

The final phase of the battle of Antietam featured two well-defined fights. First, the IX Corps' attempt to cross Antietam Creek and once across, it launched its "final attack" on Lee's right flank, south of Sharpsburg. The fighting in the first portion of the third phase involved a portion of the Union IX Corps versus a couple of regiments from Brig. Gen. Robert Toombs' brigade supplemented by a handful of men from other brigades. The second portion involved a massive frontal attack, involving most IX Corps units.

The third phase of Gettysburg was more complex, involving six separate actions. The day began with a massive Confederate attack on Culp's Hill at first light involving Johnson's division supplemented by some brigades from Rodes' and Early's divisions. They were up against the reconstituted XII Corps ensconced behind strong breastworks. A couple of brigades also fought over possession of the Bliss farm buildings, just south of Gettysburg. The fight involved Posey's and Smyth's brigades. The main event was the Pickett-Pettigrew-Trimble Charge, involving portions of four Confederate divisions against the Union II Corps, augmented by some other troops. Three cavalry fights rounded out the day: the large engagement northeast of Gettysburg involving Stuart's and Gregg's cavalry divisions, the latter aided by George Custer's brigade of Kilpatrick's division. Further south, Kilpatrick attempted to turn Lee's right flank, by unleashing Farnsworth's brigade of his own division and Merritt's brigade of Buford's division against portions of three Confederate infantry brigades from Hood's division (Robertson's, Anderson's, and Law's), but the effort failed. Finally, at Fairfield to the west, the 6th U. S. Cavalry was gutted by "Grumble" Jones cavalry brigade.

The number of units and troops engaged at Antietam during the third phase of its battle pales in relation to the third day of battle at Gettysburg.

The Union forces at Antietam involved the IX Corps crossing Antietam Creek and attacking Lee's right flank, comprised of D. R. Jones' division. A. P. Hill's division's sudden appearance helped bolster Lee's flank. Therefore, a total of six divisions fought during the last phase of Antietam. Eight Union divisions fought at Gettysburg on July 3 (three from the II Corps, two from the XII Corps, and portions of three cavalry divisions). The Confederates threw portions of seven infantry divisions (Johnson's, Rodes', Early's, Pickett's, Pettigrew's, Trimble's, and Anderson's) at the high ground. Part's of Hood's infantry division helped fend off Kilpatrick's attacks and Stuart's cavalry division increases the number of participating on July 3 to nine. Only McLaws' division was not used during the final phase. Therefore, a total of six divisions fought during the final phase at Antietam and 17 saw combat at Gettysburg.

Approximately 16,300 men fought during the third phase at Antietam (Union: 11,700; Confederate: 4,600) and 53,400 (Union: 24,900; Confederate: 28,500) at Gettysburg. While a larger proportion of Union troops battled during the third phase at Antietam (Union: 20%; Confederates: 13%), Lee threw a greater percentage of his army into battle than Meade on July 3 (Union: 26%; Confederates: 38%).

Leadership

A cloud hung over some of the senior leaders involved in the final actions at Antietam. Burnside was taken to task by McClellan for not breaking camp and following the Confederates sooner on September 15. McClellan took pains to explain his expectations to Burnside the day before the major battle. A. P. Hill and John Hood were also under a cloud as they had been placed under arrest by Stonewall Jackson for their perceived transgressions during the march, and were only recently permitted to return to their divisions.

McClellan tried to scapegoat Burnside's performance at Antietam, explaining that he should have attacked earlier in the day. However, Burnside received his attack orders shortly before 10:00 a.m. and immediately executed them. A. P. Hill has been criticized for not getting to the battlefield before 3:30 p.m., because he did not march at first light and did not take the most direct route, causing him to arrive later than anticipated, creating more suspense than was necessary. His pace was so severe, that hundreds fell out of the ranks and were unavailable to face the IX Corps when needed most.

The Union army's leadership during the third day of Gettysburg was superb. Hancock masterfully motivated his II Corps infantrymen and brought reinforcements to bear where and when needed. Similarly, Slocum shuffled his XII Corps troops from front line to rear on Culp's Hill to ensure that his men were fresh when they faced Ewell's attacks.

On the Confederate side at Gettysburg, Ewell, who had not attacked in conjunction with Longstreet on July 3, again caused grief as he attacked too soon in the morning—before Longstreet. Ewell's attacks were uncoordinated and doomed to fail. By attacking early, Meade could have shuffled troops from Culp's Hill, if the center of his line needed reinforcements.

Prior to the Pickett-Pettigrew-Trimble charge, Lee and Longstreet spent time discussing and disagreeing on the attack, but in the end, the army commander again had the final word. Longstreet was correct in expressing his concerns about the attack, and his hesitancy probably did not translate into a Confederate defeat. The defeat can be squarely placed on Lee's shoulders, who did not adequately coordinate his troops' actions and who acted rashly. He believed a massive artillery barrage followed by a determine attack could carry the day, but he was wrong. A. P. Hill also shoulders blame for his enthusiastic support for the attack and for providing eight brigades, all of which were badly cut up earlier in the battle and were in no shape for another desperate attack. He actually had two brigades that had not seen combat and should have replaced some of the more decimated units.

The cavalry leadership was a mixed bag. Stuart finally reached the battlefield on the evening of July 2 and Lee made his disappointment very clear. Stuart would fight under a cloud when he took on Gregg's cavalry division northeast of town on July 3. Gregg provided a superb screen to prevent Stuart's division from reaching Lee's army. Further south, Kilpatrick needlessly attacked Lee's right flank and all he could show for it were long casualty lists, including the death of Farnsworth.

Tactics

The final phase of each battle involved the aggressor attempting to turn the enemy's right flank. At Antietam, the IX Corps was first required to cross the Lower Bridge before it could attack the heights. Burnside and McClellan used finesse in planning the assault: while infantry stormed the Lower Bridge, a flanking movement across Antietam Creek at a downstream ford ultimately carried the day. It took longer than expected, but the tactic worked in the end. It would take several hours for the men to cross the creek and prepare for their attack on Lee's flank. The attack on Culp's Hill, Meade's right flank, was folly, as the heights were impregnable and thousands of young Southern boys became casualties because of it. Ewell resorted to hammer blows to achieve his goal, but each attempt was repulsed.

Artillery played an important role throughout both battles, but may have played the most decisive role during the third phase at Gettysburg. The Confederate artillery attempted to soften up the enemy's line with a massive artillery barrage at Gettysburg prior to the Pickett-Pettigrew-Trimble Charge, but Burnside did not use the same approach during his Final Attack at Antietam, probably because he had fewer guns and it was more difficult to bring them across Antietam Creek and into position on the high ground beyond. In both battles, the defender's artillery was unleashed when the attacker's infantry advanced, but it was much more destructive at Gettysburg because of the open, rolling terrain that exposed the attackers, compared with the deep ravines the IX Corps traversed at Antietam. Also, the Union defenders at Gettysburg had many more cannon at their disposal (about 140) than the Confederates defending Lee's right flank at Antietam (about 40). Although the Confederate defenders had fewer guns at Antietam, they were easily able to smother the three batteries that accompanied the IX Corps' charge.

The Pickett-Pettigrew-Trimble Charge at Gettysburg, like the IX Corps' Final Attack at Antietam, came up to the enemy's defensive line, and was thrown back in a similar manner. Because of the open terrain and the more determined attack at Gettysburg, the Confederates lost a much higher proportion of their men during the charge. Some units lost more than 50% of their effectives. Only Col. Harrison Fairchild's brigade at Antietam lost such a high a percentage.

Coordination

The final infantry attacks at Gettysburg and Antietam were massive endeavors requiring sound coordination for success. Willcox's division attacked on the right of Burnside's line during the Final Attack at Antietam. The terrain disrupted efforts to coordinate its two brigades' (Welsh's and Christ's) advance. First, Christ's brigade on the extreme right made progress toward the town of Sharpsburg, but when it did not see Welsh to its left, Col. Christ halted it. Welsh contended with more difficult terrain, and when it did drive forward, Christ did not join it, dissipating the power of the attack. Rodman's division on the left of the line also experienced coordination issues, as Fairchild's brigade drove forward, almost to Harpers Ferry Road before turning back. It was not fully supported by Harland's brigade on its left, and sustained heavy casualties as a result. A massive attack by Burnside's entire IX Corps could have possibly swept the Confederates from the field before A. P. Hill's division appeared, as the strength differential would have been approximately 11,000 to 2,500.

McClellan's coordination of the two major attacks at either end of the battlefield is suspect. He decided to attack first from the north at about 6:00 a.m. and then from the south (across the Lower Bridge), but he waited until almost 9:30 a.m. to give orders to launch the latter attack. The time gap allowed enemy reinforcements to flood the northern fields, helping to devastate the I Corps and Sedgwick's division (II Corps). An earlier attack on the Lower Bridge could have potentially put pressure on both ends of the line at the same time and possibly an earlier and more complete victory for McClellan. However, a case can be made for not attacking the Lower Bridge earlier, for Walker's Confederate division, numbering over 3,500 men was pulled from that sector, making it potentially easier for the IX Corps to cross Antietam Creek.

The Pickett-Pettigrew-Trimble Charge at Gettysburg, despite involving brigades from four divisions from two corps was surprisingly well coordinated. It fell apart toward the end of the charge, when two of Anderson's brigades—Lang's and Wilcox's—were launched after the rest of the charge had all but ended, leading to senseless loss of additional men.

Lee's failure to coordinate the charge on Culp's Hill and the attack on Cemetery Ridge, was most egregious. Whether such coordination would have had an impact on either charge is unknown.

Duration of Combat

The final phase the Battle of Antietam began with the first attack on the Lower Bridge at about 10:00 a.m. The bridge was taken at about 1:00 p.m. and then it took two more hours for Burnside to get his troops across Antietam Creek and into position to launch the attack against Lee's center and right flank. The Final Attack began at about 3:15 p.m. and continued until dark—about 7:00 p.m. The two sides therefore battled for about seven hours.

Gettysburg was far more complex during the final phase of the battle, as there were multiple uncoordinated actions. The attack on Culp's Hill began before dawn and continued until 11:00 a.m. Like Antietam, there was about a two hour break until 1:00 p.m. when Lee's artillery opened fire, presaging the Pickett-Pettigrew-Trimble Charge. The fighting ended well before dark. The cavalry also actions occurred in the afternoon after the major infantry combat. The fighting during the third phase probably continued for about ten hours at Gettysburg, compared with seven hours at Antietam.

Losses

The losses during the third phase at Antietam totaled 3,550 or 20% of those engaged (Union: 2,350 or 20%; Confederate: 1,200 or 21%). The losses during July 3 at Gettysburg were immense in comparison: 10,950 (Union: 2,800; Confederate: 8,150). This translates to a casualty rate of 11% for the Union troops and 28% for the Confederates.

Union Maj. Gen. Isaac Rodman was mortally wounded and Brig. Gen. Lawrence Branch was killed outright during the final phase at Antietam. At Gettysburg, Confederate Brig. Gen. Richard Garnett was killed and Brig. Gen. Lewis Armistead was mortally wounded. Brig. Gen. Elon Farnsworth, a Union cavalry brigade commander, also died during this phase of the battle.[22]

Comparing Burnside's Final Attack with the Pickett/Pettigrew/Trimble Charge

The major charge during the final phase of each battle exhibit striking similarities and merit a closer examination. The attackers, Burnside at Antietam and Longstreet at Gettysburg, fielded a similar number of men—about 13,000 for the Pickett-Pettigrew-Trimble Charge at Gettysburg and as many as 12,000 men for the IX Corps' Final Attack at Antietam. Both were aligned in a straight line stretching almost a mile in length. Both kicked off at around 3:00 p.m., and both involved an attempt to take strategically important high ground south of the two towns. It was a "winner takes all" approach for both armies and both charges ultimately failed.

Longstreet's attack at Gettysburg relied on a massive cannonade to soften the enemy's defensive line; Burnside's did not. Lee made the preliminary cannonade an important component of the Pickett-Pettigrew-Trimble Charge and he sent as many batteries as he could to batter the Union center and the artillery positions on Cemetery Hill and Little Round Top. McClellan did not send additional cannon to Burnside at Antietam, so where Lee at Gettysburg fielded almost 150 cannon, Burnside had fewer than 55. Most of Burnside's artillery remained on the opposite side of Antietam Creek, and dueled with the Confederate artillery south of town. Col. Porter Alexander intended to advance at least a dozen cannon with the attack column at Gettysburg, but was unable to do so because they were unexpectedly moved. Some did advance, but with almost empty limbers. Three Union batteries advanced with the IX Corps infantry at Antietam and probably played a larger role during the actual charge.[23]

Each infantry attack column was required to traverse open fields before reaching the enemy's position. However, Burnside's men were closer to the enemy line at the start of the charge and the foot soldiers benefitted from the deep ravines cutting through the open ground that provided a good deal of cover. The attack column at Gettysburg was forced to first traverse almost three-quarters of a mile over a rolling terrain that provided less shelter.

The final Confederate infantry attack at Gettysburg featured four divisions in two army corps; Burnside's attack also involved four divisions, but they were all part of the IX Corps, making coordination potentially smoother. The built-in advantage did not materialize, however, and the Gettysburg charge was actually better coordinated, at least, during its early and middle stages.

The entire IX Corps was not intended to make the attack, as Burnside did not wish to use those units that had been involved in earlier fighting. The attacking units did not all share the same amount of ardor. For example, Fairchild's, Welsh's, and a portion of Harland's made sustained attacks, driving D. R. Jones' division's defensive line back into Sharpsburg or across Harpers Ferry Road, but others, such as Christ's brigade and portions of Harland's, did not attack or if they did, it was somewhat half-hearted. Some of the Confederate attackers at Gettysburg gained the Union's defensive position at the stone wall at the base of Cemetery Ridge before being counterattacked by newly arriving troops. However, not all made it that far. While many of Pickett's men scaled the wall, fewer from Pettigrew's (Heth's) and Trimble's (Pender's) reached it. These troops had fought hard and well on July 1, were worn out from those experiences and were still recovering from the loss of so many comrades. In addition, the wall in front of these troops, because of the angle, was farther to the east than the one sheltering the Union troops in front of Pickett's men. Similarly, the belated attacks of Wilcox's and Lang's brigades were quickly turned back.

Some of the defenders were pushed back in both charges. At Antietam, D.R. Jones' division, was pushed back to Harpers Ferry Road and beyond and it all looked promising until A. P. Hill's division arrived to save the day. Pickett's division and part of Pender's crashed into the "Angle" at Gettysburg, sending the 71st Pennsylvania to the rear.

Unexpected counterattacks helped seal the fate of both charges. At Antietam, A. P. Hill's division arrived just in time to help blunt Burnside's attack. The initial attack of Gregg's South Carolinians hit the IX Corps' left flank. At Gettysburg, the Confederate attack columns were hit on both flanks, doing serious damage. On the left, the 8th Ohio (Carroll's brigade, Hays' division, II Corps) hit Brockenbrough's brigade (Heth's/Pettigrew's division), driving it back before barreling into the next brigade in line, Davis' (Heth's/Pettigrew's division). At the opposite end of the line, Vermonters from Stannard's brigade (Doubleday's/Rowley's division, I Corps) forced the right side of Kemper's brigade to break off from the charge to face this new threat.

The losses incurred by the attackers differed greatly. Because of the open terrain and the massed Union artillery fire, the Confederate losses at Gettysburg exceeded 50%. The IX Corps' losses at Antietam were much lower because fewer of its troops made an all out attack on the Confederate line, there were fewer defenders with fewer cannon, and because nightfall put an end to the fighting.

Table 22: Comparison of the Third Phase of the Battles (Does not include skirmishing at Antietam's Middle Bridge sector)

Issue	Maryland Campaign	Pennsylvania Campaign
Role of cavalry	Minor	Important
Large units that opened the third phase of the battle	**Confederates:** D. R. Jones' division **Union:** IX Corps	**Confederates:** Ewell's Corps **Union:** XII Corps
Other large units fighting during the third phase	**Confederates:** A.P. Hill's division **Union:** None	**Confederates:** All three of Lee's Corps **Union:** II Corps & part of the I Corps
Number of divisions engaged	**Confederates:** 2 (22%) **Union:** 4 (25%)	**Confederates:** Parts of 8 infantry (89%) & Stuart's **Union:** Parts of 8 (42%)
Number of brigades engaged	**Confederates:** 6 (15%) **Union:** 8 (18%)	**Confederates:** 18 (49%) **Union:** 18 (35%)
Number of troops engaged	**Confederates:** 4,600 (13%) **Union:** 11,700 (20%) Total: 16,300	**Confederates:** 28,500 (38%) **Union:** 24,875 (26%) Total: 53,375
Leader directing the action wounded/ mortally wounded	**Confederates:** No **Union:** No	**Confederates:** No **Union:** Yes (Hancock)
Second in command takes over the field	**Confederates:** No **Union:** No	**Confederates:** No **Union:** No

Issue	Maryland Campaign	Pennsylvania Campaign
Major goal	Crush Confederate center/right & capture Sharpsburg	Crush Union right & center
Duration of the fighting	7 hours	10 hours
Direction of major initial attack	East to west	North to south
Direction of second attack	East to west	West to east
Dubious deployment and coordination of troops	**Confederates**: No **Union**: Yes	**Confederates**: No **Union**: No
Time of initial movement toward the enemy	10:00 a.m.	6:00 a.m.
Pulling Troops from other sectors	**Confederates**: Yes **Union**: No	**Confederates**: Yes **Union**: Yes
Number of casualties	**Confederates**: 1,200 (21%) **Union:** 2,350 (20%) Total: 3,550 (20%)	**Confederates:** 8,150 (28%) **Union:** 2,800 (11%) Total: 10,950 (20%)

Chapter 18: Lee Re-crosses the Potomac River

The Maryland Campaign of 1862

Both Lee and McClellan spent the night of September 17-18 huddling with their senior officers to develop plans for the following day. Maj. Gen. William Franklin, who's VI Corps had played only a minor role in the battle, agitated to be permitted to carry Nicodemus Heights, plant artillery there and blast Lee's left flank into submission. McClellan initially agreed, but countermanded it later that evening. McClellan later testified he rescinded the order because "15,000 Pennsylvania troops would soon arrive, and that upon their arrival the attack would be ordered." McClellan subsequently chose not to renew the battle because "success of an attack on the 18th was not certain." He emphasized, "Virginia lost, Washington menaced, Maryland invaded—the national cause could afford no risks of defeat. One battle lost and almost all would have been lost." He also admitted his men were exhausted from the intense fighting and the "heaviest and most efficient batteries" had expended most of their ammunition. Reinforcements arrived through September 18 and by noon McClellan had 78,000 effectives present. Ezra Carman believed as many as 35,000 had not been committed to battle, but a number had been under artillery fire. McClellan decided to renew the fight on September 19.[1]

Lee's army was also in rough shape. One by one, he asked his senior officers about the condition of the men in their commands during the meeting on the evening of September 17. According to artillerist Col. Stephen Lee, Longstreet was "much depressed," and reported it was "as bad as could be; that he had lost terribly and his lines had been barely held and there was little better than a good skirmish line along his front." Some, like Brig. Gen. John Hood were bitter. When Lee asked, "[W]here is your splendid division you had this morning," Hood replied, "They are lying on the field where you sent them…My division has been almost wiped out." Lee considered turning McClellan's right flank, but Jackson and Stephen Lee realized the folly of such an attempt and advised against it. Lee's army welcomed at least 6,000 men after the battle—stragglers who had caught up with the army. These additions gave Lee a fighting force of over 30,000 and possibly more. McClellan's army was almost three times the size of Lee's.[2]

Lee maintained his position on September 18, except for pulling back his center about 200 yards closer to Sharpsburg. He wisely decided not to renew the fight on September 18, but "we awaited without apprehension the renewal of the attack," Lee wrote in his after-battle report. He concluded "the enemy's force would be largely and rapidly augmented, it was not prudent to wait until he should be ready again to offer battle," so he began withdrawing his troops after nightfall on September 18 to the ford "near Shepherdstown, without loss or molestation." He sent orders between 2:00 and 3:00 p.m. on September 18 to get the trains rolling across the Potomac River at Blackford's (Boteler's) Ford. Longstreet's wing began crossing after nightfall and his men completed the crossing by 2:00 a.m. on September 19. Jackson's men crossed next. Brig. Gen. Maxcy Gregg's South Carolina brigade (A. P. Hill's division) was the last infantry unit to cross the river and it was followed by Brig. Gen. Fitz Lee's cavalry brigade, which completed its crossing by 10 a.m. The army was able to quickly cross back into Virginia as the Potomac River was a mere three miles from Sharpsburg.[3]

When Union cavalry commander Brig. Gen. Alfred Pleasonton realized Lee was gone on September 19, he cautiously entered Sharpsburg and then rode toward Blackford's Ford, collecting enemy stragglers along the way. Lee probably suspected McClellan would follow, so he left two brigades totaling about 600 men along the western bank of the Potomac River and placed 33 cannon under Brig. Gen. William Pendleton on the bluffs above to discourage an enemy pursuit. Units from the Union V Corps (the 4th Michigan and 1st U. S. Sharpshooters) did cross to try to capture the guns. Pendleton realized the danger and ordered his cannons withdrawn, but the Union infantry surged forward and captured four of them and later hauled them back across the river. Pendleton worried that all of his guns were lost, so he galloped to Lee's headquarters, waking him up with the news at about midnight. Lee showed little emotion and told Pendleton that little could be done until daylight. When Stonewall Jackson heard the news he ordered A. P. Hill's Light Division to arms and marched it back toward the Potomac River on the morning of September 20.[4]

McClellan ordered Pleasonton to "push your command forward after the enemy as rapidly as possible, using your artillery upon them wherever an opportunity presents, doing them all the damage in your power without incurring too much risk to your command." Unfortunately, V Corps commander Maj. Gen. Fitz John Porter had ordered Pleasonton back to Keedysville and Williamsport. Porter recalled Pleasonton, but since the cavalryman had not yet arrived at the ford by 7:00 a.m., he sent Col. Thomas Lovell's brigade of U. S. Regulars across the river.[5]

After marching west for less than half a mile, Lovell's men encountered the advancing lead elements of A. P. Hill's division and Lovell ordered his brigade back toward the Potomac River as Col. James Barnes' 1st Brigade crossed the river at about 8:00 a.m. to reinforce the Regulars (See Map 32). Meanwhile, Hill quickly deployed his division for action in two lines of brigades and began the attack. Massed Union artillery across the Potomac River at its sharp bend south of Shepherdstown opened a blistering fire on the Confederates, hindering their attack against the vulnerable Union infantry with their backs against the river. The two sides were almost equal in size—about 3,000 men, but another Confederate division under Brig. Gen. Jubal Early also approached the isolated Union troops. Watching the action through his field glasses on the opposite side of the river, Porter realized the folly of retaining troops on the west side of the Potomac River, so he ordered them evacuated, but not before the two sides began exchanging volleys.[6]

Most of Porter's men successfully crossed the Potomac River, thus avoiding a potential bloodbath by being pinned against the river. The large, 800-man 118th Pennsylvania did not budge from its position as its commander had received orders not long before to hold his position, so he doubted the veracity of the order to evacuate delivered by an aide. Meanwhile, Hill's men approached the Pennsylvanians and encircled them on three sides. Pinned against the river, the rookies attempted to defend themselves but despaired to learn most of their guns were defective. They finally made their way to safety, but not before losing almost 300 men. This ended the Maryland Campaign.[7]

While Lee made his way to the Shenandoah Valley to rest and refit his army, McClellan remained in the area around the battlefield for six weeks. Many units of the Army of the Potomac were in rough shape. Battles had shaved their number, and supplies, especially shoes, were a major issue. Secretary of War Stanton and General-in-Chief Halleck both claimed that massive amounts of supplies were shipped to McClellan, but the latter swore he never received them. He was not about to face Lee in Virginia with an army in disarray. He finally began crossing the Potomac into Virginia after Lee on October 26, but it was too late. Stanton had already launched an investigation and Lincoln was convinced McClellan had the "slows." McClellan was removed from command on November 5, the day after the midterm elections, never to command any unit again. He would run against Lincoln under the Democratic Party banner in the 1864 presidential election and lose badly.[8]

The Pennsylvania Campaign of 1863

General Robert E. Lee, the aggressor at Gettysburg, decided to wait another day before retreating back to Virginia. He straightened his line along Seminary Ridge on July 4, shifting Lt. Gen. Ewell's II Corps from north of town to the west. Lee had put his long wagon trains in motion, beginning at 3:00 a.m. on July 4. Theirs would be a long journey, through South Mountain and then across Maryland to the Potomac River. He actually had several wagon trains that stretched a total of 57 miles. One, under Brig. Gen. John Imboden, followed a northern route. It contained the wounded and the First and Third Corps wagons, stretching over 17 miles. Two others under Maj. John Harman contained the II Corps wagons and they followed a slightly southern route. Ewell purportedly told Harman, "Get that train safely across the Potomac or [I] want to see [your] face no more!" The trains were vulnerable to enemy cavalry raids, which began almost as soon as the wagons began their long journey, and continued though July 6. Hundreds of wagons were captured or destroyed.

Lee also put his army on the road after dark on July 4 and the vanguard reached Hagerstown on July 6. A long pontoon bridge spanned the Potomac River near Falling Waters (just downstream from Williamsport) prior to the battle of Gettysburg, but no one apparently thought to guard it and it was destroyed by Union forces on the evening of July 4. By the time Lee arrived in Western Maryland, the swollen Potomac River precluded any thought of a crossing. So, he personally supervised the layout of a strong defensive line west of Hagerstown that stretched from northwest of that town, south to Downsville, where its right flank was anchored by the Potomac River. The line sat on the strong Salisbury Ridge, running in a north-south direction.

Although Meade had won a decisive victory over Lee, his army was in poor shape. The I, III, V, and XI Corps had sustained heavy casualties and only the VI Corps was fresh. Many of the men had not eaten since July 1 and supplies remained a pressing issue. At least 1,400 horses were killed and many more were sick or injured, hampering the army's movements.

Meade conducted another council of war with his corps commanders on the evening of July 4 where he asked his senior leaders four questions: 1- "Shall the army remain [at Gettysburg]"? 2- "If we remain, shall we assume the offensive?" 3- "Do you deem it expedient to move towards Williamsport through Emmitsburg?" 4- "Shall we pursue the enemy if he is retreating on his direct line of communications?" The group agreed they should remain in place until they had more definitive information on the enemy's movements and motives, and definitely to not attack Lee, but when the army did move, it should be along a parallel course. Meade later claimed his motives for these assemblages were because "I had just assumed command of the army, and felt that it was due to myself to have the opinions of high officers before I took action on matters which involved such momentous issues." While pondering his options, Meade put his cavalry on the road to threaten Lee's flanks and attack his massive wagon trains.

Word of Lee's retreat reached Meade on the morning of July 5, but his movements needed to conform to the enemy's intentions. Was Lee merely pulling back to a new defensive position where he would again take on the Union army, or was he truly retreating, probably to Williamsport, Maryland, which was along his line of communications? If the latter, Lee's march would cover 44 miles, but Meade's, using a parallel track, would be 64 miles.

Meade pushed the VI Corps south on Fairfield Road at 8:00 a.m. on July 5 and encountered Lee's rearguard near Fairfield, Pennsylvania, about six miles from Gettysburg, at about 5:00 p.m. A sharp fight ensued which resulted in bagging about 250 Confederate soldiers. Meade continued expressing concerns about Lee's motives, including the possibility of being lured into a trap where he would be defeated and Lee could sweep south and capture Washington. Nevertheless, Meade put the II, V, and XII Corps on the road, heading south that day, and later on the 5th, also the XI Corps. Meade's remaining two corps, the shattered I and III Corps remained around Gettysburg and did not march for another day or two.[9]

The Union cavalry continued their attacks on the Confederate trains. Brig. Gen. Kilpatrick launched his men up South Mountain during a treacherous storm on the night of July 4-5 and attacked a portion of the Confederate wagon train at Monterey Pass. The division commander claimed his troopers captured as many as 287 wagons and 1,300 wounded officers and men. Other cavalry fights occurred: Smithsburg (July 5), Hagerstown (July 6), Williamsport (July 6), Boonsboro (July 8), and Funkstown (July 8) as Stuart caught up with the Union cavalry. The initial fights involved Kilpatrick's and Buford's divisions attacking the wagon trains (Williamsport) and then morphed into probing Lee's flanks.

Meade's army made its way west, but too snail-like for Lincoln and Halleck, causing the latter to write on the evening of July 7: "You have given the enemy a stunning blow at Gettysburg. Follow it up, and give him another before he can reach the Potomac." Both men could not have been happy when they read Meade's telegram sent during the afternoon of July 8:

> The spirit of the army is high; the men are ready and willing to make every exertion to push forward. The very first moment I can get the different commands, the artillery and cavalry, properly supplied and in hand, I will move forward. Be assured I most earnestly desire to try the fortunes of war with the enemy on this side of the river, hoping, through Providence and the bravery of my men to settle the question, but I should do wrong not to frankly tell you of the difficulties encountered. I expect to find the enemy in a strong position, well covered with artillery, and I do not desire to imitate his example at Gettysburg, and assault a position where the chances were so greatly against success. I wish in advance to moderate the expectations of those who, in ignorance of the difficulties to be encountered, may expect too much. All that I can do under the circumstances I pledge this army to do.[10]

Halleck responded, "There is reliable information that the enemy is crossing at Williamsport. The opportunity to attack his divided forces should not be lost. The President is urgent and anxious that your army should move against him by forced marches." Meade quickly responded, "My army is and has been making forced marches, short of rations, and barefooted." He also realized the intelligence was faulty as Lee was not yet crossing the Potomac.

Map 35: Lee's Retreat from Gettysburg
A: Initial Movements (July 7-8)
B: Positions on July 13

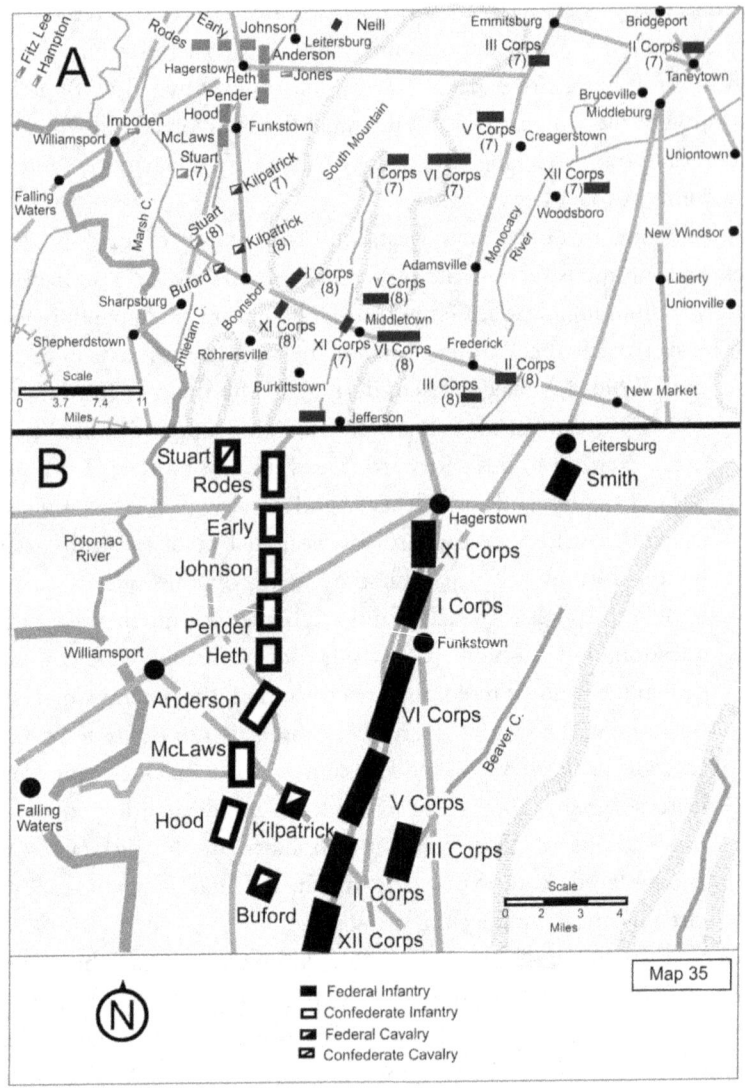

Halleck later took a more conciliatory approach, responding, "Do not understand me as expressing any dissatisfaction--on the contrary, your army has done most nobly. I only wish to give you opinions formed from information received here." Meade was able to placate Washington when he told Halleck on July 9, "the army is moving in three columns."[11]

The army's pace was anything but snail-like. On July 7, the various corps marched as many as 30 miles through the driving rain, following different paths. Meade and his quartermasters scrambled to find enough rations to feed the men on the march. Adequate horses and forage for them remained a pressing issue.

Halleck counseled caution, writing to Meade the evening of July 9, "I think it will be best for you to postpone a general battle till you can concentrate all your forces and get up your reserves and re- enforcements. I will push on the troops as fast as they arrive." By the end of July 12, the various commands were concentrated south of Hagerstown, where the men threw up breastworks. Possibly because Meade was unsure of himself as army commander, he continued relying on councils of war. He called one that evening, where the majority of those present advised against an attack. Meade's new chief of staff, Brig. Gen. Andrew Humphreys, explained how Lee's defensive line "was naturally strong, and was strongly intrenched. It presented no vulnerable points, but much of it was concealed from view…Its flanks were secure and could not be turned." Meade decided to wait, and Halleck exploded when he heard the news, shooting off the following dispatch to Meade on the night of July 13: "You are strong enough to attack and defeat the enemy before he can effect a crossing. Act upon your own judgment and make your generals execute your orders. Call no council of war. It is proverbial that councils of war never fight. Re-enforcements are pushed on as rapidly as possible. Do not let the enemy escape."[12]

It was too late, as by that time Lee was already crossing the Potomac River via fords and the pontoon bridge, effectively ending the Pennsylvania Campaign. Meade did not begin crossing the river until July 18. Kilpatrick's cavalry managed to attack Lee's rearguard at Falling Waters, however, on July 14. Custer's impetuous charge netted hundreds of prisoners and mortally wounded Brig. Gen. James Pettigrew.

Meade has been criticized for not aggressively attempting to push Lee against the Potomac River and destroy him. However, he been in command a mere handful of days prior to Lee's retreat, had lost three corps commanders (Hancock, Sickles, and Reynolds), many of his officers and men, his army was suffering from an acute loss of horses and supplies for the men, and Lee's army also occupied an exceptionally strong defensive position.[13]

Comparisons of the Two Campaigns

Lee's army was badly wounded after both major battles, but he continued holding his position for an additional day, perhaps hoping the enemy would charge his line, be repulsed, and allow him to declare victory. He was also concerned about morale and a hasty retreat back to Virginia could have damaged his men's and boosted the enemy's. When his adversary did not attack during either campaign, Lee's only option was to limp back to Virginia.

The distance to the Potomac River dictated the nature of the action after each battle. Lee was within a handful of miles from the river after the battle of Sharpsburg and he crossed without molestation on the evening of September 18-19, and into the following morning. Lee's major dilemma after Gettysburg was returning safely to Virginia from his position deep (over 40 miles) within enemy territory. His army moved quickly toward the Potomac River, beginning on July 4, but the combination of high waters because of recent rains, and a destroyed pontoon bridge, heightened the drama. Lee selected a strong position, and Meade was probably wise not to attempt to storm it, but by not attempting it, he brought down the wrath of Lincoln and many others, both civilian and military. The controversy continues to this day.

The fights following the major battles were different. McClellan, after Antietam, aggressively pushed part of the V Corps across the Potomac River, resulting in a confrontation near Shepherdstown on September 20, three days after the battle. It did not amount to much, as Maj. Gen. Fitz John Porter understood the vulnerability of his few brigades and pulled his men back to safety. McClellan decided not to press the issue and remained in Maryland for about six weeks after the battle of Antietam, much to Lincoln's chagrin. It is only a coincidence that action before the battle of Antietam occurred three days before (at South Mountain) and three days after (at Shepherdstown).

Meade also sent infantry after Lee after Gettysburg, and part of the VI Corps tangled with the Confederate rearguard about six miles west of the battlefield. He then unleashed his cavalry and they harried Lee's wagon trains moving west. Meade pursued the enemy army and was preparing to attack Lee when the latter slipped across the Potomac River. Meade, unlike McClellan, had been in command for a much shorter period of time and had a much larger percentage of his infantry involved in the fight. Of Meade's seven army corps, only one, the VI Corps was relatively fresh. During the Maryland Campaign, of McClellan's six army corps, two (V and VI Corps) were fairly fresh.

Both McClellan and Meade complained about supply-chain issues after their major battles against Lee. Both armies had lost substantial amounts of supplies, uniforms/shoes (McClellan) and food (Meade) were pressing issues. Despite these issues, Meade continued pushing toward the Potomac River for a confrontation with Lee. He could not do otherwise, as Lee's wounded army was stuck with its back against a swollen Potomac River and vulnerable to destruction. Lee was on the defensive during this period. McClellan faced a different set of conditions, as Lee had already crossed the Potomac River and to follow him would invite a battle.

Table 23: Comparison of the Aftermath of the Battles

Issue	Maryland Campaign	Pennsylvania Campaign
Lee leaves the battlefield	Waits a full day; adjusts line	Waits a full day; adjusts line
Could Lee have continued the invasion if he achieved a victory	No—Army badly wounded	No—Army badly wounded
Begins crossing Potomac River	**Confederates:** Evening of September 18 **Union:** October 26	**Confederates:** July 13 **Union:** July 17
Date of renewal of combat	September 20, 1862 (three days after the battle)	July 5, 1863 (two days after the battle)
Nature of fighting during the retreat	Rearguard action (Shepherdstown)	Rearguard action (Fairfield) & cavalry actions
Distance to Potomac River	3 miles	Over 40 miles
Did cavalry play a major role during the retreat?	Minor	Yes

PART 4: AFTER THE BATTLES: END OF THE CAMPAIGNS

Chapter 19: The Army Commanders and Their Commanders-in-Chief

The Maryland Campaign of 1862

With Lee back in Virginia and the threat to Washington mitigated, McClellan could breathe a sigh of relief. He wrote his wife, "I feel that I have done all that can be asked in twice saving the country." McClellan's sour impression of Lincoln and Halleck came into play once again, just three days after the battle, when he received a telegram from the General-in-Chief stating he was "entirely in the dark in regard to your own movements and those of the enemy. This should not be so." McClellan lashed back, "I regret that you find it necessary to couch every dispatch in a spirit of fault-finding" and ended his correspondence by complaining that Halleck had "not yet found leisure to say one word in commendation of the recent achievements of this army." Little Mac was satisfied with the end result of the campaign, but Halleck and Lincoln were not, as they wanted Lee's army destroyed, not merely driven back across the Potomac River. Upon hearing of Lee's unmolested crossing of the Potomac River, Lincoln purportedly blurted out, "McClellan drove Lee to the river and then just shooed him across."[1]

McClellan learned from Halleck on October 1 that Lincoln would be visiting his army. When he arrived, Lincoln told McClellan he was there to see the battlefield and visit the troops, but McClellan realized "the real purpose of his visit is to push me into a premature advance into Virginia." Lincoln did all that he said he would, touring the battlefield, reviewing the troops and visiting the wounded. Lincoln and McClellan met privately on October 3 and then again the following morning, until it was time for the President to return to Washington. McClellan accompanied Lincoln as far as South Mountain. Lincoln did not leave a record of the meetings, but his discontent with McClellan was evident, at least to an acquaintance from Illinois who accompanied him on his trip to Maryland. Ozias Hatch and Lincoln walked to high ground overlooking McClellan's camps and the president purportedly asked, "Do you know what this is? Hatch replied, "It is the Army of the Potomac." Lincoln then responded, "So it is called, that is a mistake; it is only McClellan's bodyguard."

Unlike Lincoln, McClellan's left his versions of the meetings. He was unhappy with the draft Emancipation Proclamation and was not shy about telling Lincoln so. They also discussed the progress of the army and McClellan recalled the only negative comment Lincoln made was that he was "too prone to be sure that everything was ready before acting." As the meeting ended, McClellan believed the President accepted his explanation of waiting to pursue Lee into Virginia, stating "he would stand by me against 'all comers.'" McClellan was therefore disheartened when he received a telegram from Gen. Halleck at 4:00 p.m. the following day, stating "the President directs that you cross the Potomac and give battle to the enemy or drive him south. Your army must move now while the roads are good." The telegram also contained possible routes and ended with an expectation that McClellan should "immediately report what line you adopt and when you intend to cross the river." McClellan suspected that once Lincoln returned to Washington other forces would put pressure on him.[2]

McClellan complied with Halleck's requests and began concentrating his army near Harpers Ferry. A raid by Maj. Gen. Jeb Stuart's cavalry into Pennsylvania complicated McClellan's timetable. Stuart was able to ride all the way to Chambersburg, Pennsylvania, eliciting Lincoln's anger. McClellan intended to advance into Virginia and head for Winchester, but the railroad between it and Harpers Ferry had been destroyed and would take some time for repairs to be made. Lack of needed supplies also hampered McClellan's advance into Virginia. On October 17, McClellan told Lincoln he would cross the river "the moment my men are shod & my cavalry are sufficiently remounted to be serviceable." Supplies began flowing to the army on October 18. The condition of his horses still concerned McClellan on October 25 and he wired Halleck, "the horses…are absolutely broken down from fatigue and want of flesh." This prompted Lincoln to write, "Will you pardon me for asking what the horses of your army have done since the battle of Antietam that fatigues anything?" After several additional delays, such as the construction of two long pontoon bridges over the Potomac River at Berlin, Maryland, the army finally began crossing into Virginia on October 26. Lincoln waited until the day after the mid-term elections

(November 5) to remove McClellan from command of the Army of the Potomac.[3]

Although Lee did not achieve the goals he set for himself during the Maryland Campaign, he learned some important lessons about his own abilities. Heretofore, Lee fervently believed his major responsibilities lie in bringing the army to battle and then letting his subordinates orchestrate a victory. Given the complexity of the battle at Sharpsburg, Lee was thrust into a new role—that of tactician and he performed it very well. His biographer called his army's actions "a model in the full employment of a small force for a defensive battle on the inner line." He would revert back to his old ways at Gettysburg, however.[4]

Lee's relationship with President Jefferson Davis remained strong, despite the setback at Antietam. Lee attempted to keep Davis in the loop with numerous communications, which the president undoubtedly appreciated. Davis ended a communication to Lee on September 28 with the sentence: "In the name of the Confederacy, I thank you and the brave men of your army for the deeds which have covered our flag with imperishable fame." He ended the letter to Lee with the valediction, "Your friend."[5]

The Pennsylvania Campaign of 1863

The Union troops' exuberance after their victory over Lee was shared by the civilian population. The *Washington Sunday Morning Chronicle* published the details of Meade's victory in its July 5 edition and went on to predict, "Lee's army is already seriously interfered with, and his escape from our army will be a matter of great difficulty." Several elected officials accompanied the army to observe Lee's demise, and Lincoln could finally feel a measure of relief. His enthusiasm began waning when he realized that Lee just might escape. These misgivings may have begun when he read Meade's congratulatory order to his troops on July 4 which included the phrase, "drive the invaders from our soil." It said nothing about going after Lee to finish the job. Lincoln exploded "My God! Is that all? Will our Generals never get that idea out of their heads? The whole country is our soil!" Calling upon the shadows of the Maryland Campaign, he uttered, "This is a dreadful reminiscence of McClellan."[6]

Lincoln grew increasingly frustrated when day after day passed without word of Lee's destruction. He finally wrote to Meade on July 13: You will follow up and attack Genl. Lee as soon as possible before he can cross the river. If you fail this dispatch will clear you from all responsibility and if you succeed you may destroy it." Meade dreaded sending Lincoln the telegram he knew he must, so about noon on July 14 he informed Lincoln, "On advancing my army this morning, I found, on reaching his lines, that they were evacuated." The message sent Lincoln into deep despair. He grieved to his oldest son, Robert, "We had them in our grasp. We had only to stretch forth our hands & they were ours."[7]

The recriminations began almost immediately. Halleck responded to Meade's communication: "I need hardly say to you that the escape of Lee's army without another battle has created great dissatisfaction in the mind of the President, and it will require an active and energetic pursuit on your part to remove the impression that it has not been sufficiently active heretofore." Meade was furious. He had won a great battle over a heretofore unbeaten foe and should have been praised, not scorned. He shot back a telegram stating, "The censure of the President conveyed in your dispatch…is, in my judgment, so undeserved that I feel compelled most respectfully to ask to be immediately relieved from command of this army." Realizing the harm Meade's resignation would do to Lincoln's reputation, Halleck quickly responded, "My telegram, stating the disappointment of the President at the escape of Lee's army, was not intended as a censure but as a stimulus to an active pursuit." Lincoln also realized he had disquieted a very sensitive officer and he wrote soothing words, indicating how grateful he was "for the magnificent success you gave the cause of the country at Gettysburg." He could not, however, allow the communication to end without a sting, "I do not believe you appreciate the magnitude of the misfortune involved in Lee's escape. He was within your easy grasp, and to have closed upon him would…have ended the war." Lincoln thought better of sending the message, and simply filed it away. Historians have debated who was right in this debate, but in Meade's mind, it was clear his army was severely wounded and Lee's army occupied a very strong position that invited a Union defeat.[8]

Some believe the Gettysburg Campaign continued even after Meade began crossing the Potomac River on July 17, for he immediately pursued the Confederate army until the end of the month, but was unable to bring it to a pitched battle.

Meade remained in command of the Army of the Potomac through the end of the war, but during the fall and winter of 1863-64, he was summoned on multiple occasions to confer with Lincoln and Halleck. Meade knew he was on thin ice and his every movement would be scrutinized. Lincoln continued pushing him into battle, which led to an almost catastrophic charge during the Mine Run Campaign in early December, a time when most armies are long into winter quarters. Lincoln finally relinquished his role as Meade's tormentor when he brought Ulysses S. Grant to command all the Union's armies in the early spring of 1864.

Lee's defeat during his second invasion of the North was a bitter blow that shook the soldiers to the core. A young Marylander recorded in his diary: "I went into the last battle [Gettysburg] feeling that victory must be ours—that such an army could not be foiled, and that God would certainly declare himself on our side. Now I feel that unless He sees fit to bless our arms, our valor will not avail." A staffer in the War Department went one step further, writing in his diary on July 26, 1863: "Gettysburg has shaken my faith in Lee as a general. To fight an enemy superior in numbers at such a terrible disadvantage of position in the heart of his own territory, when the freedom of movement gave him the advantage of selecting his own time and place for accepting battle, seems to have been a great military blunder…and the result was the worst disaster which has ever befallen our arms."

Lee shouldered full responsibility for the loss in a letter to Jefferson Davis on July 31, 1863: "No blame can be attached to the army for its failure to accomplish what was projected by me…I am alone to blame." After further reflection, Lee wrote Davis again on August 8, explicitly suggesting his removal: "I have been prompted by these reflections more than once since my return from Pennsylvania to propose to Your Excellency the propriety of selecting another commander for this army." He cited several reasons for this request. First, he noted "I have seen and heard of expression of discontent in the public journals as the result of the expedition." Lee clearly invited his removal as a way of sparing the Government the shame of further rebuke from the press. Second, he noted "the growing failure of my bodily strength. I have not yet recovered from the attack I experienced the past spring, and am becoming more and more incapable of exertion, and am thus prevented from making the personal examinations and giving the personal supervision to the operations in the field which I feel to be necessary." Lee caught malaria during the Mexican War and suffered from a variety of ailments throughout the war, including heart disease, which would kill him five years after the end of the war.[9]

Davis carefully penned his response on August 11, telling Lee, "suppose, my dear friend, that I were to admit, with all their implications, the points which you present, where am I to find that new commander who is to possess the greater ability which you believe to be required? I do not doubt the readiness with which you would give way to one who could accomplish all that you have wished, and you will do me the justice to believe that if Providence; should kindly offer such a person for our use, I would not hesitate to avail of his services." Davis ended the letter by writing: "It only remains for me to hope that you will take all possible care of yourself, that your health and strength may be entirely restored, and that the Lord will preserve you for the important duties devolved upon you in the struggle of our suffering country for the independence which we have engaged in war to maintain."[10]

Comparisons of the Two Campaigns

Lincoln's exuberance over the Army of the Potomac's victory at Antietam and Gettysburg quickly faded when he realized both army commanders had little interest in immediately pitching into Lee's wounded army. In both instances, the Union army was in rough shape, although McClellan had left much of the Army of the Potomac behind in Washington and the addition of almost 40,000 men soon after the battle could tip the balance. Two of his corps (V and VI) were already on the field and had been barely used. Meade had most of his army with him at Gettysburg and while he could have brought up some reserves, they would not be as numerous as those available to McClellan.

Lincoln's frustration with both army commanders boiled over and led to a series of telegrams from him and from Halleck. Lincoln decided to pay a personal visit to McClellan and the army during the opening days of October which did little to move Little Mac. McClellan needed supplies and he would not budge until he received them. Because Meade was still in the field, pursuing active operations against Lee after the battle, Lincoln did not visit.

Lincoln's unhappiness with McClellan and Meade stemmed from similar circumstances, but the President reserved a special wrath for the former as he believed he was putting his Democratic Party-leaning ideals ahead of his duty to the Nation. He ultimately felt compelled to remove McClellan from command. In Meade's case, the army commander was so upset by Lincoln's frustration that he almost resigned. No matter the outcome, the discontent after each campaign led to issues between the President and the commander of the Army of the Potomac. Removal of either McClellan in 1862 or Meade in 1863 would have caused considerable discontent. McClellan had his supporters in Congress and was beloved by his men; Meade had won a major victory and the optics were against removing him so quickly. Lincoln chose to weather the storm and removed McClellan, but chose to stick with Meade.

Lee was becoming a legend by Antietam and his stature only grew by the onset of the Pennsylvania Campaign. Although unsuccessful in both campaigns, Lee retained Davis' confidence as they had developed a warm personal and professional relationship. Lee was the only Confederate general who consistently won victories, usually under difficult circumstances. The two men were also close confidants. Unlike other generals, Lee never bemoaned his circumstances and always sought solutions to problems, rather than tossing them onto Davis' lap.

Chapter 20: Post-Campaign Events

The Maryland Campaign of 1862

Lee moved his army into the Shenandoah Valley after the Maryland Campaign to rebuild and resupply it. He then headed south in November and won major victories over old Union corps adversaries: Burnside (at Fredericksburg) and Hooker (at Chancellorsville). Maryland never seceded, nor did a significant number of young Marylanders take up arms and fight with "Marse Robert."

All of the Confederate columns moving north were stymied during the fall campaign and this put a damper on the South's hopes for independence.

The Union's midterm elections occurred in early November and all did not go well for the Republicans. They lost 21 seats in the House of Representatives, and the Democrats picked up 27, some from third parties. A Democrat even won the election in Lincoln's home district in Illinois. The Republican Speaker of the House, Galusha Grow of Pennsylvania, also lost his reelection bid. The Republicans lost their plurality and ability to govern, but the Unionist Party threw their seats in support of Lincoln's party, tipping the scales. The situation did not change much in the Senate, as the Republicans gained a seat and the Democrats lost one. Again, the Unionist Party with five seats, threw its support behind the Republicans and they retained control.

One of the most important outcomes of the Maryland Campaign was the Emancipation Proclamation. Lincoln developed this executive order during the summer of 1862 and when he brought it to his Cabinet, they were stunned. After a full discussion, the group encouraged Lincoln to file the document until after a major battlefield victory. To do otherwise would appear to be a dying gasp, they told him. The document abolished slaves in "states in rebellion" and permitted African American men to join the U. S. armed forces. While it appeared to quench some of Lincoln's thirst for abolition of slavery, it was also a measure to entice the states that had joined the rebellion to lay down their swords and rejoin the Union. Maryland, which was a slave state, and other border states, were unaffected by the proclamation.

President Lincoln issued his preliminary Emancipation Proclamation five days after the battle of Antietam, on September 22. It was preliminary because Lincoln clearly told the rebelling Southern States he would sign and implement it if they remained "in rebellion" on January 1, 1863. Come back into the Union and the Executive Order would not be implemented or they would not be affected by it. None budged, and the Proclamation went into effect. Its impact was immediately felt. While many celebrated, a number of soldiers felt otherwise. One summarized his comrades' feelings by noting, "They do not wish to think they are fighting for Negroes ... but to put down the Rebellion." It did not take long for most of the soldiers to come around and the war shifted from a war to keep the Union together to also include freedom for enslaved people. The Northern press generally followed their political leanings. Republican newspapers glorified the Proclamation; Democratic denigrated it; and others felt it did not go far enough.

Perhaps equally important, it put another nail into the coffin of foreign recognition. With the enactment of the Emancipation Proclamation, the war became a moral conflict to end slavery. As such, England and other countries would not wish to enter such dangerous territory. Henry Adams noted the sudden outpouring of pro-Union sentiment among the British and wrote, "The Emancipation Proclamation has done more for us here than all our former victorious and all our diplomacy."[1]

Foreign recognition that burned so brightly in England during the summer of 1862, dimmed after Lee's Maryland Campaign defeat. The issue came up again on October 28 when Lord Palmerston's Cabinet took up the issue. Some members continued supporting recognition, but the Prime Minister made his feelings known that his position had changed from "when the Confederates seemed to be carrying all before them," to "I have very much come back to our original view that we must continue merely to be lookers-on till the war shall have taken a more decided turn." He prevailed when his team subsequently voted.[2]

The Pennsylvania Campaign of 1863

The Mississippi stronghold of Vicksburg fell on July 4, setting off additional waves of celebrations across the North. The South continued losing chunks of territory and would continue to do so throughout the war.

Gone was the possibility of foreign recognition, but the hope remained of a Lincoln defeat in the following year's presidential race. In the North, the increased need for manpower to fuel the armies led to the passage of draft measures, setting off violent protests and riots in several towns, especially New York City.

Lincoln decided to bring newly promoted Lt. Gen. Ulysses S. Grant east to command the Union armies as General-in-Chief, early in 1864, and for the first time, the North had effective coordination across all its forces.

Comparisons of the Two Campaigns

Both campaigns have been called the "Turning Point of the Civil War" and a case can be made for each. This historian is firmly in the camp of the former. So much was riding on the Maryland Campaign, especially foreign recognition, the outcome of the Union's mid-term elections, and for Lincoln, the ability to roll out the Emancipation Proclamation. The war was significantly different after the Maryland Campaign, both politically and militarily. Of course Gettysburg was a pivotal battle, but not nearly as much was riding on a Confederate victory in that battle. It would, however, usher in Lee's last major attempt to invade the North by the Army of Northern Virginia.

Chapter 21: Final Thoughts/Summary

The Armies

The size and condition of the armies during the two campaigns were among the most glaring differences in the two campaigns. The Confederate army at Gettysburg was twice the size of its earlier counterpart, while McClellan's army at Antietam was only 62% of the size of Meade's at Gettysburg. These disparities affected the size of the battlefield and the complexity of the actions. McClellan's army at Antietam also had a large proportion of green units, and stories abound of troops not knowing how to form into line of battle and even load and fire their weapons. By Gettysburg, the Union army was a more professional fighting unit with a much lower percentage of new units. Lee had the advantage of having a veteran army during both campaigns, but he was better able to bulk up with new units prior to the Pennsylvania Campaign, but all had seen combat in other theaters.

The morale of the troops was probably about the same during each campaign; the Union army's was low because of frequent losses and turnover of commanders. However, the prospect of fighting on their own soil certainly buoyed the motivation of the Union soldiers in both campaigns. Lee's army in both campaigns exhibited high morale, but at least during the Maryland Campaign, a number refused to cross the Potomac River.

The armies were in worse shape during the Maryland Campaign, as many of the combatants had fought a major battle a mere two and a half weeks before Antietam and many had recently returned from the campaign around Richmond. Both armies were in better shape during the Pennsylvania Campaign because they had a month to rest before the Battle of Gettysburg.

The Leaders

The armies benefitted from skillful and accomplished senior leaders, for the most part, in both campaigns. Lee, Jackson, and Longstreet formed a talented troika and most of their divisional leaders proved up to the task at Antietam. The same can be said of the Union army at Antietam. McClellan was a seasoned officer who knew how to fight and he enhanced his army's effectiveness by surrounding himself with proven leaders. There were some weak links however: Brig. Gen. Joseph Mansfield (XII Corps) had never led troops in battle during the Civil War and his tenure with his new men was a mere two days. Maj. Gen. William Franklin (VI Corps) exhibited overly cautious behavior and Maj. Gen. Edwin Sumner (II Corps) could be rash.

At Gettysburg, an officer who had never commanded an army was thrust into this position. Meade, however, was a consummate professional who had excelled at the brigade, division, and corps command levels. He had his detractors after the battle. Assistant Secretary of War, Charles Dana, believed he lacked the "boldness that was necessary to bring the war to a close. He lacked self-confidence and tenacity of purpose." Meade was smart enough to listen to his seasoned corps commanders. However, even this proclivity was criticized. One of his brigade commanders felt Meade "treated his coprs commanders rather as friends than as inferiors." Meade undoubtedly realized he needed their support to be successful, but at times, they were over hesitant to recommend decisive actions.[1]

Lee fell short at Gettysburg for a variety of reasons, but one of the most important was his command structure. Reorganizing an army on the eve of a critically important campaign is not a good idea, but he felt compelled to do so because of the death of Stonewall Jackson. He could not find a suitable replacement, so he settled on a three-corps system, but A. P. Hill and Richard Ewell were inexperienced and required more direction than Lee was accustomed to providing. Prior to this campaign, Lee would tell Longstreet and Jackson what he desired, and they would fill in the details. In the absence of this direction, both men fumbled badly. Additionally, too many of Lee's division commanders at Gettysburg were new to their positions. Some, like Dorsey Pender, performed well; others like Henry Heth, did not.

The army commanders occasionally listened to their corps/wing commanders; sometimes not. Longstreet was consistent in his support of both invasions, but in both campaigns, believed Lee should assume a defensive position and allow the enemy to attack him. He noted after the war, "If General Lee had kept his army together [during the Maryland Campaign], he could not have been defeated." He purportedly told Lee on the night of September 13, 1862, "General, I wish we could stand still and let the damn Yankees come to us!" Longstreet was more strident in his concerns at Gettysburg, leading to conflict with Lee. McClellan at Antietam primarily took council from Porter, but Meade at Gettysburg listened to advice from all his subordinates, but subsequently formulated his own conclusions.

The cavalry during the two campaigns were vastly different. Both mounted arms were significantly smaller during the Maryland Campaign, and in the case of Pleasonton's division, were not well organized. By Gettysburg, Pleasonton commanded a cavalry corps composed of three well-trained and experienced divisions. Stuart's cavalry was also larger at Gettysburg, but remained organized as a division. Pleasonton's men were showing hints of being effective in scouting, screening, and fighting during the Maryland Campaign, but were much more advanced by Gettysburg. While Stuart's cavalry may have shown some growth, it was not as dramatic as the Union's ascension.

Lee's army at Gettysburg was a superb military unit that closely matched the size of its counterpart and brimmed with confidence of future success. Such was not the case at Antietam, where Lee's men were outnumbered, poorly equipped, and exhausted. Artilleryman, Porter Alexander wrote that Antietam "will be pronounced by military critics to be the greatest military blunder that Gen. Lee ever made. . .In the first place Lee's inferiority of force was too great to hope to do more than to fight a sort of drawn battle." Of all the outcomes, it was "the best possible outcome one could hope for."[2]

Part of Lee's setbacks resulted from underestimating his foe. In both campaigns, Lee believed his inferior sized army could strike deep into Union territory with little concern because the Union army would follow only slowly. He was incorrect in both campaigns. He also overestimated the abilities of his men. His men fought superbly during both battles, but, in the end, too much was expected of them. Had not Hooker, Mansfield, and Richardson not been wounded at Antietam, the Union army may have driven into Sharpsburg. Also, the timely arrival of A.P. Hill's division saved the day. Lee's men also fought tenaciously at Gettysburg, but in the end, Lee failed because of the shortcomings of two of his corps commanders and the timely arrival of reinforcements.

Role of Leaders, Civilian and Military, Outside of the Armies

Four men played major roles in both campaigns: President Abraham Lincoln, President Jefferson Davis, General-in-Chief Henry Halleck, and

Governor Andrew Curtin, and the behavior of all were fairly consistent in both campaigns. Davis remained a staunch supporter of Lee and the two exchanged cordial communications. Lincoln was a strong commander-in-chief. Although he tried to defer to the army commanders during the actions in Maryland and Pennsylvania, he often presented his strong views, or had them communicated through Halleck. The latter remained indecisive in both campaigns, giving general direction but unwilling to assume a larger directive role, much to Lincoln's frustration. Pennsylvania Governor, Andrew Curtin, played a large role in both campaigns. His network of spies and informants collected information, some accurate, others not so, that he forwarded to Washington. While he agitated to form a militia force to safeguard his state during the Maryland Campaign, he did just that in the Pennsylvania Campaign.

All three Union army commanders, McClellan, Hooker, and Meade, shared Lincoln's wrath for not aggressively pursuing Lee. Hooker for not following Lee fast enough as the Confederate army moved north; the other two for not aggressively confronting Lee's army after its defeat in battle. Lee enjoyed more consistent support from his commander-in-chief, but he felt the weight of the Gettysburg defeat and was much more vocal after that campaign in wishing to be removed from army command.

Travel to the Battlefields

Several factors impacted how fast the armies reached the battlefields: location of the armies at the onset of the campaigns, knowledge of the enemy's strength and location, and condition of the army.

All army commanders must be aware of the enemy's movements and strength. This information was difficult to come by during the Civil War and the resulting ambiguity impacted the Maryland and Pennsylvania Campaigns. In both cases, the Union commander (McClellan and Hooker) would not budge until he had sufficient information to make an intelligent decision. To move without it could result in the loss of Washington. In both cases, the Union cavalry commander (Pleasonton) provided insufficient intelligence. By Gettysburg, Hooker had a better system of scouts and spies, but he still was not getting the information he needed to make informed and decisive decisions.

Lee was surprised in both campaigns by the rapid approach of the Union army. He could not have known about the loss of the copy of Special Orders Number 191 during the Maryland Campaign, but by acquiescing to Stuart's request to leave the army and range further afield on his own, he set the stage for a disastrous surprise at Gettysburg. This was another of Lee's major missteps.

When the armies were put into motion, they arrived on the battlefield in less time during the Maryland Campaign, partly because the two army's starting points were relatively close to the site of the big battle. Lee's jumping off point at Leesburg, Virginia was only about 35 miles from Sharpsburg. He probably chose to cross the Potomac River primarily at White's Ford, as it was still close enough to Washington to pose a threat, but far enough away to give his men a head start as they moved north. McClellan's starting point around Washington, about 50 miles from Sharpsburg, also permitted a fairly rapid approach to the battlefield, although he was hampered by the need to reorganize his army before it could begin the journey after Lee. The armies had a harder time getting to the battlefield during the Pennsylvania Campaign, as their starting point, Fredericksburg, Virginia, was about 200 miles (as the crow flies) from Gettysburg.

In addition to distance, Lee faced another major hurdle in beginning the Pennsylvania Campaign. Whereas during the Maryland Campaign, McClellan's beaten army was sheltered and protected by the defenses of Washington and Lee could move north with impunity, at the onset of the Gettysburg Campaign, Hooker's large army blocked the Army of Northern Virginia. Hooker had been defeated at Chancellorsville, but his army had a month to recover and remained a formidable force. Lee had to carefully pull units from Hooker's front without attracting undue attention. Lee's worst-case scenario was Hooker driving south and attacking Richmond.

Once the 1862 invasion began, Lee moved quickly north to Frederick apparently, daring McClellan to venture out of the Washington defenses so he could engage his army out in the open. The Pennsylvania Campaign involved more stealth and Lee used the Blue Ridge Mountains to shield his movements north in the Shenandoah Valley.

In both campaigns, the Union army commander divided his units into wings to facilitate and better coordinate movements to the battlefields.

Nature of the marches to the battlefield

The nature of the marches differed during each campaign. The longer distances from the starting point (Fredericksburg) to final battle (Gettysburg) during the Pennsylvania Campaign demanded more frequent rests. The campaign was therefore characterized by long marches followed by periods of inactivity, at least during the early and middle parts of the march north for both armies.

The marches during the Maryland Campaign tended to be less strenuous because of shorter distances to the battlefield. It took several days for McClellan to sufficiently reorganize his army before driving it north after Lee, but once begun, there were no extensive rest periods. In contrast, Lee allowed his army to rest for several days when it reached the environs of Frederick before making extensive marches, beginning on September 10.

The final stage saw both armies make forced marches to the battlefield. During the Maryland Campaign, Longstreet's two divisions rapidly marched Hagerstown to South Mountain to reinforce D. H. Hill's division, which was attempting to block McClellan's army from forcing its way into the Pleasant Valley. Hundreds fell by the waysides, as they could not maintain the blistering pace. During the next three nights, Lee's men marched all night to reach the battlefield (Longstreet's divisions on September 14-15; Jackson's divisions on September 15-16; McLaws' and Anderson's on September 16-17).

The final phase of the Pennsylvania Campaign also witnessed a number of forced marches to Gettysburg. For example, two of Lee's divisions (Rodes' and Johnson's) marched 30 miles in two days from Carlisle to Gettysburg; the Union VI Corps made a similarly long march to the battlefield, beginning on July 1.

Travel Logistics

Confederate logistical issues tended to play a larger role during the Pennsylvania campaign, where Lee was burdened by more wagons than during the earlier invasion. This impacted not only his move to, and arrival at, the battlefields, it also constrained his range of options. During the battle, one of Lee's wagon trains stretched all the way back to Williamsport, a distance of over 50 miles. Lee explained his dilemma in his after-action report, "It had not been intended to deliver a general battle so far from our base unless attacked, but coming unexpectedly upon the whole Federal Army, to withdraw through the mountains with our extensive trains would have been difficult and dangerous."[3]

Preliminary Fights

Both campaigns featured the fall of a major Union garrison. Both McClellan and Hooker were charged with protecting Harpers Ferry and Winchester, respectively, and both fell to the Confederates. The role of Harpers Ferry in the Maryland Campaign was far more important than Winchester in the Pennsylvania Campaign, as it dramatically altered Lee's strategic plan and led to the fight at Antietam.

The Maryland Campaign featured desperate attempts to breach the South Mountain gaps by McClellan's army. Success in this endeavor would allow McClellan to fall on the dispersed pieces of Lee's army and potentially destroy each in turn. It might also lift the Harpers Ferry siege. Although the Union army was able to seize the gaps and pass through them by the morning of September 15 (two days before the battle), the troops were unable to destroy portions of Lee's army and lift the Harpers Ferry siege. The dramatic prelude to Antietam was not duplicated during the Pennsylvania Campaign.

The town of Frederick, Maryland, played a major role in both campaigns. Lee captured the town during the Maryland Campaign and issued Special Orders 191 while there. The Union armies during both campaigns pointed toward Frederick as they moved north after Lee's army. It was a good destination as it blocked the approaches to both Washington and Baltimore.

Harpers Ferry also figured prominently in both campaigns. During the Maryland Campaign, the continued presence of the garrison forced Lee to abort his plans of traveling north and instead he divided his army to minimize the risk posed by the Federal troops garrisoned there. The small town did not figure directly into the military aspect of the Pennsylvania Campaign, but Hooker wanted its garrison and repeatedly requested it. When Halleck would not comply, Hooker used it as the excuse to resign as army commander.

Gambles, Risks, and Blunders

Lee gambled several times during both campaigns, and they jeopardized his ability to realize his strategic goals. During the Maryland Campaign, Lee's preoccupation with the Union garrison at Harpers Ferry caused him to modify his invasion strategy and break his army into multiple parts. A basic tenant of war is to not divide your army in enemy territory, especially if you are outnumbered. Lee eventually divided his army into five parts, which invited their piecemeal destruction by McClellan's army. The strategy also forced Lee to move to Sharpsburg to await his army's consolidation. His intent was never to fight there, but the decision to invest Harpers Ferry and McClellan's rapid advance, played his hand. Whether the Harpers Ferry garrison was a significant threat is debatable. It did lie along Lee's line of communications and it would have put a large Union force in his rear, but did these factors override Lee's ability to drive north with his army intact, find a good battleground and give battle to McClellan on his own terms? Lee also erred in thinking he had plenty of time to reduce the Harpers Ferry garrison, as McClellan would only approach cautiously. Finding Special Orders 191 was certainly beneficial, but McClellan was already showing an unusual tendency to move quickly.[4]

After the war, many Confederates speculated on the lost opportunities. Some came to the conclusion that the loss of Special Orders 191, the mortal wounding of Stonewall Jackson, and the myriad of other events mitigating against Lee's victory during both campaigns caused it to look "as if the good Lord had ordained that we should not succeed."[5]

The Pennsylvania Campaign found Lee gambling again when he left only a third of his army—A. P. Hill's Third Corps (22,000 men) in front of Hooker's army (about 78,000 men) while the rest of his men began moving north at the start of the campaign. This was a desperate gamble that could have resulted in the destruction of a large part of his army and the loss of Richmond. Lee did halt his army's movements northwest and north periodically when it seemed as though the enemy was becoming aggressive, such as the cavalry action at Brandy Station or the thrust across the Rappahannock River by portions of the VI Corps. Driving north while Maj. Gen. John Dix's small army of almost 35,000 men was just south of

Richmond was also a major risk that could have caused Lee grief, had the force been commanded by a more aggressive leader.

Lee's greatest mistake during the Pennsylvania Campaign may have been to allow Stuart to embark on his raid in late June without firm direction about timelines and route. It caused Lee to move north without knowing the location of the Union army and resulted in the collision at Gettysburg.[6]

Battlefield Preliminaries

Lee was on the defense at Antietam and the offense at Gettysburg and this played a major part of the outcome of each battle. Outnumbered, with a third of his army still not present when the battle began at Antietam, Lee desperately hung on until the remaining units arrived. Some considered him rash for even attempting to make a stand at Antietam, but he occupied the high ground and interior lines. McClellan had most of his army available at the start of the battle, but he worried about Stonewall Jackson's route from Harpers Ferry. The most direct approach would be toward the IX Corps' left flank and this caused McClellan some anxiety. He did not know that Jackson would march his men to Shepherdstown and approach Lee's army from the rear. Some have speculated that McClellan held most of his V Corps out of the action in case Jackson's men appeared on the flank.

Meade held the interior lines at Gettysburg and was able to skillfully move troops around the field to areas in danger. Lee's exterior line forced him to occupy a more extensive area with a smaller army.

Gettysburg has been characterized as an "accident" as both sides converged on the town from different directions. Such was not the case at Antietam, where Lee chose the ground as the best place he could find to make a stand with Longstreet's three divisions and await the arrival of the remaining six divisions fighting with Jackson at Harpers Ferry.

During both campaigns, the combatants were not fully on the field at the beginning of the major engagement. This was less of a problem at Gettysburg, as both armies arrived all through July 1 and 2, so they counterbalanced each other. McClellan's army, although not fully reconstituted at the outset of the battle of Antietam, was complete enough to take on and defeat the portions of Lee's army on the battlefield when the sun rose on September 17. At that point, three of Lee's divisions, fully a third of his army, were still on the road. Two divisions arrived that morning, just in time to help parry some of McClellan's thrusts. A. P. Hill's timely arrival toward the end of the battle is the stuff of legends, but it was too close a call for Lee. Had Hill not arrived when he did, there is a good chance McClellan could have pinned Lee against the Potomac River.

Terrain played a major role in each battle. Both battlefields had rolling terrain with high ground at certain strategic spots. The southern part of the field at Antietam is more rugged, with deep ravines, than the northern area and most of the Gettysburg battlefield. Trees on both battlefields were primarily restricted to specific woodlots (e.g., East/West Woods at Antietam; Herbst/Spangler's Woods at Gettysburg). Hills and ridges characterized both battlefields and the armies used them to their best advantage. They became a focal point of most of the attacks. Distinct high ground at Gettysburg (e.g., Little Round Top, Cemetery Hill, Culp's Hill) was more prevalent and taller than their counterparts at Antietam, although the bluffs on either side of Antietam Creek and Cemetery Hill provided good artillery platforms and defensive positions for infantry.

Stone walls at Gettysburg and Antietam provided good protection for both armies. Antietam also sported ledges to protect the men. Although Lee arrived at Antietam two days before the battle, he did not order his men to dig trenches or build breastworks. The same was true of Gettysburg, with the exception of Culp's Hill, where the men of the Union XII Corps spent considerable time and effort building breastworks on the night of July 1-2, which would make their position impregnable.

Barriers were more prevalent at Antietam. The proximity of the Potomac River so close to Sharpsburg certainly played a role in both armies' tactical approaches, as did Antietam Creek. The two armies viewed the creek in different ways. For Lee, it was a way of funneling the enemy's attack column into well defined areas so the entire front did not require guarding—only those crossing spots. However, Lee didn't have the manpower on the evening of September 16 to defend all of the crossings, and the Union I Corps crossed Antietam Creek at the undefended Upper Bridge and Pry's Ford. McClellan had the opposite problem—how to get his army across this barrier. The Upper and Middle Bridges did not pose a problem, but the IX

Corps experienced significant challenges attempting to cross at the Lower Bridge. Bodies of water were not as important during the Gettysburg Campaign. While there were streams on the battlefield, such as Rock Creek and Willoughby Run, they did not pose the same challenges as Antietam Creek and the Potomac River at Antietam.

Both battlefields encompassed a small town that was held by the Confederates during the battle. Good road systems brought the combatants to both battlefields, but Gettysburg had double the number of Sharpsburg's. Some of these roads were also important for moving troops during the battles.

Tactical Plans

The aggressors' tactical plans differed in the two major battles. McClellan sought to first crush Lee's left flank by a massive attack from the north, followed later by an attack from the south against Lee's right flank. If either was successful, he intended to attack Lee's center. Lee had the advance of occupying interior lines, which allowed for an easier movement of troops to areas needing them most. Meade also enjoyed interior lines at Gettysburg and used them to his best advantage.

Lee began the battle on July 1 at Gettysburg without a tactical plan in place. He instructed his subordinates to avoid a confrontation until his entire army was assembled, but Heth blundered into Buford's cavalry west of Gettysburg, opening the battle. The attack from the north was also not planned, and while Lee had Meade's troops in a vice, it was not planned or executed particularly well. Lee's tactical plan at Gettysburg evolved through time because of changing conditions and input from his senior officers. What did not change was his desire to drive the enemy from the high ground. The Union army's tenacity, Meade's ability to move troops around the battlefield as needed and bad luck doomed most of Lee's efforts.

The execution of each aggressor's battle plans has been criticized. For example, McClellan waited almost four hours to launch his second front at the southern end of Lee's line. This permitted Lee to rush reinforcements to areas under attack, including Walker's division, which had been deployed well south of Sharpsburg. The result was a steady stream of reinforcements that helped blunt Hooker's early attacks and devastate Sedgwick's division in the

West Woods. However, a case can be made that by delaying the start of the second front, McClellan guaranteed fewer enemy troops remaining in defense of Lee's right flank. McClellan has also been criticized for allowing large units to sit idle on the battlefield, including the V and most of the VI Corps. The idea of driving straight for Lee's heart in the center of his line was never realized.

Lee has come under criticism for several of his decisions at Gettysburg. Once the armies collided, Lee attempted to coordinate the late afternoon attacks that drove the enemy from Oak Ridge and Seminary Ridges. He was unable to get the Second Corps (Ewell) and Third Corps (Hill) to attack the high ground south of Gettysburg (Cemetery and Culp's Hills). On July 2, he permitted his subordinates to modify and delay his attack plan, thus providing time for additional Union troops to arrive on the battlefield. He has also been criticized for crafting overly ambitious plans to best the Union army at Gettysburg. For example, his decision to execute an *en echelon* attack on the Union left flank on July 2 has been questioned. While it brought some advantages, it ultimately failed because there were insufficient troops available to exploit breaches made in Meade's line. Most scorn is heaped on Lee's decision to launch the Pickett-Pettigrew-Trimble Charge on July 3 and not coordinating it with Ewell's attack on Culp's Hill.

The leaders of the armies on defense have been praised for their actions during both campaigns. Lee masterfully moved his limited number of troops around the battlefield at Antietam, blunting all of McClellan's attacks. The same can be said about Meade's activities at Gettysburg.

The Three Phases of the Battles

The breakdown of the two battles into phases provides some interesting insights and a case can be made for this type of analysis. The armies battled for control of the high ground during the first phase of both battles. At Antietam, Union troops attempted to take the high ground around Dunker Church north of town, sparking combat in the Miller Cornfield, East Woods and West Woods. The combatants fought for the series of ridges west of Gettysburg and the high ground north of the town during its first day of combat. The aggressors were, in both cases, successful in achieving their goals, although Lee wanted Cemetery and Culp's Hills captured on July 1, but his corps commanders let him down. His troops did capture the town of Gettysburg.

Most of the second phase of the fight at Antietam involved two divisions from the II Corps attempting to capture Sharpsburg, but were first forced to drive the enemy from the Sunken Road and the Piper farm beyond. That fight paled in comparison with July 2 at Gettysburg, where massive numbers of troops struggled over high ground south of the town, including Little Round Top, Houck's Ridge, Cemetery Ridge, Cemetery Hill, and Culp's Hill. The fighting involved parts of the Union I, II, III, V, XI, and XII Corps while Lee used parts of all three of his corps during the second day at Gettysburg. In both battles, the aggressors failed in achieving their goals.

During the third phase of the battle of Antietam, McClellan attempted to crush Lee's weakened right flank with the fresh IX Corps. It first fought its way across Antietam Creek at the Lower Bridge and then subsequently attacked Lee's flank south of Sharpsburg in what is called the Final Attack. Only the timely arrival of A.P. Hill's division from Harpers Ferry, saved Lee's army from possible destruction. Gettysburg also involved large-scale fights south of town, including efforts to capture Cemetery Ridge in the center of the Union line and Culp's Hill on the right. A series of cavalry battles also occurred during this final phase. The aggressor again was denied victory in both battles.

The army commanders used their armies in different ways during the two campaigns. McClellan primarily used four of his six army corps at Antietam (I, II, IX, and XII), retaining the V and VI in supportive roles. At Gettysburg, perhaps because the VI Corps arrived so late on July 2, it was not thrown into the fray. Therefore, the VI Corps played a minor role in both campaigns. Lee was fairly consistent in using virtually all of his troops during both campaigns, probably because he was outnumbered in both.

Coordination

Each army's complex organizational structure demanded coordination if success was to be achieved. The two campaigns saw varied degrees of success. Lee appears to have taken an active role in coordinating his units' movements at Antietam, effectively moving troops from one sector to another to attempt to staunch the enemy's hammer blows. He adopted a different approach at Gettysburg at a time when he probably needed to be much more hands on. He had two new and untested commanders at the corps level, yet he adopted essentially a "hands off" approach when they needed precise and unambiguous direct orders. His illness during the battle could have contributed to his actions or he simply believed his new commanders, so active and aggressive at the divisional level, would rise to the occasion. The most egregious mistakes were in allowing subordinates to override his plans and for not insisting on adequate coordination among his corps commanders. For example, Ewell's Second Corps was to attack the northern hills (Cemetery and Culp's) at the same time that Longstreet launched his attack on the Union left. Ewell hesitated and did not launch his men until Longstreet's attacks were all but over. The impact of simultaneous attacks at both ends of the field can only be surmised, but they could have resulted in a different outcome. Even worse, Ewell and Longstreet were again to conduct a coordinated attack at first light on July 3. However, Longstreet was permitted to delay his attack, but Lee apparently never informed Ewell, who sent seven brigades against Culp's Hill, only to be slaughtered on its steep slopes.

Although new to army command, Meade did a fine job of moving units around to limit the enemy's successes on July 2 and 3 at Gettysburg. Some have criticized McClellan for a poor job of coordinating his units at Antietam, as his V Corps seemingly did little while the IX Corps attacked Lee's left flank. However, this unit linked the two wings of the army, and if defeated, McClellan's forces could have been cut in half.

Luck Smiles on the Defenders but not the Aggressors

In both campaigns, the army on the defense benefited from luck. At Antietam, Lafayette McLaws' division arrived from Harpers Ferry in time to blunt John Sedgwick's division's attack into the West Woods, and A.P. Hill's division arrived just in time to halt the IX Corps drive toward Sharpsburg. At Gettysburg, the timely arrival of the V Corps helped blunt Lee's hammer blows. At a micro-level, Col. Strong Vincent taking it upon himself to march his men up to Little Round Top and Col. Patrick O'Rork's drive up the same hill later on, helped save this critically important feature. Other examples are Brig. Gen. George Stannard's brigade's timely appearance to blunt the capture of Cemetery Ridge on July 2 and its attack on Brig. Gen. James Kemper's right flank the following day. The 8th Ohio's charge against the left flank of the Pickett-Pettigrew-Trimble line of attack also falls into this category.

On the other side of the coin, the II Corps was driving the enemy from the Piper farm toward Sharpsburg until Maj. Gen. Israel Richardson was wounded, halting the onslaught. The IX Corps *almost* achieved victory against Lee's right flank, but was thwarted by Hill's division's untimely arrival. At Gettysburg, the setbacks to Brig. Gen. James Archer's and Brig. Gen. Joseph Davis' brigades on July 1 due to the untimely attacks by Union troops are further examples of the aggressors' bad luck. The Confederates came very close to capturing the strategically important Little Round Top, Cemetery Hill, Cemetery Ridge, and Culp's Hill on July 2.

Some Noteworthy Actions

Both battles featured a field that changed hands several times during the conflict. The David Miller Cornfield changed hands five or six times during the desperate fighting on the morning of September 17. It certainly was in the same category as the Gettysburg Wheatfield, which also changed hands multiple times. In both cases, the aggressor was able to capture the contested area, but it had little to no tactical value.

The grand charge during the final phase of each battle is noteworthy. The IX Corps' attack south of Sharpsburg was finding success until A. P. Hill's division slammed into its front and flank, ending the attempt. The Pickett-Pettigrew-Trimble Charge at Gettysburg is better known, but was also unsuccessful, partly because of vicious attacks against each flank. One major difference was the artillery. Lee unleashed a torrent of shells toward the Union positions prior to the charge at Gettysburg, but at Antietam, the IX Corps did not have the same firepower, so the artillery played a minor role. The defender's artillery at Gettysburg had a greater impact on blunting Lee's attack, compared with Antietam.

Duration

The three-day battle of Gettysburg lasted much longer than Antietam's single day, but its lulls in the fighting were more pronounced. After the morning fight at Gettysburg on July 1, there were periodic breaks in the action as the troops rested and awaited the arrival of reinforcements. The battle on July 2 did not begin until about 4:00 p.m., and July 3 also saw long breaks in the action. The daylong action at Antietam was characterized by more continuous fighting with fewer and shorter breaks.

Losses

The proportion of each army's losses in each campaign was very similar. Using numbers from the Antietam Battlefield Board and a careful analysis by Busey and Martin on Gettysburg, the Confederates lost 10,300 (29%) at Antietam and 23,231 (32%) at Gettysburg. The Union army lost 12,780 at Antietam (22%) and 23,055 at Gettysburg (25%). Therefore, the Union army lost a smaller percentage of men during its battles than the Confederates.[7]

Both battles took their toll on general officers. At Antietam, three Union generals (Joseph Mansfield, Israel Richardson, and Isaac Rodman) and three Confederate generals (William Starke, George B. Anderson, and Lawrence Branch) were killed or mortally wounded. Three Union generals were also killed or mortally wounded at Gettysburg (John Reynolds, Samuel Zook, and Stephen Weed) and four Confederate generals (Richard Garnett, Lewis Armistead, William Barksdale, and Paul Semmes). Jesse Reno, commander of the IX Corps, died at Fox's Gap prior to Antietam, and James Pettigrew died at Falling Waters during the retreat from Gettysburg.[8]

While his army was badly wounded at the conclusion of each major battle, Lee, in both cases, chose to hold his position into the following day. He initially considered launching an attack, but also hoped the enemy would attack and be bloodied in the process. In both cases, Lee put his army on the road during the evening of the day after the battle.

Returning to Virginia

The proximity to Virginia after these major battles played a major role in the retreats/pursuits. Because Sharpsburg is only a handful of miles from the Potomac River ford at Shepherdstown, Lee was able to quickly cross without the need for bridges and he made his escape quickly and essentially unscathed. Being in south central Pennsylvania after the Battle of Gettysburg, posed major challenges to Lee as he attempted to save his army and its wagon trains. Constant attacks by Union cavalry tried the army's patience and resolve, and hundreds of wagons and men were lost. When Lee's army finally approached the Potomac River, he realized his pontoon bridge was destroyed and the river was too high to ford. This led to drama not experienced during the Maryland Campaign.

The war continued on after both campaigns. The Maryland Campaign was followed by the bloody Fredericksburg Campaign before the armies finally went into winter quarters. Meade chased Lee about during the Bristoe Station and Mine Run Campaigns after the Pennsylvania Campaign, but could not bring him to a head-to-head battle, and end the war.

Lee and His Strategic Goals

Lee failed in achieving his strategic goals in each campaign. During the Maryland Campaign, he was unable to bring McClellan into battle in Pennsylvania, did not secure abundant supplies, did not encourage Maryland to join the Confederacy, and did not woo hundreds of young Marylanders to the army.

During the Pennsylvania Campaign, Lee again failed to meet most of his stated objectives. He was able to, however, secure tons of supplies and thousands of heads of livestock.

Aftermath of Each Campaign

The war dragged on after each campaign. Lee would continue to best the Union army a couple of times after Antietam, but Gettysburg severely hampered the Army of Northern Virginia's offensive capabilities. The merry go round of Army of the Potomac leaders continued after Antietam, but finally stopped after Gettysburg, as Meade commanded the army through the end of the war.

Neither campaign impacted the outcome of Union elections, but face of the war changed after the Maryland Campaign. Lincoln's Emancipation Proclamation shifted the war aims to one of abolishing slavery, which had the effect of keeping England and France out of the war and opening the way for thousands of Black soldiers to join the Union armies.

Union Orders of Battle

Antietam

ARMY OF THE POTOMAC
Maj. Gen. McClellan

I CORPS
Maj. Gen. Joseph Hooker

First Division
Brig. Gen. John Hatch,
Brig. Gen. Abner Doubleday

First Brigade
Col. Walter Phelps

22nd, 24th, 30th, 84th New York;
2nd US Sharpshooters

Second Brigade
Brig. Gen. Abner Doubleday,
t. Col. J. William Hofmann

7th Indiana; 76th, 95th New York;
56th Pennsylvania

Third Brigade
Brig. Gen. Marsena R. Patrick

21st, 23rd, 35th, 80th New York

Fourth Brigade
Brig. Gen. John Gibbon

19th Indiana; 2nd, 6th, 7th Wisconsin

Artillery
Capt. J. Albert Monroe

Edgell's, Monroe's, Campbell's, Reynolds'
batteries

Gettysburg

ARMY OF THE POTOMAC
Maj. Gen. Joseph Hooker
Maj. Gen. George Meade

I CORPS
Maj. John Reynolds, Maj. Gen. Abner
Doubleday, Maj. Gen. John Newton

First Division
Brig. Gen. James Wadsworth

First Brigade
Brig. Gen. Solomon Meredith,
Col. William Robinson

19th Indiana; 24th Michigan, 2nd, 6th, 7th
Wisconsin

Second Brigade
Brig. Gen. Lysander Cutler

7th Indiana; 76th, 84th, 95th,
147th New York; 56th Pennsylvania

Brigade broken up by Gettysburg

See First Brigade, First Division, I Corps

Second Division
Brig. Gen. James Ricketts

First Brigade
Brig. Gen. Abram Duryee

97th, 104th, 105th New York;
107th Pennsylvania

Second Brigade
Col. William Christian, Col. Peter Lyle

26th, 94th New York; 88th,
90th Pennsylvania

Third Brigade
Brig. Gen. George Hartsuff,
Col. Richard Coulter

12th, 13th Massachusetts; 83rd New York;
11th Pennsylvania

Artillery
Thompson, Matthews' batteries

Third Division
Brig. Gen. George Meade,
Brig. Gen. Truman Seymour

First Brigade
Brig. Gen. Truman Seymour,
Col. Richard Roberts

1st, 2nd, 5th, 6th, 13th Pennsylvania
Reserves

Second Brigade
Col. Albert Magilton

3rd, 4th, 7th, 8th Pennsylvania Reserves

Second Division
Brig. Gen. John Robinson

First Brigade
Brig. Gen. Gabriel Paul, Col. Samuel
Leonard, Col. Adrian Root, Col. Richard
Coulter, Col. Peter Lyle

16th Maine; 13th Massachusetts; 94th, 104th
New York, 107th Pennsylvania

Second Brigade
Brig. Gen. Henry Baxter

12th Massachusetts; 83rd, 97th New York;
11th, 88th, 90th Pennsylvania

Brigade broken up by Gettysburg

Third Division
Maj. Gen. Abner Doubleday,
Brig. Gen. Thomas Rowley

First Brigade
Col. Chapman Biddle

80th New York; 121st, 142nd, 151st
Pennsylvania

Second Brigade
Col. Roy Stone, Col. Langhorne Wister, Col.
Edmund Dana

143rd, 149th, 150th Pennsylvania

Third Brigade Lt. Col. Robert Anderson 3rd, 4th, 7th, 8th Pennsylvania Reserves **Artillery** Simpson's, Cooper's, Ransom's batteries **II CORPS** **Maj. Gen. Edwin Sumner** **First Division** **Maj. Gen. Israel Richardson,** **Brig. Gen. Winfield Hancock** **First Brigade** Brig. Gen. John Caldwell 5th New Hampshire; 7th, 61st/64th New York; 81st Pennsylvania **Second Brigade** Brig. Gen. Thomas Meagher 29th Massachusetts; 63rd, 69th, 88th New York **Third Brigade** Col. John Brooke 2nd Delaware; 52nd, 57th, 66th New York; 53rd Pennsylvania **Artillery** Pettit's and Thomas' batteries	**Third Brigade** Brig. Gen. George Stannard. Col. Francis Randall 13th, 14th, 16th Vermont **Artillery Brigade** Col. Charles Wainwright Hall's, Cooper's, Davison's, Reynolds,' Stevens' batteries **II CORPS** **Maj. Gen. Winfield Hancock,** **Brig. Gen. John Gibbon** **First Division** **Brig. Gen. John Caldwell** **First Brigade** Col. Edward Cross, Col. H. Boyd McKeen 5th New Hampshire; 61st New York; 81st, 148th Pennsylvania **Second Brigade** Col. Patrick Kelly 28th Massachusetts; 63rd, 69th, 88th New York, 116th Pennsylvania **Third Brigade** Brig. Gen. John Zook 52nd, 57th, 66th New York; 140th Pennsylvania **Fourth Brigade** Col. John Brooke 27th Connecticut; 2nd Delaware; 64th New York; 53rd, 145th Pennsylvania

Second Division
Maj. Gen. John Sedgwick,
Brig. Gen. Oliver Howard

First Brigade
Brig. Gen. Willis Gorman

15th, Massachusetts; 1st Minnesota; 34th, 82nd New York

Second Brigade
Brig. Gen. Oliver Howard, Col. Joshua Owen, Col DeWitt Baxter

69th, 71st, 72nd, 106th Pennsylvania

Third Brigade
Brig. Gen. Napoleon Dana, Col. Norman Hall

19th, 20th Massachusetts; 7th Michigan; 42nd, 59th New York

Third Division
Brig. Gen. William French

First Brigade
Brig. Gen. Nathan Kimball

14th Indiana; 8th Ohio; 132nd Pennsylvania; 7th West Virginia

Second Brigade
Col. Dwight Morris

14th Connecticut; 108th New York; 130th Pennsylvania

Third Brigade
Brig. Gen. Max Weber, Col. John Andrews

1st Delaware; 5th Maryland; 4th New York

Second Division
Brig. Gen. John Gibbon,
Brig. Gen. William Harrow

First Brigade
Brig. Gen. William Harrow, Col. Francis Heath

19th Maine; 15th, Massachusetts; 1st Minnesota; 82nd New York

Second Brigade
Brig. Gen. Alexander Webb

69th, 71st, 72nd, 106th Pennsylvania

Third Brigade
Col. Norman Hall

19th, 20th Massachusetts; 7th Michigan; 42nd, 59th New York

Third Division
Brig. Gen. Alexander Hays

First Brigade
Col. Samuel Carroll

14th Indiana; 8th Ohio; 7th West Virginia

Second Brigade
Col. Thomas Smyth, Lt. Col. Francis Pierce

14th Connecticut; 1st Delaware; 12th New Jersey; 10th New York

Third Brigade
Col. George Willard, Col. Eliakim Sherrill, Lt. Col. James Bull

39th, 111th, 125th, 126th New York

Unattached Artillery	**Artillery Brigade** Capt. John Hazard
Frank's, Hazard's, Owen's	Rorty's; Arnold's, Brown's, Woodruff's, Cushing's batteries
The III Corps was not at Antietam	**III CORPS** **Maj. Gen. Daniel Sickles,** **Maj. Gen. David Birney**
	First Division Brig. Gen. David Birney, Brig. Gen. Hobart Ward
	First Brigade Brig. Gen. Charles Graham, Col. Andrew Tippin
	57th, 63rd, 68th, 105th, 114th, 141st Pennsylvania
	Second Brigade Brig. Gen. Hobart Ward, Col. Hiram Berdan
	20th Indiana; 3rd, 4th Maine; 86th, 124th New York; 99th Pennsylvania; 1st, 2nd US SS
	Third Brigade Col. P. Regis de Trobriand
	17th Maine; 3rd, 5th Michigan; 40th New York; 110th Pennsylvania
	Second Division **Brig. Gen. Andrew Humphreys**
	First Brigade Brig. Gen. Joseph Carr
	1st, 11th, 16th Massachusetts; 12th New Hampshire; 11th New Jersey; 26th Pennsylvania

Second Brigade
Col. William Brewster

70th, 71st, 72nd, 73rd, 74th, 120th New York

Third Brigade
Col. George Burling

2nd New Hampshire; 5th, 6th, 7th, 8th New Jersey; 115th Pennsylvania

Artillery Brigade
Capt. George Randolph,
Capt. Judson Clark

Clark's, Winslow's, Smith's Bucklyn's, Seeley's batteries

V CORPS Maj. Gen. Fitz John Porter	V CORPS Maj. Gen. George Sykes
First Division Maj. Gen. George Morell	**First Division** Brig. Gen. James Barnes
First Brigade Col. James Barnes	**First Brigade** Col. William Tilton
2nd Maine; 18th, 22nd, Sharpshooters Massachusetts; 1st Michigan; 13th, 25th New York; 118th Pennsylvania	18th, 22nd Massachusetts; 1st Michigan; 118th Pennsylvania
Second Brigade Brig. Gen. Charles Griffin	**Second Brigade** Col. Jacob Sweitzer
2nd District of Columbia; 9th, 32nd Massachusetts; 4th Michigan; 14th New York; 62nd Pennsylvania	9th, 32nd Massachusetts; 4th Michigan; 62nd Pennsylvania
Third Brigade Col. Thomas Stockton	**Third Brigade** Col. Strong Vincent, Col. James Rice
20th Maine; 16th, Sharpshooters Michigan; 12th, 17th, 44th New York; 83rd Pennsylvania	20th Maine; 16th Michigan; 44th New York; 83rd Pennsylvania

Second Division
Brig. Gen. George Sykes

First Brigade
Lt. Col. Robert Buchanan

3rd, 4th, 12th (1st & 2nd Batt.),
14th (1st & 2nd Batt.) U.S.

Second Brigade
Maj. Charles Lovell

1st/6th, 2nd/10th, 11th, 17th U.S.

Third Brigade
Col. Gouverneur Warren

5th, 10th New York

Artillery

Randol's, Weed's, Van Reed's batteries

Third Division
Brig. Gen. Andrew Humphreys

First Brigade
Brig. Gen. Erastus Tyler

91st, 126th, 129th, 134th Pennsylvania

Second Brigade
Col. Peter Allabach

123rd, 131st, 133rd, 155th Pensyvlania

Artillery

Robinson's, Barnes' batteries

Artillery Reserve
Lt. Col. William Hays

Wever's, von Kleiser's, Langner's, Kusserow's, Taft's, Graham's Miller's batteries

Second Division
Brig. Gen. Romeyn Ayres

First Brigade
Col. Hannibal Day

3rd, 4th, 6th, 12th (1st & 2nd Batt.),
14th (1st & 2nd Batt.) U.S.

Second Brigade
Col. Sidney Burbank

1st, 7th, 10th, 11th, 17th U.S

Third Brigade
Brig. Gen. Stephen Weed,
Col. Kenner Garrard

140th, 146th New York; 91st, 155th Pennsylvania

Third Division
Brig. Gen. Samuel Crawford

First Brigade
Col. William McCandless

1st, 2nd, 6th, 13th Pennsylvania Reserves

Second Brigade
Col. Joseph Fisher

5th, 9th, 10th, 11th, 12th Pennsylvania Reserves

Artillery Brigade
Capt. Augustus Martin

Walcott's, Hazlett's, Watson's Gibbs,' Barnes' batteries

VI CORPS Maj. Gen. William Franklin	VI CORPS Maj. Gen. John Sedgwick
First Division Maj. Gen. Henry Slocum	**First Division** Brig. Gen. Horatio Wright
First Brigade Col. Alfred Torbert	**First Brigade** Brig. Gen. Alfred Torbert
1st, 2nd, 3rd, 4th New Jersey	1st, 2nd, 3rd, 4th, 15th New Jersey
Second Brigade Col. Joseph Bartlett	**Second Brigade** Brig. Gen. Joseph Bartlett, Col. Emory Upton
5th Maine, 10th, 27th New York; 96th Pennsylvania	5th Maine, 121st New York; 95th, 96th Pennsylvania
Third Brigade Brig. Gen. John Newton	**Third Brigade** Brig. Gen. David Russell
18th, 31st, 32nd New York; 95th Pennsylvania	6th Maine; 49th, 119th Pennsylvania; 5th Wisconsin
Artillery Capt. Emory Upton	
Wolcott's, Porter's Hexamer's Williston's batteries	
Second Division Maj. Gen. William Smith	**Second Division** Brig. Gen. Albion Howe
First Brigade Brig. Gen. Winfield Hancock, Col. Amasa Cobb	See Third Brigade, First Division, VI Corps
6th Maine; 43rd New York; 49th, 137th Pennsylvania; 5th Wisconsin	
Second Brigade Brig. Gen. William Brooks	**Second Brigade** Col. Lewis Grant
2nd, 3rd, 4th, 5th, 6th Vermont	2nd, 3rd, 4th, 5th, 6th Vermont

Third Brigade Col. William Irwin 7th Maine; 20th, 33rd, 49th, 77th New York **Formerly Darius Couch's Division (IV Corps)**	**Third Brigade** Brig. Gen. Thomas Neill 7th Maine; 33rd, 43rd, 49th, 77th New York; 61st Pennsylvania **Third Division** Maj. Gen. John Newton, Brig. Gen. Frank Wheaton **First Brigade** Brig. Gen. Alexander Shaler 65th, 67th, 122nd New York; 23rd, 82nd Pennsylvania **Second Brigade** Col. Henry Eustis 7th, 10th, 37th Massachusetts; 2nd Rhode Island **Third Brigade** Brig. Gen. Frank Wheaton, Col. David Nevin 62nd New York; 93rd, 98th, 139th Pennsylvania
Artillery Capt. Romeyn Ayres Vanneman's, Cowan's, Martin's batteries	**Artillery Brigade** Col. Charles Tompkins McCartney's, Cowan's, Harn's Waterman's Williston's, Butler's, Martin's, Adams' batteries
IX CORPS Maj. Gen. Ambrose Burnside, Brig. Gen. Jacob Cox **First Division** Brig. Gen. Orlando Willcox **First Brigade** Col. Benjamin Christ 28th Massachusetts; 17th Michigan; 79th New York; 50th Pennsylvania	**IX Corps not at Gettysburg**

Second Brigade
Col. Thomas Welsh

8th Michigan; 46th New York; 45th, 100th Pennsylvania

Artillery

Cook's and Benjamin's batteries

Second Division
Brig. Gen. Samuel Sturgis

First Brigade
Brig. Gen. James Nagle

2nd Maryland; 6th, 9th New Hampshire; 48th Pennsylvania

Second Brigade
Brig. Gen. Edward Ferrero

21st, 35th Massachusetts; 51st New York; 51st Pennsylvania

Artillery

Durell's and Clark's batteries

Third Division
Brig. Gen. Isaac Rodman,
Col. Edward Harland

First Brigade
Col. Harrison Fairchild

9th, 89th, 103rd New York

Second Brigade
Col. Edward Harland

8th, 11th, 16th Connecticut; 4th Rhode Island

Artillery

Muhlenberg's battery

Kanawha Division
Col. Eliakim Scammon

First Brigade
Col. Hugh Ewing

12th, 23rd, 30th Ohio; McMullin's battery

Second Brigade
Col. George Crook

11th, 28th, 36th Ohio Simmonds battery

XI Corps not at Antietam

XI CORPS
Maj. Gen. Oliver Howard,
Maj. Gen. Carl Schurz

First Division
Brig. Gen. Francis Barlow,
Brig. Gen. Adelbert Ames

First Brigade
Col. Leopold von Gilsa

41st, 54th, 68th New York;
153rd Pennsylvania

Second Brigade
Brig. Gen. Adelbert Ames,
Col. Andrew Harris

17th Connecticut;
25th, 75th, 107th Ohio

Second Division
Brig. Gen. Adolph von Steinwehr

First Brigade
Col. Charles Coster

134th, 154th New York;
27th, 73rd Pennsylvania

Second Brigade
Col. Orland Smith

33rd Massachusetts; 136th New York;
55th, 73rd Ohio

Third Division
**Maj. Gen. Carl Schurz, Brig. Gen.
Alexander Schimmelfennig**

First Brigade
Brig. Gen. Alexander Schimmelfennig,
Col. George von Amsberg

82nd Illinois; 45th, 157th New York;
61st Ohio; 74th Pennsylvania

Second Brigade
Col. Wladimir Krzyzanowski

58th, 119th New York; 82nd Ohio;
75th Pennsylvania; 26th Wisconsin

Artillery Brigade
Maj. Thomas Osborn

Wiedrich's, Wheeler's Dilger's
Heckman's, Wilkeson's batteries

XII CORPS	XII CORPS
Maj. Gen. Joseph Mansfield, Brig. Gen. Alpheus Williams	Maj. Gen. Henry Slocum, Brig. Gen. Alpheus Williams
First Division Brig. Gen. Alpheus Williams, Brig. Gen. Samuel Crawford, Brig. Gen. George Gordon	**First Division** Brig. Gen. Alpheus Williams, Brig. Gen. Thomas Ruger
First Brigade Brig. Gen. Samuel Crawford, Col. Joseph Knipe	**First Brigade** Col. Archibald McDougall
10th Maine; 28th New York; 46th, 124th, 125th, 128th Pennsylvania	5th, 20th Connecticut; 3rd Maryland; 123rd, 145th New York; 46th Pennsylvania

Third Brigade
Brig. Gen. George Gordon,
Col. Thomas Ruger

27th Indiana, 2nd Massachusetts;
13th New Jersey; 3rd Wisconsin

Second Division
Brig. Gen. George Greene

First Brigade
Lt. Col. Hector Tyndale,
Maj. Orrin Crane

5th, 7th, 66th Ohio; 28th Pennsylvania

Second Brigade
Col Henry Stainrook

3rd Maryland; 102nd New York;
111th Pennsylvania

Third Brigade
Col. William Goodrich,
Lt. Col. Jonathan Austin

3rd Delaware; Purnell Legion;
60th, 78th New York

Brigade not at Antietam

Artillery
Capt. Clermont Best

Robinson's, McGilvery's, Cothran's,
Bruen's, Knap's, Hampton's, Muhlenberg's
batteries

Third Brigade
Brig. Gen. Thomas Ruger,
Col. Silas Colgrove

27th Indiana, 2nd Massachusetts;
13th New Jersey; 107th New York;
3rd Wisconsin

Second Division
Brig. Gen. John Geary

First Brigade
Col. Charles Candy

5th, 7th, 29th, 66th Ohio;
28th, 147th Pennsylvania

Second Brigade
Col. George Cobham,
Brig. Gen. Thomas Kane

29th, 109th, 111th Pennsylvania

Third Brigade
Brig. Gen. George Green

60th, 78th, 102nd, 137th, 149th New York

Lockwood's (Independent) Brigade
Brig. Gen. Henry Lockwood

1st (Potomac Home Guard), 1st
(Eastern Shore) Maryland;
150th New York

Artillery Brigade
Lt. Edward Muhlenberg

Winegar's, Atwell's, Rugg's, Kinzie's
batteries

Cavalry Division
Brig. Gen. Alfred Pleasonton

First Brigade
Maj. Charles Whiting

4th, 6th U.S.

Second Brigade
Col. John Farnsworth

8th Illinois; 3rd Indiana; 1st Massachusetts; 8th Pennsylvania

Third Brigade
Col. Richard Rush

4th, 6th Pennsylvania

Fourth Brigade
Col. Andrew McReynolds

1st New York; 12th Pennsylvania

Fifth Brigade
Col. Benjamin Davis

8th New York; 3rd Pennsylvania

Horse Artillery

Tidball's, Robertson's, Gibson's, Hains' batteries

Cavalry Corps
Brig. Gen. Alfred Pleasonton

First Division
Brig. Gen. John Buford

First Brigade
Col. William Gamble

8th, 12th Illinois; 8th New York

Second Brigade
Col. Thomas Devin

6th, 9th New York; 17th Pennsylvania; 3rd West Virginia

Reserve Brigade
Brig. Gen. Wesley Merritt

6th Pennsylvania; 1st, 2nd, 5th 6th U.S.

Second Division
Brig. Gen. David Gregg

First Brigade
Col. John McIntosh

1st Maryland; Purnell Legion, 1st Massachusetts; 1st New Jersey; 1st, 3rd Pennsylvania; Rank's battery

Third Brigade
Col. Irvin Gregg

1st Maine; 10th New York 4th, 16th Pennsylvania

Third Division
Brig. Gen. Judson Kilpatrick

First Brigade
Brig. Gen. Elon Farnsworth

5th New York; 18th Pennsylvania; 1st Vermont; 1st West Virginia

	Second Brigade Brig. Gen. George Custer 1st, 5th, 6th, 7th Michigan **Horse Artillery** **First Brigade** Capt. James Robertson Martin's, Heaton's, Pennington's, Elder's, Daniels' batteries **Second Brigade** Capt. John Tidball Randol's, Graham's, Calef's batteries

Confederate Orders of Battle

Antietam	Gettysburg
ARMY OF NORTHERN VIRGINIA Gen. Robert E. Lee	**ARMY OF NORTHERN VIRGINIA** Gen. Robert E. Lee
LONGSTREET'S WING Maj. Gen. James Longstreet	**FIRST CORPS** Lt. Gen. James Longstreet
McLaws' Division Maj. Gen. Lafayette McLaws	**McLaws' Division** Maj. Gen. Lafayette McLaws
Kershaw's Brigade Brig. Gen. Joseph Kershaw	**Kershaw's Brigade** Brig. Gen. Joseph Kershaw
2nd, 3rd, 7th 8th South Carolina	2nd, 3rd, 7th 8th , 15th, 3rd Batt. South Carolina
Cobb's Brigade Lt. Col. Christopher Sanders; Lt. Col. William MacRae	**Wofford's Brigade** Brig. Gen. William Wofford
16th, 24th, Cobb's Georgia; 15th North Carolina	16th, 18th, 24th, Georgia Cobb's, Phillips,' 3rd Georgia Sharpshooters
Semmes' Brigade Brig. Gen. Paul Semmes	**Semmes' Brigade** Brig. Gen. Paul Semmes Col. Goode Bryan
10th, 53rd Georgia; 15th, 32nd Virginia	10th, 50th, 51st 53rd Georgia
Barksdale's Brigade Brig. Gen. William Barksdale	**Barksdale's Brigade** Brig. Gen. William Barksdale Col. Benjamin Humphreys
13th, 17th, 18th, 21st Mississippi	13th, 17th, 18th, 21st Mississippi
	Cabell's Artillery Battalion Col. Henry Cabell
	Manly's, Fraser's McCarthy's, Carlton's batteries

Anderson's Division Maj. Gen. Richard Anderson	See Anderson's division under the Third Corps
Wilcox's Brigade Col. Alfred Cumming, Maj. Hilary Herbert, Capt. James Crow 8th, 9th, 10th, 11th Alabama	See Wilcox's brigade under Anderson's division
Mahone's Brigade Col. William Parham 6th, 12th, 16th, 41st 61st Virginia	See Mahone's brigade under Anderson's division
Featherston's Brigade Col. Carnot Posey 2nd (Batt.), 12th, 16th, 19th, Mississippi	See Posey's brigade under Anderson's division
Armistead's Brigade Brig. Gen. Lewis Armistead 9th, 14th, 38th, 53rd, 57th Virginia	See Armistead's brigade under Pickett's division
Pryor's Brigade Brig. Gen. Roger Pryor, Col. John Hately 14th Alabama, 2nd, 5th, 8th Florida; 3rd Virginia	**See Perry's brigade under Anderson's division**
Wright's Brigade Brig. Gen. Ambrose Wright 44th Alabama; 3rd, 22nd, 48th Georgia	See Wright's brigade under Anderson's division
Artillery Maj. John Saunders Maurin's, Phelps', Moorman's, Chapman's, Grimes	

Hood's Division Brig. Gen. John Hood	**Hood's Division** Maj. Gen. John Hood
Hood's Brigade Col. William Wofford 18th Georgia; Hampton's Legion; 1st, 4nd, 5th Texas	**Robertson's Brigade** Brig. Gen. Jerome Robertson 3rd Arkansas; 1st, 4nd, 5th Texas
Whiting's Brigade Col. Evander Law 4th Alabama, 2nd, 11th Mississippi, 6th North Carolina	**Law's Brigade** Brig. Gen. Evander Law 4th, 15th, 44th, 47th, 48th Alabama
See Anderson's brigade under D.R. Jones' division	**Anderson's Brigade** Brig. Gen. George Anderson, Lt. Col. William Luffman 7th, 8th, 9th, 11th, 59th Georgia
See Toombs' brigade under D. R. Jones' division	**Benning's Brigade** Brig. Gen. Henry Benning 2nd, 15th, 17th, 20th Georgia
	Henry's Artillery Battalion Maj. Mathias Henry, Maj. John Haskell Latham's, Bachman's, Garden's, Reilly's batteries
Evans' Brigade Brig. Gen. Nathan Evans, Col. Peter Stevens 17th, 18th, 22nd, 23rd South Carolina Holcombe Legion; Macbeth Artillery	**Brigade not at Gettysburg**
Jones' Division Brig. Gen. David R. Jones	**Pickett's Division** Maj. Gen. George Pickett
Pickett's Brigade Brig. Gen. Richard Garnett 8th, 18th, 19th, 28th, 56th Virginia	**Garnett's Brigade** Brig. Gen. Richard Garnett 8th, 18th, 19th, 28th, 56th Virginia

Kemper's Brigade Brig. Gen. James Kemper	**Kemper's Brigade** Brig. Gen. James Kemper
1st, 7th, 11th, 17th, 24th Virginia	1st, 7th, 11th, 17th, 24th Virginia
Toombs' Brigade Brig. Gen. Robert Toombs, Col. Henry Benning	See Benning's brigade under Hood's division
2nd, 15th, 17th, 20th Georgia	
Drayton's Brigade Brig. Gen. Thomas Drayton	Brigade was broken up by Gettysburg
50th, 51st Georgia; Phillips' Legion; 3rd (Batt.), 15th South Carolina	
Jenkins' Brigade Col. Joseph Walker	Brigade was not at Gettysburg
1st (Volunteers), 2nd (Rifles), 4th (Batt.), 5th, 6th South Carolina Palmetto Sharpshooters	
Jones' Brigade Col. George T. Anderson	See Anderson's brigade under Hood's division
1st (Regulars), 7th, 8th, 9th, 11th Georgia	
See Armistead's brigade under D. R. Jones' division	**Armistead's Brigade** Brig. Gen. Lewis Armistead, Lt. Col. William White, Maj. Joseph Cabell, Col. William Aylett
	9th, 14th, 38th, 53rd, 57th Virginia
Artillery	**Dearing's Artillery Battalion** Maj. James Dearing, Maj. John Read
Brown's battery	Stribling's, Caskie's, Macon's Blount's batteries

Walker's Division Brig. Gen. John Walker	Division broken up by Gettysburg
Walker's Brigade Col. Van Manning, Col. Edward Hall	Brigade broken up by Gettysburg
3rd Arkansas, 27th, 46th, 48th North Carolina; 30th Virginia; French's battery	
Ransom's Brigade Brig. Gen. Robert Ransom	Brigade not at Gettysburg
24th, 25th, 35th, 49th North Carolina, Branch's battery	
Reserve Artillery	**Artillery Reserve**
Washington Artillery Col. James Walton	**Washington Artillery Battalion** Maj. Benjamin Eshleman
Washington Artillery (1st, 2nd, 3rd, 4th Companies)	Squires, Richardson's, Miller's, Norcom's batteries
Lee's Battalion Col. Stephen Lee	**Alexander's Battalion** Col. Edward Alexander
Woolfolk's, Jordan's, Elliott's, Eubank's, Moody's, Parker's batteries	Woolfolk's, Jordan's, Fickling's Moody's, Parker's, Taylor's batteries
JACKSON'S WING Maj. Gen. Thomas Jackson	**SECOND CORPS** Lt. Gen. Richard Ewell
Ewell's Division Brig. Gen. Alexander Lawton, Brig. Gen. Jubal Early	**Early's Division** Maj. Gen. Jubal Early
Lawton's Brigade Col. Marcellus Douglass, Maj. John Lowe, Col. John Lamar	**Gordon's Brigade** Brig. Gen. John Gordon
13th, 26th, 31st, 38th, 60th, 61st Georgia	13th, 26th, 31st, 38th, 60th, 61st Georgia
Early's Brigade Brig. Gen. Jubal Early, Col. William Smith	**Smith's Brigade** Brig. Gen. William Smith
13th, 25th, 31st, 44th, 49th, 52nd, 58th Virginia	31st, 44th, 49th, 52nd, Virginia

Trimble's Brigade
Col. James Walker

15th Alabama; 12th, 21st Georgia;
21st, 1st Sharpshooters North Carolina

Hays Brigade
Brig. Gen. Harry Hays

5th, 6th, 7th, 8th, 14th Louisiana

Artillery
Maj. Alfred Courtney

Johnson's, D'Aquin's battery

A.P. Hill's Division
Maj. Gen. A.P. Hill

Branch's Brigade
Brig. Gen. Lawrence Branch

7th, 18th, 28th, 33rd, 37th North Carolina

Gregg's Brigade
Brig. Gen. Maxcy Gregg

1st (Provisional), 1st (Rifles),
12th, 13th, 14th South Carolina

Pender's Brigade
Brig. Gen. William Pender

16th, 22nd, 34th, 38th North Carolina

Field's Brigade
Col. John Brockenbrough

40th, 47th, 55th, 22nd (Batt.) Virginia

Archer's Brigade
Brig. Gen. James Archer, Col. Peter Turney

5th (Batt.) Alabama; 19th Georgia;
1st, 7th, 14th Tennessee

Hoke's Brigade
Col. Isaac Avery,
Col. Archibald Godwin

6th, 21st, 57th North Carolina

Hays Brigade
Brig. Gen. Harry Hays

5th, 6th, 7th, 8th, 9th Louisiana

Jones' Artillery Battalion
Lt. Col. Hilary Jones

Carrington's, Tanner's Green's,
Garber's batteries

See Lane's brigade under Pender's division

See McGowan's brigade under Pender's division

See Scales' brigade under Pender's division

See Brockenbrough's brigade under Heth's division

See Archer's brigade under Heth's division

Thomas' Brigade
Brig. Gen. Edward Thomas

14th, 35th, 45th, 49th Georgia

Artillery
Lt. Col. R. Walker

McIntosh's, Crenshaw's, Braxton's, Pegram's batteries

Jackson's Division
Brig. Gen. John R. Jones, Brig. Gen. William Starke, Col. Andrew Grigsby

Winder's Brigade
Col. Andrew Grigsby, Lt. Col. Robert Gardner, Maj. Hazael Williams

2nd, 4th, 5th, 27th, 33rd Virginia

Taliaferro's Brigade
Col. Edward Warren, Col. James Jackson, Col. James Sheffield

47th, 48th Alabama; 23rd, 37th Virginia

Jones' Brigade
Capt. John Penn, Capt. A. Page, Capt. Robert Withers

1st (Batt.), 21st, 42nd, 48th, Virginia

Starke's Brigade
Brig. Gen. William Starke, Col. Jesse Williams, Col. Leroy Stafford, Col. Edmund Pendleton

1st, 2nd, 9th, 10th, 15th, Coppens' Louisiana

Artillery
Maj. Lindsay Shumaker

Carpenter's, Brockenbrough's, Wooding's, Caskie's, Raine's, Poague's batteries

See Thomas' brigade under Pender's division

Johnson's Division
Maj. Gen. Edward Johnson

Walker's Brigade
Brig. Gen. James Walker

2nd, 4th, 5th, 27th, 33rd Virginia

Steuart's Brigade
Brig. Gen. George Steuart

1st (Batt.) Maryland; 1st, 3rd North Carolina; 10th 23rd, 37th Virginia

Jones' Brigade
Brig. Gen. John M. Jones

21st, 25th, 42nd, 44th, 48th, 50th Virginia

Nicholls' Brigade
Col. Jesse Williams

1st, 2nd, 10th, 14th 15th, Louisiana

Andrews' Artillery Battalion
Maj. Joseph Latimer, Capt. Charles Raine

Dement's, Carpenter's, Brown's, Raine's'

D.H. Hill's Division Maj. Gen. Daniel Hill	Rodes' Division Maj. Gen. Robert Rodes
Ripley's Brigade Brig. Gen. Roswell Ripley Col. George Doles	**Doles' Brigade** Col. George Doles
4th, 44th Georgia; 1st, 3rd North Carolina	4th, 12th, 21st, 44th Georgia
Rodes' Brigade Brig. Gen. Robert Rodes	**O'Neal's Brigade** Col. Edward O'Neal
3rd, 5th, 6th, 12th, 26th Alabama	3rd, 5th, 6th, 12th, 26th Alabama
Garland's Brigade Brig. Gen. Samuel Garland, Col. Duncan McRae	**Iverson's Brigade** Brig. Gen. Alfred Iverson
5th, 12th, 13th 20th, 23rd North Carolina	5th, 12th, 20th, 23rd North Carolina
Anderson's Brigade Brig. Gen. George B. Anderson; Col. Risden Bennett	**Ramseur's Brigade** Brig. Gen. Stephen Ramseur
2nd, 4th, 14th, 30th North Carolina	2nd, 4th, 14th, 30th North Carolina
Colquitt's Brigade Col. Alfred Colquitt	**Brigade not at Gettysburg**
13th Alabama; 6th, 23rd, 27th, 28th Georgia	
Brigade not at Antietam	**Daniel's Brigade** Brig. Gen. Junius Daniel
	2nd (Batt.), 32nd, 43rd, 45th, 53rd North Carolina
Artillery Maj. Scipio Pierson	**Carter's Artillery Battalion** Lt. Col. Thomas Carter
Hardaway's, Bondurant's, Carter's, Jones'	Reese's, Carter's Page's, Fry's
Artillery Reserve Brig. Gen. William Pendleton	**Artillery Reserve** Col. J. Thompson Brown

Nelson's Battalion Maj. William Nelson	**Nelson's Battalion** Maj. William Nelson
Kirkpatrick's, Ancell's, Huckstep's, Johnson's, Milledge's batteries	Kirkpatrick's, Massie's Milledge's
Brown's Battalion Col. J. Thompson Brown	**First Virginia Artillery Battalion** Capt. Willis Dance
Dance's, Watson's, Smith's, Hupp's, Coke's batteries	Watson's, Smith's, Cunningham's, Graham's, Griffin
Cutts's Battalion Lt. Col. Allen Cutts	
Blackshear's, Lane's, Lloyd's, Patterson's, Ross' batteries	
Jones' Battalion Maj. Hilary Jones	
Page's, Peyton's, Turner's, Wimbish's batteries	
	THIRD CORPS **Lt. Gen. A.P. Hill**
	Anderson's Division **Maj. Gen. Richard Anderson**
See Anderson's division in Longstreet's Wing	**Anderson's Division** **Maj. Gen. Richard Anderson**
See Wilcox's brigade under Anderson's division	**Wilcox's Brigade** Brig. Gen. Cadmus Wilcox
	8th, 9th, 10th, 11th, 14th Alabama
See Mahone's brigade under Anderson's division	**Mahone's Brigade** Brig. Gen. William Mahone
	6th, 12th, 16th, 41st 61st Virginia
See Featherston's brigade under Anderson's division	**Posey's Brigade** Brig. Gen. Carnot Posey, Col. Nathaniel Harris
	12th, 16th, 19th, 48th Mississippi

See Pryor's brigade under Anderson's division	**Perry's Brigade** Col. David Lang 2nd, 5th, 8th Florida
See Wright's brigade under Anderson's division	**Wright's Brigade** Brig. Gen. Ambrose Wright 2nd (Batt.), 3rd, 22nd, 48th Georgia
	Cutts's Artillery Battalion Maj. John Lane Patterson's, Wingfield's, Ross' batteries
Division not at Antietam	**Heth's Division** Maj. Gen. Henry Heth, Brig. Gen. James Pettigrew
Brigade not at Antietam	**Pettigrew's Brigade** Brig. Gen. James Pettigrew, Col. James Marshall, Maj. John Jones 11th, 26th, 47th, 52nd North Carolina
See Field's brigade under A.P. Hill's division	**Brockenbrough's Brigade** Col. John Brockenbrough 22nd (Batt.), 40th, 47th, 55th Virginia
See Archer's brigade under A.P. Hill's division	**Archer's Brigade** Brig. Gen. James Archer, Col. Birkett Fry, Lt. Col. Samuel Shepard 5th (Batt.), 13th Alabama; 1st, 7th, 14th Tennessee
See Law's Brigade for some of these regiments	**Davis' Brigade** Brig. Gen. Joseph Davis 2nd, 11th, 42nd Mississippi; 55th North Carolina
	Garnett's Artillery Battalion Lt. Col. John Garnett Maurin's, Moore's, Gandy's, Lewis' batteries

Division not at Antietam	Pender's Division Maj. Gen. William Pender
See Branch's brigade under A.P. Hill's division	**Lane's Brigade** Brig. Gen. James Lane 7th, 18th, 28th, 33rd, 37th North Carolina
See Gregg's brigade under A.P. Hill's division	**McGowan's Brigade** Col. Abner Perrin 1st (Provisional), 1st (Rifles), 12th, 13th, 14th South Carolina
See Pender's brigade under A.P. Hill's division	**Scales' Brigade** Brig. Gen. Alfred Scales 13th, 16th, 22nd, 34th, 38th North Carolina
See Thomas' brigade under A.P. Hill's division	**Thomas' Brigade** Brig. Gen. Edward Thomas 14th, 35th, 45th, 49th Georgia
	Poague's Artillery Battalion Maj. William Poague Wyatt's, Graham's Ward's, Brooke's batteries
	Artillery Reserve Col. Reuben Walker
	McIntosh's Artillery Battalion Maj. David McIntosh Rice's, Hurt's, Wallace's, Johnson's batteries
	Pegram's Artillery Battalion Maj. William Pegram, Capt. Ervin Brunson Crenshaw's, Marye's, Brander's, Zimmerman's, McGraw's batteries

Cavalry Division **Maj. Gen. James Stuart**	**Cavalry Division** **Maj. Gen. James Stuart**
Hampton's Brigade Brig. Gen. Wade Hampton	**Hampton's Brigade** Brig. Gen. Wade Hampton
1st North Carolina; 2nd South Carolina; 10th Virginia; Cobb's, Jeff Davis Legion	1st North Carolina; 2nd South Carolina;; Cobb's, Phillips', Jeff Davis Legion
Fitz Lee's Brigade Brig. Gen. Fitzhugh Lee	**Fitz Lee's Brigade** Brig. Gen. Fitzhugh Lee
1st, 3rd, 4th, 5th, 9th Virginia	1st (Batt.) Maryland; 1st, 2nd, 3rd, 4th, 5th Virginia
Robertson's Brigade Col. Thomas Munford	**Jones' Brigade** Brig. Gen. William Jones
2nd, 6th, 7th, 12th, 17th (Batt.) Virginia	6th, 7th, 11th Virginia
Regiments in other brigades at Antietam	**William H. F. Lee's Brigade** Col. John Chambliss
	2nd North Carolina, 9th, 10th, 13th Virginia
Not at Antietam	**Robertson's Brigade** Brig. Gen. Beverly Robertson
	4th, 5th North Carolina
Horse Artillery Capt. John Pelham	**Horse Artillery** Maj. Robert Beckham
Chew's, Hart's, Pelham's batteries	Breathed's, Chew's, Griffin's, Hart's, McGregor's, Moorman's batteries

APPENDICES

Appendix 1: Comparison of Casulties in the Two Campaigns

The armies lost far more men during at Gettysburg (46,286) than at Antietam (22,720). The reasons are obvious: Gettysburg was fought over three days by significantly larger armies. However, if one looks at the losses per day, Antietam exceeds Gettysburg, 22,720/day to 15,429/day. Although Gettysburg lasted three days, actual fighting occurred at only certain periods. For example, on the second day at Gettysburg, the fighting did not begin until after 3:30 p.m.

The total number of captured/missing were significantly different in the two major battles. At Gettysburg, 24% of the total losses were in this category, compared with only 8% at Antietam. If these losses are kept constant, the armies had a higher percentage of deaths at Gettysburg (22%) versus 18% at Antietam. The reverse is true at Antietam, where the wounded amounted to 83% of the casualties, compared with Gettysburg (77%).

In both campaigns, the Confederate army lost a higher percentage of its men. These differences are not solely related to whether an army was on the offensive or defensive, as the two armies traded roles in these battles, but it did not influence the ratio of losses.

The breakdown of casualty categories is also interesting. For the Confederates, a higher percentage of men were killed (27%) at Antietam (27%) than at Gettysburg (20%), and the same was true for the wounded (75% versus 57%). These percentages are skewed by the high number of men captured at Gettysburg—primarily because of the Pickett-Pettigrew-Trimble Charge.

The percentage of Union troops captured at Gettysburg (23%) far exceeds the number at Antietam (6%), primarily because of the losses incurred during the retreat to Cemetery Hill on the late afternoon/evening of July 1. The rest of the casualty categories flipped, as the Union side had fewer killed/mortally wounded at Gettysburg

(14%) compared with Antietam (17%); a higher percentage were wounded during the latter battle (77% versus 63%).

Table 25: **Comparison of Casulties in the Two Campaigns**

Issue	Maryland Campaign	Pennsylvania Campaign
Total Losses	Total: 22,720 **Killed:** 3,650 (16%) **Wounded:** 17,300 (76%) **Captured/Missing:** 1,770 (8%)	Total: 46,286 (15,428/day) **Killed:** 7,863 (17%) **Wounded:** 27,224 (59%) **Captured/Missing:** 11,199 (24%)
Losses By Army	**Confederate: 10, 320 (27%)** - K/MW: 1,550 (27%) - W: 7,750 (75%) - M/C: 1,020 (10%) **Union: 12.400 (21%)** - K/MW 2,100 (17%) - W: 9,550 (77%) - M/C: 750 (6%)	**Confederate: 23,231 (32%) or 7,744/day** - K/MW: 4,708 (20%) or 1,569/day - W: 12,693 (57%) or 4,231/day - M/C: 5,830 (23%) or 1,943/day **Union: 23,055 (25%) or 7,685/day** - K/MW: 3,155 (14%) or 1,052/day - W: 214,531 (63%) or 4,844/day - M/C: 5,369 (23%) or 1,790/day

Appendix 2: Comparison of the Loss of Corps/Wing, Division, and Brigade Commanders in the Two Campaigns

The two armies lost a significant number of senior officers during each campaign.

During the Maryland Campaign, the Confederate army lost 15 brigade-level officers and higher; the Union army lost 13.

The losses in the Confederate army were at the division level: Starke (k), Lawton (w), J. R. Jones (w), Richard Anderson (w) and brigade level: Branch(k), Garland (k), Douglass (k), G. B. Anderson (k), Cummings (w), Wright (w), Manning (w), Warren (w), Walker (w), Penn (w), and Ripley (w).

The losses for the Federals were at all levels, including two at the corps level: Mansfield (mw) and Hooker (w); four at the division level: Richardson (mw), Rodman (mw), Hatch (w), and Sedgwick (w); and seven at the brigade level: Goodrich (mw), Hartsuff (w), Meagher (w), Howard (w), Dana (w), Webber (w), and Tyndale (w).

The Confederate army again lost 15 senior leaders at Gettysburg. The Confederates did not lose any corps commanders, but lost three division commanders: Heth (w), Pender (mw), and Hood (w), and twelve brigade commanders: Archer (captured), Scales (w), Semmes (mw), Barksdale (mw), G. T. Anderson (w), Avery (mw), Garnett (mw), Armistead (mw), Kemper (w), Pettigrew (mw), Hampton (w), and Jenkins (w).

The Union army also lost 15 of its senior leaders: three of the seven corps commander went down during the fighting: Reynolds (mw), Sickles (w), and Hancock (w). Frances Barlow was wounded at the divisional level and ten brigade commanders were stricken: Meredith (w), Paul (w), Stone (w), Zook (mw), Cross (mw), Willard (mw), Vincent (mw), Weed (mw), Graham (captured), Stannard (w), Farnsworth (k).

Table 26: Comparison of the Loss of Corps/Wing, Division, and Brigade Commanders in the Two Campaigns

Issue	Maryland Campaign	Pennsylvania Campaign
Corps/Wing Commander (Maj./Lt. Gen.)	**Confederate: 0** - K/MW: 0 - W: 0 **Union: 2** - K/MW: 1 - W: 1	**Confederate: 0** - K/MW: 0 - W: 0 **Union: 2** - K/MW: 1 - W: 2
Division Commander (Maj. Gen.)	**Confederate: 4** - K/MW: 1 - W: 3 **Union: 4** - K/MW: 2 - W: 2	**Confederate: 3** - K/MW: 1 - W: 2 **Union: 1** - K/MW: 0 - W: 1
Brigade Commander (Brig. Gen.)	**Confederate: 11** - K/MW: 4 - W: 7 **Union: 7** - K/MW: 1 - W: 6	**Confederate: 10** - K/MW: 6 - W: 3 - C/M: 1 **Union: 10** - K/MW: 5 - W: 4 - C/M: 1

ENDNOTES

Chapter 1: War Comes to the North
1. Stephen W. Sears, *Lincoln's Lieutenants: The High Command of the Army of the Potomac* (Boston: Houghton Mifflin Harcourt, 2017), 188, 276; John Matsui, "War in Earnest: The Army of Virginia and the Radicalization of the Union War Effort," *Civil War History*, vol. 58 (no. 2), 185-87; John J. Hennessey, *Return to Bull Run: The Campaign and Battle of Second Manassas* (New York: Simon & Shuster, 1993), 9, 12-13.
2. Joseph L. Harsh, *Taken at the Flood: Robert E. Lee & Confederate Strategy in the Maryland Campaign of 1862* (Kent, OH: The Kent State University Press, 1999), 27.

Chapter 2: Why Lee Invaded the North in 1862 & 1863
1. U. S. War Department, *The War of the Rebellion: A Compilation of the Official Records of the Union and Confederate Armies*, 128 vols. (Washington: GPO, 1880-1901), Series I, 19, part 2, 590 (hereafter *OR*); Roy P. Basler, ed., *The Collected Works of Abraham Lincoln*, 9 vols. (New Brunswick, NJ: Rutgers University, 1953-55), vol. V, 292-97.
2. Harsh, *Taken at the Flood*, 28-32; D. Scott Hartwig, *To Antietam Creek: The Maryland Campaign of September 1862* (Baltimore, MD: Johns Hopkins University Press, 2012), 49-50.
3. *OR* 19, pt. 2, 590; Clifford Dowdey and Louis H. Manarin, *The Wartime Papers of R. E. Lee* (New York: Virginia Civil War Commissions, 1961), 292-93; James M. McPherson, *Battle Cry of Freedom: The Civil War Era* (New York: Oxford University Press, 1988), 390-91
4. *OR* 19, pt. 2, 591-92.
5. Harsh, *Taken at the Flood*, 46-47; Joseph L. Harsh, *Confederate Tide Rising: Robert E. Lee and the Making of Southern Strategy, 1861 – 1862* (Kent, OH: Kent State University Press, 1999), 67-71; John Ropes, *The Story of the Civil War* (New York: G. P. Putnam Sons, 1898), 328.
6. *OR* 19, pt. 2, 591-92; Douglas Southall Freeman, *R. E. Lee: A Biography* 4 vols. (New York: Charles Scribner's Sons, 1936), vol. 2, 350-51.
7. *OR* 19, pt. 1, 144; Bradley T. Johnson, "First Maryland Campaign," *Southern Historical Society Papers*, vol. xxii (1884), 504-05.
8. A. G. Hopkins, *American Empire: A Global History* (Princeton, NJ: Princeton University Press, 2018), 231-33; Ephraim Douglass Adams, *Great Britain and the American Civil War*, 2 vols., (New York: Longmans, Green and Co., 1925), vol. 2, 43-44; *The Times*, August 15, 1862; *New York Times*, February 11, 1862; McPherson, *Battle Cry of Freedom*), 390-91
9. Charles Marshall, *An Aide-de-Camp of Lee, Being the Papers of Colonel Charles Marshall, Sometimes Aide-de-Camp, Military Secretary, and Assistant Adjutant General on the Staff of Robert e. Lee, 1862 – 1865* (Boston: Little, Brown, 1927), 145-46. Despite the failed Confederate autumn invasions, the Democrats picked up 27 seats in the House of Representatives and one in the Senate.
10. Dowdey and Manarin, *The Wartime Papers of R. E. Lee*, 301.
11. *OR* 19, pt. 1, 144; Gary W. Gallagher, ed., *Lee: The Soldier* (Lincoln, NE: University of Nebraska Press,

1996), 7; Harsh, *Taken at the Flood*, 49; Freeman, *R. E. Lee*, vol. 2, 351. Maryland's state legislature took up the issue of secession in April 1861 and developed articles to leave the Union, but a majority of representatives did not believe they had the power to leave the Union and therefore the State remained in the Union.

12. OR 19, pt. 2, 590-91; Dowdey and Manarin, *The Wartime Papers of R. E. Lee*, 293.

13. Dowdey and Manarin, *The Wartime Papers of R. E. Lee*, 294; Harsh, *Taken at the Flood*, 75.

14. Wilbur Sturtevant Nye, *Here Come the Rebels!* (Dayton, OH: The Press of Morningside Bookshop, 1988), 3.

15. OR 25, pt. 2, 570, 713-14, 715; Jedediah Hotchkiss, *Make Me a Map of the Valley: The Civil War Journal of Stonewall Jackson's Topographer* (College Station, TX: Texas A. & M. University Press, 1973), 116; Nye, *Here Come the Rebels!* 8-9.

16. OR 25, pt. 2, 698-99, 709, 713-14, 720, 724-25; Allen C. Guelzo, *Gettysburg: The Last Invasion* (New York: Alfred A. Knopf, 2013), 32-33; John Henninger Reagan, *Memoirs, with Special Reference to Secession and the Civil War* (New York: Neale, 1905), 121-22; Freeman, *R. E. Lee*, vol. 3, 19. Gen. William Jones commanded the Confederate forces in Southwest Virginia at the time. Seddon told Jones that "a brigade or a regiment or two may be called for to join a force to be sent from here to the re-enforcement of General Bragg's army. OR 25, pt. 2, 698-99.

17. OR 27, pt. 2, 305.

18. "Letter from Major-General Henry Heth, of A. P. Hill's Corps, A. N. V." *Southern Historical Society Papers*, vol. IV (1877), 153.

19. "Letter from Major-General Henry Heth," 153; William Allan, "Memoranda of Conversations with General Robert E. Lee," in *Lee the Soldier*, Gary Gallagher, ed. (Lincoln, NE: University of Nebraska Press, 1966), 13-14.

20. OR 25, pt. 3, 930-31.

Chapter 3: The Armies and Their Leaders

1. Ezra J. Warner, *Generals in Gray: Lives of the Confederate Commanders* (Baton Rouge, LA: The Louisiana State University Press, 1959), 181-82; Ezra J. Warner, *Generals in Blue: Lives of the Union Commanders* (Baton Rouge, LA: The Louisiana State University Press, 1964), 290-9; Stewart Sifakis, *Who Was Who in the Civil War* (New York: Facts on File, 1988), 172.

2. William C. Davis, "Lee and Jefferson Davis," in *Lee the Soldier*, Gary Gallagher, ed., 295-96.

3. Ethan S. Rafuse, *McClellan's War: The Failure of Moderation in the Struggle for the Union* (Bloomington, IL: Indiana University Press, 2005), 191, 211-12; Hartwig, *To Antietam Creek*, 8-11, 52.

4. Steven R. Stotelmyer, *Too Useful to Sacrifice: Reconsidering George B. McClellan's Generalship in the Maryland Campaign from South Mountain to Antietam* (El Dorado Hills, CA: Savas Beatie, 2019), xiii-xiv; Mark Grimsley, "The Lincoln-McClellan Relationship in Myth and Memory," *Journal of the Abraham Lincoln Association*, Vol. 38, Issue 2 (Summer, 2017), 63-81; Rafuse, *McClellan's War*, 191; Thomas J. Rowland, *In the Shadow of Grant and Sherman: George B. McClellan & Civil War History* (Kent, OH: Kent

State University Press, 1998), 233-37; Basler, ed., *The Collected Works of Abraham Lincoln*, vol. 5, 149-50; Alan T. Nolan, *Lee Considered: General Robert E. Lee and Civil War History* (Chapel Hill, NC: The University of North Carolina Press, 1991), 153-160; David Welker, *The Cornfield: Antietam's Bloody Turning Point* (Philadelphia: Casemate, 2020), 16.

5. Joseph T. Glatthaar, *General Lee's Army: From Victory to Collapse* (New York: Free Press, 2008), 123-25; J. Cutler Andrews, *The South Reports the Civil War* (Princeton, NJ: Princeton University Press, 1970), 118; William Parker diary, August 16, 1861 entry, Washington and Lee College; 123-25; Edward P. Alexander, *Fighting for the Confederacy: The Personal Recollections of General Edward Porter Alexander*, Gary W. Gallagher, ed. (Chapel Hill, NC: University of North Carolina Press, 1998), 91. Although most are familiar with Lee's aggressiveness, fewer apparently are aware of his slow decision making process. Walter Taylor, a trusted member of Lee's staff wrote home, "He is too undecided and takes too long to firm his conclusions." Lee was a master of piecing together information and this may have contributed to his perceived slowness. R. Lockwood Tower, ed. *Lee's Adjutant: The Wartime Letters of Colonel Walter Herron Taylor, 1862-1865* (Columbia, SC: The University of South Carolina Press, 1995), 130-31.

6. Freeman, *R. E. Lee*, vol. 2, 340; G. Moxley Sorrel, *Recollections of a Confederate Staff Officer* (New York: Neale Publishing Company, 1917), 103; Charles R. Knight, *From Arlington to Appomattox: Robert E. Lee's Civil War Day by Day, 1861 – 1865* (El Dorado Hills, CA: Savas Beatie, 2021), 187, 193.

7. Gideon Welles, *The Civil War Diary of Gideon Welles, Lincoln's Secretary of the Navy.* William E. Glenapp and Erica L. Glenapp, eds. (Urbana, IL: The University of Illinois Press, 1987); 32; Edward Bates, "Remonstrance and notes, September 2, 1862, Library of Congress; Sears, *Lincoln's Lieutenants*, 339-341; John G. Nicolay and John Hay, *Abraham Lincoln: A History*. Seven volumes (New York: The Century Co., 1886), vol. VI, 53.

8. Jack D. Welsh, *Medical Histories of Confederate Generals* (Kent, OH: Kent State University Press, 1995), 135; W. W. Blackford, *War Years with Jeb Stuart* (New York: Charles Scribner's Sons, 1945), 230. Some historians question whether reports of Lee's illness were overblown and served to excuse his failure at Gettysburg.

9. OR 27, pt. 1, 60; Edwin B. Coddington, *The Gettysburg Campaign: A Study in Command* (New York: Scribners, 1968), 129-33.

10. Warner, *Generals in Blue*, 316; T. Harry Williams, *Lincoln and His Generals* (New York: Alfred A. Knopf, 1952), 259-61; John G. Selby, *Meade: The Price of Command, 1863-1865* (Kent, OH: The Kent State University, 2018), 16-17, 86-87; David S. Sparks, ed., *Inside Lincoln's Army: The Diary of General Marsena Rudolph Patrick, Provost Marshal General, Army of the Potomac* (New York: Thomas Yoseloff, 1964), 261; Tom Huntington, *Searching for George Gordon Meade* (Mechanicsburg, PA: Stackpole Books, 2013), 6-7; John F. Marszalek, *Commander of All of Lincoln's Armies: A Life of General Henry W. Halleck* (New

York: Belknap Press, 2004), 175; Kent Masterson Brown, *Meade at Gettysburg: A Study in Command* (Chapel Hill, NC: University of North Carolina Press, 2021), 18, 35.

11. OR 27, pt. 1, 61; Marszalek, *Commander of All of Lincoln's Armies*, 175-76.

12. Curt Anders, *Henry Halleck's War: A Fresh Look at Lincoln's Controversial General-in-Chief* (Indianapolis, IN: Guild Press, 1999, 444; Marszalek, *Commander of All Lincoln's Armies*, 129-54; Brown, *Meade at Gettysburg*, 17; Welles, *Diary of Gideon Wells*, vol. I, 363-64.

13. Sears, *Lincoln's Lieutenants*, 347-51; Hartwig, *To Antietam Creek*, 139-40. The V Corps was the exception to the two-division corps during the Peninsula Campaign, as it contained three divisions. French's new division was an odd mix of old and new troops. One brigade was totally green, a second had seen only garrison duty near Fortress Monroe and the third was composed of veterans. Although Couch's division was to operate in conjunction with the VI Corps, its orders came directly from army headquarters. It would later be officially integrated into the VI Corps.

14. Hartwig, *To Antietam Creek*, 137-39; OR 19, pt. 2, 197. The governor of each state was given a quota of troops to be provided. These troops were assembled into regiments, before being sent to the armies.

15. Hartwig, *To Antietam Creek*, 60; Warner, *Generals In Gray*, 169-70, 337.

16. Freeman, *Lee's Lieutenants*, vol. 2, 145-46, Hartwig, *To Antietam Creek*, 61-62.

17. Sears, *Lincoln's Lieutenants*, 494, 597-98, 615-16; Warner, *Generals in Blue*, 58. The I Corps was merged into the II Corps and the III Corps into the V Corps.

18. *Richmond Whig*, May 9, 1863; Freeman, *Lee's Lieutenants*, vol. 2, 689-91.

19. Freeman, *Lee's Lieutenants*, vol. 2, 698-705.

20. OR, series IV, vol. 2, 198.

21. Hartwig, *To Antietam Creek*, 138-39.

22. Bradley M. Gottfried, *Kearny's Own: The History of the First New Jersey Brigade in the Civil War* (New Brunswick, NJ: Rutgers University Press, 2005), 81-83; Samuel Toombs, *Reminiscences of the War: Comprising a Detailed Account of the Experiences of the Thirteenth Regiment New Jersey Volunteers in Camp, on the March, and in Battle* (Orange, NJ: Journal Office, 1878), 12.

23. Toombs, *Reminiscences of the War*, 13; Charles J. Mills, *Through Blood and Fire: The Civil War Letters of Major Charles J. Mills, 1862-1865*. Gregory A. Coco, ed. (Gettysburg, PA: n.p., 1982), 24; Jonathan E. Shipman to Friend Hubbard, September 14, 1862, (USAHEC).

24. W. A. Croffut and John M. Morris, *The Military and Civil History of Connecticut During the War of 1861-1865* (New York: Ledyard Bill, 1868), 260; OR 19, pt. 2, 197-98; Alpheus S. Williams, *From the Cannon's Mouth: The Civil War Letters of General Alpheus S. Williams*. Milo M. Quaife, ed. (Detroit, MI: Wayne State University Press, 1959), 126; Oliver C. Bosbyshell, *Pennsylvania at Antietam* (Harrisburg: Antietam Battlefield Memorial Commission, 1906), 149-50; Samuel Fiske, *Mr. Dunn Browne's Experiences in the Army* (Boston: Nichols & Noyes, 1866), 47-49; Hartwig, *To Antietam Creek*, 138-39.

25. *OR* 19, pt. 1, 61, 67; Hartwig, *To Antietam Creek*, 139-40; Daniel J. Vermilya, "Perceptions, Not Realities?: The Army of the Potomac in the Maryland Campaign," *The Antietam Journal*, vol. 1 (September 2021), 48; George Meade, *The Life and Letters of George Gordon Meade*, 2 vols. (New York: Charles Scribner's Sons, 1913), vol. 1, 377, vol. 2, 11; Charles Frederick Benjamin, *Memoir of James Allen Hardie, Inspector General United States Army* (Washington, DC: n.p., 1877), 38-39.

26. Hartwig, *To Antietam Creek*, 55; D. H. Hill, "Lee Attacks North of the Chickahominy," *Battles & Leaders of the Civil War*, vol. 2, 352.

27. Hartwig, *To Antietam Creek*, 57-60; D. Scott Hartwig, "Robert E. Lee and the Maryland Campaign," in *Lee the Soldier*, Gary Gallagher, ed. (Lincoln, NE: University of Nebraska Press, 1996), 334; Louise Haskell Daly, *Alexander Cheves Haskell: The Portrait of a Man* (Wilmington, NC: Broadfoot Publishing Co., 1989), 84.

28. Daniel J. Vermilya, "'Perceptions, not Realities…': The Army of the Potomac in the Maryland Campaign," Save Historic Antietam Foundation, Joseph L. Harsh Scholarship Award, 2012, 9-10.

29. D. Scott Hartwig, "Who Would Not Be a Soldier," in Gary Gallagher, ed., *The Antietam Campaign* (Chapel Hill, NC: The University of North Carolina Press, 1999), 164; Hartwig, *To Antietam Creek*, 80. Hartwig calculated 12% of Lee's men had been in five major battles, 48% in three or four and only 19% in less than one. Hartwig, *To Antietam Creek*, 81.

30. *OR* 19, pt. 2, 597-98.

31. *OR* 25, pt. 2, 473, 532; Sears, *Lincoln's Lieutenants*, 525-27.

32. Freeman, *Lee's Lieutenants*, vol. 2, 710.

33. John W. Busey and David G. Martin, *Regimental Strengths and Losses at Gettysburg* (Hightstown, NJ: Longstreet House, 1982), 16, 169.

34. Curt Johnson and Richard C. Anderson, Jr., *Artillery Hell: The Employment of Artillery at Antietam* (College Station, TX: Texas A&M University Press, 1995), 6-7, 39, 47, 95; Hartwig, *To Antietam Creek*, 83-87, 158-60; Edward Longacre, *The Man Behind the Guns: A Biography of Henry Jackson Hunt* (South Brunswick, NJ: A. S. Barnes, 1977), 119; L. Van Loan Naiswald, *Grape and Canister* (New York: Oxford University Press, 1960), 30-31; Jennings Cropper Wise, *The Long Arm of Lee: The History of the Artillery of the Army of Northern Virginia* (New York: Oxford University Press, 1950), 277-80; Charles A. Cuffel, *Durell's Battery in the Civil War* (Philadelphia: Craig, Finley & Co., 1900), 78. The historian of Durell's battery recalled Hunt as a "small grizzly man with an effeminate voice," but also "an experienced and able artillerist." Cuffel, *Durell's Battery in the Civil War*, 78.

35. Dowdey and Manarin, *The Wartime Papers of R. E. Lee*, 293-96.

36. Edward Porter Alexander, "Confederate Artillery Service," *Southern Historical Society Papers*, vol. 11 (1883), 104-05.

37. *OR* 25, pt.2, 613, 625-26; Bradley M. Gottfried, *The Artillery of Gettysburg* (Nashville, TN: Cumberland House, 2008), 253-57.

38. Van Loan Naiswald, *Grape and Canister*, 214-15; Philip M. Cole, *Civil*

War Artillery at Gettysburg: Organization, Equipment, Ammunition, and Tactics (New York: Da Capo, 2002), 55; Gottfried, *The Artillery of Gettysburg*, 249-53.

39. Henry Hunt, "The Second Day at Gettysburg," *Battles & Leaders of the Civil War*, ed. By Robert U. Johnson and Clarence C. Buell. 4 vols. (New York: T. Yoseloff, 1958-59), vol. 3, 297-99; Gottfried, *The Artillery of Gettysburg*, 85; Alexander, "Confederate Artillery Service," *Southern Historical Society Papers*, vol. 11, 104-05; Cole, *Civil War Artillery at Gettysburg*, 162; Glatthaar, *General Lee's Army*, 265-67.

40. George W. Newton, *Silent Sentinels: A Reference Guide to the Artillery at Gettysburg* (El Dorado Hills, Savas Beatie, 2005), 114-15.

41. Stephen Z. Starr, *The Union Cavalry in the Civil War*, 3 vols. (Baton Rouge, LA: Louisiana State University Press, 1979), vol. 1, 240; Hartwig, *To Antietam Creek*, 155-56; Benjamin W. Crowninshield, "Cavalry in Virginia During the War of the Rebellion," *Journal of the Military Service Institution*, vol. 12 (May 1891), 26.

42. Hartwig, *To Antietam Creek*, 88-89; Edward G. Longacre, *Lee's Cavalrymen: A History of the Mounted Forces of the Army of Northern Virginia* (Mechanicsburg, PA: Stackpole, 2002), 30, 42-44.

43. Edward G. Longacre, *Lincoln's Cavalrymen: A History of the Mounted Forces of the Army of the Potomac* (Mechanicsburg, PA: Stackpole, 2000), 101-103,

44. Laurence H. Freiheit, *Boots and Saddles: Cavalry During the Maryland Campaign of September 1862* (Iowa City, IA: Camp Pope Publishing, 2013), 444-45; Eric J. Wittenberg, *The Union Cavalry Comes of Age* (Washington, DC: Potomac Books, Inc., 2003), 4; *OR* 19, pt. 1, 814; Benjamin W. Crowninshield, *A History of the First Regiment of Massachusetts Cavalry Volunteers* (Boston: Houghton, Mifflin, 1891), 71-72.

45. Edward G. Longacre, *The Cavalry at Gettysburg: A Tactical Study of the Mounted Operations during the Civil War's Pivotal Campaign, 9 June – 14 July 1863* (Lincoln, NB: Bison Books, 1986), 20, 46, 48-54, 161-62, 165-67; Busey and Martin, *Regimental Strengths and Losses at Gettysburg*, 143; J. David Petruzzi and Steven A. Stanley, *The Gettysburg Campaign in Numbers and Losses: Synopses, Orders of Battle, Strengths, Casualties, and Maps, June 9 – July 14, 1863* (El Dorado Hills, CA: Savas Beatie, 2012), 117, 147, 149; Gottfried, *The Artillery of Gettysburg*, 251-52.

46. Starr, *The Union Cavalry in the Civil War*, vol. 1, 421; Longacre, *The Cavalry at Gettysburg*, 165.

47. *OR* 29, pt. 2, 707-08; Longacre, *Lee's Cavalrymen*, 243-44.

48. Busey and Martin, *Regimental Strengths and Losses at Gettysburg*, 315-19; Gottfried, *The Artillery of Gettysburg*, 258.

49. Ezra Carman, *The Maryland Campaign of September 1862*, Thomas Clemens, ed. 3 vols. (El Dorado Hills: Savas Beatie, 2010, 2012), vol. I, 151.

50. Frederick H. Dyer, *A Compendium of the War of the Rebellion*, 3 vols. (Des Moines, IA: The Dyer Publishing Company, 1908), vol. I, 287; Carman, *The Maryland Campaign of 1862*, vol. I, 152-53; Hartwig, *To Antietam Creek*, 142.

51. George B. McClellan, *McClellan's Own Story* (New York: Charles I. Webster and Co., 1887), 139; Carman, *The Maryland Campaign of 1862*, vol. I, 133-34, 148, 416-17, Warner, *Generals in*

Blue, 378-79; William H. Powell, *The Fifth Corps* (New York: G. P. Putnam's Sons, 1896), 6; Mark A. Snell, *From First To Last: The Life of William B. Franklin*, (Fordham University Press, New York, 2002), 8, 9, 24, 52-64, 109; Hartwig, *To Antietam Creek*, 20; Ezra A, Carman, *The Maryland Campaign of 1862*, vol. I, 148.

52. Warner, *Generals in Blue*, 57; Augustus Woodbury, *Ambrose Everett Burnside* (Providence: N. B. Williams & company, 1882), 6; Augustus Woodbury, *Major General Ambrose E. Burnside and the Ninth Army Corps: A Narrative of Campaigns in North Carolina, Maryland, Virginia, Ohio, Kentucky, Mississippi and Tennessee, During the War for the Preservation of the Republic* (Providence: Sidney S. Rider & Brother, 1867), 104; William Marvel, *Burnside* (Chapel Hill, NC: The University of North Carolina Press, 1991), 2-3, 94, 99, 111.

53. Warner, *Generals in Blue*, 309; Carman, *The Maryland Campaign of 1862*, vol. II, 112; Thomas G. Clemens, "'Too Bad, Poor Fellows:' Joseph K. Mansfield and the XII Corps at Antietam," in *Corps Commanders in Blue: Union Major Generals in the Civil War*. Ethan S. Rafuse, ed. (Baton Rouge, LA: Louisiana State University Press, 2014), 65, 67, 71.

54. Sears, *Lincoln's Lieutenants*, 486-94; Hartwig, *To Antietam Creek*, 152-53; Williams, *From the Cannon's Mouth*, 126. Isaac Rodman was the only non-West Point graduate division commander without prior experience in leading a large body of troops was.

55. Welsh, *Medical Histories of Confederate Generals*, 112, 143; Sorrel, *Recollections of a Confederate Staff Officer*, 97; Henry Kyd Douglas, "Stonewall Jackson in Maryland," *Battles & Leaders of the Civil War*, vol. 2, 620; James I. Robertson, *Stonewall Jackson: The Man, The Soldier, the Legend* (New York: Macmillan, 1997),587-88. Staff officer Henry Kyd Douglas noted that Jackson accepted the horse, "a gigantic gray mare" because "Little Sorrel" had been temporarily stolen. Douglas, "Stonewall Jackson in Maryland," 620. Staff officer Moxley Sorrel recalled that Longstreet "was in no good humor at such footwear and the need of occasionally walking in it. In fact, a wobbly carpet slipper was not a good-looking thing for a commander on the field." Sorrel, *Recollections of a Confederate Staff Officer*, 97.

56. Hartwig, *To Antietam Creek*, 152-53; Guelzo, *Gettysburg*, 20; Justus Schiebert, *Seven Months in the Rebel States during the North American War, 1863*. Joseph C. Hayes, ed. (Tuscaloosa, AL: William Stanley Hoole, 1958), 75;

57. Carman, *The Maryland Campaign*, vol. 1, 148-62.

58. Freeman, *Lee's Lieutenants*, vol. 2, 692- 706.

Chapter 4: Supplies, Morale, and the Men's Condition

1. *OR* 25, pt. 2, 597-98, 604, 612, 622, 686, 693094, 709, 712, 726, 735-36, 737-38; 205; "Address of Colonel Edward McCrady, Jr." *Southern Historical Society Papers*, vol. XIV (1886), 205; John C. Oeffinger, ed., *A Soldier's General: The Civil War Letters of Lafayette McLaws* (Chapel Hill, NC: The University of North Carolina Press, 2002), 154-55.

2. "Letter from Major-General Henry Heth," 154.

3. David E. Johnston, *The Story of a Confederate Boy in the Civil War* (Portland, OR: Glass & Prudhomme Company, 1914), 137.

4. Abner Doubleday Report of Service, "Army Generals' Reports of Civil War Service, vol. 13, 435-36, National Archives; James Wren, *Captain James Wren's Diary: From New Bern to Fredericksburg,* John M. Priest, ed. (Shippensburg, PA: White Mane, 1990), 61.

5. Hartwig, *To Antietam Creek,* 80-81, 153-54; Carl L. David, *Arming the Union* (Port Washington, NY: Kennikat Press, 1973), 41, 61, 171; Francis A. Donaldson, *Inside the Army of the Potomac,* J. Gregory Acken, ed. (Harrisburg, PA: Stackpole Books, 1998), 133.

6. Carnot Posey to wife, May 20, 1863, Carnot Posey Papers, Museum of the Confederacy; Glatthaar, *General Lee's Army,* 256-57.

7. "Letter from Major-General Henry Heth," 145-60; Nye, *Here Come the Rebels!* 4-5. An army of 70,000 men would require a daily ration of 105 tons of food; each horse required 14 pounds of hay and 12 pounds grain daily, so an army with 10,000 animals would need 156 tons each day. Hartwig, *To Antietam Creek,* 67.

8. Brown, *Retreat from Gettysburg,* 48-49; Joseph G. Bilby, *Small Arms at Gettysburg: Infantry and Cavalry Weapons in America's Greatest Battle* (Yardley, PA: Westholme, 2008), 114; OR 19, 3, 378, 472; Brown, *Meade at Gettysburg,* 58, 174.

9. Williams, *From the Cannon's Mouth,* 119; OR 19, pt. 2, 225-27; John Gibbon, *Personal Recollections of the Civil War* (New York: G. P. Putnam, 1928), 75.

10. OR 19, 2, 223-24.

11. Charles F. Johnson, *The Long Roll* (Aurora, NJ: Roycroftens, 1911), 181.

12. Marshall, *An Aide-de-Camp of Lee,* 33-34; Robertson, *Stonewall Jackson,* 576; OR 19, pt. 2, 622; OR 19, pt. 1, 860-61; Carman, *The Maryland Campaign,* vol. I, 109; Hartwig, "Robert E. Lee and the Maryland Campaign," 337; Walker, "Jackson's Capture of Harpers' Ferry," *Battles & Leaders of the Civil War,* vol. 2, 605; Cadmus Wilcox to John, September 26, 1862, LOC; Glatthaar, *General Lee's Army,* 181; Calvin L. Collier, *They'll Do To Tie To!: 3rd Ark. Infantry Regiment- CSA* (Little Rock, AR: Arkansas Civil War Centennial Commission, 1959), 81-82. Henry Halleck's biographer hypothesized that Lee lost "the equivalent of several divisions, and the men who drifted away could not be replaced." Curt Anders, 263.

13. OR 12, pt. 3, 928; OR 19, pt. 2, 592-93.

14. OR 19, pt. 2, 597-98.

15. Alexander, *Fighting for the Confederacy,* 139; Collier, *They'll Do To Tie To!,* 82.

16. Dudley Pendleton to Mama, May 7, 1862 (Duke University); William Pegram to sister, May 11, 1863 (Virginia Historical Society), William Ballinger Diary, May 18, 1863 entry (Center for American History); Glatthaar, *General Lee's Army,* 256-57.

17. Coddington, *The Gettysburg Campaign,* 27-30; Fiske, *Mr. Dunn Browne's Experiences in the Army,* 150-51; Stephen Minot Weld, *War Diary and Letters* (Boston: The Riverside Press, 1912), 213.

18. Bennett A. Clements, "Memoir of Jonathan Letterman, M.D.," *Journal of the Military Service Institution,* vol. iv, no.

15 (September 1883), 3-4; *OR* 11, pt. 1, 210-20; *OR* 11, pt. 3, 349-51; Scott McGaugh, *Surgeon in Blue: Jonathan Letterman, Civil War Doctor who Pioneered Battlefield Care* (New York: Arcade, 2013), 77.
19. *The Medical & Surgical History of the War of the Rebellion*, six volumes, (Washington, Government Printing Office, 1870) vol. 11, 214; McGaugh, *Surgeon in Blue*, 80-84.
20. William Quentin Maxwell, *Lincoln's Fifth Wheel* (New York: Longmans, Green & Co., 1956), 161.
21. Clements, "Memoir of Jonathan Letterman, M.D.," 35-39; McGaugh, *Surgeon in Blue*, 101, 106, 108, 115-18, 122
22. H. H. Cunningham, *Doctors in Gray: The Confederate Medical Service* (Baton Rouge, LA: Louisiana State University Press, 1963), 113, 116-17, , 119, 158; Dowdey and Mararin, eds., *The Wartime Papers of R. E. Lee*, 307; https://antietam.aotw.org/officers.php?officer_id=928&from=results.
23. McGaugh, *Surgeon in Blue*, 176-77, 179, 184
24. *OR* 27, pt. 2, 326-30

Chapter 5: Intelligence Gathering
1. Stansbury F. Haydon, *Aeronautics in the Union and Confederate Armies* (Baltimore, MD: Johns Hopkins Press, 1941), 284-95.
2. Edwin C. Fishel, *The Secret War for the Union: The Untold Story of Military Intelligence in the Civil War* (Boston: Houghton Mifflin Company, 1996), 214-15; *OR* 19, pt. 1, 211, 219; Thomas J. Ryan, *Spies, Scouts, and Secrets in the Gettysburg Campaign* (El Dorado Hills, CA: Savas Beatie, 2015), xi, 1-2; James V. Murfin, *The Gleam of Bayonets: The Battle of Antietam and Robert E. Lee's Maryland Campaign, September 1862* (Cranbury, NJ: Thomas Yoseloff, Publisher, 1965), 50, 54, 124-25; *Report of the Joint Committee on the Conduct of the War*, 38th Congress, 2nd Session (Washington: U. S. Printing Office, 1865), 74. Not all the newspapers exaggerated Lee's figures. The *New York Tribune* on September 8, 1862 noted, "The strength of the rebel army [is] exaggerated" and estimated an army of 60,000. Twenty years later, Pinkerton admitted that Lee had about 40,000 men at Antietam. Allan Pinkerton, *The Spy of the Rebellion: Being a True History of the Spy System of the United States Army During the Late Rebellion* (New York: G. W. Dillingham, Publisher, 1883), 567.
3. *OR* 19, pt. 1, 233; Fishel, *The Secret War for the Union*, 216-17.
4. Ryan, *Spies, Scouts, and Secrets in the Gettysburg Campaign*, xiii-xiv; Fishel, *The Secret War for the Union*, 213-14.
5. *OR* 19, pt. 2, 292, 205; Fishel, *The Secret War for the Union*, 214.
6. *OR* 19, pt. 1, 137-39; Fishel, *The Secret War for the Union*, 213-14; Ryan, *Spies, Scouts, and Secrets in the Gettysburg Campaign*, xv, 20- 21; "The Signal Corps," Antietam National Military Park (n.d.); John W. Schildt, *Roads to Antietam* (Shippensburg, PA: Burd Street Press, 1997), 115.
7. *OR* 27, pt. 2, 27; Ryan, *Spies, Scouts, and Secrets in the Gettysburg Campaign*, 224-25.
8. Ryan, *Spies, Scouts, and Secrets in the Gettysburg Campaign*, 105, 124, 196; Charles Evans, *War of the Aeronauts*, (Mechanicsburg, PA: Stackpole Books, 2002), 288-90; Fishel, *The Secret War*, 423, 442-43.
9. *OR* 27, pt. 2, 37.

10. Arthur L. Wagner, *The Service of Security and Information* (Washington DC: James J. Chapman, 1893), 148, 157-58.
11. Ryan, *Spies, Scouts, and Secrets in the Gettysburg Campaign*, 10-11; Hartwig, *To Antietam Creek*, 155.
12. Carman, *The Maryland Campaign of September 1862*, 165-66; OR 19, pt. 1, 208-09; ; OR 19, pt. 2, 602-03; Hartwig, *To Antietam Creek*, 157.
13. Freiheit, *Boots and Saddles*, 441
14. Ryan, *Spies, Scouts, and Secrets in the Gettysburg Campaign*, xii, xv, 182, 188; OR 27, pt. 3, 172; Starr, *The Union Cavalry in the Civil War*, vol. 1, 397, 399; Bradley M. Gottfried, *The Maps of the Cavalry in the Gettysburg Campaign: An Atlas of Mounted Operations from Brandy Station Through Falling Waters, June 9 – July 14, 1863* (El Dorado Hills, CA: Savas Beatie, 2020), 38.
15. Gottfried, *The Maps of the Cavalry in the Gettysburg Campaign*, 70, 88.
16. John S. Mosby, "The Confederate Cavalry in the Gettysburg Campaign," *Battles & Leaders of the Civil War*, vol. 3, 252; James Longstreet, *From Manassas to Appomattox* (Bloomington, IL: Indiana University Press, 1960), 346-47; Alan T. Nolan, "R. E. Lee and July 1 at Gettysburg," in *Lee the Soldier*, 484-87.

Chapter 6: The Two Campaigns Begin
1. *OR* 19, pt. 2, 590.
2. Hartwig, *To Antietam Creek*, 91-92; Alexander Hunter, "A High Private's Account of the Battle of Sharpsburg," *Southern Historical Society Papers*, vol. 12 (1884), 507; OR, 19, pt. 2, 169; Carman, *The Maryland Campaign of 1862*, vol. I, 86-87.
3. OR 19, pt. 2, 592-93; Joseph Harsh, *Sounding the Shallows: A Confederate Compendium for the Maryland Campaign of 1862* (Kent, OH: Kent State University Press, 2000), 155-56; Henry Robinson Berkeley, *Four Years in the Confederate Artillery: The Diary of Private Henry Robinson Berkeley* (Richmond, VA: Virginia Historical Society, 1991), 27; Wise, *The Long Arm of Lee*, 278- 79. Col. Thomas Munford and his 2nd Virginia Cavalry screened the army's march to Leesburg. He entered the town on September 2 and pushed out Union cavalry posted there. Munford then continued northeast to Edward's Ferry, and then Poolesville, Maryland, to reconnoiter and secure the opposite side of the Potomac River. Schildt, *Roads to Antietam*, 14; John Devine, ed., *Loudoun County and the Civil War* (Leesburg, VA: Loudoun County Civil War Commission, 1961), 41. A total of nine Confederate batteries were left behind at Leesburg. They traveled to Winchester to refit. Wise, *The Long Arm of Lee*, 279.
4. *Mobile Register and Advertiser*, September 28, 1862; Hartwig, *To Antietam Creek*, 94.
5. Harsh, *Taken at the Flood*, 83-84.
6. OR 19, pt. 1, 25, 36, 38-39, 117-18, 124; OR 19, pt. 2, 172-81, 208-09; OR 51, pt. 1, 785-88; Hartwig, *To Antietam Creek*, 163-65; Fishel, *The Secret War for the Union*, 211. Pleasonton was spread thin as he was ordered to undertake numerous tasks with few troopers. These included reconnoitering, guarding the fords, and screening the Union army when it began moving north. Carman, *The Maryland Campaign*, vol. 1, 165 (n. 5).
7. OR 19, pt. 1, 814-15; OR 19, pt. 2, 186; Crowninshield, *A History of the First Massachusetts Cavalry*, 71-72.

8. Henry Douglas, *I Rode with Stonewall: War Experiences of the Youngest Member of Jackson's Staff* (Chapel Hill, NC: University of North Carolina Press, 1951), 147; William Allen, *Army of Northern Virginia in 1862* (Dayton, OH: Morningside House, 1984), 326; Jubal Early, *War Memoirs, Autobiographical Sketch and Narrative of the War Between the States*, Frank E. Vandiver, ed. (Bloomington, IN: Indiana University Press, 1960), 135; Carman, *The Maryland Campaign*, vol. I, 90; John H. Worsham, *One of Jackson's Foot Cavalry, His Experiences and What he Saw during the War, 1861-1865* (Richmond, VA: Jackson, TN: McCowat-Mercer, 1964), 82; OR 27, pt. 1, 952. The rocky Potomac River substrate played havoc on the men's feet, particularly those without shoes. A North Carolina private recalled reaching the Maryland shore "worn out, wet and completed disgusted by our first impression of Maryland." Thomas D. Boone, *History of Company F, 1st North Carolina Infantry*, 36 (GNMP).

9. OR 19, pt. 2, 593-94, 595. Joseph Harsh clarified the difference between "Special Orders" and "General Orders." "Special Orders were usually employed to direct individual or small groups of persons or units and were circulated in separate parts on a need-to-know basis, whereas General Orders were promulgated when the subject matter applied to the whole or large segments of the army and usually appeared in complete form." Harsh, *Taken at the Flood*, 94.

10. OR 19, pt. 1, 520, 522; OR 19, pt. 2, 188-89, 208; Harsh, *Taken at the Flood*, 98-99. When McClellan learned of the enemy crossing, he encouraged General-in-Chief Halleck to withdraw the Harpers Ferry garrison, or at the very least, move it to Maryland Heights. McClellan would later write that the suggestion was met with "ill-concealed contempt." McClellan, *McClellan's Own Story*, 550.

11. *Report of Lewis H. Steiner, M.D., Inspector of the Sanitary Commission, Containing a Diary Kept During the Rebel Occupation of Frederick, MD and Account of the Operations of the U.S. Sanitary Commission during the Campaign in Maryland, September, 1862* (New York: Anson D. F. Randolph, 1862), 8-9

12. Schildt, *Roads to Antietam*, 21-22; *Report of Lewis H. Steiner*, 8-9; OR 19, pt. 2, 596-98, 600-01; Hartwig, *To Antietam Creek*, 108-11.

13. OR 19, pt. 2, 191-193, 196, 204; OR 19, pt. 1, 25, 38; Hartwig, *To Antietam Creek*, 170; Fishel, *The Secret War for the Union*, 213-14.

14. Schildt, *Roads to Antietam*, 34, 44; *Report of Lewis H. Steiner*, 9; OR 19, pt. 2, 601-02; Fishel, *The Secret War for the Union*, 213. Lee had hoped to enlist ex-Governor Enoch Lowe in his efforts to convince Maryland to cooperate with his army. Lowe was living in Richmond at the time and made his way toward the army but was not able to arrive in a timely manner and Lee realized "the citizens were embarrassed as to the intentions of the army, I determined to delay no longer in making known our purpose," so he released the proclamation. OR 19, pt. 2, 605

15. Schildt, *Roads to Antietam*, 34, 44; OR 19, pt. 2, 596-97, 601-02; Carman, *The Maryland Campaign*, vol. I, 106-08; *New York Herald*, September 13, 1862; *The Philadelphia Public Ledger*, September 13, 1862; John Esten Cooke, *Life of*

Stonewall Jackson (n.p.: Hansebooks, 2017), 127-28; Hartwig, "Robert E. Lee and the Maryland Campaign," 337-38; Harsh, *Sounding the Shallows*, 158. Ex. Gov. Enoch Lowe explained that the cold reception to Lee's army by Marylanders was the result of their not knowing the intent of the raid in advance. *Richmond Dispatch,* October 1, 1862.
16. OR 19, pt. 2, 203, 204, 215.
17. OR 19, pt. 2, 216, 217.
18. Hartwig, *To Antietam Creek*, 141; Carman, *The Maryland Campaign*, vol. I, 149-50.
19. OR 19, pt. 2, 211.
20. Freiheit, *Boots and Saddles*, 168; Chris J. Hartley, *Stuart's Tarheels* Chris J. Hartley, *Stuart's Tarheels: James B. Gordon and His North Carolina Cavalry* (Baltimore, MD: Butternut & Blue, 1996), 126-127. It was also called the "Moonlight and Roses Ball."
21. Bradley M. Gottfried, *Roads to Gettysburg: Lee's Invasion of the North, 1863* (Shippensburg, PA: White Mane Publishing Company, 2001), 6-9; OR 27, pt. 1, 30; OR 27, pt. 2, 859-60; OR 27, pt. 3, 859.
22. Coddington, *The Gettysburg Campaign*, 50-51, 101-02.
23. Guelzo, *Gettysburg: The Last Invasion*, 50; Basler, ed., *The Collected Works of Abraham Lincoln*, vol. 6, 257; OR 27, pt. 1, 31.
24. Gottfried, *Roads to Gettysburg*, 21-22; OR 27, pt. 1, 31-33; OR 27, pt. 3, 8, 868-69.
25. OR 27, pt. 1, 33-24, 35, 41; OR 27, pt. 2, 92, 188-89, 546; OR 27, pt. 3, 48-49, 54, 55, 233; Gottfried, *Roads to Gettysburg*, 33-39; Nye, *Here Come the Rebels!*, 70-72; Donald C. Pfanz, *Richard S. Ewell: A Soldier's Life* (Chapel Hill, NC: The University of North Carolina Press, 1998), 281; Samuel Pickens Diary, June 11, 1863 entry (Pickens Papers, University of Alabama).
26. OR 27, pt. 2, 440, 546-47; Pfanz, *Richard S. Ewell, 282*
27. OR 27, pt. 3, 69, 72, 78-79;
28. Guelzo, *Gettysburg: The Last Invasion*, 81.
29. A. M. Gambone, *Major-General Darius Nash Couch: Enigmatic Valor* (Baltimore, MD: Butternut and Blue, 2000), 138; OR 27, pt. 3, 76-77, 78-80. Lincoln actually created two departments: The Department of the Susquehanna, east of Johnstown Pennsylvania and the Laurel Hill Mountains, and the Department of the Monongahela, on the west side of them. Stanton and Curtin finally settled on a compromise: the new recruits would be paid, equipped, and trained by the Federal Government but would be kept on a standby basis so Curtin could call upon them when needed. Edwin Coddington believed this (and other) agreements were the forerunners of the National Guard. Edwin B. Coddington, "Pennsylvania Prepares for Invasion, 1863," *Pennsylvania History*, vol. 31, no. 3 (April 1964), 158.
30. Richard J. Sommers, *Challenges of Command in the Civil War: Generalship, Leadership, and Strategy at Gettysburg, Petersburg, and Beyond* (El Dorado Hills, CA: Savas Beatie, 2018), 146-47; Bradley M. Gottfried, *The Maps of Gettysburg: An Atlas of the Gettysburg Campaign, June 3 – July 13, 1863* (El Dorado Hills, CA: Savas Beatie, 2007), 8.
31. OR 19, pt. 1, 211, 219; OR 27, pt. 1, 48.

Chapter 7: The Campaigns in Midstream

1. OR 19, pt. 2, 226-27; Carman, *The Maryland Campaign*, vol. 1, 174.
2. Hartwig, *To Antietam Creek*, 123-24.
3. R. L. Dabney, *Life of Lieut.-Gen. Thomas J. Jackson*. 2 vols. (London: James Nisbet & Co., 1866) vol. 2, 302; OR, 19, pt. 2, 594, 603; Lafayette McLaws, "The Capture of Harpers Ferry," *Philadelphia Weekly Press*, September 5, 1888; Longstreet, *Manassas to Appomattox*, 201-02. According to Jackson's biographer, Lee's aggressive lieutenant balked at the audaciousness of the plan, advocating instead on dealing with McClellan first and then taking on the Harpers Ferry garrison. Lee won over Jackson and the details were fleshed out. Dabney, *Life of Lieut.-Gen. Thomas J. Jackson*. vol. 2, 302; Hartwig, "Robert E. Lee and the Maryland Campaign," 338-39.
4. OR 19, pt. 2, 209-11, 220; Hartwig, *To Antietam Creek*, 171-73, 182. George B. McClellan, *The Civil War Papers: Selected Correspondence, 1860-1865*, Stephen W. Sears, ed., (New York: Ticknor & Fields, 1989), 44. McClellan would worry about a second column of Confederates until September 13 when he was handed a copy of Lee's Special Orders No. 191. Hartwig, *To Antietam Creek*, 708 (n. 53).
5. OR 19, pt. 2, 228, 230, 247.
6. Hartwig, *To Antietam Creek*, 126.
7. Lafayette McLaws, "The Capture of Harpers Ferry," *Philadelphia Weekly Press*, September 12, 1888.
8. OR 19, pt. 2, 239, 241; OR 51, pt. 1, 805-809; Carman, *The Maryland Campaign*, vol. 1, 175. The three wings would travel over three major routes to Frederick: the Right Wing traveled on what is now Route 97, which put it between Frederick and Baltimore; the Left Wing moved along the Potomac River in what is now roughly Rt. 28; the Center Wing traveled roughly the route of I-270 from Washington to Frederick. Schildt, *Roads to Antietam*, 34.
9. Charles W. Turner, ed., *Captain Greenlee Davidson, C.S.A.: Diary and Letters, 1851 – 1863* (Verona, VA: McClure Press, 1975, 49; Hartwig, *To Antietam Creek*, 225-26, 234-35.
10. Gallagher, ed., *Lee: The Soldier*, 8; OR 19, pt. 1, 145, 839, 885
11. OR 19, pt. 2, 253-55, 277; Hartwig, *To Antietam Creek*, 195-96. The 120,000 figure came from Pennsylvania Gov. Curtin who wrote to McClellan on September 10, He attached a note from a trusted clergyman: "One of my elders, a reliable man, traveled 7 miles through their camps on Sunday. Their force around Frederick is not less than 120,000 men, and the part under Lee had not joined that army." Curtin continued that "their whole army in Maryland would exceed 200,000 men, and their intention was to march either upon Harrisburg or Baltimore, probably the latter." McClellan was inclined to believe the inflated figure of 120,000, but not the 200,000 as he did not believe there were many troops left in Virginia. OR 19, pt. 2, 247-49.
12. OR 19, pt. 1, 43, 44.
13. Hartwig, *To Antietam Creek*, 192-93; Carman, *The Maryland Campaign*, vol. 1, 176-80; OR 19, pt. 2, 249.
14. Mills, *Through Blood and Fire*, 26; John Vautier journal (USAHEC); Isaac Hall, *History of the Ninety-Seventh Regiment, New York Volunteers in the War for the Union* (Utica, NY: L. C. Childs, 1890), 83.

15. Turner, ed., *Captain Greenlee Davidson, C.S.A.*, 47-48; James F. L. Caldwell, *The History of a Brigade of South Carolinians* (Dayton, OH: Morningside Press, 1984), 41; James Kirkpatrick Diary, September 11, 1862 entry (University of Texas, Austin); Carman, *The Maryland Campaign*, vol. 1, 109; OR 19, pt. 2, 602.

16. OR 19, pt. 2, 267-69, 252-53, 269, 273-74. Gov. Curtin issued a call for 50,000 volunteers. Carman, *The Maryland Campaign*, vol. 1, 111.

17. OR 19, pt. 2, 268-69.

18. OR 19, pt. 1, 523-24, 912-13; Turner, ed., *Captain Greenlee Davidson*, 49; Caldwell, *The History of a Brigade of South Carolinians*, 42; McLaws, "The Capture of Harpers Ferry."

19. OR 19, pt. 1, 26-27, 814-19; OR 19, pt. 2, 267, 270; Hartwig, *To Antietam Creek*, 196-203.

20. OR 19, pt. 276-77.

21. OR 27, pt. 1, 38, 39-40; OR 19, pt. 2, 613; OR 27, pt. 3, 888; Longstreet, "Lee's Invasion of Pennsylvania," vol. III, 249; Gottfried, *Roads to Gettysburg*, 46- 65; Ryan, *Spies, Scouts, and Secrets in the Gettysburg Campaign*, 172. O. B. Curtis, *History of the Twenty-Fourth Michigan of the Iron Brigade, Known as the Detroit and Wayne County Regiment* (Gaithersburg, MD: Olde Soldier Books, Inc., 1988), 147. I Corps was at Kettle Run, the III and V Corps were at Catlett's Station, the VI Corps at Potomac Creek, the XI Corps at Centreville and the XII Corps at Dumfries.

22. OR 27, pt. 1, 39.

23. Ryan, *Spies, Scouts, and Secrets in the Gettysburg Campaign*, 175-81; OR 27, pt. 1, 42; Nye, *Here Come the Rebels*, 108-123; Gottfried, *Roads to Gettysburg*, 66-78.

24. OR 27, pt. 1, 43; Nye, *Here Come the Rebels*, 108-123; Gottfried, *Roads to Gettysburg*, 66-78.

25. OR 27, pt. 3, 97, 113, 134.

26. OR 27, pt. 3, 136-37.

27. OR 27, pt. 1, 1077-79.

28. OR 27, pt. 1, 138-39.

29. OR 27, pt. 1, 145.

30. OR 27, pt. 1, 45-47; Marszalek, *Commander of All Lincoln's Armies*, 173-74.

31. OR 27, pt. 1, 45, 47-8; OR 27, pt. 2, 687, 719-20; Gottfried, *Roads to Gettysburg*, 79-86; Jacob Hoke, *The Great Invasion* (New York: Thomas Yoseloff, 1959), 105-07; OR 27, pt. 3, 896; Anders, *Henry Halleck's War*, 444; Nye, *Here Come the Rebels*, 259-65; Coddington, *Gettysburg Campaign*, 147.

32. OR 27, pt. 3, 900-01; OR 19, pt. 1, 48, 49; Gottfried, *Roads to Gettysburg*, 87-95.

33. OR 27, pt. 1, 50, 52, 53; OR 27, pt. 3, 905; Gottfried, *Roads to Gettysburg*, 96-108; Edwin B. Houghton, *Campaigns of the Seventeenth Maine* (Portland, ME: Short & Loring, 1866), 75.

34. OR 27, pt. 1, 615, 911.

35. OR 27, pt. 1, 54; OR 27, pt. 3, 246, 249, 906, 912-13; Gottfried, *Roads to Gettysburg*, 109-20; John O. Casler, *Four Years in the Stonewall Brigade* (Marietta, GA: Continental Book Col, 1951), 168, 170.

Chapter 8: The Two Armies Approach the Battlefield

1. David Hunter Strother, "Personal Recollections of the War," *Harper's Magazine*, June 1866, 275; OR 19, pt. 1, 209.

2. Silas Colgrove, "The Finding of Lee's Lost Order," *Battles & Leaders of the Civil War*, vol. 2, 603; Wilber D. Jones, *Giants in the Cornfield: The 27th Indiana Infantry* (Shippensburg, PA: White Mane Publishing, 1997), 229-233; OR 19, pt. 1, 45; Hartwig, *To Antietam Creek*, 282-86.

3. OR 19, pt. 1, 45; McClellan, *Civil War Papers*, 399; Vermilya, "Perceptions, Not Realities?" 42.

4. Gallagher, ed., *Lee: The Soldier*, 8; Hartwig, *To Antietam Creek*, 298-99; OR 19, pt. 2, 287-88. Former Confederate officer William Allen interviewed Robert E. Lee in his office on February 15, 1868 on a variety of topics. One was the Maryland Campaign. The loss of Special Order No. 191 was a blow to his army's chances for success, Lee opined. "Had the Lost Dispatch not been lost, and had McClellan continued his cautious policy for two or three days longer, I (Lee) would have had all my troops reconcentrated on MD. side, stragglers up, men rested & I intended then to attack McClellan, hoping the best results from state of my troops & those of the enemy." Gallagher, ed., *Lee: The Soldier*, 8.

5. OR 19, pt. 2, 287.

6. Gallagher, ed., *Lee: The Soldier*, 8; Hartwig, *To Antietam Creek*, 298-99; OR 19, pt. 2, 287-88; Longstreet, *Manassas to Appomattox*, 220.

7. OR 19, pt. 1, 951; Douglas Southall Freeman, *Lee's Lieutenants*, 3 vols. (New York: Charles Scribner's Sons, 1942) vol. 2, 196; Freeman, *R. E. Lee*, vol. 2, 373-75; Hartwig, *To Antietam Creek*, 480-84; OR 51, pt. 2, 618-19; Carman, *The Maryland Campaign*, vol. 1, 381-83.

8. Randolph A. Shotwell, *The Papers of Randolph A. Shotwell*, J. G. De Roulac Hamilton, ed., 2 vols. (Raleigh, NC: North Carolina Historical Commission, 1929-1931), vol. 1, 340; Carman, *The Maryland Campaign*, vol. 1, 387-89; R. T. Coles, *From Huntsville to Appomattox: R. T. Coles' History of the 4th Regiment, Alabama Volunteer Infantry*, Jeffrey D. Stocker, ed. (Knoxville, TN: University of Tennessee Press, 1996), 64. Colquitt's and Rodes' brigades led D. H. Hill's division to Boonsboro and then to Sharpsburg. Carman, *The Maryland Campaign*, vol. 1, 387.

9. Carman, *The Maryland Campaign*, 395-99, 402, 403-05; OR 19, pt. 2, 296; Jacob Dolson Cox, *Military Reminiscences of the Civil War*, 2 vols. (New York: Charles Scribner's Sons, 1900), vol. 1, 297; OR 19, pt. 1, 308; McClellan, *McClellan's Own Story*, 588-89

10. Strothers, "Personal Recollections," 280; OR 51, pt. 1, 836.

11. A. L. Long, *Memoirs of Robert E. Lee* (Secaucus, NJ: Blue and Gray, 1983), 216; OR 19, pt. 1, 140, 951; OR 27, pt. 1, 829-30; Carman, *The Maryland Campaign of 1862*, vol. I, 259-60.

12. Julius White, "The Capitulation of Harpers Ferry," *Battle & Leaders of the Civil War*, vol. 2, 613; William M. Luff, "March of the Cavalry from Harpers Ferry September 14, 1862," *Illinois MOLLUS* (Chicago: A. C. McClurg and Co., 1894), vol. 2, 33-34, 40-5.

13. OR 19, pt. 2, 311, 321.

14. OR 27, pt. 3, 913-15; Gottfried, *The Maps of the Cavalry in the Gettysburg Campaign*, 70.

15. OR 27, pt. 1, 54, 55.

16. OR 27, pt. 3, 264.

17. OR 27, pt. 3, 924-25.

18. Gottfried, *Roads to Gettysburg*, 127-32; Ryan, *Spies, Scouts, and Secrets in the Gettysburg Campaign*, 225.

19. OR 27, pt. 1, 55; Gottfried, *Roads to Gettysburg*, 133-39.
20. OR 27, pt. 3, 933-35; Gottfried, *Roads to Gettysburg*, 140-148.
21. Coles, *From Huntsville to Appomattox*, 102; Nye, *Here Come the Rebels*, 272-73; M. Jacobs, *Notes on the Rebel Invasion of Maryland and Pennsylvania and the Battle of Gettysburg* (Philadelphia: J. B. Lippincott & Company, 1864), 15; OR 27, pt. 2, 366, 465, 613, Hoke, *The Great Invasion*, 171.
22. OR 27, pt. 3, 314, 335, 336, 344-47; Schildt, *Roads to Gettysburg*, 195.
23. OR 27, pt. 3, 347-48.
24. OR 27, pt. 3, 344, 345, 347, 355-58, 942-43; Charles Bachelor letter, copy in the Brake Collection, USAMHI; OR 27, pt.1, 59-60; Coddington, *The Gettysburg Campaign*, 99; Gottfried, *Roads to Gettysburg*, 162-75.
25. Hardie purportedly told Meade. "I have come to give [you] trouble." Meade, *The Life and Letters of George Gordon Meade*, vol. 2, 1-2, 11-12; Freeman Cleaves, *Meade of Gettysburg* (Norman, OK: University of Oklahoma Press, 1960), 126; Brown, *Meade at Gettysburg*, 43-44, 56-57.
26. OR 27, pt. 1, 61-62, 358, 466-67, 613; OR 27, pt. 3, 378, 942-43; Bill Hyde, *The Union Generals Speak: the Meade Hearings on the Battle of Gettysburg* (Baton Rouge, LA: Louisiana State University Press, 2003), 103; Robert Underwood Johnson and Clarence Clugh Buell, *Battles and Leaders of the Civil War*, 4 vols. (New York: Thomas Yoseloff, 1956), vol. 3, 243; Hoke, *The Great Invasion*, 238; Charles Marshall, "Events Leading Up to the Battle of Gettysburg," *Southern Historical Society Papers*, vol. 23 (1895), 226-27; James Longstreet, "Lee's Invasion of Pennsylvania," *Battles and Leaders of the Civil War*, vol. 3, 249-50.
27. OR 27, pt. 3, 401-02, 408, 409, 411, 943-94, OR 27, pt. 2, 215-16, 307, 467; Nye, *Here Come the Rebels*, 322; Coddington, *The Gettysburg Campaign*, 143-44; Brown, *Meade at Gettysburg*, 81; Gambone, *Major General Darius Nash Couch*, 147, 300-02.
28. Hoke, *The Great Invasion*, 204; OR 27, pt. 2, 358; 467, Henry Heth, *The Memoirs of Henry Heth* (Westport, CT: Greenwood Press, 1974), 173; Brown, *Meade at Gettysburg*, 92; OR 27, pt. 1, 68-69; OR 27, pt. 3, 414-15, 429, 432, 437-38; Schildt, *Roads to Gettysburg*, 405.
29. Nye, *Here Come the Rebels*, 325-26; OR 27, pt. 2, 266, 458-59, 461-67, 613, 696; OR 27, pt. 1, 482, 497, 500, 502, 531, 825; Hunt, "The Second Day at Gettysburg," 274.
30. OR 27, pt. 2, 266; Longstreet, *From Manassas to Appomattox*, 365-66; Gottfried, *Roads to Gettysburg*, 220-23.

Chapter 10: The Preliminary Fights
1. National Park Service, *John Brown's Raid* (Washington, DC: U. S. Government Printing Office, 1974), 12-13; Hartwig, *To Antietam Creek*, 206-07.
2. Harsh, *Taken at the Flood*, 146; OR 12, pt. 3, 30-1; OR 12, pt. 2, 189, 765-68; OR 19, pt. 1, 533, 757; Stephen Ambrose, *Halleck: Lincoln's Chief of Staff* (Baton Rouge: Louisiana State University Press), 82-83; McClellan, *McClellan's Own Story*, 549-50. Miles commanded the 2nd U. S. Infantry prior to the war. He was one of only 22 colonels in the U. S. army prior to the war. In commanded a reserve division during the First Bull Run Campaign, but was rumored to be drinking, and although exonerated, was removed. He

was assigned to command the Railroad Brigade in late March 1862 with the responsibility of guarding a long stretch of the B & O Railroad. He established his headquarters at Harpers Ferry. George W. Cullum, *Biographical Register of the Officers and Graduates of the U.S. Military Academy, from 1802 to 1867*, 3 vols. (New York: D. Van Nostrand, 1879), vol. 2: 266-67; *Report of the Joint Committee on the Conduct of the War*, 29-39.

3. OR 19, pt. 1, 533, 691; OR 51, pt. 1, 784; Chester G. Hearn, *Six Years of Hell* (Baton Rouge, LA: Louisiana State University Press, 1996), 130-33; Hartwig, *To Antietam Creek*, 212-17.

4. Douglas, "Stonewall Jackson in Maryland," B & L, vol. 2, 622; OR 19, pt. 1, 524, 852, 913, 953. Gen. White's arrival at Harpers Ferry set up the unwanted conflict over command of the garrison since he had seniority over Miles. White sidestepped the problem by allowing Miles to remain in command.

5. OR, 19, pt. 1, 543-44, 537, 576, 614-15, 863; Dennis E. Frye, "Through God's Blessings," *North & South Magazine*, vol. 5, no. 7 (October 2002), 71; Wayne Mahood, "Some Very Hard Stories Were Told: The 126th New York Infantry at Harpers Ferry," *Civil War Regiments*, vol. 1, no. 4 (1991)," 32; Carman, *The Maryland Campaign*, vol. 1, 238-39; William H. Nichols, *The Siege and Capture of Harpers Ferry by the Confederates, September, 1862* (Providence, RI: Rhode Island Soldiers and Sailors Historical Society, 1889), 26. A number of witnesses recalled hearing Miles give Ford discretionary orders to withdraw when he thought all was lost.

6. John G. Walker, "Jackson's Capture of Harpers' Ferry," *Battles & Leaders of the Civil War*, vol. 2, 608-09; OR, 19, pt. 1, 913, 953; Harsh, *Taken at the Flood*, 228-29; Carman, *The Maryland Campaign*, vol. 1, 242-43; Frye, "Through God's Blessings," 72; White, "The Capitulation of Harpers Ferry," 613.

7. OR, 19, pt. 1, 854, 913, 958; OR, 19, pt. 2, 607; James Dinkins, *1861 – 1865: By an Old Johnnie: Personal Recollections and Experiences in the Confederate Army* (Dayton: OH: Morningside Books, 1975), 54.

8. OR, 19, pt. 1, 854, 913, 951, 954, 958-59, 966, 980, 1,007, 1,111; OR, 19, pt. 2, 607; Carman, *The Maryland Campaign*, vol. 1, 270-71, 273, 245-57; Dennis Frye, "Drama between the Rivers: Harpers Ferry in the 1862 Maryland Campaign," in *Antietam: Essays on the 1862 Maryland Campaign*, Gary Gallagher, ed. (Kent, OH: Kent University press, 1989), 27; Harsh, *Taken at the Flood*, 273-74.

9. Carman, *The Maryland Campaign*, vol. 1, 254; Bradley M. Gottfried, *The Maps of Antietam: An Atlas of the Antietam (Sharpsburg) Campaign, Including the Battle of South Mountain September 2-20, 1862* (El Dorado Hills, CA: Savas Beatie, 2012), 104; OR, 19, pt. 1, 855-56, 951, 955, 980-81; Frye, "Through God's Blessing," 68, 74; Harsh, *Taken at the Flood*, 317; Douglas, *Stonewall Jackson in Maryland*, 606-07, 627; OR 51, pt. 2, 618-19; Caldwell, *The History of a Brigade of South Carolinians*, 43.

10. Harsh, *Taken at the Flood*, 285-86.

11. Longstreet, *From Manassas to Appomattox*, 220; Henry Thweatt Owen, "The Battle of South Mountain," Virginia Historical Society (Richmond, VA); Hartwig, *To Antietam Creek*, 339,

680; Bradley M. Gottfried, ed., *Brigades of Antietam* (Sharpsburg, MD: The Press of the Antietam Institute, 2021), 217. Owen believed the march to Fox's Gap began at 11:00 a.m., but Longstreet recalled it was just after dawn. Hartwig supported Owen's recollection.

12. Cox, *Military Reminiscences*, vol. 1, 280; Jacob D. Cox, "Forcing Fox's and Turner's Gap," *Battles & Leaders of the Civil War*, 586; Daniel Harvey Hill, "The Battle of South Mountain," *Battles & Leaders of the Civil War*, 561; OR 19, pt. 1, 1,019

13. Carman, *The Maryland Campaign*, vol. 2, 316-44; Rutherford B. Hayes, *Diary and Letters of Rutherford B. Hayes* (Freemont, OH: Ohio Historical Center, 1998), 199; Hill, "The Battle of South Mountain," 562; D. Scott Hartwig, "'My God Be Careful!' The Morning Fight at Fox's Gap," *Civil War Regiments*, vol. 5 (no. 3), 34-51; 34-51; OR 19, pt. 1, 462, 464, 469, 1, 032, 1,041-42, 1,046; Kurt Graham, "Death of a Brigade: Drayton's Brigade at Fox's Gap, September 14, 1862," http://www.angelfire.com/ga2/Phillips Legion/deathofabrigade.html; Calvin Leach Diary, Southern Historical Collection (University of North Carolina); *OR Suppl.*, vol. 3, 583

14. OR, 19, pt. 1, 267; Carman, *The Maryland Campaign*, vol. I, 345-63; Harrison J. Mills, *Chronicles of the Twenty-First Regiment New York Volunteers* (Buffalo, NY: 21st Veterans Association, 1887), 280; Samuel P. Bates, *History of the Pennsylvania Volunteers, 1861-5*. 5 vols., (Harrisburg, PA: B. Singerly, State Printer, 1869), vol. I, 369, 549; Hill, "The Battle of South Mountain," 271-72.

15. Carman, *The Maryland Campaign*, vol. I, 364-368; OR, 19, pt. 1, 252-53, 1,053; Alan T. Nolan, *The Iron Brigade: A Military History* (Lansing, MI: Historical Society of Michigan, 1983), 125-26; Alan T. Nolan and Marc Storch, "The Iron Brigade Earns its Name," *Blue and Gray Magazine*, vol. XXI, no. 6 (2004), 11-16.

16. OR, 19, pt. 1, 45.

17. OR 19, pt. 1, 858; Carman, *The Maryland Campaign*, vol. I, 300-301.

18. Carman, *The Maryland Campaign*, vol. I, 310-12; OR 19, pt. 1, 382-83, 387, 389; *Newark Daily Advertiser*, September 20, 1862; Gottfried, *Kearny's Own*, 72.

19. Carman, *The Maryland Campaign*, vol. I, 309.

20. OR 27, pt. 2, 43, 440; Charles S. Grunder and Brandon H. Beck, *The Second Battle of Winchester* (Lynchburg, VA: H. E. Howard, 1991), 24-30.

21. Grunder and Beck, *The Second Battle of Winchester*, 45; OR, 27, pt. 2, 47, 83, 547-48; L. Leon *Diary of a Tarheel Confederate Soldier* (Tocca, GA: The Confederate Reprint Co., 2014), 30-31.

22. Coddington, *The Gettysburg Campaign*, 89; Grunder and Beck, *The Second Battle of Winchester*, 51-52; OR 27, pt. 2, 49, 63, 68, 442, 517.

23. OR 27, pt. 1, 31-33; OR 27, pt. 3, 8; Starr, *The Union Cavalry*, vol. 1, 39; H. B. McClellan, *The Life and Campaigns of Major-General J.E.B. Stuart* (Boston: Houghton, Mifflin and Company, 1885), 294.

24. Robert F. O'Neill, *The Cavalry Battles of Aldie, Middleburg, and Upperville: Small but Important Riots, June 10 – 17* (Lynchburg, VA: H. E. Howard, Inc., 1993), 1- 171; Robert F. O'Neill, "Aldie, Middleburg, and Upperville,"

Gettysburg Magazine, no. 43 (July, 2010), 14- 46.
25. Ryan, *Spies, Scouts, and Secrets in the Gettysburg Campaign,* 213-14; Eric J. Wittenberg and J. David Petruzzi, "Corbit's Charge: Jeb Stuart Clashes with the 1st Delaware Cavalry at Westminister, Maryland, June 29, 1863," *Gettysburg Magazine,* no. 36 (January 2007), 9-16.

Chapter 11: The Final Marches to the Battlefield
1. Schildt, *Roads to Antietam,* 116-17; Hartwig, *To Antietam Creek,* 339.
2. Harsh, *Taken in the Flood,* 328; Carman, *The Maryland Campaign,* vol. II, 16-17; Hartwig, *To Antietam Creek,* 570; OR 19, pt. 1, 856, 857.
3. OR 51, pt. 1, 834-46; OR 19, pt. 1, 295; OR 19, pt. 2, 308; Hartwig, *To Antietam Creek,* 495-96.
4. OR, 19, pt. 1, 53; Harsh, *Taken in the Flood,* 306, 319-22; James Longstreet, "The Invasion of Maryland," *Battles & Leaders of the Civil War,* vol. II, 667;
5. Harsh, *Taken in the Flood,* 314;
6. Harsh, *Taken at the Flood,* 330-31; Hartwig, *To Antietam Creek,* 486; OR 19, pt. 1, 857-58.
7. Harsh, *Taken at the Flood,* 332-33; Von Borcke, *Memoirs,* vol. 1, 226; Blackford, *War Years with Jeb Stuart,* 148.
8. Carman, *The Maryland Campaign,* vol. 2, 20-27; OR 19, pt. 1, 41; OR 19, pt. 2, 307.
9. OR 27, pt. 2, 316, 366, 385, 424, 462, 504, 545; Eric Wittenberg, *The Devil's to Pay: John Buford at Gettysburg* (El Dorado Hills, CA: Savas Beatie, 2014), 47-48, 52-53.
10. Gottfried, *The Maps of Gettysburg,* 42; James L. Bowen, *History of the Thirty-Seventh Regiment, Mass., Volunteers in the Civil War of 1861- 1865* (Holyoke, MA: C. W. Bryan & Col., 1884), 174; Gottfried, *The Roads to Gettysburg,* 220-23.

Chapter 12: Battlefield Terrain
1. Carman, *The Maryland Campaign,* vol. 2, 1- 13.
2. Coddington, *The Gettysburg Campaign,* 331-32.

Chapter 13: Initial Encounters on the Battlefield Prior to the Battle
1. OR 19, pt. 1, 217; Carman, *The Maryland Campaign,* vol. 2, 27-29.
2. Harsh, *Taken at the Flood,* 326, 343-44; OR 19, pt. 1, 148.
3. OR 19, pt. 1, 268-69, 937; OR 51, pt. 1, 156; Carman, *The Maryland Campaign,* vol. 2, 32-37; Hartwig, *To Antietam Creek,* 621.
4. William C. Davis, *The Confederate General,* 7 vols. (Harrisburg, PA: National Historical Society, 1991), vol. V, 24-25; Bradley M. Gottfried, *Brigades of Gettysburg: The Union and Confederate Brigades at the Battle of Gettysburg* (New York: Da Capo, 2002), 604.
5. OR 19, pt. 1, 927.

Chapter 14: Battle Plans
1. Carman, *The Maryland Campaign,* vol. II, 49.
2. Harsh, *Taken at the Flood,* 344; Owen, *In Camp and Battle,* 139.
3. OR 19, pt. 1, 54; Harsh, *Taken at the Flood,* 344-45.
4. OR 19, pt. 1, 30.
5. OR 19, pt. 1, 55.
6. OR 19, pt. 1, 30, 55; Harsh, *Taken at the Flood,* 345-47; Rafuse, *McClellan's War,* 309-11.
7. Coddington, *The Gettysburg Campaign,* 359- 61; James Longstreet, "The

Mistakes of Gettysburg," *The Annals of the Civil War* (New York: Da Capo Press, 1994), 426-27; James Longstreet, "Lee in Pennsylvania," *The Annals of the Civil War* (New York: Da Capo Press, 1994), 421; Cory M. Pfarr, *Longstreet at Gettysburg: A Critical Reassessment* (Jefferson, NC: McFarland Press, 2019),41-45.
8. Jubal Early, "Causes of Lee's Defeat," *Southern Historical Society Papers*, vol. IV, 271-74; OR 27, pt. 2, 318-19, 446; Coddington, *The Gettysburg Campaign*, 363-65.
9. OR 27, pt. 2, 318-19, 350, 446; Coddington, *The Gettysburg Campaign*, 365-75;
10. OR 27, pt. 2, 308.
11. Coddington, *The Gettysburg Campaign*, 451; Brown, *Meade at Gettysburg*, 278-79, 284-85; Gibbon, *Recollections of the Civil War*, 144-45.
12. Stotelmyer, *Too Useful to Sacrifice*, 135-37.

Chapter 15: The First Phase of the Battles

1. Sears, *Lincoln's Lieutenants*, 378-80; Carman, *The Maryland Campaign of 1862*, vol. II, 43-44.
2. OR 19, pt. 1, 217-18; Carman, *The Maryland Campaign of 1862*, vol. II, 26.
3. Carman, *The Maryland Campaign of 1862*, vol. II, 39-40.
4. Harsh, *Taken at the Flood*, 364; Rufus R. Dawes, *Service with the Sixth Wisconsin Volunteers* (Madison, WI: The State Historical Society of Wisconsin, 1962), 87.
5. Dawes, *Service with the Sixth Wisconsin Volunteers*, 87-88; OR 19, pt. 1, 254; Carman, *The Maryland Campaign*, vol. II, 573, 593, 598.
6. John Vautier to John Gould, November 11, 1892 & December 5, 1892, Gould Papers; OR 51, pt. 1, 140.
7. Pharris D. Johnson, *Under The Southern Cross: Army Life with Gordon Bradwell* (Macon, GA: Mercer University Press, 1999), 89-90; Gregory White, *This Most Bloody & Cruel Drama: A History of the 31st Georgia Volunteer Infantry* (Baltimore, MD: Butternut & Blue, 1997), 49; Carman, *The Maryland Campaign*, vol. II, 57-62; OR 19, pt. 1, 968; Hall, *Ninety-Seventh Regiment*, 91-93; Carman, *Maryland Campaign*, vol. II, 58-60.
8. Carman, *The Maryland Campaign*, vol. II, 64, 65, 110; Terry L. Jones, *Lee's Tigers: The Louisiana Infantry in the Army of Northern Virginia* (Baton Rouge, LA: Louisiana State University Press, 1987), 129, 130; James Gannon. *Irish Rebels, Confederate Tigers: A History of the 6th Louisiana Volunteers* (Mason City, IA: Savas Publishing, 1998), 135-36; John Michael Priest, ed., *Captain James Wren's Diary: From New Bern to Fredericksburg* (Shippensburg, PA: White Maine Publishing Co., 1990), 73.
9. Carman, *The Maryland Campaign*, vol. II, 76-77; Dawes, *Service with the Sixth Wisconsin Volunteers*, 90-91; Lance J. Herdegen, *The Iron Brigade in Civil War and Memory: The Black Hats from Bull Run to Appomattox and Thereafter* (El Dorado Hills, CA: Savas Beatie, 2012), 251-54; Gibbon, *Personal Recollections*, 81-82. Nolan and Storch, "The Iron Brigade Earns Its Name," 20. Doubleday's division was actually composed of four brigades. In addition to Gibbon's, Phelps', and Patrick's making the charge, Col. William Hofmann's brigade was left behind along Hagerstown Pike.

10. OR 19, pt. 1, 1008, 1016-1017; Carman, *The Maryland Campaign*, vol. II, 67, 77-78; Thomas M. Rankin, *23rd Virginia Infantry* (Lynchburg, VA: H. E. Howard, Inc., 1985), 50.

11. Jerry W. Holsworth, "Uncommon Valor: Hood's Texas Brigade in the Maryland Campaign," *Blue & Gray Magazine*, August 1996, 16-19; Harsh, *Taken at the Flood*, 374; James Lile Lemon, *Feed Them the Steel: Being the Wartime Recollections of Captain James Lile Lemon, Co. A, 18th Georgia Infantry, CSA*, Mark H. Lemmon, ed., (n.p.: n.p., n.d), 34; Dawes, *Service with the Sixth Wisconsin Volunteers*, 91; Susannah J. Ural, *Hood's Texas Brigade* (Baton Rouge, LA: Louisiana State University, 2017), 124.

12. Holsworth, "Uncommon Valor," 20; Carman, *The Maryland Campaign*, vol. II, 93-103; James Casey, ed., "The Ordeal of Adoniram Judson Warner: His Minutes of South Mountain and Antietam," *Civil War History*, vol. xxvii, no. 3 (1982), 224-227; Joseph Gibbs, *Three Years in the Bloody 11th* (University Park, PA: The Pennsylvania State University Press, 2002), 182-84.

13. P. A. Work, "The 1st Texas Regiment of the Texas Brigade of the Army of Northern Virginia at the Battles of Boonsboro Pass or Gap and Sharpsburg or Antietam, MD in September 1862," copy at the ANB Library; Houston *Tri-Weekly Telegraph*, October 15, 1862. Unlike other regiments, the 1st Texas carried its regimental flag and a Confederate States banner. Both were captured in the Cornfield.

14. Carman, *The Maryland Campaign*, vol. II, 94-99; Steven R. Davis, "'. . . Like Leaves in an Autumn Wind': The 11th Mississippi Infantry in the Army of Northern Virginia," *Civil War Regiments*, vol. 2, no. 4 (1992), 288-89; Richard W. Iobst and Louis H. Manarin *The Bloody Sixth: The Sixth North Carolina Regiment Confederate States of America* (Raleigh, NC: North Carolina Confederate Centennial Commission, 1965), 95-96; Robert Eberly, Jr., *Bouquets from the Cannon's Mouth* (Shippensburg, PA: White Mane Publishing, 2005), 131; OR 19, pt. 1, 269-70, 938; OR 51, pt. 2, 150-54; Carman, *The Maryland Campaign*, vol. II, 107-109; Bates *Pennsylvania Volunteers*, vol. I, 850; Gibbs *Bloody 11th*, 183-85.

15. Carman, *The Maryland Campaign*, vol. II, 119-123, 122-23; Henry W. Thomas, *History of the Doles-Cook Brigade of the Army of Northern Virginia...* (Atlanta, GA: The Franklin Printing and Publishing Company, 1903), 470; *The Countryman* (Georgia), October 6, 1862; John Key to Ezra Carman, September 29, 1897; Williams, *From the Cannon's Mouth*, 125-26; Carman, *The Maryland Campaign of 1862*, vol. II, 115; OR 19, pt. 1, 484, 486-91; Alpheus Williams to Ezra Carman, May 16, 1877, NYPL; Bates, *Pennsylvania Volunteers*, vol. IV, 167.

16. Sears, *Lincoln's Lieutenants*, 381; Carman, *The Maryland Campaign*, vol. II, 616; Welsh, *Medical Histories of Confederate Generals*, 130; OR 19, pt. 1, 1043, 1023. The 6th Georgia with 78.4% losses vied with the 1st Texas (82.3%), although some believed the latter's losses were even greater. Carman, *The Maryland Campaign*, vol. II, 615; Bradley M. Gottfried, ed., *The Brigades of Antietam* (Sharpsburg, MD: The Press of the Antietam Institute, 2021), 297.

17. *OR* 19, pt. 1, 305-306310-312.; *National Tribune*, April 3, 1884; "Gen'l O.O. Howard's Personal Reminiscences of the War of the Rebellion." *National Tribune*, November 20, 188; Carman, *The Maryland Campaign*, vol. II, 207-08; Marion V. Armstrong, *Unfurl Those Colors! McClellan, Sumner & the Second Corps in the Antietam Campaign* (Tuscaloosa, AL: The University of Alabama Press, 2008), 191-92; Thomas K. Tate, *General Edwin Vose Sumner, USA* (Jefferson, NC: The McFarland Co., 2013), 171-72; Sgt. Jonathan Stowe, 15th Massachusetts Infantry, 2nd Corps diary entry, Sept. 17, 1862, *Civil War Times Illustrated Collection*, USAMHI; Carman, *The Maryland Campaign*, vol. II, 195; Joseph R. C. Ward, *History of the One-Hundred and Sixth Regiment Pennsylvania Volunteers, 1861-1865* (Philadelphia: Grant, Faires & Rogers, 1906), 90; Bates, *History of Pennsylvania Volunteers*, vol. 2, 701.

18. *OR* 19, pt. 1, 476, 505, 916, 920-21; Harsh, *Taken at the Flood*, 392-93; Carman, *The Maryland Campaign*, vol. II, 234, 306-21; Gottfried, *The Maps of Antietam*, 182-83; Lawrence Wilson, *Itinerary of the Seventh Ohio Volunteer Infantry, 1861-1864* (New York: The Neale Publishing Co., 1907), 211.

19. Wittenberg, *The Devil's to Pay*, 47-48, 52-53. J. David Petruzzi, "John Buford: By the Book," *American's Civil War*, vol. 18 no. 3 (July 2005), 24-27; John H. Calef, "Gettysburg Notes: The Opening Gun," *Journal of the Military Services Institute of the United States*, January/February 1907, 42-44.

20. Joseph Dickinson, "A Gettysburg Incident," *The Proceedings of the Buford Memorial Association* (New York: Privately printed, 1895), 23-25; Aaron B. Jerome, "Buford on Oak Hill," in J. Watts de Peyster, ed., *The Decisive Conflicts of the Late Civil War, or Slaveholders' Rebellion, Battles Morally, Territorially, and Militarily Decisive* (New York: McDonald and Co., Printers, 1867), 151-52; H. P. Moyer, *Seventeenth Regiment Pennsylvania Volunteer Cavalry or One Hundred and Sixty-Second in the Line of Pennsylvania Volunteer Regiments, War to Suppress the Rebellion, 1861- 1865* (Lebanon, PA: Sowers Printing Co., n.d.), 59.

21. Walter Clark, ed., *Histories of the Several Regiments and Battalions from North Carolina in the Great War, 1861-1865*, 5 vols. (Raleigh, NC: E. M. Uzzell, printer, 1901), vol. 5, 117; J. B. Turney, "The First Tennessee at Gettysburg," *Confederate Veteran* vol. 8 (1900), 535; *OR* 27, pt. 1, 927, 934; Longacre, *The Cavalry at Gettysburg*, 187-88; Albert Huntington, *8th New York Cavalry: Historical Paper* (Palmyra, NY: n.p., 1903), 14; *The National Tribune*, May 24, 1885.

22. *OR* 27, pt. 1, 646; W. H. Moon, "Beginning the Battle at Gettysburg," *Confederate Veteran*, vol. 33 (1925), 449; W. H. Bird, *Stories of the Civil War, Company C, 13th Regiment of Alabama Volunteers* (Columbiana, AL: n.p. n.d.), 7; Alan D. Gaff, "Here Was Made our Last and Hopeless Stand," *Gettysburg Magazine*, issue 2 (January 1990), 29.

23. Gottfried, *Brigades of Gettysburg*, 42-44, 616-17; Dawes, *Service with the Sixth Wisconsin*, 164-68; New York Monuments Commission for the Battlefields of Gettysburg and Chattanooga, *Final Report on the Battlefield of Gettysburg*, 3 vols. (Albany: NY: J. B. Lyon Company Printers, 1900), vol. 3, 1006.

24. *OR* 27, pt. 1, 702, 727; *OR* 27, pt. 2, 444-46, 552-53.

25. Harry W. Pfanz, *Gettysburg: The First Day* (Chapel Hill, NC: University of North Carolina Press, 2001), 161-75; John D. Vautier, "At Gettysburg," *Philadelphia Weekly Press*, November 10, 1886; George W. Grant, "The First Army Corps on the First Day at Gettysburg," *Minnesota MOLLUS*, vol. 5, 49; Berkeley, *Four Years in the Confederate Artillery*, 50; Gottfried, *Brigades of Gettysburg*, 70-72, 515-16, 528-30, 538-40.

26. *OR* 27, pt. 1, 758; Harry Pfanz, *Gettysburg—Culp's Hill and Cemetery Hill* (Chapel Hill, NC: The University of North Carolina Press, 2001), 92-93.

27. *OR* 27, pt. 268, 279; *OR* 27, pt. 2, 607, 642-643; Clark, *N.C. Regiments*, vol. 2, 343-44; vol. 3, 103-104;

28. *OR* 27, pt. 1, 704, 715, *OR* 27, pt. 2, 492; G. W. Nichols, *A Soldier's Story of His Regiment...* (Jesup, GA: n.p., 1898), 116.

29. *New York at Gettysburg*, vol. 3, 1,051; *OR* 27, pt. 1, 721, 729.

30. Octavus H. Tubbs letter, GNMP; Cyndi Dalton, *Sixteenth Maine Regiment: The Blanket Brigade* (Union, ME: Union Publishing Co., 1995), 134; Abner Ralph Small, *The Road to Richmond—The Civil War Memoirs of Major Abner R. Small of the 16th Maine*, (Berkeley, CA: University of California Press, 1959), 101; *OR* 27, pt. 1, 295; *OR* 27, pt. 2, 656-57, 661; Varina D. Brown, *A Colonel at Gettysburg and Spotsylvania* (Columbia, SC: State Co., 1931), 77.

31. *OR* 27, pt. 2, 607; David McIntosh, "Review of the Gettysburg Campaign by One Who Participated Therein," *Southern Historical Society Papers*, vol. XXXVII (January-December, 1909), 119.

32. *OR* 27, pt. 2, 317-18.

33. Pfanz, *Gettysburg: The First Day*, 336-39.

34. Busey and Martin, *Regimental Strengths and Losses at Gettysburg*, 125-27, 139-41, 284-93, 297-305.

Chapter 16: The Second Phase of the Battles

1. Carman, *The Maryland Campaign*, vol. II, 241-45; *OR* 19, pt. 1, 323, 1,037; Dyer, *A Compendium of the War of the Rebellion*, vol. I, 291.

2. *OR* 19, pt. 1, 332, 337, 1037; John B. Gordon, *Reminiscences of the Civil War* (New York: Charles Scribner's Sons, 1904), 87; Graham, "The Fifth Maryland Infantry at Antietam;" Carman Papers, NA-AS; William B. Styple, ed., *Writing and Fighting the Civil War: Soldier Correspondence to the New York Sunday Mercury* (Kearney, NJ: Belle Grove Publishing Company, 2000), 128-130.

3. Carman, *The Maryland Campaign*, vol. II, 251; *OR* 19, pt. 1, 327.

4. Carman, *The Maryland Campaign*, vol. II, 259, 271, 587; *OR* 19, pt. 1, 884-85; *OR Supplement*, vol. 3, 568; C. Irvine Walker, *The Life of Lieutenant General Richard Heron Anderson* (Charleston, SC: Art Publishing Col, 1917), 100; Thomas F. Galway, *The Valiant Hours: Narrative of "Captain Brevet," An Irish-American in the Army of the Potomac* (Harrisburg, PA: Stackpole, 1961), 40; William W. Chamberlaine, *Memoirs of the Civil War* (Washington, DC: Press of Byron S. Adams, 1912), 33; *A Historical Sketch of the Quitman Guards, Company E, Sixteenth Mississippi Regiment, Harris' Brigade: From its Organization in Holmsville...to the*

surrender of the Army of Northern Virginia (New Orleans, LA: Isaac T. Hinton, 1866), 34.

5. OR 19, pt. 1, 53-5, 281, 294-95; Carman, *The Maryland Campaign*, vol. II, 18, 172, 264, 266-67, 272; David Power Conyngham, *The Irish Brigade and its Campaigns* (New York: Fordham University Press, 1994), 305.

6. OR 19, pt. 1, 1037, 1038; Carman, *The Maryland Campaign*, vol. II, 279-80, 281, 283; Francis A. Walker, *History of the Second Army Corps in the Army of the Potomac* (New York: C. Scribner's Sons, 1886), 112-13; OR 19, pt. 1, 289; Charles A. Fuller, *Personal Recollections of the War of 1861...In the 61st New York Volunteer Infantry* (Sherburne, NY: News Job Printing House, 1906), 59.

7. Armstrong, *Unfurl Those Colors!* 246-47.

8. Carl Schurz, *Reminiscences of Carl Schurz*, 3 vols. (San Bernardino, CA: Elibron Classics, 2006), vol. 3, 20-21; OR 27, pt. 1, 27, 115, 608; Oliver O. Howard, *Autobiography of Oliver Otis Howard*, 2 vols., (New York: Baker and Taylor Co., 1907), vol. 1, 422-24; George Meade, *With Meade at Gettysburg* (Philadelphia: John C. Winston, 1930), 95; Shultz and Mingus, "Sunrise Hours at Gettysburg, July 2, 1863," *Gettysburg Magazine*, no. 56, 14, 22; Guelzo, *Gettysburg: The Last Invasion*, 221-23.

9. Coddington, *The Gettysburg Campaign*, 359-68.

10. William D. Hewitt, "The Confederate Deliberate Attack 5 P.M. July 1 to 8 P.M. July 2," in *The Most Shocking Battle I Have Ever Witness: The Second Day at Gettysburg*," Papers of the 2006 Gettysburg National Military Park Seminar (Gettysburg, PA: National Park Service, 2008), 22-24; Karlton D. Smith, "'To Consider Every Contingency:' Lt. Gen. James Longstreet, Capt. Samuel R. Johnston, and the Factors that Affected the Reconnaissance and Countermarch, July 2, 1863," in *The Most Shocking Battle I Have Ever Witness: The Second Day at Gettysburg,"* Papers of the 2006 Gettysburg National Military Park Seminar, 102-05, 109-12.

11. Pfanz, *Gettysburg: The Second Day*, 82-103, 124-48.

12. Coddington, *The Gettysburg Campaign*, 343-46.

13. Coddington, *The Gettysburg Campaign*, 381-84.

14. OR 27, pt. 1, 493; Charles H. Weygant, *History of the One Hundred and Twenty-Fourth Regiment, N.Y.S.V.* (Newburgh, NY: Journal Print House, 1877), 175, 176; Collier, *They'll Do to Tie to!* 140-41; OR 27, pt. 2, 407, 415.

15. OR 27, pt. 1, 592, 593, 651, 600-01, 623-25; John J. Pullen, *Twentieth Maine: A Volunteer Regiment in the Civil War* (Dayton, OH: Morningside House, 1997), 117-19; OR 27, pt. 2, 411, 413, 623; William C. Oates, *The War Between the Union and Confederacy and its Lost Opportunities* (New York: Neale Publishing Co., 1905), 217-222; John C. West, *A Texan in Search of a Fight* (Waco, TX: Press of J. S. Hill and Company, 1901), 94; Emerson Gifford Taylor, *Gouverneur Kemble Warren: The Life and Letters of an American Soldier, 1830-1882* (Gaithersburg, MD: Ron R. Van Sickle Military Books, 1988), 128-29. Soldiers had been detached to fill the men's canteens but they had not yet returned when the attack was launched.

16. George W. Verrill, "The Seventeenth Maine at Gettysburg and in the Wilderness," *Maine MOLLUS*,

vol. 1, 262-68; Jay Jorgensen, *Gettysburg's Bloody Wheatfield* (Shippensburg, PA: White Mane Publishing Company, 2002), 54-66; OR 27, pt. 1, 520, 610-11; Kevin E. O'Brien, "Hold Them with the Bayonet: deTrobriand's Brigade Defends the Wheatfield," *Gettysburg Magazine*, Issue 21 (July 1999), 84; Jay Jorgenson, "Anderson Attacks the Wheatfield," *Gettysburg Magazine*, Issue 14 (1996), 68-69; John L. Smith, *History of the 118th Pennsylvania Volunteers, Corn Exchange Regiment* (Philadelphia: J.L. Smith, Publisher, 1909), 244; Anonymous diary, 1st Michigan Folder, GNMP.

17. OR 27, pt. 1, 381, 386, 394; Joseph G. Bilby, *Remember Fontenoy! The 69th New York, Irish Brigade in the Civil War* (Hightstown, NJ: Longstreet House, 1995), 89; OR 27, pt. 2, 368; Augustus Dickert, *History of Kershaw's Brigade* (Newberry, SC: Elbert H. Hull Company, 1899), 241; Eric Campbell, "Caldwell Clears the Wheatfield," *Gettysburg Magazine*, Issue 3 (July 1, 1990), 37; Gottfried, *The Maps of Gettysburg*, 170-77.

18. Harry W. Pfanz, *Gettysburg: The Second Day* (Chapel Hill, NC: The University of North Carolina Press, 1987), 292, 294-95; OR 27, pt. 1, 645, 647, 649; Timothy J. Reese, *Sykes' Regular Infantry Division, 1861-1865* (Jefferson, NC: McFarland Publishing, 1990), 256.

19. OR 27, pt. 1, 574; Mac Wychoff, *A History of the Second South Carolina Infantry, 1861-1865* (Fredericksburg, VA: Sergeant Kirkland's Museum and Historical Society, 1994), 78-80; Martin A. Haynes, *History of the Second New Hampshire Regiment: Its Camps, Marches, and Battles* (Manchester, NH: Charles F. Livingston Printer, 1865), 171, 176.

20. William E. Loring, "Gettysburg," *National Tribune*, July 9, 1885; OR 17, pt. 1, 499, 502, 503, 504-505; John D. Bloodgood, *Personal Reminiscences of the War* (New York: Hunt and Eaton, 1893), 138-39; Edward R. Bowen, "Collis' Zouaves—The 114th Pennsylvania at Gettysburg," *Philadelphia Weekly Times*, June 22, 1887; J. S. McNeily, "Barksdale's Mississippi Brigade at Gettysburg," *Publications of the Mississippi Historical Society*, vol. 14 (1914), 236; Lafayette McLaws, "Gettysburg," *Southern Historical Society Papers*, vol. 7 (1879), 73; Frank E. Moran, "A Fire Zouave—Memoirs of a Member of the Excelsior Brigade," *National Tribune*, November 6, 1890.

21. OR 27, pt. 1, 543, 553-54; Cadmus Wilcox, "General C. M. Wilcox on the Battle of Gettysburg," *Southern Historical Society Papers*, vol. 6 (July – December, 1878), 99; OR 27, pt. 2, 631; Pfanz, *Gettysburg—The Second Day*, 368-75.

22. OR 27, pt. 1, 442-43, 451; Janet B. Hewett, Noah Andre Trudeau, and Bryce A. Suderow, eds., *Supplement to the Official Records of the Union and Confederate Armies*, 100 vols. (Wilmington, NC: Broadfoot Publishing Company, 1994), vol. 5, 163; Busy and Martin, *Regimental Strengths and Losses*, 39, 235; Pfanz, *Gettysburg—The Second Day*, 376.

23. William Lochren, "The First Minnesota at Gettysburg." Minnesota MOLLUS, vol. 3, 48-51; Robert W. Meinhard, "The First Minnesota at Gettysburg," *Gettysburg Magazine*, Issue 5 (July 1991), 82; OR 27, pt. 1, 475, 476; OR 27, pt. 2, 618; McNeily, "Barksdale's Mississippi Brigade at Gettysburg," 249; *New York at*

Gettysburg, vol. 2, 886, 906; Thomas L. Elmore, "the Florida Brigade at Gettysburg, *Gettysburg Magazine*, Issue 15 (July 1996), 50.
24. Coco, Gregory A. ed. *From Ball's Bluff to Gettysburg... And Beyond: The Civil War Letters of Private Roland E. Bowen, 15th Massachusetts Infantry 1861-1864*. Gettysburg, PA: Thomas Publications, 1994, 196-201; Frederick Fuger, "Cushing's Battery at Gettysburg," *Journal of the Military Service Institution of the United States*, vol. 41 (1907), 406-07; *Pennsylvania at Gettysburg*, vol. 1, 415, 550-51; Bradley M. Gottfried, "Wright's Charge at Gettysburg: Piercing the Union Line or Inflated Glory?" 77-79; OR 27, pt. 1, 267, 436, 472, 499, 559-60; OR 27, pt. 2, 626, 628; Gottfried, *Brigades of Gettysburg*, 99; George H. Scott, "Vermont at Gettysburg," *Proceedings of the Vermont Historical Society*, vol. 1 (1930), 65; Busey and Martin, *Regimental Strengths and Losses*, 129, 311.25. Pfanz, *Gettysburg—The Second Day*, 393; OR 27, pt.1, 653, 657, 662, 685; "Wofford's Georgia Brigade."26. OR 27, pt. 1, 714, 716, 718; OR 27, pt. 2, 280, 484,, 486; Pfanz, *Gettysburg: Culp's Hill and Cemetery Hill*, 237, 250-52, 255; Gottfried, *The Maps of Gettysburg*, 218-24; Jubal A. Early, *Autobiographical Sketch and Narrative of the War Between the States*, 75.27. OR 27, pt. 1, 773, 825-26, 847, 856, 860; Pfanz, *Gettysburg: Culp's Hill and Cemetery Hill*, 111-13, 211-13; OR 27, pt. 2, 506-10, 536, 538, 539; George K. Collins, *Memoirs of the 149th Regiment New York Volunteer Infantry* (Syracuse, NY: Printed Privately, 1891), 138-39.

Chapter 17: The Third or Final Phase of the Battles
1. Carman, *The Maryland Campaign of 1862*, 402-09; OR 19, pt. 1, 419, 424; OR 51, pt. 1, 844.
2. OR 19, pt. 1, 472, 473; 144; OR, 51, pt. 1, 161-165; Martin F. Schmitt, ed., *General George Crook: His Autobiography* (Norman, OK: University of Oklahoma Press, 1986), 97; OR 19, pt. 1, 472; Carman, *The Maryland Campaign*, vol. II, 412; John Amrine, *The National Tribune*, March 10, 1910; Cox, "Battle of Antietam," vol. II, 650-51; OR 19, pt. 1, 419; Cox, *Military Reminiscences*, 304-05.
3. Carman, *The Maryland Campaign*, vol. II, 415, 582; OR 19, pt. 1, 178, 443-44, 447; Lyman Jackson, *History of the Sixth New Hampshire in the War for the Union* (n.p.: n.p., 1891), 103-04; Carman, *The Maryland Campaign*, vol. II, 582; OR 19, pt. 1, 178, 443-44..
4. Carman, *The Maryland Campaign*, vol. II, 582; OR 19, pt. 1, 163, 178, 416-23, 428, 443-44; Theodore Fogle, "Bloodletting at Burnside Bridge." *America's Civil War*, September 2015, 18 Fogle,
5. Carman, *The Maryland Campaign of 1862*, 582; OR 19, pt. 1, 438.
6. Alexander Hunter, *Johnny Reb and Billy Yank* (New York: The Neale Publishing Company, 1905), 283-88; OR 19, pt. 1, 451, 453-54, 455, 905; Carman, *The Maryland Campaign*, vol. II, 435-36, 451, 453-56; Johnston, *The Story of a Confederate Boy in the Civil War*, 149-50; David Johnston to Ezra Carman, September 21, 1897, NA-AS; Alexander Hunter, "A High Private's Sketch of Sharpsburg," *Southern Historical Society Papers*, vol. XI, no. 1 (January, 1883), 14-18.

7. *OR* 19, pt. 1, 981. Two of Hill's brigades were not engaged at Antietam, and he claimed that only 2,000 men in the three other brigades actually saw action.
8. Carman, *The Maryland Campaign of 1862*, vol. II, 466-67, 473, 482,; *OR* 19, pt. 1, 991-92, 993-94, 996-97; Jacob Bauer to wife, September 20, 1862, copy at ANB Library. Caldwell, *The History of a Brigade of South Carolinians*, 46.
9. *OR* 19, pt. 1, 453-54, 456-57.
10. Carman, *The Maryland Campaign of 1862*, vol. II, 593, 598, 601, 611.
11. Carman, *The Maryland Campaign*, vol. II, 355-386; *OR* 19, pt. 1, 194, 200, 212, 239; Gottfried, ed., *The Brigades of Antietam*, 110.
12. *OR* 27, pt. 2, 308.
13. Terry Jones, ed., *Campbell Brown's Civil War: With Ewell and the Army of Northern Virginia* (Baton Rouge, LA: Louisiana State University Press, 2004). 222.
14. *OR* 27, pt. 1, 815, 817, 820, 824, 863, 864-65, 866,868; *OR* 27, pt. 2, 518, 568, 593, 601; Pfanz, *Gettysburg: Culp's Hill and Cemetery Hill*, 289, 348.; Alonzo H. Quint, *The Record of the Second Massachusetts* (Boston: James P. Walker, 1867), 180
15. Elwood Christ, *The Struggle for the Bliss Farm at Gettysburg, July 2nd and 3rd, 1863* (Baltimore, MD: Butternut & Blue, 1998), 55-87.
16. Longstreet, "Lee in Pennsylvania," 429; Longstreet, *From Manassas to Appomattox*, 385; Scotty Bowden and Bill Ward, *Last Chance for Victory: Robert E. Lee and the Gettysburg Campaign* (Cambridge, MA: Da Capo Press, 2003), 431-34.
17. Gottfried, *The Artillery of Gettysburg*, 195-208; Anthony W. McDermott and John E. Reilly, *A Brief History of the 69th Regiment, Pennsylvania Veteran Volunteers* (n.p.: n.p. n.d), 29 .
18. Bradley M. Gottfried, *Stopping Pickett: The History of the Philadelphia Brigade* (Shippensburg, PA: White Mane Publishing Co., 1999), 167-74.
19. Gottfried, *Brigades of Gettysburg*, 100-02, 166-67, 469-71; William Burns' Diary, July 3, 1863 entry, USAMHI.
20. Gottfried, *Brigades of Gettysburg*, 581, 587-88; Busey and Martin, *Regimental Strengths and Losses at Gettysburg*, 127, 129-30, 271, 297, 302, 307, 308.
21. Busey and Martin, *Regimental Strengths and Losses at Gettysburg*, 144-45, 315; Bradley M. Gottfried, *The Maps of the Cavalry in the Gettysburg Campaign* (El Dorado Hills, CA: Savas Beatie, 2020), 114-37.
22. Carman, *The Maryland Campaign of 1862*, vol. II, 582, 593, 598, 601, 611.
23. Gottfried, *The Artillery of Gettysburg*, 195; Johnson and Anderson, Jr., *Artillery Hell*, 77-81

Chapter 18: Lee Re-crosses the Potomac River
1. *Conduct of the War*, vol. 2, pt. 1, 627; William Franklin, "Notes on Crampton's Gap and Antietam," *Battles & Leaders of the Civil War*, vol. II, 597; *OR* 19, pt. 1, 65; Carman, *The Maryland Campaign of 1862*, vol. II, 501-04
2. Carman, *The Maryland Campaign of 1862*, vol. II, 504-05; *Richmond Times Dispatch*, December 20, 1896. Gen. Longstreet strenuously disagreed in calling it a "Council of War." He claimed he did meet with Lee the evening of September 17, but never did the army commander ask about the

condition of the troops as he was on the field and could observe them himself. James Longstreet to Ezra Carman, February 11, 1897, NYPL. Charles Marshall, Lee's aide, agreed with Longstreet. Charles Marshall to Ezra Carman, March 9, 1897, NYPL.
3. OR 19, pt. 1, 151.
4. Thomas A. McGrath, *Shepherdstown: The Last Clash of the Antietam Campaign, September 19-20, 1862* (Lynchburg, VA: Schroeder Publications, 2007), 50-80; Freeman, *Lee's Lieutenants*, vol. 2, 232-23; Douglas, *I Rode with Stonewall*, 181.
5. OR 19, pt. 1, 340, 346, 351, 361; OR 19, pt. 2, 331; OR 51, pt. 1, 853; McGrath, *Shepherdstown*, 92-101.
6. OR 19, pt. 1, 340, 982; McGrath, *Shepherdstown*, 117-19.
7. Gregory Acken, ed., *Inside the Army of the Potomac: The Civil War Experience of Captain Francis Adams Donaldson* (Mechanicsburg, PA: Stackpole Books, 1998), 133; Smith, *History of the Corn Exchange Regiment*, 59, 60-61, 81.
8. Stotelmyer, *Too Useful To Sacrifice*, 199-250.
9. Brown, *Meade at Gettysburg*, 307-11, 322-26, 327, 340; OR 27, pt. 1, 489, 916-17, 928, 939, 943, 970-71, 977, 993-94, 998, 1005-06; OR 27, pt. 3, 10; Hyde, *Union Generals* Speak, 128, 259-61; William Harrison Beach, *The First New York (Lincoln) Cavalry from April 19, 1861, to July 7, 1865* (New York: The Lincoln Cavalry Association, 1902), 269; Kent Masterson Brown, *Retreat from Gettysburg: Lee, Logistics, & the Pennsylvania Campaign* (Chapel Hill, NC: University of North Carolina Press, 2005), 72-74, 86, 188, 293-95; Alexander, *Fighting for the Confederacy*, 269-70; Hotchkiss, *Make Me a Map of the Valley*, 158, 159-60; Eric J.

Wittenberg, J. David Petruzzi, and Michael F. Nugent, *One Continuous Fight: The Retreat from Gettysburg and the Pursuit of Lee's Army of Northern Virginia, July 4 – 14, 1863* (El Dorado Hills, CA: Savas Beatie, 2008), 79-82, 160.
10. OR 27, pt. 1, 82-84. 988, 993-94, 998, 999, 1000
11. OR 27, pt. 1, 84-87.
12. A.A. Humphreys, *From Gettysburg to the Rapidan. The Army of the Potomac, July, 1863 to April, 1864* (New York: Charles Scribner's Sons, 1883), 6; OR 27, pt. 1, 89, 92, 146.
13. Brown, *Meade at Gettysburg*, 362-70; OR 27, pt. 1, 93-94.

Chapter 19: The Army Commanders and Their Commanders-in-Chief

1. McClellan, *McClellan's Own Story*, 613; Rafuse, *McClellan's War*, 334-35; OR 19, pt. 1, 68; Sears, *The Civil War Papers of George B. McClellan*, 475; Joseph Hartwell Barrett, *Abraham Lincoln and His Presidency*, 2 vols. (Cincinnati, OH: The Robert Clarke Co., 1904), vol. 2, 130.
2. OR 19, pt. 1, 10, 11; John Nicolay and John Hay, *Abraham Lincoln: A History*, 10 vols. (New York: Century Co., 1914), vol. VI, 175; McClellan to wife, October 2, 1862 in Sears, ed., *Civil War Papers of George B. McClellan*, 488; McClellan, *McClellan's Own Story*, 627-28.
3. Sears, ed., *The Civil War Papers of George B. McClellan*, 499; Rafuse, *McClellan's War*, 349-55; OR 19, pt. 2, 484-85; Stotelmyer, *Too Useful to Sacrifice*, 199-250.
4. Freeman, *R. E. Lee*, vol. 2, 414.
5. OR 19, pt. 2, 634.
6. *Washington Sunday Morning Chronicle*, July 5, 1863; J. R. T. Ettlinger and

Michael Burlinghame, eds., *Inside Lincoln's White House: The Complete Civil War Diary of John Hay* (Carbondale, ILL: Southern Illinois University Press, 1997), 61, 62.
7. Ettlinger and Burlinghame, eds., *Inside Lincoln's White House*, 63, 2, 63, 65; OR 27, pt. 1, 92; "Robert Todd Lincoln's Reminiscences, Given 5 January 1885," *in* An Oral History of Abraham Lincoln: John G. Nicolay's Interviews and Essays, *Michael Burlingame*, ed. (Carbondale, ILL: Southern Illinois University Press, 1996), 88, 153.
8. OR 27, pt. 1, 92-93; Basler, ed., *Lincoln's Collected Works*, vol. 6, 327-28; Brown, *Meade at Gettysburg*, 362-70.
9. Randolph H. McKim, *A Soldier's Recollections: Leaves from the Diary of a Young Confederate* (Washington, DC: Zenger Publishing, 1983), 182; Robert Garlick Hill Kean, *Inside the Confederate Government: The Diary of Robert Garlick Hill Kean,* Edward Younger, ed., (New York: Oxford University Press, 1957), 84; Douglas Southall Freeman and Grady McWhiney, *Lee's Dispatches: Unpublished Letters of General Robert E. Lee, C.S.A., to Jefferson Davis* (New York: Putnam, 1957), 109-111; OR 51, pt. 2, 752-53; Jack D. Welsh, *Medical Histories of Confederate Generals* (Kent, OH: Kent State University Press, 2013), 134-35.
10. OR 29, pt. 2, 640-41.

Chapter 20: Post-Campaign Events

1. Bell Irvin Wiley, *The Life of Billy Yank: The Common Soldier in the Union* (Baton Rouge, LA: Louisiana State University, 2008), 112; Worthington Chauncey Ford, ed., *A Cycle of Adams Letters 1861-1865*, 2 vols. (Boston: Houghton Mifflin Company, 1920), vol. I, 243; McPherson, *Battle Cry of Freedom*, 557-67.
2. Frank L. Owsley, *King Cotton Diplomacy: Foreign Relations of the Confederate State of America* (Chicago, IL: The University of Chicago Press, 1969), 351

Chapter 21: Final Thoughts

1. Charles A. Dana, *Recollections of the Civil War: With the Leaders at Washington and in the Field in the Sixties* (New York: D. Appleton and Co., 1913), 189-90; Regis de Trobriand, *Four Years with the Army of the Potomac* (Boston, MA: Ticknor & Co., 1889), 518-19.
2. Harsh, *Taken at the Flood*, 485; Longstreet, "Maryland," 673; Gallagher, ed., *Lee the Soldier*, 8, 347-48; Alexander, *Fighting for the Confederacy*, 146.
3. OR 27 (2), 318.
4. Harsh, *Taken at the Flood*, 484.
5. Ryan, *Spies, Scouts, and Secrets*, 142.
6. Taylor, *General Lee*, 125.
7. Busey and Martin, *Regimental Strengths and Losses at Gettysburg*, 125, 260; Antietam Battlefield Board (https://www.nps.gov/anti/learn/historyculture/casualties.htm)
8. Brig. Gen. Samuel Garland was killed at Fox's Gap on September 14, 1862

BIBLIOGRAPHY

Archival Sources

Antietam National Military Park Library
  Jacob Bauer to wife, September 20, 1862
  "The Signal Corps"
  P. A. Work, "The 1st Texas Regiment of the Texas Brigade of the Army of Northern Virginia at the Battles of Boonsboro Pass or Gap and Sharpsburg or Antietam, MD in September 1862."

Carman Papers, New York Public Library
  Graham, "The Fifth Maryland Infantry at Antietam."
  David Johnston to Ezra Carman, September 21, 1897
  John Key to Ezra Carman, September 29, 1897
  James Longstreet to Ezra Carman, February 11, 1897
  Charles Marshall to Ezra Carman, March 9, 1897
  Alpheus Williams to Ezra Carman, May 16, 1877

Center for American History
  William Ballinger Diary

Duke University
  Dudley Pendleton to Mama, May 7, 1862

Gettysburg National Military Park Library
  Anonymous diary, 1st Michigan Folder
  Thomas D. Boone, "History of Company F, 1st North Carolina Infantry."
  Octavus H. Tubbs letter

Gould Papers, Massachusetts Public Library
  John Vautier to John Gould, November 11, 1892 & December 5, 1892.

Library of Congress
  Edward Bates, "Remonstrance and notes."
  Cadmus Wilcox to John, September 26, 1862

Museum of the Confederacy
  Carnot Posey to wife, May 20, 1863
National Archives
  Abner Doubleday Report of Service, "Army Generals' Reports of Civil War Service."

United States Army Military History Institute (USAMHI)
  Charles Bachelor letter
  William Burns' Diary, July 3, 1863 entry, USAMHI.
  Jonathan E. Shipman to Friend Hubbard, September 14, 1862
  Sgt. Jonathan Stowe Diary
  John Vautier Journal

University of Alabama
  Samuel Pickens Diary

University of North Carolina
  Calvin Leach Diary

University of Texas (Austin, TX)
  James Kirkpatrick Diary

Virginia Historical Society
  William Pegram to sister, May 11, 1863
  Henry Thweatt Owen, "The Battle of South Mountain."

Washington and Lee College
  William Parker Diary

Newspapers

Houston Tri-Weekly Telegraph, October 15, 1862
Mobile Register and Advertiser, September 28, 1862
Newark Daily Advertiser, September 20, 1862
New York Herald, September 13, 1862
Richmond Dispatch, October 1, 1862
Richmond Times Dispatch, December 20, 1896
Richmond Whig, May 9, 1863
The Countryman (Georgia), October 6, 1862
The National Tribune, April 3, 1884, May 24, 1885

The Philadelphia Public Ledger, September 13, 1862
The Times, August 15, 1862; *New York Times*, February 11, 1862
Washington Sunday Morning Chronicle, July 5, 1863

Official Documents

Hewett, Janet B. Noah Andre Trudeau, and Bryce A. Suderow, eds. *Supplement to the Official Records of the Union and Confederate Armies*, 100 vols. Wilmington, NC: Broadfoot Publishing Company, 1994.

Report of the Joint Committee on the Conduct of the War, 38th Congress, 2nd Session. Washington: U. S. Printing Office, 1865.

U. S. Surgeon-General's Office. *The Medical & Surgical History of the War of the Rebellion*. 6 vols. Washington, Government Printing Office, 1870.

United States War Department, *The War of the Rebellion: A Compilation of the Official Records of the Union and Confederate Armies*, 128 volumes. Washington: U. S. Government Printing Office, 1880-1901.

Books

A Historical Sketch of the Quitman Guards, Company E, Sixteenth Mississippi Regiment, Harris' Brigade: From its Organization in Holmsville ...to the Surrender of the Army of Northern Virginia. New Orleans, LA: Isaac T. Hinton, 1866.

Acken, Gregory, ed. *Inside the Army of the Potomac: The Civil War Experience of Captain Francis Adams Donaldson.* Mechanicsburg, PA: Stackpole Books, 1998.

Adams, Ephraim Douglass. *Great Britain and the American Civil War.* 2 vols. New York: Longmans, Green and Co., 1925.

Ambrose, Stephen *Halleck: Lincoln's Chief of Staff.* Baton Rouge: Louisiana State University Press, 1962.

Anders, Curt. *Henry Halleck's War: A Fresh Look at Lincoln's Controversial General-in-Chief.* Indianapolis, IN: Guild Press, 1999.

Andrews, J. Cutler *The South Reports the Civil War.* Princeton, NJ: Princeton University Press, 1970

Alexander, Edward P. *Fighting for the Confederacy: The Personal Recollections of General Edward Porter Alexander.* Gary W. Gallagher, ed. Chapel Hill, NC: University of North Carolina Press, 1998.

Allen, William *Army of Northern Virginia in 1862.* Dayton, OH: Morningside House, 1984.

Armstrong, Marion V. *Unfurl Those Colors! McClellan, Sumner & the Second Corps in the Antietam Campaign.* Tuscaloosa, AL: The University of Alabama Press, 2008.

Barrett, Joseph Hartwell. *Abraham Lincoln and His Presidency.* 2 vols. Cincinnati, OH: The Robert Clarke Co., 1904.

Basler, Roy P., ed. *The Collected Works of Abraham Lincoln,* 9 vols. New Brunswick, NJ: Rutgers University, 1953-55.

Bates, Samuel P. *History of the Pennsylvania Volunteers, 1861-5.* 5 vols. Harrisburg, PA: B. Singerly, State Printer, 1869.

Beach, William Harrison. *The First New York (Lincoln) Cavalry from April 19, 1861, to July 7, 1865.* New York: The Lincoln Cavalry Association, 1902.

Benjamin, Charles Frederick. *Memoir of James Allen Hardie, Inspector General United States Army.* Washington, DC: n.p., 1877.

Berkeley, Henry Robinson. *Four Years in the Confederate Artillery: The Diary of Private Henry Robinson Berkeley.* Richmond, VA: Virginia Historical Society, 1991.

Bilby, Joseph G. *Remember Fontenoy! The 69th New York, Irish Brigade in the Civil War.* Hightstown, NJ: Longstreet House, 1995.

____. *Small Arms at Gettysburg: Infantry and Cavalry Weapons in America's Greatest Battle.* Yardley, PA: Westholme, 2008.

Bird, W. H. *Stories of the Civil War, Company C, 13th Regiment of Alabama Volunteers.* Columbiana, AL: n.p. n.d.

Blackford, W. W. *War Years with Jeb Stuart.* New York: Charles Scribner's Sons, 1945.

Bloodgood, John D. *Personal Reminiscences of the War.* New York: Hunt and Eaton, 1893.

Borcke, Heros von *Memoirs of the Confederate War of Independence.* 2 vols. Philadelphia: J. B. Lippincott & Co., 1867.

Bosbyshell, Oliver C. *Pennsylvania at Antietam.* Harrisburg: Antietam Battlefield Memorial Commission, 1906.

Bowden, Scotty and Bill Ward, *Last Chance for Victory: Robert E. Lee and the Gettysburg Campaign.* Cambridge, MA: Da Capo Press, 2003.

Bowen, James L. *History of the Thirty-Seventh Regiment, Mass., Volunteers in the Civil War of 1861-1865.* Holyoke, MA: C. W. Bryan & Col., 1884.

Brown, Kent Masterson. *Retreat from Gettysburg: Lee, Logistics, & the Pennsylvania Campaign.* Chapel Hill, NC: University of North Carolina Press, 2005.

____. *Meade at Gettysburg: A Study in Command.* Chapel Hill, NC: University of North Carolina Press, 2021.

Brown, Varina D. *A Colonel at Gettysburg and Spotsylvania.* Columbia, SC: State Co., 1931.

Busey, John W. and David G. Martin, *Regimental Strengths and Losses at Gettysburg*. Hightstown, NJ: Longstreet House, 1982.

Caldwell, James F. L. *The History of a Brigade of South Carolinians*. Dayton, OH: Morningside Press, 1984.

Carman, Ezra. *The Maryland Campaign of September 1862*, Thomas Clemens, ed. 3 vols. El Dorado Hills: Savas Beatie, 2010, 2012.

Casler, John O. *Four Years in the Stonewall Brigade*. Marietta, GA: Continental Book Co., 1951.

Chamberlaine, William W. *Memoirs of the Civil War*. Washington, DC: Press of Byron S. Adams, 1912.

Christ, Elwood. *The Struggle for the Bliss Farm at Gettysburg, July 2nd and 3rd, 1863*. Baltimore, MD: Butternut & Blue, 1998.

Clark, Walter ed., *Histories of the Several Regiments and Battalions from North Carolina in the Great War, 1861-1865*, 5 vols. Raleigh, NC: E. M. Uzzell, printer, 1901.

Cleaves, Freeman. *Meade of Gettysburg*. Norman, OK: University of Oklahoma Press, 1960.

Coco, Gregory A. ed. *From Ball's Bluff to Gettysburg... And Beyond: The Civil War Letters of Private Roland E. Bowen, 15th Massachusetts Infantry 1861-1864*. Gettysburg, PA: Thomas Publications, 1994.

Collins, George K. *Memoirs of the 149th Regiment New York Volunteer Infantry*. Syracuse, NY: Printed Privately, 1891.

Coddington, Edwin. *The Gettysburg Campaign: A Study in Command*. New York: Scribners, 1968.

Cole, Philip M. *Civil War Artillery at Gettysburg: Organization, Equipment, Ammunition, and Tactics*. New York: Da Capo, 2002.

Coles, R. T. *From Huntsville to Appomattox: R. T. Coles' History of the 4th Regiment, Alabama Volunteer Infantry*, Jeffrey D. Stocker, ed. Knoxville, TN: University of Tennessee Press, 1996.

Collier, Calvin L. *They'll Do To Tie To!: 3rd Ark. Infantry Regiment- CSA*. Little Rock, AR: Arkansas Civil War Centennial Commission, 1959.

Conyngham, David Power. *The Irish Brigade and its Campaigns*. New York: Fordham University Press, 1994.

Cooke, John Esten. *Life of Stonewall Jackson*. n.p.: Hansebooks, 2017.

Cox, Jacob Dolson. *Military Reminiscences of the Civil War*. 2 vols. New York: Charles Scribner's Sons, 1900.

Crowninshield, Benjamin W. *A History of the First Regiment of Massachusetts Cavalry Volunteers*. Boston: Houghton, Mifflin, 1891.

Croffut W. A. and John M. Morris. *The Military and Civil History of Connecticut During the War of 1861-1865*. New York: Ledyard Bill, 1868.

Cuffel, Charles A. *Durell's Battery in the Civil War.* Philadelphia: Craig, Finley & Co., 1900.

Cullum, George W. *Biographical Register of the Officers and Graduates of the U.S. Military Academy, from 1802 to 1867.* 3 vols. (New York: D. Van Nostrand, 1879.

Cunningham, H. H. *Doctors in Gray: The Confederate Medical Service.* Baton Rouge, LA: Louisiana State University Press, 1963.

Curtis, O. B. *History of the Twenty-Fourth Michigan of the Iron Brigade, Known as the Detroit and Wayne County Regiment.* Gaithersburg, MD: Olde Soldier Books, Inc., 1988.

Dabney, R. L. *Life of Lieut.-Gen. Thomas J. Jackson.* 2 vols. London: James Nisbet & Co., 1866.

Dalton, Cyndi. *Sixteenth Maine Regiment: The Blanket Brigade.* Union, ME: Union Publishing Co., 1995.

Daly, Louise Haskell. *Alexander Cheves Haskell: The Portrait of a Man.* Wilmington, NC: Broadfoot Publishing Co., 1989.

Dana, Charles A. *Recollections of the Civil War: With the Leaders at Washington and in the Field in the Sixties.* New York: D. Appleton and Co., 1913.

David, Carl L. *Arming the Union.* Port Washington, NY: Kennikat Press, 1973.

Davis, William C. *The Confederate General.* 7 vols. Harrisburg, PA: National Historical Society, 1991.

de Trobriand, Regis. *Four Years with the Army of the Potomac.* Boston, MA: Ticknor & Co., 1889.

Devine, John, ed. *Loudoun County and the Civil War.* Leesburg, VA: Loudoun County Civil War Commission, 1961.

Dickert, August. *History of Kershaw's Brigade.* Newberry, S.C.: Elbert H. Hull Company, 1899.

Dinkins, James. *1861 – 1865: By an Old Johnnie: Personal Recollections and Experiences in the Confederate Army.* Dayton: OH: Morningside Books, 1975.

Donaldson, Francis A. *Inside the Army of the Potomac.* J. Gregory Acken, ed. Harrisburg, PA: Stackpole Books, 1998.

Douglas, Henry. *I Rode with Stonewall: War Experiences of the Youngest Member of Jackson's Staff.* Chapel Hill, NC: University of North Carolina Press, 1951.

Dowdey, Clifford and Louis H. Manarin. *The Wartime Papers of R. E. Lee.* New York: Virginia Civil War Commissions, 1961.

Dyer, Frederick H. *A Compendium of the War of the Rebellion.* 3 vols. Des Moines, IA: The Dyer Publishing Company, 1908.

Early, Jubal. *War Memoirs, Autobiographical Sketch and Narrative of the War Between the States.* Frank E. Vandiver, ed. Bloomington, IN: Indiana University Press, 1960.

Eberly, Robert, Jr., *Bouquets from the Cannon's Mouth*. Shippensburg, PA: White Mane Publishing, 2005.

Ettlinger, J. R. T. and Michael Burlinghame, eds. *Inside Lincoln's White House: The Complete Civil War Diary of John Hay*. Carbondale, IL: Southern Illinois University Press, 1997.

Evans, Charles. *War of the Aeronauts*. Mechanicsburg, PA: Stackpole Books, 2002.

Fishel, Edwin C. *The Secret War for the Union: The Untold Story of Military Intelligence in the Civil War*. Boston: Houghton Mifflin Company, 1996.

Fiske, Samuel. *Mr. Dunn Browne's Experiences in the Army*. Boston: Nichols & Noyes, 1866.

Ford, Worthington Chauncey, ed. *A Cycle of Adams Letters 1861-1865*, 2 vols. Boston: Houghton Mifflin Company, 1920.

Freeman, Douglas Southall. *R. E. Lee: A Biography*. 4 vols. New York: Charles Scribner's Sons, 1936.

___. *Lee's Lieutenants*, 3 vols. New York: Charles Scribner's Sons, 1942.

___, and Grady McWhiney, *Lee's Dispatches: Unpublished Letters of General Robert E. Lee, C.S.A., to Jefferson Davis*. New York: Putnam, 1957.

Freiheit, Laurence H. *Boots and Saddles: Cavalry During the Maryland Campaign of September 1862*. Iowa City, IA: Camp Pope Publishing, 2013.

Fuller, Charles A. *Personal Recollections of the War of 1861…In the 61st New York Volunteer Infantry*. Sherburne, NY: News Job Printing House, 1906.

Gallagher, Gary W. ed., *Lee: The Soldier*. Lincoln, NE: University of Nebraska Press, 1996. University of North Carolina Press, 1998.

Galway, Thomas F. *The Valiant Hours: Narrative of "Captain Brevet," An Irish-American in the Army of the Potomac*. Harrisburg, PA: Stackpole, 1961.

Gambone, A. M. *Major-General Darius Nash Couch: Enigmatic Valor*. Baltimore, MD: Butternut and Blue, 2000.

Gannon, James. *Irish Rebels, Confederate Tigers: A History of the 6th Louisiana Volunteers*. Mason City, IA: Savas Publishing, 1998.

Gibbon, John. *Personal Recollections of the Civil War*. New York: G. P. Putnam, 1928.

Gibbs, Joseph. *Three Years in the Bloody 11th*. University Park, PA: The Pennsylvania State University Press, 2002.

Glatthaar, Joseph T. *General Lee's Army: From Victory to Collapse*. New York: Free Press, 2008.

Gordon, John B. *Reminiscences of the Civil War*. New York: Charles Scribner's Sons, 1904.

Gottfried, Bradley M. *Stopping Pickett: The History of the Philadelphia Brigade*. Shippensburg, PA: White Mane Publishing Co., 1999.

___. *Roads to Gettysburg: Lee's Invasion of the North, 1863*. Shippensburg, PA: White Mane Publishing Company, 2001.

___. *Brigades of Gettysburg: The Union and Confederate Brigades at the Battle of Gettysburg*. New York: Da Capo, 2002.

___. *Kearny's Own: The History of the First New Jersey Brigade in the Civil War*. New Brunswick, NJ: Rutgers University Press, 2005.

___. *The Maps of Gettysburg: An Atlas of the Gettysburg Campaign, June 3 – July 13, 1863*. Dorado Hills, CA: Savas Beatie, 2007.

___. *The Artillery of Gettysburg*. Nashville, TN: Cumberland House, 2008.

___. *The Maps of Antietam: An Atlas of the Antietam (Sharpsburg) Campaign, Including the Battle of South Mountain September 2-20, 1862*. El Dorado Hills, CA: Savas Beatie, 2012.

___. *The Maps of the Cavalry in the Gettysburg Campaign: An Atlas of Mounted Operations from Brandy Station Through Falling Waters, June 9 – July 14, 1863*. El Dorado Hills, CA: Savas Beatie, 2020.

___, ed. *Brigades of Antietam*. Sharpsburg, MD: The Press of the Antietam Institute, 2021.

Grunder, Charles S. and Brandon H. Beck. *The Second Battle of Winchester*. Lynchburg, VA: H. E. Howard, 1991.

Guelzo, Allen C. *Gettysburg: The Last Invasion*. New York: Alfred A. Knopf, 2013.

Hall, Isaac. *History of the Ninety-Seventh Regiment, New York Volunteers in the War for the Union*. Utica, NY: L. C. Childs, 1890.

Harsh, Joseph L. *Taken at the Flood: Robert E. Lee & Confederate Strategy in the Maryland Campaign of 1862*. Kent, OH: The Kent State University Press, 1999.

___. *Confederate Tide Rising: Robert E. Lee and the Making of Southern Strategy, 1861 – 1862*. Kent, OH: Kent State University Press, 1999.

___. *Sounding the Shallows: A Confederate Compendium for the Maryland Campaign of 1862*. Kent, OH: Kent State University Press, 2000.

Hartley, Chris J. *Stuart's Tarheels: James B. Gordon and His North Carolina Cavalry*. Baltimore, MD: Butternut & Blue, 1996.

Hartwig, D. Scott. *To Antietam Creek: The Maryland Campaign of September 1862*. Baltimore, MD: Johns Hopkins University Press, 2012.

Hayes, Rutherford B. *Diary and Letters of Rutherford B. Hayes*. Freemont, OH: Ohio Historical Center, 1998.

Haynes, Martin A. *History of the Second New Hampshire Regiment: Its Camps, Marches, and Battles*. Manchester, NH: Charles F. Livingston Printer, 1865.

Hearn, Chester G. *Six Years of Hell*. Baton Rouge, LA: Louisiana State University Press, 1996.

Hennessey, John J. *Return to Bull Run: The Campaign and Battle of Second Manassas.* New York: Simon & Shuster, 1993.

Herdegen, Lance J. *The Iron Brigade in Civil War and Memory: The Black Hats from Bull Run to Appomattox and Thereafter.* El Dorado Hills, CA: Savas Beatie, 2012.

Heth, Henry. *The Memoirs of Henry Heth.* Westport, CT: Greenwood Press, 1974.

Hoke, Jacob. *The Great Invasion.* New York: Thomas Yoseloff, 1959.

Hopkins, A. G. *American Empire: A Global History.* Princeton, NJ: Princeton University Press, 2018.

Houghton, Edwin B. *Campaigns of the Seventeenth Maine.* Portland, ME: Short & Loring, 1866.

Howard, Oliver O. *Autobiography of Oliver Otis Howard.* 2 vols. New York: Baker and Taylor Company, 1907.

Hotchkiss, Jedediah. *Make Me a Map of the Valley: The Civil War Journal of Stonewall Jackson's Topographer.* College Station, TX: Texas A. & M. University Press, 1973.

Humphreys, A.A. *From Gettysburg to the Rapidan. The Army of the Potomac, July, 1863 to April, 1864.* New York: Charles Scribner's Sons, 1883.

Hunter, Alexander. *Johnny Reb and Billy Yank.* New York: The Neale Publishing Company, 1905.

Huntington, Albert. *8th New York Cavalry: Historical Paper.* Palmyra, NY: n.p., 1903.

Huntington, Tom. *Searching for George Gordon Meade.* Mechanicsburg, PA: Stackpole Books, 2013.

Hyde, Bill *The Union Generals Speak: the Meade Hearings on the Battle of Gettysburg.* Baton Rouge, LA: Louisiana State University Press, 2003.

Iobst, Richard W. and Louis H. Manarin *The Bloody Sixth: The Sixth North Carolina Regiment Confederate States of America.* Raleigh, NC: North Carolina Confederate Centennial Commission, 1965.

Jackson, Lyman. *History of the Sixth New Hampshire in the War for the Union.* n.p.: n.p., 1891.

Jacobs, M. *Notes on the Rebel Invasion of Maryland and Pennsylvania and the Battle of Gettysburg.* Philadelphia: J. B. Lippincott & Company, 1864.

Jones, Wilber D. *Giants in the Cornfield: The 27th Indiana Infantry.* Shippensburg, PA: White Mane Publishing, 1997.

Jones, Terry L. *Lee's Tigers: The Louisiana Infantry in the Army of Northern Virginia.* Baton Rouge, LA: Louisiana State University Press, 1987.

___. ed. *Campbell Brown's Civil War: With Ewell and the Army of Northern Virginia.* Baton Rouge, LA: Louisiana State University Press, 2004.

Johnson, Charles F. *The Long Roll.* Aurora, NJ: Roycroftens, 1911.

Johnson, Curt and Richard C. Anderson, Jr., *Artillery Hell: The Employment of Artillery at Antietam.* College Station, TX: Texas A&M University Press, 1995.

Johnston, David E. *The Story of a Confederate Boy in the Civil War.* Portland, OR: Glass & Prudhomme Company, 1914.

Johnson, Pharris D. *Under The Southern Cross: Army Life with Gordon Bradwell.* Macon, GA: Mercer University Press, 1999.

Jorgensen, Jay. *Gettysburg's Bloody Wheatfield.* Shippensburg, PA: White Mane Publishing Company, 2002.

Kean, Robert Garlick Hill. *Inside the Confederate Government: The Diary of Robert Garlick Hill Kean,* Edward Younger, ed. New York: Oxford University Press, 1957.

Knight, Charles R. *From Arlington to Appomattox: Robert E. Lee's Civil War Day by Day, 1861 – 1865.* El Dorado Hills, CA: Savas Beatie, 2021.

Lemon, James Lile, *Feed Them the Steel: Being the Wartime Recollections of Captain James Lile Lemon, Co. A, 18th Georgia Infantry, CSA,* Mark H. Lemmon, ed. n.p.: n.p., n.d.

Leon, L. *Diary of a Tarheel Confederate Soldier.* Tocca, GA: The Confederate Reprint Co., 2014.

Long, A.L. *Memoirs of Robert E. Lee.* Secaucus, NJ: Blue and Gray, 1983.

Longacre, Edward. *The Man Behind the Guns: A Biography of Henry Jackson Hunt.* South Brunswick, NJ: A. S. Barnes, 1977.

___. *The Cavalry at Gettysburg: A Tactical Study of the Mounted Operations during the Civil War's Pivotal Campaign, 9 June – 14 July 1863.* Lincoln, NB: Bison Books, 1986.

___. *Lincoln's Cavalrymen: A History of the Mounted Forces of the Army of the Potomac.* Mechanicsburg, PA: Stackpole, 2000.

___. *Lee's Cavalrymen: A History of the Mounted Forces of the Army of Northern Virginia.* Mechanicsburg, PA: Stackpole, 2002.

Longstreet, James. *From Manassas to Appomattox.* Bloomington, IL: Indiana University Press, 1960.

Marszalek, John F. *Commander of All of Lincoln's Armies: A Life of General Henry W. Halleck.* New York: Belknap Press, 2004.

Marvel, William. *Burnside.* Chapel Hill, NC: The University of North Carolina Press, 1991.

McClellan, George B. *The Civil War Papers: Selected Correspondence, 1860-1865.* Stephen W. Sears, ed. New York: Ticknor & Fields, 1989.

McClellan, H. B. *The Life and Campaigns of Major-General J.E.B. Stuart.* Boston:

Houghton, Mifflin and Company, 1885.

McDermott, Anthony W. and John E. Reilly. *A Brief History of the 69th Regiment, Pennsylvania Veteran Volunteers.* n.p.: n.p. n.d.

McGaugh, Scott *Surgeon in Blue: Jonathan Letterman, Civil War Doctor who Pioneered Battlefield Care.* New York: Arcade, 2013.

McGrath, Thomas A. *Shepherdstown: The Last Clash of the Antietam Campaign, September 19-20, 1862.* Lynchburg, VA: Schroeder Publications, 2007.

McKim, Randolph H. *A Soldier's Recollections: Leaves from the Diary of a Young Confederate.* Washington, DC: Zenger Publishing, 1983.

Maxwell, William Quentin. *Lincoln's Fifth Wheel.* New York: Longmans, Green & Co., 1956.

McPherson, James M. *Battle Cry of Freedom: The Civil War Era.* New York: Oxford University Press, 1988.

Marshall, Charles. *An Aide-de-Camp of Lee, Being the Papers of Colonel Charles Marshall, Sometimes Aide-de-Camp, Military Secretary, and Assistant Adjutant General on the Staff of Robert E. Lee, 1862 – 1865.* Boston: Little, Brown, 1927.

Meade, George. *The Life and Letters of George Gordon Meade.* 2 vols. New York: Charles Scribner's Sons, 1913.

____. *With Meade at Gettysburg.* Philadelphia: John C. Winston, 1930.

Mills, Charles J. *Through Blood and Fire: The Civil War Letters of Major Charles J. Mills, 1862-1865.* Gregory A. Coco, ed. Gettysburg, PA: n.p., 1982.

Mills, Harrison J. *Chronicles of the Twenty-First Regiment New York Volunteers.* Buffalo, NY: 21st Veterans Association, 1887.

Moyer, H. P. *Seventeenth Regiment Pennsylvania Volunteer Cavalry or One Hundred and Sixty- Second in the Line of Pennsylvania Volunteer Regiments, War to Suppress the Rebellion, 1861- 1865.* Lebanon, PA: Sowers Printing Co., n.d.

Murfin, James V. *The Gleam of Bayonets: The Battle of Antietam and Robert E. Lee's Maryland Campaign, September 1862.* Cranbury, NJ: Thomas Yoseloff, Publisher, 1965.

Naiswald, L. Van Loan. *Grape and Canister.* New York: Oxford University Press, 1960.

National Park Service, *John Brown's Raid.* Washington, DC: U. S. Government Printing Office, 1974.

New York Monuments Commission for the Battlefields of Gettysburg and Chattanooga. *Final Report on the Battlefield of Gettysburg.* 3 vols. Albany: NY: J. B. Lyon Company Printers, 1900.

Nicolay, John and John Hay. *Abraham Lincoln: A History.* 10 vols. New York: Century Co., 1914.

Nichols, William H. *The Siege and Capture of Harpers Ferry by the Confederates, September, 1862.* Providence, RI: Rhode Island Soldiers and Sailors

Historical Society, 1889.

Newton, George W. *Silent Sentinels: A Reference Guide to the Artillery at Gettysburg.* El Dorado Hills, Savas Beatie, 2005.

Nolan, Alan T. *The Iron Brigade: A Military History.* Lansing, MI: Historical Society of Michigan, 1983.

___. *Lee Considered: General Robert E. Lee and Civil War History.* Chapel Hill, NC: The University of North Carolina Press, 1991.

Nicolay, John G. and John Hay. *Abraham Lincoln: A History.* 7 vols. New York: The Century Co., 1886.

Nichols, G. W. *A Soldier's Story of His Regiment...* Jesup, GA: n.p., 1898.

Nye, Wilbur Sturtevant. *Here Come the Rebels!* Dayton, OH: The Press of Morningside Bookshop, 1988.

Oates, William C. *The War Between the Union and Confederacy and its Lost Opportunities.* New York: Neale Publishing Co., 1905.

Oeffinger, John C. ed. *A Soldier's General: The Civil War Letters of Lafayette McLaws.* Chapel Hill, NC: The University of North Carolina Press, 2002.

O'Neill, Robert F. *The Cavalry Battles of Aldie, Middleburg, and Upperville: Small but Important Riots, June 10 – 17.* Lynchburg, VA: H. E. Howard, Inc., 1993.

Owen, William M. *In Camp and Battle with the Washington Artillery of New Orleans.* Boston: Ticknor & Co., 1885.

Owsley, Frank L. *King Cotton Diplomacy: Foreign Relations of the Confederate State of America.* Chicago, IL: The University of Chicago Press, 1969.

Pennsylvania Battlefield Commission, *Pennsylvania at Gettysburg: Ceremonies at the Dedication of the Monuments Erected by the Commonwealth of Pennsylvania to Mark the Positions of the Pennsylvania Commands Engaged in the Battle.* 2 vols. Harrisburg, PA: E. K. Meyers, State Printer, 1893.

Petruzzi, J. David and Steven A. Stanley. *The Gettysburg Campaign in Numbers and Losses: Synopses, Orders of Battle, Strengths, Casualties, and Maps, June 9 – July 14, 1863.* El Dorado Hills, CA: Savas Beatie, 2012.

Pfanz, Donald C. *Richard S. Ewell: A Soldier's Life.* Chapel Hill, NC: The University of North Carolina Press, 1998.

Pfanz, Harry W. *Gettysburg: The Second Day.* Chapel Hill, NC: The University of North Carolina Press, 1987.

Pfanz, Harry. *Gettysburg—Culp's Hill and Cemetery Hill.* Chapel Hill, NC: The University of North Carolina Press, 2001.

Harry W. Pfanz, *Gettysburg: The First Day.* Chapel Hill, NC: University of North Carolina Press, 2001.

Pfarr, Cory M. *Longstreet at Gettysburg: A Critical Reassessment.* Jefferson, NC: McFarland Press, 2019.

Pinkerton, Allan *The Spy of the Rebellion: Being a True History of the Spy System of the United States Army During the Late Rebellion*. New York: G. W. Dillingham, Publisher, 1883.

Powell, William H. *The Fifth Corps*. New York: G. P. Putnam's Sons, 1896.

Priest, John Michael, ed. *Captain James Wren's Diary: From New Bern to Fredericksburg*. Shippensburg, PA: White Maine Publishing Co., 1990.

Pullen, John J. *Twentieth Maine: A Volunteer Regiment in the Civil War*. Dayton, OH: Morningside House, 1997.

Quint, Alonzo H. *The Record of the Second Massachusetts*. Boston: James P. Walker, 1867.

Rafuse, Ethan S. *McClellan's War: The Failure of Moderation in the Struggle for the Union*. Bloomington, IL: Indiana University Press, 2005.

Rankin, Thomas M. *23rd Virginia Infantry*. Lynchburg, VA: H. E. Howard, Inc., 1985.

Reagan, John Henninger. *Memoirs, with Special Reference to Secession and the Civil War*. New York: Neale, 1905.

Reese, Timothy J. *Sykes' Regular Infantry Division, 1861-1865*. Jefferson, NC: McFarland Publishing, 1990.

Report of Lewis H. Steiner, M.D., Inspector of the Sanitary Commission, Containing a Diary Kept During the Rebel Occupation of Frederick, MD and Account of the Operations of the U.S. Sanitary Commission during the Campaign in Maryland, September, 1862. New York: Anson D. F. Randolph, 1862.

Robertson, James I. *Stonewall Jackson: The Man, The Soldier, the Legend*. New York: Macmillan, 1997.

Ropes, John. *The Story of the Civil War*. New York: G. P. Putnam Sons, 1898.

Rowland, Thomas J. *In the Shadow of Grant and Sherman: George B. McClellan & Civil War History*. Kent, OH: Kent State University Press, 1998.

Ryan, Thomas J. *Spies, Scouts, and Secrets in the Gettysburg Campaign*. El Dorado Hills, CA: Savas Beatie, 2015.

Schiebert, Justus. *Seven Months in the Rebel States during the North American War, 1863*. Joseph C. Hayes, ed. Tuscaloosa, AL: William Stanely Hoole, 1958.

Schildt, John W. *Roads to Antietam*. Shippensburg, PA: Burd Street Press, 1997.

Schmitt, Martin F. ed., *General George Crook: His Autobiography*. Norman, OK: University of Oklahoma Press, 1986.

Schurz, Carl. *Reminiscences of Carl Schurz*. 3 vols. San Bernardino, CA: Elibron Classics, 2006.

Sears, Stephen W. *Lincoln's Lieutenants: The High Command of the Army of the Potomac*. Boston: Houghton Mifflin Harcourt, 2017.

Selby, John G. *Meade: The Price of Command, 1863-1865*. Kent, OH: The Kent State University, 2018.

Sifakis, Stewart. *Who Was Who in the Civil War*. New York: Facts on File, 1988.

Shotwell, Randolph A. *The Papers of Randolph A. Shotwell*, J. G. De Roulac Hamilton, ed. 2 vols. Raleigh, NC: North Carolina Historical Commission, 1929-1931.

Small, Abner Ralph. *The Road to Richmond: The Civil War Memoirs of Major Abner R. Small of the 16th Maine*. Berkeley, CA: University of California Press, 1959.

Smith, John L. *History of the Corn Exchange Regiment, 118th Pennsylvania Volunteers from their First Engagement at Antietam to Appomattox*. Philadelphia, PA: J. L. Smith, 1905.

Snell, Mark A. *From First To Last: The Life of William B. Franklin*. Fordham University Press, New York, 2002.

Sommers, Richard J. *Challenges of Command in the Civil War: Generalship, Leadership, and Strategy at Gettysburg, Petersburg, and Beyond*. El Dorado Hills, CA: Savas Beatie, 2018.

Sorrel, G. Moxley. *Recollections of a Confederate Staff Officer*. New York: Neale Publishing Company, 1917.

Sparks, David S., ed. *Inside Lincoln's Army: The Diary of General Marsena Rudolph Patrick, Provost Marshal General, Army of the Potomac*. New York: Thomas Yoseloff, 1964.

Stansburg, F. Haydon, *Aeronautics in the Union and Confederate Armies*. Baltimore, MD: Johns Hopkins Press, 1941.

Starr, Stephen Z. *The Union Cavalry in the Civil War*. 3 vols. Baton Rouge, LA: Louisiana State University Press, 1979.

Stotelmyer, Steven R. *Too Useful to Sacrifice: Reconsidering George B. McClellan's Generalship in the Maryland Campaign from South Mountain to Antietam*. El Dorado Hills, CA: Savas Beatie, 2019.

Styple, William B. ed., *Writing and Fighting the Civil War: Soldier Correspondence to the New York Sunday Mercury* (Kearney, NJ): Belle Grove Publishing Company, 2000.

Tate, Thomas K. *General Edwin Vose Sumner, USA*. Jefferson, NC: The McFarland Co., 2013.

Taylor, Emerson Gifford *Gouverneur Kemble Warren: The Life and Letters of an American Soldier, 1830-1882*. Gaithersburg, MD: Ron R. Van Sickle Military Books, 1988.

Thomas, Henry W. *History of the Doles-Cook Brigade of the Army of Northern Virginia…* Atlanta, GA: The Franklin Printing and Publishing Company, 1903.

Toombs, Samuel. *Reminiscences of the War: Comprising a Detailed Account of the*

Experiences of the Thirteenth Regiment New Jersey Volunteers in Camp, on the March, and in Battle. Orange, NJ: Journal Office, 1878.

Tower, R. Lockwood, ed. *Lee's Adjutant: The Wartime Letters of Colonel Walter Herron Taylor, 1862-1865.* Columbia, SC: The University of South Carolina Press, 1995.

Turner, Charles W. ed., *Captain Greenlee Davidson, C.S.A.: Diary and Letters, 1851 – 1863.* Verona, VA: McClure Press, 1975.

Ural, Susannah J. *Hood's Texas Brigade.* Baton Rouge, LA: Louisiana State University, 2017.

Wagner, Arthur L. *The Service of Security and Information.* Washington DC: James J. Chapman, 1893.

Walker, C. Irvine. *The Life of Lieutenant General Richard Heron Anderson.* Charleston, SC: Art Publishing Col, 1917.

Walker, Francis A. *History of the Second Army Corps in the Army of the Potomac.* New York: C. Scribner's Sons, 1886.

Ward, Joseph R. C. *History of the One-Hundred and Sixth Regiment Pennsylvania Volunteers, 1861-1865.* Philadelphia: Grant, Faires & Rogers, 1906.

Warner, Ezra J. *Generals in Gray: Lives of the Confederate Commanders.* Baton Rouge, LA: The Louisiana State University Press, 1959.

____. *Generals in Blue: Lives of the Union Commanders.* Baton Rouge, LA: The Louisiana State University Press, 1964.

Weld, Stephen Minot. *War Diary and Letters.* Boston: The Riverside Press, 1912.

Welker, David. *The Cornfield: Antietam's Bloody Turning Point.* Philadelphia: Casemate, 2020.

Welles, Gideon. *The Civil War Diary of Gideon Welles, Lincoln's Secretary of the Navy.* William E. Glenapp and Erica L. Glenapp, eds. Urbana, IL: The University of Illinois Press, 1987.

Welsh, Jack D. *Medical Histories of Confederate Generals.* Kent, OH: Kent State University Press, 1995.

____. *Medical Histories of Confederate Generals.* Kent, OH: Kent State University Press, 2013.

West, John C. *A Texan in Search of a Fight.* Waco, TX: Press of J. S. Hill and Company, 1901.

Weygant, Charles H. *History of the One Hundred and Twenty-Fourth Regiment, N.Y.S.V.* Newburgh, NY: Journal Print House, 1877.

White, Gregory. *This Most Bloody & Cruel Drama: A History of the 31st Georgia Volunteer Infantry.* Baltimore, MD: Butternut & Blue, 1997.

Wiley, Bell Irvin. *The Life of Billy Yank: The Common Soldier in the Union.* Baton Rouge, LA: Louisiana State University, 2008.

Williams, Alpheus S. *From the Cannon's Mouth: The Civil War Letters of General Alpheus S. Williams*. Milo M. Quaife, ed. Detroit, MI: Wayne State University Press, 1959.

Williams, T. Harry. *Lincoln and His Generals*. New York: Alfred A. Knopf, 1952.

Wilson, Lawrence *Itinerary of the Seventh Ohio Volunteer Infantry, 1861-1864*. New York: The Neale Publishing Co., 1907.

Wittenberg, Eric J. *The Union Cavalry Comes of Age*. Washington, DC: Potomac Books, Inc., 2003.

____. *The Devil's to Pay: John Buford at Gettysburg*. El Dorado Hills, CA: Savas Beatie, 2014.

____. Wittenberg, Eric J., J. David Petruzzi, and Michael F. Nugent. *One Continuous Fight: The Retreat from Gettysburg and the Pursuit of Lee's Army of Northern Virginia, July 4 – 14, 1863*. El Dorado Hills, CA: Savas Beatie, 2008.

Wise, Jennings Cropper. *The Long Arm of Lee: The History of the Artillery of the Army of Northern Virginia*. New York: Oxford University Press, 1950.

Woodbury, Augustus. *Major General Ambrose E. Burnside and the Ninth Army Corps: A Narrative of Campaigns in North Carolina, Maryland, Virginia, Ohio, Kentucky, Mississippi and Tennessee, During the War for the Preservation of the Republic* (Providence: Sidney S. Rider & Brother, 1867.

____. *Ambrose Everett Burnside*. Providence: N. B. Williams & company, 1882.

Worsham, John H. *One of Jackson's Foot Cavalry, His Experiences and What he Saw during the War, 1861-1865*. Richmond, VA: Jackson, TN: McCowat-Mercer, 1964.

Wren, James. *Captain James Wren's Diary: From New Bern to Fredericksburg*. John M. Priest, ed. Shippensburg, PA: White Mane, 1990.

Wychoff, Mac *A History of the Second South Carolina Infantry, 1861-1865*. Fredericksburg, VA: Sergeant Kirkland's Museum and Historical Society, 1994.

Articles

Address of Colonel Edward McCrady, Jr." *Southern Historical Society Papers*, vol. XIV (1886), 183- 221.

Alexander, Edward Porter "Confederate Artillery Service." *Southern Historical Society Papers*, vol. 11 (1883), 98-113.

Allan, William. "Memoranda of Conversations with General Robert E. Lee." in *Lee the Soldier*, Gary Gallagher, ed. Lincoln, NE: University of Nebraska Press, 1966, 7-24.

Bowen, Edward R. "Collis' Zouaves—The 114th Pennsylvania at Gettysburg." *Philadelphia Weekly Times*, June 22, 1887.

Calef, John H. "Gettysburg Notes: The Opening Gun." *Journal of the Military Services Institute of the United States*, January/February 1907, 40-58.

Campbell, Eric. "Caldwell Clears the Wheatfield." *Gettysburg Magazine*, Issue 3 (July 1, 1990), 27-50.

Casey, James, ed., "The Ordeal of Adoniram Judson Warner: His Minutes of South Mountain and Antietam." *Civil War History*, vol. xxvii, no. 3 (1982), 224-227.

Clemens, Thomas G. "'Too Bad, Poor Fellows:' Joseph K. Mansfield and the XII Corps at Antietam," in *Corps Commanders in Blue: Union Major Generals in the Civil War*. Ethan S. Rafuse, ed. Baton Rouge, LA: Louisiana State University Press, 2014, 61-95.

Clements, Bennett A. "Memoir of Jonathan Letterman, M.D." *Journal of the Military Service Institution*, vol. iv, no. 15 (September 1883), 1-38.

Coddington, Edwin B. "Pennsylvania Prepares for Invasion, 1863." *Pennsylvania History*, vol. 31, no. 3 (April 1964), 157-75.

Colgrove, Silas. "The Finding of Lee's Lost Order." *Battles & Leaders of the Civil War*, ed. By Robert U. Johnson and Clarence C. Buell. 4 vols. (New York: T. Yoseloff, 1958-59), vol. 2, 603.

Cox, Jacob D. "Forcing Fox's and Turner's Gap." *Battles & Leaders of the Civil War*, vol. 2, 591-97.

Crowninshield Benjamin W. "Cavalry in Virginia During the War of the Rebellion." *Journal of the Military Service Institution*, vol. 12 (May 1891), 527-51.

Davis, Steven R. "'. . . Like Leaves in an Autumn Wind': The 11th Mississippi Infantry in the Army of Northern Virginia." *Civil War Regiments*, vol. 2, no. 4 (1992), 269-312.

Davis, William C. "Lee and Jefferson Davis." in *Lee the Soldier*, Gary Gallagher, ed., 291-305.

Dickinson, Joseph. "A Gettysburg Incident." *The Proceedings of the Buford Memorial Association*. New York: Privately printed, 1895.

Douglas, Henry Kyd "Stonewall Jackson in Maryland." *Battles & Leaders of the Civil War*, vol. 2, 620-29.

Early, Jubal, "Causes of Lee's Defeat." Southern Historical Society Papers, vol. IV, 50-66.

Elmore, Thomas L. "The Florida Brigade at Gettysburg." *Gettysburg Magazine*, number 15 (1996), pp. 45-59.

Fogle, Theodore. "Bloodletting at Burnside Bridge." *America's Civil War*, September 2015, 18.

Franklin, William. "Notes on Crampton's Gap and Antietam." *Battles &*

Leaders of the Civil War, vol. II, 591-97.

Frye, Dennis. "Drama between the Rivers: Harpers Ferry in the 1862 Maryland Campaign," in *Antietam: Essays on the 1862 Maryland Campaign*, Gary Gallagher, ed. (Kent, OH: Kent University press, 1989), 14-34.

Fuger, Frederick. "Cushing's Battery at Gettysburg." *Journal of the Military Service Institution of the United States*, vol. 41 (1907), 405-10.

Gaff, Alan D. "Here Was Made our Last and Hopeless Stand." *Gettysburg Magazine*, issue 2 (January 1990), 25-31.

"Gen'l O.O. Howard's Personal Reminiscences of the War of the Rebellion." *National Tribune*, November 20, 1884.

Gottfried, Bradley M. "Wright's Charge at Gettysburg: Piercing the Union Line or Inflated Glory?" Issue 17, (1998), 70-82.

Grant, George W. "The First Army Corps on the First Day at Gettysburg." *Minnesota MOLLUS* (vol. 5), 45-58.

Grimsley, Mark. "The Lincoln-McClellan Relationship in Myth and Memory." *Journal of the Abraham Lincoln Association*, Vol. 38, Issue 2 (Summer, 2017), 63-81.

Hartwig, D. Scott "Robert E. Lee and the Maryland Campaign." in *Lee the Soldier*, 331-55.

___. "'My God Be Careful!' The Morning Fight at Fox's Gap," *Civil War Regiments*, vol. 5 (no. 3), 27-58.

___. "Who Would Not Be a Soldier." in Gary Gallagher, ed., *The Antietam Campaign*. Chapel Hill, NC: The University of North Carolina Press, 1999, 143-68.

Hewitt, William D. "The Confederate Deliberate Attack 5 P.M. July 1 to 8 P.M. July 2," in *The Most Shocking Battle I Have Ever Witness: The Second Day at Gettysburg." Papers of the 2006 Gettysburg National Military Park Seminar* (Gettysburg, PA: National Park Service, 2008), 2- 38.

Hill, D. H. "Lee Attacks North of the Chickahominy." *Battles & Leaders of the Civil War*, vol. 2, 347-362.

___. "The Battle of South Mountain." *Battles & Leaders of the Civil War*, vol. 2, 559-82.

Holsworth, Jerry W. "Uncommon Valor: Hood's Texas Brigade in the Maryland Campaign." *Blue & Gray Magazine*, August 1996, 6-55.

Hunt, Henry "The Second Day at Gettysburg." *Battles & Leaders of the Civil War*, vol. 3, 290-312.

Hunter, Alexander "A High Private's Sketch of Sharpsburg." *Southern Historical Society Papers*, vol. XI, no. 1 (January, 1883), 14-18.

Jerome, Aaron B. "Buford on Oak Hill." in J. Watts de Peyster, ed., *The Decisive Conflicts of the Late Civil War, or Slaveholders' Rebellion, Battles Morally,*

Territorially, and Militarily Decisive. New York: McDonald and Co., Printers, 1867), 151-52.

Johnson, Bradley T. "First Maryland Campaign." *Southern Historical Society Papers*, vol. XXII (1884), 504-05.

Jorgenson, Jay." Anderson Attacks the Wheatfield." *Gettysburg Magazine* (January 1996), Issue 14, 64-76.

"Letter from Major-General Henry Heth, of A. P. Hill's Corps, A. N. V." *Southern Historical Society Papers*, vol. IV (1877), 151-53.

Lochren, William. "The First Minnesota at Gettysburg." Minnesota MOLLUS, vol. 3, 41-56.

Longstreet, James. "The Invasion of Maryland." *Battles & Leaders of the Civil War*, vol. II, 663-74.

___. "The Mistakes of Gettysburg." *The Annals of the Civil War* (New York: Da Capo Press, 1994), 619-33.

___. "Lee in Pennsylvania." *The Annals of the Civil War*, 414-46.

Loring, William E. "Gettysburg." *National Tribune*, July 9, 1885.

Luff, William M. "March of the Cavalry from Harpers Ferry September 14, 1862." *Illinois MOLLUS* (Chicago: A. C. McClurg and Co., 1894), vol. 2, 33-48.

David McIntosh, "Review of the Gettysburg Campaign by One Who Participated Therein, *Southern Historical Society Papers*, vol. XXXVII (January-December, 1909), 74- 143.

McLaws, Lafayette. "Gettysburg." In *Southern Historical Society Papers* (1879), vol. VII, 64-90.

___. "The Capture of Harpers Ferry." *Philadelphia Weekly Press*, September 5, 1888 & September 12, 1888.

McNeily, J. S. "Barksdale's Mississippi Brigade at Gettysburg." In *Publications of the Mississippi Historical Society* (1914), vol. 14, 231-265.

Marshall, Charles. "Events Leading Up to the Battle of Gettysburg." *Southern Historical Society Papers*, vol. XXIII (1895), 205-229.

Matsui, John. "War in Earnest: The Army of Virginia and the Radicalization of the Union War Effort." *Civil War History*, vol. 58 (no. 2), 185-87.

Mahood, Wayne. "Some Very Hard Stories Were Told: The 126th New York Infantry at Harpers Ferry." *Civil War Regiments*, vol. 1, no. 4 (1991), 7-41.

Meinhard, Robert W. "The First Minnesota at Gettysburg." *Gettysburg Magazine*, Issue 5 (July 1991), 79-88.

Moon, W. H. "Beginning the Battle at Gettysburg." *Confederate Veteran*, vol. 33 (1925), 449.

Moran, Frank E. "A Fire Zouave—Memoirs of a Member of the Excelsior Brigade." *National Tribune*, November 6, 1890.

Mosby, John S. "The Confederate Cavalry in the Gettysburg Campaign." *Battles & Leaders of the Civil War*, vol. 3, 251-2.
Nolan, Alan T. "R. E. Lee and July 1 at Gettysburg." in *Lee the Soldier*, 475-96.
___and Marc Storch, "The Iron Brigade Earns its Name." *Blue and Gray Magazine*, vol. XXI, no. 6 (2004), 6-50.
O'Brien, Kevin E. "Hold Them with the Bayonet: deTrobriand's Brigade Defends the Wheatfield." *Gettysburg Magazine*, Issue 21 (July 1999), 74-87.
O'Neill, Robert F. "Aldie, Middleburg, and Upperville." *Gettysburg Magazine*, no. 43 (July, 2010), 14- 46.
Petruzzi, J. David "John Buford: By the Book." *American's Civil War*, vol. 18 no. 3 (July 2005), 24-27.
"Robert Todd Lincoln's Reminiscences, Given 5 January 1885." in *An Oral History of Abraham Lincoln: John G. Nicolay's Interviews and Essays*, Michael Burlingame, ed. (Carbondale, IL: Southern Illinois University Press, 1996), 88-89.
Scott, George H. "Vermont at Gettysburg." *Proceedings of the Vermont Historical Society*, vol. 1 (1930), 51-73.
David Shultz and Scott Mingus, "Sunrise Hours at Gettysburg, July 2, 1863." *Gettysburg Magazine*, no. 56 (January 2017), 13-25.
Smith, Karlton D. "'To Consider Every Contingency:' Lt. Gen. James Longstreet, Capt. Samuel R. Johnston, and the Factors that Affected the Reconnaissance and Countermarch, July 2, 1863." in *The Most Shocking Battle I Have Ever Witness: The Second Day at Gettysburg,*" Papers of the 2006 Gettysburg National Military Park Seminar, 100-124.
Strother, David Hunter. "Personal Recollections of the War." *Harper's Magazine*, June 1866.
Turney, J. B. "The First Tennessee at Gettysburg." *Confederate Veteran* vol. 8 (1900), 535.
Vautier, John D. "At Gettysburg." *Philadelphia Weekly Press*, November 10, 1886.
Vermilya, Daniel J. "Perceptions, Not Realities?: The Army of the Potomac in the Maryland Campaign." *The Antietam Journal*, vol. 1 (September 2021), 7-50.
Verrill, George W. "The Seventeenth Maine at Gettysburg and in the Wilderness." *Maine MOLLUS*, vol. 1, 259-82.
Walker, John G. "Jackson's Capture of Harpers' Ferry." *Battles & Leaders of the Civil War*, vol. 2, 604-11.
White, Julius. "The Capitulation of Harpers Ferry." *Battles & Leaders of the Civil War*, vol. 2, 612-14.

Wilcox, C. M. "Letter." In *Southern Historical Society Papers*, vol. IV (1877), 111-117.

____. "General C. M. Wilcox on the Battle of Gettysburg." *Southern Historical Society Papers*, vol. VI (July – December, 1878), 97-104.

Wittenberg, Eric J. and J. David Petruzzi, "Corbit's Charge: Jeb Stuart Clashes with the 1st Delaware Cavalry at Westminister, Maryland, June 29, 1863." *Gettysburg Magazine*, no. 36 (January 2007), 9-16.

"Wofford's Georgia Brigade." *Atlanta Constitution*, December 8, 1897.

Internet Resources

https://antietam.aotw.org/officers.php?officer_id=928&from=results.
Kurt Graham, "Death of a Brigade: Drayton's Brigade at Fox's Gap, September 14, 1862,"
http://www.angelfire.com/ga2/PhillipsLegion/deathofabrigade.html;
Antietam Battlefield Board
 (https://www.nps.gov/anti/learn/historyculture/casualties.htm)

INDEX

Abercrombie, John, and his division, 173
Adams, Charles, 216
Alabama Units, *Infantry, 6th*, 294, 297; *13th*, 269; *15th*, 306; *47th*, 306; *48th*, 307
Aldie, VA, 143, 144, 217
Alexander, Edward (Porter), 78-79, 88, 344, 356
Alexandria, VA, 87
Alexandria and Loudoun Railroad, 142
Allen, William, 21, 22, 446 (note 4)

Anderson, George B., and his brigade, 205, 292, 297, 298, 324, 327, 396, 396
Anderson, George T., and his brigade, 205, 307, 309, 350
Anderson, Richard, and his division, 37; reputation, 65; initial actions before Antietam, 121; at Harpers Ferry, 198, 203, 210; to Sharpsburg, 224; at Antietam, 293, 295, 321, 325-26, 386; assigned to Third Corps at Gettysburg, 39, 68; movements during Pennsylvania Campaign, 135, 135, 146, 164, 180; at Gettysburg, 245, 278, 301, 305, 313, 316, 320, 340, 344, 346-47, 351, 354
Anderson, Richard [historian], 48
Anderson, Robert, 260
Antietam Creek, 159, 223, 224, 235, 247, 250, 251, 295, 330, 338, 350, 351, 353, 355, 393
Archer, James, and his brigade, assigned to Third Corps at Gettysburg, 39, 268, 269, 274, 289, 337, 340, 394
Arkansas Units, *Infantry, 3rd*, 305
Armistead, Lewis, and his brigade, 78, 355, 396
Ashby's Gap, 145
Averill, William, 58
Avery, Isaac, and his brigade, 277, 319, 327
Ayres, Romeyn, and his brigade/division, assignments, 69

B&O Railroad, 14, 98, 105, 447 (note 2)
Bachelor, Charles, 172
Ballinger, William, 79
Baltimore, MD, during the Maryland Campaign, 31, 102, 123, 174
Baltimore & Ohio Railroad, 212
Bank's Ford, 90
Banks, Nathaniel, and his corps, 10, 36
Barksdale, William, and his brigade, 199, 312, 314, 326, 327, 396
Barlow, Francis, and his regiment/division, at Antietam, 297, 298; at Gettysburg, 272, 276, 287, 319
Barnes, James, and his brigade/division, 146, 309, 362, 362
Barnsville, MD, 98, 125, 167
Bates, Edward, 28
Bartlett, Joseph, and his brigade, 210
Bauer, Jacob, 337
Bealton, VA, 111
Beauregard, P.G.T., 163

479

Beckham, Robert, and his artillery battalion, 60
Bedford, PA, 163
Benning, Henry, and his brigade, 306, 326
Berlin, MD, 372
Berryville, VA, 111, 134, 135, 146, 162, 212, 213, 218
Biddle, Chapman, and his brigade, 274, 276, 287
Big Mount, PA, 171
Big Round Top, 229, 245, 306
Big Spring, VA, 98
Bird, W., 269
Birney, and his division, assignments, 69; at Gettysburg, 181, 313
Black Horse Tavern, 181
Blackford's Ford, 166, 221, 361
Bliss farm, 341, 343, 350
Blue Ridge Mountains, 92, 106, 110, 141, 143, 144, 145, 162, 217, 385
Blocher's Knoll, 276, 287
Bolivar, MD, 206
Bolivar Heights, 197, 198, 200, 202
Boonsboro, 121, 122, 126, 153, 156, 157, 183, 203, 365
Bonneauville, PA, 181
Bowen, James, 226
Bragg, Braxton, 20, 87, 433 (note 16)
Branch, Lawrence, and his brigade, 355, 396
Brandy Station, Battle of, 110, 116, 216
Bristoe, VA 145
Bristoe Station, VA, 167
Bristoe Station, battle of, 397
Brockenbrough, John, and his brigade, 274, 340, 347, 357

Brooke, John, and his brigade, 310
Brooks, W.T., and his brigade, 210
Brookville, MD, 123
Brown, John, 196
Brown, Kent, 179
Brownsville, MD, 222
Brownsville Pass, 126, 210
Bruceville, MD, 177
Brewster, William, and his brigade, 312
Bryan, K., 307
Buckeystown, MD, 210
Buford, John, and his division, 58, 60, 172, 177, 216, 225, 238, 267-69, 278, 282, 288, 349, 365
Bull Run, First Battle of, 13, 25, 447 (note 2)
Bull Run, Second Battle of, 10, 11, 12, 13, 15, 27, 35, 47, 72, 82, 95, 284
Bull Run Mountains, 110, 145
Bureau of Military Intelligence, 88, 90
Burling, George, and his brigade, 307
Burns, William, 346

Carlisle, PA, 123, 163, 164, 167, 171, 175, 181, 183, 386
Carman, Ezra, 103, 120, 207, 240, 252, 257, 293, 294, 360
Carr, George, 320
Carr, Joseph, and his brigade, 312-13
Carroll, Samuel, and his brigade, 319, 322, 327, 357
Cashtown, PA, 176, 225, 236-38, 267
Catlett's Station, 111, 134, 445 (note 21)
Catoctin Mountain, 154

Cavetown, MD, 164
Cedar Mountain, Battle of, 27
Cemetery Hill (Gettysburg), 229, 231, 243, 390, 392; on July 1, 272, 276-80, 282, 288; on July 2, 244-45, 247, 317-21, 323, 325, 327, 340, 345, 392, 295; on July 3, 356
Cemetery Hill (Sharpsburg), 224, 231, 336
Cemetery Ridge (Gettysburg), July 1, 243-45; July 2, 299, 302, 3113, 316-18, 321, 322, 393, 394-95; July 3, 341, 343, 347, 349, 355, 357
Centreville, VA, 134, 135, 144, 150, 167, 445 (note 21)
Chain Bridge, 97
Chambersburg, PA, 126, 137, 142, 148, 162, 163, 164, 166, 168, 171, 175, 182, 226, 372
Chambliss, John, and his brigade, 59, 168
Chancellorsville, Battle of, 10, 11, 29, 31, 45, 67, 269, 272, 284, 301, 340, 378, 385
Charlestown, WV, 162, 164
Cheek's Ford, 96, 101, 121
Chester Gap, 111
Christ, Benjamin, and his brigade, 334, 336, 354, 357
Christian, William, and his brigade, 253, 254, 255, 256, 260, 285
Clarksburg, MD, 102, 125, 128
Cobb, Howell, and his brigade, 211, 292, 294
Coddington, Edwin, 443 (note 29)
Colquitt, Alfred, and his brigade, at Fox's Gap, 204, 208; to Antietam, 446 (note 8); at Antietam, 261, 263, 292, 294 leaves army, 45
Colgrove, Silas, and his brigade, 343

Columbia, PA, 167, 175
Colvill, William, 314
Connecticut Units, *Infantry, 8th*, 336; *11th*, 331, 332; *14th*, 42; *16th*, 42, 336-37
Conscription Act, 77
Cooksville, MD, 125, 128
Cornfield (Antietam), 42, 238, 250-64, 288, 293, 326, 331, 392, 395
Coster, Charles, and his brigade, 276-77, 288
Couch, Darius, and his division during Maryland Campaign, 35, 97, 123, 154, 203, 435 (note 13); relieving the Harpers Ferry garrison, 208, 211; commands the Department of the Susquehanna during the Pennsylvania Campaign, 112, 163, 177, 443 (note 29)
Cox, Jacob, and his Kanawha Division, 101, 204; at Antietam, 331, 334, 336-37
Cracklinton, MD, 123
Crampton's Gap, 132, 154, 155, 156, 157, 203, 208-11, 218
Crawford, Samuel, and his brigade/division, 76-77, 317
Crook, George, and his brigade, 205, 332, 334
Cross, Edward, and his brigade, 309, 310, 327
Culp's Hill, 229, 231, 243, 390, 392; on July 1, 244; on July 2, 245, 247, 299, 300-01, 317-21, 325, 326-27, 340, 392, 395; July 3, 341-43, 350, 352-53, 355, 394
Culpeper Court House, VA, 100, 106, 108, 110, 135, 142, 163, 216
Cumberland, MD, 163
Cumberland Valley, 129, 163

481

Cumberland Valley Railroad, 179
Curtin, Andrew, 383-84; during the Maryland Campaign, 66, 85, 103, 123-24, 129-30, 131, 132, 155, 160, 444 (note 11), 445 (note 16); during the Pennsylvania Campaign, 112, 117, 137, 139, 151, 171, 443 (note 29)
Custer, George, and his brigade, 59, 349, 367
Cutler, Lysander, and his brigade, 269, 270, 288

Damascus, MD, 125, 128
Daniel, Junius, and his brigade, 341
Davis, Benjamin "Grimes" and his cavalry, 159, 183, 202
Davis, Jefferson, 14; communication with Lee during the Maryland Campaign, 14, 15, 17, 18, 44, 50, 78, 95, 100, 101, 103; communication with Lee during the Pennsylvania Campaign, 20, 74, 95, 375-76; relations with Lee, 26, 383
Davis, Joseph, and his brigade, assigned to Third Corps at Gettysburg, 39, 45, 268, 269, 270, 285, 287, 288, 340, 347, 357, 394
Dawes, Rufus, 252, 256
de Trobriand, Regis, and his brigade, 307
Delaware Units, *Cavalry, 1st*, 217; *Infantry, 1st*, 42
Department of Ohio, 38
Department of the Monongahela, 443 (note 29)
Department of the Susquehanna, 112, 163, 443 (note 29)
Devil's Den, 229, 304-06

Devin, Thomas, and his brigade, 225, 267
Dillsburg, PA, 180
Dix, John, and his military department, 106, 108, 166, 179, 388
Doles, George, and his brigade, 276
Doubleday, Abner, and his brigade/division, 67; during the Maryland Campaign; 73, 451 (note 9); at Antietam, 235, 251-53, 255-56, 259, 286; at Gettysburg, 270, 274
Douglas, Henry Kyd, 438 (note 55)
Douglass, Marsellus, and his brigade, 253, 254, 256, 257
Downsville, MD, 363
Dranesville, VA, 91, 95, 142, 169
Drayton, Thomas, and his brigade, 205-06
Dryer, Hiram, 338
Duane, James, 330
Dumfries, VA, 134, 135, 445 (note 21)
Dunker Church, 221, 231, 241, 252, 253, 255, 256, 257, 261, 264, 287-88, 293, 330
Duryee, Abram, and his brigade, 254, 255
D'Utassy, Frederick, and his brigade, 198

Eagle Hotel, 225
Early, Jubal, and his brigade/division, at Antietam, 253, 362; assigned to Second Corps at Gettysburg, 39; movements north in Pennsylvania Campaign, 111, 143, 162, 163, 166, 168, 171, 175, 176, 166, 168, 171, 175, 176; attack on Winchester, 212, 213; initial

arrival at Gettysburg, 225; July 1 at Gettysburg, 236, 242, 244, 276, 280, 282; July 2 at Gettysburg, 300, 317, 320, 324; July 3 at Gettysburg, 345, 350, 356
East Woods, 228, 236, 238, 250, 253, 256, 257, 261, 263, 264, 281, 286, 288, 293, 326, 331, 392
Edward's Ferry, 58, 146, 166, 167, 169, 172, 441 (note 3)
Elk Ridge, 89, 196, 199
Elliott, Washington, and his brigade, 214
Ellis, A. Van Horn, 305
Ely, William, and his brigade, 214
Emancipation Proclamation, 22, 372, 378-79
Emmitsburg, MD, 162, 176, 179, 181
Engelbrecht, Jacob, 100
Evans, Nathan, and his brigade, 37, 65
Evergreen Cemetery, 299
Ewell, Richard, and his corps, 253, assignments, 67; initial movements north during the Pennsylvania Campaign, 106, 108, 110, 111, 115; during the second phase of the march to Gettysburg, 135, 136, 141, 142, 143, 145, 148; during the last phase of the march to Gettysburg; 162, 163, 165, 166, 168, 180, 182, 183; attacks on garrisons during Pennsylvania Campaign, 212, 219; Gettysburg, July 1, 225, 243-45, 247, 272, 280-81, 284, 287; Gettysburg, July 2, 200-01, 317, 320; Gettysburg, July 3, 340-01, 343, 352-53; Gettysburg aftermath, 363, 382, 392, 393-94

Ewing, Hugh, and his brigade, 337

Fairchild, Harrison, and his brigade, 336, 353, 357
Fairfax Court House, 136, 142
Fairfax Station, VA, 136, 140
Fairfield, PA, 177, 364
Falling Waters, MD, 166, 363, 367, 396
Falls Church, VA, 87, 95
Farnsworth, Elon, and his brigade, 59, 349, 352, 355
Farnsworth, John, and his brigade, 102
Ferrero, Edward, and his brigade, 333
Final Attack, 334-38, 352
Fiske, Samuel, 42
Fleetwood Hill, 216
Flint Hill, VA, 110
Ford, Thomas, and his brigade, 197, 199, 448 (note 5)
Fort Ethan Allen, 97
Fort Macon, 10
Fort Monroe, 166, 435 (note 13)
Fort Pulaski, 10
Fox's Gap, 155, 156, 203, 204-06, 218, 261, 263, 396
Franklin, William, and his corps, troubles with Washington, 36, 63 effectiveness, 69; during the Maryland Campaign, 128, 131, 203, 223; fight at Crampton's Gap, 208-11; at Antietam, 241, 331, 360, 382
Frederick, MD, 387; during the Maryland Campaign, 36, 58, 86, 102-03, 123, 124, 128, 131, 132, 150, 198, 206, 386, 444 (notes 8 and 11); McClellan's army arrives, 153;

483

during the Pennsylvania Campaign, 174, 175, 176
Fredericksburg, VA, 106, 111, 134, 385
Fredericksburg, Battle of, 29, 63, 378, 396
Fremont, John, 10
French, William, and his division, during Maryland Campaign, 35; at Antietam, 264, 292-95, 298, 322-23, 324-25, 331, 435 (note 13); during Pennsylvania Campaign, 177
Front Royal, VA, 100, 146
Frosttown Plateau/Gap, 207, 218
Fry, Birkett, and is brigade, 274
Funkstown, MD, 365

Gamble, William, and his brigade, 225, 267, 269, 277
Garland, Samuel, and his brigade, 204, 205, 261, 263, 292, 460 (note 8)
Garnett, Richard, and his brigade, 207, 355, 396
Geary, John, and his division, 69, 341
General Orders, 442 (note 9), 62, 111, 115; 66, 174; 67, 174; 71, 146, 151; 73, 171, 185; 102, 96, 115; 139, 80; 147, 80; 150, 80; 155, 76, 78, 120, 150
Georgia Units, *Infantry, 2nd*, 331, 334; *6th*, 263; *10th*, 210; *18th*, 259; *20th*, 331; *27th*, 263; *50th*, 331-32
Gibbon, John, and his brigade/division, 208, at Antietam, 255-56, 255, 256, 261; at Gettysburg, 245, 313, 345
Gilmer, J. F., 19
Gloskoski, Joseph, 89
Goose Creek, 142, 145, 166

Gordon, John, and his brigade, 171, 175, 276, 294
Gordonsville, VA, 106
Goshen, MD, 123
Gorman, Richard, and his brigade, 265
Gourd Vine Church, 110
Graham, Charles, and his brigade, 312, 327
Grant, Ulysses S., 10, 11, 375, 380
Gregg, David, and his division, 58, 60, 143, 172, 177, 216; at Gettysburg, 182, 349, 352
Gregg, Maxcy, and his brigade, 337, 357, 361
Greencastle, PA, 164, 168, 169
Greenwood, PA, 166, 168, 176
Greene, George, and his division/brigade; assignments, 69; at Antietam, 263, 264, 267, 293; at Gettysburg, 300, 320, 323
Griffin, Charles, and his division, 36
Grigsby, A. J., and his brigade, 253
Grow, Galusha, 378
Guild, Lafayette, 81-82
Gum Springs, VA, 142, 144, 145, 167, 167

Hagerstown, MD, during the Maryland Campaign, 121, 126, 129-30, 153-54, 157, 159, 183, 203, 386; during the Pennsylvania Campaign, 162, 164, 171, 363, 365, 367
Hall, Norman, and his brigade, 313
Halltown, VA, 198, 200
Halleck, Henry, 173, 446 (note 12), health, 33; interactions with McClellan, 28, 33, 85-86, 104-05, 128, 362, 371-72, 442 (note 10); interactions with Hooker, 29, 33,

140, 141, 173; interactions with Meade, 33, 365, 367, 374; worried about the security of Washington, 35; military intelligence, 97; army's movements north during the Pennsylvania Campaign, 108; interactions with Gov. Curtin, 137, 155; preliminary combat, 196, 197, 218, 387

Hampton, Wade, and his brigade, 59; during the Maryland Campaign, 132, 154; during the Pennsylvania Campaign, 168, 217

Hancock, Winfield, and his division/corps, commands II Corps at Gettysburg, 66; effectiveness, 69; movements during the Pennsylvania Campaign, 134, 135, 140, 142, 144, 145, 167, 172, 177; reaches battlefield, 182; Battle of Gettysburg, 280-81, 299, 302, 313-14, 323-24, 344-45, 349, 350, 352, 364, 368

Hanover, PA, 179, 180, 217

Hanover Junction, VA, 43

Hardie, James, 173-74, 447

Harland, Edward, and his brigade, 336, 357

Harpers Ferry, 89; during the Maryland Campaign, 89, 96, 120, 121, 124, 126, 131, 159, 183, 337, 372, 387, 442 (note 10), 444 (note 3); during the Pennsylvania Campaign, 29, 149, 173, 174

Harrisburg, PA, during the Maryland Campaign, 15, 23, 104, 123, 129, 131, 444 (note 11); during the Pennsylvania Campaign, 19, 139, 142, 162, 167, 175, 177, 180, 248; siege of, 196-203, 208, 218

Harman, John, 363

Harrison, 88, 175

Harrison's Landing, VA, 10

Harrow, William, and his brigade, 313, 316

Harsh, Joseph, 12, 242, 442 (note 9)

Hartranft, John, 333

Hartsuff, George, and his brigade, 253, 255, 256, 260

Hartwig, Scott, 66, 122, 154

Hatch, John, and his division, 207

Hatch, Ozias, 371-72

Hayes, Rutherford, 205

Hays, Alexander, and his division, assignments, 69, at Gettysburg, 343, 345, 347

Hays, Harry, and his brigade, at Antietam, 253, 255; at Gettysburg, 277, 319, 277, 319

Hay, John, 28

Heidlersburg, PA, 175

Herndon Station, VA, 142

Herr Ridge, 231, 268-69

Heth, Henry, and his division, assigned to Third Corps at Gettysburg, 39, 68; movements north during Pennsylvania Campaign, 146, 164, 166, 171, 180; at Gettysburg, 225, 236, 238, 242-43, 267-69, 272-74, 276, 278, 282, 284-85, 287-88, 340, 344, 346, 357, 382, 391

Hewitt, Sylvester, 199;

Hill, A.P., and his division/corps; reputation, 65, 382; assignments, 39, 67; army's need for supplies; 72, 74; movements during Maryland Campaign, 160; at Harpers Ferry, 202, 226; at Antietam, 337-38, 351, 354, 357, 361,-62, 383, 389, 394-95;

485

initial movements north during Pennsylvania Campaign, 106; movements toward Gettysburg during the second phase, 135, 135, 141, 142, 145, 146; movements toward Gettysburg during the final phase, 164, 166, 169, 171, 180; June 30-July 1, 238, 245, 247, 267, 278, 280, 284, 287; July 2, 300, 321, 323; July 3, 340, 352

Hill, D. H., and his division, reputation, 65; assigned to Longstreet's wing at Antietam, 37; perceptions of Confederate infantry, 43; early stages of the Maryland Campaign, 98, 103, 121, 124, 126; Special Orders 191, 153, 155; fights at South Mountain, 155, 204, 205, 261-62, 282; march to Sharpsburg, 156, 221, 446 (note 8); at Sharpsburg, 288, 292-93, 298, 321, 386; not at Gettysburg, 67

Hillsborough, VA, 198

HMS Trent, 16

Hofmann, William, and his brigade, 451 (note 9)

Hood, John, and his division, reputation, 65; at Fox's Gap, 206; activities at Sharpsburg before the fighting, 221, 235-36; at Antietam, 253, 257, 259-61, 263, 282, 288, 360; preparing for the Pennsylvania Campaign, 20, 39, 67; movements north during Pennsylvania Campaign, 143, 162, 166, 169, 179, 182; at Gettysburg, 226, 245, 301, 304-05, 307, 313, 320-21, 326, 350-51

Hooker, Joseph, 29, 69; given command of the I Corps prior to the Maryland Campaign, 36, 62; fight at South Mountain, 203, 206, 208; 222; at Antietam, 235, 240, 250-51, 262, 283, 285-86, 292, 331, 353, 390; given command of Army of the Potomac, 79; army on the eve of the Pennsylvania Campaign, 66; preparing for the Pennsylvania Campaign, 20, 21, 29, 51, 62; interactions with Halleck/Lincoln, 29, 31, 108, 110, 116, 136, 140, 143, 144, 146, 173; military intelligence, 88, 89, 111, 142, 144, 166; movements during the Maryland Campaign, 101, 102, 128, 223; movements north during the Pennsylvania Campaign, 106, 108, 135, 136, 148, 150, 164, 167; resigns as army chief, 173-74

Hotchkiss, Jedediah, 19

Houck's Ridge, 231, 305-06, 309, 321, 323, 326, 393

Howard, Oliver, and his brigade/corps, effectiveness, 69; at Antietam, 265; movements during the Pennsylvania Campaign, 111, 134, 135, 142, 145, 164, 167, 169, 171, 172, 176, 179; reaches the Gettysburg battlefield, 182, 225; during the Battle of Gettysburg, 272, 274, 281, 283, 284, 300, 325

Howe, Albion, and his division, 69

Huey, Pennock, and his brigade, 59

Humphreys, Andrew, and his division, 35, 67; assignments, 69, 181; at Gettysburg, 313-14, 367

Hunt, Henry, 47, 49, 51, 52, 181, 252, 345, 436 (note 34)

Hunter, Alexander, 336

Hunterstown, MD, 217

Hyattstown, MD, 174

Illinois Central Railroad, 25
Imboden, John, and his brigade, 60, 182, 363
Indiana Units, *Infantry, 19th*, 255, 256, 260, 261; *20th*, 305
Ingalls, Rufus, 73, 174
Irish Brigade, at Antietam, 295, 298
Iron Brigade (see Gibbon for Antietam), 79; at Gettysburg, 269, 270, 274, 276, 287, 288
Irwin, William, and his brigade, 267
Iverson, Alfred, 273

Jackson, (Stonewall) Thomas, initial service in the Shenandoah Valley, 10; wing commander at Antietam, 37, 102, 281-82; injury, 65, 103, 438 (note 55); advises Lee, 247, 368, 381, 444 (note 3); movements to Harpers Ferry, 98, 121-22, 124, 125, 126, 130; worries McClellan, 240, 389; Special Orders 191, 153; Harpers Ferry siege, 156, 198, 200, 202, 203, 219; his men return to Lee's army from Harpers Ferry, 160, 221; at Antietam, 252-53, 257, 263-64, 284, 286-88; at Chancellorsville, 11, 67; impact of death, 67, 68, 79, 244, 280, 282, 388; prior to the Pennsylvania Campaign, 19; reputation, 29, 63, 351
James River, 10, 27, 141
Jefferson, MD, 154, 169, 210
Jenkins, Albert, and his brigade, 60, 111, 137, 142, 164, 168, 176, 212, 213

Jenkins, Micah, and his brigade, 45, 332
Johnson, S.R., 245, 301-02
Jones, D.R., and his division, 37, reputation, 65; size of unit, 48; arrives at Sharpsburg, 157, 221, at Antietam, 293, 331, 334, 338, 351, 357
Jones, J.R., and his division, reputation, 65; preliminary fights, 219; heads to Sharpsburg, 221, 224; at Antietam, 235, 253, 256, 260, 263, 282, 286-86
Jones, Samuel, 20
Jones, William, and his brigade, 59, 92, 168, 216, 248, 349-50, 349, 433 (note 16)
Johnson, Bradley, 16
Johnson, Charles, 336
Johnson, Curt, 48
Johnson, Edward, and his division, assigned to Second Corps at Gettysburg, 39, 67; movements north in Pennsylvania Campaign, 111, 143, 162, 163, 166, 168, 171, 175, 176, 180, 184, 212, 214; at Gettysburg, 225, 280, 317, 320, 323, 343, 350-51, 386
Johnston, Joseph, 13, 25, 87
Johnston S. R., 245, 248

Kearny, Philip, 36
Keedysville, MD, 157, 159, 208, 221, 223, 362, hospital at, 81
Kemper, James, and his brigade/division, 37, 207, 336, 357, 394
Kennedy, John, 310
Kershaw, Joseph, and his brigade, 199, 309, 310, 312

487

Kettle Run, VA, 445 (note 21)
Kilpatrick, Hugh, and his brigade/division, 59, 60, 92, 143, 172, 177, 180, 217; at Gettysburg, 182, 349, 352; after Gettysburg, 365, 367
Kimball, Nathan, and his brigade, 41, 293, 294
King, Rufus, 36
Kingsburg, Henry, 332
Knipe, Joseph, 163, 169, 262
Knoxlyn Ridge, 268
Knoxville, TN, 63
Kuhn, John, 276

Lamar, Jefferson, 211
Lane, James, and his brigade, 277, 340
Lang, David, and his brigade, 313-14, 316, 340, 347, 354
Law, Evander, and his brigade, 182, 235, 259, 260, 301, 304, 306, 326, 350
Lawton, Alexander, and his division, reputation, 65; preliminary fights, 219; heads to Antietam, 221, 224; at Antietam, 235, 253, 259, 263, 282, 286, 288
Lee, Fitzhugh, and his brigade, during the Maryland Campaign, 58, 59, 97, 102, 132, 157, 235, 361; during the Pennsylvania Campaign, 168
Lee, Robert E., 27, 446 (note 12), 447 (note 2); in command of the Army of Northern Virginia, 12, 33; offensive philosophy, 14, 373, 248, 434 (note 5); planning for the Maryland Campaign, 15, 17, 18, 23, 43-44, 442 (note 14), 443 (note 15), 444 (notes 3 & 4); determines to fight at Sharpsburg, 159, 226, 368; tactics during battle of Antietam, 240, 241, 246, 288, 293, 336; strength at Antietam, 440 (note 2); during Battle of Antietam, 264, 282, 286, 325, 326, 334, 337; after Antietam, 360-63; at Chancellorsville, 11, 12; planning for the Pennsylvania Campaign, 19, 20, 22, 45; before Gettysburg/arrives, 242, 243, 272, tactics at Gettysburg, 243-46, 247, 274, 278, 280, 285, 300-01, 304, 317, 323-24, 343-49, 352, 356; during Battle of Gettysburg, 274, 282, 287, 320, 341, after Gettysburg, 363, relations with Davis, 25, 31, 375-6; 373, 375-76; Ill/injured, 27-29, 29, 31-32, 434 (note 8); need for supplies, 74, 75, 77; organization/reorganization of the army, 39-40; condition of army, 77, 78, 150; communications with Davis during the Maryland Campaign, 50, 78, 95, 100, 101, 103, 120, 373; communications with Davis during the Pennsylvania Campaign, 163; reputation/men's perspectives, 79; military intelligence, 86, 88-89, 92; movements north during the Pennsylvania Campaign, 108, 110, 112, 115, 148; misjudges enemy/predicts moves, 116, 156, 157; gambles, 116, 120; summary of getting to the battlefields, 188-93; arrives at Gettysburg, 225; after Gettysburg, 373
Lee, Stephen, 241, 252, 264, 360

Lee, W.H.F. (Rooney), and his brigade, 59
Leesborough, MD, 102
Leesburg, VA, 385; during the Maryland Campaign, 15, 16, 95, 96, 97, 105, 123, 441 (note 3); during the Pennsylvania Campaign, 145, 148, 164
Leister, Lydia, 246
Lemon, James, 259
Letterman, Jonathan, 80, 81, 82
Liberty, MD, 98, 177
Liddell, P, 236
Light's Ford, 198
Lightfoot, James, 297
Lincoln, Abraham, 10, 11, 12, 13, 362; after Battle of Antietam, 22; decides on who will command the army, 27-30; worried about the security of Washington, 35-36, 46, 108, 115; relations with McClellan, 31, 132, 371-73, 376-77; 383-84; visits McClellan, 371-72; relations with Hooker, 29, 31, 135, 140, 383-84; relations with Meade, 32, 365, 373-74; 383-84; military intelligence, 97; after the campaigns, 376, 378-79, 380
Lincoln, Robert, 374
Little Round Top, 181, 229, 231, 243, 245, 301-02, 304, 305, 306-07, 310, 317, 326, 345, 356, 393-94
Littlestown, PA, 177, 179
Lockwood, Henry, and his brigade, 45, 322
London, 16
Long, Armistead, 278
Longstreet, James, reputation, 29, 63, 384; wing commander at Antietam, 37, 458 (note 2); units supervised by, 38-39, 67; injury, 65, 438 (note 55); military intelligence, 88, 175; march to South Mountain, 155, 203-04, 382, 449 (note 11); march to Sharpsburg, 221; loses part of ordnance train, 159, 184; during Maryland Campaign before Antietam, 96, 100, 120-21, 126; initial movements north during Pennsylvania Campaign, 106, 108, 115; final movements toward Gettysburg, 135, 142, 145, 148, 149, 162, 163, 166, 169, 180, 182; at Gettysburg, 226, 243; July 1, 244-45, 300; July 2, 245-47, 301-02, 304-05, 317, 320, 322-24, 394; July 3, 247, 340-41, 343-44, 346, 352, 356
Loudoun Heights, 121, 130, 196, 200, 202
Louisiana Units, *Infantry, 15th*, 256
Lovell, Thomas, and his brigade, 362
Lovettsville, VA, 121, 198
Lowe, Enoch, 442 (note 14), 443 (note 15)
Lowe, Thaddeus, 85
Lower Bridge, 225, 235, 242, 288, 330-34, 353-54, 355, 390, 393
Luray, VA, 100
Lutheran Theological Seminary, 248

McCandless, William, and his brigade, 317
McClellan, George, 25, 26, 27; in command of the Union army early in 1862, 10, 13, 31; relations with Lincoln, 26, 31, 371-73, 376-77; position during the Second Bull Run Campaign/assigned Army of the Potomac, 27-28, 97; interactions

with Halleck, 28, 33, 104, 371-72, 442 (note 10); attempts to protect Washington, 35, 102, 116, 150; reorganization of the army, 35-36, 41, 43, 57, 62-64, 100; condition of army, 76-77; military intelligence, 85, 86, 87, 89, 91, 122-23, 125, 126, 131; interactions with Gov. Curtin, 104; movements toward Lee's army, 104, 105, 114, 123, 125, 128, 131, 157, 159, 183, 222-24; reaches Frederick, 153; Summary of getting to the battlefields, 188-93; preliminary battles, 200, 202, 208, 211; decides to engage Lee at Antietam, 226; after Antietam, 376

McConnellsburg, PA, 137, 145, 162, 164

McCrady, Edward, 72

McDowell, Irvin, 10, 25, 36

McIntosh, David, 272, 280, 336

McLaws, Lafayette, and his division, reputation, 65; assigned to Longstreet's wing at Antietam and his corps at Gettysburg, 37, 39, 67; condition of army, 72, 77; early activities during the Maryland Campaign, 101; siege of Harpers Ferry, 121, 122, 124, 125-26, 154, 198, 200; fight at Crampton's Gap/in Pleasant Valley, 155, 160, 203, 210, 211; Lee worries about his command, 156; to Sharpsburg, 222, 224, 265; at Antietam, 264-65, 286, 288, 295, 301, 386, 394; movement north during the Pennsylvania Campaign, 106, 143; at Gettysburg, 226, 245, 281, 301-02, 309-10, 312, 320-21, 351

McNeil, Hugh, 23

McPherson's Ridge, 231, 268-69, 270, 272, 279, 287

McRae, D.K., and his brigade, 261

McReynolds, Andrew, and his brigade, 111, 212, 214

Magilton, Albert, and his brigade, 160

Mahone, William, and his brigade, 326, 340

Maine Units, *4th*, 305, 307; *10th*, 263; *16th*, 277; *17th*, 307; *19th*, 313-14; *20th*, 306

Malvern Hill, Battle of, 48, 242

Manassas, VA, 164

Manchester, MD, 177, 180, 181

Mansfield, Joseph, and his corps, 63; effectiveness, 69; march to Sharpsburg, 102, 125, 128, 131, 203 222; at Antietam, 235, 250-51, 262-63, 281, 283, 286, 288, 298, 330, 382

Marshall, Charles, 17, 77-78

Martinsburg, WV, 90, 100, 122, 124, 125, 126, 130, 197, 198, 212, 213, 218

Maryland Heights, 122, 124, 130, 183, 196, 197, 199, 200, 202, 442 (note 10)

Maryland Units, *Cavalry, 1st (USA) Infantry, 1st Battalion*, 18; *2nd*, 332-33

Marsh Creek, 182, 245

Massachusetts Units, *Cavalry, 1st*, 58, 97; *Infantry, 15th*, 265, 316; *19th*, 313; *29th*, 298, *37th*, 226

Meade, George, fight at Frosttown Plateau/Gap, 206-07; at Antietam, 235, 251-52, 257, 259, 286; placed in charge of the army, 30, 31, 173-74; interactions with Lincoln/Halleck, 31, 32, 33, 374-77;

490

condition of the army during the Pennsylvania Campaign, 75, 179; before Gettysburg, 238, 243, 246-47, 280-81, 299-301; at Gettysburg, 381, 382, 384; July 2, 302, 304, 314, 316-17, 319-22, 324, 326; July 3, 344, 349, 351-53, 354; follows Lee, 364-65, 367-69
Meagher, Thomas, and his brigade, 297, 298
Mechanicsburg, PA, 176
Mercersburg, PA, 137, 164
Merritt, Wesley, and his brigade, 349
Michigan Units, *Infantry, 1st*, 309; *4th*, 361; *24th*, 274;
Middle Bridge, 221, 235, 327, 330, 338-40, 390, 337-40
Middlebrook, MD, 123
Middleburg, VA, 144, 145, 217
Middletown, MD, 121, 124, 125, 169, 177, 204, 206
Miles, Dixon, 100, 128, 196-97, 199, 200, 202, 203, 208, 447 (notes 2), 448 (note 5)
Miller, David, 265
Millwood, VA, 212
Milroy, Robert, and his division, 111, 135, 136, 148, 163, 212, 213, 214, 218
Mine Run Campaign, 375, 397
Miner, Brinkerhoff, 89
Minnesota Units, *Infantry, 1st*, 314, 327
Mississippi River, 10
Mississippi Units, *Infantry, 11th*, 261;
Monocacy Aqueduct, 89, 167, 169, 173
Monocacy River, 131, 198

Monterey Pass, 177
Moor, Augustus, 204
Morrell, George, and his division, 285
Morris, Dwight, and his brigade, 41, 293-94
Muddy Branch, MD, 97
Munford, Thomas, and his brigade, preliminary activities during Maryland Campaign, 102, 132, 154, 210, 441 (note 3); during the Pennsylvania Campaign, 143
Myer, Albert, 88

Nagle, James, and his brigade, 332-33
Nevin, David, and is brigade, 317
New Guilford, PA, 182
New Hampshire Units, *Infantry, 2nd*, 312; *6th*, 333
New Jersey Units, *Infantry, 13th*, 41, 42
New Market, MD, 125
New Orleans, 10
Newton, John, and his brigade/division, 210
New York Herald, 144
New York Units, *Artillery*, Smith's, 305; *Infantry, 9th*, 77, 336; *42nd*, 313; *51st*, 333; *61st/64th*, 297; *82nd*, 316; *124th*, 305; *140th*, 307, 326; *149th*, 320
New Windsor, MD, 177
Newport News, VA, 38
Nicodemus Heights, 252, 360
North Carolinia Units, *5th*, 263; *26th*, 274; *55th*, 269;
North Woods, 228, 252, 262
Northrup, Lucius, 74
Nye, Wilbur, 19

O'Neal, Edward, and his brigade, 273, 341
O'Rorke, Patrick, 307, 394
Oak Hill, 225, 229, 272
Oak Ridge, 229, 270, 272-73, 276-77, 287, 392
Ohio Units, *Infantry, 8th*, 295, 357; *23rd*, 205
Ohio & Mississippi Railroad, 25
Orange and Alexandria Railroad, 72, 134, 135, 142, 144, 148, 167
Offut's Crossroads, MD, 123

Palmerston, Henry John, 16, 379
Pardee Field, 341
Parham, William, and his brigade, 210
Parker, Joel, 139
Parr Ridge, 123, 124, 125
Patrick, Marsena, and his brigade, 87, 88, 255, 256, 257, 260, 261
Peach Orchard, 245, 299, 302, 304-05, 309, 310-12
Pegram, William, 79, 272
Pender, Dorsey, and his brigade/division, assigned to Third Corps at Gettysburg, 39, 68; movements north to Gettysburg, 141, 146, 164, 166, 171, 180; at Gettysburg, 225, 242, 272, 276, 277-78, 282, 287, 289, 340, 344, 346, 357, 382
Pendleton, Dudley, 79
Pendleton, Edmund, 256
Pendleton, William, 48, 50-51, 52, 96, 361
Peninsula Campaign, 82, 435 (note 13)

Penn, Davidson, and his brigade, 253
Pennsylvania Units, *3rd Reserves*, 26; *4th Reserves*, 261; *13th Reserves*, 254; *26th Pennsylvania Emergency*, 169; *46th*, 262; *51st*, 333; 262; *69th*, 345, 347; *71st*, 346; *99th*, 305; *118th*, 362; *132nd*, 41; *124th*, 42; *128th*, 262
Perrin, Abner, and his brigade, 277
Pettigrew, James, and his brigade, assigned to Third Corps at Gettysburg, 39, 45; at Gettysburg, 179, 225, 236-8, 267, 268, 274, 347, 357; after Gettysburg, 367, 396
Phelps, Walter, and his brigade, 255, 256, 257, 259
Philadelphia, PA, during the Maryland Campaign, 15, 23; during the Pennsylvania Campaign, 19, 142, 167, 175
Pickett, George, and his division, 20, assigned to Longstreet's corps at Gettysburg, 39, 67; movements north to Gettysburg, 166, 168, 179, 182
Pickett-Pettigrew-Trimble Charge, 343-49, 350, 352, 353, 354, 355, 356-58, 392, 394, 395
Pierce, Franklin, 26
Pinkerton, Allan, 85, 87, 440 (note 2)
Pipe Creek Circular, 180, 243, 247
Piper farm, 298-9, 327, 392
Pittsburgh, PA, 179
Pleasant Valley, 122, 124, 126, 154, 157, 197, 198, 203, 206, 211, 218 222, 386
Pleasonton, Alfred, and his division/corps, during the Maryland Campaign, 57, 91, 95, 123, 128,

204, 338, 361; collects military intelligence during the Maryland Campaign, 97, 102, 116, 441 (note 6); movements during the Pennsylvania Campaign, 20, 59, 60-61, 92, 136; collects military intelligence during the Pennsylvania Campaign, 108, 116, 136, 148, 149; fight for the Blue Ridge Mountain gaps, 141, 142, 143, 144, 145, 146, 148, 162; screening the Union army during the Pennsylvania Campaign, 177; performance, 384
Plum Run, 313-16
Poffenberger, Joseph, 235, 240, 253
Point of Rocks, MD, 198
Poolesville, MD, 58, 89, 97, 102, 167, 169, 441 (note 3)
Polk, J. M., 260
Pope, John, 10, 15, 27-28, 36, 63, 97
Porter, Fitz John, and his corps, troubles with Washington, 36, 63; effectiveness, 69; movements north during the Maryland Campaign, 126, 223; at Antietam, 340, 362, 368, 382
Posey, Carnot, and his brigade, 73, 316-17, 326, 343, 350
Potomac Creek, 445 (note 21)
Potomac River, 368; during early part of the Maryland Campaign, 15, 58, 122, 123, 157, 198, 221, 248, 337, 361-64, 442 (note 8); during the Pennsylvania Campaign, 21, 136, 142, 143, 145, 164, 166, 169, 172
Potter, John, 333
Powers' Hill, 304
Pry's Ford, 235

Pryor, Roger, and his brigade, 295, 325

Railroad Brigade, 448 (note 2)
Ransom, Robert, and his brigade, 45
Rappahannock River, 106, 108, 111, 388
Reagan, John, 20
Red Hill, 89, 247
Reel Ridge, 298
Reno, Jesse, and his corps, 200, 204, 206, 396
Reynolds, John, and his division/corps, 30; assignments during the Maryland and Pennsylvania Campaigns, 66, 129, 155; effectiveness, 69; movements during the Pennsylvania Campaign, 111, 134, 135, 142, 145, 167, 169, 172, 179; reaches battlefield, 182, 225; at Gettysburg, 243, 267-70, 272-73, 276-77, 280-82, 283, 284, 285-86, 289, 299-300, 316, 322, 368, 396
Rhode Island Units, *Cavalry, 1st,* 144; *Infantry, 4th,* 336-37
Richardson, Israel, and his division, march to Sharpsburg, 157, 223; 295, 297-98, 322-23, 324, 327, 383, 394, 396
Richmond, VA, 10, 13, 25; during the Maryland Campaign, 16, 18; during the Pennsylvania Campaign, 106, 442 (note 14)
Richmond Whig, 38
Ricketts, James, and his division, 235, 251-52, 253, 255, 259
Ridgeville, MD, 123, 125, 128, 131
Ripley, James, 160

Ripley, Roswell, and his brigade, 205, 261, 263

Robertson, Beverly, and his brigade, 59, 92, 168, 247

Robertson, Jerome, and his brigade, 304, 305, 306, 350

Robinson, John, and his division, assignments, 69, at Gettysburg, 270, 272, 273, 277, 287

Rock Creek, 181, 225, 229

Rockville, MD, 102, 123, 175

Rodes, Robert, and his brigade/division, during the Maryland Campaign, 96; fight at Frosttown Plateau/Gap, 207; to Antietam, 446 (note 8); at Antietam, 292-94, 297, 324; assigned to Second Corps at Gettysburg, 39, 67; movements north in Pennsylvania Campaign, 111, 136, 143, 162, 163, 166, 167, 168, 171, 175, 176, 212, 213, 386; preliminary fights prior to Gettysburg, 216, 217; at Gettysburg, 225; July 1, 242-43, 272-73, 276-77, 282, 285, 289, 317; July 2/3, 319, 325, 341, 350-51

Rodman, Isaac, and his division, 332-34, 336-37, 354-55, 396, 438 (note 54)

Rose farm, 307

Rose woods, 307, 309

Roulette farm, 293, 295

Rowser's Ford, 172

Russell, Charles, 200

Ryan, Thomas, 92, 136

Salisbury Ridge, 363

Sangster's Station, VA, 144

Sanitary Commission, 81

Scales, Alfred, and his brigade, 277

Scammon, Eliakim, and his brigade/division, 334

Schenck, Robert, and his corps, 36, 173

Schurz, Carl, and his division/corps, assignments, 69

Schimmelfennig, Alexander, 272, 276, 287

Scott, T. A., 137

Scott, Winfield, 25

Seddon, James, 19

Sedgwick, John, and his division/corps, 66; effectiveness, 69; at Antietam, 264-65, 281-82, 284, 286, 288, 292, 324, 331, 354, 391, 394; movements during the Pennsylvania Campaign, 108, 111, 134, 135, 140, 144, 145, 167, 169, 173, 174, 177, 182; at Gettysburg, 226, 300

Seminary Ridge, 182, 229, 231, 236, 268, 276, 277-80, 287, 312-13, 317, 343-44, 349, 363, 393

Semmes, Paul, and his brigade, 210, 310, 327, 396

Senaca Creek, 123

Seven Days Battles, 26

Seven Pines, Battle of, 25, 35

Seymour, Horatio, 139

Seymour, Truman, and his brigade, 207, 251, 253, 254

Sharpe, George, 88

Sharpsburg Lutheran Church, 90

Sharpsburg Ridge, 242

Shenandoah River, 202

Shenandoah Valley, during the Maryland Campaign, 14, 15, 96; during the Pennsylvania Campaign, 19, 21, 115, 134, 137, 140, 146, 212; after the campaigns, 378

Shepherdstown, WV, 124, 143, 164, 166, 221
Shepherdstown Ford, 322, 396
Sherfy house, 310
Sherrill, Eliakim, and his brigade, 327
Shippensburg, PA, 164, 171
Sickles, Daniel, and his corps, 66; effectiveness, 69; movements during the Pennsylvania Campaign, 111, 134, 135, 145, 167, 169, 172, 177; reaches battlefield, 182; at Gettysburg, 299-300, 302-04, 305, 307, 310, 313, 320, 324, 364, 368, 393
Sigel, Franz, and his corps, 36
Signal Corps, 88-98
Slaughter Pen, 305-06, 307
Slocum, Howard, and his division/corps, 66; effectiveness, 69; movements during Pennsylvania Campaign, 134, 136, 142, 145, 169, 173, 176, 179; reaches battlefield, 182; fight at Crampton's Gap, 210; Battle of Gettysburg, 273-74, 299-300, 319, 324-26, 341, 343, 350, 352, 364, 390, 392-93
Smith, William, and his brigade, 341, 343
Smyth, Thomas, 350
Smithsburg, MD, 164, 365
Smoketown, MD, hospital at, 81
Snavely's Ford, 288, 333
Solomon's Gap, 197
Sorrel, Moxley, 438 (note 55)
South Carolina Units, *Infantry, 2nd*, 310; *3rd*, 309; 7th, 309
South Mountain, 58, 169, 177, 198, 292, 387
Spangler's Meadow, 343

Special Orders, 442 (note 9), 3, 36; 103, 10; 188, 100; 191, 58, 93, 121, 124, 132, 153, 203, 384, 388, 446 (note 4); 197, 80
Sperryville, VA, 110
St. James Church, 216
Stafford Court House, 134
Stahel, Julius, and his division, 59, 144
Stanton, Edwin, 30, 103, 112, 139, 362, 363, 443 (note 29)
Stannard, George, and his brigade, 45, 316, 347, 349, 357, 394
Starke, William, and his brigade, 256, 257, 285, 289, 396
Steiner, Lewis, 101, 102
Stephenson's Depot, 148, 213-14, 218, 219
Steuart, George, and his brigade, 320, 341
Stevens, Isaac, 36
Stevens, Thaddeus, 168
Stevensburg, VA, 108
Stone, Roy, and his brigade, 274, 276
Stony Hill, 307, 309-10
Stowe, Jonathan, 265
Stuart, James Brown, 93; responsibilities and organization during the Maryland Campaign 57, 58, 59, 60, 116; activities during the Maryland Campaign, 91, 97, 105, 121, 155; after Maryland Campaign, 372; organization & responsibilities during the Pennsylvania Campaign, 22, 60-61, 116; early activities during the Pennsylvania Campaign, 92, 108, 110; fight for the Blue Ridge Mountain gaps, 141, 142, 146, 148; raid during Pennsylvania

Campaign, 167, 172, 175, 176, 180, 181-82, 185, 388; cavalry fights prior to Gettysburg, 216, 217; at Gettysburg, 182, 349, 352; after Gettysburg, 365; performance, 384

Sturgis, Samuel, and his division, 10, 206, at Antietam, 332-34

Sugar Loaf Mountain, 89, 97, 128, 131, 132

Suffolk, siege of, 45

Sumner, Edwin, 63, 69; events/ movements during Maryland Campaign, 102, 125, 128, 131, 203 222; at Antietam, 241, 250, 264-65, 283-84,86, 288, 293-95, 321, 322, 324, 326, 338, 382, 392-93

Sunken Road, 42, 249, 264, 292-99, 321, 325, 326, 327, 392

Susquehanna River, 167, 171, 175, 177

Sweitzer, Jacob, 309, 310

Sykes, George, and his division/ corps, 66; effectiveness, 69; movements during the Maryland Campaign, 101, 102, 157, 223; at Antietam, 338; movements during the Pennsylvania Campaign, 134, 142, 144, 145, 169, 172, 177, 179, 182; at Gettysburg, 300, 310, 324, 362 364, 393

Taneytown, MD, 177

Taylor, Walter, 121, 280, 434 (note 5)

Tennallytown, 97, 102

Texas Units, *Infantry, 1st*, 260, 305; *4th*, 236, 260; *5th*, 236, 307

Thomas, Edward, and his brigade, 340

Thoroughfare Gap, 145, 148, 167

Tilton, William, and his brigade, 309

Toombs, Robert, and his brigade, 331, 350

Torbert, Alfred, and his brigade, 210

Two Taverns, PA, 273-74

Traveler, 27

Tredegar Iron Works, 49

Trimble, William, and his brigade/ division, 198, 346, 347, 357

Turner's Gap, 124, 154, 156, 159, 203, 204, 206, 208, 218,250

Urbana, MD, 105, 131

Union Mills, MD, 179, 181

Uniontown, MD, 177, 181

United States Units, *Artillery, Calef's*, 268; *Campbell's*, 257, 260; *Hazlett's*, 307; *Robertson's*, 59; *Tidball's*, 59; *Weir's*, 313; *Cavalry, 2nd*, 25; *6th*, 349; *Infantry, 1st Sharpshooters*, 361; *2nd*, 447 (note 2)

Upper Bridge, 225, 231, 235, 242, 390

Upperville, VA, 59, 145, 217

Valley of Death, 317

Vautier, John, 253

Vicksburg, MS, 10, 12, 20, 379

Vincent, Strong, and his brigade, 146, 306, 307, 326, 327

Virginia Central Railroad, 72

Virginia Units, *Artillery, Brockenbrough's battery*, 49; *Cavalry, 2nd*, 441 (note 3); *5th*, 204; *Infantry, 17th*, 336

Von Steinwehr, Adolph, and his division, 272, 276

Wadsworth, James, and his division, assignments, 69; at Gettysburg, 225, 269-70, 287

Walker, James, and his brigade, at Antietam, 214, 253-54, 256, 257; at Gettysburg, 341

Walker, John, and his division, reputation, 65; assigned to Longstreet's wing at Antietam, 37; condition of the army, 77; siege of Harpers Ferry, 121, 122, 124, 126, 198, 199-200; activities before the battle of Antietam, 222, 265; at Antietam, 247, 253, 265, 267, 281-82, 286, 288, 330, 354, 391

Walker, Joseph, and his brigade, 332

Ward, Hobart, and his brigade, 305, 306

Ward, William, and his brigade, 198

Warfield Ridge, 182, 228, 231, 301

Warren, Gouvernor, 304, 306, 326

Warrenton, VA, 144

Washington DC, 13, 31; during the Maryland Campaign, 14, 15; during the Pennsylvania Campaign, 134, 140

Washington Sunday Morning Chronicle, 373

Waynesboro, MD, 164

Webb, Alexander, and his brigade, 345, 346

Weber, Max, and his brigade, 126, 293-94

Weed, Stephen, and his brigade, 307, 327, 396

Wells, Gideon, 27, 33

Welsh, Thomas, and his brigade, 334, 336, 354, 357

West Woods, 221, 229, 250; fight for, 264-67, 293, 294, 325, 330-31, 392

Westminster, MD, 74, 82, 176, 217

Wheatfield, 229, 305, 307-10, 395

White, Julius, 100, 125, 130, 197, 198, 448 (note 4)

White Oak Church, VA, 90

White Post, VA, 115

White's Ford, 96, 100, 385

Wilcox, Cadmus and his brigade/ division, 37; condition of his unit, 78, 313-14, 316, 340, 347, 354

Willard, George, and his brigade, 45, 314, 316, 326

Willcox, Orlando, and his division, 205; at Antietam, 334, 336, 354

Williams, Alpheus, and his division, 42; condition of army, 75; at Antietam, 262, 267

Williamsport, MD, 90, 124, 125, 132, 136, 168, 198, 362-64, 365, 386, 362, 364-5, 386

Willoughby Run, 229, 269, 274

Winchester, VA, 100, 111, 121, 134, 135, 136, 142, 143, 148, 162, 197, 372; fight for, 212-15, 218, 219, 387, 441 note 3)

Winchester & Potomac Railroad, 214

Wisconsin Units, *Infantry*, *2nd*, 255 255, 256, 257; *6th*, 252, 255, 256, 257; *7th*, 255, 256, 260, 261

Wolf Run Shoals, VA, 136, 140

Woodville, VA, 110

Wofford, William, and his brigade, 235, 259, 260

Wool, John, 100, 123, 130, 197

Wright, Ambrose, and his brigade, 316-17, 344, 345, 346

Wright, Horatio, and his division/
corps, assignments, 69
Wrightsville, PA, 167, 175

York, PA, 166, 175, 176, 183
York River, 165

Zook, Samuel, and his brigade, 309,
310, 327, 396

www.ingramcontent.com/pod-product-compliance
Lightning Source LLC
Chambersburg PA
CBHW051415290426
44109CB00016B/1305